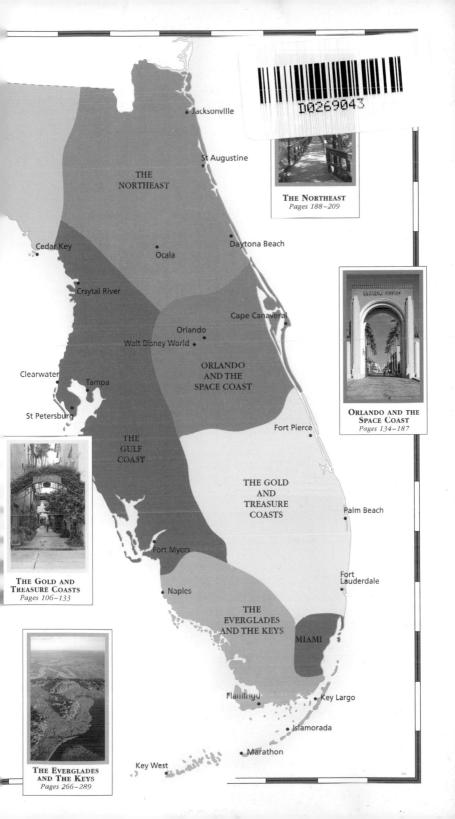

Jacksonville

St Augustine

**THE
NORTHEAST**

Cedar Key

Daytona Beach

Ocala

Crsytal River

Cape Canaveral

Orlando

Walt Disney World

**ORLANDO
AND THE
SPACE COAST**

Clearwater

Tampa

St Petersburg

Fort Pierce

**THE
GULF
COAST**

**THE GOLD
AND
TREASURE
COASTS**

Palm Beach

Fort Myers

Fort
Lauderdale

Naples

**THE
EVERGLADES
AND THE KEYS**

MIAMI

Flamingo

Key Largo

Islamorada

Marathon

Key West

D026904 3

EYEWITNESS *TRAVEL GUIDES*

FLORIDA

DK EYEWITNESS *TRAVEL GUIDES*

FLORIDA

DORLING KINDERSLEY
LONDON • NEW YORK • MUNICH
MELBOURNE • DELHI
www.dk.com

A DORLING KINDERSLEY BOOK

www.dk.com

PROJECT EDITOR Emily Hatchwell
ART EDITORS Janice English, Robert Purnell
EDITORS Freddy Hamilton, Jane Oliver,
Naomi Peck, Andrew Szudek
DESIGNERS Jill Andrews, Frank Cawley, Dawn Davies-Cook,
Eli Estaugh, Simon Oon, Edmund White

CONTRIBUTORS
Ruth and Eric Bailey, Richard Cawthorne, David Dick, Guy Mansell,
Fred Mawer, Emma Stanford, Phyllis Steinberg, Ian Williams

PHOTOGRAPHERS
Max Alexander, Dave King, Stephen Whitehorne, Linda Whitwam

ILLUSTRATORS
Richard Bonson, Richard Draper,
Chris Orr & Assocs, Pat Thorne, John Woodcock

Reproduced by Colourscan, Singapore
Printed and bound by L. Rex Printing Company Limited, China

First published in Great Britain in 1997
by Dorling Kindersley Limited
80 Strand, London WC2R 0RL
Reprinted with revisions 1999, 2000, 2001, 2002

Copyright 1997, 2002 © Dorling Kindersley Limited, London
A Penguin Company

A CIP CATALOGUE RECORD IS AVAILABLE FROM THE BRITISH LIBRARY.

ISBN 0 7513 4681 0

This book makes reference to various trademarks, marks
and registered marks owned by the Disney Company
and Disney Enterprises, Inc.

THROUGHOUT THIS BOOK, FLOORS ARE REFERRED TO IN ACCORDANCE WITH
AMERICAN USAGE, IE THE "FIRST FLOOR" IS AT GROUND LEVEL.

**The information in every
DK Eyewitness Guide is checked annually**.
Every effort has been made to ensure that this book is as up-to-date as
possible at the time of going to press. Some details, however, such as
telephone numbers, opening hours, prices, gallery hanging arrangements
and travel information are liable to change. The publishers cannot accept
responsibility for any consequences arising from the use of this book, nor
for any material on third party websites, and cannot guarantee that any
website address in this book will be a suitable source of travel information.
We value the views and suggestions of our readers very highly. Please
write to: Senior Publishing Manager, DK Eyewitness Travel Guides, Dorling
Kindersley, 80 Strand, London WC2R 0RL.

Previous pages: Roller coaster at Busch Gardens near Tampa

CONTENTS

A Tiffany window in
St Augustine *(see p199)*

INTRODUCING FLORIDA

MIAMI AREA BY AREA

**Rollerbladers, a common feature
of Florida's seaside resorts**

Dolphins entertaining the crowds at Sea World *(see pp164–7)*

A woman taking in the view from
a snow-white Florida beach

U-peel shrimp, a classic dish

Tourists enjoying the traditional
Key West sunset *(see p286)*

Villa Vizcaya, Miami

HOW TO USE THIS GUIDE

THIS GUIDE HELPS you get the most from your visit to Florida. It provides expert recommendations as well as detailed practical information. *Introducing Florida* maps the whole state and sets Florida in its historical and cultural context. *Miami Area by Area* and the six regional chapters describe all the important sights, using maps, pictures, and illustrations. Features cover topics from architecture to food and sport. Hotel and restaurant recommendations can be found in *Travelers' Needs*, while the *Survival Guide* includes tips on everything from transportation to safety.

MIAMI AREA BY AREA

Miami is divided into three sightseeing areas. Each has its own chapter, which opens with a list of the sights described. A fourth chapter, *Farther Afield*, covers outlying sights. All sights are numbered and plotted on an *Area Map*. Descriptions of each sight follow the map's numerical order, making sights easy to locate within the chapter.

Sights at a Glance lists the chapter's sights by category: Museums and Galleries, Streets and Neighborhoods, Historic Buildings, for example.

All pages relating to Miami have red thumb tabs.

1 Area Map
For easy reference, the sights are numbered and located on a map. Sights are also shown on the Miami Street Finder on pages 96–101.

A locator map shows where you are in relation to other areas of the city center.

2 Street-by-Street Map
This gives a bird's-eye view of the heart of each sightseeing area.

A suggested route for a walk is shown in red.

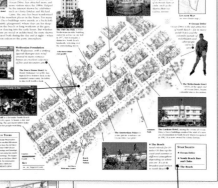

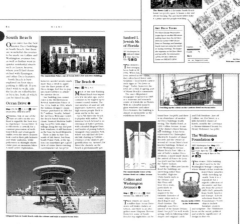

Stars indicate the sights that no visitor should miss.

3 Detailed information
All the sights in Miami are described individually, with addresses, opening hours and other practical information. The key to the symbols used in the information block is found on the back flap.

THE GOLD AND TREASURE COASTS

Narrow passages formed in Spanish galleons used to bring silver ashore, the Gold and Treasure coasts today are two of the state's visitors' magnets. The promise of winter sunshine once lured just the well-to-do but now entices millions of holidaymakers.

1 Introduction
The landscape, history and character of each region is described here, showing how the area has developed over the centuries and what it offers to the visitor today.

FLORIDA AREA BY AREA

Apart from Miami, Florida has been divided into six regions, each of which has a separate chapter. The most interesting cities, towns, and places to visit in each area are numbered on a *Pictorial Map*.

Exploring the Gold and Treasure Coasts

Each region of Florida can be quickly identified by its color coding, shown on the inside front cover.

2 Pictorial Map
This shows the main road network and gives an illustrated overview of the whole region. All entries are numbered, and there are also useful tips on getting around by car and public transportation.

3 Detailed information
All the important towns and other places to visit are described individually. They are listed in order, following the numbering given on the Pictorial Map. Within each town or city there is detailed information on important buildings and other sights.

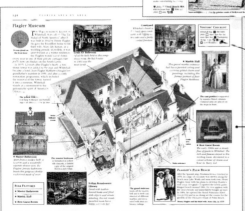

Flagier Museum

The Visitors' Checklist provides all the practical information you will need to plan your visit to all the top sights.

4 Florida's top sights
These are given two or more full pages. Historic buildings are dissected to reveal their interiors; art galleries have color-coded floor plans to help you locate the best exhibits; theme parks are shown in a bird's-eye view, with the top attractions picked out.

INTRODUCING
FLORIDA

Putting Florida on the Map

FLORIDA, WITH A POPULATION of about 14 million, is the southernmost state of the continental US, jutting down toward the Caribbean between the Atlantic Ocean and the Gulf of Mexico. The Florida peninsula measures about 430 miles (690 km) north to south, and the state as a whole covers an area of 58,560 sq miles (151,714 sq km) – roughly the same size as England. The state capital is Tallahassee, a comparatively small city in the Panhandle – the narrow strip of land extending west along the shore of the Gulf of Mexico. Florida's principal international gateways, however, are Miami and Orlando.

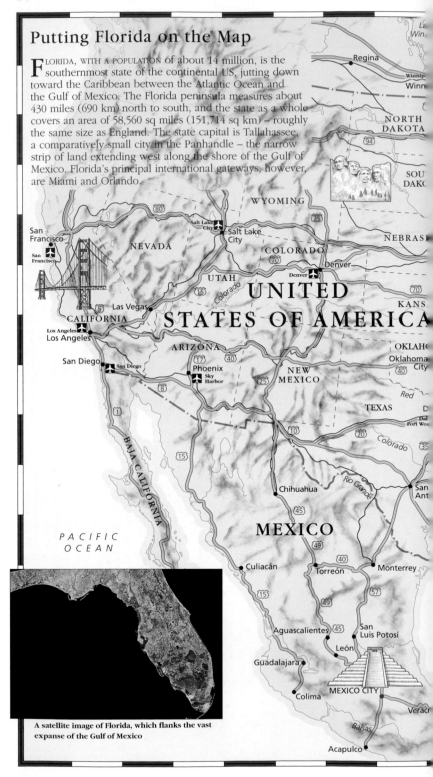

A satellite image of Florida, which flanks the vast expanse of the Gulf of Mexico

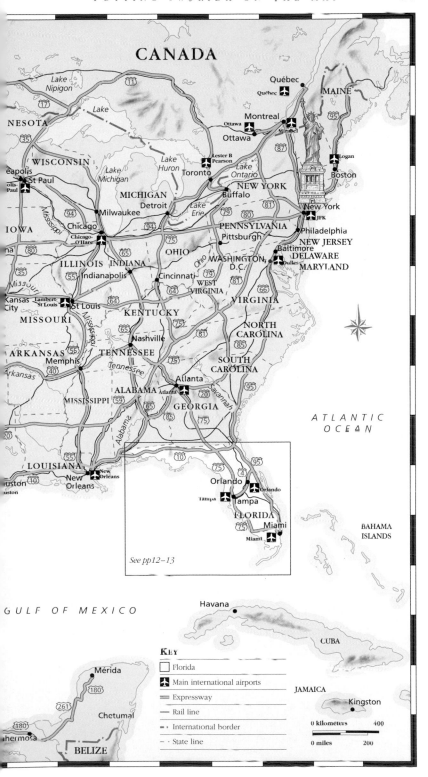

CANADA

Lake Nipigon

Lake

NESOTA

WISCONSIN

Lake Huron

Lake Michigan

Québec

Québec

MAINE

Ottawa

Montreal

Mirabel

Ottawa

Lester B Pearson

Toronto

Lake Ontario

NEW YORK

Buffalo

Logan

Boston

eapolis

olis-Paul

St Paul

MICHIGAN

Detroit

Lake Erie

New York

IOWA

Chicago

Chicago-O'Hare

Milwaukee

JFK

na

ILLINOIS INDIANA

Indianapolis

OHIO

Ohio

Cincinnati

PENNSYLVANIA

Pittsburgh

Philadelphia

NEW JERSEY

Baltimore

DELAWARE

Dulles

WASHINGTON, D.C.

MARYLAND

Kansas City

Lambert St Louis

St Louis

MISSOURI

KENTUCKY

WEST VIRGINIA

VIRGINIA

NORTH CAROLINA

ARKANSAS

Memphis

Arkansas

TENNESSEE

Tennessee

Nashville

SOUTH CAROLINA

MISSISSIPPI

Alabama

ALABAMA

Atlanta

Atlanta

GEORGIA

Savannah

ATLANTIC OCEAN

LOUISIANA

uston

New Orleans

New Orleans

Orlando

Tampa

Orlando

Tampa

FLORIDA

Miami

Miami

BAHAMA ISLANDS

See pp12–13

GULF OF MEXICO

Havana

CUBA

KEY

☐ Florida

✈ Main international airports

▬ Expressway

— Rail line

•—• International border

-- State line

Mérida

Chetumal

hermosa

BELIZE

JAMAICA

Kingston

0 kilometers   400

0 miles   200

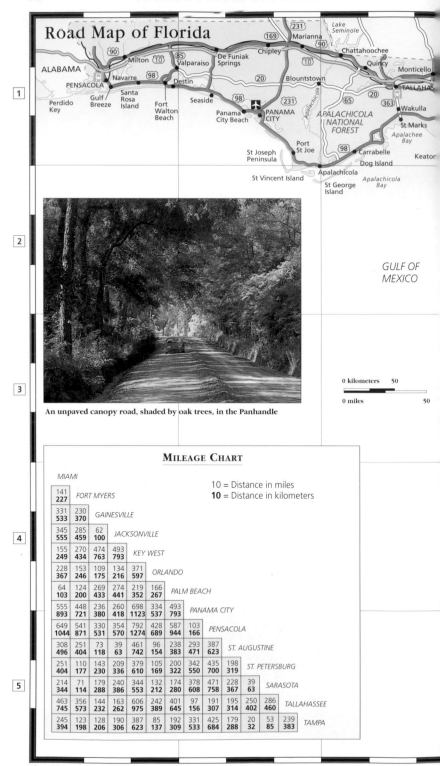

Road Map of Florida

ALABAMA

Perdido Key · Gulf Breeze · Santa Rosa Island · PENSACOLA · Navarre · 98 · Milton · 10 · Valparaiso · 85 · De Funiak Springs · Destin · Fort Walton Beach · Seaside · 98 · Panama City Beach · PANAMA CITY · 231 · St Joseph Peninsula · Port St Joe · St Vincent Island · Apalachicola · St George Island · 20 · Blountstown · Chipley · 169 · Marianna · 231 · 90 · 10 · Chattahoochee · Quincy · Monticello · APALACHICOLA NATIONAL FOREST · 65 · 20 · TALLAHAS · 363 · Wakulla · St Marks · Apalachee Bay · 98 · Carrabelle · Dog Island · Keator · Apalachicola Bay · Lake Seminole · 90

GULF OF MEXICO

An unpaved canopy road, shaded by oak trees, in the Panhandle

0 kilometers   50

0 miles   50

MILEAGE CHART

10 = Distance in miles
10 = Distance in kilometers

MIAMI													
141 **227**	FORT MYERS												
331 **533**	230 **370**	GAINESVILLE											
345 **555**	285 **459**	62 **100**	JACKSONVILLE										
155 **249**	270 **434**	474 **763**	493 **793**	KEY WEST									
228 **367**	153 **246**	109 **175**	134 **216**	371 **597**	ORLANDO								
64 **103**	124 **200**	269 **433**	274 **441**	219 **352**	166 **267**	PALM BEACH							
555 **893**	448 **721**	236 **380**	260 **418**	698 **1123**	334 **537**	493 **793**	PANAMA CITY						
649 **1044**	541 **871**	330 **531**	354 **570**	792 **1274**	428 **689**	587 **944**	103 **166**	PENSACOLA					
308 **496**	251 **404**	73 **118**	39 **63**	461 **742**	96 **154**	238 **383**	293 **471**	387 **623**	ST. AUGUSTINE				
251 **404**	110 **177**	143 **230**	209 **336**	379 **610**	105 **169**	200 **322**	342 **550**	435 **700**	198 **319**	ST. PETERSBURG			
214 **344**	71 **114**	179 **288**	240 **386**	344 **553**	132 **212**	174 **280**	378 **608**	471 **758**	228 **367**	39 **63**	SARASOTA		
463 **745**	356 **573**	144 **232**	163 **262**	606 **975**	242 **389**	401 **645**	97 **156**	191 **307**	195 **314**	250 **402**	286 **460**	TALLAHASSEE	
245 **394**	123 **198**	128 **206**	190 **306**	387 **623**	85 **137**	192 **309**	331 **533**	425 **684**	179 **288**	20 **32**	53 **85**	239 **383**	TAMPA

A   B   C

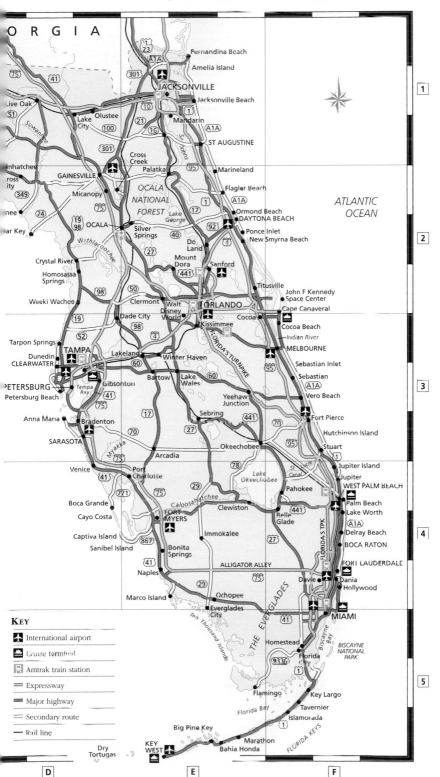

GEORGIA

Fernandina Beach
Amelia Island
JACKSONVILLE
Jacksonville Beach
Live Oak
Lake City Olustee
Mandarin
 St Augustine
inhatchee
Cross Creek
Palatka
Marineland
GAINESVILLE
Micanopy
OCALA NATIONAL FOREST
Flagler Beach
Ormond Beach
DAYTONA BEACH
Ponce Inlet
New Smyrna Beach
OCALA
Silver Springs
Lake George
De Land
Crystal River
Mount Dora
Sanford
Titusville
Homosassa Springs
Weeki Wachee
Clermont
Walt Disney World
ORLANDO
Dade City
Kissimmee
Cocoa
John F Kennedy Space Center
Cape Canaveral
Cocoa Beach
Indian River
Tarpon Springs
TAMPA
Dunedin
CLEARWATER
Lakeland
Winter Haven
MELBOURNE
Sebastian Inlet
Sebastian
PETERSBURG
Petersburg Beach
Tampa Bay
Gibsonton
Bartow
Lake Wales
Vero Beach
Anna Maria
Bradenton
Yeehaw Junction
Fort Pierce
SARASOTA
Sebring
Hutchinson Island
Venice
Arcadia
Okeechobee
Stuart
Port Charlotte
Lake Okeechobee
Jupiter Island
Jupiter
WEST PALM BEACH
Boca Grande
Cayo Costa
FORT MYERS
Clewiston
Pahokee
Palm Beach
Lake Worth
Captiva Island
Sanibel Island
Immokalee
Belle Glade
Delray Beach
BOCA RATON
Bonita Springs
ALLIGATOR ALLEY
FORT LAUDERDALE
Naples
Davie
Dania
Hollywood
Marco Island
Ochopee
THE EVERGLADES
MIAMI
Everglades City
Ten Thousand Islands
Homestead
Florida City
BISCAYNE NATIONAL PARK
Biscayne Bay
Flamingo
Key Largo
Florida Bay
Tavernier
Islamorada
FLORIDA KEYS
Big Pine Key
Marathon
Bahia Honda
KEY WEST
Dry Tortugas

ATLANTIC OCEAN

KEY

- International airport
- Cruise terminal
- Amtrak train station
- Expressway
- Major highway
- Secondary route
- Rail line

1
2
3
4
5

D   E   F

Miami

THE METROPOLIS often referred to simply as
Miami, or Greater Miami, is more accurately called Dade County. It covers 2,000 sq
miles (3,220 sq km) and incorporates many
districts and several cities. In this book, Miami
has been divided up into three sightseeing
areas: Miami Beach, including the resort of
South Beach; Downtown and Little Havana,
more traditionally urban areas; and the leafy
suburbs of Coral Gables and Coconut Grove.

Coral Gables: Miami's most desirable residential district, laid out around a series of cana

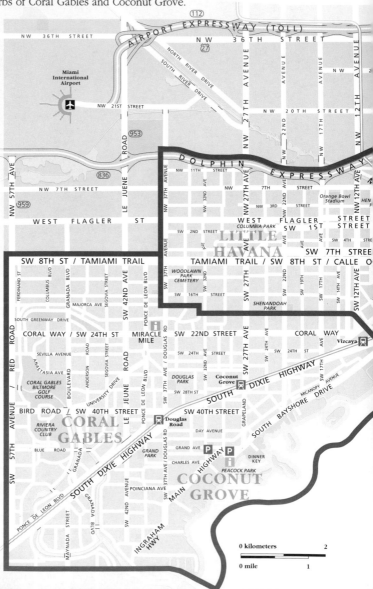

Miami Beach: a city in its own right, linked by causeways to the mainland

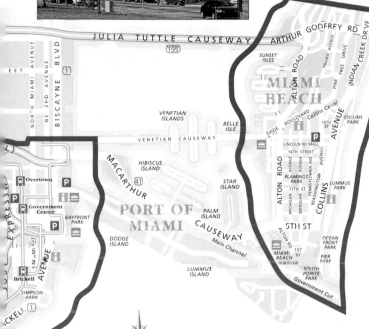

JULIA TUTTLE CAUSEWAY · ARTHUR GODFREY RD

195

SUNSET ISLES

PRAIRIE AVENUE
PINE TREE DRIVE
INDIAN CREEK DRIVE

MIAMI BEACH

ALTON ROAD

EET
NORTH MIAMI AVENUE
NE 2ND AVENUE
BISCAYNE BLVD
1

VENETIAN ISLANDS

BELLE ISLE

Collins Canal
DADE BOULEVARD
19TH ST
COLLINS PARK

VENETIAN CAUSEWAY

COLLINS AVENUE

LINCOLN RD MALL
16TH STREET

MACARTHUR

HIBISCUS ISLAND

41

STAR ISLAND

Overtown
P

ALTON ROAD

AVENUE
FLAMINGO PARK
11TH ST
PENNSYLVANIA AVE
MICHIGAN AVENUE
MERIDIAN AVENUE
WASHINGTON AVENUE
LUMMUS PARK

COLLINS

Government Center
BAYFRONT PARK

PORT OF MIAMI

PALM ISLAND
CAUSEWAY
Main Channel

5TH ST

DODGE ISLAND

ALTON RD

OCEAN FRONT PARK

EXPRESSWAY
SW MIAMI AVE
AVENUE

LUMMUS ISLAND

MIAMI BEACH
1ST ST
PIER PARK

Brickell

SIMPSON PARK

SOUTH POINTE PARK
Government Cut

CKELL
1

Downtown: the visual and commercial focus of the metropolis, with high-rises spanning the Miami River

KEY

✈	International airport
🚇	Metrorail station
🚤	Water taxi boarding point
P	Parking
ℹ	Information
=	Expressway
=	Metrorail line

A PORTRAIT OF FLORIDA

F OR THE MAJORITY OF FLORIDA'S *40 million-plus annual visitors, the typical travel poster images of Florida – sun, sea, sand, and Mickey Mouse – are reason enough to jump on the next plane. The Sunshine State deserves its reputation as the perfect family vacation spot, but Florida is much richer in its culture, landscape, and character than its stereotypical image suggests.*

It is easy to turn a blind eye to what lies beyond the Florida coast, where the beaches are varied and abundant enough to satisfy every visitor – whether you want simply to relax beneath azure skies or make the most of the state's fine sports facilities. However, great rewards await those who put aside their suntan lotion and beach towels to explore.

Beach buggie, Daytona Beach

The lush forests, the rolling hills of the north, the colorful displays of bougainvillea and azaleas in spring shatter the myth that Florida's landscape is totally dull and flat. Wherever you are, it is only a short trip from civilization to wild areas, such as the Everglades, which harbor an extraordinary diversity of plant and animal life, and where alligators and snakes are living reminders of the inhospitable place that Florida was not much more than 100 years ago. By world standards the state was a late developer (most of its historic districts date only from the early 1900s), but Florida boasts the nation's oldest town: St. Augustine, where a rare wealth of well-preserved buildings provide a glimpse of life in the 18th century.

Both climatically and culturally, Florida is a state divided – a bridge between temperate North America and tropical Latin America and the Caribbean. In the north, roads are lined with stately live oak trees and people speak with a southern drawl,

The unspoiled, watery landscape near Flamingo in Everglades National Park

◁ A typical scene in South Beach, Miami, where in-line skates and minimal clothing are the norm

A local resident enjoying some leisurely fishing off Naples pier, on the shores of the Gulf of Mexico

while, in the south, shade from the subtropical sun is cast by palm trees, and the inhabitants of Miami are as likely to speak Spanish as English.

PEOPLE AND SOCIETY

The state "where everyone is from somewhere else," Florida has always been a cultural hodgepodge. The Seminole Indians, who arrived in the 17th century, have been in Florida longer than any other group. They live mostly on reservations, but you see them by the roadside in some southern areas, selling their colorful, handmade crafts. The best candidates for the title of "true Floridian" are the Cracker farmers, whose ancestors settled in the state in the 1800s; their name comes perhaps from the cracking of their cattle whips or the cracking of corn to make grits. Unless you explore the interior, you probably won't meet a Cracker; along the affluent, heavily populated coast, you'll rub shoulders mainly with people whose roots lie in more northerly states.

North Americans have poured into Florida since World War II; the twentieth most populous state in the US in 1950, Florida is now ranked fourth. The largest single group to move south has been the retirees, for whom Florida's

Miami Cubans playing dominos

climate and lifestyle of leisure (plus its tax concessions) hold great appeal after a life of hard work. Retirees take full advantage of Florida's recreational and cultural opportunities. You'll see many seniors playing a round of golf, fishing, or browsing around one of Florida's state-of-the art shopping malls. While super-rich communities like Palm Beach fit the conservative and staid image that some people still have of Florida, the reality is very

A stand selling clothes made by Seminole Indians

different. An increasing number of the new arrivals are young people, for whom Florida is a land of opportunity, a place to have fun and enjoy the good life. It is this younger generation that has helped turn Miami's South Beach, where beautiful bodies pose against a backdrop of Art Deco hotels, into one of the trendiest resorts in the US.

A refreshing ride in one of Florida's popular water parks

There has also been massive immigration from Latin America, and Miami has a large Cuban community. Here, salsa and merengue beats fill the air while exuberant festivals fill the calendar. The ethnic diversity is also celebrated in the local food: as well as genuine re-creations of Caribbean and other ethnic dishes, you can enjoy the exciting and innovative dishes that have emerged with the craze for cross-cultural cuisine.

Oranges, Florida's juiciest crop

source of revenue has been agriculture: citrus fruits, vegetables, sugar, and cattle. Citrus grows mainly in central Florida, where fruit trees can stretch as far as the eye can see. High-tech industry is significant too, while the proximity of Miami to Latin America and the Caribbean has made it the natural route for US trade with the region. Florida's warm climate has also generated high-profile moneyspinners: spring baseball training draws teams and lots of fans south, while the fashion trade brings models by the dozen and plenty of glamour to Miami.

ECONOMICS AND TOURISM

Economically, Florida is not in bad shape compared with other US states. For most of its history, the state's main

It is tourism that fills the state's coffers. The Walt Disney World Resort may appear to dominate the tourist industry, but Florida makes the most of all its assets: its superb beaches, its location within easy striking distance of the Bahamas and the Caribbean (the state's cruise industry is flourishing), and its natural habitats. After decades of unbridled development, Florida has finally learned the importance of safeguarding its natural heritage. Vast areas of land have already disappeared beneath factories, condos, and cabbage fields, but those involved in industry and agriculture are acting more responsibly, and water use is now being strictly monitored. Florida's natural treasures, from its swamps to its last remaining panthers, are now protected for posterity.

Flamingos, seen in some parks and a popular icon

The Landscape of Florida

FLORIDA'S LANDSCAPE is relentlessly low-lying, the
highest point in the state being just 345 ft (105 m)
above sea level. The rare, rolling hills of the Panhandle
provide some of the loveliest countryside in the state,
whose flat peninsula is otherwise dominated by grass-
land and swamp, punctuated by forests and thousands
of lakes. Great swathes of the natural landscape have
had to surrender to the onslaught of urban development and agriculture – second only to tourism as the
state's main economic resource. However, you can still
find areas that are surprisingly wild and unpopulated.

*Wetlands consist mainly of
tree-covered swamps, like this
cypress swamp, and more
open, grassy marshes.*

Pensacola

Tallahassee

APALACHICOLA
NATIONAL
FOREST

Panama
City

0 kilometers   50

0 miles   50

Gainesville

Withla

Sandy beaches
account for over
1,000 miles (1,600 km)
of Florida's coastline. In
contrast to the coral sand
on the Atlantic side, the
fine quartz sand in the
Panhandle is so white
that legend has it that
unscrupulous traders
sold it as sugar during
World War II.

St Petersburg

FLORIDA'S SINKHOLES

Many of Florida's 30,000 lakes and ponds started out as a
sinkhole, or "sink." This curious phenomenon, which occurs
mainly in northern Florida, is a result of the natural erosion
of the limestone that forms the bedrock of much of the state.
Most sinkholes form gradually, as the soil sinks slowly into
a depression. Others appear much more dramatically, often
after heavy rain, when an underground cavern collapses
beneath the weight of the
ground above. The largest
recorded sinkhole occurred in
Winter Park in 1981. It swal-
lowed half a dozen cars and a
house, and formed a crater
more than 300 ft (90 m) in
diameter. There is no sure way
to predict sinkhole development, and many homeowners
take out sinkhole insurance.

Barrier islands,
formed by the piling
up of drifting sand, ring
much of Florida's coast.

KEY

▢	Main urban areas
▢	Main wetland areas
▢	Main forested areas
– –	Intracoastal Waterway
▼	Cattle
🐟	Fish and seafood
🍊	Citrus fruit
⚘	Sugar cane
⬈	Tobacco
⬈	Peanuts

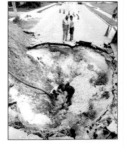

**City workers surveying a sink-
hole in the middle of a road**

The Intracoastal Waterway is a natural but dredged channel, whose main section along the east coast is a continuation of a route that begins farther north in Maryland; some of the Florida sections were dredged back in the 1880s. It is a popular boating route (see p342).

Cattle were shipped from Florida to market in Cuba under the Spanish. Today, Florida is second only to Kentucky in the raising of beef cattle in the southeastern states, its industry based largely on the Brahma, a hardy breed of cattle originally from India. The state's principal cattle ranching country lies along the Kissimmee River, and the town of Kissimmee is known as the "cow capital of Florida" (see p177).

Forest, mostly pine, covers 50 percent of the state's land area, but more than half of this is grown for commercial use.

Florida's citrus industry produces over 70 percent of the citrus fruits consumed in the US. Oranges are grown mainly for their juice, for which the state is famous.

Sugar cane thrives on the rich soil south of Lake Okeechobee (see p124). Once reliant on migrant laborers from the Caribbean, who cut the cane by machete, the industry is now largely mechanized.

cksonville

● Daytona Beach

● Orlando

● Fort Pierce

Lake Okeechobee

● Palm Beach

saltatchee

t Myers

● Naples

Miami Canal

● Fort Lauderdale

● MIAMI

Tamiami Canal

EVERGLADES

The Florida Keys are a chain of fossilized coral islands, many of which are tiny and uninhabited.

Urban growth is the inevitable result of the constant influx of migrants from other US states and abroad, as well as of the general movement from rural to urban areas. The southeastern coast of Florida is almost completely built up – as seen at Delray Beach, which straddles the Intracoastal Waterway on the Gold Coast.

FLORIDA KEYS

Key West

Wildlife and Natural Habitats

FLORIDA'S GREAT VARIETY of habitats and wildlife is due in part to the meeting of temperate north Florida with the subtropical south. Other factors include the state's humidity, sandy soils, low elevation, and proximity to the water. Some plants and animals can live in several habitats, while others can survive only in one. The bird life in Florida is particularly rich in winter, when migratory birds arrive from the colder northern states.

A tropical hardwood hammock in southern Florida

COASTAL AREAS

Florida's coasts are rich in wildlife despite the often exposed conditions. Apart from wading birds, many animals remain hidden during the day. Some lie buried in the sand, while others, such as turtles, leave the water only in darkness. Salt marshes and lagoons, protected from the ocean by dunes, are a particularly rich habitat.

Saltwater lagoons are fertile territory for fish and shellfish.

Horseshoe crabs emerge from the ocean in great hordes, usually in spring. They congregate on the beaches to breed.

Ocean

Shrubs on the dunes are "pruned" by the ocean's salty spray and bent by the wind.

Limestone bedrock

Clay, sand, and shells

The bald eagle, an endangered species found by the ocean and in some inland areas, has a wing-span of 7 ft (2 m).

Dunes, shaped by the wind and waves, shift all the time but are stabilized by the roots of sea oats and other plants.

The sea grape, which grows on dunes mainly in southeast Florida, is named after the oval fruit that hangs in grapelike clusters.

PINE FLATWOODS

These woods, where pines tower over an understory of plants and shrubs, cover about half of Florida and are often interspersed with swamps and other habitats. They thrive when swept by fire periodically, and the plants and animals that live here have adapted to survive the difficult conditions.

Saw palmetto, as well as shrubs such as wax myrtle, do well in the open woodlands.

Slash pine is the most common tree in the flatwoods.

Clay and sand

Sand

White-tailed deer are solitary creatures. Those in Florida are smaller than the white-tailed deer found in more northerly states of the US.

Pygmy rattlesnakes are well camouflaged to blend easily into a back-ground of grass and scrub.

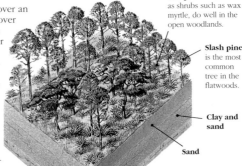

The red-bellied woodpecker nests in dead trees and may use the same nest in successive years.

FRESHWATER SWAMPS

Many swamps have been drained to make way for agriculture or development, but they are still found all over Florida. They are often dominated by cypress trees, which are well suited to the watery conditions, requiring little soil to grow. The dwarf cypress is the most common species, the larger giant or bald cypress tree being rare these days.

White ibis find ample food in freshwater marshes and swamps. They nest in large colonies in high trees or among reeds.

Peat

The bobcat *has a distinctive short tail, facial ruff, and spotted coat.*

Cypress trees often form a "dome." The trees at the water's edge are shorter than those at the center.

Sawgrass

Cypress knees are special roots that supply oxygen to the tree, which would otherwise die in the wet soil.

Water and organic matter

Anole lizards *are usually green but can change to dark brown, depending on body heat or levels of stress.*

Water lilies *are the most spectacular freshwater flowering plants. The large leaf is a common resting site for frogs.*

HARDWOOD FORESTS

These are among the most verdant habitats in the state. Hardwood-dominated forests are called "hammocks." Unlike the tropical hardwood hammocks of southern Florida, those in the north are dominated by the splendid live oak tree, interspersed with other species such as hickory and magnolia.

Spanish moss, like other epiphytes or air plants, grows on (but does no harm to) its host tree.

Wild turkeys *are easily recognized by their colored plumage and "beard."*

Magnolia, *one of the oldest known flowering plants, is characterized by its showy ornamental flowers and aromatic bark.*

Cabbage or sabal palm

Sand and clay

Live oak

Hammocks occur mainly in patches or narrow bands along rivers.

Opossums *are proficient climbers, with hands, feet, and tail well adapted to grasping thin branches.*

Armadillos *are mainly nocturnal. When threatened they roll into a ball, the hard armor protecting the soft body from predators such as bobcats.*

Hurricanes in Florida

Hurricane Hunters logo

A HURRICANE IS A TROPICAL CYCLONE with wind speeds of at least 74 mph (119 km/h). One in ten of the hurricanes to occur in the North Atlantic hits Florida – which means an average of one of these big storms every two years. The hurricane season runs from June 1 to November 30, but the greatest threat is from August to October. The Saffir-Simpson Hurricane Scale, which measures the winds and ocean flooding expected, categorizes hurricanes from one to five; category five is the worst, with winds of over 155 mph (249 km/h). Hurricane names come from a recognized alphabetical list of names, which rotates every six years. Originally, only women's names were used, but since 1979 both men's and women's names have been alternated.

Monument to the 1935 hurricane *(see p280)*

The areas of Florida most likely to be hit by a hurricane are the southeast coast, including the Florida Keys, the west coast of the Everglades, and the western Panhandle.

THE LIFE OF A HURRICANE
The development of a hurricane is influenced by several factors – primarily heat and wind. First the sun must warm the ocean's surface enough for water to evaporate. This rises and condenses into thunderclouds, which are sent spinning by the earth's rotation. The hurricane moves forward and can be tracked using satellite images like this one. On hitting land, the storm loses power because it is cut off from its source of energy – the warm ocean.

A boat lifted out of the water onto Miami's Rickenbacker Causeway by the force of the hurricane

A tent camp, set up to house some of the 250,000 left temporarily homeless by Hurricane Andrew

An apartment building after its façade was ripped off by Andrew's ferocious winds

HURRICANE ANDREW
On August 24, 1992 Hurricane Andrew devastated South Florida. It measured only "4" on the Saffir-Simpson Scale (less than the 1935 hurricane that hit the Florida Keys), but it was the country's costliest ever natural disaster, causing $25 billion worth of damage. Astonishingly, only 15 people died in Florida (and 23 in the country as a whole) from the direct effects of Hurricane Andrew.

The Eye

Encircled by the fastest winds, the "eye" at the heart of the storm is a calm area. Once the eye has passed by, the winds return to their full force.

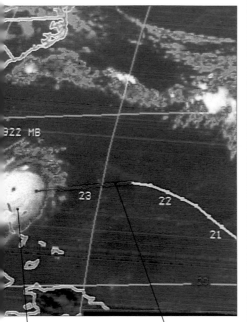

322 MB

23 22 21

A typical hurricane is 300 miles (480 km) wide and can rise 50,000–60,000 ft (15,250–18,300 m) above the ocean. It moves forward at a speed of 10–45 mph (15–70 km/h).

Many hurricanes, including Andrew, form off Africa and then move west across the Atlantic.

THE STORM SURGE

Most damage and deaths during a hurricane are a result not of wind and rain but of flooding from the storm surge. This wall of water is whipped up by fierce winds near the eye of the storm and then crashes onto the shore; it can span over 50 miles (80 km) and reach a height of 20 ft (6 m) or more.

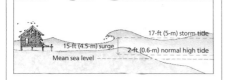

17-ft (5-m) storm tide
15-ft (4.5-m) surge   2-ft (0.6-m) normal high tide
Mean sea level

MONITORING A HURRICANE

Using satellites, computer models, and radar, the National Hurricane Center in Miami can detect a hurricane long before it reaches Florida. The most detailed information, however, is provided by pilots known as Hurricane Hunters, who fly in and out of the hurricane gathering data.

The damage from a hurricane is greatly reduced by preparedness: television and radio bulletins keep the public informed, and everyone is encouraged to plan the route of the storm on special hurricane tracking maps.

Trees bent by hurricane force winds

1 Hurricane Alerts

The issuing of a Hurricane Watch is the first indication that a hurricane could hit Florida. This means that a storm may arrive within 36–48 hours. A Hurricane Warning heralds the storm's likely arrival within 24 hours. Airports are likely to close during these alerts.

Traditional hurricane alert flag

2 Evacuation

Emergency management officials may issue evacuation orders via the local news media before a hurricane hits. People living in high-rise buildings, mobile homes, and low-lying areas are particularly vulnerable. Signs bearing the hurricane symbol direct people along safe routes. The Red Cross shelters those with nowhere else to go.

Evacuation sign

3 The All Clear

After a hurricane dissipates or moves on, the all clear is given for people to return home. However, safety is still a concern after the storm because of downed power lines, flooding, and cleanup-related accidents.

Shipwrecks and Salvage

T HE WATERS OFF FLORIDA are littered with thousands of
shipwrecks that have accumulated over hundreds
of years. Many sank during storms at sea, while others
were tossed onto the reefs off the Keys. The salvaged
wrecks picked out on the map are those that have had
a large amount of their cargo recovered. Spain's treasure
ships are the greatest prize among salvagers, just as they
were once the favored target of pirates. In museums
all over Florida everyday objects and treasure offer an
insight into the lives and riches of the Spanish.

Lighthouses
*Since the 1800s, lighthouses
like the one at Jupiter have
helped ships stay on course.*

The *Atocha*
*Florida's best-known
Spanish wreck, which sank in
1622, was located by Mel Fisher
(see p110) in 1985 after a 16-year
search. The treasure, worth an
estimated $300 million, included
coins, gold bars, and jewelry.*

The Florida Keys
were ideal territory for
"wreckers" *(see p289),*
who rescued and then
sold the cargo from
ships that foundered
on the nearby reef.

*From
Mexico*

Salvaging Treasure
*Salvaging has always
required ingenuity. This
manuscript from 1623
shows a Spanish technique
invented to rescue sunken
treasure in the Keys.*

Havana

Havana, the Cuban capital,
was the main assembly
point for Spanish fleets en
route home.

Spanish ships sailing from the
New World would pick up the
Gulf Stream and tradewinds
near Florida to aid their journey back across the Atlantic.

MEXICO

*From
South
America*

KEY

🚢 Salvaged
wreck

🚢 Unsalvaged
wreck

↗ Shipping
route

TREASURE SEEKERS

It took Mel Fisher more than 100 court hearings to establish his right to keep the treasures of the *Atocha*. Federal law states that wrecks located up to 3 miles (5 km) offshore belong to the state in whose waters they are found, but the law is unclear when it comes to ships lying outside that limit. Amateurs who find coins with metal detectors on land can keep what they find, but in Florida a license is required to remove anything from an offshore wreck within its jurisdiction.

A treasure hunter on the beach

WHERE TO SEE SPANISH TREASURE IN FLORIDA

Maritime Museum of the Florida Keys see p278

McLarty Treasure Museum see p110

Mel Fisher's Maritime Museum see p288

Mel Fisher's Treasure Museum see p110

Museum of Man in the Sea see p224

St. Lucie County Historical Museum see p111

A Spanish treasure fleet that sank here in 1715 *(see p110)* is still being salvaged. Amateurs scour nearby beaches for coins that are sometimes washed up after a storm.

To Spain

Spanish Ships
Caravels and galleons transported treasure back to Spain. These ships could carry a crew of about 200. The chests of gold and silver were usually kept under guard in a room on the lower deck.

Blackbeard
Notorious for his cruelty – and also for his habit of setting fire to hemp cords attached to his hat in order to intimidate his victims – Blackbeard preyed on Spanish ships in the early 18th century. He was killed by the British Navy in 1718.

BAHAMAS

Hispaniola and nearby Tortuga were favorite haunts of French and English pirates, who would launch attacks on Spanish ships from here.

TORTUGA

0 kilometers 200

0 miles 200

CARIBBEAN SEA

HISPANIOLA

Florida's Architecture

BUILDINGS IN FLORIDA are perhaps most interesting as a reflection of the way in which the state was settled. Early pioneers built simple homes, but aspirations grew from the railroad era onward. Entrepreneurs, eager to lure people south, imitated styles with which northerners would be familiar. This trend, plus the speed of settlement, meant that Florida never really developed an indigenous style. But the Sunshine State has some quirky and memorable architecture, often inspired by the need to adapt to the warm climate.

High-rise architecture in downtown Jacksonville

FLORIDA'S VERNACULAR STYLE

The early pioneers of the 1800s built houses whose design was dictated mainly by the climate and the location: the most identifiable common elements are the devices to maximize natural ventilation. Local materials, usually wood, were used. Original "Cracker" homes, so named after the people who built and lived in them *(see p18)*, don't survive in great numbers, but the vernacular style has influenced Florida's architecture ever since.

A chickee, the traditional simple home of Florida's native Indians

The brick chimney replaced the original one, which was made of mud and sticks.

A dog trot, or open walk-through, was often added if, as here, the original house was extended.

The roof, here made of cypress shingle, was usually steeply pitched.

***The McMullen Log House**, a pine log cabin completed in 1852, is a typical Cracker dwelling. It is now preserved in Pinellas County Heritage Village.* (See p238.)

Overhanging eaves shade both the porch and the windows.

THE GILDED AGE

From the 1880s, the railroads and tourism brought new wealth and ideas from outside the state. The love affair with Mediterranean Revivalism began and can be seen in Flagler's brick hotels in St. Augustine. Wood was still the favored material, though, and was used more decoratively – most famously in Key West. Other concentrations of Victorian houses are found in Fernandina Beach *(see p192)* and Mount Dora *(see p206)*.

A tower fulfilled a decorative more than a practical purpose.

Ventilation was still a primary concern, hence the generous number of windows.

Verandas that wrapped around the house were quite common.

Gabled roofs were popular and could be high enough to fit in an attic.

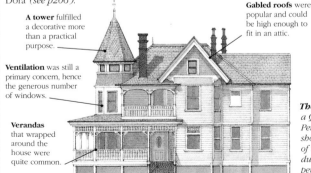

Moorish tower, Tampa Bay Hotel

***The McCreary House**, a Queen Anne home in Pensacola dated c.1900, shows the refinement of vernacular styles during the Victorian period.* (See p217.)

THE FANTASY OF THE BOOM YEARS

The most notable buildings of the period 1920-50 set out to inspire romantic images of faraway places. Each new development had a theme, spawning islands of architectural styles from Moorish to Art Deco – the latter in Miami's South Beach district (see pp58–63). Mediterranean Revivalism dominated, however. Its chief exponents were Addison Mizner in Palm Beach (see pp114–17) and George Merrick in Coral Gables (see pp78–81).

The Art Deco Greystone Hotel in Miami's South Beach

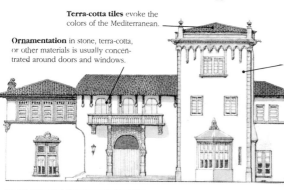

Terra-cotta tiles evoke the colors of the Mediterranean.

Ornamentation in stone, terra-cotta, or other materials is usually concentrated around doors and windows.

Balconies, turrets, and irregular roof levels are all recurrent features.

Palm Beach mansions are primarily Spanish Revival in style. This one on South Ocean Boulevard was built by Julius Jacobs, one of Mizner's chief designers, in 1929.

POSTWAR ARCHITECTURE

Many of Florida's most striking modern buildings are either shopping malls or public buildings, such as theaters or sports stadiums, which are often as impressive for their scale as for their design. More of a curiosity are the new towns of Seaside and Disney's Celebration (see p150), which have arisen out of nostalgia for small-town America and as a reaction to the impersonal nature of the modern city.

Van Wezel Performing Arts Hall in Sarasota (see p254)

Large sash windows allow abundant sunlight and sea breezes to enter the house.

Seaside, a piece of award-winning town planning in Florida's Panhandle, has houses with picket fences and other quaint pseudo-Victorian features. (See p222.)

A veranda on the second floor offers a shady place to sit or enjoy the ocean views.

Wood, characteristic of vernacular architecture in Florida, is the favored material in Seaside.

Neon signs along International Drive, Orlando

THE HIGHWAY

In the 20th century, the flood of visitors and settlers speeding south along Florida's highways has spawned buildings unique to the road. Alongside the drive-in banks and restaurants are buildings shaped like ice-cream cones or alligators – designed to catch the eye of the motorist driving past at speed. Such outlandishness, aided too by colorful neon signs, breaks up the monotonous strip of motels and fast food outlets.

Spectator Sports in Florida

FLORIDA OFFERS A FINE CHOICE of sports entertainment. The greatest variety and number of events can be seen in Miami *(see p94)* and the southeast, but there are games to watch wherever you are in the state. The spring is the busiest time in most fields of sports. Professional teams are relatively new in Florida, and their popularity is often exceeded by that of their college counterparts; collegiate competitions can easily draw crowds of over 80,000 highly partisan fans. Participation sports are described on pages 340–43.

College football match at the Gator Bowl in Jacksonville

FOOTBALL

FLORIDA PRESENTLY boasts three teams in the National Football League (NFL): the Miami Dolphins, the Tampa Bay Buccaneers, and since 1995, the Jacksonville Jaguars. The Miami Dolphins are the most successful, having appeared five times in the Super Bowl. They won in 1973, completing the first ever unbeaten, no-tie season in NFL history – a feat yet to be repeated. The home game season runs from September to December *(see p94)*.

Florida holds more college bowl games than any other state. The best teams are the Seminoles of Tallahassee, the Hurricanes out of Miami, and the Gators from Gainesville; their rivalry is fierce.

Around New Year's Day there is a glut of important and popular college games. The three favorites are the Citrus Bowl in Orlando, the Orange Bowl Classic in Miami, and the annual Gator Bowl clash in Jacksonville.

BASEBALL

SINCE WORLD WAR I, Florida's warm climate has made it a favorite spring training site for major league baseball teams. They each return to the same town every year, pumping millions of dollars into the local economy and bringing much prestige. The towns identify strongly with their visitors, whose names are often borrowed by the local Florida State League teams.

Training starts in late February, and in March the teams take part in friendly games in the so-called **Grapefruit League**. These games, which take place throughout the week, attract huge crowds, with fans often coming from outside the state. For dates and tickets contact the individual stadiums in advance.

Set up in 1993, the Florida Marlins were the state's first major league baseball team. Second to enroll were the Tampa Bay Devil Rays, who are based at St. Petersburg's Tropicana Field stadium *(see p339)*. The baseball season runs from April to August.

GRAPEFRUIT LEAGUE: WHO PLAYS WHERE

Atlanta Braves
Walt Disney World.
📞 *(407) 939-1500.*

Baltimore Orioles
Fort Lauderdale.
📞 *(954) 776-1921, (800) 236-8908.*

Boston Red Sox
Fort Myers. 📞 *(941) 334-4700.*

Houston Astros
Kissimmee.
📞 *(407) 933-2520.*

LA Dodgers
Vero Beach.
📞 *(561) 569-6858.*

Minnesota Twins
Fort Myers. 📞 *(800) 338-9467.*

New York Yankees
Tampa. 📞 *(813) 879-2244.*

Philadelphia Phillies
Clearwater. 📞 *(727) 441-9941.*

St. Louis Cardinals
Jupiter.
📞 *(561) 775-1818.*

A complete list is available from the Florida Sports Foundation (see p343).
W www.flasports.com

HORSE RACING AND POLO

FLORIDA BOASTS the country's second largest thorough-bred industry, centered on Ocala *(see p208)*. The Miami region is home to the most famous races, including the prestigious Florida Derby in March and the Breeder's Cup in November, both staged at

LA Dodgers baseball team, at Vero Beach for spring training

Gulfstream Park in Hallandale. In the spring you can see horses being trained at Hialeah Park (see p 18) in Miami. Racing also takes place at Tampa Bay Downs during the winter months.

Polo is particularly popular along the Gold Coast, where the top tournament is the Challenge Cup, held in January in West Palm Beach (see p122). With horses galloping over a field as big as nine football fields, and players hitting balls at up to 110 mph (176 km/h), games can be very exciting. At half-time, spectators join in the traditional divot-stamping ritual, in which the scuffed-up turf is stamped flat.

Horse racing at Gulfstream Park, Florida's premier venue

RODEOS

ARCADIA IS THE main center for professional competition, with two big rodeos a year (see p261), but in February and July crowds also flock to Kissimmee for the Great Silver Spurs Rodeo. Participants from all over the US compete for big purses and top national rankings in bronco riding and other contests. Numerous amateur rodeos can be seen in Davie (see p133) and Kissimmee (see p177), all year round.

JAI ALAI

FLORIDA'S GAME of jai alai, a kind of pelota that originated in Europe, is virtually unique in the US (see p133).

Jai alai, claimed by its fans as the oldest and fastest game in the world

Matches take place on a three-walled court, where players use a curved wicker basket to catch and hurl the ball, generating speeds in excess of 150 mph (240 km/h). The back wall is made of granite to absorb the resultant force.

Games are usually played by eight teams of one or two players. After the first point the winners stay on to meet the next team. This goes on until one team has seven points. An evening usually consists of 14 such games.

Jai alai is played all year round in indoor stadiums known as frontons. One of the main attractions is the chance to gamble, and millions are wagered every year.

MOTOR RACING

AUTO AND MOTORCYCLE racing are big in Florida. The season starts in February at the Daytona International Speedway (see p204), one of the world's fastest tracks, with two very popular races. The Rolex 24, like its older brother at Le Mans, runs all day and all night, and the Daytona 500 is a season highlight for the National Association of Stock Car Auto Racing (NASCAR).

The Daytona 500, first held in 1959

Other big races take place in Hialeah (Miami), Homestead, Pensacola, and Sebring (near Orlando). Hot rods come to Gainesville in March for the Gatornationals, the top drag-racing event on the Atlantic seaboard. Motorcycles also race at Daytona.

BASKETBALL

PROFESSIONAL basketball is fairly new in Florida, with the NBA's Orlando Magic and the Miami Heat; the WNBA's Orlando Miracles are the women's pro team. Florida's college basketball teams have a widespread following. Watch the local papers for schedules. The season runs from October to April.

Orlando in action

GOLF AND TENNIS

GOLF TOURNAMENTS abound in Florida, birthplace of golf ace Jack Nicklaus. Top of the bill are the Bay Hill Invitational in Orlando and the PGA Tournament Players Championship in Ponte Vedra Beach near Jacksonville; both are held at the end of March.

Tennis is another big favorite. Key Biscayne's Crandon Park is famous for its annual Lipton International Players Championship in March, which pulls huge crowds.

FLORIDA THROUGH THE YEAR

WITH ITS WARM CLIMATE, Florida is a year-round destination, but the difference in the weather between north and south means it has two distinct tourist seasons. In south Florida (including Orlando) the busiest time is from October to April, when tourists come to enjoy the mild winters. Most will have left well before summer arrives, when it can be uncomfortably hot. Orlando's

Jouster at Sarasota fair

theme parks still attract families with kids on school vacations, but in summer the Panhandle sees the biggest crowds. Be warned that prices in the relevant tourist season can be double those charged during the rest of the year. Whatever time of year you visit, you are bound to encounter a festival of some kind, but apart from national holidays *(see p35)*, few of these are Florida-wide. For a full list contact the local tourist office.

SPRING

IN LATE FEBRUARY, college students invade Florida for the Spring Break. They pour in by the thousands from all over the US. For the next six weeks Florida's coastal resorts are bursting, putting pressure on accommodations, particularly in Daytona Beach and Panama City Beach.

Baseball training *(see p30)* is also a big attraction in the spring. In the north, feast your eyes on the blooming azaleas and dogwood trees.

Daytona Beach swarming with pleasure seekers on Spring Break

MARCH

Medieval Fair *(last weekend in Feb)*, Sarasota. Celebrating the Middle Ages with food and festivities.
Sanibel Shell Fair *(first week)*. Shell collectors and artists come to Sanibel Island *(see pp264–5)*.
Florida Strawberry Festival *(first week)*, Plant City near

Little Havana's Calle Ocho, hub of the party at Carnival Miami

Tampa. Strawberry shortcake and country music.
Motorcycle Races "Bike Week" *(early Mar)*, Daytona Beach *(see pp204–205)*. Bikers converge from all over, on vintage and modern bikes.
Carnival Miami *(second Sunday)*. A nine-day street party in Miami's Latin district *(see pp74–5)*.
St. Augustine Arts and Crafts Festival *(last weekend)*. Skilled craft artists offer their wares at the city's historical sites.
Festival of the States *(late Mar–early Apr)*, St. Petersburg. Three weeks of parades, balls, jazz, and fireworks.
Winter Park Art Festival *(mid Mar)*. Greater Orlando's arts and fine crafts in quaint downtown Winter Park.

APRIL

Antique Boat Festival *(first weekend)*, Mount Dora *(see p206)*. Antique boats race on the lake as visitors attend exhibitions in the pretty town.
Springtime Tallahassee *(all month)*. One of the South's biggest festivals, this extended

extravaganza features parades, balloon races, great food, and a variety of live music.
Easter *(Mar/Apr)*. Celebrate sunrise services at the Castillo de San Marcos *(see pp200–201)* and take carriage rides around St. Augustine.
Conch Republic Celebration *(late Apr–early May)*, Key West. Party all week with parades, bed races, dancing, and other events honoring the town's founding fathers.

MAY

SunFest *(first week)*, West Palm Beach. A week-long mix of cultural and sports events.

Emblem of the Conch Republic

Isle of Eight Flags Shrimp Festival *(first weekend)*, Fernandina Beach. Sample the local shrimp and other seafood delicacies while you peruse the craft stands.
Destin Mayfest *(third weekend)*. Locals and visitors alike flock to the sound of live jazz on the Destin Harborwalk.

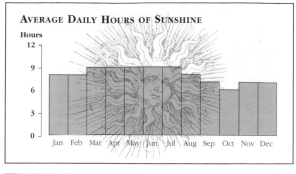

AVERAGE DAILY HOURS OF SUNSHINE

Hours

12 — 9 — 6 — 3 — 0

Jan Feb Mar Apr May Jun Jul Aug Sep Oct Nov Dec

Sunshine Chart
The chart gives figures for the entire state. The west coast near St. Petersburg, which boasts an average of 361 days of sunshine per year, enjoys more sun than elsewhere, but blue skies are a fairly consistent feature everywhere. Even in southern Florida's wetter summer months, the clouds generally disperse quickly.

Young boy in patriotic colors at a Fourth of July celebration

SUMMER

TEMPERATURES and humidity rise as summer progresses, with only Atlantic breezes and almost daily afternoon storms to bring some relief. Florida's hurricane season (*see pp24–5*) is also underway. Travelers on a tight budget can make the most of the off-season hotel prices in the south.

The big summer holiday is Independence Day on July 4, which is celebrated with street pageants, fireworks extravaganzas, barbecues, picnics, and mass cooling off in the water.

JUNE

Monticello Watermelon Festival (*all month*), Monticello (*see p229*). The harvest is celebrated in back-country style with barbecues and hoedowns.
Goombay Festival (*first weekend*), Coconut Grove, Miami (*see p82*). A Bahamian party offering a parade, great food, and Caribbean music

Fiesta of Five Flags (*early Jun*), Pensacola. Two weeks of festivities include parades, marathons, and fishing rodeos as well as the reenactment of Tristan de Luna's beach landing in 1559.
Downtown Venice Street Craft Festival (*mid-Jun*). Quiet, romantic Venice spruces up its downtown streets for this very popular crafts bazaar.

JULY

America Birthday Bash (*Jul 4*), Miami. The city sounds off with fireworks at midnight, preceded by picnics and fun and games for all the family, in the biggest Independence Day celebration in south Florida.
Silver Spurs Rodeo (*early Jul, Feb*), Kissimmee (*see p177*). The state's oldest and wildest rodeo (arena currently under renovation).
Hemingway Days Festival (*mid-Jul*), Key West. The city offers up a week of author signings, short story contests,

theatrical productions, and a very entertaining Hemingway look-alike competition.
Florida International Festival (*late Jul –early Aug*), Daytona Beach. This world-famous music festival features pop, jazz, and classical music.

AUGUST

Boca Festival Days (*all month*), Boca Raton. This celebration features an arts-and-craft fair, barbershop quartet performances, and a sand castle building contest.
Annual Wausau Possum Festival (*first Saturday*), Wausau. This town north of Panama City Beach honors the marsupial with activities such as greased pole climbing and corn-bread baking, and offers the chance to sample possum-based dishes.
Carrollwood Twilight Arts and Crafts Festival (*first weekend*), Tampa. The city's fast-paced lifestyle slows a little for this large art show.

Bearded contenders at the Hemingway Days Festival look-alike contest

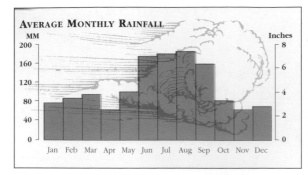

AVERAGE MONTHLY RAINFALL

MM		Inches
200		8
160		6
120		
80		4
40		2
0		0

Jan Feb Mar Apr May Jun Jul Aug Sep Oct Nov Dec

Rainfall Chart
The chart gives figures for the whole state. The north-south climatic divide means that, for example, October is the driest month in the Panhandle but the wettest in the Keys. The rule is that southern Florida is wetter than the north in summer (when short, sharp downpours are the norm), while in winter it's the reverse.

FALL

T HE TEMPERATURES begin to cool, and although storms are still a threat, the weather is pleasant. The fall months are usually quiet: the beaches, attractions, and highways are all much less crowded.

Thanksgiving, on the fourth Thursday in November, is the highlight of fall for many, when families come together to eat turkey and pumpkin pie. It is followed by the biggest shopping day of the year and commercially launches the countdown to Christmas.

SEPTEMBER

Las Olas Art Fair *(early Sep)*, Fort Lauderdale. Las Olas Boulevard is the main drag for this street fair offering art displays, tasty food, and music.
St. Augustine's Founding Anniversary *(Saturday nearest 8th)*. This period-dress reenactment of the Spanish landing in 1565 is held near the spot where the first settlers stepped off their ships.

Sleek craft on display at the Fort Lauderdale Boat Show

OCTOBER

Destin Fishing Rodeo *(all month)*. The "World's Luckiest Fishing Village" welcomes hordes of competitive anglers for this frenzy of fishing that includes a two-day seafood festival in the first week.
Jacksonville Jazz Festival *(mid-Oct)*. This is an unusual combination of art and craft exhibitions mixed with three days of international jazz stars competing and performing.

Boggy Bayou Mullet Festival *(mid-Oct)*, Valparaiso and Niceville. These twin cities near Fort Walton Beach celebrate the local fish with fine food, arts, and entertainment.
Fort Lauderdale Boat Show *(late Oct)*. The largest in-water boat show in the world draws yachting enthusiasts to four separate city locations.
Fantasy Fest *(last week)*, Key West. This wild, week-long Halloween celebration features gay festivities, masked balls, a costume contest, and lively street processions.
Johns Pass Seafood Festival *(last weekend)*, Madeira Beach. This popular festival attracts seafood lovers to Johns Pass Village *(see p238)*.
Guavaween *(last Saturday)*, Tampa. This zany Halloween parade pokes fun at the life and history of the city, especially at an early attempt to grow guavas in the area.

NOVEMBER

Apalachicola Seafood Festival *(first weekend)*. The fishing fleet is blessed, net-making lessons are given, and oyster-shucking-and-eating contests are held at Florida's oldest and biggest seafood festival.
Orange Bowl Festival *(early Nov–late Feb)*, Miami. This youth festival presents over 20 sports and cultural events.
Festival of the Masters *(second weekend)*, Walt Disney World. Artists from across the country show their work in Downtown Disney *(see p162)*.
Miami Book Fair International *(mid-Nov)*. Publishers, authors, and bookworms congregate in downtown Miami for this cultural highlight.

Costumed revelers out on the streets for Key West's Fantasy Fest

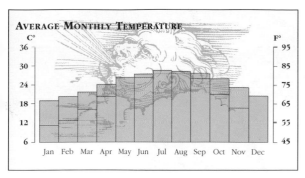

AVERAGE MONTHLY TEMPERATURE

C°		F°
36		95
30		85
24		75
18		65
12		55
6		45

Jan Feb Mar Apr May Jun Jul Aug Sep Oct Nov Dec

Temperature Chart
This chart gives the average temperature in Miami and Jacksonville, the higher level being the figure for Miami. In the north, even in winter, the evenings are only mildly chilly, and snow is very rare, although it's too cold for swimming. In southern Florida, the hot summer temperatures are exacerbated by the high humidity.

WINTER

WINTER MONTHS are full of excitement in anticipation of Christmas and New Year's. The flood of "snowbirds" from the north intensifies. The celebrities arrive too, some to relax, others to perform during the state's busiest entertainment season. The crowds multiply at Walt Disney World and the Magic Kingdom is at its most colorful.

DECEMBER

Winterfest Boat Parade
(early Dec), Fort Lauderdale. Boats decked with lights cruise the Intracoastal Waterway in a magical nighttime display.
King Orange Jamboree Parade *(Dec 31)*, Miami. Huge event to herald the New Year, parodied the previous night by the outrageous King Mambo Strut in Coconut Grove.

Santa on the Intracoastal Waterway for a sunny Florida Christmas

JANUARY

Orange Bowl *(New Year's Day)*, Miami. Fans of college football flock to the eponymous stadium *(see p95)* for the big postseason game.
Greek Epiphany Day *(Jan 6)*, Tarpon Springs. Ceremonies, feasts, and music at the Greek Orthodox Cathedral *(see p237)*.

Pirates arriving for mock invasion at Tampa's annual Gasparilla Festival

Art Deco Weekend *(mid Jan)*, Miami Beach. Take tours and dance to 1930s music at this street party in the stunning Art Deco district *(see pp58–65)*.

FEBRUARY

Gasparilla Festival *(second Monday)*, Tampa. A boisterous party, with boat parades and locals in appropriate dress, in memory of the pirates who ravaged the coast *(see p249)*.
Speed Weeks *(first three weeks)*, Daytona Beach. These motor races build up to the famous Daytona 500 on the final Sunday *(see pp204–205)*.
Florida Citrus Festival *(mid-Feb)*, Winter Haven near Orlando. The citrus harvest is honored at this country fair.
Coconut Grove Arts Festival *(mid-Feb)*, Miami *(see p82)*. This avant-garde art show is one of the country's largest.
Florida State Fair *(mid-Feb)*, Tampa. Carnival rides, corn on the cob, big-name performers, and even alligator wrestling can be enjoyed at this big fair.

Miami Film Festival *(mid-Feb)*. The Film Society of America hosts a broad array of films over ten days *(see p337)*.
Swamp Cabbage Festival *(last weekend)*, La Belle, east of Fort Myers. This celebration features rodeos and dancing, and you can sample delicacies made from the edible heart of the honored state tree.

PUBLIC HOLIDAYS

New Year's Day (Jan 1)
Martin Luther King Day (3rd Mon, Jan)
President's Day (3rd Mon, Feb)
Memorial Day (last Mon, May)
Independence Day (Jul 4)
Labor Day (1st Mon, Sep)
Columbus Day (2nd Mon, Oct)
Election Day (1st Tue, Nov)
Veterans Day (Nov 11)
Thanksgiving (4th Thu, Nov)
Christmas Day (Dec 25)

The History of Florida

AT FIRST GLANCE, Florida appears to be a state with little history, but behind the state's modern veneer lies a long and rich past, molded by many different nationalities and cultures.

Until the 16th century, Florida supported a large indigenous population. Many of its tribes had complex political and religious systems that demonstrated a high degree of social organization. However, after Ponce de León first sighted "La Florida" in 1513, Spanish colonization quickly decimated the Indians through warfare and disease. French explorers troubled the Spanish initially, but a real threat to their control came only much later. In 1742 English colonists from Georgia defeated the Spanish, and thus acquired Florida through the Treaty of Paris in 1763. Florida was returned to Spain in 1783, but numerous boundary disputes and the War of 1812 soon followed; Andrew Jackson captured Pensacola from the British in 1819, and the official US occupa-

Henry Flagler

tion took place in 1821. American attempts to remove the Seminoles from Florida led to conflicts that lasted for over 65 years. Soon after the Seminole Wars came the Civil War, by the end of which, in 1865, the state was in ruins. But Florida soon recovered. Entrepreneurs like Henry Flagler built a network of railroads and luxurious hotels that attracted wealthy tourists from the north. Tourism flourished during the early 20th century and by 1950 had become Florida's top industry.

As the state opened up, agriculture expanded and migrants flooded in. The recession of the 1920s and 1930s was only a short hiatus in the state's growth, and between 1940 and 1990 the population increased sixfold.

Today, Florida is home to a sizeable Hispanic community, with a strong Cuban presence as well as many other ethnic groups. Economic inequalities have led to social problems and the state's relentless urbanization has put a severe strain on the environment, but Florida is still booming.

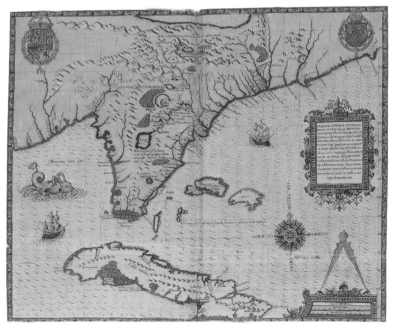

Theodore de Brys' 16th-century map of Florida, one of the earliest in existence

◁ An early postcard from Florida, a popular vacation destination in the 1920s

Prehistoric Florida

Stone tool

FLORIDA WAS ONCE part of the volcanic chain that formed the Caribbean islands. This eroded over millions of years and was submerged. When the land finally reemerged, Florida was connected to North America.

Humans first arrived in Florida after the last Ice Age and formed distinct tribes. Some developed from nomadic hunter-gatherer societies to ones with permanent settlements along Florida's bountiful rivers and rich seaboard. A high degree of religious and political organization was common to many groups by around AD 1000 and was manifested especially in the building of burial and temple mounds.

EARLY TRIBAL CONTACTS

— *Areas in contact*

Human Effigy Vessel
This painted, ceramic burial urn dates from AD 400–600. Such vessels were often very ornate and usually depicted birds and animals. "Kill holes" were often made in the pots to allow the soul of the pottery to accompany that of the dead.

Pots were often incised. This added to the surface area of the vessel and increased its resistance to heat, as well as making it more aesthetically pleasing.

Copper headdress plates were made of hammered copper that came from as far away as the Great Lakes.

FLORIDA'S PREHISTORIC TRIBES

Agriculture and burial mounds, traits shared with groups elsewhere in the southeast US, were associated with the Timucua and other tribes in north Florida. Southern tribes, such as the Calusa, and Tequesta, left a legacy of wood carvings and midden mounds, which indicate a diet based on fish and shellfish.

MARCO ISLAND'S SECRET

Calusa wood carving

In 1896, a unique discovery was made on Marco Island *(see p270)*. Many Calusa Indian artifacts of perishable organic material were found perfectly preserved in swampland. However, once out of the protective mangrove sludge the objects quickly crumbled away. Today, sadly just one or two of these extraordinary pieces, which include ceremonial items such as carvings and masks, survive.

Fired Bowl
Made c. AD 800, this ceramic bowl probably had a ceremonial use. Markings help archaeologists to identify the pot's makers.

TIMELINE

c. 10,000 Palaeo-Indian stone tools are first made by Florida's earliest inhabitants

Atlatls *or throwing sticks, part of the tool-kit after 6000 BC*

10,000 BC	9000 BC	8000 BC	7000 BC	6000 BC	5000 B

The skeleton of a mastodon, an Ice Age animal that once lived in Florida

c. 7500 The temperature rises and people start to hunt smaller animals like deer and include more plant foods in their diet

c. 5000 The first semipermanent settlements are built along the St. Johns River, creating large midden mounds

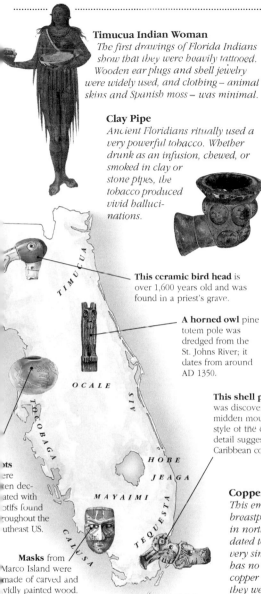

Timucua Indian Woman
The first drawings of Florida Indians show that they were heavily tattooed. Wooden ear plugs and shell jewelry were widely used, and clothing – animal skins and Spanish moss – was minimal.

Clay Pipe
Ancient Floridians ritually used a very powerful tobacco. Whether drunk as an infusion, chewed, or smoked in clay or stone pipes, the tobacco produced vivid hallucinations.

This ceramic bird head is over 1,600 years old and was found in a priest's grave.

A horned owl pine totem pole was dredged from the St. Johns River; it dates from around AD 1350.

This shell pendant was discovered in a midden mound. The style of the carved detail suggests a Caribbean connection.

ts
ere
en dec-
ated with
otifs found
roughout the
utheast US.

Masks from Marco Island were made of carved and vidly painted wood.

WHERE TO SEE PREHISTORIC FLORIDA

Historical museums all over the state contain items relating to Florida's prehistory. Most notable is the Natural History Museum in Gainesville (*see p209*). Temple mound sites at Crystal River and Fort Walton Beach both have museums attached – Crystal River (*p236*) is in a particularly attractive setting.

Crystal River's *Indian complex consists of well-preserved midden and temple mounds.*

Copper Goods
This embossed copper breastplate, discovered in north Florida and dated to around AD 1300, is very similar to one from Georgia. Florida has no copper reserves, the presence of copper objects is thought to indicate that they were once traded as prestige goods.

c. **1000** Northern Florida sees a shift from a basic hunter-gatherer economy to one of cultivation. The settled communities develop more complex societies, and the first burial mounds are built

c. **1000** Political systems and religious practices develop, and temple mounds are built. Increased contact with tribal groups outside Florida

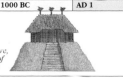

000 BC	3000 BC	2000 BC	1000 BC	AD 1	AD 1000

c. **3000** From this time, Florida enjoys a climate that is similar to today's

c. **2000** The first crude pottery appears in Florida

A temple structure, built on top of a burial mound

c. **800** First evidence of corn crops being grown in north Florida

Spanish Florida

SPANISH FLEET SEA ROUTES

— *Sea routes*

AFTER JUAN PONCE DE LEON first sighted Florida in 1513, several Spanish conquistadors attempted unsuccessfully to find gold and colonize the region. The French were the first to establish a fort in 1564, but it was soon destroyed by the Spanish: the Gulf Stream carried Spanish treasure ships from other New World colonies past Florida's coast, and it was vital that "La Florida" not fall into enemy hands. The Spanish introduced Christianity, horses, and cattle. European diseases, in addition to the brutality of the conquistadors, decimated local Indian populations. Britain, eager to expand her American colonies, led several raids into Florida in the 1700s, in an attempt to supplant Spanish rule.

Spanish crucifix

El Adelantado IUAN PONCE Descubridor de la Florida.

Ribault's column, erected in 1562 *(see p193)*, marked the French claim to north Florida.

Juan Ponce de León
While searching for gold, Ponce de León found land that he named Pascua Florida, *after the Feast of Flowers (Easter).*

Corn, native to Florida, was a staple crop for the Indians.

FORT MOSE

Runaway slaves escaping the harsh conditions in the British Carolinas fled to Florida, where, as in other Spanish colonies, slaves enjoyed certain rights. The Spanish saw the advantage of helping Britain's enemies and in 1738 created Fort Mose, near the garrison town of St. Augustine, for the runaways. This fort, with its own militia and businesses, is regarded as North America's first independent black community.

Black militiaman in the Spanish colonies

FLORIDA'S FIRST SETTLEMEN
The Huguenot René de Laudonnière founded "La Caroline," Florida's first successful European settlement, in 156 Another Frenchman, Le Moyne, painte the Indians greeting the colonizers.

TIMELINE

1513 Ponce de León discovers Florida. He tries to establish a Spanish colony eight years later, but is unsuccessful

Hernando de Soto's signature

1622 The Spanish ships *Atocha* and *Santa Margarita* sink during a hurricane

c.1609 *A History of the Conquest of Florida* is published by Garcilasso Inca del Vega

1520	1540	1560	1580	1600	1620

1528 Pánfilo de Narváez lands in Tampa Bay in search of El Dorado, the land of gold

1539 Hernando de Soto arrives at Tampa Bay with 600 men, but he dies by the Mississippi River three years later

1566 The Jesuits arrive in Florida

1565 Pedro Menéndez de Avilés founds San Agustín (St. Augustine) after defeating the French

Cross-section of the Atocha

Hernando de Soto
De Soto was the most ruthless of the conquistadors. His search for gold led to the massacre of many Indians; only a third of his own party survived.

Silver and Gold Hair Ornament
Indian artifacts made of precious metals fueled the Spanish myth of El Dorado. In fact, the metals came from Spanish wrecks.

René de Laudonnière surveys the offerings of the Indians.

Athore, the chief of the Timucua, shows the French colonizers his tribe worshiping at Ribault's column.

WHERE TO SEE SPANISH FLORIDA

In St. Petersburg, the De Soto National Memorial marks the spot where de Soto landed (*see p253*). A reconstruction of Fort Caroline (*p193*) lies just outside Jacksonville. However, the best place to see the Spanish legacy is in St. Augustine (*pp196–9*) and its imposing Castillo de San Marcos (*pp200–201*).

Nuestra Senora de la Leche *is a shrine in St. Augustine founded by de Avilés in 1565.*

Sir Francis Drake
Spain's power in the New World colonies worried the British. Drake, an English buccaneer, burned down St. Augustine in 1586.

Codice Osune
This 16th-century manuscript depicts members of Tristan de Luna's expedition to Florida. In 1559, a hurricane destroyed his camp at Pensacola Bay, defeating his attempts at colonization.

1670 The Treaty of Madrid defines the Spanish claim to the New World

The pirate Blackbeard's flag

1718 Blackbeard, who terrorized the east coast of Florida, is killed off North Carolina

1740 The British, based in Georgia, besiege the Castillo de San Marcos

1763 Under the Treaty of Paris, Britain gets Florida and returns recently captured Cuba to Spain

| 1640 | 1660 | 1680 | 1700 | 1720 | 1740 | 1760 |

1687 The first eight slaves fleeing the British plantations in the Carolinas arrive in Florida

1702 The British raze St. Augustine to the ground

1693 The Spanish establish Pensacola, which is permanently settled five years later

Castillo de San Marcos, St. Augustine

1756 Castillo de San Marcos is completed

The Fight for Florida

Hide boot

A PLENTIFUL SUPPLY of hides and furs, and the opportunity to expand the plantation system, attracted the British to Florida. After taking control in 1763, they divided the colony in two. Florida was subsidized by Britain and so stayed loyal during the American Revolution. However, Spain regained West Florida in 1781 and then East Florida was handed back two years later. American slaves fled to Florida creating antagonism between Spain and the US. This was exacerbated by Indian raids to the north and an Indian alliance with the runaway slaves. General Andrew Jackson invaded Spanish Florida, captured Pensacola, and even occupied West Florida, thus provoking the First Seminole War.

BRITISH FLORIDA 1764–83

☐ *East Florida*

▨ *West Florida*

Fort George was the main British fortification at Pensacola.

A drummer kept the marching beat, and led soldiers into battle.

The Spanish Caste System
Few Spanish women came to the colonies, so Spanish men often took black or Indian wives. A hierarchical caste system emerged – with those of pure Spanish blood at the top.

Brazier
Used for warmth during northern Florida winters, a brasero *could also smoke out mosquitos in summer.*

THE CAPTURE OF PENSACOLA

In 1781, after a month-long siege, the Spaniard Bernardo de Gálvez defeated the British and captured Pensacola for Spain. His victory undoubtedly helped the bid for independence made by the American colonies.

TIMELINE

1776 American Revolution leaves Britain's reserves heavily depleted, and British loyalists begin to abandon Florida

1783 Under the Second Treaty of Paris, Britain recognizes American independence, gains the Bahamas and Gibraltar, and returns Florida to the Spanish, who start to colonize it in earnest

1785–1821 Several Spanish-American border disputes occur

| 1765 | 1770 | 1775 | 1780 | 1785 |

British soldier in the American Revolution

1781 Under de Gálvez, the Spanish land at Pensacola and capture West Florida

1782 US Congress chooses the bald eagle as the emblem of the new republic

National emblem

General Jackson

An ambitious soldier, Andrew Jackson led many raids into Florida and eventually conquered it. His successes made him the ideal candidate to become Florida's first American governor in 1821 and, later, the seventh US president.

William Bartram's Illustrations

In 1765, William Bartram was appointed the royal botanist in America. He documented Florida's wildlife and her indigenous peoples.

Bernardo de Gálvez, the 27-year-old Spanish governor of Louisiana, was wounded in action in the battle for Pensacola.

Political Cartoon

This cartoon shows the horse America throwing his master. British loyalists in East Florida were dismayed by the loss of the Colonies after 1783, and soon chose to leave Florida.

WHERE TO SEE THE FIGHT FOR FLORIDA

The Kingsley Plantation *(see p193)* near Jacksonville is the state's oldest surviving plantation house. Pensacola's historic Seville District *(p216)* was laid out by the British during their occupation, and St. Augustine *(pp196–9)* contains several buildings dating from this era; they include the British Government House, and the charming Ximenez-Fatio house, from the second period of Spanish rule.

***Kingsley Plantation** occupies a lovely setting at the mouth of the St. Johns River.*

The Slave Trade

Slavery fueled the plantation system. The journey from Africa to America could take months, and slaves were so tightly packed on board ship that many died en route.

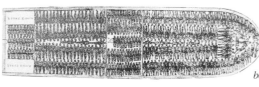

1803 The US buys Louisiana and pushes east, creating Florida's present western boundary. The US claims West Florida

1800 Spain cedes West Florida's Louisiana territories to the French

1808 A law banning the slave trade is enacted by the US Congress, but it is widely ignored

Slave manacles

1817 First Seminole War begins

1795	1800	1805	1810	1815

1795 Spain cedes territory north of the 31st parallel to the US

The Patriots of East Florida's flag

1812 American patriots capture Amelia Island, demanding that the US annex East Florida from the Spanish. Their attempt fails but instills the feeling that Florida should belong to America

1819 To settle Spain's $5-million debt to the US, all Spanish territories east of the Mississippi (including Florida) are ceded to the US

Antebellum Florida

Pelican, by Audubon

AFTER FLORIDA BECAME PART of the US in 1821, American settlement proceeded apace, and the plantation system was firmly established in north Florida. The settlers wanted good land, so the Federal government tried to remove all Indians to west of the Mississippi; resulting conflicts developed into the Second and Third Seminole Wars. After Abraham Lincoln, an opponent of slavery, was elected president in 1860, Florida became the third state to secede from the Union. During the ensuing Civil War it saw little action; Florida's chief role was to supply food to the Confederates, especially beef and salt.

INDIAN LANDS 1823–32

☐ *Indian reservation land*

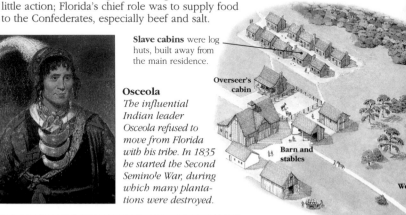

Slave cabins were log huts, built away from the main residence.

Overseer's cabin

Barn and stables

We

Osceola
The influential Indian leader Osceola refused to move from Florida with his tribe. In 1835 he started the Second Seminole War, during which many plantations were destroyed.

UNCLE TOM'S CABIN

In 1852, Harriet Beecher Stowe, a religious northerner who spent her later years in Florida, published a novel that helped to change the face of America. *Uncle Tom's Cabin* is a tale about a slave who, having rescued a white child, is sold to a sadistic master and is eventually flogged to death. It was hugely successful and furthered the cause of the antislavery lobby. During the Civil War, President Lincoln joked that Mrs. Stowe was the "little woman who started this big war."

135,000 SETS, 270,000 VOLUMES SOLD.

UNCLE TOM'S CABIN

FOR SALE HERE.

The Greatest Book of the Age. **Poster for *Uncle Tom's Cabin***

Cotton
The principal cash crop on plantations was cotton. It required intensive labor and the work was grueling – especially picking the cotton off the spiny bushes.

TIMELINE

1821 Jackson becomes governor of the territory of Florida

1823 Treaty of Moultrie Creek requires the Seminoles to move from north to central Florida

1832 Under the Treaty of Payne's Creek, 15 Seminole chiefs cede their land in Florida to the US and agree to move west

1835 Second Seminole War begins

Early horse-drawn trai

1820	1825	1830	1835	1840

Osceola refusing to sign 1832 treaty

c.1824 The Indian village of Talasi is chosen as the site of the new state capital and is renamed Tallahassee

1832 JJ Audubon, the naturalist, visits Key West

1842 Second Seminole War ends

1829 General Jackson becomes President of the US

1836 The first railroads in Florida begin operating

Paddlesteamer
During the Seminole and Civil Wars, steamboats were used to transport troops and supplies to the interior.

Chief Billy Bowlegs
In 1855, a group of surveyors pillaged Indian land. Chief Billy Bowlegs retaliated, starting the Third Seminole War. He surrendered in 1858; however, other Seminoles retreated into the Everglades.

...odwood House was built ...a grand style that befitted its wealth and importance within the local community.

WHERE TO SEE ANTEBELLUM FLORIDA

Gamble Plantation *(see p252)* sheds light on the lifestyle of a wealthy plantation owner, while at Bulow Plantation *(p202)* and Indian Key *(p280)* you can see the ruins of communities destroyed by the Seminoles. The Museum of Science and Discovery *(p194)* in Jacksonville contains Civil War artifacts, including some from the US army steamboat *Maple Leaf*. Key West's East Martello Tower *(p286)* and Fort Zachary *(p288)*, and Fort Clinch *(p192)*, in the northeast, are fine examples of 19th-century forts.

The East Martello Tower *was built by Union forces to defend Key West's Atlantic coast.*

Laundry

Privy

Guest House

...pring ...ouse

The kitchen was in a separate building because of the risk of fire.

Battle of Olustee
In February 1864, Union forces, including two Negro regiments, were defeated by Confederate troops in the northeast. Some 10,000 men fought in the six-hour battle, 2,000 were injured and 300 died.

...LANTATION LIFE

...tebellum plantations such as Goodwood *(see p229)*, ...constructed here, were almost self-sufficient. They ...d their own laws, and some housed over 200 ...ves who tended cotton, corn, and other crops.

---

345 On July 4 Florida becomes the 27th state ...join the United States of America. The ...pitol building in Tallahassee is completed

1848 John Gorrie invents an ice-making machine

1855 Third Seminole War begins; three years later 163 Indians surrender (including Billy Bowlegs) and are forcibly removed from Florida

1861 Civil War begins

1865 The northern army is defeated at the Battle of Natural Bridge. The Civil War ends in the same year

...345	1850	1855	1860	1865

STATE OF FLORIDA

Florida's first state seal

1852 Harriet Beecher Stowe publishes the antislavery epic, *Uncle Tom's Cabin*

1860s Scottish merchants found Dunedin on Florida's west coast

Confederate Civil War bond

Florida's Golden Age

AFTER THE CIVIL WAR Florida's economy was devastated, but its fine climate and small population meant it was a land ripe for investment. The railroad barons Henry Flagler and Henry Plant forged their lines down the east and west coasts of Florida during the late 1880s and '90s, and tourists followed in increasing numbers, stimulating the economy. A diverse agricultural base also sheltered Florida from the depression of the 1890s that ravaged other cotton-producing states. Fortunes were made and fine mansions were built. Blacks were less fortunate; most lost the right to vote, Ku Klux Klan violence grew, and segregation was the norm.

José Martí, Cuban hero

GROWTH OF THE RAILROADS

— *Railroads by 1860*

— *Railroads by 1890*

— *Overseas Railroad by 1912*

Steamboat Tourism
Before the advent of the railroads, tourists explored Florida's interior by paddlesteamer. Steamboats plied scenic rivers such as the Oklawaha and the St. Johns.

Cigar labels were miniature works of art, and the design would often depict a topographical scene. The cigar industry took off in Florida in the late 1800s.

Jacob Summerlin
After the Civil War, Jacob Summerlin, the "King of the Crackers" (see p18), made his fortune by selling beef to Spanish Cuba. His wild cattle were descended, ironically, from animals that had been introduced to Florida by the conquistadors.

GRAND HOTELS

Both Plant and Flagler built opulent palaces for rich tourists who used the railroads to escape the northern winters; these "snowbirds" would spend the winter season in style, in towns like Tampa and St. Augustir

TIMELINE

A Ringling Brothers' circus act

1869 The first black Cabinet member is appointed as Secretary of State in Florida

1870 More than 100 blacks are killed by the Ku Klux Klan in Jackson County

1885 Vincente Ybor transfer his cigar industry to Tampa

1892 In the electio only 11 percent of black remain eligible to vo

1870	1875	1880	1885	18

1884 Ringling brothers set up their traveling circus

1891 The Cuban, José Martí, makes a speech in Tampa to drum up support for his independence movement

1868 Vote granted to all male American citizens aged 21 and over, including blacks

1870s Steamboats start to take tourists, as well as goods, into the interior of Florida

1886 Flagler starts construction of the Florida East Coast Railroad

Rail Travel
Many rich tourists had private railroad cars. Today Henry Flagler's is at his former Palm Beach home (see p120)

(see p120)

Where to See the Golden Age

St. Augustine *(see pp196–9)* boasts several of Flagler's buildings, including what is today the Lightner Museum. The Tampa Bay Hotel is now the Henry B. Plant Museum *(p244)*, and Fernandina has some fine examples of steamboat architecture *(p192)*. On Pigeon Key *(p282)* you'll find Flagler's Overseas Railroad construction camp.

Spanish-American War
When America joined Cuba's fight against Spain in 1898, Florida boomed. Thousands of troops converged on Tampa, Miami, and Key West, and money from the nation's coffers poured in to support the war effort.

__Flagler College__ in St. Augustine was once Henry Flagler's magnificent Ponce de Leon Hotel.

The Tampa Bay Hotel,
built by Henry Plant in 1891, operated as a hotel until 1932. It had 511 rooms, and during the Spanish-American War served as the officers' quarters.

Gilded Rocking Chair
Representative of the decorative excesses of the 19th century, this rocking chair from the Lightner Museum (see p199) is elaborately embellished with scrolls and swans.

(see p199)

The Birth of a Nation
On its release in 1915, this epic film provoked a resurgence of violence by the Ku Klux Klan in Florida.

e Hillsborough
ver and nearby
mpa Bay helped
n Tampa into one
the three largest
ulf ports by 1900.

Driving on the sand at Daytona Beach

1895	1900	1905	1910	1915

1895 Blossoming citrus groves are hit by the "Great Freeze." Julia Tuttle sends some orange blossoms to Flagler in Palm Beach to persuade him to continue his railroad to Miami

1905 The University of Florida is established at Gainesville

1918 Prohibition starts in Florida

1898 Teddy Roosevelt and his Rough Riders arrive in Tampa en route to fight in the Spanish-American War in Cuba

1912 Flagler steams into Key West

1903 Alexander Winton sets a 68-mph (109-km/h) land speed record on the hard sand at Daytona Beach

1915 Dredging doubles the size of Miami Beach

1916 Florida's cotton crop is wiped out by the boll weevil

orange blossom

Boom, Bust and Recovery

Early Pan Am poster

L IKE THE REST OF THE US, Florida saw times of both rapid growth and depression during the first half of the 20th century. Excited by the rampant development during the 1920s land boom, northerners poured in, many as "Tin Can Tourists" in their Model T Fords. Then, in 1926, three years before the Wall Street Crash, a real estate slump ruined many in the state. But economic recovery came earlier than in the rest of the US, with the the growth of tourism and the introduction of federal schemes; many unemployed fled to Florida from the north looking for work. During and after World War II, the state continued to prosper; in the 1950s it was boosted by the launch of the NASA space program.

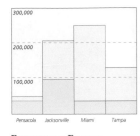

POPULATION FIGURES

☐ *1920*   ☐ *1950*

Land Boom
At the height of the boom, prime land could fetch $26,000 per acre. A great many northerners were bankrupted after unwittingly investing in swampland far from the waterfront.

Hurricane of 1926
On September 18 a hurricane hit South Florida, destroying 5,000 homes. Locals said the winds "blowed a crooked road straight."

THE AMERICAN DREAM IN FLORID
Florida's warm winter climate and economic upswing attracted floods of northerners. Many who first came as visitors returned to settle, a foreign immigrants also favored the state. It w a land of opportunity with rapid urban growt and industries that provided good jobs – even t young could expect a good standard of living

TIMELINE

1928 The Tamiami Trail between Tampa and Miami is officially opened

1929 The first commercial flight between Miami to Havana is made by Pan American World Airways

1931 Ernest Hemingway buys a house in Key West

1935 Hurricane destroys Flagler's Overseas Railroad

| 1920 | 1925 | 1930 | 1935 | 1 |

1931 Hialeah Park race track opens after pari-mutuel betting *(see p133)* is legalized

Horse race at Hialeah Park

1926 Florida land prices crash, two banks collapse, and a hurricane hits the southeast and the Everglades, devastating Miami

1939 Gangster Al Capone retires to an estate on Palm Island in Miami

Tin Can Tourists
Each winter, this new breed of tourist loaded up their cars and headed south. They stayed en masse in trailer parks sharing their canned food and enjoying the Florida sun.

WHERE TO SEE BOOMTIME FLORIDA
The Wolfsonian Museum *(see p65)* and Miami Beach's Art Deco buildings *(pp56–65)* shouldn't be missed. Mizner's whimsical Palm Beach legacy *(pp114–19)* is also worth visiting. Frank Lloyd Wright's college in Lakeland *(p252)* is very impressive; Henry Ford's winter home in Fort Myers *(p262)* is more modest.

Miami Beach contains a striking assortment of recently restored Art Deco buildings.

Zora Neale Hurston
Zora wrote about the lives of rural blacks. Her best known novel, Their Eyes Were Watching God, *was written in 1937.*

Roosevelt's New Deal
The president's New Deal, which allowed farmers to borrow money, helped Florida to recover from the Great Depression. Writers and photographers documented the policy's effects.

World War II
Florida was a training ground for many thousands of troops from 1941–5. War reduced tourism, but the camps helped the economy.

Citrus Industry
Florida became the largest citrus producer in the country, helping it to survive the Depression of the 1930s

---

947 President Truman opens Everglades National Park

Racing car in the Daytona 200

1954 The first span of the Sunshine Skyway bridge over Tampa Bay opens

1959 Lee Perry wins the first Daytona 200 race at the Daytona Speedway

1945	1950	1955	1960

1945 On December 5, the disappearance of Flight 19 starts the myth of the Bermuda Triangle

1958 The first Earth satellite, *Explorer I,* is launched from Florida after NASA chooses Cape Canaveral as the site of its satellite and rocket programs

942 In February, German U-boats torpedo a tanker just off the coast of Florida, in full view of bathers

NASA logo

The Sixties and Beyond

Theme park dolphin

Since 1960, FLORIDA has flourished. Tourism has expanded at an unprecedented rate, and countless hotels have been built to cater to all budgets. Theme parks like Walt Disney World and the Kennedy Space Center, home to NASA's space program, have brought both worldwide fame and crowds of visitors to the Sunshine State. The population has also grown rapidly, through migration from within the US and from abroad; modern Florida is home to many ethnic groups. African-Americans were helped by the Civil Rights movement in the 1960s, but today there is tension between them and the large Hispanic community, which includes the biggest Cuban population outside Cuba. The negative effects of development have led to increased steps to protect natural resources: conservation has become a major issue.

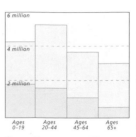

STATE POPULATION FIGURES

☐ 1960   ☐ 2000

Conservation
One way Floridians can support the conservation movement is by buying a special license plate. Money raised goes to the cause depicted.

The Cuban Exodus
Over 300,000 Cubans have fled to Florida since Castro took over Cuba in 1959. Early arrivals came on "freedom flights," but later refugees had to make the perilous trip by sea on flimsy rafts.

Steam forms when water floods the launchpad at blast off.

Martin Luther King
The Civil Rights movement reached Florida in the 1960s. Martin Luther King Jr., the movement's most prominent leader, was arrested while on a march in St. Augustine in 1964.

SPACE SHUTTLE
To replace the rockets used in Apollo missions, NASA designed a thermally protected space shuttle that wouldn't burn up on reentry into the earth's atmosphere. The first manned shuttle was launched in 1981 *(see pp186–7).*

TIMELINE

1964 Martin Luther King Jr. is arrested and imprisoned in St. Augustine

Alan Shepherd, NASA astronaut

1969 Apollo II is launched from Cape Canaveral. Buzz Aldrin and Neil Armstrong are the first men to walk on the moon

1973 Dade County is officially bilingual, and English-Spanish road signs are erected

1977 Snow falls on Miami in January

| 1965 | 1970 | 1975 |

1962 Cuban missile crisis

1961 Alan Shepherd becomes the first US man in space

1967 Orange juice becomes Florida's state beverage

1971 The Magic Kingdom, Walt Disney's first venture in Florida, opens in Orlando at a cost of $700 million

1976 Florida the first US s to restore th death penal

Cinderella Castle, in the Magic Kingdom

The external tank is the only part of the shuttle that is not reused.

Miami Vice
Miami has a reputation for crime and violence. This was graphically portrayed in the 1980s' TV show, Miami Vice.

Naturalization
Becoming a US citizen is the dream of many immigrants. Mass ceremonies see thousands pledge an oath of allegiance together.

Blast off catapults the shuttle into orbit. About 7.3 million lbs (3.3 million kg) of thrust is produced.

Florida's Elderly
Just under 20 percent of Florida's population is over 65 years old. Many retirees are attracted to the state by its low taxes and easy, outdoors lifestyle.

WHERE TO SEE MODERN FLORIDA

Florida has plenty of fine modern architecture, from the skyscrapers in downtown Miami *(see pp68–73)* and Jacksonville *(see p194)* to the Florida Aquarium in Tampa *(see p248)*. To see a more nostalgic approach to modern architecture, visit Seaside in the Panhandle *(see p222)*.

Downtown Miami's *modern skyscrapers create a distinctive and impressive city skyline.*

Caribbean Cruises
Tourism is big business in Florida, and cruises in state-of-the-art ships are an increasingly popular vacation choice.

0 125,000 Cubans arrive in Florida in the Mariel boatlift, which begun by Fidel Castro and lasts for five months

1981 The maiden voyage of the Space Shuttle is launched

1990 General Noriega, the former ruler of Panama, faces drugs charges in Miami

1992 Hurricane Andrew wreaks havoc in south Florida

George Bush

2000 George Bush wins controversial presidential elections

| 0 | 1985 | 1990 | 1995 | 2000 |

Key West itself the Republic" one week

Symbol of the Conch Republic

1986 The space shuttle *Challenger* explodes, killing all seven crew members

1993 The Task Force on Tourist Safety is created

1994 Another influx of Cubans arrives in Florida

1998 Worst tornado storm in Florida's history kills 42 and injures more than 250

MIAMI AREA
BY AREA

Miami at a Glance

MIAMI HAS BEEN CALLED the Magic City because what was merely a trading outpost a century ago now sprawls for 2,000 sq miles (5,200 sq km) and boasts a population of two million. Visitors are most likely to remember Miami for its fun-filled South Beach, for its lustrous beaches, and for the Latin and Caribbean culture that permeates daily life. Greater Miami is home to more than two million residents, and it draws close to nine million visitors each year. As in any urban area, safety guidelines are important.

Little Havana, the original heart of the city's Cuban community, is Miami's most welcoming neighborhood. Life in the streets is fun, with domino games and buzzing cafés. (See pp74–5.)

The Biltmore Hotel epitomizes Coral Gables, the exclusive minicity developed during the 1920s real estate boom. Tales of celebrity guests and Mafia murders add to the mystique of the luxurious hotel. (See pp78–81.)

CORAL GABLES AND COCONUT GROVE
(see pp76–85)

The "International Villages" are clusters of ethnic architecture, from French to Chinese, hidden away along the shady streets of Coral Gables. A tour of them will provide a taste of Miami's loveliest suburb. (See pp78–9.)

Coconut Grove Village is a small, friendly area where the focus is on entertainment. Enjoy a relaxing amble or shop in the daytime, before heading for the restaurants and bars, which come to life in the evening. (See p82.)

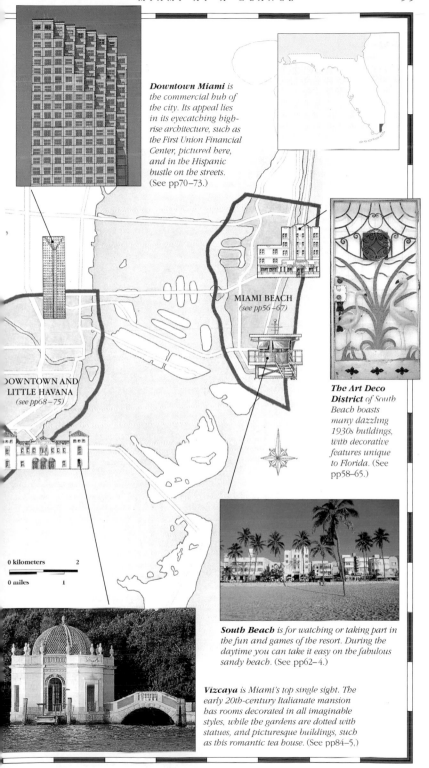

Downtown Miami is the commercial hub of the city. Its appeal lies in its eyecatching high-rise architecture, such as the First Union Financial Center, pictured here, and in the Hispanic bustle on the streets. (See pp70–73.)

MIAMI BEACH
(see pp56–67)

DOWNTOWN AND LITTLE HAVANA
(see pp68–75)

The Art Deco District of South Beach boasts many dazzling 1930s buildings, with decorative features unique to Florida. (See pp58–65.)

0 kilometers   2

0 miles   1

South Beach is for watching or taking part in the fun and games of the resort. During the daytime you can take it easy on the fabulous sandy beach. (See pp62–4.)

Vizcaya is Miami's top single sight. The early 20th-century Italianate mansion has rooms decorated in all imaginable styles, while the gardens are dotted with statues, and picturesque buildings, such as this romantic tea house. (See pp84–5.)

MIAMI BEACH

NOW OFTEN REFERRED TO as the American Riviera, Miami Beach was a sandbar accessible only by boat a century ago. It was the building of a bridge to the mainland in 1913 that enabled real estate investors like millionaire Carl Fisher to begin developing the island. The resort they created from nothing took off in the 1920s, becoming a spectacular winter playground. The devastating hurricane of 1926 and the 1929 Wall Street Crash signaled the end of the boom, but Miami Beach bounced back in the 1930s with the erection of hundreds of Art Deco buildings, only to decline again after World War II. In another metamorphosis, Miami Beach is on the rise once again. As a result of a spirited preservation campaign, South Beach (the southern part of Miami Beach) has been given a new lease of life. It boasts the world's largest concentration of Art Deco buildings, whose funky colors are no less arresting than the local population of body builders, fashion models, and drag queens. Anything goes in South Beach, where the mood veers between the chic and the bohemian, hence its nickname SoBe – after New York's hip SoHo district. The Art Deco hotels along Ocean Drive are everyone's favorite haunt but there are other diversions, from trendy shops to higher-brow art museums. The district north of SoBe tempts few people, but what the two areas do share is a superb sandy beach, unbroken mile after mile.

Sea horse on the façade of the Surfcomber Hotel

SIGHTS AT A GLANCE

Museums and Galleries
Bass Museum of Art **9**
Sanford L. Ziff Jewish Museum **3**
The Wolfsonian Foundation **5**

Streets and Neighborhoods
Central Miami Beach **10**
Collins and Washington Avenues **4**
Española Way **6**
Lincoln Road Mall **7**
Ocean Drive **1**

Beaches
The Beach **2**

Monuments
Holocaust Memorial **8**

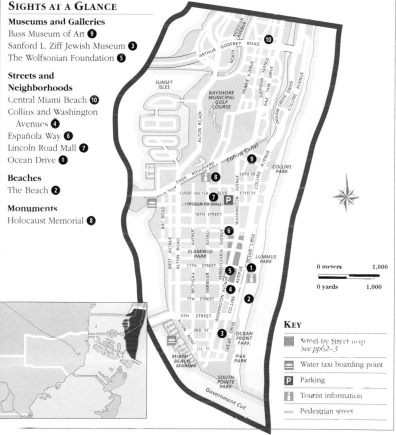

KEY

	Street-by-Street map *See pp62–3*
	Water taxi boarding point
P	Parking
i	Tourist information
	Pedestrian street

◁ **The Marlin Hotel, a classic South Beach establishment, illuminated in colorful neon**

Ocean Drive: Deco Style

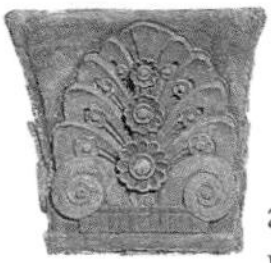
Deco detail, South Beach

THE CREAM of South Beach's Art Deco District, which consists of some 800 preserved buildings, is found on Ocean Drive. Its splendid array of buildings illustrates Miami's unique interpretation of the Art Deco style, which took the world by storm in the 1920s and '30s. Florida's version, often called Tropical Deco, is fun and jaunty. Motifs such as flamingos and sunbursts are common, and South Beach's seaside location inspired features more befitting an ocean liner than a building. Using inexpensive materials, architects managed to create an impression of stylishness for what were, in fact, very modest hotels. The best of the buildings along Ocean Drive are illustrated here and on pages 60–61.

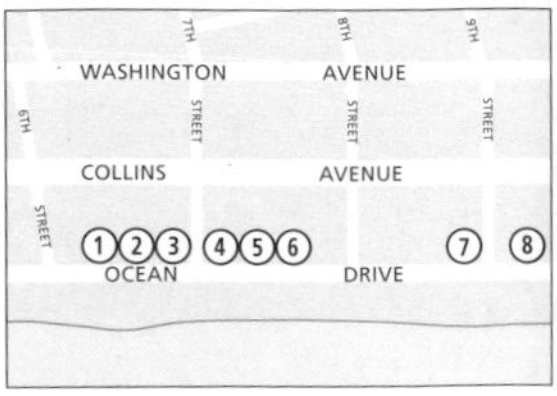

OCEAN DRIVE: 6TH TO 9TH STREETS

White, blue, and green were popular colors in the 1930s and '40s; they echo Miami's tropical vegetation and the ocean.

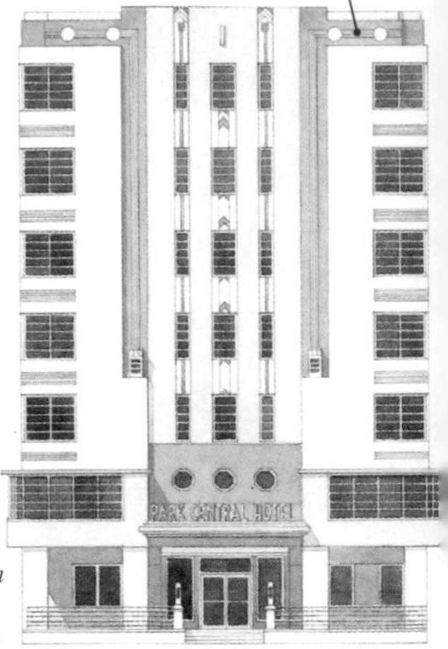

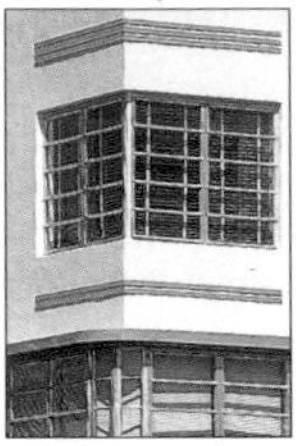
Windows are often continuous around corners.

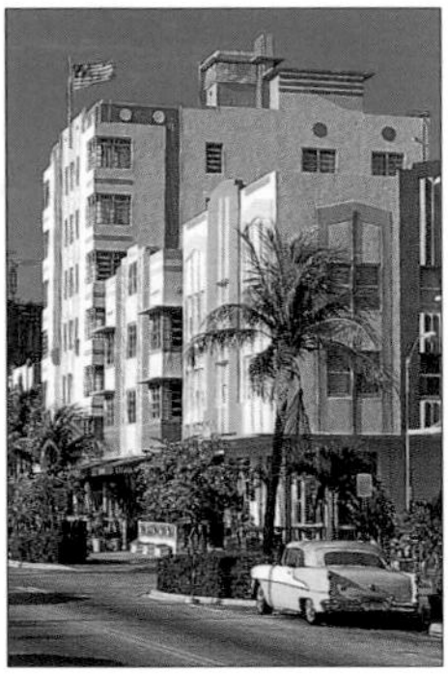
View along Ocean Drive

① ***Park Central*** *(1937)*
Henry Hohauser, the most famous architect to work in Miami, designed this hotel. It has fine etched windows.

Angular edges exemplify the influence of Cubism.

Bands of windows give plenty of light and, when open, encourage the circulation of cooling sea breezes.

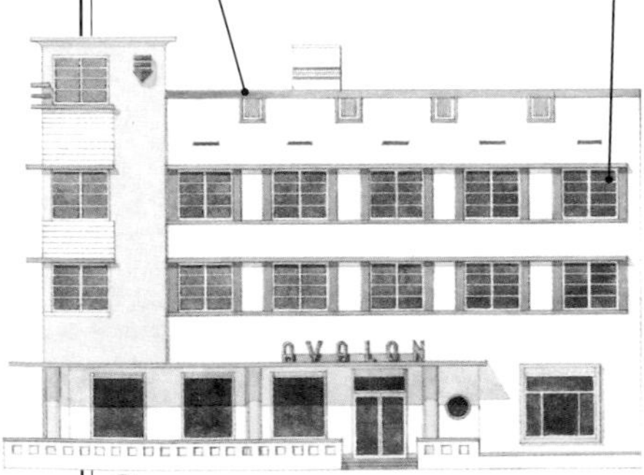

④ ***Avalon*** *(1941)*
The Avalon is a fine example of Streamline Moderne. The lack of ornamentation and the asymmetrical design are typical, as is the emphasis on horizontal as opposed to vertical lines.

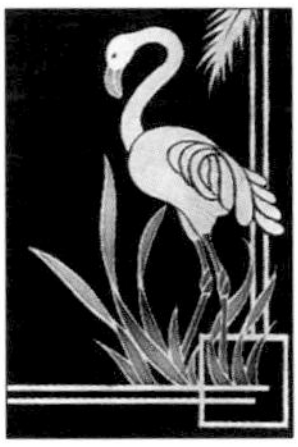
A flamingo is etched into glass doors in the Beacon's lobby.

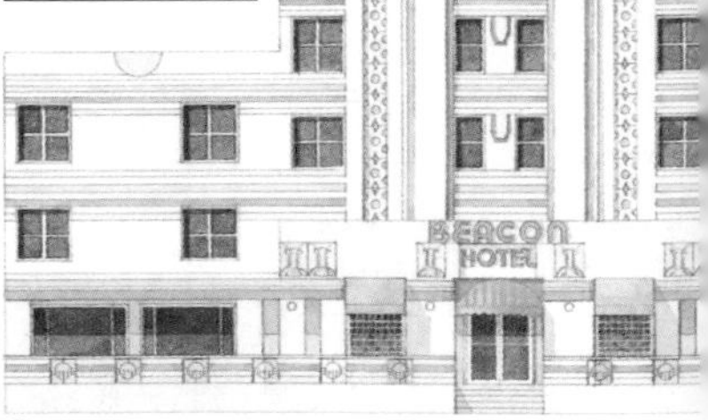

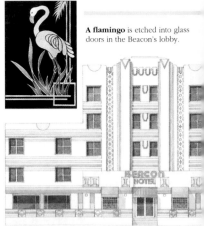

⑤ ***Beacon*** *(1936)*
The traditional abstract decoration above the ground floor windows of the Beacon has been brightened by a contemporary color scheme, an example of Leona Horowitz's Deco Dazzle (see p65).

ART DECO: FROM PARIS TO MIAMI

The Art Deco style emerged following the 1925 Exposition Internationale des Arts Décoratifs et Industriels Modernes in Paris. Traditional Art Deco combined all kinds of influences, from Art Nouveau's flowery forms and Egyptian imagery to

Deco-style postcard of the Avalon Hotel

the geometric patterns of Cubism. In 1930s America, Art Deco buildings reflected the belief that technology was the way forward, absorbing features that embodied the new Machine Age and the fantasies of science fiction. Art Deco evolved into a style called Streamline Moderne, which dominates along Ocean Drive. Few buildings in South Beach stick to just one style. Indeed it is the creative mix of classic Art Deco details with streamlining and tropical motifs that has made the architecture along Ocean Drive unique.

The Berkeley Shore, behind Ocean Drive on Collins Avenue, has classic Streamline Moderne features such as this stepped parapet.

Color has been used to give the idea of vertical fluting.

Circles, as decoration or as windows, were inspired by the portholes used in ship design.

The lobby of the Majestic has splendid brass elevator doors.

Bas-relief friezes are a recurrent decorative element on Ocean Drive façades.

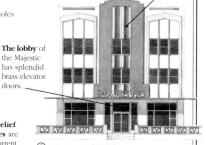

② **Imperial** (1939)
The design of the Imperial echoes that of the earlier Park Central next door.

③ **Majestic** (1940)
This hotel was the work of Albert Anis, the architect also responsible for the nearby Avalon and Waldorf hotels.

Racing stripes are typical of Streamline Moderne.

"Eyebrows" flat overhangs above the windows – are ideal for providing shade against the unrelenting Miami sun.

This ornamental lighthouse is one of the most evocative examples of Ocean Drive's "architecture for the seashore."

Neon lighting was frequently used to highlight hotel signs and architectural features, so that they could be enjoyed after dark.

Porthole windows

⑥ **Colony** (1935)
One of Henry Hohauser's finest hotels, the Colony has Ocean Drive's most famous neon sign and an interesting mural in the lobby.

⑦ **Waldorf Towers** (1937)
The maritime influence on the design of the Waldorf and some other hotels led to the coining of the phrase "Nautical Moderne."

Ocean Drive: Deco Style

THREE PRINCIPAL ART DECO styles exist in South
Beach: traditional Art Deco, the more futuristic
Streamline Moderne, and Mediterranean Revival,
which is derivative of French, Italian, and Spanish
architecture. The unusual injection of Mediterranean
Revival influences along Ocean Drive is noticeable
mainly between 9th and 13th streets.
Here too you will find some of South
Beach's most classic Art Deco
buildings.

**OCEAN DRIVE:
9TH TO 13TH STREETS**

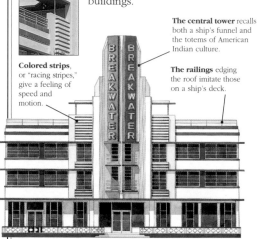

The central tower recalls
both a ship's funnel and
the totems of American
Indian culture.

Colored strips,
or "racing stripes,"
give a feeling of
speed and
motion.

The railings edging
the roof imitate those
on a ship's deck.

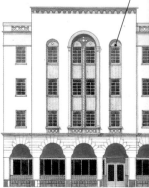

The window arches and
columned porch are evocative
of Mediterranean architecture.

⑧ *Breakwater (1939)*
*The Breakwater, by Anton Skislewicz, is a classic
Streamline Moderne hotel with its racing stripes and a
striking central tower. It also has one of Ocean Drive's
better interiors, with etched glass and a terrazzo floor.*

⑨ *Edison (1935)*
*Hohauser (see p58) experimented
here with Mediterranean Revivalism,
although he was preceded by the
architect of the nearby Adrian.*

The sign for the Leslie
hotel is simple, like the
building – in contrast
with the more exube-
rant Carlyle next door.

Flat roofs are the norm along
Ocean Drive, but these are
often broken by a tower or
other vertical projection.

**Corner
windows**

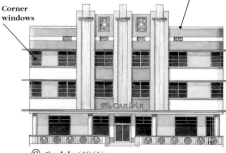

⑫ *Leslie (1937)*
*This classic Art Deco hotel's coat of
bright yellow paint is typical of the
color schemes currently in favor
along Ocean Drive (see p64).*

⑬ *Carlyle (1941)*
*With its three stories and three vertical columns,
the Carlyle makes use of the classic Deco divisions,
sometimes known as the "holy three." Most hotels
along Ocean Drive have three floors.*

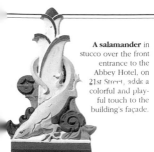

A salamander in stucco over the front entrance to the Abbey Hotel, on 21st Street, adds a colorful and playful touch to the building's façade.

PRESERVING SOUTH BEACH

The campaign to save the Art Deco architecture of South Beach began in 1976, when Barbara Capitman (1920–90) set up the Miami Design Preservation League – at a time when much of the area was destined to disappear under a sea of high-rises. Three years later, one square mile (2.5 sq km) of South Beach became the first 20th-century district in the country's National Register of Historic Places. Battles still raged against developers throughout the 1980s and '90s, when candlelit vigils helped save some buildings.

Barbara Capitman in 1981

Vertical fluting occurs frequently along Ocean Drive.

"Eyebrow" overhangs shade the windows.

Terra-cotta tiles

Reinforced concrete was the most common building material used along Ocean Drive, with walls generally covered in stucco.

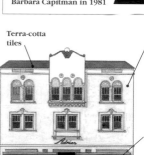

A veranda is a prerequisite for most Ocean Drive hotels.

⑩ **Clevelander** *(1938)*
This hotel's architect, Albert Anis, used classic Deco materials – such as glass blocks in the hotel's bar, now a top South Beach nightspot.

⑪ **Adrian** *(1934)*
With its subdued colors and chiefly Mediterranean inspiration, the Adrian stands out among neighboring buildings.

The frieze recalls the abstract designs of the Aztecs.

The terrazzo floor in the bar is a mix of stone chips and mortar – a cheap version of marble that brought style at minimal cost.

The corners of the building are beautifully rounded.

⑭ **Cardozo** *(1939)*
A late Hohauser work and Barbara Capitman's favorite hotel, this is a Streamline masterpiece, in which the detail of traditional Art Deco is replaced with curved sides, aerodynamic racing stripes, and other expressions of the modern age.

⑮ **Cavalier** *(1936)*
With its sharp edges, this traditional Art Deco hotel provides quite a contrast to the later Cardozo next door.

Street-by-Street: South Beach

Decoration on the Netherlands Hotel

The Art Deco district of South Beach, which runs from 6th to 23rd streets between Lenox Avenue and Ocean Drive, has attracted more and more visitors since the 1980s. Helped by the interest shown by celebrities such as Gloria Estefan and Michael Caine, the area has been transformed into one of the trendiest places in the States. For many visitors the Deco buildings serve merely as a backdrop for a hedonistic playground, where days are for sleeping, lying on the beach, or long workouts at the gym, evenings for dancing into the early hours. But whether your passions are social or architectural, the route shown can be enjoyed both during the day and at night – when a sea of neon enhances the party atmosphere.

The Old City Hall, a 1920s Mediterranean-style building, ended its service as city hall in 1977, but it remains a distinctive South Beach landmark, towering over the surrounding streets.

Wolfsonian Foundation
The Wolfsonian, with a striking Spanish Baroque-style relief around its main entrance, houses an excellent collection of fine and decorative arts 5

The Essex House Hotel, by Henry Hohauser *(see p58)*, has typical Deco features such as the rounded corner entry. Its lobby is also well worth a look.

The News Café is a favorite South Beach haunt *(see p330)*, open 24 hours a day and always buzzing. The sidewalk tables make it a prime spot for people-watching.

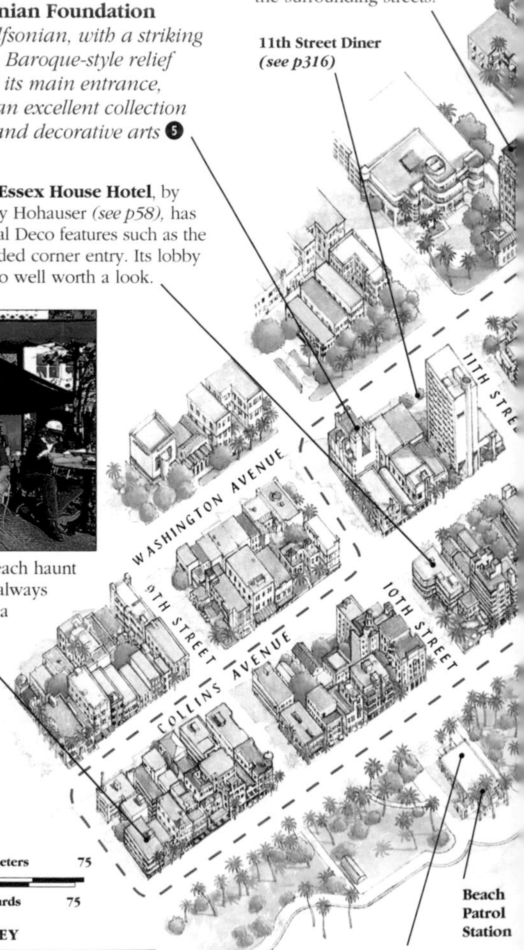

11th Street Diner ***(see p316)***

Beach Patrol Station

Art Deco Welcome Center

0 meters 75
0 yards 75

Key

– – Suggested route

Art Deco Tours

The Miami Design Preservation League offers 90-minute walking tours from the Art Deco Welcome Center (1001 Ocean Drive) Thursdays and Saturdays; bicycle tours every third Sunday morning; audio tours available daily; also the Art Deco Weekend (see p35). *For information call the Art Deco Welcome Center at (305) 672-2014.*

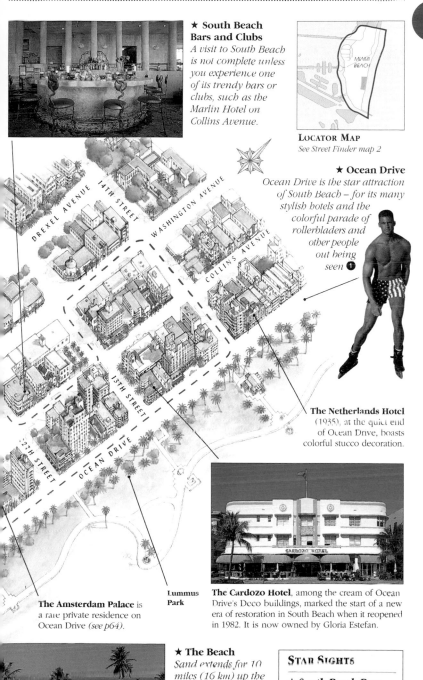

★ South Beach Bars and Clubs
A visit to South Beach is not complete unless you experience one of its trendy bars or clubs, such as the Marlin Hotel on Collins Avenue.

LOCATOR MAP
See Street Finder map 2

★ Ocean Drive
Ocean Drive is the star attraction of South Beach – for its many stylish hotels and the colorful parade of rollerbladers and other people out being seen ❶

The Netherlands Hotel
(1935), at the quiet end of Ocean Drive, boasts colorful stucco decoration.

The Cardozo Hotel, among the cream of Ocean Drive's Deco buildings, marked the start of a new era of restoration in South Beach when it reopened in 1982. It is now owned by Gloria Estefan.

Lummus Park

The Amsterdam Palace is a rare private residence on Ocean Drive *(see p64)*.

★ The Beach
Sand extends for 10 miles (16 km) up the coast. The beach changes atmosphere depending on where you are, being at its broadest and liveliest in South Beach ❷

STAR SIGHTS

★ **South Beach Bars and Clubs**

★ **Ocean Drive**

★ **The Beach**

South Beach

OCEAN DRIVE has the best known Deco buildings in South Beach. There are wonderful discoveries to be made on Collins and Washington Avenues too, as well as farther west in quieter residential streets, such as Lenox Avenue, where you'll find doors etched with flamingos and other Deco features.

South Beach, or SoBe, is best explored on foot since parking is difficult. If you don't wish to walk, join the locals on rollerblades or bicycles, both of which can be rented locally.

Ocean Drive ❶

Map 2 F3, F4. 🚌 C, H, K. ℹ️ 1001 Ocean Drive, (305) 672-2014.

SPENDING TIME at one of the bars or cafés on the waterfront is arguably the best way to experience Ocean Drive. It is effectively a catwalk for a constant procession of well-toned flesh and avant-garde outfits; even the street cleaners look cool in their pith helmets and white uniforms, while police officers in skintight shorts cruise past on mountain bikes. A more active

The Amsterdam Palace, one of Ocean Drive's few non-Deco buildings

exploration, however, needn't involve much more than a stroll to appreciate the finer points of Art Deco design; feel free to pop into hotel lobbies to admire the interior decor.

One building you cannot enter is the Mediterranean Revival Amsterdam Palace at No. 1114, built in 1930, which the late fashion designer Gianni Versace purchased in 1993 for $3.7 million. Nearby, behind the Art Deco Welcome Center, the Beach Patrol Station is a classic Nautical Moderne building *(see p59)*, with ship's railings along the top and porthole windows; it still functions as the base for local lifeguards.

There is little to lure you south of 6th Street, but from South Pointe Park, at the tip, you can sometimes get a good view of cruise liners entering Government Cut *(see p73)*.

The Beach ❷

Map 2. 🚌 FM, L, H, S.

MUCH OF THE SAND flanking Miami Beach was imported a few decades ago, and it continues to be replenished to counter coastal erosion. The vast stretches of sand are still impressive, however, and in tourist season people flock to swim and lie in the sun.

Up to 5th Street the beach is popular with surfers. The immense beach beyond is an extension of SoBe's persona, with colorful lifeguard huts and hordes of posing bathers. Alongside runs Lummus Park, where you still find Jewish folk chatting in Yiddish – evidence of the district's pre-gentrification era. Around 21st Street the clientele on the beach is predominantly gay.

Lifeguard huts in South Beach, with the colors and style to match Ocean Drive

Sanford L. Ziff Jewish Museum of Florida ❸

301 Washington Ave. **Map** 2 E4.
📞 (305) 672-5044. 🚌 FM, H, W.
🕐 10am–5pm Tue–Sun.
⊙ Jewish hols. 🈳 ♿ 🎫
W www.jewishmuseum.com

THIS MUSEUM occupies the first synagogue built in Miami Beach, in 1936. When large numbers of Jews arrived in the 1930s, they often faced fierce anti-Semitism – local hotels carried such signs as "No Jews or Dogs." Today, Jews are a vital, if aging, part of Miami Beach's community.

The once dilapidated synagogue reopened in 1995 as a museum and research center of Jewish life in Florida. With its colorful stained-glass windows and other Deco features, the building is almost as memorable as the exhibitions staged here.

The unmistakable tower of the Delano Hotel on Collins Avenue

Collins and Washington Avenues ❹

Map 2. 🚌 W, C, H, L. ℹ️ 1920 Meridian Ave, (305) 672-1270.

THESE STREETS are much scruffier than Ocean Drive: stores sell kinky clothes or tattoos, and there is an altogether more Hispanic flavor. However, some of South Beach's top nightclubs can be

CHANGING COLORS IN SOUTH BEACH

Art Deco buildings were originally very plain, typically in white with only the trim in bright colors; the paint never extended to the backs of the buildings since money was too tight in the 1930s to allow anything more than a jazzy façade. In the 1980s, designer Leonard Horowitz created the "Deco dazzle" by smothering some 150 buildings in color. Purists express dismay at this reinvention of the look of South Beach, but advocates argue that the Deco details are better highlighted than ever. Both color schemes are used these days.

Touching up the color on the Cardozo Hotel on Ocean Drive

found here (see p95), and there is an abundance of modest Art Deco buildings worth seeing. The Marlin Hotel, at 1200 Collins Avenue, is one of the district's finest Streamline buildings. It has been rejuvenated by Christopher Blackwell, founder of Island Records and the owner of several of Ocean Drive's best known buildings. Behind, at 1300 Washington Avenue, Miami Beach Post Office is one of SoBe's starker Deco creations; a mural inside shows the arrival of Ponce de León (see p40) and his battle with the native Indians.

North up Collins past Lincoln Road the buildings are interesting rather than beautiful. High-rise 1940s hotels such as the Delano and Ritz Plaza still bear Deco traits, particularly in their towers inspired by the futuristic fantasies of comic strips such as *Buck Rogers* and *Flash Gordon*. The strikingly non-Deco interior of the luxury Delano Hotel (see p297) is well worth seeing, with its billowing white drapes and original Gaudí

and Dali furniture. Just off Collins, on 21st Street, is a little-heralded cluster of hotels, notably the Governor, a chrome-trimmed beauty by Henry Hohauser (see p58).

The Wolfsonian Foundation ❺

1001 Washington Ave. **Map** 2 E3.
📞 (305) 531-1001. 🚌 C, H, K, W
🕐 11am–6pm Mon–Sat, noon–5pm Sun. ● Wed. 🎫 free entry 6–9pm on Thu. 🈳 ♿ 🎫
W www.wolfsonian.fiu.edu

THIS STURDY 1920s building (see p62) used to be the Washington Storage Company, where Miami's wealthy stored their valuables while traveling up north. Now it holds a superb collection of decorative and fine arts from the period 1885–1945, primarily from North America and Europe. Selections from the Foundation's 70,000 objects include furniture, posters, and sculpture, and focus on the social, political, and aesthetic significance of design in that era.

Electric kettle (1909) in the Wolfsonian

Española Way, a leafy Mediterranean-style shopping street

Española Way ❻

Map 2 E2. 🚌 *C, K, H, W.*

Between Washington and Drexel Avenues, Española Way is a tiny, pretty enclave of Mediterranean Revival buildings, where ornate arches, capitals, and balconies adorn salmon-colored, stuccoed frontages. Built from 1922–5, it is said to have been the inspiration for Addison Mizner's Worth Avenue in Palm Beach *(see pp114–15)*.

Española Way was meant to be an artists' colony but instead became an infamous red-light district. Over the last couple of decades, however, its intended use has been resurrected in its dozen or more boutiques and offbeat art galleries *(see p93)*.

Lincoln Road Mall ❼

Map 2 E2. 🚌 *H, S, C.* **ArtCenter South Florida** 📞 *(305) 674-8278.* 🕐 *5–10pm Wed–Fri, 2–10pm Sat.* ⬤ *Thanksgiving, Dec 25, Jan 1.* ♿ 🕸 *www.artcentersf.org*

What is now the most up-and-coming cultural corner of South Beach has had a roller-coaster history. Developer Carl Fisher *(see p57)* envisaged it as the "Fifth Avenue of the South" when it was planned in the 1920s, and its stores did indeed become the height of fashion. Four decades later, Morris Lapidus (designer of the Fontainebleau Hotel) turned the street into one of the country's first pedestrian

malls, but this did not prevent Lincoln Road's decline in the 1970s; the industrial concrete pavilions that Lapidus introduced may not have helped.

The street's revival was initiated by the setting up of the ArtCenter South Florida here in 1984. Between Lenox and Meridian Avenues there are three exhibition areas and some dozen studios that double as work-in-progress and selling space, as well as other independent galleries *(see p93)*. Many people will probably find the art too experimental for their living rooms.

The galleries are usually open in the evenings. Then the mall comes alive, as theater-goers frequent the restored Art Deco Lincoln and Colony theaters *(see p94)*, and those searching for a less intense

alternative to Ocean Drive can hang out at voguish restaurants and cafés such as the Van Dyke at 846 – Lincoln Road's answer to the News Café *(see p62)*. At night, too, the Streamline Moderne Sterling Building at No. 927 looks terrific, its glass blocks emanating a wondrous blue glow.

Holocaust Memorial ❽

1933–45 Meridian Ave. **Map** 2 E1. 📞 *(305) 538-1663.* 🚌 *A, FM, G, L.* 🕐 *9am–9pm daily.* ♿ 🕸 *www.holocaustmmb.org*

Miami Beach has one of the largest populations of Holocaust survivors in the world, hence the great appropriateness of Kenneth Treister's gut-wrenching memorial, finished in 1990. The centerpiece is an enormous bronze arm and hand stretching skyward, representing the final grasp of a dying person. It is stamped with a number from Auschwitz and covered with nearly 100 life-size bronze statues of men, women, and children in the throes of unbearable grief. Around this central plaza is a tunnel lined with the names of Europe's concentration camps, a graphic pictorial history of the Holocaust, and a granite wall inscribed with the names of thousands of victims.

The Holocaust Memorial

Winers and diners outside the Van Dyke Café, Lincoln Road Mall

**Coronation of the Virgin (c.1492)
by Domenico Ghirlandaio**

Bass Museum of Art ⑨

2121 Park Ave. **Map** 2 F1. 📞 *(305) 673-7530.* 🚌 *K, G, L, S.* ⏰ *10am–5pm Tue–Sat (1–9pm on 2nd & 4th Wed of every month), 1–5pm Sun.* ⚫ *public hols.* 🚫 Ø. ♿ ⓦ www. bassmuseum.org

THIS MAYAN-INFLUENCED Deco building was erected in 1930 as the city's library and art center. As a museum it came of age in 1964 when philanthropists John and Johanna Bass donated their own art collection, made up mainly of European paintings, sculpture, and textiles from the 15th to 17th centuries.

Gallery space is divided between permanent and temporary exhibitions. Highlights include a few Renaissance works, paintings from the northern European schools, featuring pictures by Rubens and Dürer, and giant 16th-century Flemish tapestries. Among the modern works are lithographs by Fernand Léger and Toulouse-Lautrec.

SHOOTING FASHION IN MIAMI BEACH

Thanks to its combination of Art Deco buildings, palm trees, beach, and climate, South Beach is one of the world's most popular places for fashion shoots. About 1,500 models live here, but this doesn't include the thousands of hopefuls who flock here uninvited during the season and stroll about looking cool in the bars and on the beach. The season runs from October to March, when the weather in Europe and northern America is too cold for outdoor shoots.

Stroll around SoBe in the early morning and you cannot fail to spot the teams of directors, photographers, make-up artists, and their assistants as well as, of course, the models themselves. Ocean Drive is the top spot for shoots, but you can surprise a team at work even in the quieter back streets.

Photographer and crew shooting a model in Miami Beach

Central Miami Beach ⑩

Map 2 F1. 🚌 *G, J, L, S, T, FM, C.*

MIAMI BEACH north of 23rd Street, sometimes called Central Miami Beach, is a largely unprepossessing sight, with endless 1950s and '60s high-rise apartments separating the Atlantic from busy Collins Avenue. A boardwalk running all the way from 23rd to 46th Street overlooks a narrow beach, frequented primarily by families.
The most eye-catching sight in the area is the **Fontainebleau Hotel** (pronounced "Fountainblue" locally). When driving up Collins Avenue to 44th Street, be sure to avoid driving right through the wall across the road: it is painted with a trompe l'oeil arch and image of the Fontainebleau, which in reality is hidden behind.

Completed in 1954, the curvaceous Fontainebleau is apparently the nearest the architect Morris Lapidus (b.1903) could get to his client's wishes for a modern French château style. The hotel's dated grandeur still impresses, particularly the lobby with Lapidus's signature bow ties on the tiles and the pool complete with waterfall. The hotel was an ideal setting for the James Bond film *Goldfinger* in the 1960s.

From the Bayside Market-place *(see p 72)* you can take a tour on any of several cruise boats available. The tours provide a more leisurely view of many of the million-aires' mansions of Biscayne Bay *(see p71)*. There is also Water Taxi shuttle from the Marketplace to the hotels.

Trompe l'oeil view of the Fontainebleau Hotel, Central Miami Beach

DOWNTOWN AND
LITTLE HAVANA

WHEN THE DEVELOPMENT of Miami took off with the arrival of the Florida East Coast Railroad in 1896, the early city focused on one square mile (2.5 sq km) on the banks of the Miami River, site of the present downtown area. Wealthy industrialists from the northern US set up banks and other institutions and built winter estates along Brickell Avenue. This is now the hub of Miami's financial district that was spawned by a banking boom in the 1980s. Downtown's futuristic skyscrapers, bathed nightly in neon, demonstrate the city's status as a major financial and trade center.

Even after World War II, Miami was still little more than a resort. It was largely the arrival of Cuban exiles

Brass state seal, Dade County Courthouse

from 1959 onward *(see p50)* that turned Miami into a metropolis. The effect of this Cuban influx is visible most clearly on the streets both Downtown and just across the river in Little Havana. The chatter, faces, shop signs, and food make both districts feel more like an Hispanic city with an American flavor than the other way around.

Downtown and Little Havana are enjoyable as much for their atmosphere as for their sights. Downtown has the Metro-Dade Cultural Center, with one of Florida's best historical museums, but tourists are catered to primarily at the shopping and entertainment mall of Bayside Marketplace, which is also a starting point for relaxing boat trips around Biscayne Bay.

SIGHTS AT A GLANCE

Museums and Galleries
Metro-Dade Cultural Center **2**

Historic Buildings
US Federal Courthouse **1**

Modern Architecture
Brickell Avenue **5**

Neighborhoods
Little Havana **6**

Shops and Restaurants
Bayside Marketplace **3**

Boat Trips
Biscayne Bay Boat Trips **4**

KEY

▨	Street-by-Street map *See pp70–71*
Ⓡ	Metrorail station
⛴	Water taxi boarding point
Ⓟ	Parking
ℹ	Tourist information

0 kilometers   2
0 miles   1

◁ **The striking NationsBank building towering over the Miami River, Downtown**

Street-by-Street: Downtown

DOWNTOWN'S SKYLINE IS SUBLIME. It undoubtedly looks best from a distance, particularly at night, but the architecture can also be enjoyed close-up. The raised track of the Metromover gives a good overall view; or you can explore at ground level, allowing you to investigate the handsome interiors of some of Downtown's public buildings.

The commercial district that lurks beneath the flash high-rises is surprisingly downscale, full of cut-price jewelry and electronics stores, but the Latin street life is vibrant: cafés specialize in Cuban coffee and street vendors sell freshly peeled oranges, Caribbean-style. Flagler Street, Downtown's main thoroughfare, is the best place to get the Hispanic buzz. Visit during weekday office hours; the streets can be unsafe at night.

The Downtown Skyline is a monument to the banking boom of the 1980s. There is an excellent view of it from the MacArthur Causeway.

US Federal Courthouse
This detail from the mural inside the courtroom depicts Miami's transformation from a wilderness to a modern city ❶

Dade County Courthouse has an impressive lobby, with ceiling mosaics that feature this copy of the earliest version of Florida's state seal, complete with mountains.

0 meters   150

0 yards   150

KEY

— — — Suggested route

STAR SIGHTS

★ **Metro-Dade Cultural Center**

★ **NationsBank Tower**

★ **Metro-Dade Cultural Center**
This large complex, with a Mediterranean-style central courtyard and fountains, contains the only museum in downtown Miami ❷

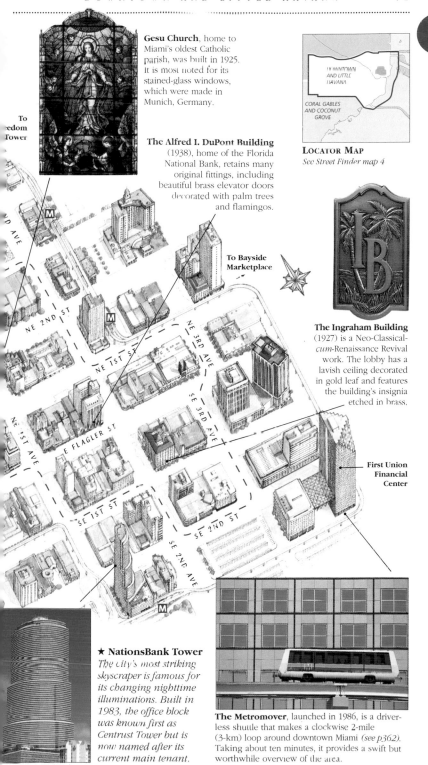

Gesu Church, home to Miami's oldest Catholic parish, was built in 1925. It is most noted for its stained-glass windows, which were made in Munich, Germany.

To Freedom Tower

The Alfred I. DuPont Building (1938), home of the Florida National Bank, retains many original fittings, including beautiful brass elevator doors decorated with palm trees and flamingos.

LOCATOR MAP
See Street Finder map 4

To Bayside Marketplace

The Ingraham Building (1927) is a Neo-Classical-*cum*-Renaissance Revival work. The lobby has a lavish ceiling decorated in gold leaf and features the building's insignia etched in brass.

First Union Financial Center

★ **NationsBank Tower**
The city's most striking skyscraper is famous for its changing nighttime illuminations. Built in 1983, the office block was known first as Centrust Tower but is now named after its current main tenant.

The Metromover, launched in 1986, is a driverless shuttle that makes a clockwise 2-mile (3-km) loop around downtown Miami *(see p362).* Taking about ten minutes, it provides a swift but worthwhile overview of the area.

Downtown

DOWNTOWN's grand early 20th-century buildings, scattered among more modern high-rises, are very evocative of the confidence of those boom years. The Mediterranean Revival and Neo-Classical styles were both popular. A fine example of the latter is Freedom Tower (1925) on Biscayne Boulevard, modeled very loosely on the Giralda in Seville. At first home to the now-defunct *Miami News*, its role and name changed in the 1960s when it became the reception center for Cubans fleeing from Castro *(see p50)*. It now stands empty.

Downtown also has a few Deco buildings, such as Burdines on Flagler Street *(see p92)*.

Freedom Tower (1925)

US Federal Courthouse **❶**

301 N Miami Ave. **Map** 4 E1.
C (954) 356-7451. **M** Arena/State Plaza. **◯** 8am–5pm Mon–Fri.
● public hols. **&**

THIS IMPOSING Neo-Classical building, finished in 1931, has hosted a number of high-profile trials, including that of Manuel Noriega, the former Panamanian president, in 1990. It has a pleasant, thoroughly Mediterranean courtyard, but the main attraction (for the casual visitor at least) is the mural entitled *Law Guides Florida's Progress (see p70)* on the second floor; this was designed by Denman Fink, famous for his work in Coral Gables *(see p80)*. Public access to the courthouse is often restricted, especially during important cases.

Metro-Dade Cultural Center **❷**

101 West Flagler St. **Map** 4 E1.
C (305) 375-3000. **M** Government Center. **🚌** 21, 77. **◯** 10am–5pm Tue–Fri (9pm on 3rd Thu of month), noon–5pm Sat & Sun. **🌐** **&**
W www.miamiartmuseum.org

DESIGNED BY the celebrated American architect Philip Johnson in 1982, the Metro-Dade Cultural Center is an art gallery, museum, and library.

Visitors from out of town will probably find the Historical Museum of Southern Florida, which concentrates on pre-1945 Miami, of most interest. There are informative displays on the Spanish colonization and Seminole culture among other topics, but it is the old photographs that really bring Miami's history to life: these capture everything from the hardships endured by the early pioneers to the fun and games of the Roaring Twenties.

The Miami Art Museum of Dade County, across the plaza from the historical museum,

Bathers in 1920s Miami, displayed in the Historical Museum

plans to develop a permanent collection, but at present holds only short-term exhibitions, chiefly of post-1945 American art; these are well worth a visit.

Bayside Marketplace **❸**

401 Biscayne Blvd. **Map** 4 F1.
C (305) 577-3344. **M** College/ Bayside. **🚌** C, S, 16, 48, 95.
◯ 10am–10pm Mon–Thu, 10am–11pm Fri & Sat, 11am–9pm Sun.
● Thanksgiving, Dec 25. **&**

BY FAR THE MOST popular spot among tourists Downtown (as well as the best place to park in the area), Bayside Marketplace is an undeniably fun complex. It curves around Miamarina, where a plethora of boats, some private, some offering trips around Biscayne Bay, lie docked.

With its numerous bars and restaurants – among them a remarkable-looking Hard Rock Café *(see p330)* complete with a guitar erupting from its roof – Bayside is a good place to eat as well as shop. The food court on the first floor does not serve *haute cuisine* but is fine for a fast-food meal. Bands often play in the waterfront esplanade.

The nearby Bayfront Park is austere by comparison. At its center the Torch of Friendship commemorates President John F. Kennedy, surrounded by the coats of arms of Central and South American countries; a plaque from the city's exiled Cuban community thanks the United States for allowing them to settle here.

Boats moored in Miamarina in front of Bayside Marketplace

Biscayne Bay Boat Trips ❹

Bayside Marketplace. **Map** 4 F1.
Ⓜ *College/Bayside.* ▦ *C, 5, 16, 48,
95.* **Island Queen Cruises** *(305) 379-
5119.* **Tours** *(305) 577-3344.* **Water
Taxi** *(954) 467-6677.*

T HE WORLD'S BUSIEST cruise
port and a sprinkling of
exclusive private island communities occupy Biscayne Bay
between Downtown and
Miami Beach. Since racing
along MacArthur Causeway in
a car provides only a brief
glimpse of this area, cruises
from Bayside Marketplace
offer a better, more leisurely
view. "Estates of the Rich and
Famous" tours run by Island
Queen Cruises and other
companies leave regularly
and last about 90 minutes.

Tours begin by
sailing past the
port, situated
on Dodge and
Lummus islands.
The port contributes
more than $5 billion a
year to the local economy,
handling over three million
cruise passengers annually.
The mammoth ships make an
impressive sight when they're
in dock or heading to or from
port (usually on weekends).

Near the eastern end of
MacArthur Causeway you
pass the US Coastguard's fleet
of high-speed craft, used to
intercept drug smugglers and
illegal aliens. Opposite lies
unbridged Fisher Island,
separated from South Beach
by Government Cut, a deep
water channel dredged in
1905. A beach for Blacks in
the 1920s, Fisher Island has
ironically become a highly
exclusive residential enclave,

The Atlantis, the most famous building along Brickell Avenue

with homes costing rarely less
than $500,000. The tour con-
tinues north around Star, Palm,
and Hibiscus islands, which
were all man-made
in the second
decade of the
20th century,
when real estate
lots were sometimes
sold "by the gallon."
Mansions in every possible
architectural style lurk beneath
lush tropical foliage, among
them the former homes of
Frank Sinatra and Al Capone,
as well as the present abodes
of such celebrities as Gloria
Estefan and Julio Iglesias.

Other boat trips from
Bayside Marketplace include
nighttime cruises, deep-sea
fishing excursions, and even
gondola rides. The Water Taxi
also provides a shuttle service
along the mainland shore,
linking Bayside Marketplace
with various hotels, as well
as a request service between
Bayside and Miami Beach
Marina, at the eastern end of
MacArthur Causeway.

**Biscayne Bay
tour boat sign**

ISLAND QUEEN

Brickell Avenue ❺

Map 4 E2– E4. Ⓜ *various stations.*
Ⓡ *Metrorail (Brickell).* ▦ *6, 8, 24,
48, B.* ℹ *701 Brickell Ave, Suite
2700, (305) 539-3034.*

I N THE EARLY 20th century, the
building of palatial mansions
along Brickell Avenue earned
it the name Millionaires' Row.
Nowadays, its northern section
is Miami's palm-lined version
of New York's Wall Street – its
international banks enclosed
within flash, glass-sided blocks
reflecting each other and the
blue sky. South of the bend
at Southwest 15th Road comes
a series of startling apartment
houses glimpsed in the opening credits of television series
Miami Vice. Created in the
early 1980s by an iconoclastic
firm of Postmodernist architects called Arquitectonica,
the buildings may no longer
be strictly *à la mode,* but
they still manage to impress.

The most memorable is the
Atlantis (at No. 2025), for its
"skycourt" – a hole high up in
its façade containing a palm
tree and Jacuzzi. The punched-
out hole reappears as an
identically sized cube in the
grounds below. Arquitectonica
also designed the Palace, at
No. 1541 and the Imperial, at
No. 1627. Described as "architecture for 55 mph" (that is,
best seen when traveling past
in a car), these exclusive
residences were designed to
be admired from a distance;
they are out-of-bounds to
casual visitors.

One of the lavish mansions seen during a Biscayne Bay boat tour

Little Havana ❶

Map 3. 🚌 *11 from Downtown,
8, 24 from Coral Gables.*
El Crédito Cigar Factory 1106 SW
8th St. ☎ *(305) 858-4162.* ○ *8am–
6pm Mon–Fri, 1–4pm Sat.*
● *public hols.*
Cuban Museum of the Americas
Lowe Art Museum, UM Coral Gables.
Map 5 A5. ☎ *(305) 284-5500.* 🖥
www.lowemuseum.org

Cubans live all over Greater Miami, but it is the 3.5 sq miles (9 sq km) making up Little Havana that, as its name suggests, have been their surrogate homeland since they first started fleeing Cuba in the 1960s *(see p50)*. Other Hispanic groups have now settled here too.

Your time in Little Havana is best spent out in the streets, where the bustling workaday atmosphere is vibrant. A salsa beat emanates from every other shop; posters advocate a continuation of the armed struggle against Castro; *bodegas* (canteens) sell Cuban specialties such as *moros y cristianos (see p315)*, while wrinkled old men knock back thimblefuls of *café cubano.*

Little Havana's principal commercial thoroughfare and sentimental heart is Southwest 8th Street, better known as **Calle Ocho**. Its liveliest stretch, between 11th and 17th Avenues, is best enjoyed on foot, but other points of interest are more easily explored by car.

Founded in Havana in 1907 and moved to Miami in 1968,

Cubans enjoying a game of dominoes in Máximo Gómez Park

El Crédito Cigar Factory, near the corner of Calle Ocho and 11th Avenue, is small but authentic. You are welcome to watch the handful of cigar rollers at work. The leaves are grown in the Dominican Republic – reputedly from Cuban tobacco seeds, the world's best. Local smokers, mainly non-Cuban, come to buy boxes of the wide range of cigars on sale *(see p93)*.

Southwest 13th Avenue, south from Calle Ocho, is known as **Cuban Memorial Boulevard** and is the district's nationalistic focal point. The eternal flame of the Brigade 2506 Memorial remembers the Cubans who died in the Bay of Pigs invasion of Cuba in 1961. Every year people gather here on April 17 to remember the disastrous attempt to overthrow Fidel Castro's regime.

Beyond, other memorials pay tribute to Cuban heroes Antonio Maceo and José Martí, who fought against Cuba's Spanish colonialists in the 1800s *(see pp46–7)*.

At intervals along Calle Ocho between 12th and 17th Avenues, more recent Latin celebrities such as Julio Iglesias and Gloria Estefan are honored with stars on the pavement in Little Havana's version of Hollywood's Walk of Fame.

At the corner of 14th Avenue, older male Cubans match their wits over dominoes in tiny **Máximo Gómez Park** – also known as Domino Park. According to

Waitress at the Versailles

The eternal flame commemorating the Bay of Pigs invasion

a list of rules, players can be banned from the park for spitting, shouting, or foul language.

North of Calle Ocho at West Flagler Street and Southwest 17th Avenue, **Plaza de la Cubanidad** has a map of Cuba sculpted in bronze; José Martí's enigmatic words alongside translate as "the palm trees are sweethearts that wait." Behind, a flourish of flags and banners advertises the headquarters of Alpha 66, Miami's most hardline grouping of anti-Castro Cubans, whose supporters take part in military exercises in the Everglades – although most realize an armed invasion of Cuba will never happen.

The **Cuban Museum of the Americas**, located at the University of Miami's Lowe Art Museum in Coral Gables *(see p81)*, holds a collection of more than 500 works by Cuban artists, historical and political memorabilia, and Afro-Cuban lore.

Much farther west, at 3260 Calle Ocho, lies **Woodlawn Cemetery**. You can ask for directions to the memorials to the unknown Cuban freedom fighter in plot 31, with Cuban and US flags flying alongside, or to the unheralded tomb of Gerardo Machado, an infamous Cuban dictator of the 1930s.

Finish off a tour of Little Havana with a snack or full meal at the nearby **Versailles** restaurant *(see p318)*; this is a cultural and culinary bastion of Miami's Cuban community.

Miami's Cuban Community

THE CUBAN COMMUNITY in Miami is unusually cohesive, thanks to a shared passion for its homeland and a common hatred for Fidel Castro and his dictatorship. The exiles, as they often call themselves, come from all walks of life. Early immigrants were largely wealthy white (and rightwing) professionals, who now sit on the boards of some of Miami's biggest companies and live in the city's stylish and upscale suburbs. The so-called Marielitos, who came in 1980 (see p50), were mostly working class, like many of those who have arrived since. Some second-generation Cubans, such as pop star Gloria Estefan, now have very successful careers. Nowadays these professionals are often dubbed "yucas," or Young, Up and-coming Cuban-Americans.

The Cuban presence is felt in every layer of Miami society – seen in everything from the food to the Spanish spoken on the street, and visible everywhere from Little Havana to elite Coral Gables.

Gloria Estefan

Images of Old Cuba
Murals, such as this one of the Cuban resort of Varadero, symbolize the nostalgia and love for the homeland felt by Cubans of all generations. Many hope to return to the island one day.

Political Action
Cubans in Miami eagerly follow events in Cuba. They often take to the streets to wave the Cuban flag and protest against the Castro regime or the US government's Cuban policy.

Salsa music, recorded by Cubans in Miami and popular in the city

CUBAN CULTURE IN MIAMI
The Cubans have brought their music, their religion, their whole way of life to Miami. They are nominally Catholic, but many Cubans adhere to Santería, an unusual blend of Catholic beliefs and the animist cults taken to Cuba by African slaves during the colonial period.

A Cuban-style hole in the wall café, where coffee, snacks, and conversation are enjoyed.

A religious shop or *botánica* in Little Havana selling the paraphernalia of Santería

CORAL GABLES AND COCONUT GROVE

CORAL GABLES, one of the country's richest neighborhoods, is a separate city within Greater Miami, and feels it. Aptly named the City Beautiful, its elegant homes line winding avenues shaded by banyans and live oaks; backing up to hidden canals, many have their own jetties. Regulations ensure that new buildings use the same architectural vocabulary advocated by George Merrick when he planned Coral Gables in the 1920s *(see p80)*. As well as exploring Merrick's legacy, you can peer into some of Miami's most stylish shops. Coconut

Fireman's head, Salzedo Street

Grove is Miami's oldest community. Wreckers *(see p289)* lived here from the mid-1800s, but the area attracted few people until the 1880s, when Ralph Monroe *(see p82)* persuaded some friends to open a hotel. It was staffed by Bahamians and frequented by Monroe's intellectual friends. Ever since, the area has had a mixed flavor, with posh homes just a stone's throw from the blighted, so-called Black Coconut Grove. Affordable restaurants and shops draw weekend and evening crowds, making Coconut Grove the liveliest district in Miami after South Beach.

SIGHTS AT A GLANCE

Museums and Galleries
Lowe Art Museum **6**
Museum of Science and Space
   Transit Planetarium **11**

**Streets and
Neighborhoods**
Coconut Grove Village **7**
Miracle Mile **1**

Historic Buildings
The Barnacle **8**
Biltmore Hotel **5**
Coral Gables City Hall **2**
Coral Gables Merrick
   House **3**
Venetian Pool **4**
Vizcaya pp84–5 **12**

Churches
Ermita de la Caridad **10**

Marinas
Dinner Key **9**

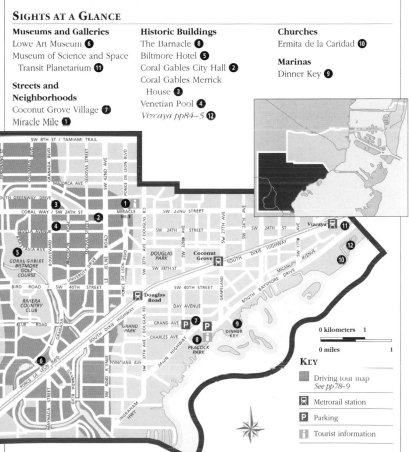

KEY

Driving tour map
See pp78–9

Metrorail station

Parking

Tourist information

0 kilometers 1

0 miles 1

◁ **Tower of the Biltmore Hotel, an unmistakable landmark in Coral Gables**

Coral Gables Driving Tour

THIS DRIVING TOUR wends its way along Coral Gables' lush and peaceful lanes connecting the major landmarks of George Merrick's 1920s planned city (*see pp80–81*). As well as much-admired public buildings like the Biltmore Hotel, it takes in two of the original four grand entrances and six of Merrick's Disneyesque international "villages."

It is quite possible to visit all the sights on the tour in one busy day. Allow time to get lost; Coral Gables is very confusing for a planned city. Signs for streets, named after Spanish places that Merrick allegedly pulled out of a dictionary, are often hard to spot, lurking on white stone blocks in the grass.

Alhambra Water Tower ③
This folly, built in 1925, was the work of Denman Fink (see p80).

Coral Gables Congregational Church ⑦
Coral Gables' first church, built by Merrick in Spanish Baroque style, has an elaborate bell tower and portal.

Venetian Pool ⑥ is a beautiful public swimming pool embellished with Venetian-style buildings.

Biltmore Hotel ⑧
One of the most stunning hotels in the country, the Biltmore has been beautifully restored to its 1920s grandeur.

The Lowe Art Museum ⑩ boasts an excellent collection, including some fine European and Native American art.

French City Village ⑪
This is one of seven international villages that were built to add variety to the mostly Mediterranean-style city.

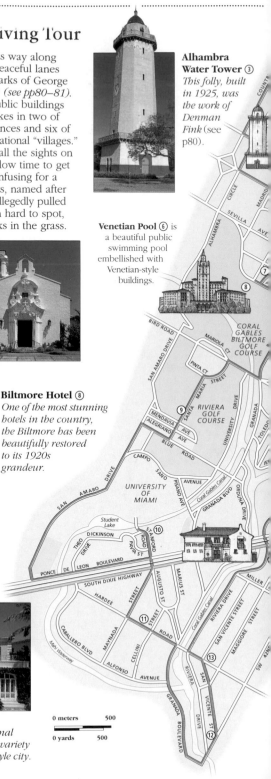

0 meters   500

0 yards   500

The Granada Entrance ① is a copy of the gate to Granada in Spain.

The Country Club Prado Entrance ②, complete with ornamental pillars, is the most elegant of the grand entrances.

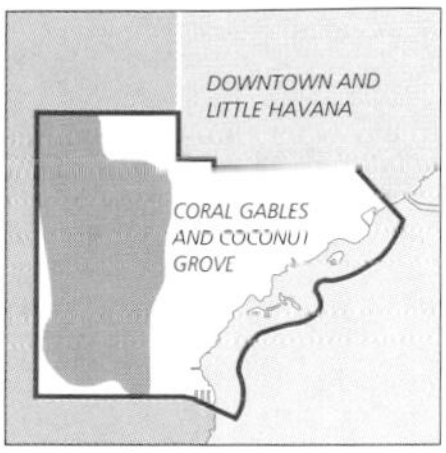

Locator Map
See Street Finder, map 5

Coral Way ④
Live oaks and Spanish-style houses line one of Coral Gables' loveliest and oldest streets.

Coral Gables Merrick House ⑤ was once the home of George Merrick and is now a museum.

Coral Gables City Hall ⑯ has a decorative interior, featuring murals painted in the 1920s and '50s.

Key

Expressway

Tour route

Metrorail line

Miracle Mile ⑰
Conservative bridal, fashion, and jewelry stores set the tone along the district's most important shopping street.

Tips for Drivers

Tour length: *14 miles (23 km).*
Starting point: *Anywhere, but the route is best done in a counterclockwise direction.*
Stopping-off points: *There are some highly rated restaurants off Miracle Mile (see p80), and you can enjoy an English-style tea at the Biltmore if you book 24 hours in advance. Or, you can take a dip at the Venetian Pool.*
When to go: *Wednesdays and Sundays are the best days to visit because of the hours of the Coral Gables Merrick House, Lowe Art Museum, and the Biltmore tours (see pp80–81). Avoid the rush hours (7–9:30am, 4:30–6:30pm).*

A private boat moored on one of Coral Gables' canals

Finding the Sights

① Granada Entrance
② Country Club Prado Entrance
③ Alhambra Water Tower
④ Coral Way
⑤ Coral Gables Merrick House
⑥ Venetian Pool
⑦ Coral Gables Congregational Church
⑧ Biltmore Hotel
⑨ Colonial Village
⑩ Lowe Art Museum
⑪ French City Village
⑫ Dutch South African Village
⑬ French Country Village
⑭ Chinese Village
⑮ French Normandy Village
⑯ Coral Gables City Hall
⑰ Miracle Mile

Galleried rotunda inside the Colonnade Building on Miracle Mile

Miracle Mile ❶

Coral Way between Douglas and Le Jeune roads. **Map** 5 C1. 🚇 *Metrorail (Douglas Rd) then bus J or 40.*

IN 1940, A DEVELOPER hyped Coral Gables' main shopping street by naming it Miracle Mile (the walk along one side and down the other being the mile in question). Along its length, colorful canopies adorn shops as prim and proper as their clientele *(see p92)*. High prices and competition from out-of-town malls mean the street is rarely busy.

The Colonnade Building, at No. 169, was built in 1926 by George Merrick as the sales headquarters for his real estate business. Its superb rotunda is now a lobby for the deceptively modern and very impressive Colonnade Hotel. The Doc Dammers' Saloon *(see p330)* contains evocative photographs of Coral Gables' heyday. Nearby, at Salzedo Street and Aragon Avenue, the Old Police and Fire Station Building, built in 1939, features a wonderful pair of sculpted firemen.

Coral Gables City Hall ❷

405 Biltmore Way. **Map** 5 C1. ☎ *(305) 446-6800.* 🚇 *Metrorail (Douglas Rd).* 🚌 *24.* ⏱ *8am–5pm Mon–Fri.* ⬤ *public hols.* ♿

BUILT IN 1928, Coral Gables City Hall epitomizes the Spanish Renaissance style favored by Merrick and his colleagues. Its semicircular façade even has a Spanish-style coat of arms, which was designed for the new city of Coral Gables by Denman Fink, George Merrick's uncle. Fink was also responsible for the mural of the four seasons that decorates the dome of the bell tower: winter is represented as an old man, the other seasons as young women. Above the stairs, a mural that illustrates Coral Gables' early days, *Landmarks of the Twenties*, was the work of John St. John in the 1950s; he artificially aged it by chain-smoking and exhaling onto the paint as it dried.

Coat of arms on Coral Gables City Hall

Coral Gables Merrick House ❸

907 Coral Way. **Map** 5 B1. ☎ *(305) 460-5361.* 🚌 *24.* ⏱ *1–4pm Wed & Sun.* 🚫 ♿

MAKE THE EFFORT to visit the Merrick family home to appreciate the comparatively modest background of Coral Gables' creator. However, its opening hours are limited.

When Reverend Solomon Merrick brought his family to Florida from New England in 1899, they settled in a wooden cabin south of the growing city of Miami. They later added a much larger extension and named the house Coral Gables, thinking the local oolitic limestone used to build it was coral because of the fossilized marine life it contained.

Now a museum, the emphasis is as much on the family as on Solomon's famous son, George. Some of the furniture was owned by the Merricks, and there are family portraits and paintings by George's mother and his uncle. The grounds have been reduced in size, but the small garden is awash with tropical trees and plants.

GEORGE MERRICK'S DREAM CITY

The dream of George Merrick was to build a new city. With the help of Denman Fink as artistic advisor, Frank Button as landscaper, and Phineas Paist as architectural director, he conjured up a wholly planned aesthetic wonderland. Its architecture was to be part-Spanish, part-Italian – in Merrick's words "a combination of what seemed best in each, with an added touch of gaiety to suit the Florida mood." The dream spawned the biggest real estate venture of the 1920s, costing around $100 million. Some $3 million a year was spent on advertising alone, with posters promoting idyllic canal scenes while they were still on the drawing board. The 1926 hurricane *(see p48)* and the Wall Street crash left Merrick's city incomplete, but what remains – together with subsequent imitations – is a great testament to his imagination.

Portrait of George Merrick, on display in his family home

Venetian Pool, ingeniously created in the 1920s out of an old coral rock quarry

Venetian Pool **4**

2701 De Soto Blvd. **Map** 5 B2.
(305) 460-5356. Metrorail (S Miami) then bus 72. mid-Jun–mid-Aug: 11am–7:30pm Mon–Fri; Apr–May & Sep–Oct: 11am–5:30pm; Nov–Mar: 10am–4:30pm; all year: 10am–4:30pm Sat & Sun. Mon Sep–May, Thanksgiving, Dec 24–25, Jan 1.
www.venetianpool.com

THIS MAY BE the most beautiful swimming pool in the world. Worth visiting whether you like to swim or not, it was fashioned from a coral rock quarry in 1923 by Denman Fink and Phineas Paist. Pink stucco towers and loggias, candy-cane Venetian poles, a cobblestone bridge, caves, and waterfalls surround the clear, spring-fed waters. The pool was originally one of the most fashionable social spots in Coral Gables: see the photographs in the lobby of beauty pageants staged here during the 1920s.

Biltmore Hotel **5**

1200 Anastasia Ave. **Map** 5 A2.
(305) 445-1926. Metrorail (S Miami) then bus 72. Sun pm.
www.biltmorehotel.com

CORAL GABLES' outstanding single building was completed in 1926. In its heyday, when it hosted celebrities such as Al Capone (who had a speakeasy here), Judy Garland, and the Duke and Duchess of Windsor, guests hunted fox in the vast grounds (now a golf course) and were punted along canals in gondolas. The Biltmore served as a military hospital during World War II, when its marble floors were covered in linoleum, and it remained a veterans' hospital until 1968. Following a $55-million restoration in 1986 the hotel went bankrupt in 1990, but then opened its doors again two years later.

A 315-ft (96-m) near replica of Seville Cathedral's Giralda tower, which was also the model for Miami's Freedom Tower *(see p72)*, rises from the hotel's imposing façade. Inside, Herculean pillars line the grand lobby, while from the terrace behind you can survey the largest hotel swimming pool in the US. The Biltmore's famous swimming instructor, Johnny Weismuller, known for his role as Tarzan, set a world record here in the 1930s.

Weekly tours of the hotel depart from the desk.

Lowe Art Museum **6**

1301 Stanford Drive. **Map** 5 A5.
(305) 284-3535. Metrorail (University). 52, 56, 72. 10am–5pm Tue–Sat, noon–5pm Sun, noon 7pm Thu Mon, Thanksgiving, Dec 25, Jan 1.
www.lowemuseum.org

THIS MUSEUM is located in the middle of the campus of the University of Miami, founded in 1925 thanks to a $5 million donation from George Merrick. Among the 8,000 permanent exhibits are impressive Renaissance and Baroque works, and an excellent collection of Native American art. The entire collection from the Cuban Museum of the Americas is now housed here, with more than 500 original artworks, Afro-Cuban lore, and historical memorabilia. Ancient art from Latin America and Asia, and 20th-century photography are also well represented.

Han dynasty horse, Lowe Art Museum

South view of the Biltmore Hotel, Coral Gables' most famous landmark

Coconut Grove Village ❼

Map 6 E4, F4. 🚇 Metrorail (Coconut Grove). 🚌 42 from Coral Gables, 48 from Downtown.

A FABLED HIPPY hangout in the 1960s, these days the focal point of Coconut Grove cultivates a more salubrious air. Well-groomed young couples wining and dining beneath old-fashioned streetlamps now typify what is often known simply as "the village." Only the odd snake charmer and neck masseur, plus a few New Age shops, offer glimpses of alternative lifestyles. Come at night or on the weekend to see the Grove at its best.

The village's nerve center is at the intersection of Grand Avenue, McFarlane Avenue, and Main Highway, where you'll find Johnny Rockets, a great 1950s-style burger bar, and the hyped-up **CocoWalk**. This outdoor mall *(see p92)* is Coconut Grove's busiest spot. Its courtyard is full of cafés and souvenir stands, while on upper floors a band often plays. There are also family restaurants *(see p318)*, a movie theater, and nightclub.

A short distance east along Grand Avenue, a stylish mall called the **Streets of Mayfair** *(see p92)* is worth visiting as much for its striking ensemble of Spanish tiles, waterfalls, and foliage as for its shops. But in order to better appreciate

CocoWalk open-air mall in Coconut Grove Village

Coconut Grove's relaxed café lifestyle, head along the side-streets of Commodore Plaza and Fuller Street.

For a different atmosphere, browse among the food stands of the colorful **Farmers' Market**, held on Saturdays at McDonald Street and Grand Avenue. Farther along Grand Avenue are the simple homes of the local Bahamian community. This neighborhood comes alive during Coconut Grove's exuberant Goombay Festival *(see p33)*, but be cautious at other times.

A five-minute stroll south along Main Highway takes you through a shady, affluent neighborhood where palms, bougainvillea, and hibiscus conceal handsome clapboard villas. At 3400 Devon Road is the picturesque **Plymouth Congregational Church**,

which appears to have been built a lot longer ago than 1916. It is usually locked, but the ivy-covered façade and setting are the main attraction.

Monroe, designer of the Barnacle, painted by Lewis Benton in 1931

The Barnacle ❽

3485 Main Highway, Coconut Grove. **Map** 6 E4. 📞 (305) 448-9445. 🚌 42, 48. ⏰ 9am–4pm Fri–Sun. ⬤ Thanksgiving, Dec 25, Jan 1. 🈴

H IDDEN FROM Main Highway by tropical hardwood trees, the Barnacle is Dade County's oldest home. It was designed and occupied by one Ralph Monroe, a Renaissance man who made his living from boat building and wrecking *(see p289)*. As well as being a botanist and photographer, he was an avid environmentalist and had a strong belief in the importance of self-sufficiency.

When first constructed in 1891 the house was a bunga-low, built of wood salvaged from wrecks and inventively laid out to allow air to

---

circulate (essential in those pre-air-conditioning times). Then, in 1908, Monroe jacked the building up and added a new ground floor to make room for his expanding family.

Inside the two-story house visitors can explore rooms stuffed with old family heirlooms and wonderful dated practical appliances, such as an early refrigerator. The hour-long tours of the property also take in Monroe's clapboard boathouse, full of his tools and workbenches. Alongside, you can see the rail track that Monroe used to winch boats out of the bay.

Dinner Key **9**

S Bayshore Drive. **Map** 6 F4.
🚇 Metrorail (Coconut Grove). 🚌 48.

IN THE 1930s, Pan American Airways transformed Dinner Key into the busiest seaplane base in the US. It was also the point of departure for Amelia Earhart's doomed round-the-world flight in 1937. You can still see the airline's sleek Streamline Moderne-style *(see p59)* terminal, which houses Miami City Hall; the hangars where seaplanes were once harbored are now boatyards. For a glimpse of how some people

The Space Transit Planetarium, venue for star and laser shows

enjoy their leisure time, take a walk among the yachts berthed in what is the most prestigious marina in Miami.

Ermita de la Caridad **10**

3609 S Miami Ave. **Map** 3 C5.
📞 *(305) 854-2404.* 🚇 Metrorail (Vizcaya). 🚌 12, 48. ⏱ 9am–9pm daily. ♿

THIS PECULIAR conical church, erected in 1966, is a very holy place for Miami's Cuban exiles – a shrine to their patron saint, the Virgin of Charity. A mural above the altar (which faces Cuba rather than being oriented eastward) illustrates the history of the Catholic church in Cuba, showing the Virgin and her shrine on the island. (The church is hard to find: take the first turn north of the Mercy Hospital.)

Deco detail on Miami City Hall façade, Dinner Key

Museum of Science and Space Transit Planetarium **11**

3280 S Miami Ave. **Map** 3 C5.
📞 *(305) 854-4247.* 🚇 Metrorail (Vizcaya). 🚌 48. ⏱ 10am–6pm daily. ⊘ Thanksgiving, Dec 25. 📷 ♿ Ⓦ www.miamisci.org

CHILDREN WITH inquiring minds love this Museum and its newest addition, The Bird of Prey Wildlife Center. The museum has many fun, interactive games, and adults may be interested in the moving letters written by victims of Hurricane Andrew, which hit in 1992 *(see p24)*, or by the Internet room.

Your ticket covers admission to the Space Transit Planetarium, which puts on impressive star shows daily and laser shows on weekends. Plans are in place for creating the first international "Science Center of the Americas" in association with the Smithsonian Institution.

The Ermita de la Caridad, right on the edge of Biscayne Bay, which attracts many Cuban worshipers

Vizcaya ❷

Light fixture

Florida's grandest residence was completed in 1916 as the winter retreat for millionaire industrialist James Deering. His vision was to replicate a 16th-century Italian estate, but one that had been altered by succeeding generations. Hence, Vizcaya and its opulent rooms come in a blend of styles from Renaissance to Neo-Classical, furnished with the fruits of Deering's shopping sprees around Europe. The formal gardens combine beautifully the features of Italian and French gardens with Florida's tropical foliage.

Deering would constantly enquire of his ambitious architect: "Must we be so grand?" fearing that Vizcaya would be too costly to support. After his death in 1925, it proved to be so until 1952, when it was bought by Dade County. The house and gardens were opened to the public soon afterward.

★ **Deering Bathroom**
Deering's elaborate bathroom has marble walls, silver plaques, and a canopied ceiling reminiscent of a Napoleonic campaign tent.

Seahorse weathervane

Pulcinella
The 18th-century English statue of Pulcinella, in the intimate Theater Garden, is one of many European sculptures in the grounds of the villa.

The Dining Room resembles a Renaissance banquet hall, complete with tapestries and a 16th-century refectory table.

★ **Music Room**
This Rococo room is arguably the loveliest in the house. It is lit by a striking chandelier of multicolored glass flowers.

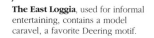

The East Loggia, used for informal entertaining, contains a model caravel, a favorite Deering motif.

STAR FEATURES

★ **Music Room**

★ **Deering Bathroom**

★ **Gardens**

★ **Gardens**
Formal gardens like those at Vizcaya are a rarity in Florida. The Mount provides a lovely view down the symmetrical Center Island to the South Terrace of the villa.

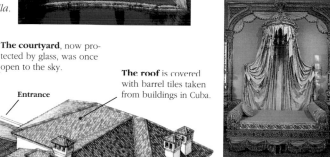

The courtyard, now protected by glass, was once open to the sky.

Entrance

The roof is covered with barrel tiles taken from buildings in Cuba.

Cathay Bedroom
Overwhelmed by the luxurious canopied bed, the Cathay Bedroom is decorated with chinoiserie, which was immensely popular in Europe in the 18th century.

The Living Room is a grand Renaissance hall with the curious addition of an organ, made especially for Vizcaya.

The Swimming Pool is visible outside but is reached from a grotto beneath the house.

Deering Sitting Room
The ceiling decoration of this Neo-Classical room features a seahorse, one of Vizcaya's recurrent motifs.

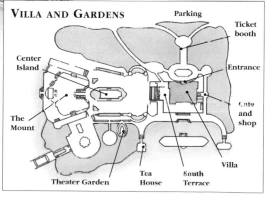

VILLA AND GARDENS

Parking

Ticket booth

Center Island

Entrance

The Mount

Gate and shop

Theater Garden

Tea House

South Terrace

Villa

FARTHER AFIELD

THE AREAS north of Miami Beach and Downtown and south of Coral Gables are seldom very scenic, but they are well worth exploring for the great beaches and fun family attractions, as **Palms in Fairchild Tropical Garden** well as some really bizarre sights.

Much of northern Miami has a reputation for poverty and danger, in particular Liberty City and Overtown. Avoid these areas, and follow the safety tips on page 348. Be careful, too, when driving through Hialeah or visiting Opa-Locka or Little Haiti – atmospheric neighborhoods but ones that are likely to appeal mainly to the more adventurous sightseers.

Southern Miami's dull, nondescript suburbs eventually give way to mile after mile of citrus orchards and nurseries. These flatlands were at the epicenter of Hurricane Andrew in 1992 (*see p24*), and the natural landscape still looks mauled in places. Many of this area's attractions, which consist primarily of zoos, parks, and gardens, were very badly damaged. These have mostly reopened, although restoration work continues in many cases.

SIGHTS AT A GLANCE

Historic Buildings
Ancient Spanish Monastery **2**
Coral Castle **15**

Museums and Galleries
American Police
  Hall of Fame **5**
Gold Coast
  Railroad Museum **12**
Weeks Air Museum **11**

Parks, Gardens, and Zoos
Charles Deering Estate **10**
Fairchild Tropical Garden **8**
Miami Metrozoo **13**
Miami Seaquarium **6**
Monkey Jungle **14**
Parrot Jungle **9**

Beaches
Key Biscayne **7**
North Beaches **1**

Neighborhoods
Little Haiti **4**
Opa-Locka **3**

10 miles = 16 km

KEY

▪	Main sightseeing areas
▫	Urban area
=	Expressway
=	Major highway
=	Secondary route
—	Rail line
▣	Amtrak station
✈	Airport

◁ **The 12th-century cloisters of the Ancient Spanish Monastery in northern Miami**

North Beaches ❶

Collins Avenue. 🚌 K or S from South Beach or Downtown.

Beach at Haulover Park, under the protective eye of a lifeguard

THE BARRIER ISLANDS north of Miami Beach are occupied mainly by exclusively posh residential areas and unlovely resorts, strung out along Collins Avenue. Package tourists often get stuck here when many would probably prefer South Beach. Still, there are lots of inexpensive accommodations and a long sandy beach.

A peaceful strip of sand between 79th and 87th Streets separates Miami Beach from

Surfside, a simple community very popular with French Canadians. At 96th Street Surfside merges with **Bal Harbour**, a stylish enclave known for some flashy hotels

and one of the swankiest malls around *(see p92)*. Northward is the pleasant **Haulover Park**, with a marina on the creek side and dune-backed sands facing the ocean.

Ancient Spanish Monastery ❷

16711 W Dixie Hwy, N Miami Beach. 📞 (305) 945-1462. 🚌 H from South Beach, 3 from Downtown. 🕙 10am–4pm daily, 1–5:30pm Sun. ● public hols. 🚫 ♿ 🌐 www.spanishmonastery.com

THESE MONASTERY cloisters have an unusual history. Originally built in 1133–41 in Spain, in 1925 they were bought by newspaper tycoon William Randolph Hearst, who had their 35,000 stones packed into

crates. An outbreak of foot-and-mouth disease led to the crates being opened (for the packing straw to be checked), and the stones were repacked incorrectly. Once in New York, they remained there

until 1952, when it was decided to piece together "the world's largest and most expensive jigsaw puzzle." The cloisters resemble the original version, but there is still a pile of unidentified stones in one corner of the gardens.

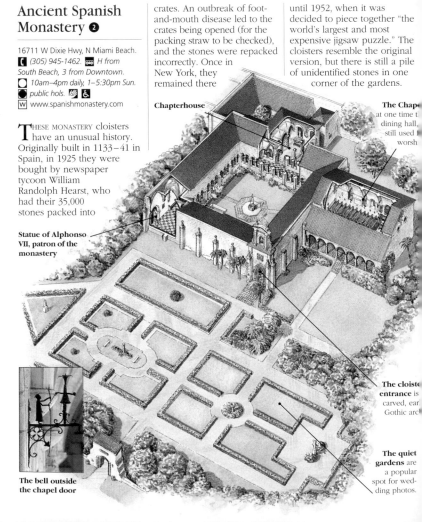

Chapterhouse

The Chape at one time t dining hall, still used f worsh

Statue of Alphonso VII, patron of the monastery

The cloiste entrance is carved, ear Gothic arc

The quiet gardens are a popular spot for wedding photos.

The bell outside the chapel door

Arabian-style dome of the City Hall in Opa-Locka

Opa-Locka ❸

Junction of NW 27th Ave & NW 135th St, 10 miles (16 km) NW of Downtown.
E, from Sunny Isles Blvd.

NICKNAMED THE "Baghdad of Dade County," Opa-Locka was the brainchild of aviator Glenn Curtiss. Taking his inspiration from the tales of *The Arabian Nights*, he created his own fantasy city, financing the construction of more than 90 Moorish buildings during the 1920s boom (*see pp48–9*).

Nowadays, Opa-Locka is a depressed area; it would not be wise to stray far from the restored City Hall (at Opa-Locka and Sharasad boulevards). All in pink with minarets, domes, and keyhole arches, this is the best example of the remaining Moorish-style architecture. Otherwise, Opa-Locka's fantasy lives on mainly in shops with names such as Ali Baba Appliances and streets called Caliph or Sultan.

Little Haiti ❹

46th to 79th Streets, E of I-95.
9 or 10 from Downtown.

EVER SINCE THE 1980s, many Haitian refugees have settled in this part of Miami. It is a visibly impoverished but colorful community, and fairly safe if you stick to the main streets, 54th Street and NE 2nd Avenue.

The **Caribbean Marketplace**, at NE 2nd Avenue and 60th Street, has a few craft stalls, but more interesting are the surrounding shops painted dazzling colors. High-decibel Haitian music blares out of some; others are *botánicas* stocking herbal potions and saints' ephemera (*see p75*); more sell "Caribbean-style" chicken and plantains.

American Police Hall of Fame ❺

3801 Biscayne Blvd. (305) 573-0070. 3, 16. 10am–5:30pm daily. Dec 25.

FEW VISITORS are unmoved by the Hall of Fame's vast marble memorial, engraved with the names of over 5,000 American police officers who have died in the line of duty. Yet some of the exhibits, while fascinating, are gory and sensationalist. The *Robo-Cop* mannequin, brass knuckles, and weapons disguised as lipstick and an umbrella are innocuous enough. Some visitors, however, may find the prospect of strapping themselves into an electric chair or inspecting the gas chamber harder to stomach.

1930s police car, American Police Hall of Fame

Miami Seaquarium ❻

4400 Rickenbacker Cswy, Virginia Key. (305) 361-5705. B from Brickell Ave. 9:30am–6pm daily. www.miamiseaquarium.com

IF YOU'RE VISITING Orlando's Sea World (*see pp164–7*), you may not want to bother with the 35 acre Miami Seaquarium, but the sea lion, dolphin, and killer whale shows are surefire crowd pleasers. The new "Swim with the Dolphins" program draws the largest crowds twice daily, Wednesday through Sunday. Other attractions include viewing areas for manatees, sharks, a mangrove swamp full of pelicans, and a coral reef aquarium.

Key Biscayne ❼

7 miles (11 km) SE of Downtown.
B. Bill Baggs Cape Florida SRA (305) 361-5811. daily.

THE VIEW OF Downtown from Rickenbacker Causeway, connecting the mainland to Virginia Key and Key Biscayne, is one of Miami's best. Views aside, Key Biscayne has some of the city's top beaches. Most impressive is the beach in **Crandon Park** in the upper half of the key, which is 3 miles (5 km) long and enormously wide, with palm trees and picnic areas. At the key's southern end, the **Bill Baggs Cape Florida State Recreation Area** has a shorter beach joined to more picnic areas by boardwalks across dunes. The lighthouse near the tip, built in 1825, is undergoing restoration.

A mix of mini-malls and oceanfront apartments line Crandon Boulevard between the two parks. More scenic are the posh residences around Harbor Drive on the bay side.

Mural advertising a religious shop (*botánica*) in Little Haiti

Fairchild Tropical Garden ❽

10901 Old Cutler Rd. 🆔 *(305) 667-1651.* 🚌 *65 from Coconut Grove.* ⭕ *9:30am–4:30pm daily.* ⬤ *Dec 25.* 🌳 ♿ **Mattheson Hammock Park** 🅲 *(305) 665-5475.* ⭕ *6am to sunset daily.* Ⓦ *www.ftg.org*

T HIS HUGE and dizzyingly beautiful tropical garden, established in 1938, doubles as a major botanical research institution. Around a series of man-made lakes stands one of the largest collections of palm trees in the world (550 of the 2,500 known species) as well as an impressive array of cycads – relatives of palms and ferns that bear unusual giant red cones. There are countless other wonderful trees and plants, including a comical-looking sausage tree.

During 40-minute tram tours, guides describe how plants are used in the manufacture of medicines and perfumes (the flowers of the ylang-ylang tree, for example, are used in Chanel No. 5). Allow another two hours to explore on your own.

Next door to the Fairchild Tropical Garden is the waterfront Mattheson Hammock Park, which is still recovering from the beating it received from Hurricane Andrew. There are walking and cycling trails through mangrove swamps, but most visitors head for the Atoll Pool, an artificial salt-water swimming pool encircled by sand and palm trees right alongside Biscayne Bay.

Parrot Jungle ❾

11000 SW 57th Ave. 🅲 *(305) 666-7834.* 🚇 *Metrorail (South Miami) then bus 57.* ⭕ *9:30am–6pm daily.* 🌳 ♿ Ⓦ *www.parrotjungle.com*

O VER 1,100 BIRDS populate this beautifully maintained tropical garden. Some are caged, some roam wild, while others perform tricks such as riding roller skates in the ever-popular Trained Bird Show. Other attractions include a jungle trail past ponds infested with alligators and turtles.

A new Parrot Jungle is now being created on Watson Island in Biscayne Bay.

Charles Deering Estate ❿

16701 SW 72nd Ave. 🅲 *(305) 235-1668.* ⭕ *9am–5pm daily.* 🌳 📷 ♿ ⬤ *Thanksgiving.* Ⓦ *www.co.miami-dade.fl.us/parks/deering.com*

W HILE HIS BROTHER James enjoyed the splendor of Vizcaya *(see pp84–5),* Charles Deering had his own stylish winter retreat on Biscayne Bay, which he used regularly between 1916 and 1927. His 400-acre (162-ha) estate,

The Charles Deering Estate, devastated by Hurricane Andrew

including a Mediterranean Revival mansion, was acquired by the state in 1985.

Several of the estate's buildings, including the main house and a 19th-century inn called Richmond Cottage, were damaged by Hurricane Andrew but have been restored and opened to the public.

The grounds, however, are the main attraction here, although they too were ravaged by Andrew's 160-mph (258-km/h) winds. They include mangrove and rockland pine forests, a salt marsh, and what is supposed to be the largest virgin coastal tropical hardwood hammock on the US mainland. There is an extensive fossil site on the grounds and guided canoe tours on the weekend.

The tranquil, palm-fringed lakes of the Fairchild Tropical Garden

A Bengal tiger in front of a mock Khmer temple at Miami Metrozoo

STILL RUN by the family that founded it back in 1933, Monkey Jungle's best selling point is that human visitors are caged while the animals roam free. You walk through a caged area with Java macaques clambering above you, or you can observe South American monkeys at close quarters in a simulated rainforest. Other primates, including gorillas and gibbons, are kept conventionally in cages.

Demonstrations showing the various capabilities of macaques, chimpanzees, and other species take place regularly throughout the day.

Weeks Air Museum ⓫

14710 SW 128th St, adjacent to Tamiami Airport. 【 (305) 233-5197. ☐ 10am–5pm daily ● Thanksgiving, Dec 25. 🅆 ⓰
🆆 www.weeksairmuseum.com

THIS MUSEUM is dedicated to the preservation of old aircraft. A new hangar proudly displays American, German, and Russian World War II fighters, along with ejector seats, machine-gun turrets, and so forth.

There is also a fascinating section on an American all-black fighter squadron formed in 1941, at a time when the assumption was that African-Americans were incapable of flying combat aircraft.

A display re-creates a World War II US military encampment in the South Pacific.

Gold Coast Railroad Museum ⓱

12450 SW 152nd St, Perrine. 【 (305) 253-0063. 🚈 Metrorail (Dadeland North) then Zoo Bus. ☐ 11am–3pm daily. 🅆 ⓰
🆆 www.goldcoast-railroad.org

LOCATED NEXT to the Miami Metrozoo, this unusual museum is a must-see for railroad enthusiasts. Highlights include the presidential railroad car "Ferdinand Magellan," two California Zephyr cars, and three old Florida East Coast Railway steam locos. There's even a 2-foot gauge railroad for children to ride.

Miami Metrozoo ⓭

12400 SW 152nd St, Perrine. 【 (305) 251-0400. 🚈 Metrorail (Dadeland North) then Zoo Bus. ☐ 9:30am–5:30pm daily. 🅆 ⓰
🆆 www.metro-dade.com/parks

THIS GIANT ZOO is one of the country's best. Animals are kept in spacious landscaped habitats, separated from humans by moats. Highlights include lowland gorillas, Malayan sun bears, and white Bengal tigers. The Petting Zoo offers elephant rides, and the Wildlife Show demonstrates the agility of big cats.

Take the 20-minute ride on the monorail for an overview, and then visit what you like; or take the monorail to Station 4 and then walk back.

Monkey Jungle ⓮

14805 SW 216th St, Cutler Ridge. 【 (305) 235-1611. 🚈 Metrorail (Dadeland South) then bus 1, 52 or Busway Max to Cutler Ridge Mall, then taxi. ☐ 9:30am–5pm daily. 🅆 ⓰
🆆 www.monkeyjungle.com

A macaque, one of the most active primates at Monkey Jungle

Crescent moon sculpted from rock at Coral Castle

Coral Castle ⓯

28655 S Dixie Hwy, Homestead. 【 (305) 248-6344. 🚈 Metrorail (Dadeland South) then bus Busway Max. ☐ 9am–6pm daily. ● Dec 25. 🅆 ⓰
|🆆| www.coralcastle.com

FROM 1920 TO 1940, a Latvian named Edward Leedskalnin single-handedly built this series of giant castle-like sculptures out of coral rock, using tools assembled from automobile parts. He sculpted most of the stones 10 miles (16 km) away in Florida City, moving them again on his own to their present site. Some, such as a working telescope, represent their creator's great passion for astrology. Others, such as the heart-shaped table, remember a Latvian girl who refused to marry him.

SHOPPING IN MIAMI

MIAMI'S SHOPS range from the ultra chic to the quirky and colorful, reflecting the nature of the city. Being made up of neighborhoods, Miami offers a choice of districts to shop in. Serious shoppers will probably gravitate toward the malls, which attract visitors from all over Latin America and the Caribbean. Some of these double as entertainment centers *(see p332)*, often staying open until 11pm, but most of the stores tend to keep normal hours.

Gucci logo, Bal Harbour Shops

If your shopping tastes are more offbeat, head for Coconut Grove or South Beach, where shops are aimed at a totally different market. Here, wild leather gear, motorized skateboards, cardboard art, and the like are offered, and you can pick up fun souvenirs too. Most stores in Coconut Grove stay open late, especially on weekends. Stores in South Beach keep irregular hours, with most opening up late in the day; some don't get going until 11am or noon.

WHERE TO SHOP

SOUTH BEACH is a fun place to shop, but the most relaxed shopping area is Coconut Grove. It has numerous boutiques concentrated in a small area and boasts two malls *(see p82):* **CocoWalk**, whose two dozen jewelry, gift, and clothing stores play second fiddle to cafés and restaurants, and the **Streets of Mayfair** – where pricey boutiques are suitable mainly for window-shopping.

Bayside Marketplace *(see p72)* aims to entertain but has a wide range of stores, with all kinds of gift emporia and fashion stores. Otherwise, shop Downtown only if you're after cut-price electronics and jewelry, although **Burdines** department store, founded in 1898, is of more general interest. **Omni International Mall**, to the north, has lost out to Bayside Marketplace but has a good choice of shops as well as its own movie theater.

Entirely different in tone is Coral Gables, with its demure stores along Miracle Mile *(see p80)* and its posh art galleries.

Dedicated shoppers head for Miami's famous malls. **Bal Harbour Shops** is a fascinatingly snooty mall in a tropical garden setting whose tone is set by wealthy old ladies and security staff in uniforms with the tag "Bahamian gendarme." **Aventura Mall**, also in North Miami, is impressive only for its size: it has over 200 shops including four department stores, one of which is Macy's.

Typical window-dressing in a South Beach boutique

FASHION AND JEWELRY

MIAMI HAS EVERYTHING, from top designer to discount clothes. In Bal Harbour Shops, jewelers and fashion stores with household names such as Tiffany & Co., Gucci, and Cartier stand alongside shops like J. W. Cooper, specializing in Western gear. By contrast, **Loehmann's Fashion Island**, in nearby Aventura, deals in cut-rate designer clothes. More good deals can be had in the 100 odd discount stores of Downtown's Fashion District – on 5th Avenue between 24th and 29th Streets. The **Seybold Building**, also Downtown, is famous for its cut-rate gold, diamonds, and watches.

In South Beach, stores on Lincoln Road and Washington Avenue deal primarily in leather and "disco dolly" outfits, but there are more chic stores too. The boutiques along Miracle Mile in Coral Gables are more consistently upscale: **J. Bolado**, for made-to-measure clothes, is typical.

GIFTS AND SOUVENIRS

BAYSIDE MARKETPLACE is reliable gift-buying territory, with shops such as the **Warner Brothers Studios Store** and the **Disney Store**, and a gaggle of pushcarts laden with espadrilles, ties,

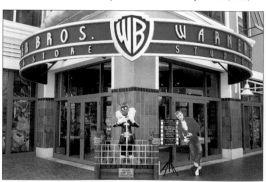

Warner Brothers Studios Store, a kids' favorite at Bayside Marketplace

Cigarmaker in action at El Crédito Factory

and other items. In Coconut Grove, alongside numerous shops selling T-shirts and sunglasses are shops specializing in anything from oriental crafts to condoms. In North Miami Beach visit **Edwin Watts Golf Shop**; this is the place to go for everything golf, including discounts on greens fees.

Burdines is not a classic hunting-ground for souvenirs, but you can sometimes pick up unusual items, such as genuine artifacts from the wreck of the *Atocha* salvaged by Mel Fisher *(see p26)*.

Chrisalyn in Miami Beach offers unusual gifts, from lamps to necklaces. They often have Victorian-style jewelry for sale.

South Beach is probably the best place for fun mementos and gifts. The **Art Deco**

Welcome Center on Ocean Drive has a small but good choice, including T-shirts, posters, and models of Ocean Drive buildings, in addition to a few genuine Art Deco antiques. The shop also maintains an impressive selection of pertinent books.

The best place for cigars is **El Crédito Cigar Factory** in Little Havana *(see p74)*. A mix of tourists and businessmen come to buy the cigars that are made by hand at the factory; the best brand is called La Gloria Cubana.

A good shop for edible souvenirs, such as Florida jellies and sauces, is **Epicure** in South Beach, although tourists are not targeted by this gourmet supermarket.

Craft stalls are set up in Española Way *(see p66)* on weekends, but Miami is generally not a good place to buy locally made crafts. Fine art is a much easier proposition. Española Way itself has a few avant-garde galleries, but you'll find a greater concentration

of better quality fine art along Lincoln Road. Most of the two dozen or so galleries, including the South Florida Art Center *(see p66)*, feature contemporary paintings, sculpture, ceramics, and furniture in provocative or Pop Art style. The art in Coral Gables' galleries is more traditional.

BOOKS AND MUSIC

I F MIAMI gives you a taste for Latin American music, you'll find a good choice at **Casino Records** in Little Havana. Try **Esperanto Music** in Miami Beach for a large selection of Latin and world music.

Books & Books in Coral Gables is everyone's favorite bookshop, with shelves from floor to ceiling and a good selection of travel and arts titles. For books about Florida, don't fail to visit the Indies Company gift shop in the Historical Museum of Southern Florida *(see p72)*, whose stock of books covers every imaginable

A ceramic Art Deco hotel

subject relating to the state. You'll find branches of chain bookstores, such as B. Dalton, in most shopping malls.

ENTERTAINMENT IN MIAMI

A FLEET OF STRETCH LIMOS parked outside the hottest nightclubs attests to the fact that South Beach is one of the trendiest places on the planet. For many people the chance to party in style is one of the city's chief attractions. Most people make for the nightclubs, which are perhaps surprisingly laid-back, and these are also good spots for live music. For anyone not into celebrity-spotting or dancing, Miami offers a good range of cultural and sports events. The city used

Miami Dolphins player in action

to be thought of as something of a cultural desert, but its performing arts scene is now buoyant. The winter season is the busiest, when Miami attracts many world-famous artists. If you are lucky, your visit may coincide with one of the city's colorful and large-scale festivals *(see pp32–5)*.

The easiest way to purchase tickets for most cultural or sports events is to call Ticketmaster *(see p339)*. Otherwise, contact the individual stadium or theater direct.

INFORMATION

THE TWO ESSENTIAL sources of information are the Weekend section of Friday's edition of the *Miami Herald*, and the free and more comprehensive *New Times*, which is published every Wednesday. For hot tips about the latest spots, read Tara Solomon's column in the *Miami Herald*. The vibrant gay nightlife of South Beach is covered in detail in several free and widely available magazines.

PERFORMING ARTS

MAJOR TOURING companies perform at the **Dade County Auditorium**, the **Jackie Gleason Theater of the Performing Arts** (known as TOPA) in South Beach, and Downtown's **Gusman Center for the Performing Arts**, a 1920s theater with a fabulous ornate Moorish interior. The Broadway Series (November to April) in the Jackie Gleason Theater leads Miami's drama scene. More intimate spots include the **Coconut Grove**

Playhouse, which stages a mix of Off-Broadway hits and more avant-garde local work, and the **Actors' Playhouse**, in Coral Gables, for new shows and old favorites.

The much-respected **Miami City Ballet** performs classical and contemporary work, often at the Jackie Gleason Theater, and you can sometimes see the dancers rehearse at the company's base in Lincoln Road. Also in South Beach, the Ballet Flamenco La Rosa, part of the **Performing Arts Network** group of dance companies, is well worth seeing; they often appear at the **Colony Theatre**.

Miami's most acclaimed classical orchestra is Michael Tilson Thomas's New World Symphony, made up of graduates from the country's most prestigious music schools; it performs at the **Lincoln Theatre** from October to May. The Concert Association of Florida *(see p336)* organizes most of Miami's top concerts, and keep an eye out for performances by the Florida Philharmonic *(see p336)*.

Hialeah Park, famous for its horse-racing and flamingos

SPECTATOR SPORTS

BOTH THE Miami Dolphins football team and the Florida Marlins baseball team compete at the **Pro Player Stadium**. The University of Miami's Hurricanes, one of Florida's top college football squads, draws almost equally large crowds; they play at the **Orange Bowl Stadium**. The Miami Heat plays basketball and the Florida Panthers ice hockey at the **Miami Arena**.

For a more typically Florida scene, catch a game of jai alai *(see p31)* at the **Miami Jai Alai Fronton** near the airport. Betting is *de rigueur* both here and at the **Hialeah Park** racetrack. See pages 30–31 for details of seasons.

LIVE MUSIC

MOST BARS on Ocean Drive offer live music, typically Latin jazz, reggae, or salsa, but there are better places. The Normandy Fountain Café in

The Coconut Grove Playhouse, which can draw New York shows

The stage show at Club Tropigala, designed to evoke the 1950s

North Miami Beach *(see p316)* is a mecca for jazz lovers. Another good place is **Tobacco Road**, Miami's oldest club, which presents anything from rock to Latin jazz nightly.

Or try one of the city's famous Latin floor shows, featuring Las Vegas-style extravaganzas with sparkling showgirls, a live band, and couples of all ages dancing salsa. **Club Tropigala** in the Fontainebleau Hotel is the best known for eating and dancing, but **Café Nostalgia**, in Little Havana is more evocative of Old Cuba – watch an old Cuban film before dancing into the small hours.

NIGHTCLUBS

TWO AREAS IN Greater Miami buzz after dark: Coconut Grove, mainly for wining and dining, and South Beach, with its far more hip scene. Here the bars along Ocean Drive and nearby streets are busy all day, and the nightclubs get going only after midnight.

New clubs are opening up all the time, so ask around for tips on SoBe's latest hot spots. Favorite places are: **Bash**, which was started by Sean Penn and Mick Hucknall and is a popular place for celebrity-spotting; **Chaos** offers an upscale scene—each Sunday

the club turns into a different city, London, Rio, or Paris; the ultra-trendy **Liquid**, with a chic crowd strutting to house, funk, soul, and hip-hop; and **Opium Gardens**, a huge open-air place with outrageous Sunday tea dances.

Many clubs have a gay night. Others advertise themselves as exclusively gay, but the scene is usually mixed. **Salvation** draws a heavily gay crowd and has a lighted dance floor, which makes anyone a dance diva. **Twist**, with a Key West-style terrace, is a very popular gay bar and has a dance floor too.

One of the four bars at the Clevelander on Ocean Drive

DIRECTORY

PERFORMING ARTS

Actors' Playhouse
280 Miracle Mile.
Map 5 1C.
(305) 444-9293.

Coconut Grove Playhouse
3500 Main Highway.
Map 6 E4.
(305) 442-2662.

Colony Theatre
1040 Lincoln Rd.
Map 2 D2.
(305) 674-1026.

Miami/Dade County Auditorium
2901 W Flagler St.
(305) 545-3395.

Gusman Center for the Performing Arts
174 E Flagler St. **Map** 4 E1.
(305) 374-2444.

Jackie Gleason Theater of the Performing Arts
1700 Washington Ave.
Map 2 E2.
(305) 673-7300.

Lincoln Theatre
541 Lincoln Rd.
Map 2 E2.
(305) 673-3330.

Miami City Ballet
905 Lincoln Rd. **Map** 2 E2.
(305) 532-4880.

Performing Arts Network
555 17th St. **Map** 2 E2.
(305) 672-0552.

SPECTATOR SPORTS

Hialeah Park
2200 E 4th Ave, Hialeah.
(305) 885-8000.

Miami Arena
721 NW 1st Ave.
(305) 530-4400.

Miami Jai Alai Fronton
3500 NW 37th Ave.
(305) 633-6400.

Orange Bowl Stadium
1501 NW 3rd St.
Map 3 1B.
(305) 643-7100.

Pro Player Stadium
2269 NW 199th St.
(305) 620-2578.

LIVE MUSIC

Café Nostalgia
2212 SW 8th St.
(305) 541-2631.

Club Tropigala
Fontainebleau Hilton,
4441 Collins Ave.
(305) 672-7469.

Tobacco Road
626 S Miami Ave.
Map 4. E2.
(305) 374-1198.

NIGHTCLUBS

Bash
655 Washington Ave.
Map 2 E4.
(305) 538-2274.

Chaos
743 Washington Ave.
Map 2 E4.
(305) 674-7350.

Liquid
1439 Washington Ave.
Map 2 F3.
(305) 532-9154

Opium Gardens
136 Collins Ave.
Map 2 E5.
(305) 531-5535.

Salvation
1771 West Ave. **Map** 2 D3.
(305) 673-6508.

Twist
1057 Washington Ave.
Map 2 E3.
(305) 538-9478.

MIAMI STREET FINDER

THE MAP REFERENCES given with all sights, shops, and entertainment venues described in the Miami chapter refer to the five pages of maps in this section. The key map below shows the area of the city that is covered, with the three major sightseeing districts color-coded pink. All the principal sights men-tioned in the text are marked, as well as useful information, such as transit stops, tourist offices, and post offices; a full list is given in the key. Map references are also given for Miami's hotels *(see pp296–9),* restaurants *(see pp316–19),* and bars and cafés *(see p330)* included in the Travelers' Needs section.

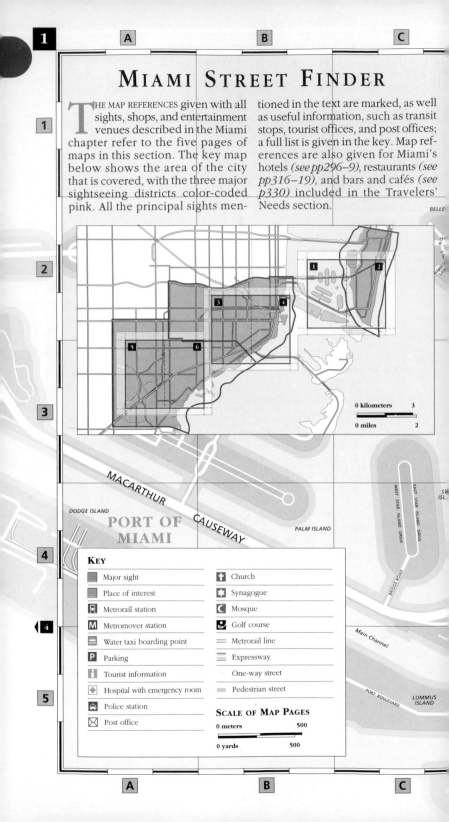

0 kilometers 3
0 miles 2

MACARTHUR CAUSEWAY

DODGE ISLAND

PORT OF MIAMI

PALM ISLAND

WEST STAR ISLAND DRIVE

EAST STAR ISLAND DRIVE

BRIDGE ROAD

Main Channel

PORT BOULEVARD

LUMMUS ISLAND

KEY

▪ Major sight		✝ Church	
▪ Place of interest		✡ Synagogue	
▪ Metrorail station		☾ Mosque	
M Metromover station		⛳ Golf course	
▪ Water taxi boarding point		= Metrorail line	
P Parking		≡ Expressway	
▪ Tourist information		— One-way street	
✚ Hospital with emergency room		▬ Pedestrian street	
▪ Police station			
⊠ Post office			

SCALE OF MAP PAGES

0 meters 500
0 yards 500

D   E   F

WEST 25TH STREET
W 23RD ST
Sunset Lake
BAYSHORE MUNICIPAL GOLF COURSE
WEST 24TH STREET
WEST 23RD STREET
WEST 22ND STREET
SUNSET DRIVE
BAY AVE
LAKE AVE
WEST 21ST STREET
24TH TER
24TH ST
Lake Pancoast
FREE
DRIVE
PINE
23RD AVENUE
22ND
COLLINS AVENUE
21ST ST
MIAMI BEACH DRIVE

NORTH BAY ROAD
ALTON ROAD
MERIDIAN
NORTH
PRAIRIE
23RD ST
AVENUE
AVENUE

20TH STREET
WASHINGTON COURT
PARK AVENUE
LIBERTY
Bass Museum of Art
MIAMI BEACH DRIVE
COLLINS AVENUE
COLLINS PARK

AVENUE
ROAD
AVENUE
19TH STREET
MICHIGAN AVENUE
BOULEVARD
DADE
Holocaust Memorial
MERIDIAN CT
19TH STREET
CONVENTION CENTER DRIVE
Miami Beach Convention Center
WASHINGTON AVENUE
19TH STREET
20TH
COLLINS

LAND VIEW PARK
18TH STREET
WEST
18TH STREET
18TH STREET

PURDY
BAY
17TH STREET
HANK MEYER BOULEVARD
City Hall
Jackie Gleason Theater
17TH STREET
JAMES AVENUE
Delano Hotel

LINCOLN COURT
AVENUE
AVENUE
AVENUE
Colony Theater
LINCOLN ROAD
MALL
Lincoln Theater
LINCOLN ROAD
Delano Hotel

WEST
ROAD
ALTON ROAD
South Florida Art Center
LINCOLN TERRACE
16TH STREET
LENOX
MICHIGAN
JEFFERSON
AVENUE
AVENUE
16TH STREET
AVENUE

15TH TER
15TH STREET
15TH STREET
15TH STREET

FLAMINGO WAY
14TH COURT
14TH TER
ESPANOLA WAY
Warsaw Ballroom

13TH TER
14TH STREET
MERIDIAN
14TH PLACE
EUCLID
14TH ST
AVENUE

MONAD TER
13TH STREET
FLAMINGO PARK
13TH STREET
Miami Beach Post Office
13TH ST
OCEAN DRIVE

12TH STREET
MEMORIAL FIELD
D'EXEL
WASHINGTON
12TH ST
Marlin Hotel
Cardozo Hotel
Amsterdam Palace

11TH STREET
PENNSYLVANIA
Old City Hall
11TH ST
Cleveland Hotel
AVENUE
LUMMUS PARK

10TH STREET
Wolfsonian Foundation
10TH
Clevelander Hotel

FL
Art Deco Welcome Center

9TH STREET
9TH ST
COLLINS

ROAD
AVENUE
8TH STREET
8TH ST
News Café

ALTON
WEST
7TH STREET
AVENUE
COLLINS AVENUE

South Shore Hospital
6TH STREET
AVENUE
AVENUE
AVENUE
AVENUE
6TH ST
Park Central Hotel

5TH   STREET

MIAMI BEACH

US Coast Guard Base
LENOX
ALTON
4TH STREET
MICHIGAN
JEFFERSON
MERIDIAN
EUCLID
4TH STREET
AVENUE
OCEAN DRIVE

3RD STREET
3RD STREET
Sanford L Ziff Jewish Museum

Miami Beach Marina
ROAD
2ND STREET
WASHINGTON
2ND STREET
COLLINS AVENUE
OCEAN FRONT PARK

1ST STREET
1ST STREET
PIER PARK

COMMERCE STREET
Joe's Stone Crab Restaurant
BISCAYNE STREET

NAROY STREET
INLET BOULEVARD

SOUTH POINTE PARK

D   E   F

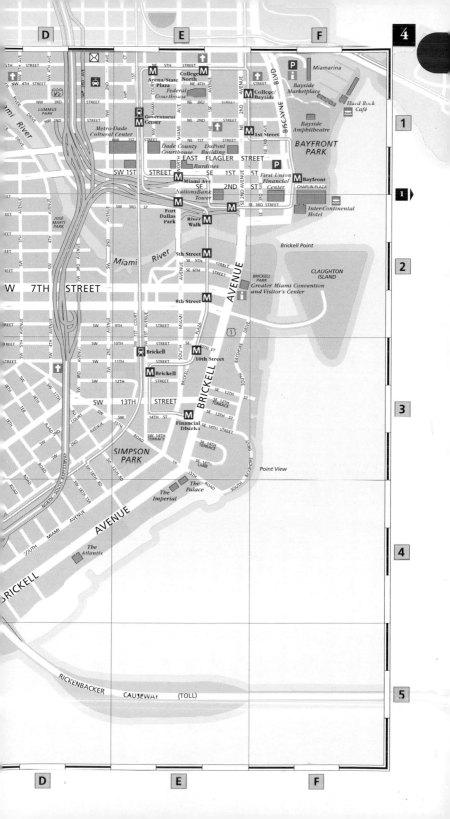

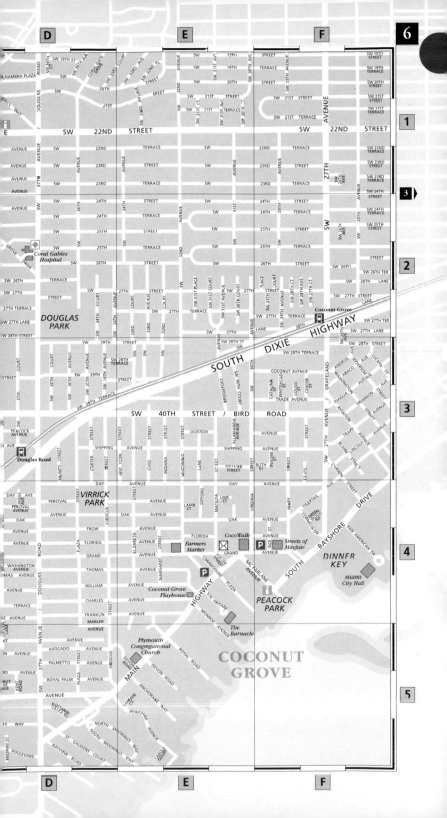

FLORIDA AREA
BY AREA

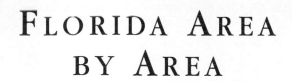

Florida at a Glance

W ALT DISNEY WORLD ASIDE, Florida is best known for its
beaches; there are so many of these that everyone
should be able to find one to suit his taste. Most tourist
attractions, from state-of-the-art museums to historic
towns, are also found along the coast. The joy of
Florida, however, is that inland destinations are within
easy reach. It is well worth venturing away from the
hubbub of the coast to explore some of the state's richest
natural landscapes and get the full flavor of Florida.

Canoeing is very popula
the Panhandle, where r
such as the Suwannee
frequently flanked by
vegetation. (See p2

**THE
PANHANDLE**
(see pp210–231)

TH
NORTH
(see pp18

Beaches in the
Panhandle boast the
finest sand in Florida,
washed by the warm
waters of the Gulf of
Mexico. Resorts like
Panama City Beach
throng with people
in the summer.
(See pp222–3.)

THE
GULF CO
(see pp232

Busch Gardens, which
combines a wildlife park
with roller coasters and
other rides, is the top
large-scale family attraction outside Orlando.
(See pp250–51.)

0 kilometers   75

0 miles   75

The Ringling Museum of Art boasts one of the
state's top art collections and has a handsome
courtyard filled with copies of Classical statuary,
including this Lygia and the Bull. (See pp256–9.)

Castillo de San Marcos is a 17th-century Spanish fort in Florida's oldest town, St. Augustine. Its well-preserved state is due to both its design and its 13-ft (4-m) thick walls. (See pp200–201.)

Orlando's theme parks are Florida's principal attraction away from the coast. Here, you can escape into a man made fantasy world, where an extraordinary array of shows and rides provide the entertainment. Most famous is Walt Disney World (see pp138–63), but Universal Studios (see pp168–73), pictured here, and Sea World (see pp164–7) draw their own vast crowds.

Daytona Beach (*see pp203–205*)

Kennedy Space Center (*see pp182–7*)

ORLANDO AND THE SPACE COAST (*see pp134–187*)

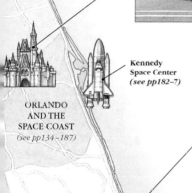

The Gold Coast is full of luxurious homes. In Palm Beach you can visit the 1920s home of Henry Flagler, and marvel at the mansions and yachts along the Intracoastal Waterway (See pp114–21.)

THE GOLD AND TREASURE COASTS (*see pp106–133*)

THE EVERGLADES AND THE KEYS (*see pp266–289*)

John Pennekamp Coral Reef State Park (*see pp278–9*)

Everglades National Park, a vast expanse of prairie, swamp, and mangrove that teems with wildlife, is as wild as Florida gets. It is just a short drive from Miami. (See pp272–7.)

THE GOLD AND TREASURE COASTS

N AMED AFTER BOOTY *found in Spanish galleons wrecked along their shores, the Gold and Treasure coasts today are two of the state's wealthiest regions. The promise of winter sunshine once lured just the well-to-do but now entices millions of vacationers.*

Vacations center on the pencil-thin barrier islands that extend right along the coast, squeezed between prime beaches and the Intracoastal Waterway *(see p28)*. The Treasure Coast, stretching from Sebastian Inlet down to Jupiter Inlet, is relatively undeveloped, with great sweeps of wild, sandy beaches and affluent but unshowy communities.

Wedged between the Atlantic and the Everglades, the 60-mile (97-km) Gold Coast extends from just north of West Palm Beach down to Miami. Before being opened up by Flagler's East Coast Railroad in the late 19th century, this part of Florida was a wilderness populated only by Indians and the occasional settler. Today, except for golf courses and scattered parks, it is unremittingly built up. The Gold Coast divides into two counties. In Palm Beach County, rich northerners, most of whom have made their fortunes elsewhere, flaunt their privileged lifestyle in million-dollar homes and on croquet lawns and polo fields.

The winter resorts of Palm Beach and Boca Raton offer the most memorable glimpses of how affluent Americans spend their time and money. Broward County, synonymous with Greater Fort Lauderdale, is one huge metropolis. Its relentless urbanization is relieved by waterways and beaches: including in Fort Lauderdale itself, one of several local resorts that let their hair down more than their stuffy Palm Beach County counterparts.

Looking out toward the Atlantic Ocean from the top of Jupiter Inlet Lighthouse

◁ One of the verdant alleyways along Worth Avenue, Palm Beach's exclusive shopping street

Exploring the Gold and Treasure Coasts

MOST VISITORS COME here for a stay-put beach vacation. North of Palm Beach you can expect an unspoiled, uncrowded littoral, while to the south you'll find condos, sunbeds, and lots of company. Coastal parks rich in bird life provide reminders of how the land looked in its virgin state. Cultural sightseeing comes fairly low on the agenda, but West Palm Beach's superb Norton Museum of Art and the exclusive town of Palm Beach should not be missed. The more active can play golf, shop, and fish – the main reason to head inland is for the excellent fishing on Lake Okeechobee. All along the coast, hotel rooms are hard to come by and twice the price from December to April; by contrast, in summer most of the resorts are very quiet.

Boca Raton's Old Town Hall, the work of Addison Mizner *(see p116)*

SIGHTS AT A GLANCE

KEY

▬▬▬	Expressway
▬▬▬	Major highway
▬▬▬	Secondary route
▬▬▬	Scenic route
≋	River
☀	Vista

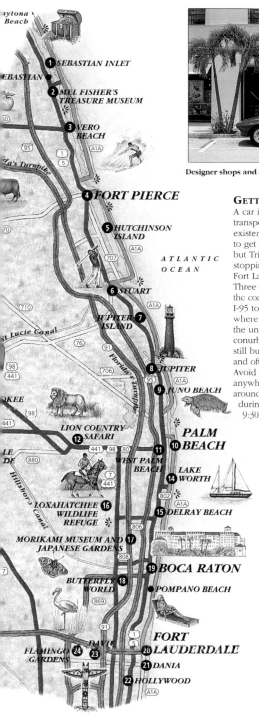

Designer shops and cars in exclusive Palm Beach

GETTING AROUND

A car is absolutely essential, as public transportation is either limited or non-existent. Amtrak basically offers ways to get to (rather than around) the area, but Tri-Rail *(see p360)* has services stopping at towns and airports between Fort Lauderdale and West Palm Beach. Three main highways run the length of the coast. Use the fast moving, multilaned I-95 to travel any distance. Avoid US 1 where possible: it trawls slowly through the unscenic center of every significant conurbation. Route A1A can be slower still but is normally far less congested and often delivers picturesque views. Avoid traveling on major roads anywhere along the Gold Coast and around the Treasure Coast's main centers during rush hours (weekdays 7:30–9:30am and 4:30–7pm).

SEE ALSO

Fort Lauderdale's popular beach, offering a wealth of water sports

Sebastian Inlet ❶

Road map F3. Indian River Co.
🚉 *Sebastian.* 🛈 *700 Main St,
(561) 589-5969.*

AT SEBASTIAN INLET, the Atlantic Ocean mingles with the brackish waters of the Indian River section of the Intracoastal Waterway *(see p21)*. The **Sebastian Inlet State Recreation Area** spans this channel and, with its 3 miles (5 km) of pristine beaches, is one of the most popular state parks in Florida.

A tranquil cove on the northern side of the inlet is an ideal place to swim – avoiding the waves that make the southern shores (on Orchid Island) one of the best surfing spots on Florida's east coast. Competitions take place on many weekends, and there are boards for rent. The park is famous for its fishing too, and the inlet's mouth is invariably very crowded with fishing boats. The two jetties jutting out into the Atlantic Ocean on either side are also crammed with anglers, while more lines dangle in the limpid waters of the Indian River.

At the southern end of the park, the **McLarty Treasure Museum** takes an in-depth look at the history surrounding the loss of a Spanish Plate Fleet in 1715. On July 31 a hurricane wrecked 11 galleons on the shallow reefs off the coast between Sebastian Inlet and Fort Pierce. The ships were en route from Havana back to Spain, riding the waters of the warm Gulf Stream, and laden with booty from Spain's New World colonies. About a third of the 2,100 sailors lost their lives, while the survivors set up a camp where the McLarty Treasure Museum now stands.

Immediately following this tragedy, some 80 percent of the cargo was salvaged by the survivors, helped by local Ais Indians. The fleet then lay undisturbed until 1928, when one of the wrecks was rediscovered. Salvaging resumed in the early 1960s; since then, millions of dollars worth of treasures have been recovered. Finds on display include gold and silver coins but feature mostly domestic items such as rings, buttons, and cutlery.

Spanish plate, McLarty Museum

🐚 **Sebastian Inlet SRA**
9700 S A1A, Melbourne Beach. 📞 *(321) 984-4852.*
🕙 *daily.* 📷 ♿

🏛 **McLarty Treasure Museum**
1380 N Route A1A. 📞 *(561) 589-2147.* 🕙 *10am-4:30pm daily* 📷 ♿

Mel Fisher's Treasure Museum ❷

Road map F3. Indian River Co. 1322 US 1, Sebastian. 📞 *(561) 589-9875.*
🚉 *Sebastian.* 🕙 *daily.* ⚫ *Easter, Thanksgiving, Dec 25, Jan 1.* 📷 ♿
🌐 www.melfisher.com

ONE OF THE GREAT rags-to-riches stories is presented at this amazing museum. Billed as "The World's Greatest Treasure Hunter," Mel

The late Mel Fisher, treasure hunter and founder of the Museum

Fisher died in 1998, but his treasure-hunting "Golden Crew" team of divers lives on.

The museum in downtown Sebastian contains treasures from different wrecks, including the 1715 fleet (which his team has been salvaging for decades), and goodies from the *Atocha (see p26)*. There are dazzling jewels, a gold bar (with the challenge to lift it), as well as more everyday items. In the Bounty Room, you can buy original Spanish *reales* or facsimiles of historic jewelry.

Vero Beach ❸

Road map F3. Indian River Co.
🏠 *18,000.* 🚉 🛈 *1216 21st St,
(561) 567-3491.*

THE MAIN TOWN of Indian River County, Vero Beach, and in particular its resort community on Orchid Island, is a seductive, well-heeled place. Mature live oaks line the residential streets, and buildings are restricted to no more than four stories. Pretty boarded houses along Ocean Drive contain galleries, boutiques, and antique shops.

The **Center for the Arts** in Riverside Park on Orchid Island puts on high-profile exhibitions, but the town is most famous for its beaches and two hotels. The Driftwood Resort, in the heart of oceanfront Vero Beach, began life in 1935 as a beach house. It was created out of reclaimed wood and driftwood by a local eccentric and filled with an amazing array of bric-a-brac, which you can still see today. Seven miles (11 km) north at

Catching the waves at the Gold Coast's Sebastian Inlet

Wabasso Beach, one of the best of the superb shell-strewn sands all along Orchid Island, is the Vero Beach Resort *(see p301)*. Disney's first Florida hotel outside Orlando, this is a model of measured elegance – with hardly a (Mickey) mouse in sight.

The **Indian River Citrus Museum**, on the mainland, is dedicated to the area's chief crop. All kinds of items to do with the citrus industry are displayed, including some old photographs, harvesting equipment, and brand labels.

🏛 Center for the Arts
3001 Riverside Park Drive. **(** *(561) 231-0707.* **●** *Thanksgiving, Dec 25, Jan 1* **&**

🏛 Indian River Citrus Museum
2140 14th Ave. **(** *(561) 770-2263.* **○** *Tue–Fri.* **●** *public hols.* **&**

Fort Pierce ❹

Road map F3. St. Lucie Co.
👥 *39,500.* **✈ ❑ ℹ** *2300 Virginia Ave, (561) 462-1535.*

NAMED AFTER a military post built during the Second Seminole War *(see pp44–5)*, Fort Pierce is not considered a tourist mecca. The town's biggest draw is its barrier islands, reached by way of two causeways that sweep across the Intracoastal Waterway.

Take the North Beach Causeway to reach North Hutchinson Island. Its southern tip is occupied by the **Fort Pierce Inlet State Recreation Area**, which includes the town's best beach, backed by dunes and popular with surfers. Just

Vero Beach's Driftwood Resort, built of reclaimed wood

to the north, on the site of a World War II training school, is the **UDT-SEAL Museum**. From 1943 to 1946, more than 3,000 US Navy frogmen of the Underwater Demolition Teams (UDTs) trained here, learning how to disarm sea mines and beach defenses. By the '60s, they had become an elite advance fighting force known as SEALs (Sea, Air, Land commandos). The museum explains the frogmen's roles in World War II, Korea, Vietnam, and Kuwait. Outside are several SEAL delivery vehicles, which are torpedo-like submarines used to carry people but not bombs and explosives.

Half a mile (0.8 km) away is Jack Island – actually a peninsula on the Indian River. This mangrove-covered preserve teems with bird life and is crossed by a short trail leading to an observation tower. Situated on the southern

causeway linking Fort Pierce to Hutchinson Island is the **St. Lucie County Historical Museum**. This has an enjoyable array of displays, which include finds from the 1715 wrecks in the Galleon Room and reconstructions of a Seminole camp and an early 20th-century general store. You can also look around the adjacent "cracker" home *(see p28)*, built in 1907, which was transported in its entirety to its present site in 1985.

Frogman, UDT-SEAL Museum

🚱 Fort Pierce Inlet SRA
905 Shorewinds Drive, N Hutchinson Island. **(** *(561) 468-3985.* **🌊 &** *limited.*

🏛 UDT-SEAL Museum
3300 N Route A1A. **(** *(561) 595-5845.* **○** *Jan–May: daily; May–Dec: Tue–Sun.* **●** *public hols.* **🌊 &**

🏛 St. Lucie County Historical Museum
414 Seaway Drive. **(** *(561) 162-1795.* **○** *Tue–Sun.* **●** *public hols.* **🌊 &**

A 1937 brand label from central Florida using the Indian River name

INDIAN RIVER'S CITRUS INDUSTRY

Citrus fruits were brought to Florida by the Spanish in the 16th century: each ship was purportedly required to leave Spain with 100 citrus seeds for planting in the new colonies. Conditions in Florida proved ideal, and the fruit trees flourished, particularly along the Indian River between Daytona and West Palm Beach, which became the state's most important citrus-growing region. In 1931, local farmers created the Indian River Citrus League to stop growers outside the area from describing their fruit as "Indian River." One third of Florida's citrus crop and 75 percent of its grapefruit yield is produced here. The majority of the oranges are used to make juice; the oranges are especially sweet and juicy because of the warm climate, soil conditions, and rainfall.

Gilbert's Bar House of Refuge Museum, on the Atlantic shore of Hutchinson Island

Hutchinson Island ❺

Road map F3. St. Lucie Co/Martin Co. 🏛 5,000. 🛈 1910 NE Jensen Beach Blvd, (561) 334-3444.

EXTENDING MORE THAN 20 miles (32 km), this barrier island is most memorable for the cornucopia of breathtaking beaches. In the south of the island, sun-worshipers head for Sea Turtle Beach and the adjacent Jensen Beach Park, close to the junction of routes 707 and A1A. Stuart Beach, at the head of the causeway across the Indian River to Stuart, is well frequented too.

By Stuart Beach is the **Elliott Museum**, created in 1961 in honor of inventor Sterling Elliott, some of whose quirky contraptions are on show. Most space here is devoted to a sparkling collection of antique cars, reconstructions of 19th- and early 20th-century rooms and local history displays.

Continuing south for about a mile (1.6 km), you reach **Gilbert's Bar House of Refuge Museum**. Erected in 1875, it is one of ten such

shelters along the east coast, established by the Lifesaving Service (predecessors of the US Coast Guard) for shipwreck victims. The stark rooms in the charming clapboard house show how hard life was for the early caretakers, who often stayed only a year.

A replica of an 1840s "surf boat" used on rescue missions sits outside. Beyond the refuge is **Bathtub Beach**, the best on the island. The natural pool formed by a sandstone reef offshore makes it a safe and popular swimming spot, especially for families.

🏛 **Elliott Museum**
825 NE Ocean Blvd. 🅲 (561) 225-1961. ⭘ daily. ⬤ Easter, Jul 4, Thanksgiving, Dec 25, Jan 1. 🎫 ♿
🏛 **Gilbert's Bar House of Refuge Museum**
301 SE MacArthur Blvd. 🅲 (561) 225-1875. ⭘ daily. ⬤ Easter, Thanksgiving, Dec 25, Jan 1. 🎫 ♿

Stuart ❻

Road map F3. Martin Co. 🏛 17,000. 🛈 1650 S Kanner Highway, (561) 287-1088.

THE MAGNIFICENT causeway across the island-speckled Indian River from Hutchinson Island offers a fine approach to Martin County's main town. Ringed by affluent waterfront enclaves and residential golf developments, Stuart has a fetching, rejuvenated downtown area, which is bypassed

by the busy coastal highways. To the south of Roosevelt Bridge, along Flagler Avenue and Osceola Street, there's a short riverside boardwalk, a smattering of pretty 1920s brick and stucco buildings, and a number of art galleries. In the evenings, live music emanates from buzzing and artfully decorated restaurants and bars.

The Florida scrub jay, a resident of Jupiter Island's sand pine scrub

Jupiter Island ❼

Road map F4. Martin Co. 🏛 200. 🛈 800 N US 1, (561) 746-7111.

MUCH OF THIS LONG, thin island is a well-to-do residential neighborhood, but there are also several excellent public beaches.

Toward Jupiter Island's northern end, **Hobe Sound National Wildlife Refuge** beckons with more than 3 miles (5 km) of beach, mangroves, and magnificent unspoiled dunes. The other half of the refuge, a strip of pine scrub flanking the Intracoastal Waterway, is a haven for birds, including the Florida scrub jay. There is a nature center by the junction of US 1 and A1A.

Blowing Rocks Preserve, a short distance farther south, has a fine beach. During storms, holes in the shoreline's limestone escarpment shoot water skyward – hence the name.

🦋 **Hobe Sound National Wildlife Refuge**
13640 SE Federal Hwy. 🅲 (561) 546-6141. 🎫 to the beach. **Beach** ⭘ daily. **Nature Center** 🅲 (561) 546-2076. ⭘ Mon–Fri. ⬤ public hols.

The brightly painted Riverwalk Café, St. Lucie Street, downtown Stuart

ENVIRONS: Named after a man who was shipwrecked nearby in 1696, **Jonathan Dickinson State Park** comprises habitats as diverse as mangrove swamps, pine flatwoods, and a cypress-canopied stretch of the Loxahatchee River. As well as walking and horseback riding trails, there are canoes for rent and boat trips along the river; manatees, alligators, ospreys, and herons are often sighted along the way.

Jupiter Inlet Lighthouse as seen from Jupiter Beach Park

✕ Jonathan Dickinson State Park
16450 SE Federal Hwy ☎ (561) 546-2771. ⬭ daily. ⬭ ⬭ limited.

Jupiter ❽

Road map F4. Palm Beach Co. ⬭ 35,000. ⬭ 800 N US 1, (561) 746-7111.

THE SMALL town of Jupiter is best known for its pristine beaches and for the spring-training camps of the Montreal Expos and the St. Louis Cardinals. The **John D. MacArthur Beach** on Singer Island is one of the state's best. The **Florida History Center and Museum** has exhibits relating to the area's original inhabitants, the Hobe Indians, and the English settlers who arrived here during the 18th century.

🏛 Florida History Center and Museum
805 N US 1. ☎ (561) 747-6639. ⬭ Tue–Sun. ⬭ public hols. ⬭

✕ John D. MacArthur State Park
Singer Island (cross the Intracoastal Waterway on Blue Heron Blvd, turn north on Ocean Blvd. ⬭ daily.

ENVIRONS: Close by, on the south side of Jupiter Inlet, is a beautiful county park, **Jupiter Beach Park**. It is easily accessible and has a superb beach of chocolate-colored sand, complete with lifeguards; it is also a mecca for anglers and pelicans. There are picnic pavilions, tables, a children's play area, rest rooms, and a fishing jetty. There is a good view across to scenic **Jupiter Inlet Lighthouse**, dating from 1860 and the oldest structure in the county, which you can climb for a wider perspective. The old oil house at its base is now a small museum. In addition to the Lighthouse, there is an added bonus for Sunday visitors: the 1896 Dubois House Museum,

operated by the Loxahatchee Historical Society and furnished in turn-of-the-century pioneer style, offers free tours. Nearby is the huge **Carlin Park**, operated by the Parks and Recreation Department of Palm Beach County. It offers playing fields, picnic areas, tennis courts, rest rooms, and a guarded beach.

⬭ Jupiter Inlet Lighthouse
Beach Rd at US 1. ☎ (561) 747-8380. ⬭ Sun–Wed. ⬭ public hols. ⬭
⬭ Carlin Park
400 Florida Hwy, A1A S ☎ (561) 624-0065 ⬭ daily. Lifeguards on duty from 9am to 5:20pm..

Juno Beach ❾

Road map F4. Palm Beach Co. ⬭ 2,700. ⬭ 1555 Palm Beach Lakes Blvd, (561) 471-3995.

THE PRISTINE SANDS by Juno Beach, a small community that stretches north to Jupiter Inlet, are one of the world's most productive nesting sites for loggerhead turtles. In Loggerhead Park, nestled between US 1 and Route A1A, the fascinating **Marine-life Center** is an eco-science center and nature trail. Injured turtles, perhaps cut by boat propellers or snagged on fishing lines, recuperate in tanks. A path leads through undisturbed sand dunes to the beach where turtles nest during the summer. Advance reservations are a must.

✕ Marinelife Center
14200 US 1 ☎ (561) 627-8280. ⬭ Tue–Sun. ⬭ Dec 25. ⬭
⬭ www.marinelife.org

FLORIDA'S SEA TURTLES

Florida's central east coast is the top sea turtle nesting area in the US. From May to September female turtles lumber up the beaches at night to lay about 100 eggs in the sand. Two months later the hatchlings emerge and dash for the ocean, again under the cover of darkness. Sea turtles, including Florida's most common species, the loggerhead, are threatened partly because hatchlings are disoriented by lights from buildings.

The approved way to see a turtle laying eggs is to join an organized turtle watch. These nocturnal expeditions are popular all along the coast: call local chambers of commerce, such as the one in Juno Beach, for details.

A loggerhead hatchling's first encounter with the sea

Palm Beach

LITERALLY AND METAPHORICALLY insular, Palm Beach has long provided an eye-opener on serious American wealth. Henry Flagler, pioneer developer of South Florida *(see p121)*, created this winter playground for the rich at the end of the 19th century. In the 1920s, the architect Addison Mizner *(see p116)* gave the resort a further boost and transformed the look of Palm Beach by building lavish Spanish-style mansions for its seasonal residents.

Tiffany & Co.'s clock

As recently as the 1960s, the town virtually closed down in summer – even traffic lights were dismantled. Nowadays, Palm Beach stays open all year, but it is still essentially a winter resort. In purportedly the richest town in the US, visitors can observe the *beau monde* as they idle away the hours in some of the state's most stylish shops and restaurants or make their way to private clubs and glamorous charity balls.

Via Roma's grand entrance belies the charming alleyway beyond

Stylish Worth Avenue, shopping mecca for the very rich

Worth Avenue

For an insight into the Palm Beach lifestyle, Worth Avenue is compulsive viewing. While their employers toy over an Armani dress or an antique Russian icon, chauffeurs keep the air conditioning turning over in the Rolls Royces outside. Stretching four fabulous blocks from Lake Worth to the Atlantic Ocean, it is the town's best known thoroughfare.

Worth Avenue, as well as the architecture of Addison Mizner, first became fashionable with the construction of the exclusive Everglades Club, at the western end, in 1918. This was the result of the collaboration between Mizner and Paris Singer, the heir to the sewing machine fortune, who had first invited the architect down

to Florida. Originally intended as a hospital for officers shell-shocked during World War I, it never housed a single patient, and instead became the town's social hub. Today, the building's loggias and Spanish-style courtyards are still a very upscale, members-only enclave.

Across the street, and in stark contrast to the club's rather plain exterior, are Via Mizner and Via Parigi, lined with colorful shops and restaurants. These interlinking pedestrian alleys were created by Mizner in the 1920s, and are Worth Avenue's aesthetic highlights. Inspired by the backstreets of Spanish villages, the lanes are a riot of

Water fountain, Via Mizner

arches, tiled and twisting flights of steps, bougainvillea, fountains, and pretty courtyards. Overlooking the alleys' entrances are the office tower and villa that Mizner designed for himself. The tower's first floor originally housed display space for his ceramics business and was the avenue's first commercial unit. Connecting the two buildings is a walkway that forms the entrance to Via Mizner's shopping area. The other vias off Worth Avenue are more modern but, built in the same style and decorated with flowers and attractive window displays, they are nonetheless charming. Don't miss Via Roma or the courtyards joining Via de Lela and Via Flora.

Worth Avenue in 1939, captured by society photographer Bert Morgan

Shopping on Worth Avenue

Necklace by Lindsay Brattan

THE EPITOME of Palm Beach, Worth Avenue and the alleyways that connect with it contain some 250 exquisitely designed clothing boutiques, art galleries, and antique shops. The shop fronts, ranging in style from Mizner's signature Spanish look to Art Deco, form an eclectic yet homogeneous and pleasing mix. The artful window displays of Florida's most famous shopping street look their best when brightly lit up at night. Some windows flaunt wonderfully ironic symbols of wealth, such as fake caviar on toast or a life-sized model of a butler. In 1979, a Rolls Royce fitted with a bulldozer blade symbolically broke the ground for The Esplanade, an open-air mall at the Avenue's eastern end. It is this sort of showy display that typifies Worth Avenue and distinguishes it from other prestigious shopping areas.

WORTH AVENUE'S EXCLUSIVE SHOPS

Worth Avenue boasts a spectacular mix of glitzy shops. Jewelry stores abound, including those specializing in high quality imitations, and you'll also find elegant ready-to-wear houses, fancy gift shops, designer boutiques, and luxury department stores.

Cartier has the ultimate in gifts and souvenirs. Choose from gold jewelry, pens and, of course, their signature watches.

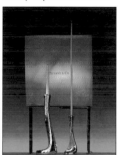

Tiffany & Co. is one of the most famous names on Worth Avenue. Best known for its jewelry (including exclusive designs by Paloma Picasso) and silverware, it also sells perfume and leather goods.

Saks Fifth Avenue, located in the elegant Esplanade mall, has two floors of luxury apparel from lingerie to designer menswear.

Greenleaf and Crosby jewelers, in Palm Beach since 1896, has a Deco frontage.

Ungaro's is one of Worth Avenue's designer boutiques. His womenswear is typically classy, chic, and bold. The window displays here are changed every week during the winter season.

The Meissen Shop has the world's largest collection of antique Meissen porcelain.

Exploring Palm Beach

THE SPIRIT AND IMAGINATION of Addison Mizner infuses the whole of Palm Beach. As well as those buildings he designed himself, he influenced the look of countless others. Mizner's architecture, described by a biographer as a "Bastard-Spanish-Moorish-Romanesque-Gothic-Renaissance-Bull-Market-Damn-the-Expense Style," gave his contemporaries plenty of ideas to work from. Palm Beach is full of the splendid creations of men such as Marion Wyeth, Maurice Fatio, and Howard Major, all active in the 1920s, as well as more recent imitations. Gazing at the luxurious mansions of the rich and famous in the exclusive "suburbs" is an essential activity in Palm Beach.

A panel, representing drama, of the mural in the Four Arts Library

Exploring Palm Beach

After the opulence of Worth Avenue, the atmosphere along the mainly residential streets to the north is more restrained. Leafy Cocoanut Row features some luxurious private homes, but along South County Road, which runs parallel, Mizner's influence is more in evidence – in the street's eclectic architecture, such as the immaculately restored Town Hall, built in 1926. Nearby is the attractive Mizner Memorial Park, where the centerpiece is a fountain and narrow pool flanked by palm trees, and Phipps Plaza – a quiet, shady close containing some delightful buildings with tiled windowsills and flower-decked gates. Mizner himself designed the fine coral house

Mizner Memorial Fountain

at No. 264. Also memorable is Howard Major's tropical cottage (1939), which features delicate Chinese influences.

If you have time to spare, it's worth strolling along some of the streets to the west of South County Road, where you'll find a mix of Mizneresque houses and early 20th-century bungalows set in shady gardens. In contrast, the most imposing street in this area is Royal Palm Way. Its rank of palm trees makes a fine approach to Royal Palm Bridge, which is an excellent platform for gawking at the luxury yachts on Lake Worth. This is particularly worthwhile in December, when they are decked out in colored lights for the annual boat parade.

🏛 Society of the Four Arts

Four Arts Plaza. 📞 (561) 655-7226.
Library and Gardens ☐ mid-Apr–Oct: Mon–Fri; Nov–Apr: Mon–Sat.
Galleries ☐ Oct–Apr: daily (Sun pm only). ● public hols. ♿

Founded in 1936, the Society of the Four Arts incorporates two libraries, exhibition space and an auditorium for lectures, concerts, and films.

The galleries and auditorium were originally part of a private club designed by Mizner, but Maurice Fatio's Italianate Four Arts Library building is far more striking. The murals in its loggia represent art, music, drama, and literature. The lovely grounds behind include a formal Chinese garden and a lawn dotted with modern bronze sculptures.

MIZNER'S SPANISH FANTASY

Addison Mizner (1872–1933) came to Palm Beach from New York in 1918 to convalesce after an accident. An architect by profession, he soon began to design houses, and in the process changed the face of Palm Beach and, essentially, Florida *(see p29)*. By adapting the design of old Spanish buildings to suit his environment, Mizner created a new style of architecture. He incorporated features such as loggias and external staircases to accommodate the region's high temperatures, and his workmen covered walls in condensed milk and rubbed them with steel wool to fake centuries-old dirt.

Addison Mizner in the mid-1920s

Addison Mizner became a multimillionaire, successful because of both his architectural vision and his ability to ingratiate himself into his prospective clients' milieu. He later turned his attention to Boca Raton *(see pp126–7)*, but the collapse of the Florida land boom at the end of the 1920s hit him heavily, and by the end of his life Mizner had to rely on friends to pay his bills.

Via Mizner *(see p114)*, a classic example of Mizner's work

⋔ Hibel Museum of Art, Edna Hibel Gallery

701 Lake Ave, Lake Worth. █ (561) 533-6872. ◯ Mon–Sat. ● Public hols. ♿ ⅏ www.hibel.org

Typical works of Edna Hibel, born in Boston in 1917 and still a resident of neighboring Singer Island (see p123), are idealized, sugary portraits of mothers and children from around the world. She paints on all kinds of surfaces, ranging from wood and silk to crystal and porcelain.

The museum, founded in 1977, holds over 1,000 of the artist's creations.

Brittany and Child (1994) by Edna Hibel (oil, gesso, and gold on silk)

⋔ The Breakers

1 South County Rd. █ (561) 655-6611. ✈ Wed pm. ♿ ⅏ www.thebreakers.com

Rising above Florida's oldest golf course, this mammoth Italian Renaissance structure is the third hotel on the site: the first Breakers, built in 1895, burned down in 1903. Its replacement went the same route in 1925, destroyed by a fire supposedly started by a guest's curling iron. Miraculously, the present Breakers was built in less than a year. The hotel has always been a focal point for the town's social life, hosting numerous galas in its magnificent ballrooms.

Palm Beach's grandest hotel is refreshingly welcoming to nonresidents: feel free to watch a game of croquet, have a milkshake in its old-fashioned soda shop, or nose around the lobby (with its hand-painted ceiling) and the palatial public rooms.

For a more in-depth look, take the weekly guided tour

Stretch limos waiting for business outside the Breakers Hotel

with the "resident historian." South of the hotel are three 19th-century wooden mansions, all that remain of **Breakers Row**. These were originally rented out to Palm Beach's wealthier visitors for the winter season.

⋔ Palm Beach suburbs

Palm Beach's high society normally hides away behind appropriately high hedges in multimillion-dollar mansions. Some of these were built by Mizner and his imitators in the 1920s, but since then hundreds of others have proliferated, in all kinds of styles, from Neo-Classical to Art Deco.

The most easily visible ones can be seen sitting on a ridge along South Ocean Boulevard, nicknamed "Mansion Row." At the top end, the Georgian residence at No. 126 belongs to Estée Lauder. No. 720, built by Mizner for himself in 1919, was for a time owned by John Lennon. Eight blocks beyond, Mar-a-Lago (No. 1100) is Palm Beach's grandest residence, with 58 bedrooms, 33 bathrooms, and three bomb

shelters. Built by Joseph Urban and Marion Wyeth in 1927, it was bought in 1985 by millionaire Donald Trump, who converted it into a private club with dues of $50,000.

The homes in the northern suburbs are more secluded. North County Road passes Palm Beach's biggest domestic property at No. 513, while No. 548 was reportedly on the market recently for $75 million. Beyond, No. 1095 North Ocean Boulevard was used as a winter retreat by the Kennedy family until 1995.

Glimpsing how the other half lives is discouraged by a minimum speed limit of 25 mph (40 km/h). This makes cycling an attractive option. Bikes are easy to rent (see p119), and there are various bicycle routes. The most scenic of these is the 3-mile (5-km) Lake Trail, which doubles as an exercise track for the locals. It runs from Worth Avenue virtually to the island's northern tip, hugging Lake Worth and skirting the backs of mansions; its prettiest section is north of Dunbar Road.

Mar-a-Lago, the most extravagant home in the Palm Beach suburbs

A Tour of Palm Beach

Circled by the main thoroughfares of South County Road and Cocoanut Row, this tour links up all the major sights of central Palm Beach, including Henry Flagler's impressive home, Whitehall. The section of the tour along Lake Drive South forms part of the scenic Palm Beach bicycle trail, which flanks Lake Worth and extends into the suburbs *(see p117)*. Although intended to be followed by car, parts (or all) could equally be done by bicycle, on foot, or even on skates. These alternatives get around the problem of Palm Beach's zealous traffic cops who patrol the streets in motorized golf carts.

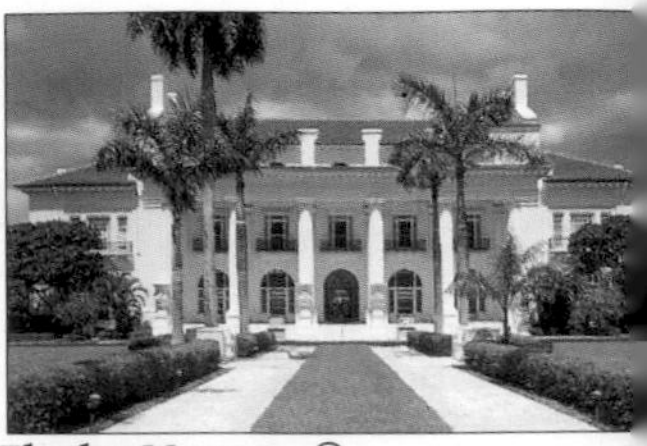

Flagler Museum ①
Formerly Flagler's private winter residence, "Whitehall" opened to the public in 1959. Beautifully restored, most of its furniture is original.

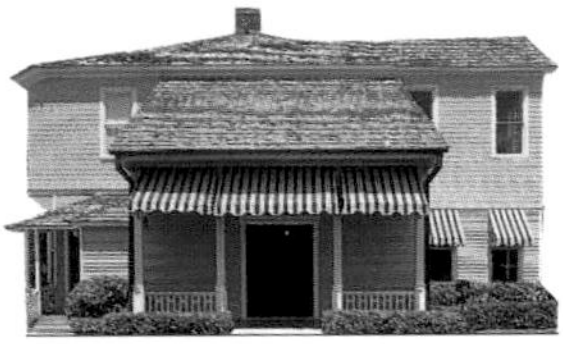

Sea Gull Cottage ②
Built in 1886, this is Palm Beach's oldest building. It was Flagler's first winter home.

Royal Poinciana Chapel ③ was built by Flagler for his guests in 1896.

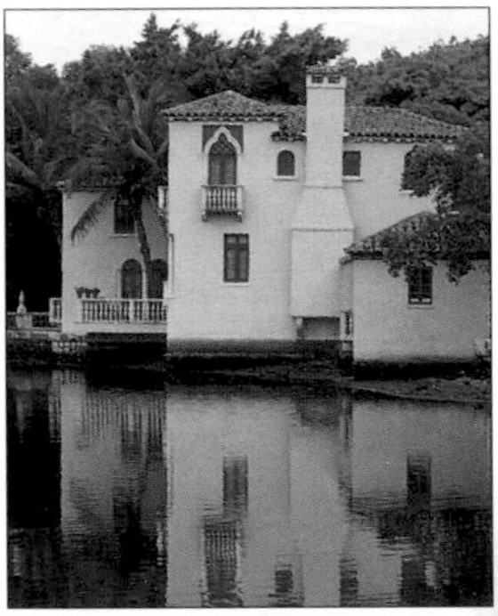

Casa de Leoni ⑤
No. 450 Worth Avenue is one of Mizner's most enchanting buildings. It set a trend for the Venetian Gothic style.

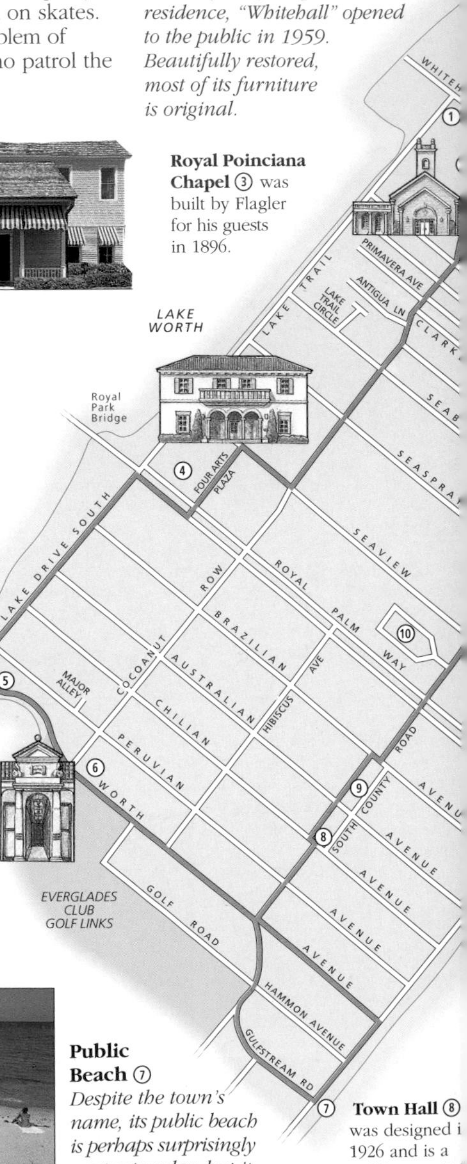

0 meters 250

0 yards 250

Key

Route of tour

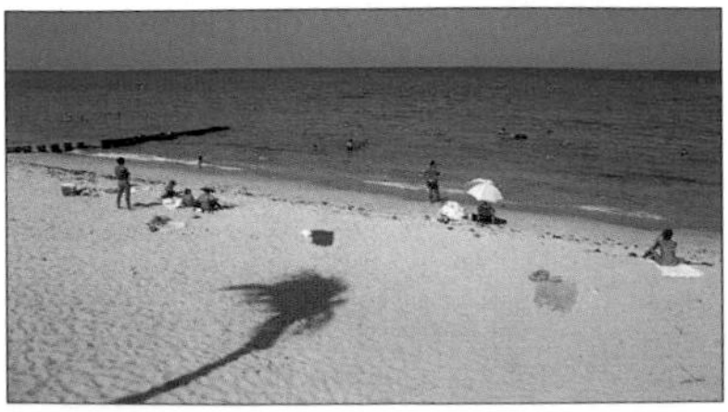

Public Beach ⑦
Despite the town's name, its public beach is perhaps surprisingly unspectacular, but it is free and open to all.

Town Hall ⑧ was designed i 1926 and is a well-known Pa Beach landmar

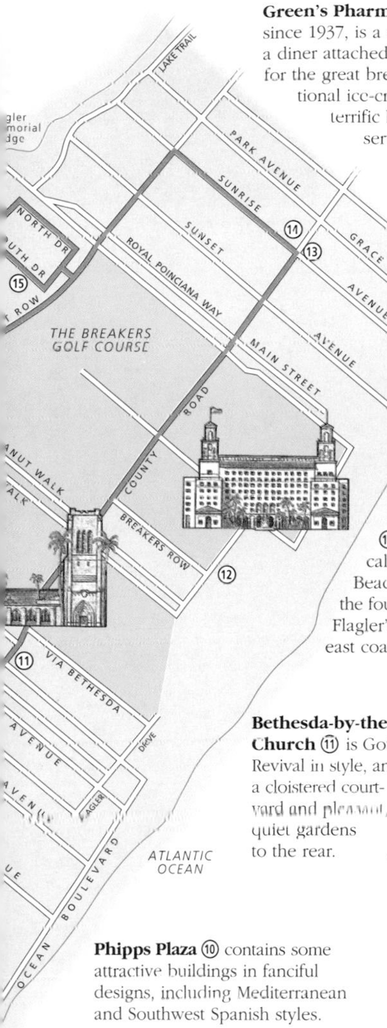

Green's Pharmacy (13), open since 1937, is a drugstore with a diner attached. People come for the great breakfasts, the traditional ice-cream sodas, and terrific burgers – all served in a lively atmosphere.

The Breakers (12), originally called the Palm Beach Inn, was the fourth of Henry Flagler's impressive east coast hotels.

Bethesda-by-the-Sea Church (11) is Gothic Revival in style, and has a cloistered courtyard and pleasant, quiet gardens to the rear.

Phipps Plaza (10) contains some attractive buildings in fanciful designs, including Mediterranean and Southwest Spanish styles.

Visitors' Checklist

Road map F4. Palm Beach Co. 👥 *10,000.* ✈ *3 miles (5 km) W.* 🚆 *Amtrak and Tri-Rail, 201 S Tamarind Ave, West Palm Beach, (800) 872-7245.* 🚌 *201 S Tamarind Ave, West Palm Beach, (800) 231-2222.* 🚍 *41, 42 from West Palm Beach.* ℹ *45 Cocoanut Row, (561) 655-3282.* 🎉 *Artigras (Feb).*

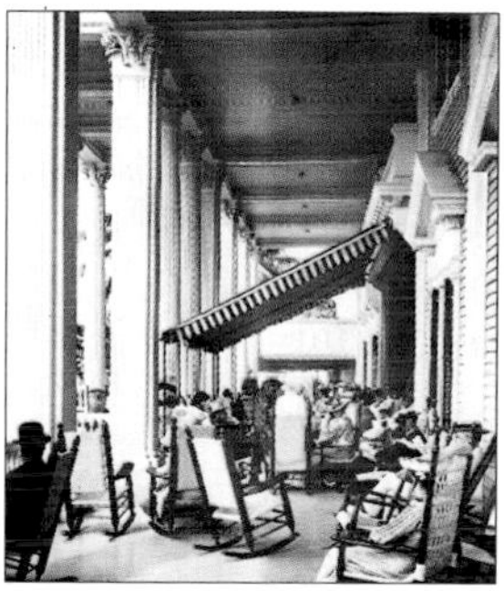

Old Royal Poinciana Hotel (15)
This lavish 2,000-room, wooden hotel was a winter retreat for the very rich. It burned down in 1935; today only the greenhouse cupola survives.

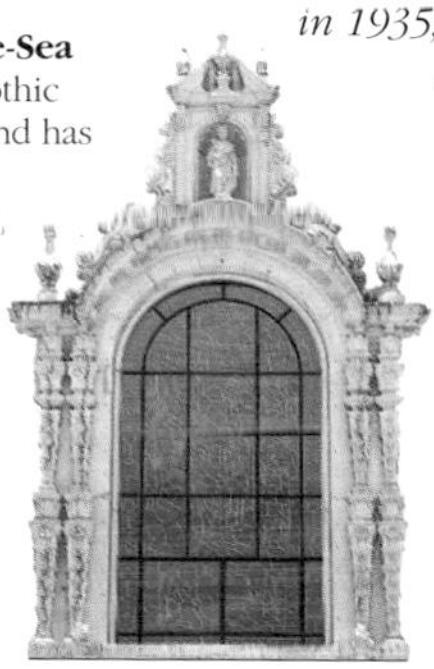

St. Edward's Church (14)
Completed in 1927, St. Edward's was built in a Spanish Revival style and features a decorative, cast stone Baroque bell tower and entrance.

Tips for Drivers

Tour length: *4.5 miles (7 km).*
Starting point: *Anywhere.*
The tour is best followed in a clockwise direction since Worth Avenue is one way, running from east to west. The Palm Beach Bicycle Trail Shop, 223 Sunrise Ave, tel (561) 659-4583 (open daily), is a good starting point if you want to rent a bicycle, tandem, or skates.
Parking: *Stock up on quarters (25c) for parking meters. There are also lots of spaces to park free for an hour, but remember not to overstay.*

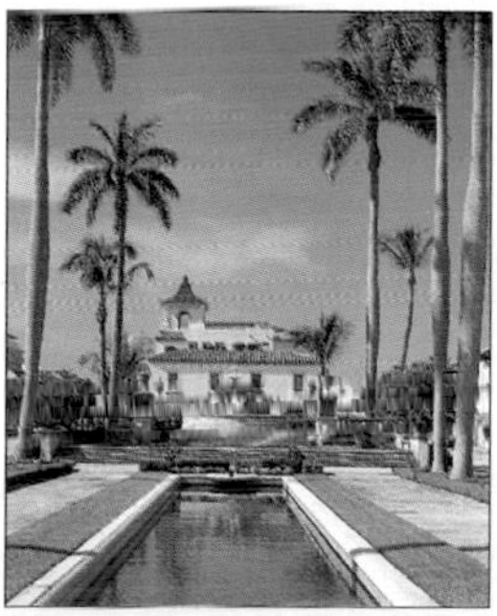

The Memorial Park fountain in downtown Palm Beach (9)

Finding the Sights

(1) Flagler Museum *(see pp120–21)*
(2) Sea Gull Cottage
(3) Royal Poinciana Chapel
(4) Society of Four Arts *(see p116)*
(5) Casa de Leoni
(6) Worth Avenue *(see pp114–5)*
(7) Public Beach
(8) Town Hall *(see p116)*
(9) Memorial Park *(see p116)*
(10) Phipps Plaza *(see p116)*
(11) Bethesda-by-the-Sea Church
(12) The Breakers *(see p117)*
(13) Green's Pharmacy
(14) St. Edward's Church
(15) Old Royal Poinciana Hotel
(16) Hibel Museum of Art *(see p117)*

Flagler Museum

Bronze detail on the front door

This 55-ROOM MANSION, known as Whitehall, was "more wonderful than any palace in Europe" after it was built in 1902 by Henry Flagler. He gave the home to his wife, Mary Lily Kenan, as a wedding present. It was intended only as a winter residence; the Flaglers traveled down every year in one of their private railroad cars *(see p47)*, now on display on the South Lawn.

In 1925, 12 years after Flagler's death, a ten-story tower was added to the rear and Whitehall became a hotel. Jean Flagler Matthews bought her grandfather's mansion in 1959 and, after costly restoration that included the removal of the tower, turned it into a museum. Whitehall stands as a monument to the indomitable spirit of America's Gilded Age.

Louis XV Ballroom
Of all the balls held in this sumptuous room, the Bal Poudré in 1903 was the most lavish.

The yellow roses bedroom had matching wallpaper and furnishings – an innovation for its time.

Swiss billiard room

★ **Master Bathroom**
Apart from a sunken bath, a toilet, and a wonderful separate shower unit, the Flaglers' private bathroom boasts this gorgeous double washstand made of onyx.

The master bedroom is furnished in yellow silk damask, a faithful copy of the original Rococo-style fabric.

Italian Renaissance Library
Lined with leather-bound books and fille with objects and orna detailing, this red, woc paneled room has a somewhat intimate fe

---

STAR FEATURES

★ **Master Bathroom**

★ **Marble Hall**

★ **Best Guest Room**

Salon
*Silk wall-coverings
and draperies
adorn this ornate
Louis XIV-style
music room.*

VISITORS' CHECKLIST

Whitehall Way. 📞 (561) 655-
2833 🕐 10am–5pm Tue–Sat,
noon–5pm Sun. ● Thanksgiving,
Dec 25, Jan 1. 📷 ♿ limited.
🎧 normally available. 📷
W www.flagler.org

★ Marble Hall
*This grand marble entrance
hall has a painted ceiling and
contains gilded chairs and
paintings, including this
formal portrait of Jean
Flagler Matthews.*

The east portico is supported
by massive fluted columns.
Outsized urns are placed on
the steps in front.

**Louis
XVI
salon**

★ Best Guest Room
*The early 1900s saw a steady
flow of guests to Whitehall. The
rich and famous stayed in this
inviting room, decorated in a
color scheme of cream and
Rose de Barry red.*

Main entrance

The grand staircase
leads off the marble
hall and is itself con-
structed of different
marbles and deco-
rated with intricate
bronze railings.

FLAGLER'S PALM BEACH

After the Spanish ship *Providencia* was wrecked in
1878, its cargo of coconuts was strewn along the
beach near Lake Worth and soon took root. Henry
Flagler, busy with his plans to develop Florida's
east coast *(see pp46–7)*, spotted the lovely palm
fringed beach around 1890. He was smitten with
the area's beauty and immediately bought up land.
In 1894, he opened the Royal Poinciana Hotel
(see p119) and in so doing set the course for the
growth of the exclusive resort of Palm Beach.

Henry Flagler and his third wife, Mary Lily, in 1910

High-rises towering over the still waters of Lake Worth in West Palm Beach

West Palm Beach ⓫

Road map F4. Palm Beach Co.
🏠 *78,000.* 🚉 🚆 *Amtrak & Tri-Rail.*
🚌 ℹ️ *1555 Palm Beach Lakes Blvd,*
(561) 471-3995.

AT THE END of the 19th century, Henry Flagler *(see p121)* decided to move the unsightly homes of Palm Beach's workers and service businesses to the mainland, out of sight of the tourists. He thus created West Palm Beach, which has been the commercial center of Palm Beach County ever since.

The city has succeeded in forging a stronger identity for itself in recent decades, but it still plays second fiddle to its infinitely more glamorous (and considerably smaller) neighbor. The sleek high-rises of downtown West Palm Beach lure only business people, while to the north lies the historic but depressed Northwest neighborhood; the outskirts of the city consist mainly of characterless residential and golfing developments.

West Palm Beach may not be the place to spend your entire holiday, but it enjoys a fine setting by scenic Lake Worth, and its small clutch of attractions are well worth making forays to visit – in particular the excellent Norton Museum of Art, rated the top museum in the southeastern US by *The New York Times.*

THE SPORT OF KINGS

Nothing better encapsulates Palm Beach County's upper-class more than the popularity of polo. From December to April, and especially on Sunday afternoons, you can follow the crowds in their blazers and boaters to clubs in West Palm Beach (the grandest), Boca Raton, and Lake Worth; together, they host some of the world's top polo championships. Tickets are cheap, and during the game you may well be treated to a jovial running commentary. Spectators often bring a champagne picnic. For information about dates call the clubs at West Palm Beach, (561) 793-6327; Boca Raton, (561) 994-1876; or Lake Worth, (561) 965-2057.

Close quarters polo action, popular entertainment along the Gold Coast

🏛 South Florida Science Museum
4801 Dreher Trail N. 📞 *(561) 832-1988.* ⏰ *daily.* ● *Thanksgiving, Dec 25.* 🅿️ 🚹 ♿ 🌐 *www.sfsm.org*
This science museum, like many in Florida, is aimed at children. There are plenty of hands-on exhibits to teach visitors about subjects such as light, sound, color, and the weather. You can have a go at creating your own clouds and even touch a mini-tornado. The best time to visit is on a Friday evening, when you can also look through a giant telescope in its observatory and watch laser light shows in the Aldrin planetarium.

🏛 Norton Museum of Art
1451 South Olive Ave. 📞 *(561) 832-5196.* ⏰ *Mon–Sun Dec–Mar.* ● *Mon Apr–Nov, public hols.* 🅿️ ♿ 🌐 *www.norton.org*
This museum has possibly the finest art collection in the state; it also attracts traveling exhibitions. The museum was established in 1941 with about 100 canvases belonging to Ralph Norton, a Chicago steel magnate who had retired to West Palm Beach. He and his wife had wide-ranging tastes, which is reflected in the art on display.

The collection falls into three main fields. First among these are the French Impressionist and Post-Impressionist art, which include paintings by Cézanne, Braque, Picasso, Matisse, and Gauguin, whose moving work *Agony in the*

Garden is the most famous painting in the museum. *Night Mist* (1945) by Jackson Pollock is another proud possession, forming part of the Norton's impressive store of 20th-century American art; this gallery also features some fine works by Winslow Homer, Georgia O'Keeffe, Edward Hopper, and Andy Warhol.

The third principal collection comprises an outstanding array of artifacts from China, including tomb jades dating from about 1500 BC and ceramic figures of animals and courtiers from the T'ang Dynasty (4th–11th centuries AD). There is also much fine Buddhist carving, in addition to more modern sculptures by Brancusi, Degas, and Rodin.

Agony in the Garden by Paul Gauguin (1889)

A rare Florida panther at the Dreher Park Zoo

✕ Palm Beach Zoo at Dreher Park

1301 Summit Blvd. ☎ *(561) 547-9453.* ○ *daily.* ● *Thanksgiving.* 🖼 🛗 w www.palmbeachzoo.org

This little zoo is as appealing to youngsters as the nearby South Florida Science Museum. Of the 100 or more species represented, most interesting are the endangered Florida panther and the giant tortoises, which can live for up to 200 years. At the re-created South American plain you can see llamas, rheas, and tapirs from an observation deck, follow a boardwalk trail through exotic foliage, or cruise around a lake alive with a huge population of pelicans.

ENVIRONS: A more pleasant alternative to staying in West Palm Beach (and a considerably cheaper option than Palm Beach) is to find accommodations north across the inlet at **Singer Island** or **Palm Beach Shores**. These are relaxing, slow-paced communities, and the wide beach is splendid, but marred by a skyline of apartment buildings.

Boating and fishing are popular activities here. Palm Beach Shores has sport-fishing boats for charter, as well as boats offering cruises around Lake Worth. The Manatee Queen is a catamaran *(see p338)* offering tours of the mansions along the Intracoastal Waterway.

At the north end of Singer Island is **John D. MacArthur Beach State Park**. Here, a dramatic boardwalk bridge meanders across a mangrove-lined inlet of Lake Worth to a hardwood hammock and a lovely beach. Brochures from the Nature Center pick out plants and wading birds, and in the summer guided nighttime walks show you nesting loggerhead turtles *(see p113).*

The Gardens mall, 2 miles (3 km) inland in Palm Beach Gardens has fragrant walkways and glass elevators that link the nearly 200 shops and appetizing food court.

✕ John D. MacArthur Beach State Park

A1A, 2 miles (3 km) N of Riviera Bridge. ☎ *(561) 624-6950.* ○ *daily; Nature Center:* ● *Tue.* 🖼 🛗 🅿 **The Gardens** 3101 PGA Blvd. ☎ *(561) 622-2115.* ○ *daily.* ● *Easter Sun, Thanksgiving, Dec 25.* 🛗

Lion Country Safari ⑫

Road map F4. Palm Beach Co. Southern Blvd W, Loxahatchee. ☎ *(561) 793-1084.* 🚉 *West Palm Beach.* 🚌 *West Palm Beach.* ○ *daily.* 🖼 🛗 w www.lioncountrysafari.com

TWENTY MILES (32 km) inland from West Palm Beach, off US 441, this park is the area's big family attraction.

There are two parts: First, you can drive through a 500-acre (200-ha) enclosure and observe lions, giraffes, rhinos, and other wildlife at close quarters. (If you have a convertible car you can rent a vehicle with a hard roof.) Second, there's a zoo and amusement park. Along with aviaries, petting areas, and islands inhabited by monkeys, there are fairground rides, boat tours, and a park populated by plastic dinosaurs. A camping area is also available. All parts of this park get very busy on weekends.

Antelope resting in the shade at Lion Country Safari

A fisherman enjoying early evening angling on Lake Okeechobee

Lake Okeechobee ⑬

Road map E4, F4. 🚌 *Palm Trans bus to Pahokee, (561) 233-1166.* 🛈 *115 E Main St, Pahokee, (561) 924-5579.* **Roland Martin** 【 *(863) 983-3151.* 🅦 *www.pahokee.com*

MEANING "BIG WATER" in the Seminole language, Okeechobee is the second largest freshwater lake in the US, covering 750 sq miles (1,942 sq km). The "Big O," as the lake is often called, is famous for its abundance of fish, particularly largemouth bass. Roland Martin or any of the many marinas will rent you a boat, tackle, bait, picnic food, or a guide and chartered boat. Nearby **Clewiston** offers the best facilities, with three marinas and a choice of decent motels.

If you're not an angler, your time in Florida is better spent elsewhere. The bird life is rich along the shore, but the lake is too big to be scenic, and a high encircling dike, which protects the country-side from floods, prevents views from the road. **Pahokee** is one of the few places to offer easy lakeside access, and it boasts possibly the best sunsets in Florida, after the Gulf Coast.

The grim and hardworking communities at the lake's southern end are dependent on sugar for their prosperity. Half the sugarcane in the country is grown in the plains around Belle Glade and

Welcome to BELLE GLADE HER SOIL IS HER FORTUNE

A Lake Okeechobee sugar town proclaims its wealth

Clewiston ("America's Sweetest Town"), where the rich soil is darker than chocolate.

The federal government plans to return 100,000 acres (40,500 ha) of sugarcane land south of Lake Okeechobee to marshland, in order to cleanse and increase the water available to the Everglades. Not surprisingly, the plan is unpopular locally.

Lake Worth ⑭

Road map F4. Palm Beach Co. 🏃 *30,000.* 🚌 🛈 *811 Lucerne Ave, (561) 582-4401.*

LAKE WORTH is a civilized, unpretentious community. On its barrier island side there is normally a jolly, public beach scene; on the mainland, a dozen or more antique shops set the tone along Lake and Lucerne Avenues, the heart of Lake Worth's low-key downtown area. Here, you'll find an Art Deco movie theater converted into an exciting space for art exhibitions, the Edna Hibel Gallery *(see p 117)*, and the **Museum**

of the City of Lake Worth,. All that a local history museum should be, this one is packed full of old photos and everyday items from toasters to cameras. It also has displays the culture of some local immigrants.

🏛 **Museum of the City of Lake Worth**
414 Lake Ave. 【 *(561) 586-1700.* ○ *Mon–Fri.* ● *public hols.*

Delray Beach ⑮

Road map F4. Palm Beach Co. 🏃 *50,000.* 🚆 *Amtrak and Tri-Rail.* 🚌 🛈 *64 SE 5th Ave, (561) 278-0424.* **Ramblin' Rose** 【 *(561) 243-0686.*

THE MOST WELCOMING place between Palm Beach and Boca Raton, Delray Beach has an upscale but unsnobby air. Stars and stripes everywhere celebrate its national award for "civic-mindedness."

The long stretch of sedate beach, with direct access and good facilities, is magnificent, and between November and April the Ramblin' Rose river-boat offers daily cruises along the Intracoastal Waterway.

Delray's heart lies inland, along Atlantic Avenue – an inviting street softly lit at night by old-fashioned lamps and lined with palm trees, chic cafés, antique shops, and art galleries. Alongside lies Old School Square, with a cluster of handsome 1920s buildings. Nearby, snug **Cason Cottage** has been meticulously restored to the way it might have looked when the house was first built in about 1915.

🏚 **Cason Cottage**
5 NE 1st St. 【 *(561) 243-0016.* ○ *Tue–Fri.* ● *public hols.* ♿

A peaceful springtime scene by the ocean at Delray Beach

Loxahatchee National Wildlife Refuge ⑯

Road map F4. Palm Beach Co.
10216 Lee Rd. ☎ *(561) 734-8303.*
🚌 *Delray Beach.* 🚍 *Delray Beach.*
Refuge ◯ *daily.* ● *Dec 25.* 📷 ♿
☑ **Visitor Center** ◯ *Nov–Apr: daily;*
May–Oct: Wed–Sun. ● *Dec 25.*

THIS 221-SQ MILE (572-sq km) refuge, which contains the most northerly remaining part of the Everglades, has superb and abundant wildlife. The best time to visit is early or late in the day, and ideally in winter, when many migrating birds from the north make their temporary home here.

A blue heron standing alert in the wildlife refuge at Loxahatchee

The visitor center, off Route 441 on the refuge's eastern side, 10 miles (16 km) west of Delray Beach, has a good information center explaining the Everglades' ecology; it is also the starting point for two memorable trails. The half-mile (0.8-km) Cypress Swamp Boardwalk enters a magical natural world, with guava and wax myrtle trees and many epiphytes *(see p276)* growing beneath the canopy. The longer Marsh Trail passes by marshland, whose water levels are manipulated to produce the best possible environment for waders and waterfowl. On a winter's evening it's a bird-watcher's paradise, with a cacophony of sound from

A schoolboy's bedroom, Japanese style, at the Morikami Museum

herons, grebe, ibis, anhingas, and other birds. You may also spot turtles and alligators.

Those with their own canoes can embark on the 5.5-mile (9-km) canoe trail. There is also an extensive program of guided nature walks.

Morikami Museum and Japanese Gardens ⑰

Road map F4. Palm Beach Co. 4000 Morikami Park Rd, ☎ *(561) 495-0233.*
🚌 *Delray Beach.* 🚍 *Delray Beach.*
◯ *Tue –Sun.* ● *public hols.* 📷 ♿
ⓦ *www.morikami.org*

THE COUNTRY'S ONLY museum devoted exclusively to Japanese culture is located on land donated by a farmer named George Morikami; he was one of a group of Japanese pioneers who established the Yamato Colony (named after ancient Japan) on the northern edge of Boca Raton in 1905. With the help of money from a development company owned by Henry Flagler *(see pp120–21),* they hoped to grow rice, tea, and silk. The project never took off, however, and the colony gradually petered out in the 1920s.

Displays in the Yamato-kan villa, on a small island in a lake, tell the settlers' story and also delve into past and present Japanese culture. There are interesting recon-

structions of a bathroom, a schoolboy's bedroom, and eel-and-sake restaurants. Formal Japanese gardens surround the villa, and paths lead into serene pinewoods.

A new building across the lake holds exhibitions on all matters Japanese, a café serving Japanese food, and a traditional tea house where tea ceremonies are performed once a month. Also, origami workshops are offered.

Butterfly World ⑱

Road map F4. Broward Co.
3600 W Sample Rd, Coconut Creek.
🔲 *(954) 977-4400.* 🚌 *Deerfield Beach (Amtrak & Tri-Rail).* 🚍 *Pompano Beach.* ◯ *daily (Sun pm only).*
● *Thanksgiving, Dec 25.* 📷 ♿
ⓦ *www.butterflyworld.com*

WITHIN GIANT walk-through aviaries brimming with tropical flowers, thousands of dazzling butterflies from all over the world flit about, often landing on visitors' shoulders. Since they're effectively solar powered, the butterflies are most active on warm, sunny days, so plan your visit accordingly. There are also cabinets of emerging pupae and a collection of mounted insects as fascinating as you're ever likely to see – including morpho butterflies, with their incredible metallic blue wings, and beetles and grasshoppers the size of an adult hand. Outside, you can wander around the extensive gardens.

A blue morpho at Butterfly World

Boca Raton 🔟

IN 1925, AN ADVERTISEMENT for Boca Raton announced: "I am the greatest resort in the world." Although the city imagined by the architect Addison Mizner *(see p116)* did not materialize in his lifetime, Boca Raton has today become one of Florida's most affluent cities. Corporate headquarters and high-tech companies are located here, and executives in a national survey have judged it Florida's most enticing place to live. What must attract them are the country clubs, plush shopping malls, and gorgeous beachfront parks, not to mention desirable homes inspired, if not built, by Mizner.

Vivid Spiderman artwork at the Museum of Cartoon Art

Peach-pink Mizner Park, one of Boca's shopping malls

Exploring Boca Raton

After initiating the development of Palm Beach, Addison Mizner turned his attention to a sleepy pineapple-growing settlement to the south. However, instead of his envisaged masterpiece of city planning, only a handful of buildings were completed by the time Florida's property bubble burst in 1926 *(see p48)*. Boca, as it is often called today, remained little more than a hamlet until the late 1940s.

The nucleus of Mizner's vision was the ultra-luxurious Cloister Inn, finished in 1926 with his trademark Spanish details. It stands off the eastern end of Camino Real, which was intended as the city's main thoroughfare, complete with a central canal for gondolas. The hotel is now part of the greatly expanded and exclusive **Boca Raton Resort and Club** *(see p299)*. Nonresidents can visit only on a weekly tour arranged by the Boca Raton Historical Society, which is based at the **Town Hall** on Palmetto Park Road. A few rooms here have simple displays concerning local history.

Just opposite, built in a style that apes Mizner's work, is the open-air **Mizner Park**. This is perhaps the most impressive of Boca's dazzling malls that provide the best illustrations of the city's rarefied lifestyle. Even more Mizneresque is the nearby **Royal Palm Plaza**, nicknamed the Pink Plaza, with chic boutiques tucked away in hidden courtyards.

The verdant and historic **Old Floresta** district, about a mile (1.6 km) west of the town hall, contains 29 Mediterranean-style homes built by Mizner for his company directors. It is a pleasant area to explore.

🏛 Boca Raton Museum of Art

801 W Palmetto Park Rd. [(561) 392-2500. ◯ Tue–Sun. ● public hols. 🖼 ⅙
W www.bocamuseum.org

The highlight of this compact art gallery is the small Mayers Collection of late 19th- and early 20th-century art. Work by Modigliani, Léger, Giacometti, and Degas, plus Picasso and Matisse, form its core.

🏛 International Museum of Cartoon Art

201 Plaza Real. [(561) 391-2200. ◯ Tue–Sun. ● Dec 25, Jan 1. 🖼 ⅙
W www.cartoon.org

This modern exhibition space in Mizner Park opened in 1996 as home to the International Museum of Cartoon Art. The collection was created in 1974 and numbers some 160,000 pieces dating from the 18th century on, gathered from all over the world. The work ranges from political cartoons to comic strip heroes like Peanuts and Spiderman.

There is also a theater and the Laughter Center, which demonstrates how humor is good for you.

🏛 Sports Immortals Museum

6830 N Federal Hwy. [(561) 997-2575. ◯ daily, times vary on weekends. ● Dec 25, Jan 1. 🖼 ⅙
Among the 10,000 sports mementos at this museum are Babe Ruth's baseball bat and Muhammad Ali's boxing robes.

Boca's attractive town hall, designed by Addison Mizner and built in 1927

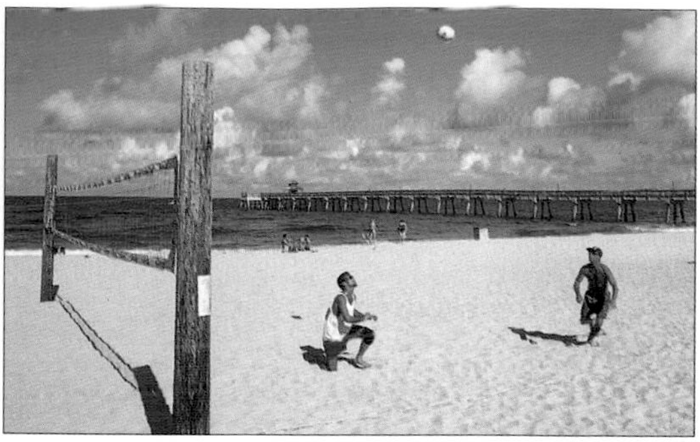

Deerfield Beach, a quiet coastal resort within easy reach of Boca Raton

Visitors' Checklist

Road map F4. Palm Beach Co. 👥 67,000. 🚆 *Tri-Rail, Yamato Rd, (800) 874 7245; Amtrak, 1300 W Hillsboro Blvd, Deerfield Beach, (800) 872-7245.* ℹ *1555 Palm Beach Lakes Blvd, (561) 471-3995.* **Boca Raton Historical Society,** ☎ *(561) 395-6766 for tours.* 🎉 *Boca Festival (Aug).*

The most prized item is a rare cigarette card worth an astonishing $600,000: the card was withdrawn when the baseball player depicted objected to any association with tobacco.

🏖 The Beaches

North of Boca Raton's inlet stretches a seductively long, undeveloped, dune-backed beach, reached via beachside parks. The most northerly of these, **Spanish River Park**, is also the most attractive, with pleasant picnic areas shaded by pines and palm trees. Its loveliest spot is a lagoon on the Intracoastal Waterway next to an observation tower. At **Red Reef Park** you can stroll along the boardwalk on top of the dunes and snorkel around an artificial reef *(see p340)* just offshore. Maybe because of the exorbitant parking fees, the sands are usually uncrowded.

🐦 Gumbo Limbo Nature Center

1801 North Ocean Blvd. ☎ *(561) 338-1473.* ○ *daily.* ● *Dec 25.* ♿ [W] www.fau.edu/gumbo

This first-rate, highly informative center lies next to the Intracoastal, within Red Reef Park. The boardwalk winds through mangroves and a tropical hardwood hammock to a tower, which offers sensational panoramic views.

Environs: High-rise development continues unabated south along Route A1A. Slow-paced **Deerfield Beach** is the area's most inviting community, thanks to its fishing pier and its fine, shell-flecked beach, backed by a palm-lined promenade. Five miles (8 km) south, **Pompano** is forever tied to its status as "swordfish capital of the world," corroborated by photos of giant catches displayed on its pier.

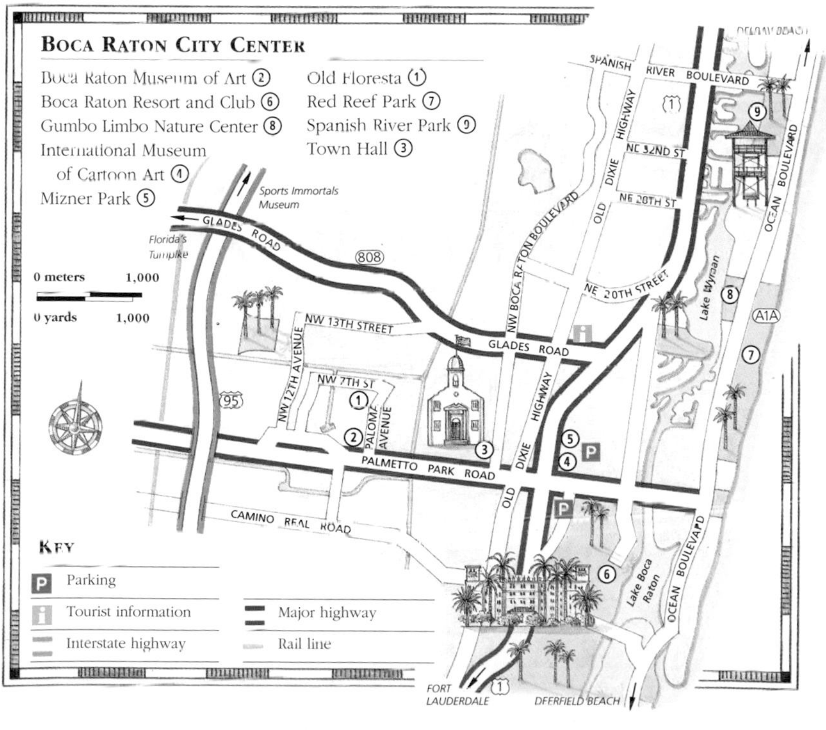
Boca Raton City Center
Boca Raton Museum of Art ②
Boca Raton Resort and Club ⑥
Gumbo Limbo Nature Center ⑧
International Museum of Cartoon Art ④
Mizner Park ⑤
Old Floresta ①
Red Reef Park ⑦
Spanish River Park ⑨
Town Hall ③
0 meters 1,000
0 yards 1,000
Sports Immortals Museum
Florida's Turnpike
Glades Road
808
Spanish River Boulevard
Highway
Dixie
Old
NE 32nd St
NE 28th St
NW Boca Raton Boulevard
NE 20th Street
Lake Wyman
Ocean Boulevard
A1A
NW 13th Street
NW 12th Avenue
NW 7th St
Palomo Avenue
95
Palmetto Park Road
Camino Real Road
Lake Boca Raton
Fort Lauderdale
Deerfield Beach
Key
Parking
Tourist information
Interstate highway
Major highway
Rail line

Fort Lauderdale ⑳

D URING THE SECOND Seminole War *(see p44),*
Fort Lauderdale consisted of little more than
three forts. By 1900, it had become a busy trading post on the New River, which meanders
through what has become a sprawling city.

Today, Greater Fort Lauderdale wears many
hats: it is an important business and cultural
center, a popular beach resort, and a giant
cruise port. But it is still the city's waterways
(see p131) that define its unique character.

Appel's *Big Bird with Child*, Museum of Art

Exploring Downtown
Fort Lauderdale
Downtown Fort Lauderdale,
with its modern, sleek, glass-
sided office buildings, presents
the city's business face. The
Riverwalk follows a 1.5-mile
(2.4-km) stretch of the New
River's north bank and links
most of the city's historical
landmarks and cultural institutions. This promenade starts
near Stranahan House, built on
the site of the city's first trading post, and passes through
a strip of parkland to end up
by the Broward Center for the
Performing Arts *(see p336).*

Old Fort Lauderdale extends
along Southwest 2nd Avenue.
It is made up of an attractive
group of early 1900s' buildings administered by the Fort
Lauderdale Historical Society,
which is based at the Fort
Lauderdale Historical Museum.
The King-Cromartie House,
built in 1907 on the south bank
of the river, was transported
by barge to its present site in
1971. Its modest furnishings
reflect the basic living conditions of Florida's early settlers.
Behind the home is a replica
of the city's first schoolhouse,
which opened in 1899.

The clutch of cafés and restaurants in old brick buildings
along adjacent Southwest 2nd
Street are buzzing at lunchtime and in the early evening.

A narrated hop-on hop-off
trolley tour is an easy way to
get to know the heart of the
city. The tour links Fort
Lauderdale's downtown
area and the beach,
taking in all the
principal sights.

⛪ Old Fort
Lauderdale
Museum of
History
219 SW 2nd Ave.
📞 *(954) 463-4431.*
🕐 *Tue–Sat.*
● *Jul 4 , Dec 25,*
Jan 1. 📷 ♿
The New River
Inn in Old Fort
Lauderdale was built
of concrete in 1905. Now
an informative local history
museum, it contains various
exhibits that chart the area's
history and the growth of the
city up to the 1940s. A small
theater shows amusing silent
films that were made during
the 1920s heyday of south
Florida's film industry.

The shady Riverwalk, winding along the north bank of the New River

🏛 Museum of Art

1 E Las Olas Blvd. ☎ *(954) 763-6464.*
⏱ *Tue–Sun* 🚫 *public hols.* 💶 ♿
ⓦ *www.museumofart.org*

This fine museum, housed in an impressive postmodern building, is best known for its large assemblage of works of CoBrA art. The name CoBrA derives from the initial letters of Copenhagen, Brussels, and Amsterdam, the capitals of the home countries of a group of expressionist painters worked from 1948–51. The museum displays works by Karel Appel, Pierre Alechinsky, and Asger Jorn, the movement's leading exponents. The new William Glackens Wing features this American Impressionist's work.

🏛 Museum of Discovery and Science

401 SW 2nd St. ☎ *(954) 467-6637.* ⏱ *daily.*
● *Dec 25.* 💶 ♿
ⓦ *www.mods.org*

Boasting the highest attendance figures for any museum in the state, this is one of the largest and best museums of its kind in Florida. Here, all kinds of creatures appear in re-created Florida "ecoscapes," and you can take a simulated ride to the moon or watch specially trained rats play basketball. In the IMAX® theater, films like *The Living Sea* are projected on to a 60-ft (18-m) high screen. This is also one of the few places in the world to show 3-D IMAX films where the audience uses special glasses and personal headsets for 360-degree sound. On weekends there are special evening screenings of these films.

🚾 Stranahan House

335 SE 6th Ave. ☎ *(954) 524-4736.*
⏱ *Wed–Sun.* ● *public hols; Jul–Aug hours vary.* 💶 ♿ *limited.*

The oldest surviving house in the city is a handsome pine and oak building, built by the pioneer Frank Stranahan in 1901. It became the center of Fort Lauderdale's community, serving as a trading post, meeting hall, post office, and bank. Even more evocative of the early days than the furnishings inside are the old photos of Stranahan trading with the local Seminoles *(see p271)*. Goods such as alligator hides, otter pelts, and egret plumes – all used in the fashions of the day and in great demand – were brought by the Seminoles from the nearby Everglades in their dugout canoes.

Las Olas Boulevard

Despite a constant stream of traffic, the section of Las Olas Boulevard between 6th and 11th Avenues amounts to Fort Lauderdale's most picturesque and busiest street. A winning mix of formal, casual, and chic boutiques and eateries line this thoroughfare, where you can pick up anything from a fur coat to modern Haitian art.

If you're not a serious shopper, visit in the evenings when the sidewalks overflow with drinkers and diners, and you can take a ride in a horse-drawn Surrey carriage.

Heading toward the beach, the boulevard crosses islands where you can get a closer look at a more lavish Fort Lauderdale lifestyle *(see p131)*.

0 kilometers   1

0 miles   1

KEY

🚌 Greyhound bus station

⚓ Boat trip boarding point

🅿 Parking

▬ Major highway

Stranahan House on the New River, Broward County's oldest residence

Exploring Fort Lauderdale: Beyond Downtown

EVEN IF YOU MISS the signs proclaiming "Welcome to Fort Lauderdale – Yachting Capital of the World," it won't take you long to recognize the real focus of the city. For tourists and residents alike, the appeal of Fort Lauderdale lies, above all, in its attractive and buzzing beaches and in the waterways that branch from the city's historical lifeblood – the New River.

Cyclists and pedestrians enjoying the shady beachfront promenade

The Beach

Until the mid-1980s, when the local authorities began to discourage them, students by the thousand would descend on Fort Lauderdale for the Spring Break. Today, the city's image has been restored; its excellent beach is still the liveliest along the Gold Coast – especially at the end of Las Olas Boulevard, where in-line skaters cruise past a few unsophisticated bars and souvenir shops, faint recollections of more decadent days along "The Strip."

Elsewhere, beachside Fort Lauderdale is more like the family resort it's promoted to be; South Beach Park has the most pleasant strip of sand.

A break in training at the pool, at the Swimming Hall of Fame

🏛 International Swimming Hall of Fame

1 Hall of Fame Drive. **[** (954) 462-6536. ◯ daily. 🖼 🔥

If you ever wanted to know about the history of Oman's aquatic sports or the evolution of diving positions, this is the place to come. This amazingly detailed museum has an odd but fun mix of exhibits, from ancient wooly swimsuits to amusing mannequins of stars, such as Johnny "Tarzan" Weismuller, holder of 57 world swimming records.

In the famous swimming pools behind, coaches make Olympic hopefuls swim gruelling lengths while attached to one end of the pool by a giant rubber cord. Spectators are welcome to attend these training sessions as well as aquatic competitions and events.

🚇 Bonnet House

900 N Birch Rd. **[** (954) 563-5393. ◯ Wed–Sun. ● public hols. 🖼 🔥 compulsory, 10am–2pm Wed–Fri, noon–3pm Sat, Sun.

This oddly furnished house, close to the waterfront, is by far the most enjoyable piece of old Fort Lauderdale. It stands amid idyllic tropical grounds, where the bonnet water lily, from which the house took its name, once grew.

Frederic Bartlett, an artist, built this cozy, plantation-style winter home himself in 1920, and examples of his work, especially murals, are everywhere. He and his wife Evelyn Lilly, also a painter, shared a passion for all things natural: hence the swans and monkeys that inhabit the grounds, the carousel animals in the palm-filled courtyard, the greenhouse full of orchids, and the collection of shells.

✦ Hugh Taylor Birch State Recreation Area

3109 E Sunrise Blvd. **[** (954) 564-4521. ◯ daily. 🖼 🔥

These 180 acres (73 ha), part of 3 miles (5 km) of barrier island that Chicago lawyer Hugh Taylor Birch bought in 1894, amount to one of the Gold Coast's few undeveloped oases of greenery. Visitors come to rent canoes on the lagoon, wander along a trail through a tropical hammock, and, above all, to exercise along a scenic circular road.

Jewelry stalls and neon lights at the Swap Shop of Fort Lauderdale

ENVIRONS: Bargain-hunters will love the **Swap Shop of Fort Lauderdale**, covering an incredible 75 acres (30 ha). This place is an American version of an oriental bazaar, with whole rows devoted to jewelry, sunglasses, and other trinkets. Many of the 12 million annual visitors are lured by the carnival and the free circus, complete with clowns and elephants. The parking lot becomes a huge drive-in movie theater in the evenings.

🏪 Swap Shop of Fort Lauderdale

3291 W Sunrise Blvd. **[** (954) 791-7927. ◯ daily. 🔥

The Jungle Queen, Fort Lauderdale's most famous cruise boat

The Waterways

Around the mouth of the New River lie dozens of parallel, arrow-straight canals. The area is known as **The Isles**, after the rows of slender peninsulas created from mud when the canals were dug in the 1920s. This is the most desirable place to live in the city: looming behind lush foliage and luxurious yachts are ostentatious mansions worth millions of dollars. Their residents, such as Wayne Huizenga, owner of the Blockbuster video empire and local baseball and football teams, are chiefly rich businesspeople.

The islands flank the Intracoastal Waterway, which also crosses **Port Everglades**. Hardly scenic but fascinating nevertheless, this is the world's second-largest cruise port after Miami, as well as a destination for container ships, oil tankers, destroyers, and submarines.

The best panorama of the waterways from dry land is from the revolving bar at the top of the tower of the Hyatt Regency Pier 66 Hotel on South East 17th Street. But the mansions, yachts, and port can really only be properly viewed from the water. You can take your pick from all kinds of boat trips. The **Jungle Queen** is an old-fashioned riverboat that chugs up the New River to a private island styled as an Indian village; there are daytime trips, taking three hours, and evening cruises that include a vaudeville show and barbecue dinner.

Ninety-minute **Carrie B** riverboat tours depart from the Riverwalk, pass various

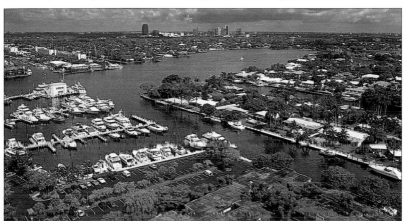

A water taxi on the New River

mansions, browse around the port, and then visit the warm waters of a power plant discharge where large numbers of manatees *(see p236)* gather.

Water Taxis, operating like shared land taxis, go up New River to Downtown and anywhere from the port north to Commercial Boulevard. Call about ten minutes before you want to be picked up, and travel on flat-fee single tickets or bargain day passes. You can rent boats from the Bahia Mar Yachting Center and Pier 66 Marina.

Finally, day-long trips to the Bahamas and daytime or evening "cruises to nowhere" are big business for **SeaEscape** and other cruise companies *(see pp338–9)*. Entertainment on board comes primarily in the form of casino action and cabaret shows.

USEFUL ADDRESSES

Carrie B
The Riverwalk at SE 5th Avenue.
(954) 768-9920.

Jungle Queen
Bahia Mar Yachting Center,
A1A, Fort Lauderdale Beach.
(954) 462-5596.

SeaEscape
Port Everglades Terminal 1.
(954) 537-2703.

Water Taxi
651 Seabreeze Boulevard,
A1A, Fort Lauderdale Beach.
(954) 467-6677.

View over Fort Lauderdale's waterways from the top of the Hyatt Regency Pier 66 Hotel

A garuda statue from Bali, at the Graves Museum in Dania

Dania ㉑

Road map F4. Broward Co.
🚶 13,000. 🚌 Hollywood. 🚃 Hollywood. 🛈 Dania, (954) 926-2323.

Dᴀɴɪᴀ BLENDS seamlessly into the coastal conurbation. Some locals visit the town only to watch a game of jai alai, but the other main attraction is the **John U. Lloyd Beach State Recreation Area**, a chunk of virgin barrier island that contrasts acutely with nearby Port Everglades *(see p131)*. From the park's northern tip, you can watch ships come and go; to the south stretches one of the Gold Coast's loveliest beaches: more than 2 miles (3 km) in length and backed by pine trees. You can rent canoes to explore the scenic, mangrove-lined creek that runs through the heart of the park.

The **South Florida Museum of Natural History**, inland, appeals to all ages. Overtly educational displays explaining, for example, the formation of the Keys, are mixed with more entertaining exhibits such as models of dinosaurs and replicas of Tutankhamun's treasures.

Just a few blocks north lies an array of some 150 antique shops. Despite their rather soulless location running alongside traffic-ridden US 1, they make entertaining browsing.

🌴 **John U. Lloyd Beach SRA**
6503 N Ocean Drive. 📞 *(954) 923-2833.* ◯ *daily.* 🅿 ♿

🏛 **South Florida Museum of Natural History**
481 S Federal Highway. 📞 *(954) 925-7770.* ◯ *Tue–Sun.* ◯ *Easter, Thanksgiving, Dec 25, Jan 1.* 🅿 ♿ W www.gravesmuseum.org

Hollywood ㉒

Road map F4. Broward Co.
🚶 126,000. 🚃 Amtrak and Tri-Rail. 🚌 🛈 330 N Federal Highway, (954) 923-4000.

Fᴏᴜɴᴅᴇᴅ ʙʏ a Californian in the 1920s, this sizeable and unpretentious resort is the destination for the majority of the 300,000 French Canadians who migrate to Greater Fort Lauderdale every winter. Gallic restaurants and cafés located on Hollywood's seaside Broadwalk, serve delicious *pommes frites* and *crêpes* to customers reading Québecois newspapers.

The pleasant promenade makes Hollywood unusually pedestrian-friendly for the state of Florida, with traffic limited to a steady stream of skaters and cyclists. Alongside the Broadwalk extend miles of meticulously maintained sands, which prove very popular with locals and visitors alike.

Each morning dozens of Hollywood's predominantly elderly visitors assemble for a light aerobics class at the outdoor Theater Under the Stars on the waterfront. They return later to the same place in order to listen to the open-air evening concerts.

ENVIRONS: At the crossroads of Routes 7 and 448, on the western edge of Hollywood resort, is the **Seminole Indian Hollywood Reservation**. Covering 480 acres (194 ha), it is Florida's smallest Indian reservation. Like other reservations in the state it is largely autonomous *(see p271)*, and billboards advertising cut-price tobacco along the roadside are grim clues to its exemption from state cigarette taxes.

Sun worshipers enjoying the pristine sands of Hollywood Beach

Fortunes being made at the Seminole Indian Bingo near Hollywood

You may prefer to avoid the rather sorry **Native Indian Village**, with its craft stands and alligator displays set up for tourists, in favor of the huge 24-hour **Seminole Indian Bingo and Poker Casino** across the road. The reservations are also exempt from state gambling laws, and in the cavernous bingo hall as many as 1,400 players compete for five-figure cash prizes. Even if you don't play a game yourself, the rows of women surrounded by sandwiches, counters, and cards make an intriguing spectacle. Games begin four times a day. Have a look, too, at the frenetic Lightning Room, where you can watch those who wish to dabble in speed bingo lose hundreds of dollars at a time.

🏠 **Native Indian Village**
3551 N State Rd 7.
📞 (954) 961-4519.
🕐 daily. ⬤ Dec 25. 🎦 ⚿

🏠 **Seminole Indian Bingo and Poker Casino**
4150 N State Rd 7.
📞 (954) 961-3220. 🕐 24 hours
⬤ Dec 25 ⚿

Davie ㉓

Road map F4, Broward Co.
🏛 70,000. ✈ Fort Lauderdale.
🚌 Fort Lauderdale. 🛈 4185 Davie Rd, (954) 581-0790.

CENTERED ON Orange Drive and Davie Road, and surrounded by paddocks and stables, the bizarre town of Davie adheres to a strictly Old West theme. Cacti grow outside the town hall's wooden huts, and the local McDonald's even has a corral at the back. Drop in on Grif's Western Wear, a cowboy supermarket at 6211 South West 45th Street, to stock up on saddles, cowboy hats, and boots. The only way to sample the town's real flavor, however, is to see bronco busting, bull-riding, and steer wrestling in a rodeo

Stetsons for sale at Grif's Western Wear shop in Davie

at the **Davie Arena**. These heart-stopping displays of cowboy skill normally take place on Wednesday nights from around 7:30pm (but call beforehand to check); there are also professional rodeos held every month.

🐎 **Davie Arena**
6591 Orange Drive. 📞 (954) 797-1166. 🕐 for rodeos only. ⚿

Flamingo Gardens ㉔

Road map F4. Broward Co. 3750 Flamingo Rd, Davie. 📞 (954) 473-2955. ✈ Fort Lauderdale. 🚌 Fort Lauderdale. 🕐 daily. ⬤ Mon (Jul–Oct), Thanksgiving, Dec 25. 🎦 📷 ⚿ Ⓦ www.flamingogardens.org

THESE BEAUTIFUL gardens started out in 1927 as a weekend retreat for the Wrays, a citrus-farming family. You can tour their lovely 1930s home, furnished in period style, but the gardens are the attraction here. Tram tours pass groves of lemon and kumquat trees, live oaks, banyan trees, and other exotic vegetation.

The gardens are also home and hospital to many Florida birds, including the rare bald eagle (see p22) and flamingos. Many species of ducks, gulls, doves, and waders – including the roseate spoonbill (see p215) – inhabit a splendid walk-through aviary split into habitats such as cypress forest and mangrove swamp.

JAI ALAI – A MERRY SPORT

This curious game originated some 300 years ago in the Basque Country (jai alai means "merry festival" in Basque) and was brought to the US in the early 1900s via Cuba. Florida has eight of the country's ten arenas, or "frontons."

Watching a game of jai alai makes for a cheap night out (if you don't bet). The program explains both the scoring and the intricacies of pari-mutuel betting, where those who bet on the winners share in the total amount wagered. People yell and cheer loudly during the points, since many will have put money on the outcome. Games take place in Dania five times a week: call (954) 927-2841 for details. The rules of the game are explained on page 31.

Jai alai player poised for a hit

ORLANDO AND THE SPACE COAST

WITH EVERYTHING *from roller coasters to performing killer whales and a well-known mouse with very big ears, Orlando is a family-oriented fantasyland and the undisputed theme park capital of the world, attracting over 34 million visitors every year.*

Orlando started out as an army post, Fort Gatlin, which was established during the Seminole Wars *(see pp44–5)*. The story goes that the fort was later renamed after a soldier called Orlando Reeves, who was hit by a Seminole arrow in 1835. A town developed, but even through the first half of the 20th century Orlando and neighboring towns like Kissimmee were only small, sleepy places dependent on cattle and the citrus crop.

Everything changed in the 1960s. First of all came the job opportunities associated with the space program at Cape Canaveral. Then Walt Disney World started to take shape: its first theme park, the Magic Kingdom, opened in 1971. Since then, Disney claims that over 500 million visitors have made the pilgrimage to what it modestly calls the world's most popular vacation destination. Its success has generated a booming entertainment industry in Greater Orlando, as more and more attractions appear on the scene, all eager to cash in on the captive market.

Scenically, aside from dozens of lakes, the region is rather dull, with Greater Orlando sprawling gracelessly among the flat agricultural lands. Along the Space Coast, the communities on the mainland shore hold little appeal. However, the barrier islands across the broad Indian River boast 72 miles (116 km) of stunning sandy beaches, and there are two enormous nature preserves rich in bird life. Amid all this, set in a preserved marshy vastness beneath giant skies, in surprising harmony with nature, is the Kennedy Space Center, from where shuttles are launched dramatically out of the earth's atmosphere.

The expansive and unspoiled watery landscape of Merritt Island on the Space Coast

◁ The imposing entrance to Universal Studios, one of Orlando's top theme parks

Exploring Orlando and the Space Coast

THE REASON so many vacationers come to Orlando is because of its theme parks, the big ones being at Walt Disney World, Sea World, and Universal Studios. It is said that in their environs, in Walt Disney World, around International Drive and in Kissimmee, there are over 80,000 hotel rooms, more than in the whole of New York. If you have time to spare, visit Cypress Gardens or Splendid China: elsewhere they would be the leading attractions. At night, experience the razzmatazz at the entertainment complexes of Church Street Station and Disney's Pleasure Island. To see Orlando's other side, spend some time in the upscale suburb of Winter Park.

Just 50 miles (80 km) away, the Space Coast is an easy day trip from Orlando. Here, beaches range from empty, wild sands to the buzzing surfing mecca of brash Cocoa Beach. And Kennedy Space Center competes sharply with Orlando's theme parks for excitement.

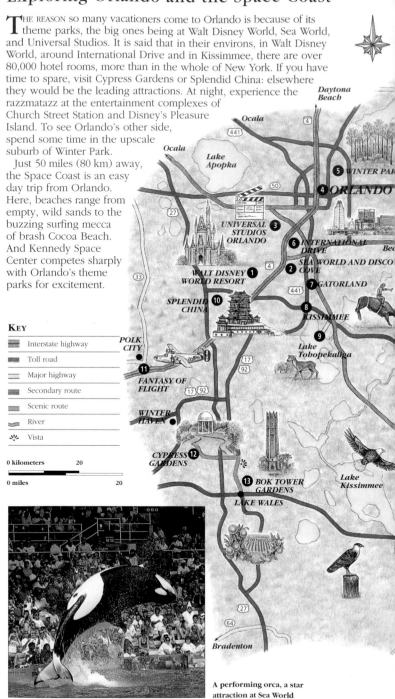

KEY

▭▭▭	Interstate highway
▭▭▭	Toll road
▭▭▭	Major highway
▭▭▭	Secondary route
▭▭▭	Scenic route
〜	River
※	Vista

0 kilometers 20

0 miles 20

Daytona Beach

Ocala

Ocala

Lake Apopka

5 WINTER PARK

4 ORLANDO

3 UNIVERSAL STUDIOS ORLANDO

6 INTERNATIONAL DRIVE

1 WALT DISNEY WORLD RESORT

2 SEA WORLD AND DISCOVERY COVE

7 GATORLAND

10 SPLENDID CHINA

8 KISSIMMEE

9 Lake Tohopekaliga

POLK CITY

11 FANTASY OF FLIGHT

WINTER HAVEN

12 CYPRESS GARDENS

13 BOK TOWER GARDENS

LAKE WALES

Lake Kissimmee

Bradenton

A performing orca, a star attraction at Sea World

Rockets from the early days of space exploration, at the Kennedy Space Center

GETTING AROUND

If you are exploring beyond the theme parks, rent a car. With an extensive network of divided highways, driving is relaxing and fast: from Walt Disney World, downtown Orlando is half an hour's drive north and Cypress Gardens an hour south. If you are spending your whole vacation on Disney property, see page 139 for transit options. Many hotels offer free shuttle bus services to the theme parks, and Lynx buses (see p363) serve most tourist destinations in Greater Orlando. The Space Coast is an hour east from Orlando on Route 528 (Bee Line Expressway). I-95 is the main north-south route along the coast, Route A1A connects the beaches on the barrier islands

SIGHTS AT A GLANCE

SEE ALSO

Walt Disney World® Resort 1

COVERING 43 SQ MILES (69 sq km), Walt Disney World Resort is the largest entertainment complex on earth. Its main draw is its theme parks: Animal Kingdom, Epcot, Magic Kingdom, and Disney-MGM Studios. It is also a self-sufficient vacation spot, supplying everything from hotels to golf courses. With under a quarter of its land so far developed, every year some new wonder arrives – Disney's Animal Kingdom is the biggest new attraction. Peerless in its imagination and attention to detail Walt Disney World Resort is also a hermetic bubble cocooned from the real world. Everything runs like clockwork, and nothing shatters the theme parks' illusions and their workings are even secreted in underground tunnels. Unless you're an unreformable cynic, Walt Disney World Resort will amaze you.

USEFUL NUMBERS

General information
☎ *(407) 824-4321.*

Accommodation information/reservations
☎ *(407) 934-7639.*

Dining reservations
☎ *(407) 939-3463.*
[W] http://disney.go.com

See p163 for further information.

WHEN TO VISIT

THE BUSIEST TIMES of the year are Christmas, Easter, June to August, and the last week in February until Easter. At these times, the parks begin to approach capacity – some 90,000 people in the Magic Kingdom alone. However, all the rides will be operating and the parks open for much longer. At off peak times, 10,000 guests a day might visit the Magic Kingdom, only one water park may be operating and certain attractions may be closed for maintenance. The weather is also a factor – in July and August, hot and humid afternoons are regularly punctuated by torrential thunderstorms. Between October and March, however, the temperatures and humidity are both more comfortable and permit a more energetic touring schedule.

LENGTH OF VISIT

WALT DISNEY WORLD is at least a week of entertainment. To enjoy it to the full, give the Magic Kingdom and Epcot two days each, leaving a day for Disney-MGM Studios and Animal Kingdom. Set aside three nights to see Fantasy in the Sky, IllumiNations and Fantasmic! firework displays.

TICKETS AND PASSES

THERE ARE NINE types of passes available for visitors. For most, one of the multi-day park hopper passes will suffice but one of the best is the Length of Stay pass, available only to Disney Hotel guests. Non-Disney guests visiting for more than ten days should consider an annual pass,

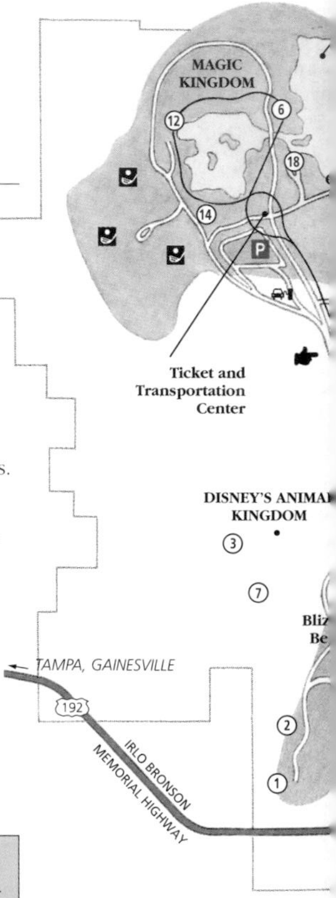
MAGIC KINGDOM
6
12
18
14
Ticket and Transportation Center
3
7
TAMPA, GAINESVILLE
192
IRLO BRONSON MEMORIAL HIGHWAY
2
1

WALT DISNEY WORLD RESORTS *(see pp303-4)*

1 All-Star Music
2 All-Star Sports
3 Animal Kingdom Lodge
4 Beach Club
5 Caribbean Beach
6 Contemporary Resort
7 Coronado Springs
8 Disney Institute
9 Disney's BoardWalk
10 Port Orleans-Riverside
11 Fort Wilderness Resort
12 Grand Floridian Resort
13 Old Key West
14 Polynesian Resort
15 Port Orleans – French Quarter
16 WDW Dolphin
17 WDW Swan
18 Wilderness Lodge
19 Yacht Club

KEY

[P] Parking
Gas station
Golf course
Monorail
Major highway
Interstate highway
Secondary route
Theme park entrance

which costs little more than a 7-day park hopper *(see p163)*. Passes are available at Disney stores, the airport and the Tourist Information centre on I-Drive *(see p176)*. In addition, Disney stores around the world sell some passes, which are sometimes included in package deals.

GETTING AROUND

A N EXTENSIVE, efficient transportation system handles an average of 200,000 guests each day. Even if you stay outside Walt Disney World Resort, many nearby hotels offer free shuttle services to and from the theme parks, but you can check this when you make your reservation.

The transportation hub of Walt Disney World is the **Ticket and Transportation Center** (TTC). Connecting it to the Magic Kingdom are two monorail services. A third monorail links the TTC to Epcot. Ferries run from the TTC to the Magic Kingdom across the Seven Seas Lagoon.

Ferries connect the Magic Kingdom and Epcot with the resorts in their respective areas, while buses link everything in Walt Disney World, including direct links to the Magic Kingdom. Residents and pass holders can use the entire transportation system for free, while one-day tickets entitle holders to use the monorails and ferries between the TTC and the Magic Kingdom.

DISABLED TRAVELERS

W HEELCHAIRS can be borrowed at the park entrance and special bypass entrances allow disabled guests and carers to board rides without waiting in line. Staff, however, are not allowed to lift guests or assist with lifting for safety reasons.

VERY YOUNG CHILDREN

T HE WAITING and walking involved in a theme park visit can exhaust young children quickly so it's a good idea to borrow a stroller, available at every park entrance. If it's missing when you leave a ride, don't worry; simply take any other as they are all the same. Tying a food-stained cloth around your pushchair handle, however, personalises it quite effectively.

SAFETY

T HE RESORT's excellent safety record and first rate security force mean problems are rare and dealt with promptly. Cast members are trained to watch out for young unaccompanied children and escort them to lost children centres.

PARKING

V ISITORS TO THE Magic Kingdom must park at the TTC and make their way by public transportation; Epcot and Disney-MGM Studios have their own parking lots. Parking is free for Disney Resort residents – others must pay, but only once a day regardless of how many times they move their vehicle. The lots are very large, so make a note of where you leave your vehicle.

ADVANTAGES OF STAYING IN THE RESORT

L ODGING IN THE resorts (hotels and villa complexes) and Walt Disney World Swan and Dolphin (operated independently but Disneyesque in every other respect) are of a very high standard. However, even the lowest-priced places are more expensive than many hotels outside Walt Disney World. Beyond Disney quality, your money also buys:
• Proximity to parks and free use of Disney's transport.
• Early entry into the theme parks (up to 90 minutes).
• Guaranteed admission to the theme parks even when the parks are otherwise full.
• The possibility of dining with your favorite Disney character in your hotel.
• The delivery of shopping purchases made anywhere in Walt Disney World Resort

Note that the hotels near Disney Village Marketplace (not run by Disney) offer few of the above privileges.

Map labels

ORLANDO AND SANDFORD INTERNATIONAL AIRPORT

Downtown Disney

Exit 27

EPCOT

(536)

Typhoon Lagoon

Orlando International Airport

(4)

DISNEY-MGM STUDIOS

Exit 26B

's Wide of Sports

Exit 25B

KISSIMMEE, Celebration Florida

TAMPA

10

15

13

8

5

| 0 meters | 500 |
| 0 yards | 500 |

☒ Magic Kingdom Resort Area
☒ Disney Village Resort Area
☒ Epcot Resort Area
☒ Studio Resort Area

TOP TIPS

• After a thunderstorm, the water parks are often almost empty – even at the busiest times of the year.
• Disney parks fill rapidly after the first hour of opening. Until then, you can frequently just walk onto rides for which you'll have to line up for later.

The Magic Kingdom

Reappearing in similar form in California, Japan, and France, the Magic Kingdom is the essential Disney theme park. Cartoon characters and nostalgic visions of how the world (and particularly America) once was and how it might be again fill its relentlessly cheerful 107 acres. The park is made up of seven "lands" evoking a particular theme or era, such as the Wild West, Colonial America, and the future. Binding the park together are stunning parades, musical street performers and three-dimensional Disney characters ready to greet their guests.

Fantasyland's landmark castle

TACKLING THE PARK

Disney hotel guests have early entry privileges on three days a week – Monday, Thursday and Saturday – so avoid the park on those days unless you're a Disney hotel guest. If you are, plan to reach the entrance turnstiles two hours before the official opening time. This will allow you to enjoy Fantasyland and Tomorrowland for an hour and a half before the rest of the park opens. On arrival you will be given a leaflet showing the lands and rides and listing show and parade times. A notice board at the top of Main Street also shows this and, additionally, gives a

list of waiting times at various attractions. Getting around the Park is relatively easy as the lands radiate from the central hub, in front of Cinderella's Castle.

The major attractions are situated at opposite sides of the park, which means that you will have to walk more than you might expect to avoid long waits in line. There are also other, more novel forms of transport. Main Street has a series of vehicles which, true to the Disney story-telling ideal, serve to tell the story of transport from the horse drawn tram to the motor car. A steam train makes a twenty minute circuit of the park, stopping at Main Street, Frontierland and Mickey's Toontown Fair.

TIPS

• If you're an early entry guest, plan to wait at the rope barrier next to Peter Pan and It's a Small World about 15 – 20 minutes before the official opening time.

• If you want to visit Splash Mountain first, board the train at Main Street before the park has opened. On opening time, the train will pull out and stop in Frontierland about 7 minutes later. The station is next to Splash Mountain and Big Thunder.

• In order to reduce the number of guests in the attractions prior to closing, much of the internal queuing areas are roped off so the lines of waiting guests still appear long from the outside.

• The best place to see all the parades is Frontierland, although during peak periods you will still have to find a spot about 45 minutes before the parade.

• Daytime parades run from Splash Mountain area to Town Square and the night-time parades in the opposite direction.

EATING AND DRINKING

Food is mostly fast, with a range of quick service places. For a reasonable meal, however, try The Liberty Tavern or the Crystal Palace for quieter dining. Cinderella's Royal Table in the castle has a regal ambience and the food is not too bad. The nicest place to eat sandwiches (the only thing on the menu) is Aunt Polly's on Tom Sawyer Island.

MAIN STREET, USA

This is a Disney fantasy of a small-town, Victorian America that never was. As you enter Main Street, you pass beneath Main Street Station from where you can ride the train around the park. Trains run every ten minutes. Beneath the station are lockers where, for a small fee, you can store

valuables and bags. As you enter the town square, City Hall lies to your left and is the place to visit first for any information, such as which shows are running and what special events might be happening. Main Street itself is a magnificent melange of color, shapes and music, all in astonishing detail. Town Square Photography, to the right as you enter the square, can sort out any film problems you have but the main shops are, as you would expect, along Main Street.

At night, this area assumes a magical ambience as thousands of lights bring a warm glow to the spotlessly clean paving. It's also an excellent place to see the Main Street Electrical Parade, a shimmering fantasy of music, live action and illuminated floats.

ADVENTURELAND

Lush foliage, evocative drumbeats and colonial buildings combine to conjure images of Africa and the Caribbean. Crossing a wooden bridge from the central hub, Adventureland is a fusion of the exotic and the tropical.

The Jungle Cruise boat ride, which takes guests around an animatronically animated setting of deepest Africa is very popular due, in most part, to the entertainment value of the "boatman" whose often wacky humour can't fail to amuse. However, the shooting at

◁ **Guests riding the Magic Carpets of Aladdin, Adventureland**

1 DAY ITINERARY

If you really want to cover the Magic Kingdom in one day, be warned, it's a daunting task, particularly in the summer.

1. *After leaving the turnstiles, head immediately for the central hub. If the entire park is open turn right and head for **Space Mountain**. If there are ropes across areas at the hub, wait at the rope entrance to Tomorrowland then head for Space Mountain at rope drop. Those who like thrills should ride whilst others can head for **Buzz Lightyear**.*
2. *After Space Mountain, head for **Alien Encounter** if you have no young children. Otherwise, head for **Fantasyland** through Tomorrowland (keep the speedway on your right and turn left at the Mad Hatter's Teacups) and ride the many **Adventures of Winnie the Pooh**.*
3. *After Winnie, turn left and head across Dumbo towards **Peter Pan's Flight** and ride.*
4. *Exit left, head to Liberty Square and visit **Haunted Mansion** on the right.*
5. *Exit Haunted Mansion to the right and continue to **Splash Mountain**. If the wait is in excess of half an hour, get a FASTPASS, turn right and cross to **Big Thunder Mountain Railroad**.*
6. *Take the exit from Big Thunder and cross the bridge bearing right to **Pirates of the Caribbean**. Ride.*
7. *Return to Splash Mountain and ride, backtrack to the **Jungle Cruise**. If the time slot is right, ride, otherwise see the **Tiki Birds Show**.*
8. *Good time for lunch. Eat light at a fast food restaurant.*
9. *Walk off lunch at the **Swiss family Treehouse** in Adventureland.*
10. *Cross the central hub to Tomorrowland and obtain a FASTPASS ticket for **Buzz Lightyear**.*
11. *Visit the **Timekeeper**, **Astro Orbiter** and the **Carousel of Progress**.*
12. *Return to ride Buzz Lightyear.*
13. *Cross central hub to **Frontierland**, and find a spot to stake out for the **afternoon parade**.*
14. *You will now have ridden and seen the top attractions in the Magic Kingdom. This is a good time to rest before the **Main Street Electrical Parade**. If the park is closing early, view the parade from the Town Square. If it's open late it's a good idea to see the parade from Main Street on the Tomorrowland side so that, when the parade has passed, you can return to the attractions in Tomorrowland, Mickey's ToonTown and Fantasyland.*
15. *Finally, stake out the bench that's almost opposite Minnie and Mickey's house in Mickey's ToonTown to see the **fireworks** in comfort.*

---

some of the animals seems curiously out of place in today's conservation conscious society, although the boatman is at pains to show he's only "scaring" them.

The recently much improved **Enchanted Tiki Birds** is an amusing and cleverly animated attraction, and is a pleasant way to spend twenty minutes out of the heat. Featuring characters from Aladdin and The Lion King, it's certainly worth a visit, just to see the walls change shape.

The **Pirates of the Caribbean** is an entertaining and remarkably detailed voyage where you cruise through crumbling, underground prisons, past fighting galleons of the 16th Century, and past scenes of debauchery and mayhem. Although not as good as the version in Disneyland Paris, the Audioanimatronic® effects are still extremely well done and the ride is certainly a firm favourite with park visitors. At the exit, there is one of the most interesting stores in the park selling essential Disneyland accessories.

FRONTIERLAND

SET IN HOLLYWOOD-inspired Wild West, this land abounds with raised walkways and trading posts. The **Diamond Horseshoe Saloon Revue** is a walk in, fast-paced comedy and dance show while the **Country Bear Jamboree** provides a completely audio animatronic animal show, much liked by youngsters and a welcome respite from a hot summer's day. Opposite Big Thunder Mountain is the landing stage where a raft can be taken to Tom Sawyer's Island.

Complete with a fort, swinging bridges, waterfalls and tunnels, it's a child's dream adventure playground.

A stunningly conceived and superbly executed journey through America's Wild West on an out of control mine train, **Big Thunder Mountain Railroad** remains one of the Park's enduring attractions. In roller coaster terms, it's a relatively gentle experience, although the rear cars provide a wilder ride than the front. It also acquires large lines of people from early in the day, so this is a ride to be enjoyed sooner, rather than later.

SHOWS AND PARADES

Don't miss seeing at least one of each of these amazing events. The shows – Legend of the Lion King and the Diamond Horseshoe Saloon Revue are the two live action presentations – are superb in their own right but the parades are unique. Floats of towering proportions surrounded by a multitude of actors and dancers travel on a set route between Frontierland and the Town Square in Main Street. There is always an afternoon parade and during the peak holiday season two evening parades called the Main Street Electrical Parade, usually at 7pm and 9pm. The evening also features Fantasy in the Sky – a Tinkerbell led extravaganza of fireworks and music.

An outstanding attraction which threatens to get you far wetter than it actually does is **Splash Mountain**. This is the epitome of what Disney does best, with a seamless integration of music, special effects and beautifully crafted creatures. This, combined with a multitude of small drops prior to the big one make this one of the finest flume rides in the world. Absolutely guaranteed to make you want to do it again, this ride develops long queues early on and remains that way until closing.

LIBERTY SQUARE

THE SMALLEST OF all the lands, Liberty Square is set in post-colonial America and hosts three attractions: the **Liberty Square Riverboat**, **Hall of Presidents** and **The Haunted Mansion**. This conveys you through a spook-ridden mansion and graveyard whilst an evocative melody drifts through dead tree branches and ghostly dogs. Entertaining rather than scary, this ride loads quickly and rarely has long lines. Board the Liberty Square Riverboat, a mock paddle steamer, and you can cruise gently through America's nineteenth-century past whilst refuge from the crowds and heat can be found in the Hall of Presidents, an audio animatronic presentation.

FANTASYLAND

DOMINATED BY THE soaring spires of Cinderella's Castle, this land forms the core of the Magic Kingdom. The delightfully designed attractions engender a feeling of amazement in even the most cynical and this land is usually the first destination for kids. **Dumbo** proves a compelling draw for young children whilst the **Carousel** (a genuine 1917 restoration) seems to entice both old and young onto its gallopers. **Snow White's Adventures** is a basic tracked ride, which tells the story that may be

slightly frightening for very young children. **Peter Pan's Flight**, however, is deservedly popular combining the feeling of flying with the delight of perfectly matched music and movement.

Opposite is **It's Small World**, a water borne journey through a series of animated tableaux accompanied by a rather persistent melody which, if you're not careful, you'll find hard to get out of your head for the rest of the day. The newest attraction, **The Many Adventures of Winnie the Pooh**, incorporates the latest in ride vehicle technology, lighting and multi-channel sound effects, producing an attraction which deserves its FASTPASS status.

The only show, **Legends of the Lion King**, offers a welcome respite from relentless walking and embodies the usual high performance standards associated with Disney. **Ariel's Grotto** hosts the interestingly named 'interactive fountain' and greeting area. Here, small children can play in a pelagic environment, meet the Little Mermaid herself and get totally soaked.

MICKEY'S TOONTOWN FAIR

THIS LAND APPEALS mainly to children. Here, Mickey's and Minnie's houses await, together with the opportunity to have your picture taken with Mickey himself. Both the houses are walk through attractions but Mickey's is actually a queuing area for the Judge's Tent where you can meet Mickey Mouse "in the flesh". An alternative

character encounter can be found at the **Toontown Hall of Fame**. There are three entrances, but lines move very slowly and a great deal of time can be lost waiting to see one of the characters. The **Barnstormer** at Goofy's Wiseacre's Farm is the only 'thrill' ride as such, but hardly lives up to its name. **Donald's Boat**, a playground and fountain, offers yet further opportunities for the very young to get very wet.

TOMORROWLAND

SOME YEARS AGO Disney revamped the facades and added new attractions to revitalise Tomorrowland. Whether it has been entirely successful is largely a matter of opinion, but there's still plenty here to enjoy. **Space Mountain** is the fastest ride where you shoot through tight bends and sharp drops in stygian blackness against projections of asteroids and the like. The effects of traveling through space are excellent, but the ride, though wilder than Big Thunder Mountain, may seem tame for seasoned thrillseekers.

The ExtraTERRORestrial Encounter is a seriously terrifying attraction which employs every psychological and special effects trick in the book to make you feel as though you're at the mercy of a rampaging alien. It's excellent for fear addicts but often too severe for children, even older ones.

Handling large crowds with ease, **Walt Disney's Carousel of Progress** is a sit down attraction where the auditorium rotates around a central stage. It examines domestic life through the ages and, although rather quaint, is a firm favourite, particularly late in the evening.

A 360-degree Circle-Vision trip through time, **The Time-keeper** has proved very popular. A standing attraction, it draws large crowds but takes 1000 people a showing. A wonderful place to escape the afternoon heat.

The Tomorrowland Transit Authority is a serene, quiet and interesting ten minute ride which uses linear induction drives. This journey through Tomorrowland affords some·of the best views in the park and an opportunity to relax after a great deal of walking. Almost never busy, it travels through Space Mountain and offers

views inside several other attractions as well.

Most recent of Tomorrowland's Innovations Is **Buzz Lightyear's Space Ranger Spin**. This superb and highly addictive journey through comic books sets you in a two seater car, fitted with laser cannons, electronic scoreboards and a control which allows you to rotate the car rapidly for a better aim. A very fast loader, it's one of the best rides in the park.

Shooting at the targets with a red laser beam which evokes bangs, crashes, pings and rapid increases in your scores. This has become one of the few rides that children tear their parents away from, such is its popularity.

TIPS

• Lines at attractions are shorter during parade times.
• Watch the fireworks from the top of Main Street (near the hub) and then enjoy the rides until the later evening parade, which is always less crowded.
• At the end of the evening there are often long queues for the monorail, so take the farther entrance marked 'Resorts' to get back to the TTC.
• The benches in Mickey's Toontown Fair opposite Mickey's house yard provide an excellent vantage point from which to watch the fireworks.
• A little known shortcut from Mickey's Toontown Fair to Tomorrowland is just to the right of the train station.

RIDES AND SHOWS CHECKLIST

This chart is designed to help you plan what to visit the Magic Kingdom. The rides and shows are listed alphabetically within each Land.

		QUEUES	HEIGHT / AGE RESTRICTION	BUSIEST TIME TO RIDE	FASTPASS	LOADING SPEED	MAY CAUSE MOTION SICKNESS	RATING OVERALL
ADVENTURELAND								
R	JUNGLE CRUISE	●		11am–5pm	→	❷		▼
R	PIRATES OF THE CARRIBBEAN	○		noon–4pm		❶		◆
S	ENCHANTED TIKI BIRDS	○				❶		▼
FRONTIERLAND								
R	BIG THUNDER MOUNTAIN RAILROAD	●	1.2m	10am–7pm		❶	✓	★
R	SPLASH MOUNTAIN	●	1.2m	10am–7pm	→	❶		★
S	COUNTRY BEAR JAMBOREE	○				❶		▼
S	DIAMOND HORSESHOE SALOON REVUE	○				❶		▼
LIBERTY SQUARE								
R	HALL OF PRESIDENTS	▶				❶		▼
R	HAUNTED MANSION	○				❶		★
R	LIBERTY SQUARE RIVERBOAT	○				❶		◆
FANTASYLAND								
R	DUMBO THE FLYING ELEPHANT	●		9am–7pm		❸		▼
R	IT'S A SMALL WORLD	○				❶		▼
R	THE MANY ADVENTURES OF WINNIE THE POOH	●		10am–6pm	→	❸		★
R	PETER PAN'S FLIGHT	●		9am–9pm		❸		★
R	SNOW WHITE'S ADVENTURES	●		9am–5pm		❸		▼
S	LEGEND OF THE LION KING	●				❶		★
MICKEY'S TOONTOWN FAIR								
R	GOOFY'S BARNSTORMER	○				❷	✓	◆
TOMORROWLAND								
R	BUZZ LIGHTYEAR'S SPACE RANGER SPIN	●		10am–6pm	→	❷	✓	★
R	EXTRATERRORESTRIAAL ALIEN ENCOUNTER	●	1.2m	10am–6pm		❶		★
R	SPACE MOUNTAIN	●	1.4m	9am–7pm	→	❷	✓	★
S	THE TIMEKEEPER	○				❶		▼

Key: Ride – R　Show – S;　Waiting Times Good – ○　Average – ▶　Bad – ●;　Overall Rating Good – ▼ Excellent – ◆　Outstanding – ★　Loading Speed Fast – ❶　Leisurely – ❷　Slow – ❸

Epcot

Epcot, an acronym for the Experimental Prototype Community of Tomorrow, was Walt Disney's dream of a technologically replete, living community. It was intended to represent a utopian vision of the future but upon its opening in 1982 several changes had been made to the original dream and Epcot opened as an educational center and permanent world's fair.

The 250 acre park is divided into two distinct halves; Future World with an emphasis on entertainment and education and World Showcase which represents the art, culture and culinary expertise of different countries around the globe.

The France Pavillion in World Showcase

TACKLING THE PARK

Epcot is two and a half times the size of the Magic Kingdom which means that at least two days are needed to see the Park in its entirety. World Showcase is not normally open until 11am so the early-morning crowds fill Future World and then gradually migrate to the rope between the two parks waiting for World Showcase to open. As with everything Disney, arriving early is the key to a successful visit. If you are entitled to early entry privileges, arrive one hour and forty minutes before the official opening time.

Although there are really only a small number of rides in Future World, the newest of these, Test Track, is also the one besieged from the outset. To reach Test Track, bear left through the huge Innoventions East building. It sometimes helps to think of Future World as a clock face; if the turnstiles are at six o'clock then Test Track is at 11 o'clock – the equivalent of walking from the entrance to the Magic Kingdom right through to Splash Mountain.

After leaving Test Track, retrace your steps back through Innoventions East and cross immediately through Innoventions West, emerging to see Honey, I Shrunk the Audience on the left at one o'clock, to continue the clock analogy. After this, return to Spaceship Earth (at six o'clock) and ride. Though this seems like a lot of back-tracking, you will have covered the main attractions very quickly and will feel a little glow of satisfaction when you see the lines snaking out of the entrances later in the day.

World Showcase holds far more interest for adults than children. However, there are Kidcot Fun Spots in several pavilions where kids can draw and have fun and the diversionary tactic of buying each child a 'Passport' to have stamped can prove a blessing. There are minor rides – usually boat rides – in some pavilions and several others show films. The dining at some pavilions is excellent and can be booked ahead through your hotel. The transportation

ILLUMINATIONS: REFLECTIONS OF EARTH

The one Epcot show that you mustn't miss is the nightly IllumiNations. Presented near closing time around World Showcase Lagoon, it is a rousing *son et lumière* show on an unbelievably extravagant scale with lasers, fire- and waterworks and a symphonic soundtrack that highlight the 11 featured nations. Best viewing spots are a seat on the veranda at the Cantina de San Angel in Mexico, the outside restaurant balcony in Japan and the International Gateway bridge near the United Kingdom.

◁ **The unmistakable globe of Spaceship Earth, the focal point of Future World**

system in the park is not very efficient (you'll always get where you want faster by walking) so good, comfortable shoes are essential. There is also not much shade so be sure to wear a hat.

Future World

The first area to be encountered by guests arriving at the main turnstiles, Future World comprises a series of huge, modernistic buildings around the outside, the access to which is through Innoventions East and West. Some buildings house a single ride attraction while others afford the opportunity to browse various exhibits – usually hands-on – and enjoy smaller rides within the main pavilion. Most of the attractions here are sponsored by major manufacturers, which will be evident from the signs.

Pin Trading
This answer to many a parent's prayer was introduced when Disney noticed that lapel pins it had produced for special events were re-selling at several times the market value. In a flash of inspiration, they created Pin Stations, small booths in every park selling only the hundreds of different pins that Disney produce. They usually cost $6 – $15 each. Following this up with a stroke of genius, they also created Pin Traders – cast members who could be persuaded to swap pins with guests and surmounted the whole idea with a set of very simple trading rules, which cast members could break in favour of the guest. This has captured the imagination of children and teenagers who happily spend hours tracking down the pin they don't have and swapping another for it. Disney hotel guests are presented with their first set of pins free on arrival, to start the ball rolling, and the concept has been so successful with both guests and cast members that Disney have no plans to end it.

Top 10 Attractions

1. Test Track
2. Honey, I Shrunk the Audience
3. Spaceship Earth
4. The Living Seas
5. Body Wars
6. Universe of Energy
7. Maelstrom
8. Wonders of China
9. Impressions of France
10. IllumiNations

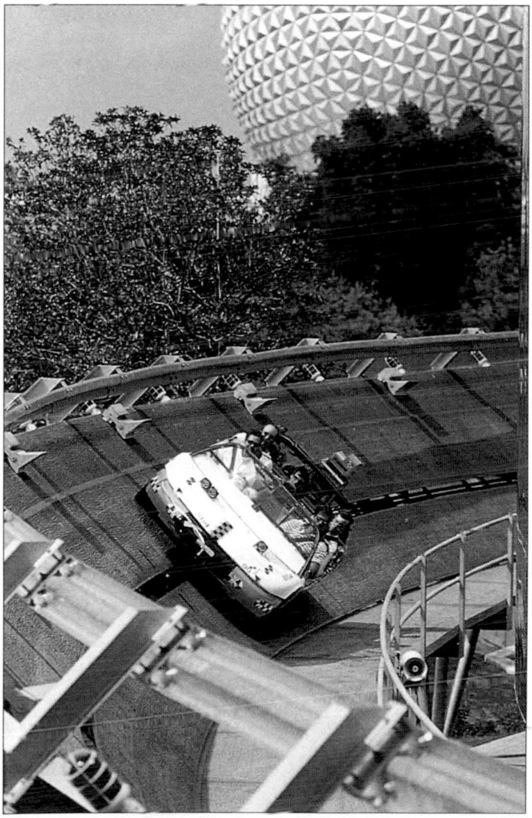

Test Track, one of the most popular rides at Epcot

Spaceship Earth
Housed in a massive, seven-and-a-half-thousand-ton geodesic sphere, this continuously loading ride conveys you gently past superbly crafted tableaux and animatronic scenes portraying mankind's progress in technology. Almost as interesting as the ride is the dome which cunningly re-circulates rainwater into the World Showcase Lagoon.

Innoventions
Both buildings, East and West, form a hands-on exhibition of products of the close future which, through ties to Sega and other technology manufacturers, is constantly updated. However, time is needed to make the most of Innoventions and many of the games have now moved to Downtown Disney, with the result that the theme has become more adult.

FUTURE WORLD CONT...

Universe of Energy

A passably entertaining film is enlivened by some fascinating technology. The entire theatre rotates before breaking into self powered, moving sections, each seating over a 100 people which then proceed to take you through a prehistoric landscape, inhabited by some fairly convincing antediluvians.

The Living Seas

The technology behind this attraction is quite stunning in its own right, but the reason most come here is to visit Sea Base Alpha, Epcot's most ambitious research project. A pre-show presentation prepares you for your journey to the bottom of the ocean, after which you take the "hydrolators" to the sea bed. There you board a continuously moving train of small cars which carry you past astonishing views of sharks, dolphins, giant turtles and manatees. Disembarkation brings you to the base itself, where you can browse through exhibits, get close up to the manatees and watch the sea life through transparent walls.

Wonders of Life

A rambling, noisy pavilion dealing, as its name suggests, with the functioning of the human body. **The Making**

of Me is a pleasant film about the events preceding childbirth whilst **Cranium Command** is a highly amusing and often overlooked animatronic presentation about the operation of the brain. **Body Wars** – Epcot's first simulator thrill ride – takes you through the human body, having first miniaturised you. This, however, although very popular, is a violent and jerky simulator ride which induces motion sickness in quite a few people.

Test Track

The most popular ride in Epcot, long lines form quickly at park opening time and increase rapidly because of frequent malfunctions. Test Track uses the most sophisticated ride vehicle technology available placing you in a simulator that moves on tracks at high speed. Essentially, you are the passengers in a six seater prototype sports car being tested prior to going into production. Although the ride puts you through brake tests, hill climbs, sharp turns, near crashes and paint spraying bays, the climax is the outside lap of the ride where the vehicle exceeds 66mph on a raised roadway around the outside of the Test Track building. So advanced is the technology that the ride is kept running 24 hours a day, as the start up procedure is

so lengthy. However, the system has frequent stops – usually because the advanced safety systems have cut in and halted the entire run. While this is obviously reassuring in some ways, the ride is so popular that the lines outside continue to grow until, by the evening, you can expect a wait of between 90 minutes and two hours for this 4 minute ride. The ride itself, however, is so good you will want to ride it again and again. Be aware that the FastPass machines outside the entrance have normally exhausted their allocation by lunchtime. After the ride, you can wander at leisure through what appears to be a large General Motors showroom.

The Imagination Pavilion

The Imaginaton Pavilion houses two attractions: the astonishingly funny Honey; I Shrunk the Audience! and the Journey into Your Imagination ride.

Honey, I Shrunk the Audience should not be missed. Seamlessly integrating Disney's own unique 3-D film technology with special effects, this show will have you rolling in the aisles with laughter, then trying to escape from something beneath your seat.

The **Journey into Your Imagination** ride is a very upbeat and light-hearted

---

CELEBRATION FLORIDA

Materializing out of former swampland adjacent to Walt Disney World, Celebration is a new town with old values. Inspired partly by the romantic streets of Charleston in South Carolina, Disney is attempting to re-create the wholesome small-town atmosphere that many middle-aged Americans remember and miss. The residents will experience a cookie-jar world of friendly neighbors and corner grocery stores.

People began moving here in 1996, the first of an expected total of 20,000 inhabitants. The pedestrian-friendly streets, the nostalgic architecture (designed by some respected architects), and the hospital that treats both "wellness" and illness seem tailor-made for fugitives from the fear and drudgery of modern city life – people who aren't daunted by Celebration's strict rules, which set out, for example, that visible curtains must be white or off-white and that streetside shrubbery must be approved by Disney. In some ways, however, Celebration is like any other town: the public is free to visit and look around.

trip in search of ideas in the arts and sciences. However, it is overcomplicated and overlong. You move past several different animated scenes which present optical illusions and sound effects.

The Land
Ecology and conservation form the main themes and permeate the three attractions housed around the fast food restaurant. As a consequence, these attractions become much busier during lunch-times. Lion King characters lead **The Circle of Life**, a hymn to conservation expressed through film and animation **Food Rocks** is a saccharin coated animatronic presentation about nutrition (with comic characters such as Chubby Cheddar and Neil Moussaka) while **Living with the Land** is a cruise through the past, present and future of US farming. The Land pavilion also offers a walking tour to accompany the boat ride which is certainly worth taking for those interested.

ONE-DAY ITINERARY

1. Arrive 1 hour 40 minutes before the official opening time on an early entry day or an hour before on a normal day.

2. Head straight towards Test Track, ride, collect FastPass ticket for later then backtrack to the opposite side of Future World for Honey, I Shrunk the Audience.

3. Leave and head back towards the entrance and ride Spaceship Earth.

4. From there, turn right and head towards Wonders of Life. Ride Body Wars.

5. Turn right out of Wonders of Life and see show at Universe of Energy.

6. Head towards World Showcase and wait for the rope drop on the left.

7. At rope drop, head to Mexico. Ride El Rio del Tiempo.

8. Leave to the right and go to Norway. Ride The Maelstrom.

9. This is almost certainly time to eat and you now have the major attractions behind you. After recuperating, visit China (movie), France (movie) and Canada (movie).

10. Return to Future World and visit The Land pavilion. Experience all three attractions there.

11. Leave the Land pavilion to the left and head for The Living Seas.

12. Exit Living Seas to the right, pass through both Innoventions East and West and return to the Wonders of Life pavilion where you can see Cranium Command and The Story of Life.

It's now a good time to head back to your hotel and return by 7.00pm to book a good spot to see IllumiNations.

RIDES AND SHOWS CHECKLIST

This chart is designed to help you plan what to visit at Epcot. The rides and shows are listed alphabetically in Future World and World Showcase.

	WAITING TIME	HEIGHT / AGE RESTRICTION	BUSIEST TIME TO RIDE	FASTPASS	MAY CAUSE MOTION SICKNESS	RATING OVERALL
FUTURE WORLD						
BODY WARS	●	1.2m	10am–2pm		✓	▼
CIRCLE OF LIFE	○		noon–2pm			▼
CRANIUM COMMAND	○					◆
FOOD ROCKS	○		noon–2pm			▼
HONEY, I SHRUNK THE AUDIENCE	●		10am–5pm	➡		★
JOURNEY INTO YOUR IMAGINATION	◗		11am–2pm			◆
LIVING WITH THE LAND	◗		noon–2pm			◆
SPACESHIP EARTH	●		9am–noon			★
THE MAKING OF ME	○					▼
TEST TRACK	●	1.2m	All day	➡	✓	★
UNIVERSE OF ENERGY	◗		10am–1pm			◆
THE LIVING SEAS	○		11am–3pm			◆
WORLD SHOWCASE						
EL RIO DEL TIEMPO	○		noon–3pm			▼
IMPRESSIONS DE FRANCE	○					▼
MAELSTROM	●		11am–5pm			▼
THE AMERICAN ADVENTURE	○					◆
O CANADA!	○					◆
WONDERS OF CHINA	○					★

Key: Waiting Times Good – ○ Average – ◗ Bad – ●;
Overall Rating Good – ▼ Excellent – ◆ Outstanding - ★

WORLD SHOWCASE

THE TEMPLES, churches, town halls, and castles of these 11 pavilions or countries are sometimes replicas of genuine buildings, sometimes merely in vernacular style. But World Showcase is much more than just a series of architectural set pieces. Every pavilion is staffed by people from the country it represents, selling high-quality local products as well as surprisingly good ethnic cuisine.

At set times (which are given on the guidemap) native performers stage live shows in the forecourts of each country: the best are the excellent acrobats at China and the bizarre and comic Living Statues at Italy. Only a couple of pavilions include rides, while a number have stunning giant-screen introductions to their country's history, culture, and landscapes. A few even have art galleries, though these often go unnoticed.

Double-decker buses do the rounds of the lake's 1.3-mile (2-km) perimeter, but it is usually quicker to walk. There are also ferries across World Showcase Lagoon, linking Canada to Morocco and Mexico to Germany.

Mexico

A Mayan pyramid hides the most remarkable interior at World Showcase. Stalls selling sombreros, ponchos, and papier-mâché animals *(piñatas)*, and musicians fill a plaza bathed in a purple twilight. The backdrop to this is a rumbling volcano.

The tranquil **El Río del Tiempo** ("The River of Time") boat ride passes through Audio-Animatronics and cinematic scenes of Mexico past and present while the restaurant here offers the best viewing spot for IllumiNations later in the day.

Norway

The architecture here includes replicas of a stave church (a medieval wooden church) and Akershus Castle (a 14th-century fortress above Oslo harbor), arranged attractively around a cobblestone square.

You can buy trolls and sweaters and other native crafts, but the essential element here is **Maelstrom**, a short but exhilarating journey down fjords in a longboat, into troll country, and across an oil rig-flecked North Sea – before docking at a fishing port. The ride is followed by a short film about Norway.

China

In this pavilion the *pièce de résistance* is the half-size replica of Beijing's well-known landmark, the Temple of Heaven. The peaceful scene here contrasts with the more rowdy atmosphere in some of the nearby pavilions.

For entertainment, there is **Wonders of China**, a Circle-Vision film (shown on nine screens all around the audience simultaneously), which makes the most of the country's fabulous, little-seen ancient sites and scenery. Note that you must stand throughout the film.

The pavilion's extensive shopping emporium sells everything from Chinese lanterns and painted screens to tea bags. Unfortunately, the restaurants are disappointing.

Germany

The happiest country in World Showcase is a mixture of gabled and spired buildings gathered around a central square, St. Georgsplatz. They are based on real buildings from all over Germany, including a merchants' hall in Freiburg and a Rhine castle. If you have children, try to time your visit so that it coincides with the hourly chime of the glockenspiel in the square.

An accordionist sometimes plays, and the shops are full of quirky or clever gifts such as beautifully crafted wooden dolls. However, you really need to dine here to get the full flavor of Germany.

Italy

The bulk of Italy's relatively small pavilion represents Venice: from gondolas moored alongside candycane poles in the lagoon to the tremendous versions of the towering redbrick campanile and the 14th-century Doge's Palace of St. Mark's Square; even the fake marble looks authentic. The courtyard buildings behind are Veronese and Florentine in style, and the Neptune statue is a copy of a Bernini work.

The architecture is the big attraction, but you should also stop off to eat in one of the restaurants or browse around the shops where you can pick up pasta, amaretti, wine, and so forth.

The American Adventure

The American pavilion is the centerpiece of World Showcase, but it lacks the detail and charm found in most of the other countries. However, Americans usually find **The American Adventure** show, which takes place inside the vast Georgian-style building, very moving. For foreigners it will provide an interesting insight into the American

---

WORLD SHOWCASE: BEHIND THE SCENES

If you'd like more than just a superficial view of Walt Disney World, its behind-the-scenes tours may appeal. In World Showcase, two-hour Hidden Treasures tours provide a closer look at the architecture and traditions of the countries featured in the park, while in the Gardens of the World tours the creation of the World Showcase gardens is explained; you are even given tips on how to create a bit of Disney magic back home. These tours cost around $25 per person. If you have $160 and seven hours to spare, you might want to sign up for the Backstage Magic tour, which includes all three theme parks. One of the highlights is the visit to the famous tunnel network beneath the Magic Kingdom. For information on all Disney tours call (407) WDW-TOUR/(407) 939-8687.

psyche. The show is an openly patriotic yet thought-provoking romp through the history of the United States up to the present day. It incorporates tableaus on screen and some excellent Audio-Animatronics figures, particularly of the author Mark Twain and the great 18th-century statesman, Benjamin Franklin.

 Japan
This is a restrained, formal place with a traditional Japanese garden, a Samurai castle, and a pagoda modeled on a seventh-century temple in Nara – whose five levels represent earth, water, fire, wind, and sky.

The Mitsukoshi department store, a copy of the ceremonial hall of the Imperial Palace in Kyoto, offers kimonos, wind chimes, bonsai trees, and the chance to pick a pearl from an oyster. However, Japan really only comes to life in its restaurants.

Morocco
Morocco's appeal lies in its enameled tiles, its keyhole-shaped doors, its ruddy fortress walls, and the twisting alleys of its *medina* (old city), which is reached via a reproduction of a gate into the city of Fez. The use of native artists gives the show a greater sense of authenticity.

Morocco offers some of the best handmade crafts in World Showcase. The alleys of the old city lead you to a bustling market of little stores selling carpets, brassware, leatherware, and shawls, with belly dancing and couscous in the Restaurant Marrakesh.

France
A Gallic flair infuses everything in the France pavilion from its architecture (including a one-tenth scale replica of the Eiffel Tower, Parisian Belle Epoque mansions, and a rustic village main street) to its upscale stores (perfume, wine, and berets). French food can be sampled in a couple of restaurants and a patisserie selling croissants and cakes.

A film entitled **Impressions de France** is the main enter-

tainment. The film, shown on five adjacent screens and set to the sounds of French classical music, offers a whirlwind tour through the country's most beautiful regions.

 United Kingdom
The Rose and Crown Pub is the focal point in this pavilion. It serves traditional English fare such as Cornish pasties, fish and chips, and even draft bitter – chilled to suit American tastes. Pleasant gardens surround the pub, as well as a medley of buildings of various historic architectural styles. These include a castle based on Hampton Court, an imitation Regency terrace, and a thatched cottage.

There is not much to do here in this pavilion other than browse around the shops, which sell everything from quality tea and china to sweaters, tartan ties, teddy bears, and toy soldiers. The terrace in the Rose and Crown, however, offers good views of IllumiNations.

 Canada
A log cabin, 30-ft (9-m) high totem poles, a replica of Ottawa's Victorian-style Château Laurier Hotel, a rocky chasm, and ornamental gardens make up the large but rather staid Canadian pavilion.

The country in all its diversity, and particularly its grand scenery, comes to life much better in the Circle-Vision film **O Canada!** (though China's Circle-Vision film is even better). The audience stands in the middle of the theater and turns around to follow the film as it unfolds on no fewer than nine screens.

Shops at Canada sell a range of Indian and Inuit crafts, as well as various edible specialties, including wine.

EATING AND DRINKING

Dining well is fundamental to visiting Epcot and particularly World Showcase. Some of the latter's pavilions have decent fast-food places, but the best restaurants (including those listed below unless otherwise stated) require reservations. Call (407) 939-3463 as soon as you know when you'll be at Epcot. Book early in the day, using the TV monitors of the WorldKey Information Satellite *(see p148)*. Most restaurants serve lunch and dinner; try unpopular hours such as 11am or 4pm if other times are unavailable. Lunch is usually about two-thirds of the price of dinner, and children's menus are available at even the most upscale restaurants.

Recommended in World Showcase are.
Mexico: the San Angel Inn serves interesting but pricey Mexican cuisine. It is the most romantic place to dine at Epcot.
Norway: Akershus offers a good-value *koldtbord* (buffet) of Norwegian dishes in a castle setting.
Germany: the Biergarten has a beer hall atmosphere, with a cheap and plentiful buffet and hearty oompah-pah music.
Italy: L'Originale Alfredo di Roma restaurant is enormously popular and engagingly chaotic, with sophisticated dishes.
Japan: you can eat communally, either in the Teppanyaki Dining Rooms around a grilling, stir-frying chef, or at the bar of Tempura Kiku for sushi and tempura (no reservations).
France: there are three top-notch restaurants here: the upscale Bistro de Paris (dinner only); Chefs de France, the most elegant restaurant in Epcot, with *haute cuisine* by acclaimed French chefs; and the terraced Au Petit Café (no reservations possible) for steaks, escargots, and crêpes.

Recommended in Future World are:
The Land: the revolving Garden Grill passes a re-created rainforest, prairie, and desert while Disney characters entertain.
The Living Seas: at the expensive Coral Reef you can both eat fish and watch fish through a transparent, underwater wall.

Disney-MGM Studios

D ISNEY-MGM STUDIOS opened in 1989, not only as the third and smallest theme park in Walt Disney World Resort but also as a fully fledged working film and TV production facility. The park combines top-notch shows and rides, based on Disney and Metro-Golden-Mayer films (to which Disney bought the rights), with educational and entertaining shows and tours that allow visitors to glimpse "inside the magic", that is, how films and TV shows are made. Tours are the only way to see the working parts of the Studios. Like Universal Studios, Disney-MGM Studios gears itself toward adults and teenagers, but it has a more nostalgic feel about it.

Mann's Chinese Theater located on Hollywood Boulevard

TACKLING THE PARK

T HIS PARK is not laid out in the same way as the other theme parks, although Hollywood Boulevard acts as a sort of 'Main Street USA' with the purpose of fun-nelling guests towards the attractions. Over the past few years, Disney has expanded the breadth and scope of the attractions here, building some of the finest in Orlando. The entertainment schedule changes frequently and streets can be closed off during the visit of a celebrity or a live filming session. Although most of this happens in winter, it's a good idea to find out times, locations, and events as soon as you enter the park from Guest Services, on the left of the main entrance.

As with the other theme parks, arriving early is the key to avoid waiting a long time in line. It's also worth bearing in mind that some attractions are particularly intense and can frighten young children.

At about 3pm, Disney-MGM Studios holds its afternoon parade. The open plan of the park means that guests may get hot while waiting for the parade, which is always based on one of the recent animated movies from Disney.

At night, **Fantasmic!** takes place. This superb event is held once a night during the slow season and twice during peak periods. Seating 10,000 people at a time, you will need to turn up at least two hours before, however, to get a good seat!

HOLLYWOOD BOULEVARD

D ELIGHTFUL ART DECO styled buildings vie with a replica of Mann's Chinese Theater to present an image of Hollywood that never was. It's here that your picture will be taken and you might well see some of the cast members acting as reporters or police, chasing celebrities. More importantly, it is on the Boulevard that the cast mem-bers will try to direct you to the Hollywood Stunt Spectacular – a live action show using many of the stunts from the Indiana Jones films. However, the top attractions are in the opposite direction.

Halfway up the boulevard, Sunset Boulevard breaks to the right, leading to the two most popular rides in the Park, The Twilight Zone Tower of Terror and the Rock 'n Roller Coaster Starring Aerosmith.

At the junction between Hollywood and Sunset Boulevards lies one of the ubiquitous pin stations where budding traders can ambush cast members and swap badges. At the top of Hollywood Boulevard lies the Central Plaza, dominated by the replica of Mann's Chinese Theater, where you can experience **The Great Movie Ride**. This is one of the few attractions where the queuing is almost as good as the ride itself. Here, huge ride vehicles carrying 60 guests apiece track silently past the largest movie sets ever built for a Disney ride. As always, the vast experience of Disney in

TIPS

• Guests who wish their offspring to see the Disney animators at work should enrol them for a day course at the Disney Institute. Although pricey, the course is great and an unforgettable experience.
• The best place to watch the afternoon parade is on the bench nearest the popcorn and drinks stand opposite 'Sounds Dangerous'. You still, however, have to get there first.
• During the parades, most of the other attractions are quiet, but almost impossible to reach if you're not on the correct side.
• In the boiler room of the Twilight Tower of Terror, take any open gateway to the lifts – don't worry if others are not. You'll get a better seat and a better view.

the movie industry has been brought to bear and created the most realistic sets imaginable. Combined with real live action sequences, this is an enjoyable ride which ends on a very upbeat and optimistic note.

SUNSET BOULEVARD

L IKE HOLLYWOOD BOULEVARD, Sunset Boulevard is a rose-tinted evocation of the famous Hollywood street in the 1940s. Theaters and store-fronts (some real, some fake) have been re-created with characteristic attention to detail, and is dominated at one end by the Hollywood Tower Hotel. This lightning-ravaged, decrepit Hotel is the spot for Orlando's scariest ride – **The Twilight Zone Tower of Terror** – in which you're strapped into the service elevator for a voyage inspired by the 1950s TV show *The Twilight Zone*™. The pre-show area is a library into which you are ushered by a melancholic bell cap. From here you enter what appears to be the boiler room of the hotel and you walk through to the lifts – apparently freight elevators fitted with plank seats. The elevator doors sometimes open to allow glimpses of ghostly corridors, but it's hard to concentrate on anything other than the ghastly 13-story plunge that everyone knows will come

The Twilight Zone Tower of Terror is particularly spectacular at night

– but not exactly when. When you arrive on the thirteenth floor the elevator actually trundles horizontally across the hotel. Once you are in the drop shaft you get dropped no fewer than seven times.

This is a masterpiece of ride technology and imagination. The original single drop has been expandedd to seven and, during the first drop, enormously powerful engines actually pull you down faster than free fall.

You can also enjoy the fleeting view of the whole park and indeed outside the park (a break with Disney tradition) before you begin the terrifying descent. This ride is not to everyone's taste, but die-hard enthusiasts and novices alike pack this ride from the outset.

A triumph of noise over everything else, the **Rock 'n Roller Coaster Starring Aerosmith** accelerates you to nearly 60mph in 2.8 seconds in the dark and pulls 5G in the first corkscrew, of which there are several. The pre-show, a rather lame affair, links a recording session of the band Aerosmith to the ride. From here you queue up at two doors. For those that like the front seats, you can get to

these via the lower ramp. Replete with loops, corkscrews and steep drops, the Rock 'n Roller Coaster also employs a fully synchronised and very loud soundtrack as it hurls you towards the neon-lit equivalent of oblivion.

Elsewhere on Sunset Boulevard, don't forget to look out for Mickey Mouse, who is usually signing autographs at the Beverly Sunset Theater. Sunset Boulevard also houses the entrance to the **Theater of the Stars**, which shows a live stage show at indicated times and combines live action with animation and a great musical score. The shows change periodically. Sunset Boulevard is also where you will find the entrance to **Fantasmic!**

FANTASMIC!

The evening show at Disney-MGM Studios tends to exhaust super-latives. It is, quite simply, the finest event of its kind in Florida. Combining music, lasers, fan fountain projection, animation and a cast of over a hundred actors and dancers, Fantasmic! manages to choreograph the entire event with split second accuracy to music, fire-works and lighting. Set on an island in a lagoon, the story concerns the ongoing battle between good and evil. Illuminated boats, flying floats and a lake which bursts into flames are but some features of this enchanting event which plays to audiences of 10,000 per showing.

Unfortunately, the show is exceptionally popular, and this means that to get a good seat you'll have to be there at least two hours before it starts. Even in the quietest time of the off peak season, all 10,000 places are taken up to 30 minutes before the show starts. However, this truly is one event you will never forgive yourself for missing.

ANIMATION COURTYARD

THE BIG APPEAL of Animation Courtyard is the chance to have a glimpse behind the scenes during the creation of Disney's Audio-Animatronics®.

The **Magic of Disney-Animation** tour at the Studios begins with a display of Walt Disney's many Oscar® awards and original "cels" – drawings that each represent a frame in an animated film. After a film in which actor Robin Williams introduces you to how cartoons are created, you enter the working studios. Here, you are separated from the Disney animators by windows, but video monitors explain what you are seeing at each stage – such as the development of the story line in the Story Room or the refining of the cartoon images in the Ink and Paint departments.

Inspired by the animated feature film *The Little Mermaid*, the song and dance show **Voyage of The Little Mermaid** is enacted by cartoon, live and Audio-Animatronic® characters. Lasers and water effects are used to create the feel of an underwater grotto. It helps if you know the film, but the show remains one of the most popular in the park. It appeals to all ages, but young children sometimes find the lightning storm scary.

SOUND STAGES

LIKE THE Magic of Disney Animation tour, the Sound Stages provide an opportunity to see how things are done in the working part of the studios. Films called *The Making of...*, which explain how the latest Disney releases were created, are often technically complex but fascinating. If time is short, you should concentrate on the Studios Backlot Tour.

The 25-minute **Backstage Pass to "101 Dalmatians"** tour devoted to the film *101 Dalmatians* starts with the chance for you to meet several puppy dalmatians with their trainer. Farther in, you're shown how the puppet puppies are made and operated. A number of props used in the film are also on display.

Although it never fails to be entertaining, the half-hour **Disney-MGM Studios Backlot Tour** best comes to life when a film is actually being shot. A tram ride takes you for a peek at the wardrobe, camera, props, and lighting departments as well as the suburban homes used as outdoor sets for TV shows. The most memorable part is Catastrophe Canyon, where the tram ends up in the midst of a flood and explosions.

The walking part of the tour is more informative. With audience participation, it demonstrates some of the special effects used in making films; battle scenes at sea are re-created using models in a water tank. You also get to look in on three sound stages, where, if you're lucky, a TV show, commercial, or movie might be being filmed.

NEW YORK STREET

THE BRICKS AND STONE in this version of New York are in fact just painted on plastic and fiberglass, the buildings' façades simply propped up with girders. Washing on the line outside a brownstone, a Chinese laundry, and the Empire State Building (painted in forced perspective to make it appear tall) add authenticity to the Big Apple. The streets were once closed to visitors, but you can now wander around freely – even though the set is still used for filming.

The Hunchback of Notre Dame: A Musical Adventure is a show based on the animated film *The Hunchback of Notre Dame*, released by Disney in 1996.

If you've got young children, don't miss the imaginative **Honey, I Shrunk the Kids Movie Set Adventure** playground with 30-ft (9-m) high blades of grass, a slide made from a roll of film, and an ant the size of a pony. The tunnels, slides, and other props keep children amused for hours. Being small, the play area can get very crowded, so it's best to go early.

In **Jim Henson's Muppet™ Vision 3-D**, a highly enjoyable, slapstick 3-D movie (starring the Muppets), trombones, cars, and rocks launch themselves at you out of the screen; they are so realistic that children often grasp the air expecting to touch something.

Audio-Animatronics characters and special effects, such as a cannon blowing holes in the walls of the theater, provide the fourth dimension.

EATING AND DRINKING

It is definitely worth going to the trouble of making a reservation at three of the full-service restaurants at Disney-MGM Studios, though more for their atmosphere than their food. You can reserve a table by calling (407) 939-3463/WDW-DINE, or by going directly to the Dining Reservation Booth, at the crossroads of Hollywood and Sunset boulevards, or to the restaurants themselves.

The civilized, costly Hollywood Brown Derby replicates the Original Brown Derby in Hollywood, where the stars met in the 1930s – right down to the celebrities' caricatures on the walls and the house specialties of Cobb Salad and grapefruit cake. Kids usually prefer the Sci-Fi Dine-In Theater Restaurant, a 1950s drive-in where customers sit in mini-Cadillacs under a starry sky to watch old science-fiction movies, while munching on popcorn and burgers. In the '50's Prime Time Café you are served by maternal waitresses in 1950s kitchens with the TV tuned to period sitcoms; the food, such as meatloaf and pot roast, is homey.

The best place to eat without a reservation is the self-service Art Deco-themed cafeteria Hollywood & Vine, where you can choose from a varied menu that includes pasta, salads, seafood, ribs, and steaks.

ECHO LAKE

THE INTEREST here focuses on three shows and one thrill ride, Star Tours, but children also enjoy the sight of a great green dinosaur. The shows reveal tricks of the trade used in making movies and TV shows.

Selected members of the audience act as audio artists or "Foley" artists (Foley is the name of the sound effects system used in Hollywood) in **Sounds Dangerous**. They add thunder, lightning, and other sounds to a short film, which is then played back to the audience. The show is narrated by popular comedic actor Drew Carey who stars as a police detective who goes undercover.

In **SuperStar Television** a few lucky guests are chosen to be filmed on a talk show and in celebrated American sitcoms such as *I Love Lucy* and *Cheers*. Due to special effects, it seems as though the novices are actually on screen with the real actors.

SHOPPING

Most of the best shops are on Hollywood Boulevard, which stays open half an hour after the rest of the theme park has closed. Mickey's of Hollywood is the big emporium for general Disney merchandise. Celebrity 5 & 10 has a range of affordable movie souvenirs, such as clapper boards and Oscars®, as well as books and posters. Much pricier is Sid Cahuenga's One-Of-A-Kind, where you can buy rare film and TV memorabilia such as genuine autographed photos (of Boris Karloff and Greta Garbo, for example), or famous actors' clothes. Limited-edition "cels" in Animation Gallery in Animation Courtyard will make an even bigger dent in your wallet; the same shop sells good Disney posters and books too.

You should be at the front of the line at least half an hour in advance to have a chance of being filmed.

The storyline of the sensational ride **Star Tours** is based on the *Star Wars* films. Your spaceship, a flight simulator akin to those used to train astronauts, takes a wrong turn and has to evade meteors and cope in an intergalactic battle. What you see on screen seems unbelievably real since your craft jolts in synchronicity with the action. The large-scale show **Indiana Jones™ Epic Stunt Spectacular!** re-creates well-known scenes from the Indiana Jones movies to deliver lots of big bangs and daredevil feats to thrill the audience. Death-defying stuntmen leap between buildings as they avoid sniper fire and sudden explosions. As an educational sideline, the stunt director and real stunt doubles demonstrate how some action sequences are realized. Try to arrive early if you want to take part as an extra in the show

RIDES, SHOWS AND TOURS CHECKLIST

This chart is designed to help you plan what to visit at Disney-MGM Studios. The rides, shows and tours are listed alphabetically within each area.

		WAITING TIME	HEIGHT / AGE RESTRICTION	BEST TIME TO RIDE	FAST-PASS	MAY CAUSE MOTION SICKNESS	RATING OVERALL
HOLLYWOOD BOULEVARD							
R	**GREAT MOVIE RIDE**	○		Any			★
SUNSET BOULEVARD							
R	**ROCK 'N' ROLLER COASTER**	●	1.2m	►11	➡	✓	◆
R	**TWILIGHT ZONE TOWER OF TERROR**	●		►11	➡	✓	★
ANIMATION COURTYARD							
T	**MAGIC OF DISNEY ANIMATION**	◗		Any			◆
S	**VOYAGE OF THE LITTLE MERMAID**	●		Any	➡		◆
SOUND STAGES							
T	**DISNEY-MGM STUDIOS BACKLOT TOUR**	○		Any			★
T	**THE MAKING OF . . .**	◗		Any			◆
NEW YORK STREET							
S	**JIM HENSON'S MUPPET™ VISION 3-D**	●		Any			★
S	**THE HUNCHBACK OF NOTRE DAME**	○		Any			◆
ECHO LAKE							
S	**INDIANA JONES™ EPIC STUNT SPECTACULAR!**	●		Any			◆
S	**SOUNDS DANGEROUS**	◗		Any			▼
S	**STAR TOURS**	◗	1.1m	►11	➡	✓	★
R	**SUPERSTAR TELEVISION**	○		Any			▼

Key: Ride – R Show – S Tour – T; Waiting Times Good – ○ Average – ◗ Bad – ●; Overall Rating Good – ▼ Excellent – ◆ Outstanding – ★ Time to Ride: Anytime – Any Before 11am – ►11

Disney's Animal Kingdom

THE LARGEST OF THE THEME PARKS Disney's Animal Kingdom is five times the size of the Magic Kingdom. It is rather unique in that there are real animals to see, not just animatronic creatures, and consequently every visit is likely to be different. The park is loosely based on the real, the mythical, and the extinct and some areas are accessible only through safari-type tours.

TACKLING THE PARK

THE PARK IS DIVIDED into seven lands: The Oasis, Safari Village, Dinoland USA, Camp Minnie-Mickey, Africa, Asia, and a land (not yet named) of legend and myth. Navigation within the park is also quite different from other parks. When you first pass through the turnstiles, you enter **The Oasis** – a foliage festooned area offering several routes to the park's central hub, Safari Village. The Oasis contains many little surprises, most of which are missed by visitors who race through to reach the attractions. Time spent waiting quietly at the various habitats will be well rewarded. For thrill-ride seekers, the park offers few traditional thrills, however, the "rides" they do have are outstanding and get very crowded.

SAFARI VILLAGE

AS YOU EMERGE into the open space of the village, the **Tree of Life** looms – this is a massive, fourteen story structure that is the signature landmark of the park. It holds sway over a pageant of brightly colored shop fronts and a multitude of pools and

Colorful camouflage at Animal Kingdom

gardens, each holding a variety of wildlife. The main shops, baby care and first aid post all face the Tree of Life.

Under its branches lie the bridges that cross to the other lands and within the trunk itself is the **Tough to be a Bug** show. This 3D theatre presentation is outstanding and not to be missed. Even teenagers think the show is "cool" and see it repeatedly. Nearby is the **River Cruise**, but skip this if you have to wait in line, as the cruise offers little in the way of variety.

CAMP MINNIE-MICKEY

DESIGNED PRIMARILY for guests to meet Disney characters, this land also has the park's two live stage productions. Lines for the **Character Trails** (at the end

of which the youngsters meet with the characters) can, predictably, become very long and sometimes become entwined with the lines waiting for the stage shows.

A very popular show, the **Festival of the Lion King** encourages cheering and singing like no other. Superbly staged, the downside is that the open-air theatre, although shaded, can become hot in the summer – try to see it early or last thing. **Pocohontas and Her Forest Friends At Grandmother Willow's Grove** lacks the punch of the Festival of the Lion King but is a favourite with little girls. The music is pleasant enough but the general feel is somewhat sugary. The theatre itself is small and lines frequently long.

AFRICA

ENTERED THROUGH the village of Harambe, Africa is the largest of the lands. The architecture is closely modelled on a Kenyan village and conceals Disney cleanliness behind a façade of simple, run down buildings and wobbly telegraph poles.

The **Kilimanjaro Safaris** is the park's busiest attraction, though it gets quieter in the afternoon. Guests board open sided trucks driven into an astonishing replica of the East African landscape. During this 20-minute drive over mud holes and creaking bridges you have the opportunity to see many African animals including hippos, rhinos, lions, and elephants, all roaming apparently free and undisturbed. It isn't unusual for a white rhino to get close enough to sniff the truck!

Affording an excellent opportunity to see Gorillas close up, the **Pangani Forest Exploration Trail** can get rather congested with guests exiting the Safaris. It gets less busy in the late

Animals roaming freely can be seen on the Kilimanjaro Safaris

afternoon and you can actually spend some time watching the animals.

A pleasant open train ride takes you to the **Conservation Station**. Purely educational, a visit can take about 90 minutes and is probably best suited to a time when you need a break from the main park.

ASIA

THIS LAND FEATURES gibbons, exotic birds and tigers set in a recreation of post-colonial Indian ruins. **Kali River Rapids** offers you a chance to get completely drenched. This short ride presents some of the most striking and detailed surroundings in the park, which you may miss as yet another wave saturates the parts still merely damp.

Tapirs, Komodo dragons and giant fruit bats can be found on the **Maharaja Jungle Trek**, the climax of which has to be the magnificent Bengal tigers roaming the palace ruins. Through glazed walled sections of the palace, you can get within arm's length of the tigers.

At the **Flights of Wonder at the Caravan Stage** birds perform fascinating and complex manoeuvres showing the natural survival techniques used by the birds in the wild.

DINOLAND USA

THIS LAND GIVES YOU the chance to witness dinosaurs live and die before your very eyes. On the popular ride **Dinosaur**, guests board a mobile motion simulator which bucks and weaves trying to both ensnare and avoid carnivorous dinosaurs. This is a pretty wild ride, and most of it is in the dark – best liked by older children. For family entertainment try **Tarzan Rocks!**, which runs four times a day at the **Theatre in the Wild**.

The Boneyard is a playground for young children, keeping them amused and sandy. However, beware the summer sun while digging for dinosaur bones.

The Rest of the Walt Disney World® Resort

THERE IS A LOT MORE to Walt Disney World than just its theme parks. At the last count, it also included 27 resorts, a campground, three water parks, nearly 300 places to eat, a variety of nightclubs, a nature preserve, a shopping village, and half a dozen golf courses. Remember that opening hours vary over the year, and outdoor attractions may closed due to the weather.

THE WATER PARKS

THE MOST POPULAR places to recuperate after a day in a theme park are the three beautifully designed and well-supervised water parks. Each has beaches and pools, plus slides and water coasters. Once you have a ticket, all rides are free. One-day hopper passes provide admission to any of the water parks.

In summer, the water parks can get very crowded and may close their lots by noon. Most parks open at 9 or 10am and in summer close at around 7pm. The parks may close for renovation in winter, so call ahead.

Blizzard Beach
(*(407) 560-3400.*
The improbable theme here is an Alpine ski resort. Cable cars take you up Mount Gushmore, topped by a snowy ski jump, from where you can take daredevil rides such as Summit Plummet and Slush Gusher. At a height of 120 ft (37 m), Summit Plummet is claimed to be the tallest speed slide in the world.

Typhoon Lagoon
(*(407) 560-4141.*
Re-creating a tropical resort in the aftermath of a storm, Typhoon Lagoon is beautifully landscaped with gardens, a river for floating in inner tubes through caves, a rainforest, and a huge lagoon with waves. You can go white water rafting and snorkel in a reef with real exotic fish and harmless small sharks.

River Country
(*(407) 824-2760.*
This is the smallest and oldest water park in Walt Disney World and can be quite awkward to get to. Nevertheless, the park is delightfully pretty. It has been designed to resemble a back woods swimming hole with rope swings and water flumes.

The centerpiece is a naturalistic cove, crossed by wooden bridges and fed by chutes of water gushing like waterfalls from pine trees and rocks.

FORT WILDERNESS RESORT AND CAMP-GROUND
(*(407) 824-3784.*

FIRST AND FOREMOST, the forest is a campground with nearly 800 sites with full hookups, but there are also 120 log cabins with all the amenities (even maid service). Horseback riding trails, bike trails, swimming and fishing, and forest walks, are some of the activities available. To get there, park your car at the entrance and take a bus, or arrive by boat from the Magic Kingdom (see p143).

WALT DISNEY WORLD AFLOAT

Cruise liners *Disney Magic* and *Disney Wonder*, which set sail in 1998, are 25 percent bigger than the average ocean liner. As well as the usual facilities each ship has almost an entire deck dedicated to children. The ships sail from Port Canaveral in Florida to Nassau in the Bahamas, and from there to Disney's private island, Castaway Cay. Package deals usually comprise some time at Walt Disney World and time at sea. For more details call (407) 566-7000.

ROMANCE DISNEY STYLE

Already the most popular honeymoon destination in the United States, Walt Disney World Resort is a wedding venue. Should you decide on a Disney wedding, you and your spouse-to-be could arrive at the wedding pavilion in Cinderella's glass coach to be greeted by the Mad Hatter; after the ceremony, you could be whisked away in a limousine chauffeured by Mickey Mouse, to prepare for your honeymoon at one of the nearby Disney resorts. If this doesn't appeal, more traditional ceremonies are also available. Special co-ordinators can arrange everything from gown design to bachelor parties. Call (407) 828-3400 for wedding information, and (407) 827-7200 for honeymoon packages.

Winter Summerland

Located next to Blizzard Beach, these two miniature golf courses have different themes: a snow-covered Florida beach, and a tropical Christmas fantasy.

WDW RESORTS

NON-RESIDENTS can dine and shop in any of the Disney resorts. The ones located on the monorail can be reached easily from the Magic Kingdom and Epcot and provide the option of taking a break from the theme parks during the day; they are also a popular place to eat and have fun in the evening.

Most of the resorts follow a theme and are sights in their own right. At the **Polynesian Resort** coconut palms and tropical plants help re-create a South Pacific island, while the Victorian-styled **Grand Floridian Resort & Spa** provides a convincing imitation of a grand 19th-century railroad hotel. These two resorts, both near the Magic Kingdom, are more popular than most.

Opened in 1996, **Disney's BoardWalk Inn** is modeled after a 1920s-style waterfront village, it features a board-walk and a green, with shops, restaurants, old-fashioned dance halls, and nightclubs – as well as a hotel and villas (*see pp303–304*).

The **Disney Institute** (*see p304*) promotes the idea that you can combine a vacation with self-improvement. Its hotel-with-campus is aimed at adults and families with older children, and the courses cover 60 activities from film production to rock climbing. Any resident of WDW Resort is welcome to sample a day at the Institute, which costs about $50. Individual resorts are described in the listings on pages 303–304, their restaurants on pages 322–23.

SPORTS

AT FORT WILDERNESS, Disney Village Marketplace and at all the lakeside resorts, you can rent jet skis and all kinds of boats. You can water ski on the Seven Seas Lagoon and Bay Lake, and fishing trips are also available. Every resort has sports and fitness facilities, but these are for residents only.

Known also as the "Magic Linkdom," WDW Resort has six golf courses, five of which are championship level; reservations are recommended.

Car racing fans can see professional races at the Walt Disney World Speedway, just south of the Magic Kingdom.

Golf Reservations
((407) 824 2270.

Disney's Wide World of Sports
((407) 363-6600.
This massive sports complex covers over 200 acres (80 ha). There are facilities for over 30 sports ranging from basket-ball and football to sumo wrestling. Its football fields and baseball stadium are used for professional competitions. There is also a track-and-field complex, a golf driving range, and 12 clay tennis courts.

AFTER DARK

AFTER THE THEME PARKS close, consider not only relaxing at a resort but checking out Disney's prime after-dark entertainment area or taking in a dinner show.

Downtown Disney
((407) 828-3058.
Downtown Disney has three distinct areas: Pleasure Island, Disney Village Marketplace, and Disney's West Side.

Every visitor should experience the sheer size and slick razzle-dazzle of **Pleasure Island**. The wide range of clubs offer music to suit all tastes from a 1970s disco to a club with a revolving dance floor. An improvised comedy club, the Comedy Warehouse is hugely popular, and at the eccentric Adventurers Club the offbeat para-phernalia on the walls sometimes comes to life. "A full-blown New Year's Eve cele-bration every night" takes the form of fireworks and a rousing song and dance performance outdoors. Allow

West End Stage show, Pleasure Island

a whole evening to do Pleasure Island justice; a single admission ticket allows entry to all of the clubs there. The **Disney Village Marketplace** is a very pretty outdoor mall. You needn't spend valuable Disney time during the day here, but it is a pleasant place to browse around in the evening. There are over a dozen shops, including The World of Disney, which is the largest emporium selling Disney merchandise in Walt Disney World Resort (and that's saying something).

The most recent addition to Downtown Disney is **Disney's West Side**. The attractions here include the House of Blues, serving up live blues and jazz, and Bongo's Cuban Café, a restaurant and club created by Gloria Estefan. There is also a 24-screen theater and a circus, where the famous Cirque du Soleil perform their shows.

Dinner Shows
C *(407) 939-3463.*
These shows shouldn't tempt you to leave the theme parks

early, but they are still good fun. You will probably need to book about three months in advance to secure seats.

Electrical Water Pageant
Every night a set of illuminated sea creatures appears briefly on a flotilla of barges in front of the hotels around the Seven Seas Lagoon and in Bay Lake, in a little-publicized but charming spectacle. The pageant usually begins outside the Polynesian Resort at 9pm and ends at the Contemporary Resort about an hour later.

ESSENTIAL INFORMATION

TYPES OF PASSES

YOU CAN BUY one- day, one-park tickets, but if you're staying for more than three days consider the following:
Park Hopper Pass: entitles one-day admission to each theme park on any four or five days.
All-in-One Hopper Pass: offers unlimited access to theme parks, water parks, and Pleasure Island on any five, six, or seven days.
Length of Stay Pass: exclusively for WDW Resort hotel guests; unlimited admission to theme parks, Pleasure Island, water parks, and Sports complex. Prices are determined by the length of your stay.
Annual Pass and Premium Annual Pass: valid for 365 days from first day of use. Child ticket pricing applies to ages 3 through 9.

BUSIEST DAYS

EACH OF THE theme parks is busy on certain days. The busiest days are as follows:
Magic Kingdom: Monday, Thursday and Saturday.
Epcot: Tuesday, Friday and Saturday.
Disney-MGM Studios: Wednesday and Sunday.

OPENING HOURS

WHEN THE theme parks are busiest, opening hours are the longest, typically

9am to 10/11pm or midnight. In less busy periods, hours are usually 9am to 6/7/8pm. Call to check. The parks open at least 30 minutes early for pass holders and guests at any of the WDW hotels and resorts.

THE IDEAL SCHEDULE

TO AVOID the worst of the crowds and the heat:
• Arrive as early as possible and visit the most popular attractions first.
• Take a break in the early afternoon, when it's hottest and the parks are busiest.
• Return to the parks in the cool of the evening to see parades and fireworks.

COPING WITH LINES

LINES TEND TO BE shortest at the beginning and end of the day, and during parade and meal times.
• Lines for the rides move slowly, but the wait for a show is rarely longer than the show itself.
• The "FastPass" allows visitors to reserve time at 19 of the most popular attractions rather than waiting in line.

WDW RESORT DINING

YOU SHOULD MAKE reservations in advance for any full-service restaurant in Walt Disney World Resort, especially in the theme parks and above all in Epcot. Whether

or not you are staying at one of the resorts, reservations can be made 60 days in advance. Some tables are held back for same-day reservations, so make your reservation as early in the morning as possible. For restaurants, see pages 322–3.

WDW RESORT WITH YOUNG CHILDREN

IF YOU'VE COME with pre-school-age kids:
• Focus mainly on the Magic Kingdom.
• Walt Disney World Resort can be physically and emotionally tiring so try to adapt your schedule accordingly.
• Rent a stroller, available at all the theme parks.
• In a system called "switching off," parents can enjoy a ride one at a time while the other parent stays with the child – without having to line up twice.

MEETING MICKEY

FOR MANY YOUNGSTERS, the most exciting moment at WDW Resort is meeting the Disney characters. You will spot them in all the theme parks, but you can have more relaxed encounters in a number of restaurants (usually at breakfast). Each theme park and many of the resorts also offer "character dining," though you must call ahead of time to make a reservation.

SeaWorld and Discovery Cove ❷

IN SCALE AND SOPHISTICATION, the world's most popular marine-life adventure park, opened in 1973, is a match for any of Orlando's other theme parks. While eager to promote its educational, research, and conservation programmes, the park delivers out-and-out entertainment too. SeaWorld's answer to the Disney mouse is Shamu, actually several orcas, and the Shamu Adventure show tops the bill. Some of the attractions, which allow you to touch or feed the marine life, are unsurpassed. Next to SeaWorld is Discovery Cove, a new all-inclusive park, where guests have the opportunity to swim with dolphins, rays and other fascinating sea animals.

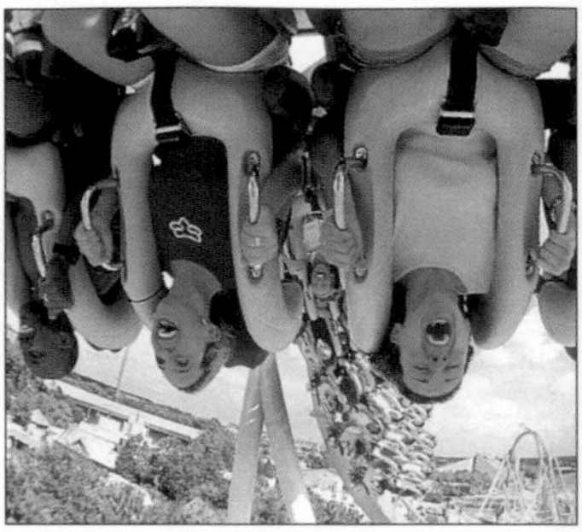

Thrillseekers hanging onto Kraken, an award-winning rollercoaster ride at SeaWorld

TACKLING THE PARK

SEAWORLD is usually less crowded than Orlando's other theme parks. Most of the presentations are walk through exhibits or sit down stadium shows. The stadiums seat so many that finding a good spot is seldom a problem and you will normally get a good seat by arriving 15 minutes before the show starts. Bear in mind that if you sit near the front you may get wet. SeaWorld's more gentle pace means that visiting after 3pm affords a cooler and less crowded experience. It is also worth noting that the shows are timed so that it's all but impossible to leave one show just in time for another. This is done to reduce crowding but it is possible to get a seat in the Clyde and Seamore (Sea Lion and Otter) show by leaving from the Shamu stadium four minutes early (while the performers are taking their bows.) At peak times, find a seat early for the Sea Lion and Otter show, performed in a small stadium, and see Wild Arctic, Terrors of the Deep, Journey to Atlantis and Kraken either early or during the Shamu or water-skiing shows.

Young children enjoy meeting the actors in furry suits who play the parts of Shamu and Crew – a killer whale accompanied by a penguin, pelican, dolphin, and an otter. You can normally find them near SeaWorld's exit at around closing time.

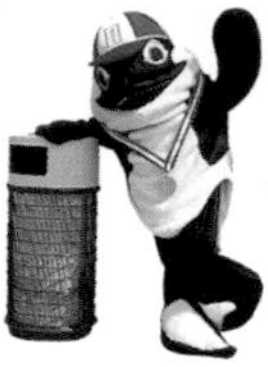

Shamu, the park's official mascot

For an overview of the park and a great view, take the six-minute ride up the 400-ft (122-m) Sky Tower.

If you have any problems or queries, go to Guest Relations, situated near the exit gate.

TOP 10 ATTRACTIONS

1. KRAKEN
2. TERRORS OF THE DEEP
3. JOURNEY TO ATLANTIS
4. WILD ARCTIC
5. PENGUIN ENCOUNTER
6. SHAMU ADVENTURE
7. CLYDE AND SEAMORE TAKE PIRATE ISLAND
8. The ATLANTIS WATER SKI SHOW
9. SHAMU'S HAPPY HARBOUR
10. FIREWORKS

ATTRACTIONS

THREE METICULOUSLY landscaped outdoor habitats, including two that allow you to feed and pet the marine life, are incorporated in **Key West at SeaWorld**. Dolphin

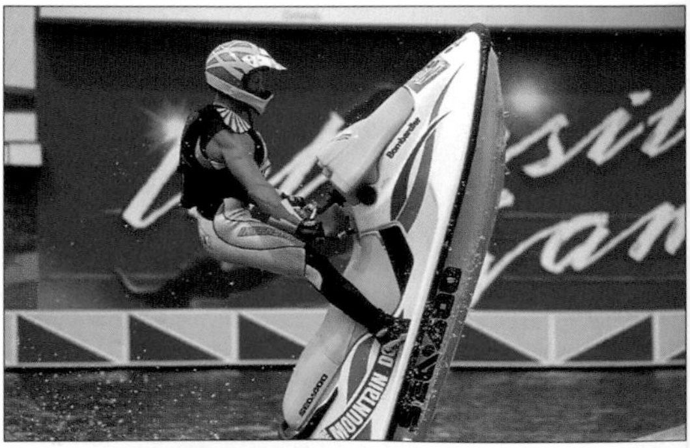

World-class waterskier performing at one of SeaWorld's water-ski shows

Cove, a wave pool in the style of a Caribbean beach, offers underwater viewing of Bottlenose dolphins and the chance to pat and even feed them. You can also touch magnificent stingrays, of which there are around 200 in Stingray Lagoon; stroking them is more enjoyable than it sounds. Turtle Point is home to rescued loggerhead, hawksbill, and green sea turtles, which are too injured to survive on their own in the wild.

Pacific Point Preserve recreates the rugged north

FIREWORKS

An absolutely stunning finale to a day in SeaWorld is the laser fireworks show. The show uses water curtain holographic projection techniques similar to IllumiNations at Epcot. SeaWorld's fireworks show, however, scores particularly highly because of its provision of a huge, lakeside stadium in which you can sit and watch the fireworks in relative comfort. The best views of this spectacular event are to be had from the 6th or 7th rows back in the centre.

Pacific coast in the form of a large, rocky pool. Here, you can watch harbor seals, South American fur seals, and Californian sea lions (the ones making the noise) basking on the rocks and gliding elegantly through the water.

Most of the other wildlife at SeaWorld is viewed through glass. **Manatees: The Last Generation?** offers a splendid underwater view of these ungainly, doleful and irresistibly appealing herbivores (see p236). The exhibit is strongly educational and includes a film show.

In the altogether more upbeat **Penguin Encounter**, a moving walkway takes you past a frozen landscape where a large colony of penguins demonstrate their comical waddling and elegant swimming. The gawky puffins are also a delight to watch.

Billed as the world's largest collection of dangerous sea creatures, **Terrors of the Deep** is understandably pop-

Amazing dolphins are put through their paces

ular. Moray eels, barracuda, and pufferfish are the hors d'oeuvre before a main course of sharks, whose toothy grins are just a short distance away from your head as you walk through a plastic tunnel inside their aquarium.

Shamu: Close Up!, next to Shamu Stadium, is a research and breeding facility where you can study killer whales behaving more or less as they would in the wild; ten of them have actually been born in the park so far. **Wild Arctic** is a high-tech ride simulating a helicopter flight through blizzards and avalanches.

TOP TIPS

• *Sea World allows guests to feed many of the animals, but restrict both the type and amount of food, which has to be purchased from them. If this is something you would like to do, check with guest services as soon as you enter the park for feeding times and food availability.*

• *Build your schedule around the four main presentations: Atlantis Water Ski, Shamu Killer Whale, Sea Lion and Otter, and Whale and Dolphin shows.*

• *Bring a waterproof plastic bag for your camera as - especially during the Shamu and Dolphin shows - people on the first twelve rows can get splashed by corrosive salt water.*

• *Journey to Atlantis is guaranteed to get you wet, so reserve this for the hottest part of the day.*

SEAWORLD'S SERIOUS SIDE

The buzzwords at the nonprofit SeaWorld Hubbs Research Institute are Research, Rescue, and Rehabilitation – the "three Rs." Florida's SeaWorld has helped thousands of whales, dolphins, turtles, and manatees in difficulty. The animals are nursed and, if necessary, operated on in the park's rehabilitation center. Those that recover sufficiently are released back into the wild. SeaWorld runs several popular tours, which offer a glimpse of this work. The Sharks! tour, for example, takes you behind the scenes at Terrors of the Deep. Inquire at Guest Relations when you enter the park.

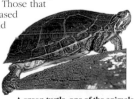

A green turtle, one of the animals rehabilitated at SeaWorld

VISITORS' CHECKLIST

Road map E2. Orange Co. 7007 SeaWorld Drive, intersection of I-4 and Bee Line Expressway.
🏢 (407) 351-3600. 🚌 8, 42 from Orlando. ⏰ minimum hours 9am–7pm daily; until 11pm in summer. 🎦 ♿ 🅿️ 🚻
🌐 www.SeaWorld.com

Dolphin Cove, where everyone can touch and feed the dolphins

You arrive at Base Station Wild Arctic, created around an old expedition ship, and encounter the animals that live there: polar bears, walruses, harbor seals, and beluga whales. Sea-World's new **Journey to Atlantis**, a water coaster with a mythological twist, and **Kraken**, a winner of the annual Orlando roller-coaster competition, are hot tickets.

Discovery Cove, adjacent to SeaWorld and separately ticketed, is a reservations-only park (see p167) and worth a one-day visit of its own.

Shows and Tours

THE EXCITEMENT of seeing a killer whale erupt out of the water carrying one of the Sea World trainers on its nose is hard to overstate. In **Shamu Adventure** stunts such as this are supplemented by a giant video screen, which provides close-ups of the action and footage of the beasts in the wild. The show also features the killer whales performing an amazing "underwater ballet." There are five Shamus, which take turns to perform, as well as a Baby Shamu.

Key West Dolphin Fest is remarkable due to the speed and agility of its performing Bottlenose dolphins and false killer whales. During the show, the mammals play with their trainers as well as interacting with members of the audience. The highlight of the show, however, is the dolphins' synchronized leaps over a rope.

The **Clyde and Seamore Take Pirate Island** show, held in the Sea Lion and Otter Stadium, features two sea lions (Clyde and Seamore), otters, and walrus in a swashbuckling adventure of lost loot, pirate ships, and hilarity on the high seas.

The Atlantis Water Ski Show competes with the waterski extravaganza at Cypress Gardens (see p179). The show incorporates speed boats, jet skis, and very impressive waterskiing stunts, including skiing in pyramid formation. The highlight of the show is a mach-speed competition with super aquabatics, gymnastics, and high-energy stunts.

Cirque de la Mer is a nontraditional circus, blending dramatic special effects, music, and acrobatics. **Pets on Stage** features talented cats, birds, dogs, and pigs, all of which have been rescued from animal shelters.

Shamu Rocks America, held at Shamu Stadium, features the SeaWorld trainers and killer whales in a night-time rock 'n' roll show, complete with drenching salt-water waves and dazzling theatrical effects. Other exhibits include **Shamu's Happy Harbor**, a 3-acre play area for smaller kids; **Dolphin Nursery** for new dolphin moms and their calves; and **Caribbean Tidepool**, which encourages close examination of tropical fish, starfish, sea anemones, and other under-water denizens.

The **Adventure Express Tour** offers exclusive guided park tours, reserved seats, feeding opportunities, and back-door access to rides.

Sea lions basking on the rocks at Pacific Point Preserve

Eating, Drinking, and Shopping

Bimini Bay Café, by the lake, is the park's only full-service restaurant and offers steaks, grilled fish, and seafood dishes. The Smokehouse Chicken & Ribs and Waterfront Sandwich Grill, for fast food, are also located at the lakeside. The best place for sandwiches is the Deli in the Anheuser-Busch Hospitality Center; snack bars and kiosks are located throughout the park. For entertainment while you eat, try the Aloha Polynesian Luau Dinner and Show, with traditional Hawaiian music, dancing, and food. Reservations are a must. Souvenirs are mainly soft toys and Shamu memorabilia: Shamu's Emporium has the largest selection; Coconut Traders has items made in Key West and samples of Florida food.

Exploring Discovery Cove

Just across the road from its big sister, Discovery Cove is a quiet revolution in terms of Florida's Theme parks. With a capacity of only 800 guests a day (the car park is limited to only 500 cars) and an entry price that makes all but lottery winners blink, the park offers some exceptional and unforgettable experiences, the most vaunted of which is a 60 minute opportunity to swim with Atlantic Bottlenose dolphins. Although expensive, forgoing the Dolphin experience can reduce the cost of a visit by half. However, Discovery Cove represents many people's lifelong dreams and is extremely popular. It is advisable, therefore, to book tickets well in advance.

Swimming with dolphins, the highlight of a visit to Discovery Cove

TACKLING THE PARK

Discovery Cove abounds with lush vegetation, thatched beach huts, and waterfalls. Intimate and beautifully constructed, you may be forgiven for thinking that the park is like your own private island. The level of service here also reflects that of any good hotel.

The package prices ($199 per person with no child reductions) include the Dolphin experience (children below 6 are not allowed to participate), valet parking, all equipment, a free snorkel, one main meal and seven days unlimited admission to Sea World. Reservations are required and entry to the park is through a 'hotel' reception where you are greeted by a personal guide, given a photo ID card and taken on a familiarisation tour. There are free lockers and towels and an almost concierge-like feel to the service.

ATTRACTIONS

Inside the park there are five main areas: Coral Reef, the Aviary, Ray Lagoon, the Tropical River and Dolphin Lagoon. Coral Reef abounds with grottos and a ship wreck, as well as affording the opportunity to swim alongside threateningly large sharks separated from you by a substantial transparent pliexi-glass wall. In the park's encircling 'river', guests enter an aviary and can feed the birds with food provided by the staff whilst in Ray Lagoon guests can snorkel quietly over large rays, which can grow up to 5 ft (1.5 m) long. At the Dolphin Lagoon, forty minutes orientation is followed by 30 minutes wading and swimming with these magnificent and highly intelligent mammals. Although cameras are not allowed here it is worth considering splitting your party for the Dolphin experience as that will enable you to take photos of each other from the shore. There are waterfalls, bathing pools and little niches throughout the park connected by beaches. There is only one restaurant, which is self service, but the food standard is high. Cameras are welcome but guests are asked to remove jewellery and other impedimenta so as to avoid distracting the sea life. Guests with disabilities are welcome and specially-made outdoor wheelchairs with oversized tires for easy manoeuvring on the beach are also offered.

Aerial view of Discovery Cove

Universal Studios Orlando ❸

ONCE A SINGLE MOVIE park, competing with the other area attractions, Universal Studios now boasts two major theme parks, a village and entertainment complex and the first of its many planned hotels. Together, Universal Studios Park, Islands of Adventure and Universal City Walk present a formidable reason to spend time away from Disney. Situated off exits 29 and 30B from I4, Universal's car parking takes the multi-storey approach, bringing guests through Universal City Walk on a series of moving walk ways to a fork where they choose between the two parks.

Universal Globe marking the entrance to Universal Studios Park

TACKLING THE PARKS

THE BUSIEST times of the year at Universal Studios Orlando are the same as at Walt Disney World (see p138); weekends are normally quieter than weekdays.

When the parks are open until late, two full days are just about long enough to see everything at the two parks. When the parks close early – the only disadvantage of visiting in off season – you really need three or four days. If you are staying in the area for over ten days, consider an annual pass: just visit Guest Services, the place for all queries, as you leave. At off peak times, you can often redeem your day pass at the end of the day for a pass entitling you to a second day free.

Lines at Universal can, if anything, be longer and slower moving than at Walt Disney World: up to two hours for the best rides. At peak times, combat the lines by arriving early (the gates open an hour before the official opening time) and by doing as many of the popular rides (see p169) as possible. You won't be able to do them all early, so ride the others just before the park closes.

You are unlikely to have to wait in line very long for shows but you should arrive 15 minutes early in tourist season to make sure of getting a seat. Those with no displayed schedule run continuously and you will rarely have to wait longer than the show's duration. Note that lines for rides close to big shows grow considerably when the performances end.

Most rides are likely to be too intense for young children and some have minimum height restrictions; the exception to this is ET Adventure. The attractions designed to appeal to youngsters are A Day in the Park with Barney, Fievel's Playland, The FUNtastic World of Hanna-Barbera, the Nickelodeon Studios, and Seuss and Jurassic Park Islands in Islands of Adventure.

On a very busy day, you might consider indulging in the four-hour VIP Tour. This provides priority admission to six attractions, as well as a walk around the back lot and a few sound stages.

Board showing the shooting schedule

UNIVERSAL STUDIOS PARK

THE ENTRANCE TO Universal Studios Park is known as **Front Lot** because it is made to look like the front lot of a working Hollywood film studio from the 1940s. The shooting schedule notice board near the turnstiles, with details of shows being filmed, is real enough, however. Immediately inside the park, the palm-lined Plaza of the Stars has

The imposing entrance archway to Universal Studios

Face to face with King Kong on Universal's Kongfrontation ride

several shops *(see p171)*, but do not linger here on arrival: instead you should head off immediately to the main attractions before the lines reach their peak.

Except for the Boneyard, a repository of interesting old movie props such as a pram from *The Flintstones* and fake plastic topiary from *Edward Scissorhands*, **Production Central** is the least aesthetic section of the park. Maps show the studios' main sound stages here, but these are actually off limits to those not on a VIP Tour. Production Central's one ride, **The FUNtastic World of Hanna-Barbera**, is great fun. Messrs Hanna and Barbera are the creators of such world-famous cartoon characters as the Flintstones, Yogi Bear, and Scooby Doo. During the ride, you seem to chase Dick Dastardly and the others right into the cartoons as your seat moves violently in time with the action on the screen.

The Slime Geyser erupting outside Nickelodeon Studios

VISITORS' CHECKLIST

Road map E2. Orange Co.
1000 Universal Studios Plaza,
exits 29 or 30B on I-4.
📱 *(407) 363-8000.* 🚌 21, 37,
40 from Orlando. ⏰ minimum
opening hours 9am–6pm daily;
extended evening opening in
summer and on public hols.

Alfred Hitchcock: The Art of Making Movies begins with a collage of the director's 53 movies, including 3-D clips of *Dial M for Murder* and *The Birds*. It then reveals various cinematic tricks, such as how the famous shower scene from *Psycho* was created by using selective camera angles.

In **Hercules and Xena, Wizards of the Screen** you can see how the popular shows *Xena: Warrior Princess* and *Hercules* are made. The highlight is the use of live action and special effects to give you the chance to fight gods and other mythical creatures as if in a real episode.

The **Nickelodeon Studios Tour** visits the production center of Nickelodeon, an extremely popular American TV network exclusively for young people. Also aimed at children, the tour lets you have a peek at a couple of sound studios (but be warned that there is no assurance that anything will be happening), and finishes with several messy party games in the Game Lab. Children will definately enjoy the Slime Geyser outside, which erupts in a shower of green slime every ten minutes or so.

NEW YORK

THIS BACK-LOT AREA has more than 60 facades, some of which replicate real buildings, others which reproduce those that have appeared only on screen. There are cut-outs of the Guggenheim Museum and New York Public Library, cleverly creating an illusion of depth and distance. Macy's, the famous department store, is there, as is Louie's Italian Restaurant, where a shootout took place in the original *Godfather* movie. The storefronts, warehouses, and even the cobblestones have been painted to appear old in a process called "distressing."

Here also is New York's top attraction, **Kongfrontation**. On this ride, you enter a subway station to take an aerial tramway across the East River. Below are the streets of 1970s Manhattan, pulverized by King Kong. Soon the largest ever computer-animated figure – with an arm span of over 50 ft (15 m) – is shaking the tramway, swatting helicopters, and breathing his banana breath all over you. In truth, most passengers find the ride more fun than scary.

Twister pits visitors against Mother Nature at her most ferocious inside a huge compound containing a simulated tornado: you will experience the terrifying power of the elements as you stand within 20 ft (6 m) of the five story-high funnel of winds.

Visitors braving the force of a simulated tornado in Twister

HOLLYWOOD

HOLLYWOOD BOULEVARD and Rodeo Drive are the most attractive streets in Universal Studios. While ignoring actual geography, these sets pay tribute to Hollywood's golden age from the 1920s to the 1950s – in the famous Ciro's and Mocambo nightclubs, the luxurious Beverly Wilshire Hotel, the top beauty salon Max Factor, and the movie palace, Pantages Theater.

The Brown Derby was a restaurant shaped like a hat where the film glitterati once congregated; Universal's own version is a fun hat shop. Schwab's Pharmacy, where hopefuls hung out sipping sodas and waiting to be discovered, is brought back to life as an old-fashioned ice-cream parlor. Notice, too, the Hollywood Walk of Fame, with the names of stars embedded in the sidewalk, just as in the real Hollywood Boulevard.

The Gory, Gruesome & Grotesque
Horror Make-Up Show

The top attraction in Hollywood is **Terminator 2: 3-D**. This ride uses the latest in 3-D film technology and robotics, together with explosive live stunts, to catapult the audience into the action alongside the star of the *Terminator* films, Arnold Schwarzenegger. A typical sequence, combining film and live action, has a Harley-Davidson "Fat Boy" dramatically bursting off the screen and on to the stage.

The Gory, Gruesome & Grotesque Horror Make-Up Show is the funniest of the semieducational attractions at Universal Studios. Scenes from films such as *The Exorcist*, *The Fly*, and *An American Werewolf in London* are

Hollywood Boulevard, a fine example of the park's superbly created sets

shown, and the bloodied, automated masks used in these films demonstrate how the special effects are realized.

EXPO CENTER

THE INSPIRATION behind Expo Center's architecture is the Los Angeles 1984 Olympics Games and Expo '86 in Vancouver. The focus here is on the rides and shows.

Back to the Future The Ride is a fantastic and popular attraction and the second most intense in Orlando (*Spiderman* in the Islands of Adventure has now inherited that crown). No knowledge of the *Back to the Future* films is needed to enjoy this journey in a time-traveling sports car. The car's movements are synchronized to the action on a mammoth wraparound screen, making it seem as though you really are plunging over a flow of molten lava, skimming ice fields, and flying right into the

mouth of a dinosaur. Adjacent to this ride is the park's newest attraction, **Men In Black**, an incredibly addictive ride in which you join Will Smith in a four-person simulator battling aliens using laser weapons and smoke bombs. Each person has their own cannon, and the scores reflect the team's ability to destroy aliens on a massive scale. In contrast, everyone should ride the enchanting, if rather tame, **ET Adventure** based on Steven Spielberg's 1982 movie. You are off to ET's home planet on a flying bicycle, soaring over a twinkling cityscape before arriving at a world inhabited by ET look-alikes.

In the **Animal Actors Stage**, animal look-alikes take the parts of canine superstars such as Lassie and Beethoven and demonstrate how they are trained for film work. Among other creatures, a skunk, a cat, a horse, a chimp, and birds also perform tricks.

Back to the Future The Ride – one of Universal's most thrilling rides

A Day in the Park with Barney appeals only to young children. A musical show set in a magical park, it features a lovable Tyrannosaurus Rex called Barney – hero of *Barney & Friends*, a top pre-school age TV show.

Fievel's Playland is inspired by the popular animated films *An American Tail* and *An American Tail: Fievel Goes West*. Fievel is a mouse, and the playground's props, such as a cowboy hat, boots, glasses and a tea cup, are oversized – just as they would seem to the movie's star rodent.

Universal's Terminator 2: 3-D, a state-of-the-art attraction

SAN FRANCISCO/AMITY

MOST OF THIS area is based on San Francisco, notably the city's Fisherman's Wharf district. Chez Alcatraz, for instance, is a snack bar closely modeled on the ticket booths for tours to Alcatraz island.

San Francisco's big draw is **Earthquake – The Big One**, a ride with an educational angle. First, the audience is shown how earthquakes can be simulated using detailed models, and how actors can be superimposed onto dramatic scenes. Then you find yourself riding a subway train in the movie *Earthquake*. A tremor measuring 8.3 on the Richter scale starts, a tidal wave descends, an oil tanker erupts and trains collide. When it's all over, you can

Beetlejuice show's sign

watch as the entire set puts itself back together again.

Amity, the other half of this corner of the park, is named after the fictional village in New England that was setting for *Jaws*. **The Jaws** ride starts off as a serene cruise around Amity Harbor, but soon the deadly dorsal fin appears, and then the giant great white shark is lunging at your boat, tearing through the water at terrifying speed. Of more limited appeal is **Beetlejuice's Graveyard Revue**. Derived from the 1988 film *Beetlejuice*, this is a noisy song and dance show. Stunts are performed in **The Wild, Wild, Wild West Stunt Show** which is a largely slapstick affair involving lots of fake punches and plenty of

high dives. During the finale the whole set blows up but in general, the show does not really live up to its title.

EATING, DRINKING AND SHOPPING

The food in Universal Studios is generally good. The Hard Rock Café is the largest in the world but there are plenty of other options. Advance reservations are advisable for Lombard's Landing, specializing in fish dishes, and the Studio Stars Restaurant which serves Californian and Italian cuisine and has a good-value buffet. Mel's Drive-In is the place to go for fast food and shakes; the wonderful 1950s diner is straight out of the 1973 movie *American Graffiti*.

Most of the shops stay open after official closing times, and you can buy a full range of themed souvenirs from them. In the Front Lot you will find Universal Studios Store, with everything from fake Oscars to oven mitts with the Universal logo, and On Location, where a signed photo of your favourite movie star costs hundreds of dollars. Most of the attractions have their own store: in Hitchcock's 3-D Theater you can buy Bates Motel soap.

MEETING THE STARS

Actors in wonderful costumes wander the streets playing the likes of Ghostbusters, Jake and Elwood from *The Blues Brothers*, Frankenstein, the Flintstones, and legends of the silver screen such as Marilyn Monroe and the Marx Brothers; they tend to congregate in the Front Lot.

Daily during the high season, and twice a week in off season, you can eat with the stars at a Character Breakfast in the park an hour prior to the scheduled opening time. Reservations are required: call (407) 354-6339 to reserve.

Actress playing screen star Marilyn Monroe

Exploring The Islands of Adventure

Islands of Adventure logo

One of the world's most techno-logically advanced theme parks, Islands of Adventure demands a day's visit of its own. The themed islands include Jurassic Park, with an educational, interactive Discovery Center, The Lost Continent, with the revolutionary Duelling Dragons coasters, and Marvel Super Hero Island, featuring Spiderman, the Incredible Hulk, Captain America, and Dr. Doom. Seuss Landing Island caters for young visitors, its Cat in the Hat ride serving as an introduction to the Seuss characters, while Popeye, Bluto, and Olive Oyl are the comic strip stars of Toon Lagoon Island.

The river ride in Jurassic Park River Adventure

TACKLING THE PARK

THERE IS NO transport system within the park other than small boats which criss-cross the lake. A day will suffice to experience all the attractions, provided that you arrive at opening time. Several hotels in the area have early entry privileges on some days which allow guests onto a couple of the islands an hour before the official opening time. As with any theme park, a clearly organised schedule is essential if you are to make the most out of your visit.

THE ISLANDS

THE ENTRANCE to the park is marked by the Pharos Lighthouse which sounds a bell every few minutes. The first island you encounter moving clockwise is the

Marvel Super Hero Island where the theme draws from the Marvel Comics' Super Hero stable of characters. The Incredible Hulk Coaster, probably the best coaster in Florida, is a green leviathan that accelerates you to over 40mph in two seconds before inverting you at 100 ft (30 m) above the ground as a prelude to diving into several watery looking holes in the ground.

Storm Force is just a faster and more intense version of Disney's Mad Hatter's Tea Party ride, which incredibly fast-spinning and might induce motion sickness. Dr Doom's Fearfall, although somewhat daunting to watch, is actually a remarkably pleasant ride in which you are strapped into seats surrounding a pillar and then catapulted into the air. Next to Dr Doom is The Amazing Adventures of Spiderman, a complex ride which achieves a stunning integration of 3D film technology together with motion simulation as well live special effects.

Toon Lagoon Island, where cartoons transmute into reality, hosts two wet rides and scheduled performances of the riotous Pandemonium Cartoon Circus. Opposite is Popeye and Bluto's Bilge-Rat Barges, a white-water raft ride that includes an encounter with a giant octopus. Me Ship the Olive, a play area for young children overlooks the raft ride and provides water canons to soak riders on the rafts below. Dudley Do-Right's Ripsaw Falls, the adjacent flume ride, is loosely based on the Rocky and Bullwinkle cartoons. It combines a pleasant cruise with an excellent final drop in which you appear to submerge.

Jurassic Park Island, based on the films of the same name, boasts exotic vegetation and offers some shade. The Jurassic Park River Adventure, is an exquisitely crafted cruise through the Jurassic Park compound where you encounter Hadrosaurs, Stegosaurs and others before 'accidentally' being diverted as a consequence of a 'raptor' breakout. The ride ends with an 85-ft (25-m) drop into a lagoon which doesn't get you too wet. Camp Jurassic, a playground area for pre-teenage children, is situated near the Pteranodon Flyers. This ride flies pairs of riders over Jurassic Park Island on an 80 second journey. The Triceratops Encounter offers an opportunity to visit the Jurassic Park 'research' center where youngsters can tickle a 24-ft (7-m) Triceratops which responds when patted. The Discovery Center is an interactive natural history exhibit where guests can view the results of mixing DNA from various species, including themselves.

The Lost Continent Island is an island of myth, legend and the supernatural. The Flying Unicorn is a very pleasant and non threatening introduction to roller coasting for young children. However, for the coaster addicts, Duelling Dragons is the ride of choice. Two coasters – Fire and Ice – battle it out to see who will arrive back first. The entrance is the longest and darkest set of tunnels imaginable, but a short cut allows exiting riders to sample the other Dragon without having to wait in line again.

Stage shows include The Eight Voyages of Sinbad, where stunts, flames and explosions will amuse fans of television's Xena: Warrior Princess and Hercules. Poseidon's Fury: Escape from the Lost City, is a show where the battle between Poseidon

and Zeus is superbly executed through a myriad of extraordinary special effects.

Seuss Landing Island is based on the Seuss children's books, and appeals mainly to

Incredible Hulk Coaster, Super Hero Island

the youngest and those familiar with the popular Seuss books: Sylvester McMonkey McBean's Very Unusual Driving Machines provides a gentle, elevated ride around the island while If I Ran The Zoo is another youngsters playground. Caro-Suess-El is a merry-go-round with Dr Seuss characters as the horses. On the ride One Fish Two Fish Red Fish Blue Fish, you have the added excitement of trying to catch fish while avoiding water jets. For those with no experience of Seuss, The Cat in the Hat is a somewhat bewildering journey through a manic display of cat-like characters on a whirling couch.

Universal CityWalk

Universal City-Walk's logo

A 30-acre entertainment complex of restaurants, night clubs, shops and cinemas, Universal CityWalk offers the visitor the opportunity to continue their Universal experience long after the parks have closed. The gateway to all of Universal's entertainment offerings, CityWalk's design was inspired by many of popular culture's innovators, such as Bob Marley, Thelonius Monk and Motown.

visitor the opportunity of hearing live music from today's finest performers.

CityWalk boasts specialty shops and state-of-the-art cinemas and its outdoor stages and common areas are the setting for live concerts, art festivals, cooking demonstrations, celebrity personal appearances and street performances. A sparkling lagoon running through the complex provides visitors with a picturesque location to sip a cool drink in the late afternoon sun or to take a moonlight stroll.

THE COMPLEX

THE APPEAL of CityWalk is primarily to adults, and popular music and dance lovers are extremely well catered for. The complex is open 4pm–2am and while there is no entrance fee, each club makes a small cover charge. An All-Club pass can be purchased which may also include a movie.

CityWalk offers a dazzling array of restaurants that range from Emeril's (a top TV chef) to the famous Hard Rock Café. For sports fans, the Nascar Café and NBA Restaurant provide athletic offerings and the Motown café the nostalgia. Bob Marley – A Tribute to Freedom is an exact replica of this famous musician's home. The

complex is also home to several nightclubs including City Jazz and The Groove Dance Club which afford the

The Hard Rock Café and music venue, Universal City Walk

Downtown Orlando, dominated by the SunTrust Center

Orlando ❹

Road map E2. Orange Co.
🏠 *200,000.* ✈ 🚉 🚌 ℹ *75 S
Ivanhoe Blvd, (407) 425-1234.*
🌐 *www.gotoorlando.com*

UNTIL THE 1950s, Orlando was not much more than a sleepy provincial town. Its proximity to Cape Canaveral and the theme parks, however, helped change all that.

Downtown Orlando, where glass-sided high-rises mark a burgeoning business district, really beckons only at night. This is when tourists and locals flock to Church Street Station and, to a lesser degree, to the bars and restaurants on Church Street and Orange Avenue, Orlando's main street.

During the daytime, take a stroll in the park around **Lake Eola**, three blocks east of Orange Avenue. This is one

Fountain at the center of the rose garden, Harry P. Leu Gardens

of the few places where you'll get a taste of Orlando's (comparatively) early history. Overlooking the lake are a few of the wood-built homes of the town's earliest white settlers; some of these have been converted into B & Bs.

Anyone in need of a more serious antidote to the theme parks should head into the quieter residential areas just north of Downtown, where there are a number of parks and museums. If you are short of time, Winter Park should be your priority.

♣ Loch Haven Park
N Mills Avenue at Rollins St.
Orlando Museum of Art 📞 *(407) 896-4231.* 🕐 *Tue–Sun.* ⚫ *public hols.* 📷 ♿ 🌐 *www.omart.org*
Loch Haven Park, 2 miles (3 km) north of Downtown, has a trio of small museums. The most highly regarded of these is the Orlando Museum of Art, which has three collections on permanent display: pre-Columbian artifacts, with animal figurines from Nazca in Peru; African art; and American paintings of the 19th and 20th centuries. The museum also hosts major international exhibitions.

♣ Harry P. Leu Gardens
1920 N Forest Ave. 📞 *(407) 246-2620.* 🕐 *daily.* ⚫ *Dec 25.* 📷 ♿
The Harry P. Leu Gardens offer 50 acres of serenely beautiful gardens in which to stroll. Elements such as Florida's largest rose garden are

formal, while elsewhere you find mature woods of spectacular live oaks, maples, and bald cypresses, festooned with Spanish moss; in winter, seek out the mass of blooming camellias. You can also tour the early 20th-century **Leu House** and its gardens, which a local businessman, Harry P. Leu, donated to the city of Orlando in 1961, perhaps as a tax write-off.

🏛 Maitland Art Center
231 W Packwood Ave, 6 miles (9 km) N of Downtown. 📞 *(407) 539-2181.* 🕐 *daily.* ⚫ *public hols.* 📷 ♿
🌐 *www.maitartctr.org*
This art center in the leafy suburb of Maitland occupies studios and living quarters designed in the 1930s by artist André Smith as a winter retreat for fellow artists. Set around courtyards and gardens, the buildings are delightful, with abundant use made of Mayan and Aztec motifs. The studios are still used, and there are exhibitions of contemporary American arts and crafts.

Decoration inspired by the Aztecs, at the Maitland Art Center

🎵 Church Street Station
129 W Church St. 📞 *(407) 422-2434.* 🕐 *daily.* 📷 *one fee for all shows.*
Created in the 1970s from an area of dilapidated hotels and shops, this entertaining nightlife complex pulls a big crowd. Top of the bill are three live musical shows performed from about 7pm until after midnight; each one re-creates a different era with appropriate antique furnishings. A Dixieland jazz band plays in **Rosie O'Grady's Good Time Emporium**, decked out with etched glass mirrors from British pubs; can-can girls dance on the bartops and slick, waistcoated bartenders join in the songs. The triple-tiered, golden oak

Cheyenne Saloon and Opera House *(see p330)* recalls the Wild West, with barmen in Stetsons, a country and western band, and line dancing; the Victorian-style, wrought-iron palace of the **Orchid Garden Ballroom** presents live rock and roll, with music from the 1950s to the 1990s. A single fee provides admission to all the live shows.

The rest of the complex, including street entertainment by acrobats and jugglers, can be enjoyed for free. There's **Phineas Phogg's**, a good dance club with a ballooning theme (restricted to those of 21 years of age and over), and also 50 one-of-a-kind shops selling anything from hats to Gothic statuary in the **Exchange Shopping Emporium**. The Buffalo Trading Co. nearby keeps an excellent stock of western gear.

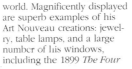

Detail from Tiffany's Four Seasons window

The best place to eat is Lili Marlene's *(see p321)*, which boasts a dining table that once belonged to Al Capone.

Winter Park ❺

Road map E2. Orange Co.
🏠 *25,000*. 🚉 🚌 🛈 *150 N New York Ave, (407) 644-8281.* **Scenic Boat Tour** 📞 *(407) 644-4056.* 📷

GREATER ORLANDO'S most refined neighborhood took off in the 1880s, when wealthy northerners began to build winter retreats here. The aroma of expensive perfume and coffee emanates from classy stores and cafés along its main street, Park Avenue, while at the country club up the road members all in white enjoy a game of croquet. At the northern end of Park Avenue, the **Charles Hosmer Morse Museum of American Art** holds probably the finest collection of works by Louis Comfort Tiffany (1848–1933) in the world. Magnificently displayed are superb examples of his Art Nouveau creations: jewelry, table lamps, and a large number of his windows, including the 1899 *The Four*

Main door of Knowles Memorial Chapel, Rollins College

Seasons. This is a staggering fusion of glass, gold leaf, lead, enamel, paint, and copper. The galleries also exhibit pieces from the same period by luminaries such as Frank Lloyd Wright.

At the southern end of Park Avenue is **Rollins College**, with a delightful arboreal campus dotted with Spanish-style buildings erected in the 1930s. Noteworthy is the Knowles Memorial Chapel, whose main entrance features a relief of a meeting between the Seminoles and the Spanish conquistadors. The college's **Cornell Fine Arts Museum** has over 6,000 works of art, including an impressive collection of Italian Renaissance paintings.

To see where the wealthy Winter Park residents live, take the narrated **Scenic Boat Tour**. Between 10am and 4pm, boats depart hourly from the east end of Morse Boulevard and chug around nearby lakes and along interconnecting canals overhung with hibiscus, bamboo, and papaya. The lakes are surrounded by magnificent live oaks, cypress trees, and huge mansions with green, sweeping lawns.

🏛 **Charles Hosmer Morse Museum of American Art**
445 Park Ave N. 📞 *(407) 645-5311.*
⭕ *Tue–Sun.* ⚫ *public hols.* 📷 ♿
🌐 www.morsemuseum.org
🏛 **Cornell Fine Arts Museum**
1000 Holt Ave. 📞 *(407) 646-2526.*
⭕ *Tue–Sun.* ⚫ *public hols.* ♿ 🌐
www.rollins.edu/cfam

Crowds enjoying the street entertainment at Church Street Station

One of the gentler rides at Wet'n Wild on International Drive

International Drive ❻

Road map E2. Orange Co.
🚉 *Orlando.* 🚌 *Orlando.* ℹ️ *Gala Center, 8723 S International Drive, (407) 363-5872.*

ONLY A STONE'S THROW from Walt Disney World, and anchored by Universal Studios and Sea World at either end, International Drive is here solely because of the theme parks. "I Drive," as everyone knows it, is a tawdry 3-mile (5-km) ribbon of restaurants, hotels, shops, and theaters. In the daytime, when everyone is at the theme parks, I Drive is deserted; after dark, however, it becomes a lively neon strip with everything open late.

I Drive's biggest and most popular attraction is **Wet'n Wild**, billed as the world's first water park when it opened in 1977. Unlike Disney's water parks *(see pp160–61)*, Wet'n Wild excels in its eight big-thrill rides such as Bomb Bay and Der Stuka – terrifyingly fast descents down near-vertical slides. Waterskiing on your knees or trying to stay on the bucking, automated Robo Surfer requires more skill. There is also the watery Kid's Playground and a few gentle rides, but Disney's water parks better serve families with young children. In the summer Wet'n Wild is open as late as 11pm, offering half-price admission.

Filled with fantastic objects, illusions and film footage of strange feats, **Ripley's Believe It or Not!** is I Drive's other quality attraction. It is one of a worldwide chain of museums that was born out of the 1933 Chicago World Fair's so-called Odditorium – the creation of a famous American broadcaster and cartoonist, Robert Ripley, who traveled the globe in search of the weird and wonderful. You can't miss Orlando's Ripley's Believe It or Not! – it is housed in a building that appears to be falling into one of Florida's infamous sink-holes *(see p20)*. **Wonder Works** offers interactive family fun with a simulated earthquake and lazer tag games. **The Mercado**, a Spanish-style outdoor shopping mall, has courtyards, fountains, 48 gift shops, several restaurants, and free entertainment in the evenings. Right next door is **Titanic–The Exhibition,** the world's first permanent Titanic attraction, with artifacts, movie memorabilia, and full-scale re-creations of the ship's rooms and grand staircase. Two blocks from the mall you'll find Orlando's excellent Official Visitor Information Center, which has coupons for many of Orlando's attractions, hotels, and restaurants; you can save money by stopping off here *(see p346).*

🏊 **Wet'n Wild**
6200 I-Drive. ✆ *(407) 351-1800.* ○ *daily.* 📷 ♿

🎪 **Ripley's Believe It or Not!**
8201 I-Drive. ✆ *(407) 363-4418.* ○ *daily.* 📷 ♿

🎭 **The Mercado**
8445 S I-Drive. ✆ *(407) 345-9337.* ○ *daily.* ● *Dec 25.* ♿

Wonder Works
8201 I-Drive. ✆ *(407) 351-8800.*

Gatorland ❼

Road map E3. Orange Co. 14501 S Orange Blossom Trail, Kissimmee. ✆ *(800) 393-5297.* 🚉 *Kissimmee.* 🚌 *Kissimmee.* ○ *daily.* 📷 ♿ 🅦 www.gatorland.com

On sale at Gatorland

THIS GIANT WORKING farm, open since the 1950s, has a license to raise alligators for their hides and meat. Gatorland's breeding pens, nurseries, and rearing ponds hold thousands of alligators, from infants that would fit into the palm of your hand to 12-ft (4-m) monsters. The alligators can be observed from a boardwalk and tower as they bask in the shallows of a cypress swamp. Gatorland's other attractions are more contrived: they include

The unmistakable sinking home of Ripley's Believe It or Not!

The gaping jaws of an alligator mark the entrance to Gatorland

a few depressed animals in cages, an alligator wrestling show, and a Gator Jumparoo, in which the animals leap out of the water to grab chunks of chicken; there are also handling demonstrations of Florida's poisonous snakes.

You can try 'gator nuggets or ribs at the restaurant or buy a can of gator chowder.

One of the typically offbeat shops in Kissimmee's Old Town

Kissimmee ⑧

Road map E3. Osceola Co.
🏛 41,000. 🚍 🚌 ℹ 1925 E Irlo Bronson Memorial Hwy, (407) 847-5000. **Old Town** 5770 W Irlo Bronson Mem. Hwy. 📞 (407) 396 4888.

IN THE EARLY 1900s, cows freely roamed the streets of this cattle boom town. Now, the only livestock you are likely to see are those that appear in the twice-yearly rodeo at Kissimmee's Silver Spurs Arena (see p31), or at the more down-to-earth rodeos held every Friday night at the **Kissimmee Arena**. Kissimmee means "Heaven's Place" in the language of the Calusa Indians (see pp38–9), but the reason most people visit is to make use of the glut of cheap motels close to Walt Disney World. They are strung out along the traffic-ridden US 192, amid chain restaurants and countless billboards advertising the latest attractions, shopping malls, and dinner shows. The latter are the chief appeal of Kissimmee after dark.

After a day in a theme park, however, you might prefer to visit Kissimmee's **Old Town**. This re-created pedestrian street of early 20th-century buildings has eccentric shops offering psychic readings, tattoos, Irish linen, candles, and so forth. There is also a moderately entertaining haunted house and a small fairground with antique equipment.

The **Flying Tigers Warbird Restoration Museum**, by the Kissimmee municipal airport, is also enjoyably quirky. It is visited by old timers who remember piloting the World War II aircraft that undergo meticulous repair here. You can take a guided tour of the hangar to hear about the finer points of airplane reconstruction. For a sizable fee you can take a spin in a 1934 biplane.

🛩 **Kissimmee Arena**
1010 Suhls Lane. 📞 (407) 933-0020. ◻ for shows. 🅿 ♿
🏛 **Flying Tigers Warbird Restoration Museum**
231 N. Hoagland Blvd. 📞 (407) 933-1942. ◻ daily. ● Dec 25. 🅿 ♿

DINNER SHOWS

For great family fun (if you still have the energy after the parks have closed), consider going to a dinner show (see p337). Orlando boasts around a dozen – excluding Disney's two shows (see p162) – strung along I Drive or off US 192 near Kissimmee. Tickets cost $30–35 for an adult and about $20 for children, but discounts are available with coupons from the Orlando Visitor Center. The following are the best.

Capone's Dinner Show: A 1931 Chicago speakeasy offers mobsters and Italian food. 📞 (407) 397-2378.

Arabian Nights: A gaudy equestrian extravaganza in a giant indoor arena. 📞 (407) 239-9223.

Colossal Studios Pirate's Dinner Adventure: A lavish show set around a pirates' ship, with boat races, acrobatics, and a tour of the studios beforehand. 📞 (407) 248-0590.

King Henry's Feast: Fun and games in a recreation of King Henry VIII's banquet hall. 📞 (407) 351-5151.

Medieval Times: Jousting knights get top billing at this colorful and dramatic show. 📞 (407) 396-1518.

Wild Bill's Wild West Dinner Extravaganza: Indian and can-can dancers entertain in a stockade fort. 📞 (407) 351-5151

A star of Wild Bill's Wild West Dinner Extravaganza

Lake Toho ⑨

Road map E3. Osceola Co. 3 miles
(5 km) S of Kissimmee. 🚉 *Kissimmee.*
🚌 *Kissimmee.* ⛴ *from Big Toho
Marina on Lakeshore Blvd, downtown
Kissimmee .*

AT THE headwaters of the
Florida Everglades, Lake
Tohopekaliga (or Toho, as
the locals call it) is famous for
its wide variety of exotic
wildlife. Cypress Island, in the
middle of the lake, is a
private nature preserve
for animals such as
emus and llamas.
There are several
eagles nesting on
the lake, as well as
other birds such as
ospreys, herons, and
egrets. The lake,
however, is open for
everyone: Go sport
fishing with a local
guide, take one of
the many boat trips
around the lake and the
Kissimmee River, or just
spend a quiet afternoon with
a picnic lunch.

**Terra-cotta warrior
at Splendid China**

Splendid China ⑩

Road map E3. Osceola Co. 3000
Splendid China Blvd, Kissimmee.
📞 *(407) 396-7111.* 🚉 *Kissimmee.*
🚌 *Kissimmee.* ○ *daily.* 📷 ♿

ORLANDO'S MOST cultural,
adult-oriented theme park
is wonderfully peaceful (do
not expect any crowds),
although some may find it too
sedate. Opened in 1993 at a
cost of $100 million, its 76
acres are a virtual duplication

of a similar park in Shenzhen,
China. Allow half a day for a
thorough visit.

There are no thrills or rides,
but you can walk or take a
tram to scaled-down replicas
of China's most famous landmarks, each of which is decorated with hundreds of toy
people and animals. The Great
Wall reappears half-a-mile
(1-km) long, made from 6.5
million bricks; the Leshan
Grand Buddha Statue, 236 ft
(72 m) tall in China, is still
magnificent in its 35-ft (11-m)
version. A sizeable portion of
the army of 8,000 terra-cotta
warriors discovered in China
in the 1970s is re-created
at a third of its original
size, while Beijing's
enormous Forbidden
City is reduced by a
factor of 15.

Once you tire of
the models – and 55
can indeed be a little
overwhelming – you can take
a seat in one of the theaters
for a display of traditional
Chinese skills, such as martial
arts and the imitation of bird-
songs; the Chongqing Acrobats
are the most entertaining.

Suzhou Gardens, at the
park's entrance, is a full-scale
reconstruction of the eastern
Chinese town of Suzhou as it
would have looked 700 years
ago; its latticework buildings
and pagoda were constructed
using period techniques, without nuts and bolts. There are
souvenir shops selling bonsai
trees and Chinese tea. The
Suzhou Pearl Restaurant, like
most of the others in the park,
serves Chinese food.

**Amateur pilot in simulated combat
at Fantasy of Flight**

Fantasy of Flight ⑪

Road map E3. Polk Co. 1400 Broadway
Blvd SE, Polk City. 📠 *(863) 984-3500.*
🚉 *Winter Haven.* 🚌 *Winter Haven.*
○ *daily.* ● *Thanksgiving, Dec 25.*
📷 ♿ 🅆 *www.fantasyofflight.com*

WHERE FANTASY OF FLIGHT
may have the edge over
Florida's many other aviation
attractions is that it provides
the very sensations of flying.
A series of vivid walk-through
exhibits takes you into a World
War II B-17 Flying Fortress
during a bombing mission,
and into World War I trenches
in the middle of an air raid.

For an extra fee you can
ride a World War II fighter
aircraft simulator in a dogfight
over the Pacific. In the cockpit,
you will be given a preflight
briefing and receive advice
from the control tower about
takeoff, landing, and the
presence of enemy aircraft.
A hangar full of mint antique
airplanes contains the first

Beijing's Forbidden City, reduced to more manageable dimensions at Splendid China

widely used airliner in the US, the 1929 Ford Tri-Motor, which appeared in the film *Indiana Jones and the Temple of Doom*, and the Roadair 1, a combined plane and car that flew just once, in 1959.

Cypress Gardens ⑫

Road map E3. Polk Co. 2641 South Lake Summit Drive, Winter Haven.
📞 *(863) 324-2111.* 🚌 *Winter Haven.*
🚉 *Winter Haven.* 🕐 *daily.* 📷 ♿
🌐 www.cypressgardens.com

FLORIDA'S FIRST theme park, opened in 1936, Cypress Gardens relies on the unlikely twin elements of flowers and waterskiing to attract the crowds. Set beside a massive cypress-fringed lake, 8,000 varieties of plants make the park a floral wonderland and unquestionably romantic. It is especially popular with

A water-ski pyramid, climax of the show at Cypress Gardens

the older generation. A luscious botanical garden makes up about a third of the grounds. Plants, all painstakingly labeled, range from a 1,600-year-old cypress tree to numerous epiphytes *(see p276)*, a very rare doubleheaded palm, and a gigantic banyan tree. You can either explore on foot or take the scenic Botanical Boat Cruise, which weaves along the garden's waterways. It stops for visitors to take photographs of the park's most famous view: "Southern Belles" in garish hooped dresses, usually posing beside a lilied lagoon, a tumbling waterfall, or the sugary

Neo-Classical "Love Chapel." Other sections of the park are devoted to impressive large-scale floral displays. Around two-and-a-half million chrysanthemum blooms appear in November, and the following month hordes of poinsettias burst into color.

Splendid topiaries can be seen during much of the year. For the Spring Flower Festival these include butterflies, fish, birds, and an Easter bunny. During the summer Victorian Garden Party you will see a horse and cart, a steamship, a carousel, and ladies and gentlemen in stylish attire. In the formal, plantation-style gardens, amusing topiaries of the gardeners themselves "work" amid the heady scents of rose, herb, fruit, and vegetable allotments.

Cypress Gardens calls itself the water-ski capital of the world. Its water-ski shows, which originated from revues put on during World War II for soldiers stationed in the area, take place at least three times a day. The sometimes graceful, sometimes dramatic stunts involve barefoot skiing, jumps, and somersaults off ramps. Do not miss the highlight of the show, a gravity-defying pyramid of ten or more skiers that undoubtedly justifies the hype.

If you have set aside an entire day to see everything, you will also have time for the butterfly conservatory and for a ride on the park's intriguing hydraulically lifted aerial viewing platform. If you still have the energy, there are also reptiles, exotic birds, and Russian circus acts.

Bok Tower Gardens ⑬

Road map E3. Polk Co. 1151 Tower Blvd, Lake Wales. 📞 *(863) 676-1408.*
🚌 *Winter Haven.* 🚉 *Lake Wales.*
🕐 *daily.* 📷 ♿
🌐 www.boktower.org

EDWARD W. BOK arrived in the US from Holland in 1870 at the age of six, and subsequently became an influential publisher. Shortly before his death in 1930, he presented

these 128 acres of beautiful woodland gardens to the American public "for the success they had given him."

Sitting at the highest spot in peninsular Florida – a dizzying 298 ft (91 m) above sea level – they center on the Singing Tower, which soars above the treetops and shelters Bok's grave at its base. You cannot climb the tower, but try to attend its 45-minute live carillon concert, rung daily at 3pm.

Yeehaw Junction ⑭

Road map E3. Osceola Co. 5570 South Kenansville Drive, Yeehaw Junction 34972. 📞 *(407) 436-1054.*
🕐 *daily.* 📷 ♿ 🌐 www.yeehawjunction.com

YEEHAW JUNCTION was once known only as a watering hole for lumbermen and cowboys driving herds of cattle from the center of the state to the reservations and plantations of the coast. Located at the crossroads of Florida's Turnpike and the scenic Highway 441, the Desert Inn is a good place to stop. The restaurant serves gator- and turtle burgers; and there is a gift shop and a large outdoor area for festivals and barbeques.

The 1880s wooden building, listed on the National Registry of Historical Places, offers a fascinating look into Cracker Country history for busloads of tourists and for bluegrass festival aficionados.

The striking, pink marble Singing Tower at Bok Tower Gardens

Canaveral National Seashore and Merritt Island ⓯

Road map F2. Brevard Co.
🚌 *Titusville.*
W www.nbbd.com/godo/cns

THESE ADJACENT preserves on the Space Coast share an astounding variety of fauna and a wide range of habitats, including saltwater estuaries, marshes, pine flatwoods, and hardwood hammocks, all due to the meeting of temperate and subtropical climates here. You can often see alligators, as well as endangered species such as manatees, but the bird life makes the greatest visual impact.

Many visitors simply head straight for the beach. The **Canaveral National Seashore** incorporates Florida's largest undeveloped barrier island beach – a magnificent 24-mile (39-km) strip of sand backed by dunes strewn with sea oats and sea grapes. Apollo Beach, at the northern end, is accessible along Route A1A, while Playalinda Beach is reached from the south, along Route 402; no road connects the two. The beaches are fine for sunbathing, but swimming conditions can be hazardous, and there are no lifeguards.

An alligator in the wild

Behind Apollo Beach, Turtle Mound is a 40-ft (12-m) high rubbish dump of oyster shells created by Timucua Indians *(see pp38–9)* between AD 800 and 1400. Climb the boardwalk

to the top for a view over Mosquito Lagoon, flecked with a myriad mangrove islets. Route 402 to Playalinda Beach provides memorable views too – of the Kennedy Space Center's shuttle launch pads, rising eerily out of the watery vastness. This route also crosses **Merritt Island National Wildlife Refuge**, which covers an area of 220 sq miles (570 sq km). Most of the refuge lies within Kennedy Space Center and is out of bounds.

By far the best way to experience the local wildlife at first hand is to follow the 6-mile (10-km) Black Point Wildlife Drive. An excellent leaflet, available at the track's start near the junction of routes 402 and 406, explains such matters as how dikes control local mosquito populations (although you should still come armed with insect repellent in summer). Halfway along the drive you can stretch your legs by following the 5-mile (8-km) Cruickshank Trail, which starts nearby and has an observation tower.

East along Route 402 towards Playalinda, the Merritt Island Visitor Information Center has excellent displays on the habitats and wildlife within the refuge. A mile (1.5 km) farther east, the Oak Hammock and Palm Hammock trails have short boardwalks across the marshland for bird watching and photography.

⚥ Canaveral National Seashore
Route A1A, 20 miles (32 km) N of Titusville or Route 402, 10 miles (16 km) E of Titusville. ▌ *(321) 267-1110.* ◯ *daily.* ● *for shuttle launches.* 📷
⚥ Merritt Island National Wildlife Refuge
Route 406, 4 miles (6.5 km) E of Titusville. ▌ *(321) 861-0667.* ◯ *daily.* ● *for shuttle launches.*

SPACE COAST BIRD LIFE

The magnificent and abundant bird life of the Space Coast is best viewed early in the morning or shortly before dusk. Between November and March, in particular, the marshes and lagoons teem with migratory ducks and waders, as up to 100,000 arrive from colder northern climes.

Sandhill crane

Brown pelican

Royal tern

Black skimmer

View from Black Point Drive, Merritt Island National Wildlife Refuge

Kennedy Space Center ⓰

See pp182–7.

US Astronaut Hall of Fame ⑰

Road map E2. Brevard Co. Junction of Route 405 and US 1. ☎ (321) 269-6100. ⊞ Titusville. ◯ daily. ● Dec 25. ⬚ ⬚
ⓦ www.astronauts.org

THIS HALL OF FAME is both educational and entertaining. It commemorates the early astronauts and has many of their personal items on display. A full-size mock shuttle shows a film of a shuttle's space flight, and the flight simulator riders undergo G-forces equal to those experienced by fighter pilots.

The US Space Camp, on the same site, runs courses for youngsters, with such activities as trying out weightlessness.

"Tico Belle," the prize exhibit at the Warbird Air Museum

Valiant Air Command Warbird Air Museum ⑱

Road map E2. Brevard Co. 6600 Tico Road, Titusville. ☎ (321) 268-1941. ⊞ Titusville. ◯ daily. ● Thanksgiving, Dec 25, Jan 1. ⬚ ⬚
ⓦ www.vacwarbirds/org

AT THIS MUSEUM an enormous hangar houses military planes from World War II and later, all lovingly restored to flying condition. The pride of

Porcher House, on the edge of Cocoa's leafy historic district

the collection is a working Douglas C-47 called Tico Belle: the aircraft saw service during World War II before becoming the official carrier for the Danish royal family.

Every March there is an air show, with mock dogfights.

Cocoa ⑲

Road map E3. Brevard Co.
🚶 20,000. ⊞ 🛈 Cocoa Beach, (321) 459-2200.

COCOA IS THE most appealing community among the sprawling conurbations along the Space Coast mainland. Its historic district, near where Route 520 crosses the Indian River to Cocoa Beach, is an attractive enclave known as Cocoa Village – with buildings dating from the 1880s (some of which house unpretentious boutiques), replica gas street-lamps, and brick sidewalks.

In Delannoy Avenue, on the eastern edge of the village, is the Classical Revival Porcher House, built of coquina stone (see p201) in 1916 by a leading citrus plantation owner. The

interior is unexciting, but note the spade, heart, diamond, and club carvings on its portico wall: Mrs. Porcher was an extremely avid bridge player.

Cocoa Beach ⑳

Road map F3. Brevard Co. 🚶 14,000.
⊞ Cocoa. 🛈 400 Fortenberry Rd, (321) 459-2200.

THE SPACE COAST'S big, no-frills resort calls itself the east coast's surfing capital. Surfing festivals and bikini contests set the tone, along with win-your-weight-in-beer competitions on the pier. Motels, chain restaurants, and the odd strip joint characterize the main thoroughfare.

These are all eclipsed by the **Ron Jon Surf Shop**. This neon palace has surf boards galore (for sale and for rent) and a huge T-shirt collection. In front of its flashing towers, beach bum sports figures are frozen in modern sculpture.

🏠 **Ron Jon Surf Shop**
4151 N Atlantic Ave. ☎ (321) 799-8820. ◯ daily: 24 hours. ⬚

The Ron Jon Surf Shop in Cocoa Beach, with everything for the surfing or beach enthusiast

Kennedy Space Center ⓰

NASA insignia

SITUATED ON MERRITT ISLAND, just an hour's drive east of Orlando, the Kennedy Space Center is the only place in the western hemisphere where humans are launched into space. It was from here, with the launch of Apollo 11 in July 1969, that President Kennedy's dream of landing a man on the moon was realized. The center is the home of NASA (National Aeronautics and Space Administration), whose manned Space Shuttle *(see pp186–7)* can regularly be seen lifting off from one of the launch pads. With a scale and popularity comparable to Orlando's other theme parks, the recently revamped Visitor Complex aims to both inform and entertain.

★ **Apollo/Saturn V Center**
A Saturn V rocket, of the kind used by the Apollo missions, is the showpiece here. There is also a reconstructed control room where visitors experience a simulated launch (see p185).

Spacemen
Staff dressed up as spacemen may put in a surprise appearance at any time, providing ideal photo opportunities for children.

Astronaut Encounter

Children's Play Dome

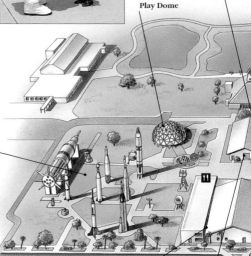

★ **Rocket Garden**
You can walk through a group of towering rockets, each of which represents a different period of space flight's history.

Nature's Technology Universe Theater

Exploration in the New Millennium

Entrance

STAR FEATURES

★ **Apollo/Saturn V Center**

★ **Rocket Garden**

★ **Bus Tours**

★ **IMAX® Films**

VISITOR COMPLEX

All visitors to the Kennedy Space Center must stop at the Visitor Complex, which was established in 1966 to offer bus tours of the area. It is now an extensive attraction with many exhibits.

W www.kennedyspacecenter.com

★ KSC Bus Tour
A bus tour makes a circuit of the center's launch pads, passing the Vehicle Assembly Building and the "crawlerway," along which the shuttle is slowly maneuvered into position.

VISITORS' CHECKLIST

Road map F2. Brevard Co. Off Route 405, 6 miles (9.5 km) E of Titusville. **(** (321) 449-4444. **🚌** Titusville. **○** 9am to dusk daily. **●** Dec 25. The center closes occasionally due to operational requirements. Always call ahead. **🗷 ♿** all the exhibits are accessible; wheelchairs and strollers are available at Information Central. **🍴 🎁 (** (321) 867-4636 for schedule of launches. **W** www.ksc.nasa.gov

★ IMAX® Films
At the Galaxy Center, huge IMAX® theaters run films about space exploration. Footage from the shuttle missions offers some breathtaking views of Earth from space (see p184).

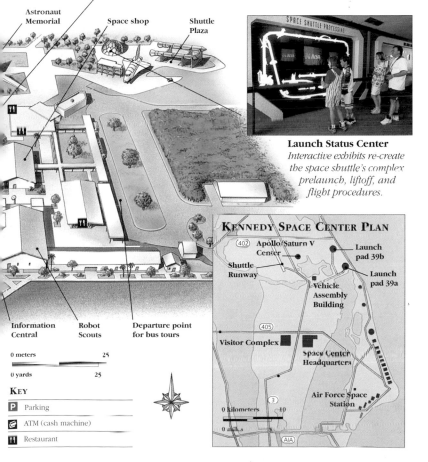

Astronaut Memorial

Space shop

Shuttle Plaza

Launch Status Center
Interactive exhibits re-create the space shuttle's complex prelaunch, liftoff, and flight procedures.

Information Central

Robot Scouts

Departure point for bus tours

0 meters 25

0 yards 25

KEY

P Parking

🏧 ATM (cash machine)

🍴 Restaurant

KENNEDY SPACE CENTER PLAN

(402) **Apollo/Saturn V Center**

Launch pad 39b

Shuttle Runway

Launch pad 39a

Vehicle Assembly Building

(405)

Visitor Complex

Space Center Headquarters

Air Force Space Station

(3)

0 kilometers 10

0 miles

(A1A)

Exploring the Kennedy Space Center

BUILT IN 1967 FOR astronauts and their families to view space center operations, today the Visitor Complex is host to more than 2 million tourists each year. The 131-sq mile (340-sq km) facility offers guests a full-day, comprehensive space experience, including excellent IMAX® films at the Visitor Complex, live-action shows, astronaut encounters, and the Apollo/Saturn V Center – the climax of the narrated, video-enhanced bus tour. The go-at-your-own pace tour enables visitors to stop and explore each of the three major destinations. One all-inclusive admission ticket takes visitors on the KSC Tour, both IMAX® space films, and all exhibits.

Kids enjoy the Robot Scouts at the Galaxy Center

VISITOR COMPLEX

THE PLACE where everyone heads first is the **Galaxy Center**, where two back-to-back IMAX® theaters put on stunning films on screens more than five stories high. For some people this is the highlight of their visit.

Top of the bill is *The Dream is Alive*, filmed by shuttle astronauts and narrated by Walter Cronkite. The film provides an insider's view, with in-flight footage gathered during a number of space missions; the thrills and basics of everyday life in space, and shows the awesome beauty of space flight. *L5: First City in Space*, the first film to accurately depict a future space settlement through the use of actual NASA footage and data. Three-D computer graphics transport you to an imaginary city in outer space; highlights from this film include a flight past Mars and a landing on a comet.

The 300-seat Universe Theater at the Visitor Complex shows the inspirational film *Quest for Life*, which highlights the need for future space exploration to search for life in our galaxy. The **NASA Art Gallery**, inside the Galaxy Center, offers more than 200 artworks by such famous artist as Andy Warhol, Robert Rauschenberg, and Annie Leibovitz. Kids will probably prefer the latest planetary explorer robots revealed in **Robot Scouts** or coming face-to-face with a real astronaut in the **Astronaut Encounter** show.

In Shuttle Plaza you can climb aboard and enjoy a close-up view of **Explorer** – a replica of the Space Shuttle. The **Launch Status Center** alongside has displays of genuine flight hardware and rocket boosters, plus a number of shows illustrating various space-related topics. Nearby, a "Space Mirror" tracks the movement of the sun, reflecting its light onto the names inscribed on the **Astronaut Memorial**. This honors the 16 astronauts, from the Apollo 1 to the Space Shuttle Challenger missions, who have died in the service of space exploration.

Exploration in the New Millennium offers a film, lecture, and informative exhibits on what the future holds for space exploration. Guests can see and touch a piece of a Mars meteorite.

The *Explorer*, a life-size replica of the Space Shuttle

TIMELINE OF SPACE EXPLORATION

1958 First American satellite, the *Explorer 1*, is launched (Jan 31)	**1962** John Glenn orbits the earth in *Mercury* spacecraft	**1969** Neil Armstrong and Buzz Aldrin (*Apollo 11*) walk on the moon (Jul 24) **1966** *Gemini 8* makes first space docking (Mar 16)	*Buzz Aldrin*	**197** Space S. *Enterp* tested a a Boein (Fe
1955	1960	1965		197
1961 On May 5, Alan Shepherd becomes the first American in space. Kennedy commits nation to moon landing *John Glenn*		**1965** Edward White is the first American to walk in space (Jun 3)	**1968** *Apollo 8* orbits the moon (Dec 24) **1975** American *Apollo* and Russian *Soyuz* vehicles dock in orbit (Jul 17)	

KSC EXHIBITS AND BUS TOUR

THE ENTRANCE GATE, modeled after the International Space Station, welcomes guests to the Visitor Complex. Once inside the Complex, there is a fascinating walk-through exhibit, which shows visitors a comprehensive history of the major missions that provided the foundation for the space program. The all-glass rotunda leads to the **Hall of Discovery**, which showcases key figures from the early days of rocketry. In the **Mercury Mission Control Room**, visitors view from an observation deck the actual components and consoles from which the first eight manned missions were monitored. Footage and interviews with some of the personnel are highlights of this area. Next, the **Hall of History** displays some of the authentic Mercury and Gemini spacecraft so visitors can relive some of the excitement and intensity of early space exploration.

The Vehicle Assembly Building, which dominates the flat landscape

Rockets on display at the Cape Canaveral Air Station

KSC Tour buses leave every few minutes from the Visitor Complex and offer an exceptional tour of the space center's major facilities. The tour encompasses three major facilities at the space center: the LC 39 Observation Gantry, the Apollo/Saturn V Center, and the International Space Station Center. The tour takes guests into secured areas, where guides explain the inner workings of each of the facilities. Visitors can take as long as they wish to explore each sight.

There are three additional special-interest tours: **Cape Canaveral: Then & Now Tour**, which is an historic tour of the Mercury, Gemini, and Apollo launch pads; the **NASA Up Close Tour**, an insider's view of the entire space shuttle program; and the **KSC Wildlife Tour** for groups of 15 or more, which offers a guided tour of Merritt Island Wildlife Refuge. Special tours to see actual rocket launches may also be arranged by booking in advance at the Complex.

SPACE CENTER TOUR

EACH SELF-GUIDED TOUR can take between two and six hours to fully explore the three facilities on the KSC Tour. You'll get a bird's-eye view of the launch pads from the 60-ft (18-m) observation tower at the first stop, the **LC 39 Observation Gantry**. Back on the ground, a film and exhibits tell the story of a shuttle launch.

At the **International Space Station Center** guests can walk through and peer inside the facility where each space station is readied for launch.

The **Apollo/Saturn V Center** features an actual 363-ft (110-m) Saturn V moon rocket. You'll see the historic launch of Apollo 8, the first manned mission to the moon in the Firing Room Theater, followed by a film at the Lunar Theater, which shows actual footage of the moon landing. The only place in the world where guests can dine next to a genuine moon rock is also here, at the Moon Rock Cafe.

1981 *Columbia* the first shuttle in (Apr 12)	**1983** The first American woman goes into space, aboard Space Shuttle *Challenger* (Jun 18)	**1988** *Discovery*, the first shuttle since the *Challenger* disaster, is launched (Sep 29) *Atlantis–Mir insignia (June 1995)*			**2001** Dennis Tito pays US$20 million to spend one week on board an International Space Center
1980		**1985**	**1990**		**1995**
Space Shuttle Columbia	**1984** First American woman, Kathryn Sullivan, walks in space (Oct 11)	**1986** The *Challenger* explodes, killing all its crew (Jan 28)	**1990** Hubble telescope is launched (Apr 24) **1995** The *Atlantis* docks with Russian *Mir* space station (Jun 29)		**1996** *Mars Pathfinder* sent to gather data from the surface of Mars **1998** John Glenn returns to space as oldest astronaut

The Space Shuttle

BY THE LATE 1970s, the cost of sending astronauts into space had become too much for the American space budget; hundreds of millions of dollars were spent lifting the Apollo missions into space, with little more than a scorched command module ever returning to Earth. The time had come to develop reusable spacecraft made for years of service, whose main cost after production would lie in maintenance. The answer was the Space Shuttle *Columbia*, which was launched into space on April 12, 1981 *(see pp50–51)*. The shuttle's large cargo capacity allows it to take all kinds of satellites and probes into space, and it will be used to lift materials for the construction of the International Space Station.

Shuttle in Space
In orbit, the shuttle's cargo doors are opened. The Hubble telescope was one of its payloads.

Flight Deck
The shuttle is built like an aircraft, but its flight deck is even more complex. You can get some idea of how it is navigated at the Launch Status Center (see p183).

Tracks enable the tower to be moved away before liftoff.

Crawlerway
This double pathway, 100 ft (30 m) wide, is specially designed to withstand the weight of the shuttle as it is taken to the launch pad by gigantic crawlers. The rock surface overlies a layer of asphalt and a 7 ft (2 m) bed of crushed stone.

The Crawler backs away once the shuttle is in place.

SHUTTLE CYCLE

The Space Shuttle has three principal elements: the main Orbiter spacecraft (with its three engines), an external tank of liquid hydrogen and oxygen fuel, and two solid-fuel booster rockets, which provide the extra thrust needed for liftoff. Like earlier rockets, the shuttle reaches orbit in stages.

1 Prelaunch
The external tank and rocket boosters are fitted to the Orbiter in the Vehicle Assembly Building. Then it is moved to the launch pad.

2 Launch
After a final che[ck] the shuttle blast[s] using its own th[ree] engines and its t[wo] booster rockets.

The service tower gives access for fueling and cargo installation.

The access arm is a corridor through which the astronauts board the shuttle.

Orbiter

Solid Rocket Booster

The flame trench channels the burning gases away from the vehicle.

THE SHUTTLE LAUNCHES

Since the shuttle made its maiden voyage in 1981, there have been many missions shared between the *Columbia*, *Challenger*, *Discovery*, *Atlantis*, and *Endeavour* vehicles. Though the program was severely crippled when the *Challenger* exploded shortly after liftoff in 1986, there are now up to eight launches a year. To view the launches within the Space Center you will need to purchase tickets from the Visitor Complex. Outside the center, there are prime, free viewing sites on US 1 at Titusville and on A1A at Cocoa Beach and Cape Canaveral.

Shuttle clearing the launch tower

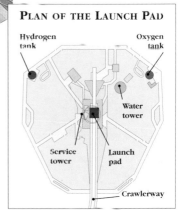

Shuttle Landing
Once it has reentered the atmosphere, the shuttle glides with its engines off on its way back to the Space Center. It lands on the runway at 220 mph (360 km/h).

Vent for spent gases

Steel pedestals

SHUTTLE LAUNCH
The launch pad is made of 2 million cu ft (56,000 cu m) of reinforced concrete, supported by six steel pedestals. The flame trench is flooded with cooling water when the engines ignite, producing an immense cloud of steam.

PLAN OF THE LAUNCH PAD

Hydrogen tank

Oxygen tank

Water tower

Service tower

Launch pad

Crawlerway

3 Separation
Two minutes later, the boosters separate and are parachuted back to earth. At eight minutes, the external tank detaches.

4 Orbital Operations
Using its own engines, the shuttle maneuvers itself into orbit and begins its operations. The mission may last between 7 and 18 days, flying at an altitude of 115–690 miles (185–1,110 km).

5 Reentry
The shuttle reenters the atmosphere backward, using its engines to decelerate. It turns nose-first as it descends into the stratosphere and uses parachutes to stop.

THE NORTHEAST

THE CHARMS OF THE NORTHEAST *are more discreet than the glitz of Miami or the thrills of Orlando. Just a few miles from busy interstate highways, salty fishing villages, overgrown plantations, and quaint country towns recall old-time Florida. Fabulous beaches lure sun-worshipers, while the historic town of St. Augustine can claim to be the longest inhabited European settlement in the US.*

The state's recorded history begins in the Northeast, on the aptly named First Coast. Juan Ponce de León first stepped ashore here in 1513 *(see p40)* and Spanish colonists established St. Augustine, now a well-preserved town guarded by the mighty San Marcos fortress – one of the region's highlights.

The Northeast also saw the first influx of pioneers and tourists during the 19th-century steamboat era *(see p46)*. At this time, Jacksonville was the gateway to Florida, with steamboats plying the broad St. Johns River and its tributaries. In the 1880s, Henry Flagler's railroad opened up the east coast, and wealthy visitors flocked to his grand hotels in St. Augustine and Ormond Beach. Those in search of the winter sun headed farther south too.

Broad sandy beaches flank the popular resort of Daytona, which has been synonymous with car racing ever since the likes of Henry Ford and Louis Chevrolet raced automobiles on the beach during their winter vacations. Daytona is also the favorite place for students to spend the spring break: this is as lively as it gets in the Northeast.

Venturing inland, west of the St. Johns, is the wooded expanse of the Ocala National Forest; the woods then thin out to reveal the rolling pastures of Marion County's billion-dollar thoroughbred horse industry. Nearby, charming country towns and villages such as Micanopy have been virtually bypassed by the 20th century.

St. Augustine's splendid Lightner Museum, occupying the former exclusive Alcazar Hotel

◁ **The boardwalk trail at Blue Spring State Park, located next to the St. Johns River**

Exploring the Northeast

T HE FIRST COAST is a well-traveled route, unfurling along the Atlantic shore in a 120-mile (193-km) string of beaches and resorts, interrupted by dunes and marshland popular with bird-watchers. Resorts run the gamut from decorous Fernandina Beach to action-packed Daytona Beach. Between these two extremes lies the historic jewel of St. Augustine. Strike inland, and the Ocala National Forest offers dozens of hiking trails, boating, and fishing on spring-fed lakes. Snorkeling and diving are also popular pursuits in crystal-clear springs. Many of the region's Victorian homes are now bed-and-breakfast inns, which make a pleasant change from hotels and provide a more homey base for exploring.

SIGHTS AT A GLANCE

Blue Spring State Park ⑮
Bulow Plantation State
  Historic Site ⑩
Daytona Beach ⑫
Daytona International Speedway ⑬
Fernandina Beach ❶
Fort Caroline National Memorial ❹
Gainesville ㉓
Jacksonville pp194–5 ❺
Jacksonville Beaches ❻
Kingsley Plantation ❸
Little Talbot Island ❷
Marineland Ocean Resort ❽
Marjorie Kinnan Rawlings State
  Historic Site ㉑
Micanopy ㉒
Mount Dora ⑰
Ocala ⑳
Ocala National Forest ⑱
Ormond Beach ⑪
Ponce de Leon Inlet Lighthouse ⑭
St. Augustine pp196–201 ❼
Sanford ⑯
Silver Springs ⑲
Washington Oaks State Gardens ❾

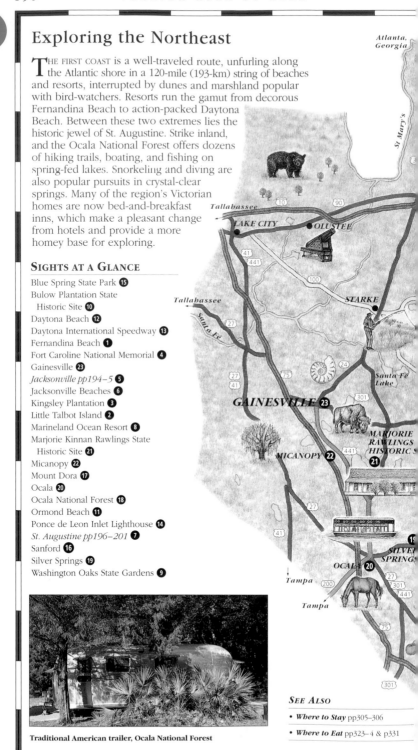

Traditional American trailer, Ocala National Forest

SEE ALSO

• **Where to Stay** pp305–306

• **Where to Eat** pp323–4 & p331

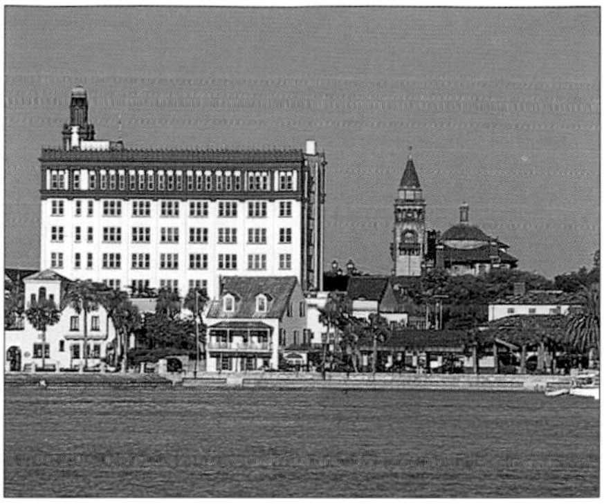

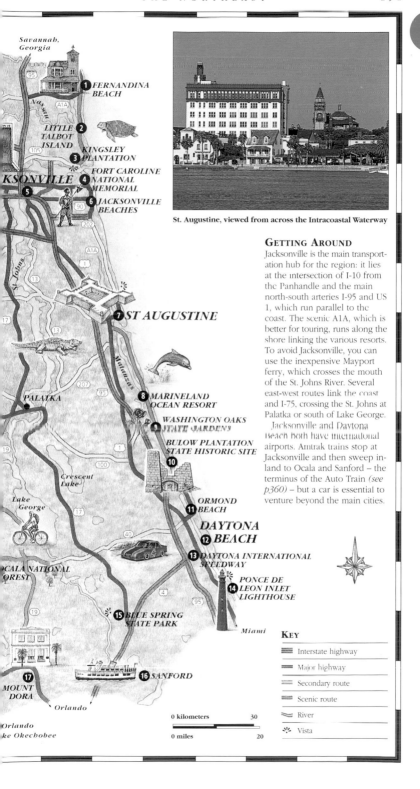

St. Augustine, viewed from across the Intracoastal Waterway

Getting Around

Jacksonville is the main transportation hub for the region: it lies at the intersection of I-10 from the Panhandle and the main north-south arteries I-95 and US 1, which run parallel to the coast. The scenic A1A, which is better for touring, runs along the shore linking the various resorts. To avoid Jacksonville, you can use the inexpensive Mayport ferry, which crosses the mouth of the St. Johns River. Several east-west routes link the coast and I-75, crossing the St. Johns at Palatka or south of Lake George.

Jacksonville and Daytona Beach both have international airports. Amtrak trains stop at Jacksonville and then sweep inland to Ocala and Sanford – the terminus of the Auto Train *(see p360)* – but a car is essential to venture beyond the main cities.

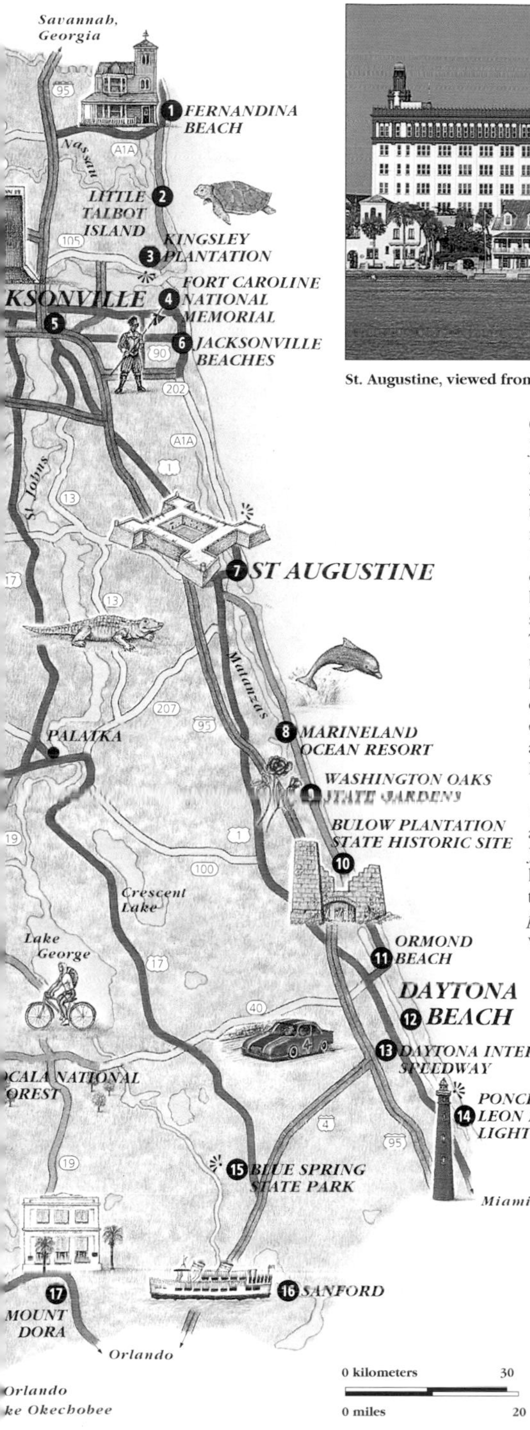

Savannah, Georgia
95
1 FERNANDINA BEACH
Nassau
A1A
2 LITTLE TALBOT ISLAND
105
3 KINGSLEY PLANTATION
4 FORT CAROLINE NATIONAL MEMORIAL
JACKSONVILLE
5
6 JACKSONVILLE BEACHES
90
202
A1A
1
St Johns
13
7 ST AUGUSTINE
17
13
Matanzas
207
95
PALATKA
8 MARINELAND OCEAN RESORT
9 WASHINGTON OAKS STATE GARDENS
BULOW PLANTATION STATE HISTORIC SITE
10
19
1
100
Crescent Lake
Lake George
17
11 ORMOND BEACH
12 DAYTONA BEACH
40
13 DAYTONA INTERNATIONAL SPEEDWAY
OCALA NATIONAL FOREST
14 PONCE DE LEON INLET LIGHTHOUSE
4
95
19
15 BLUE SPRING STATE PARK
Miami
16 SANFORD
17 MOUNT DORA
Orlando
Orlando
Lake Okechobee
0 kilometers 30
0 miles 20

Key

- Interstate highway
- Major highway
- Secondary route
- Scenic route
- River
- Vista

Fernandina's Beech Street Grill with Chinese Chippendale motifs

Fernandina Beach ❶

Road map E1. Nassau Co. 🏛 *10,000.*
🚉 *Jacksonville* 🚌 *Jacksonville.*
ℹ *102 Centre St, (904) 261-3248.*

THE TOWN OF Fernandina Beach on Amelia Island, just across the St. Mary's River from Georgia, was renowned as a pirates' den until the early 1800s. Its deep-water harbor attracted a motley crew of foreign armies and adventurers, whose various allegiances earned Amelia Island its soubriquet, the Isle of Eight Flags. Today, Fernandina is better known as a charming Victorian resort and Florida's primary source of sweet Atlantic white shrimp: more than two million pounds (900,000 kilos) are caught by the shrimping fleet each year.

The original Spanish settlement was established at Old Fernandina, a sleepy backwater just north of the present town. In the 1850s the whole town moved south to the eastern terminus of Senator David Yulee's cross-Florida railroad. The move, coupled with the dawn of Florida tourism in the 1870s *(see pp46–7),* prompted the building boom that created the much-admired heart of today's Fernandina, the 50-block **Historic District**.

The legacy of Fernandina's golden age is best seen in the Silk Stocking District, which occupies more than half of the Historic District and is so-named for the affluence of its original residents. Sea captains and timber barons built homes here in a variety of styles: Queen Anne houses decorated with fancy gingerbread detailing and turrets jostle graceful Italianate residences and fine examples of Chinese Chippendale, such as the Beech Street Grill *(see p323).*

Watching the shrimp boats put into harbor at sunset is a local ritual; the fleet is commemorated by a monument at the foot of downtown Centre Street, where chandleries and naval stores once held sway. These weathered brick buildings now house antique shops and upscale gift shops. The 1878 Palace Saloon, however, still serves a wicked Pirate's Punch at the long mahogany bar adorned with hand-carved caryatids.

Down on 3rd Street, the 1857 Florida House Inn *(see p323)* is the state's oldest tourist hotel, and a couple of blocks farther

Peg Leg, of Fernandina Beach

south, the **Amelia Island Museum of History** occupies the former jail. Guides talk visitors through the island's turbulent past – from the time of the first Indian inhabitants to the early 1900s. Period items and archaeological finds are used to illustrate the 90-minute tours. Guided tours of the town are also offered (book ahead).

🏛 **Amelia Island Museum of History**
233 S 3rd St. 📞 *(904) 261-7378.*
⭕ *Mon–Sat.* ⬤ *public hols.* 🎟
♿ *compulsory; two tours daily.*
🌐 *www.ameliaisland.com/museum*

ENVIRONS: Thirteen miles (21 km) long and only 2 miles (3 km) wide at its broadest point, **Amelia Island** was first settled by the Timucua tribe in the second century BC. The rich fishing grounds and abundant hunting suggest that the island may have supported around 30,000 Indians, although few signs remain of their presence. There's still excellent fishing, and the island also offers five golf courses and one of Florida's rare opportunities to ride horses along the beach. The splendid sands are backed by dunes that can reach 40 ft (12 m) high in places.

The northern tip of the island is occupied by the 1,121-acre (453-ha) **Fort Clinch State Park**, with trails, beaches, and campsites, as well as a 19th-century brick fort built to guard the Cumberland Sound at the mouth of the St. Mary's River. Construction of the fort, an irregular brick pentagon with massive earthworks, 4.5-ft (1.5-m) thick walls, and a battery of Civil War cannons, took from 1847 until the 1860s.

Today, the park's rangers wear Civil War uniforms. They are joined by volunteers on the first full weekend of each month in re-enactments, when a wide variety of duties are re-created; candlelit tours are given on the Saturday.

♣ **Fort Clinch State Park**
2601 Atlantic Ave. 📞 *(904) 277-7274.*
⭕ *daily.* 🎟 ♿ *limited.* ⒶΔ

Amelia Island's Atlantic shore, in easy reach of Fernandina Beach

Little Talbot Island State Park ❶

Road map E1. Duval Co. 12157 Heckscher Drive, Jacksonville. (*(904) 251-2320.* 🚊 *Jacksonville.* 🚌 *Jacksonville.* ⬜ *daily.* 🏖 🚹 *limited.* ⛺

MUCH OF AMELIA ISLAND and the neighboring islands of Big Talbot, Little Talbot, and Fort George to the south remains undeveloped and a natural haven for wildlife.

Little Talbot Island State Park has a good family camp ground, trails through coastal hammocks and marshlands, and great fishing. Expect to see anything from otters and marsh rabbits to fiddler crabs, herons, and laughing gulls. Bobcats hide out in the woods, manatees bob about in the intracoastal waters, and in summer turtles lay their eggs on the beach *(see p113)*. In autumn, northern right whales travel here to calve offshore.

View along a trail through marsh-land on Little Talbot Island

Kingsley Plantation ❸

Road map E1. Duval Co. 11676 Palmetto Ave, Fort George. (*(904) 251-3537.* 🚊 *Jacksonville.* 🚌 *Jacksonville.* ⬜ *daily.* 🔴 *Dec 25.* 🚹

LOCATED IN THE Timucuan Ecological and Historic Preserve, Kingsley Plantation is the oldest plantation house in Florida. Built in 1798 at the northern end of Fort George Island, it takes its name from Zephaniah Kingsley, who moved here in 1814. He amassed 32,000 acres

Ruins of the original slave cabins unique to the Kingsley Plantation

(12,950 ha) of land, stretching from Lake George near the Ocala National Forest north to the St. Mary's River. This area used to encompass four major plantations; the Kingsley plantation itself had as many as 100 slaves working in the fields where cotton, sugar-cane, and corn were cultivated.

Kingsley was a rather liberal thinker for his time, supporting slavery while also advocating a more lenient "task-system" for his slaves. He married a freed slave, Anna Jai, and they lived in the clapboard planta-tion house *(see p43)* until 1839.

Described at the time as "a very nice commodious house," Kingsley's relatively simple home has been restored and now contains a visitor center. The building is topped by a small rooftop parapet called a "widow's walk," once used to survey the surrounding fields. Nearby are the barn and sepa-rate kitchen house, but the plantation is best known for the 23 slave cabins located in woods near the entrance gate. Built of durable tabby *(see p282)*, these basic dwellings have survived the years, and one has been restored.

Fort Caroline in 1564 by Theodore de Bry

Fort Caroline National Memorial ❹

Road map E1. Duval Co. 12713 Fort Caroline Rd, Jacksonville. (*(904) 641-7155.* 🚊 *Jacksonville.* 🚌 *Jacksonville.* ⬜ *daily.* 🔴 *Dec 25.* 🚹 ⓦ www.nps.gov/foca

THE ACTUAL SITE of Fort Caroline was washed away when the St. Johns River was dredged in the 1880s. At Fort Caroline National Memorial, a reconstruction of the original 16th-century defenses clearly illustrates the style of the first European forts in the New World. Information panels around the site explain the fort's violent history, which began shortly after French settlers arrived in June 1564.

In the attempt to stake a claim to North America, three small French vessels carrying 300 men sailed up the St. Johns and made camp 5 miles (8 km) inland. René de Goulaine de Laudonnière led the French, who were helped by local Timucua Indians to build a tri-angular wooden fort, named La Caroline in honor of Charles IX of France *(see p40)*. A year later, with the settlers close to starvation, reinforcements under Jean Ribault arrived. The Spanish, however, took the fort, crushing the French land claims.

In the park is a replica of the stone column erected by Jean Ribault.

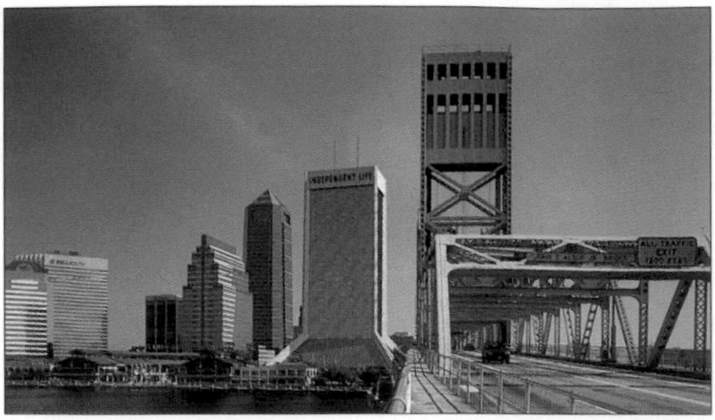

The glass and steel skyline that dominates Jacksonville's north bank

Jacksonville 5

Road map E1. Duval Co. 👥 *1,075,000.* ✈ 🚆 🚌 ℹ *3 Independent Drive, (904) 798-9148.*

JACKSONVILLE, the capital of the First Coast of Florida, was founded in 1822. Named after General Jackson *(see p43)*, the town boomed as a port and rail terminus in the late 1800s. Today, the more sedentary but just as lucrative financial businesses fuel the impressive downtown commercial district, which you can view from the Skyway or ASE *(see p363)*.

This, Florida's largest city in area, spans the St. Johns River, which flows through it and provides a focus for visitors. Most people head for the pedestrian areas that flank the river banks and are connected by water taxi services *(see p363)*, although other sights are dotted around the city.

The **Jacksonville Landing** shopping and dining complex is located on the north bank of the St. Johns, while on the south, the pleasant 1.2-mile (2-km) long **Riverwalk** connects the Jacksonville Historic Center and the impressive Museum of Science and History.

Riverside, on the opposite bank, is home to the famous Cummer Museum of Art. This large residential district, which contains a wonderful array of Revival-style architecture popular up to the 1920s, is best explored by car.

🏛 Museum of Science and History

1025 Museum Circle Drive. ☎ *(904) 396-7062.* 🕒 *daily.* 🎫 ♿

This ever-expanding museum houses an eclectic collection of exhibits and provides a user-friendly guide to local history. The 12,000 year-old material culture of the local Timucua Indians *(see pp38–9)* and their predecessors is illustrated with tools, arrowheads, pottery, and other archaeological finds.

There are sections dealing with the ecology and history of the St. Johns River and the *Maple Leaf*, a Civil War steam-

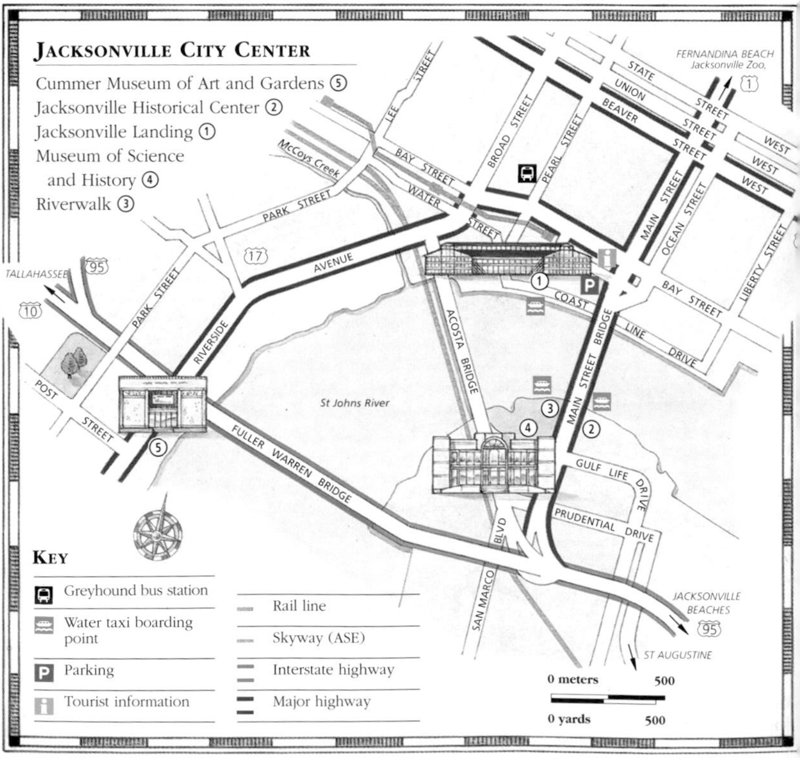
JACKSONVILLE CITY CENTER
Cummer Museum of Art and Gardens 5
Jacksonville Historical Center 2
Jacksonville Landing 1
Museum of Science and History 4
Riverwalk 3
FERNANDINA BEACH
Jacksonville Zoo,
STATE
UNION
BEAVER
STREET
STREET
STREET
WEST
WEST
WEST
LEE STREET
BROAD STREET
PEARL STREET
MAIN STREET
OCEAN STREET
LIBERTY STREET
McCoys Creek
BAY STREET
WATER STREET
PARK STREET
AVENUE
TALLAHASSEE
PARK STREET
RIVERSIDE
COAST
LINE
DRIVE
BAY STREET
ACOSTA BRIDGE
MAIN STREET BRIDGE
POST STREET
St Johns River
FULLER WARREN BRIDGE
GULF LIFE DRIVE
PRUDENTIAL DRIVE
BLVD
SAN MARCO
JACKSONVILLE BEACHES
ST AUGUSTINE
KEY
Greyhound bus station
Water taxi boarding point
Parking
Tourist information
Rail line
Skyway (ASE)
Interstate highway
Major highway
0 meters 500
0 yards 500

ship that sank in 1864, a host of entertaining hands-on gadgets in the exhibition hall, and the Alexander Brest Planetarium. This also runs state-of-the-art 3-D laser shows.

🏛 Jacksonville Historical Center

Southbank Riverwalk. **❗** *(904) 398-4301.* ◐ *Mon–Sat.* ● *public hols.* ♿

At the foot of the Main Street Bridge, the Jacksonville Historical Center is a modest museum that charts local history using information panels, artifacts, old photographs, and video footage. One section of the center salutes the silent movie era, when the city was the world's Winter Film Capital and a rotund movie projectionist from the state of Georgia named Oliver Hardy got his first acting break in 1913.

Rare white rhinos at the famous Jacksonville Zoo

✹ Jacksonville Zoo

8605 Zoo Parkway. **❗** *(904) 757-4462.* ◐ *daily.* ● *Thanksgiving, Dec 25.* 🈂 ♿ Ⓦ www.jaxzoo.org

Opened in 1914, Jacksonville Zoo lies north of the city, off I-95. Its outmoded cages have recently been replaced with natural habitats where some 600 animals, from anteaters to zebras, are on view. Lions, elephants, and kudu roam the African veldt, while diminutive dik-dik deer, African crocodiles, and porcupines can be found along the zoo's Okavango Trail. Other attractions include an aviary, a petting zoo, and a Florida wetlands area.

For a broader picture, take the 15-minute miniature train journey that loops around half of the 73-acre site.

🏛 Cummer Museum of Art and Gardens

829 Riverside Ave. **❗** *(904) 356-6857* ◐ *Tue–Sun.* ● *public hols.* 🈂 ♿ Ⓦ www.cummer.org

This excellent museum stands in exquisite formal gardens that lead down to the St. Johns River. Its twelve galleries exhibit a small but satisfying collection of both decorative and fine arts. These range from Classical and pre-Columbian sculpture and ceramics through Renaissance paintings to the Wark Collection of jewel-like early Meissen porcelain.

Other notable pieces include the tiny *Entombment of Christ* (c.1605) by Rubens, and a striking collection of Japanese netsuke. There's also work by American Impressionists and such 19th- and 20th-century artists as John James Audubon.

Jacksonville Beaches ❻

Road map E1. Duval Co, St. Johns Co. 🚗 *Jacksonville.* 🚌 *Jacksonville RH1, BH2, BH3.* ℹ *110 Beach Blvd, Jacksonville Beach, (904) 249-3868.*

SOME 12 MILES (19 km) east of downtown Jacksonville, half a dozen beaches stretch 28 miles (45 km) north and south along the Atlantic shore linked by the A1A. In the south, Ponte Vedra Beach is known for its sports facilities, particularly golf. Jacksonville Beach itself is the busiest and brashest spot and is home to **Adventure Landing**, a year-round enter-

Swimmers enjoy the freshwater lakes of Kathryn Abbey Hanna Park

tainment complex and summer season water park. Heading north, Neptune Beach and Atlantic Beach are both quieter and are popular with families.

By far the nicest spot is the **Kathryn Abbey Hanna Park**, with its 1.5 miles (2.5 km) of fine white sand beach, woodland trails, freshwater lake fishing, and swimming, picnic, and camping areas. The park lies just south of the quaint town of **Mayport**, one of the oldest fishing villages in the US, still with its own shrimping fleet. The St. Johns ferry *(see p191)* links the town to the north bank of the broad St. Johns river.

🏖 Adventure Landing

1944 Beach Blvd. **❗** *(904) 246-4386.* ◐ *daily.* 🈂 ♿

♣ Kathryn Abbey Hanna Park

500 Wonderwood Drive. **❗** *(904) 249-4700.* ◐ *daily.* 🈂 ♿ ⚠

Shrimp boats moored at the picturesque docks of Mayport on the St. Johns

Street-by-Street: St. Augustine ❼

★ **Flagler College**
Tiles and other Spanish touches were used in the architecture of this former Flagler hotel.

A MERICA'S OLDEST continuously occupied European settlement was founded by Pedro Menéndez de Avilés *(see p40)* on the feast day of St. Augustine in 1565. The town burned down in 1702 but was soon rebuilt in the lee of the mighty Castillo de San Marcos; many of the picturesque, narrow streets of the old town, lined by attractive stone buildings, date from this early period.

When Henry Flagler *(see p121)* honeymooned in St. Augustine in 1883, he was so taken by the place that he returned the following year to found the Ponce de Leon Hotel, now Flagler College, and soon the gentle trickle of visitors became a flood. St. Augustine has been a major stop on the tourist trail ever since.

Zorayda Castle
This house contains many artifacts, but the future of the building remains uncertain.

★ **Lightner Museum**
Cleopatra *(c.1890)* by Romanelli is one of the exhibits from Florida's Gilded Age on display here.

The Cordoba Hotel became Flagler's third hotel in town in 1888.

Oldest Store Museum
Groceries, domestic appliances, and hardware crowd this re-created 19th-century store.

To Oldest House

STAR SIGHTS

★ **Flagler College**

★ **Lightner Museum**

★ **Ximenez-Fatio House**

★ **Ximenez-Fatio House**
This was built as a private house in 1797. Later, a second floor with an airy veranda was added, and in the mid-1800s it became a boarding house.

Plaza de la Constitution

The heart of the Spanish settlement is this leafy square flanked by Government House and the Basilica Cathedral.

> ## VISITORS' CHECKLIST
>
> Road map E1. St. Johns Co.
> 🏠 16,000. 🚌 100 Malaga St,
> (904) 829-6401. ℹ 10 Castillo
> Drive, (904) 825-1000. 🎭 Arts
> & Crafts Spring Festival.
> 🌐 www.oldcity.com

To City Gate

City Gate

Dating from the 18th century, this city entrance leads to the Old Town via historic George Street.

The Peña-Peck House, dating from the 1740s, is the finest First Spanish Period home in the city.

Bridge of Lions

Marble lions guard the bridge built across Matanzas Bay in 1926.

0 meters	50
0 yards	50

KEY

— — — Suggested route

Spanish Military Hospital

This reconstruction of a ward re-creates the spartan hospital conditions available to Spanish settlers in the late 1700s.

Exploring St. Augustine

Tʜᴇ ʜɪsᴛᴏʀɪᴄ ʜᴇᴀʀᴛ of St. Augustine is compact and easy to explore on foot. Part of the fun is escaping off the busy main streets and wandering down shady side turnings, peering into courtyards, and discovering quiet corners where cats bask in the sunshine and ancient live oaks trail curtains of gray-green Spanish moss. Horsedrawn carriage tours are a popular way to get around and depart from Avenida Menendez, north of the Bridge of Lions. Miniature tourist trains follow a more extensive route around the main sights while their drivers narrate an anecdotal history of St. Augustine.

The blacksmith at work in the Spanish Quarter Museum

St. George Street, the historic district's main thoroughfare

A Tour of St. Augustine
Pedestrian St. George Street is the focus of the historic district, with a collection of shops and some of St. Augustine's main attractions, including the excellent Spanish Quarter Museum. Set back two blocks from the waterfront, the street leads from the old City Gate to the town square, the Plaza de la Constitution. Attractive, cobblestone Aviles Street, which runs south from this square, also has several interesting colonial buildings.

There is a very different feel along King Street, west of the plaza. Here, the Lightner Museum and Flagler College are housed in hotels built by Henry Flagler (see pp46–7) during St. Augustine's heyday, in the late 19th century.

♛ The Oldest Wooden Schoolhouse
14 St. George St. ☏ (904) 824-0192
◗ daily. ● Dec 25. ▦ ♿
Built some time before 1788, this is purportedly America's oldest wooden schoolhouse. Walls made of rough planks

of cypress and red cedar are held together by wooden pins and cast-iron spikes, and the house is encircled by a massive chain designed to anchor it to the ground in high winds.

♛ Spanish Quarter Village
33 St. George St. ☏ (904) 825-6830.
◗ daily. ● Dec 25. ▦ ♿
This entertaining and informative working museum offers a step back in time to the simple lifestyles of the mid-18th century garrison town. It is housed in seven reconstructed buildings, laid out in a grassy compound planted with citrus trees and vegetable gardens.

Staff members in period costume explain the purpose of household items in the spartan homes, and various craft demonstrations reveal the intricacies and sheer hard work needed to produce even basics such as clothing. Sparks fly in the blacksmith's shop, one of the best shows in town, and a taverna is set up with hand-blown glasses, earthenware pitchers, and casks of Cuban rum, along with games like dominoes and dice.

♛ Peña-Peck House
143 St. George St. ☏ (904) 829-5064. ◗ daily. ▦ ♿
This graciously restored house was built in the 1740s for the Spanish Royal Treasurer, Juan de Peña. In 1837 it became the home and office of Dr. Seth Peck, and the Peck family continued to live here for almost 100 years. The house is furnished in mid-19th century style, and many of the objects displayed are family heirlooms.

♛ Government House Museum
48 King St. ☏ (904) 825-5079.
◗ daily. ● Dec 25. ▦ ♿
Government House, which overlooks the Plaza de la Constitution, is adorned with Spanish-style loggias copied from a 17th-century painting of the original building. Inside a small local history museum displays archaeological and colonial artifacts including silver and gold coins salvaged from Spanish treasure ships.

The Oldest Wooden Schoolhouse, built in the 1700s

♨ Spanish Military Hospital

3 Aviles St. 📞 *(904) 825-6808.*
⭘ *daily.* ● *Dec 25.*
The Spanish Military Hospital offers a rare glimpse into the care afforded soldiers in the late 1700s. Rooms include an apothecary and a simple cot-lined ward. On display is a list of surprisingly patient-friendly hospital rules, medical instruments, and suitably gory accounts of medical practices.

🏛 Oldest Store Museum

4 Artillery Lane. 📞 *(904) 829-9729.*
⭘ *daily.* ● *Dec 25.* 📷 ♿
🖾 www.oldcity.com/oldstore
This unashamedly early 1900s nostalgic museum houses a veritable cornucopia of antique hardware and food. The collection's 100,000 odd items include box cameras, chewing tobacco, and eccentric looking apple-peelers.

♨ Ximenez-Fatio House

20 Aviles St. 📞 *(904) 829-3575.*
⭘ *Thu–Sun.* ● *public hols.* ♿
limited. 🖾 www.oldcity.com/ximenez
The lovely Ximenez-Fatio House was originally built in 1797 as the home and store of a Spanish mer-chant. Today, run by the National Society of Colonial Dames, this museum re-creates the genteel boarding house that it became in the 1830s, when invalids, developers, and adventurers first visited Florida to escape the harsh northern winters. Each room is decorated in a particular theme with period furnishings and artworks.

Tiffany stained-glass window

♨ Oldest House

14 St. Francis St. 📞 *(904) 824-2872.*
⭘ *daily.* ● *public hols.* 📷 ♿
🖾 www.oldcity.com/oldhouse
Also known as the Gonzalez-Alvarez house, this building's development can be traced through almost 300 years. There is even evidence that the site was first occupied in the early 1600s, though the existing structure postdates the English raid of 1702 *(see p41).*

The coquina walls *(see p201)* were part of the original one-story home of a Spanish artilleryman, Tomas Gonzalez,

The Gonzalez Room, named after the first residents of the Oldest House

who lived here. A second story was added during the English occupation of 1763–1783. Each room has been restored and furnished in a style relevant to the different periods of the house's long and well-documented history.

🏛 Lightner Museum

75 King St. 📞 *(904) 824-2874.*
⭘ *daily.* ● *Dec 25.* 📷 ♿
🖾 www.lightnermuseum.org
Formerly the Alcazar Hotel, set up by Henry Flagler, this three-story Hispano Moorish building was an inspired choice for a museum devoted to the country's Gilded Age. The setting was selected by the Chicago pub-lisher Otto C. Lightner, who transferred his extensive collections of Victorian fine and decorative arts to St. Augustine in 1948. There's a glittering display of superb glass (including work by Louis Tiffany), furnishings, sculpture, and paintings, plus mechanical musical instru-ments and toys. The recently restored Grand Ballroom houses an eclectic exhibit of "American Castle" furniture.

♨ Flagler College

King St at Cordova St.
📞 *(904) 829 6481* ⭘ *daily.*
♿ 🖾 www.flagler.edu
This building started out as the Ponce de Leon Hotel, another of Henry Flagler's splendid endeavors. When it opened in 1888 it was heralded as "the world's finest hotel." A rather dapper statue of Flagler him-self still greets visitors, but

only the college dining room and the elegant marble-clad foyer in the rotunda are open to the public. Here, the gilded and stuccoed cupola is deco-rated with symbolic motifs representing Spain and Florida: notably the golden mask of the Timucuan *(see pp38–9)* sun god, and the lamb symbolizing Spanish knighthood. You can also visit the Flagler Room with its odd illusionary paintings executed circa 1887.

🏛 Zorayda Castle

83 King St. 📞 *(904) 824-3097.*
● *indefinitely.*
This former private residence is a one-tenth scale replica of part of the Alhambra palace in Granada, Spain. It was built in 1883, with 40 win-dows differing in size, shape, and color.

Although the building is not open to the public, you can look through the hedges that surround the house and view the intricate detail and exceptional colors displayed in the windows, walls, and eaves.

Moorish tracery and Arabic motifs decorating the Zorayda Castle

Castillo de San Marcos

DESPITE ITS ROLE as protector of the Spanish fleets en route back to Europe, St. Augustine was guarded for over a century only by a succession of wooden forts. The Spanish colonizers finally began to build a stone fortification in 1672, after suffering repeated pirate attacks and the attentions of Sir Francis Drake *(see p41)*.

The resulting Castillo de San Marcos, which took 23 years to finish, is the largest and most complete Spanish fort in the US. Constructed of coquina, it is a textbook example of 17th-century military architecture, with layers of outer defenses and walls up to 19 ft (6 m) thick.

After the US gained Florida in 1821, the castillo was renamed Fort Marion. It was used chiefly as a military prison and storage depot for the rest of the 19th century.

Mortars
Often highly decorated and bearing the royal coat of arms, these short-barreled weapons fired large, heavy projectiles on a curved trajectory. Bombs could thus clear obstacles or land on ships' decks.

The Plaza de Armas is ringed by rooms that were used to contain stockpiles of food and weapons.

★ Guard Rooms
No Spanish soldiers actually lived in the fort. During guard duty (usually 24-hour shifts), they would cook, eat, and shelter in these reinforced vaults.

The moat, which once encircled the entire fort, was usually kept dry. During sieges livestock was kept there.

★ Glacis and Covered Way
Across the moat, a walled area known as the "covered way" shielded soldiers firing on the enemy. Leading up to the wall, a slope (the "glacis") protected the fort from cannon fire.

The ravelin guarded the entrance from enemy attack.

The inner drawbridge and portcullis, built of ironclad pine beams, were the fort's final defenses.

COQUINA

This sedimentary limestone rock, formed by billions of compacted seashells and corals, had the consistency of hard cheese when waterlogged and was easy to quarry. It hardened as it dried but could still absorb the impact of a cannonball without shattering. During the siege of 1740, the English attackers fired projectiles that buried themselves in the fort's coquina walls. Legend has it that they were then dug out and fired back.

The thick coquina walls of the powder magazine

VISITORS' CHECKLIST

1 Castillo Drive, St. Augustine.
(904) 829-6506. 8:45am–5:15pm (last admission 4:45pm) daily. Dec 25. limited. call ahead for details.
W www.nps.gov/casa/

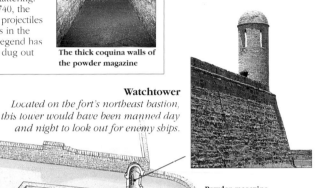

Watchtower
Located on the fort's northeast bastion, this tower would have been manned day and night to look out for enemy ships.

British room

Chapel

Powder magazine

Water battery

Sea wall

★ Gun Deck
From here, cannons could reach targets up to 3 miles (5 km) away. Strategic positioning made a deadly crossfire.

The shot furnace, built in 1844 by the US Army, was designed to heat up cannon balls. The red-hot "shot" could set enemy ships on fire.

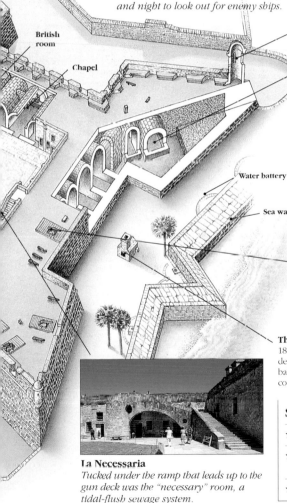

La Necessaria
Tucked under the ramp that leads up to the gun deck was the "necessary" room, a tidal-flush sewage system.

STAR FEATURES

★ **Guard Rooms**

★ **Glacis and Covered Way**

★ **Gun Deck**

Marineland Ocean Resort

Road map E2. Flagler Co. 9507 Ocean Shore Blvd, Marineland. **(** *(904) 460-1275.* St. Augustine. daily. Dec 25.
W www.marineland.net

A POPULAR ATTRACTION and resort, Marineland started life as a film facility in the late 1930s and can claim to be the original Florida marine park. Perennial favorites – the sea lion and dolphin shows – are scheduled regularly, and you can see divers feed sharks and moray eels in the Oceanarium.

Andrew, the hurricane that devastated Florida, also almost destroyed this park. It was placed on the National Register of Historic Places, and Marineland has been rebuilt, exhibits reconstructed, and the park, which many consider the epitome of a Florida tourist site, has been saved.

The 1938 Marineland complex, a pleasing blend of old and new

Washington Oaks State Gardens

Road map E2. Flagler Co. 6400 N Ocean Shore Blvd, 2 miles (3 km) S of Marineland. **(** *(904) 446-6780.* St. Augustine. daily.

BENEATH A SHADY canopy of oaks and palms, 400 acres (162 ha) of former plantation land have been transformed into lovely gardens planted with hydrangeas, azaleas, and ferns. There is also a rose garden and trails through a coastal hammock to the

Ruins of the 19th-century sugar mill at Bulow Plantation

Matanzas River. Across the A1A a boardwalk leads to the beach, which is strewn with coquina boulders *(see p201)* and tidal pools that have been eroded out of the soft stone.

Bulow Plantation Ruins State Historic Site

Road map E2. Flagler Co. Old Kings Rd, 3 miles (5 km) S of SR 100. **(** *(904) 517-2084.* Daytona Beach. daily.

SOMEWHAT OFF the beaten track west of Flagler Beach, the ruins of this 19th-century plantation stand in a dense hammock where sugar cane once grew. The site is part of the 4,675 acres (1,890 ha) of land adjacent to a creek that Major Charles Bulow bought in 1821. His slaves cleared half this area and planted rice and cotton as well as sugar cane. The plantation, known as Bulowville, was abandoned after Indian attacks during the Seminole Wars *(see pp44–5)*.

Today, Bulow Creek is a state canoe trail, and you can rent canoes to explore this lovely backwater. On its banks are the foundations of the plantation house, and from here it's a ten-minute stroll through the forest to a clearing where the ruins of the old sugar mill still stand. These resemble the mysterious remains of some long-lost ancient South American temple.

Ormond Beach

Road map E2. Volusia Co. 50,000. Daytona Beach. 126 E Orange Ave, Daytona Beach (904) 255-0415.
W www.ormondbeach.org

ORMOND BEACH was one of the earliest winter resorts on Henry Flagler's railroad *(see pp46–7)*. No longer standing, his fashionable Ormond Hotel boasted a star-studded guest list including Henry Ford and John D. Rockefeller.

Rockefeller bought a house just across the street from the hotel in 1918 – prompted by overhearing that another guest was paying less; despite

The Rockefeller Room in The Casements, Ormond Beach

his immense wealth, the millionaire chief of Standard Oil guarded his nickels and dimes closely. His winter home, **The Casements**, has been restored and today functions as a museum and cultural center. Inside are examples of Rockefeller-era memorabilia, which include the great man's high-sided wicker beach chair with glazed portholes. There's also a period-style room and a rather incongruous Hungarian arts and crafts display.

A short walk from The Casements, the **Ormond Memorial Art Museum** is set in

Old Flagler engine, Ormond Beach

a small but charming tropical garden. Shady paths wind around lily ponds inhabited by basking turtles and flanked by stands of bamboo and lush vegetation. The museum itself hosts frequently changing exhibitions of works by contemporary Florida artists.

🏛 The Casements
25 Riverside Drive. **📞** (904) 676-3216. **◯** Mon–Sat. **◯** public hols. **♿ ✆**
🏛 Ormond Memorial Art Museum
78 E Granada Blvd. **📞** (904) 676-3347. **◯** daily. **◯** public hols. **🎫 ♿**

Daytona Beach ⑫

Road map E2. Volusia Co. **👥** 64,000. **✈ 🚌 ℹ** 126 E Orange Ave, (904) 255-0415.

EXTENDING SOUTH from Ormond Beach is brash and boisterous Daytona Beach. As many as 200,000 students descend on the resort for the Spring Break (see p32), even though Daytona has tried to discourage them. Its famous 23-mile (37-km) beach is one of the few in Florida where cars are allowed on the sands, a hangover from the days when motor enthusiasts raced on the beaches (see p205).

Daytona is still a mecca for motorsports fans. The nearby speedway (see p204) draws huge crowds, especially during the Speedweek in February and the Motorcycle Weeks in March and October.

Downtown Daytona, known simply as "Mainland," lies across the Halifax River from the beach. Most of the action, though, takes place on the beach, which is lined with a wall of hotels. The old-fashioned Boardwalk is both nostalgic and tacky, with concerts in the bandstand, arcades, go-karts, cotton candy, and fast food. The gondola skyride glides above Ocean Pier, while down on the beach itself, jet skis, windsurfers, buggies, and beach bicycles can be rented.

Across the Halifax River, in the restored downtown area, the **Halifax Historical Society Museum** occupies a 1910 bank building decorated with fancy pilasters and murals. Local history displays include a model of the Boardwalk in about 1938, with chicken-feather palm trees, a Ferris wheel, and scores of miniature people.

West of downtown, exhibits at the excellent **Museum of Arts and Sciences** cover a broad range of subjects. The Florida prehistory section is dominated by the 13-ft (4-m) skeleton of a giant sloth, while Arts in America features fine and decorative arts from 1640–1920. Additionally, there are notable Cuban and African collections and a planetarium.

Miss Perkins (c. 1840) by J Whiting
Stock, Museum of Arts and Sciences

Gamble Place is run by the same museum. Built in 1907 for James N. Gamble, of Procter & Gamble, this primitive hunting lodge sits on a bluff above Spruce Creek, surrounded by open porches. The furnishings inside are all period pieces. Tours are by reservation only through the museum; these also take in the Snow White House, which was built in 1938 for Gamble's great-grandchildren, and is an exact copy of the one in the 1937 Disney classic.

🏛 Halifax Historical Society Museum
252 S Beach St. **📞** (904) 255-6976. **◯** Tue–Sat. **◯** public hols. **🎫 ♿**
🅦 www.halifaxhistorical.org
🏛 Museum of Arts and Sciences
1040 Museum Blvd. **📞** (386) 255-0285. **◯** Tue–Sun. **◯** public hols. **🎫 ♿ Gamble Place**

Cars cruising the hard-packed sands of Daytona Beach

Daytona International Speedway ⓭

Road map E2. Volusia Co. 1801 W
International Speedway Blvd. 📞 *(904)
254-2700.* 🚌 *Daytona.* 🚍 *9 from
bus terminal at 209 Bethune Blvd.*
◯ *daily.* ● *Dec 25.* 🎦 ♿
Ⓦ *www.daytonaintlspeedway.com*

D AYTONA'S VERY OWN "World
Center of Racing," the
Daytona International Speedway, attracts thousands of race
fans and visitors every year.
People come from around the
world to attend the eight major
racing weekends held annually
at the track – which can hold
over 110,000 spectators. The
Speedway is host to
NASCAR (National
Association for
Stock Car Auto
Racing) meets –
the Daytona 500
being the most
famous – and sports car,
motorcycle, and go-karting
races. There is a full program
of events such as charity
bike-a-thons, vintage car
rallies, superbike spectaculars,
and production car tests.

**1953 red Corvette in the
Klassix Auto Museum**

Tickets for each Daytona 500
are sold out a year in advance,
but visitors can relive the experience at DAYTONA USA, the
ultimate motorsports attraction
in the visitor center. A film
featuring behind-the-scenes
action and spectacular in-car
camera shots filmed during a
recent Daytona 500 is one of
the state-of-the-art exhibits
here. Visitors can test their
own stock cars using computers, design and
take part in a
simulated inter-
active pit stop,
and try their skill
at race commen-
tary. A half-hour
tram tour around the speedway track is available on days
when no races take place.

ENVIRONS: The nearby **Klassix
Auto Museum** has an impressive collection of Corvettes,
one for each year since 1953.
There are also vintage motorcycles, racing memorabilia,
and the Batmobile on display.
🏛 **Klassix Auto Museum**
2909 W International Speedway Blvd.
📞 *(904) 252-3800.* ◯ *daily.* 🎦 ♿
Ⓦ *www.klassixauto.com*

The Daytona 500, held each February at Daytona International Speedway

Ponce de Leon Inlet Lighthouse ⓮

Road map E2. Volusia Co. 4931 S
Peninsula Drive. 📞 *(904) 761-1821.*
◯ *daily.* ● *Dec 25.* 🎦 ♿
Ⓦ *www.ponceinlet.org*

T HIS IMPOSING red brick
lighthouse dates from 1887
and guards the entrance to a
hazardous inlet at the tip of the
Daytona peninsula. Recently
restored, the lighthouse tapers
skyward for 175 ft (53 m), its
beacon is visible 19 miles (30
km) out to sea, and there are
far-reaching views from the
windswept observation deck
reached by a 203-step spiral
staircase. One of the former
keepers' cottages at its base
has been restored to its 1890s
appearance, another holds the
small Museum of the Sea, and
a third contains a magnificent
17-ft (5-m) high Fresnel lens.

DAYTONA INTERNATIONAL SPEEDWAY

LAKE LLOYD

Williamson Beltway

DAYTONA
BEACH

W International Speedway Blvd ㉒

I-4
I-95

KEY

☐ Visitor's center

☐ Track

☐ Grandstand

☐ Winton tower

0 meters   500

0 yards   500

**The striking Ponce de Leon Inlet
lighthouse south of Daytona Beach**

The Birthplace of Speed

Daytona's love affair with the car started in 1903, when the first timed automobile runs took place on the sands at Ormond Beach, the official "Birthplace of Speed." That year, Alexander Winton achieved a land speed record of 68 mph (109 km/h). The speed trials were enormously popular and attracted large crowds. Wealthy motor enthusiasts gathered at Henry Flagler's Ormond Hotel (see p202), and included the likes of Harvey Firestone and Henry Ford. Speed trials continued until 1935, when Malcolm Campbell set the last world record on the beach. Stock cars began racing at Ormond Beach in 1936, and the first Daytona 200 motorcycle race took place there the following year. Development forced the racetrack to be moved in 1948; in 1959 Daytona International Speedway opened and racing on the beach was abandoned altogether.

1936 Harley-Davidson

RACING ON THE BEACH

In 1902, a guest at the Ormond Hotel noticed just how easy it was to drive his car on the hard sandy beach. He organized the first speed trials, which continued for the next 32 years.

***Ransom E. Olds' Pirate** was the first car to race on Ormond Beach in 1902. The first official race was held in 1903, when Olds challenged Alexander Winton and Oscar Hedstrom on a motorcycle. Winton won in his car,* Bullet No 1.

*The **Bluebird Streamliner** was driven to a new world record for the measured mile by Malcolm Campbell at Ormond Beach in 1935. Powered by a Rolls-Royce engine, the car reached speeds of just over 276 mph (444 km/h).*

THE "WORLD CENTER OF RACING"

In 1953 Bill France, who had entered the inaugural stock car race, saw that the growth of Daytona Beach would soon put an end to the beach races. He proposed the construction of Daytona International Speedway, today one of the world's leading race tracks.

***Go-karts** look like the fun machines that you can race on vacation, but the karts that compete at Daytona manage speeds of over 81 mph (130 km/h).*

***Lee Petty** won the first Daytona 500 at Daytona International Speedway in 1959, beating Johnny Beauchamp, his fellow competitor, by a mere 2 ft (50 cm). The 500-mile (800-km) competition was watched by a crowd of 41,000 and involved 59 cars.*

Blue Spring State Park ⑮

Road map E2. Volusia Co. 2100 W French Ave, Orange City.
📞 *(904) 775-3663.* ⬜ *daily.* 🚫 ♿
🌐 www.dep.state.fl.us/parks

ONE OF THE country's largest first-magnitude artesian springs, Blue Spring pours out around 100 million gal (450 million liters) of water a day. The temperature of the water is at a constant 68° F (20° C), and consequently the park is a favorite winter refuge for manatees *(see p236).* Between the months of November and March, when the manatees escape the cooler waters of the St. Johns River, you can see them from the park's elevated boardwalks. Snorkeling or scuba diving are available in the turquoise waters of the spring head, as is canoeing on the St. Johns. **Thursby House**, atop one of the park's ancient shell mounds, was built in the late 19th century.

ENVIRONS: About 2 miles (3 km) north as the crow flies is wooded **Hontoon Island State Park**. Reached by a free passenger ferry from Hontoon Landing, the island has an 80-ft (24-m) observation tower, camping and picnic areas, and a nature trail. Canoes and fishing skiffs can also be rented.

In 1955 a rare wooden owl totem made by the ancient local Timucua Indians *(see pp38–9)* was found here.

🏕 **Hontoon Island State Park**
2309 River Ridge Rd, De Land.
📞 *(904) 736-5309.* ⬜ *daily.* 🚫

FLORIDA'S BUBBLING SPRINGS

Most of Florida's 320 known springs are located in the upper half of the state. The majority are artesian springs, formed by waters forced up deep fissures from underground aquifers (rock deposits containing water). Those that gush over 100 cu ft (3 cu m) per second are known as first-magnitude springs.

Filtered through the rock, the water is extremely pure and sometimes high in salts and minerals. These properties, plus the sheer beauty of the springs, have long attracted visitors for recreational and health purposes.

Juniper Springs in Ocala National Forest, adapted for swimmers in the 1930s

Sanford ⑯

Road map E2. Seminole Co.
🏘 *45,000.* ⓘ *400 E 1st St, (407) 322-2212.* 🚂 *inc Auto Train.* 🚌 *Lynx buses from Orlando (see p363).*

BUILT DURING the Seminole Wars *(see pp43–5),* Fort Mellon was the first permanent settlement on Lake Monroe. Sanford was founded nearby in the 1870s. It became a major inland port thanks to the commercial steamboat services, which eventually also brought Florida's adventurous early tourists *(see p46).*

Restored downtown Sanford dates from the 1880s, the height of this Steamboat era. Several of the lovely old red brick buildings (a rarity in Florida) house antique shops, and the area can easily be explored on foot in a couple of hours. Today's visitors are more likely to arrive on the Auto Train *(see p360)* than by river, but short pleasure cruises are still available.

Sanford town sign

Mount Dora ⑰

Road map E2. Lake Co. 🏘 *11,000.*
🚂 *Sanford.* ⓘ *341 Alexander St, (352) 383-2165.*

SET AMONG THE citrus groves of Lake County, this town is one of the prettiest Victorian settlements left in the state. Its name comes from both the relatively high local elevation of 184 ft (56 m) and the small lake on which it sits. The town was originally known as Royellou, after Roy, Ella, and Louis, the children of the first postmaster.

Mount Dora's attractive tree-lined streets are laid out on a bluff above the lakeshore, and a 3-mile (5-km) historic tour map is available from the chamber of commerce. The tour takes a scenic route around quiet neighborhoods of late 19th-century clapboard homes and the sympathetically restored downtown historic district, with its tempting array of stores and antique shops.

On Donnelly Street, the splendid Donnelly House, now a Masonic Hall, is a notable example of ornate Steamboat architecture, adorned with pinnacles and a cupola.

Children playing in front of Thursby House, Blue Spring State Park

Shingles and gingerbread decoration on Donnelly House, Mount Dora

Nearby, the small Royellou Museum depicts local history in the old fire station, which later became the town jail. Down on Lake Dora, fishing and water sports are available.

🏛 **Royellou Museum**
450 Royellou Lane. 【 (352) 383-0006. ◯ Thu–Sun. ● Thanksgiving, Dec 25, Jan 1. 🚻 limited.

Ocala National Forest ⑱

Road map E2. Lake Co/Marion Co. ◯ daily. 💰 to camp site & swimming areas. 🚻 🅰 **Visitor Center** 3199 NE Co. Rd. 【 (352) 236-0288. **Juniper Springs canoe rental** (352) 625-2808. ☒ www.onf.net

BETWEEN OCALA and the St. Johns River, the world's largest sand pine forest covers 366,000 acres (148,000 ha), crisscrossed by spring-fed rivers and numerous hiking trails. It is one of the last refuges of the endangered Florida black bear and also home to many more common animals such as deer and otter. Birds, including bald eagles, ospreys, barred owls, the non-native wild turkey, and many species of waders (which frequent the river swamp areas), can all be spotted here.

Dozens of hiking trails vary in length from boardwalks and short loop trails of under a mile (1.5 km) to a 66-mile (106-km) stretch of the cross-state National Scenic Trail (see p343). Bass-fishing is popular on the many lakes scattered through the forest, and there are swimming holes, picnic areas, and camp grounds at recreation areas such as Salt Springs, Alexander Springs, and Fore Lake.

Canoe rental is widely available; the 7-mile (11-km) canoe run down Juniper Creek from the Juniper Springs Recreation Area is one of the finest in the state, but book in advance. Bird-watching is particularly good along the Salt Springs Trail, and wood ducks congregate on Lake Dorr.

You can pick up information and guides at the main visitor center on the western edge of the forest, or at the smaller centers at Salt Springs and Lake Dorr, both on Route 19.

Silver Springs ⑲

Road map E2. Marion Co. 5656 E Silver Springs Blvd. 【 (352) 236-2121. ◯ daily. 💰 🚻 limited. ☒ www.silversprings.com

GLASS-BOTTOMED boat trips at Silver Springs have been revealing the natural wonders of the world's largest artesian spring since 1878.

Today, Florida's oldest commercial tourist attraction offers not only the famous glass-bottomed boat rides but Jeep safaris and "Jungle Cruises," which travel through the Florida outback, where the early Tarzan movies starring Johnny Weismuller were filmed. Wild Waters, located next to the springs, is a lively family-oriented water park.

ENVIRONS: On a quieter note, at **Silver River State Park**, 2 miles (3 km) southeast, you can take a lovely 15-minute walk along a trail through a hardwood hammock and a cypress swamp area, leading to a swimming hole in a bend of the crystal clear river.

🦌 **Silver River State Park**
7165 NE 7th St, Ocala 【 (352) 236-7140. ◯ daily. 💰 🚻

The Jungle Cruise, one of many attractions at Silver Springs

The Young Shepherdess (1868) by Bougereau, Appleton Museum

Ocala ⓴

Road map D2. Marion Co.
🏛 65,000. 🚗 🚌 🚹 *Chamber of Commerce, 110 E Silver Springs Blvd, (352) 629-8051.*

SURROUNDED BY undulating pastures edged by mile upon mile of white wooden fences, Ocala is the seat of Marion County and center of Florida's thoroughbred horse industry. The grass hereabouts is enriched by the subterranean limestone aquifer *(see p206)*, and the calcium-rich grazing helps to contribute to the light, strong bones of championship horses. Florida's equine industry has produced more than 37 champions, including five Kentucky Derby winners.

There are over 400 thoroughbred farms and specialized breeding centers around Ocala. Many are open for visits, which are usually free of charge. Expect to see Arabians, Paso Finos, and miniature ponies on the farms; contact the Ocala Chamber of Commerce for up-to-date information regarding farm visits.

The other reason to stop off in this area is to visit the **Appleton Museum of Art**, east of Ocala. Built in 1984 of Italian marble by the industrialist and horsebreeder Arthur I. Appleton, the museum houses stunning art from around the world. His eclectic collection includes pre-Columbian and European antiquities, Oriental and African pieces, and Meissen porcelain and is known for its strong core of mainstream 19th-century European art.

🏛 **Appleton Museum of Art**
4333 NE Silver Springs Blvd. 🅲 *(352) 236-7100.* 🅾 *daily.* ⬤ *public hols.* 🅿 ♿

Marjorie Kinnan Rawlings State Historic Site ㉑

Road map D2. Alachua Co. S CR 325, Cross Creek. 🅲 *(352) 466-3672.* 🚌 *Ocala.* 🅾 *grounds daily; house Thu–Sun.* ⬤ *Aug–Sep.* 🅿 ♿ 🅿

THE AUTHOR Marjorie Kinnan Rawlings arrived in the tiny settlement of Cross Creek, which she was later to describe fondly as "a bend in a country road," in 1928. Her rambling farmhouse remains largely unchanged, nestling in a well-tended citrus grove where chickens peck and ducks waddle up from the banks of Orange Lake.

The writer remained here through the 1930s and then visited on and off until her death in 1953. The local scenery and characters fill her autobiographical novel,

Herlong Inn, stick collection

Cross Creek (1942), while the big scrub country to the south inspired her Pulitzer prize-winning novel *The Yearling* (1938), a coming-of-age story about a boy and his fawn.

Guided tours around the site explore the Cracker-style homestead, built in the 1880s, which has been imaginatively preserved and contains original Rawlings' furnishings: bookcases full of contemporary writings by authors such as John Steinbeck and Ernest Hemingway, a secret liquor cabinet, a typewriter, and a sunhat on the veranda. Lived-in touches like fresh flowers make it look as though the owner has just popped out for a stroll around the garden.

Micanopy ㉒

Road map D2. Alachua Co. 🏛 650.
🚹 *30 East University Ave, Gainesville, (352) 374-5260.*

ESTABLISHED IN 1821, Florida's second oldest permanent white settlement was a trading post on Indian lands, originally known as Wanton. Renamed Micanopy in 1826, after an Indian chief, this time-warp village is now as decorous as they come and a haven for filmmakers and antique lovers. Planted with live oaks trailing Spanish moss, the main street, Cholokka Boulevard, is lined with Victorian homes and a strip of historic, brick-fronted shops stuffed with bric-a-brac and craft galleries. Here, too, is the grandest building in Micanopy, the imposing red-brick antebellum **Herlong Mansion**, supported by four massive Corinthian columns. Built by a 19th-century lumber baron, today it serves as a bed and breakfast *(see p306)*.

Micanopy's picturesque cemetery, established in 1825, is located on a canopied street off Seminary Road, en route to I-75. Shaded by spreading live oaks and majestic cedars, and covered with a carpet of velvety moss, it is a tranquil oasis well worth seeking out.

The airy porch where author Marjorie Kinnan Rawlings once wrote

Gainesville

Road map D2. Alachua Co.
🏛 *97,000.* ✈ 🚌 ℹ *300 East
University Avenue, (352) 334 7100.*

A UNIVERSITY TOWN, the cultural capital of north central Florida and home of the Gators football team, Gainesville is a comfortable blend of town and gown. In the restored downtown historic district are brick buildings that date from the 1880s to the 1920s, several of which house cafés and restaurants. The campus is dotted with fraternity houses and two important museums.

Leave plenty of time for the first of these, the excellent **Florida Museum of Natural History**. The natural science collections contain over 10 million fossil specimens, plus superb butterfly and shell collections. There are displays dedicated to the various Florida environments and an anthropological journey through the state's history up to the 19th century. Also on campus, the striking **Samuel P. Harn Museum of Art** is one of the largest and best-equipped university art museums in the country. Its permanent collection of fine art and crafts includes Asian ceramics, African ceremonial objects, Japanese woodcuts, and European and American paintings.

🏛 **Florida Museum of Natural History**
Hull Rd at SW 34th St. 📞 *(352) 392-1721.* ⏲ *daily.* ⬤ *Dec 25.* ♿
🌐 www.flmnh.ufl.edu

🏛 **Samuel P. Harn Museum of Art**
Hull Road (off SW 34th St.). 📞 *(352) 392-9826.* ⏲ *Tue–Sun.* ⬤ *public hols.* ♿ 🌐 www.arts.ufl.edu/harn

ENVIRONS: Just southwest of town, the lovely **Kanapaha Botanical Gardens** are at the height of their beauty from June to September, although visitors in springtime are rewarded by masses of azaleas in bloom. A trail circles the sloping 62-acre site, whose beauty was first noted by the naturalist William Bartram *(see p43)* in the late 1800s. The paths meander beneath vine-covered arches and through bamboo groves. Other distinct areas include a desert garden, a lakeside bog garden, and a colorful hummingbird garden.

Gainesville's soft drink

🌿 **Kanapaha Botanical Gardens**
4700 SW 58th Drive (off Route 24). 📞 *(352) 372-4981.* ⏲ *Fri–Wed.* ⬤ *Dec 25.* 🎦 ♿

Lichen-stained gravestones in Micanopy's atmospheric cemetery

ENVIRONS: During the 17th century one of the largest and most successful Spanish cattle ranches in Florida was located to the north of present-day Micanopy. Cattle, horses, and hogs once grazed on the lush grass of **Payne's Prairie State Preserve**, where a small herd of wild American bison can sometimes be seen, as well as more than 200 species of local and migratory birds.

Passing through the preserve is the pleasant 17-mile (27-km) **Gainesville–Hawthorne State Trail**, a rail trail used by hikers, riders, and cyclists.

🦌 **Paynes Prairie State Preserve**
US 441, 1 mile (0.5 km) N of Micanopy.
📞 *(352) 466-3397.* ⏲ *daily.* 🎦 ♿
🌐 www.afn.org/~pprairie

Giant Amazonian water lilies, the late summer highlight of the bog garden in Kanapaha Botanical Gardens

THE PANHANDLE

HERE IS A SAYING IN FLORIDA *that "the farther north you go, the farther south you get." Certainly, the Panhandle has a history and sensibility closer to that of the Deep South than to the lower part of the state. Not only geography and history but climate and even time (the western Panhandle is one hour behind the rest of the state) distinguish this intriguing region from other parts of Florida.*

The Panhandle was the site of the first attempt by the Spanish at colonizing Florida and much subsequent fighting by colonial powers. A community was set up near present-day Pensacola in 1559, predating St. Augustine, but was abandoned after a hurricane. It later re-emerged and was the main settlement in the region until the 1820s, when Tallahassee was chosen as the capital of the new Territory of Florida (*see p44*). The site of the new city, equidistant from St. Augustine and Pensacola, was a compromise – the precise location reputedly being the meeting point of two scouts sent out on horseback from the two cities. Today, Tallahassee is a dignified state capital with elegant architecture but a small-town air. Thanks to the lumber and cotton trade, the 1800s saw spells of prosperity, but the region was bypassed by the influx of wealth that came to other parts of Florida with the laying of the railroads.

Tourism in the Panhandle is a more recent development, even though its fine white-sand beaches are unparalleled in the state. This stretch of coast has become increasingly popular with vacationers from the Deep South, but it is still often overlooked by overseas visitors. At the eastern end of the Panhandle, in the area known as the "Big Bend," the family resorts give way to quaint historic coastal towns like Cedar Key – a laid-back fishing village reminiscent of old-time Key West. Inland, large preserves and parks incorporating forests, springs, and navigable rivers provide the main attraction.

One of the Panhandle's many dazzling quartz sand beaches, near Pensacola

◁ Tallahassee's Old Capitol Building, in the shadow of its modern replacement

Exploring the Panhandle

M OST VISITORS TO THE Panhandle head straight for the famous beach resorts that stretch in an arc between Pensacola and Panama City Beach. Ideal for family vacations, resorts such as Fort Walton Beach and Destin offer all kinds of accommodations as well as activities ranging from water sports and deep-sea fishing to golf and tennis. While most attention is focused on the coast, the rest of the Panhandle should not be ignored – the resorts can be used as a good base for forays into the hilly, pine-forested interior, where it is possible to escape the crowds. Excellent canoeing can be enjoyed on the Blackwater and the Suwannee rivers, while near Tallahassee you will find some of Florida's prettiest countryside, crossed by unspoiled canopied roads.

Quietwater Beach, near Pensacola on Santa Rosa Island

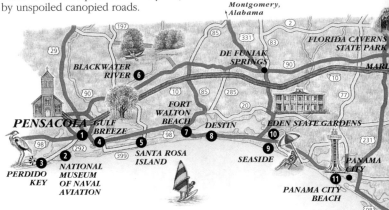

SIGHTS AT A GLANCE

The elegant, plantation-style mansion at Eden State Gardens

GETTING AROUND

Although the Amtrak line runs through the region, following the line of I-10, a car is essential for exploring the Panhandle. There are two main driving routes: the fast but dull I-10, which streaks from Pensacola to Tallahassee and then on to the Atlantic Coast; and US 98, which parallels the coast all the way from Pensacola to the so-called "Big Bend," where it links up with the main north-south Gulf Coast highway, US 19. Country roads in the Panhandle are generally quiet, but be on the alert for logging trucks pulling out of concealed forest exits.

Waterfront buildings at the popular harbor of Destin

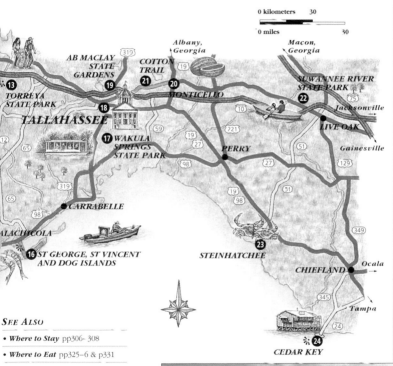

0 kilometers 30

0 miles 30

Albany, Georgia

Macon, Georgia

AB MACLAY STATE GARDENS (319) **COTTON TRAIL** (19)

19 **21** **20** **MONTICELLO** **SUWANNEE RIVER STATE PARK**

13 **22**

TORREYA STATE PARK **18** (10) *Jacksonville* (75)

TALLAHASSEE

(12) (65) (59) **17 WAKULLA SPRINGS STATE PARK** (19) (27) **PERRY** (51) *Gainesville*

(98) (27) (129)

(319) (19) (98) (51)

(65)

(98) **CARRABELLE**

ALACHICOLA (349)

16 ST GEORGE, ST VINCENT AND DOG ISLANDS **23**

STEINHATCHEE **CHIEFLAND** *Ocala*

(345) *Tampa*

(24)

24

CEDAR KEY

SEE ALSO

- **Where to Stay** pp306–308

- **Where to Eat** pp325–6 & p331

KEY

	Interstate highway
	Major highway
	Secondary route
	Scenic route
	River
	Tram

Pelicans enjoying the peace and quiet of Apalachicola

Street-by-Street: Pensacola ❶

T HE CITY'S FIRST SETTLERS were a party of Spanish colonists, led by Tristan de Luna *(see p41)*, who sailed into Pensacola Bay in 1559. Their settlement survived only two years before being wiped out by a hurricane. The Spanish returned, but Pensacola changed hands frequently: in the space of just over 300 years the Spanish, French, English, Confederate, and US flags all flew over the city. Pensacola took off in the 1880s, when much of the present downtown district was built. This area features a diverse collection of architectural styles, ranging from quaint colonial cottages to elegant Classical-Revival homes built during the late 19th-century timber boom. The route shown here focuses on the area known as Historic Pensacola Village *(see p216)*.

Lavalle House
The simple plan and bright color scheme of this early 19th-century two-room cottage was designed to appeal to its French Creole immigrant tenants.

Civil War Soldiers Museum
Exhibits here focus on the life of the ordinary soldier and include medical equipment, antique weaponry, and contemporary accounts of the Battle of Gettysburg.

The Museum of Industry
recalls Pensacola's timber and maritime trades using a reconstructed sawmill and ship's chandlery.

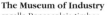

★ TT Wentworth Museum
A broad collection of Florida memorabilia, such as this 1870s bed, fill this unusual museum.

Pensacola Museum of Art
The old city jail, dating from 1908, was converted into a museum in the 1950s. This William Nell landscape is among the broad array of art exhibited.

A British officers' compound has been excavated in this parking lot. The exposed foundations form part of the city's Colonial Archaeologic Trail *(see p216)*.

Steamboat House
Dating from the mid-19th-century steamboat era (see p46), this delightful house echoes the shape of a riverboat. It comes complete with veranda "decks."

VISITORS' CHECKLIST

Road map A1. Escambia Co.
360,000. 5 miles (8 km) N.
980 E Heinburg St, (850) 433-4966. 505 W Burgess Rd, (850) 476-4800. 1401 E Gregory St, (850) 434-1234.
Fiesta of Five Flags (Jun).

★ Seville Square
Shaded by live oaks and magnolia trees, Seville Square lies at the heart of the Seville District, which was laid out by the British in the 1770s.

Fountain Square centers around a fountain decorated with plaques showing local features.

0 meters 200
0 yards 200

Dorr House, a fine Greek-Revival mansion, is the last of its kind in western Florida.

KEY

– – – Suggested route

★ Museum of Commerce
A fully equipped print workshop is one of the many interesting exhibits in the museum's cleverly constructed late-Victorian streetscape.

STAR SIGHTS

★ TT Wentworth Museum

★ Seville Square

★ Museum of Commerce

Exploring Pensacola

SEVERAL HISTORIC DISTRICTS provide the most interesting areas to explore in Pensacola. Foremost is the old downtown district, Historic Pensacola Village, centered on pretty Zaragoza Street. Farther north, in the North Hill Preservation District, you can stroll past the homes built by prominent local professionals and merchants during the 19th-century timber boom. Between the two, Palafox Street is a busy commercial district with a number of distinctive buildings dating from 1900–20.

Downtown Pensacola is linked by two bridges to its barrier island resort satellite, Pensacola Beach *(see p222)*. While sightseeing is focused on the mainland, visitors often stay in hotels by the beach, now largely recovered from the onslaught of 1995's Hurricane Opal.

Cell doors now standing open, Pensacola Museum of Art

Guides in 19th-century costume in Historic Pensacola Village

🏛 Historic Pensacola Village

Tivoli House, 205 E Zaragoza St. 📞 *(850) 595-5985.* ⏰ *Tue–Sat.* ● *public hols.* 🏛 ♿ 🅿

This collection of museums and historic houses is located in Pensacola's oldest quarter, called the Seville District. You can enjoy an unhurried stroll through the village's streets which offer a taste of the city as it was in the 19th century.

For a more in-depth look, you should take one of the guided tours that depart twice daily from Tivoli House on Zaragoza Street; in tourist season, tour guides liven up the proceedings by dressing in period costume. The tours visit the simply furnished French Creole Lavalle House (1805) and the gracious Dorr House (1871). Other properties, while not included on the tour, are open to visitors. A single ticket, available from Tivoli House, covers the tour and entrance to all village properties over two days. You

will need this ticket to visit the Museum of Industry and Museum of Commerce. Housed in a late 19th-century warehouse, the Museum of Industry on Church Street provides an informative introduction to Pensacola's early development. Exhibits cover brick-making, fishing, transportation, and the lumber trade.

Forming a backdrop to Zaragoza Street's Museum of Commerce is a Victorian street scene complete with reconstructed stores including a printer's shop with a working press, a pharmacy, a saddlery, and an old-time music store.

Overlooking leafy Seville Square is Old Christ Church, built in 1832 and the oldest church building in Florida still standing on its original site. It is currently being restored.

🏛 TT Wentworth Florida State Museum

330 Jefferson St. 📞 *(850) 595-5990.* ⏰ *Mon–Sat.* ● *public hols.* 🏛 ♿

This museum is laid out in the former City Hall, an imposing Spanish Renaissance Revival building. The founder's eclectic collections include West Florida memorabilia and

weird and wonderful oddities from all over the world. These run the gamut from arrowheads and a shrunken head from pre-Columbian times to a 1930s telephone exchange and old Coca-Cola bottles.

The museum contains well thought-out historical displays and dioramas illustrating points along Pensacola's Colonial Archaeological Trail, which links remains of fortifications dating from 1752–1821; you can pick up a leaflet explaining the trail's sites.

A ticket to Historic Pensacola Village includes admission to the TT Wentworth too.

🏛 Pensacola Museum of Art

407 S Jefferson St. 📞 *(850) 432-6247.* ⏰ *Tue–Sat.* ● *Jul 4, Thanksgiving, Dec 25, Jan 1.* 🏛 ♿ W www.artsnwfl.org/pma

The cells of the old city jail, complete with steel-barred doors, have taken on a new life as whitewashed galleries for this Museum. Frequently changing exhibitions draw on the museum's broad-based collections, which include pre-Columbian pottery, 19th-century satinware glass, and Roy Lichtenstein's Pop Art.

The Spanish Renaissance-style home of the TT Wentworth Museum

🏛 Civil War Soldiers Museum

108 S Palafox Place. 📞 *(850) 469-1900.* ⭘ *Tue–Sat.* ⬤ *Thanksgiving, Dec 25, Jan 1.* 🏷 ♿
Ⓦ www.cwmuseum.org

Designed to appeal both to experts of the Civil War and to the amateur enthusiast (but biased a bit toward the former), this museum is devoted to the main characters and campaigns of the Civil War *(see pp44–5).*

A soundtrack of marching songs, period weaponry, uniforms, and field kits illustrate different aspects of what, in many southern states, is sometimes still called the War of Northern Aggression. Among the exhibits are an officer's liquor chest, snipers' glasses, and even a gruesome medical section.

🏠 North Hill Preservation District

This historic district (stretching for about ten blocks from Wright Street, north of Pensacola Historic Village) features elegant late 19th- and early

McCreary House in the North Hill Preservation District

20th-century houses. They were built on the site of former British and Spanish forts, and even now cannon balls are occasionally dug up in their tree-shaded gardens. All the houses are privately owned. Among the most striking is the veranda-fronted McCreary House *(see p28)* on North Baylen Street, close to the intersection with De Soto Street.

National Museum of Naval Aviation ❷

See pp218–19.

Perdido Key ❸

Road map A1. Escambia Co. Route 292, 12 miles (19 km) W of Pensacola. 🚌 *Pensacola.* 🚍 *Pensacola.* ℹ️ *1401 E Gregory St, Pensacola, (850) 492-4660, (800) 328-0107.*

A 30-MINUTE DRIVE southwest from Pensacola are the pristine shores of Perdido Key, which regularly features in the list of the top 20 US beaches. There are bars and

The extensive, unspoiled sands at Johnson Beach on Perdido Key

restaurants and facilities for water sports, fishing, and diving, or you can simply swim or soak up the sun.

The whole eastern end of the island is accessible only by foot. The road runs as far as the **Johnson Beach Day Use Area**, just east of the bridge from the mainland, from where a boardwalk leads down to the main beach. The sands extend for some 6 miles (10 km) on both gulf and bay sides, and there are facilities for visitors and a ranger station.

On the mainland opposite Perdido Key, **Big Lagoon State Recreation Area** combines stretches of sandy beach with salt-marsh areas offering excellent bird-watching and hiking. You can enjoy sweeping views of the coast from an observation tower.

🏖 Johnson Beach Day Use Area

Johnson Beach Rd, off Route 292. 📞 *(850) 492-7278.* ⭘ *daily.* ⬤ *Dec 25.* 🏷 ♿
✕ Big Lagoon SRA
12301 Gulf Beach Highway. 📞 *(850) 492-1595.* ⭘ *daily.* 🏷 ♿

FLORIDA'S LUMBER BOOM

In the 19th century, the demand for lumber and naval stores including tar and turpentine played an important part in northern Florida's development. Its vast stands of live oaks were particularly popular with shipbuilders for their disease- and decay-resistant wood. Flourishing lumber towns such as Cedar Key *(see p231)* were established, and the fortunes made during the lumber boom of the 1870s–80s were transformed into Pensacola's elegant homes, including Eden Mansion *(see p223).*

By the 1930s, most of Florida's mature hardwood forest had been destroyed, and other building materials and forms of fuel had begun to replace wood. The lumber mills closed, leaving thousands unemployed.

Loggers in the 19th century, who worked long hours of hard manual labor

National Museum of Naval Aviation ②

Beechcraft GB-2 insignia

THIS VAST MUSEUM is set among the runways and hangars of the country's oldest naval air station, founded in 1914. More than 150 aircraft and spacecraft, as well as models, artifacts, technological displays, and works of aviation-related art trace the history of flight – from early wing-and-a-prayer wood and fabric biplanes to the latest state-of-the-art rocketry. Even those who are not great aviation fans will enjoy flying with the Blue Angels display team in the IMAX® theater or testing themselves in the training cockpits. Veteran pilots at the information desk field questions and lend first-hand authenticity to guided tours.

★ Blue Angels
Four former Blue Angels A-4 Sky-hawks are suspended in a dramatic diamond formation from the ceiling of the seven-story glass atrium.

The USS *Cabot* Flight Deck is a life-sized reconstruction of an aircraft carrier deck, complete with a lineup of famous World War II fighter planes.

Sunken Treasures displays two aircraft recovered from Lake Michigan, where they sank during training in World War II.

Flying Tigers
The painted jaws of these World War II fighters were the trademark of the Volunteer Flying Tiger pilots who fought in the skies over China and Burma.

Spirit of Naval Aviation Monument

GALLERY GUIDE
The museum occupies two floors, or "decks," which are divided into two wings joined by an atrium. The west wing is devoted almost entirely to World War II carrier aircraft, while the south wing is more broadly historical. More aircraft can be found on the lawns surrounding the museum.

F-14 Tomcat

Entrance

The IMAX® theater shows dramatic in-flight footage seven times daily.

STAR FEATURES
★ Blue Angels
★ Flight Simulator

Biplane
Early aircraft include World War I training planes and biplanes once favored by circus barnstormers.

K47 Airship
America's "K" type airships performed vital maritime patrol duties during World War II.

The Space Capsule Display has a Skylab Command Module as its centerpiece, alongside several tons of gadgetry and a moon rock.

★ Flight Simulator
The motion-based flight simulator is just one of more than 100 interactive displays designed to convey the complexity and wonder of aviation.

Cockpit trainers provide hands-on lessons on how to fly an aircraft.

Coast Guard Helicopter
A fully equipped rescue helicopter pays tribute to the contribution made by the Coast Guard services to the story of naval aviation.

KEY TO FLOOR PLAN
- WWII/Korean War aircraft
- Early aircraft
- Modern aircraft
- Theater
- Interactive exhibits
- Displays
- Art gallery
- Nonexhibition space

FORT BARRANCAS

Enclosed by water on three sides, the strategic Naval Air Station site was fortified by Spanish colonists in 1698. The original ramparts, built on a bluff (*barranca* in Spanish) overlooking Pensacola Bay, were replaced by a more substantial fort in 1781, and major additions were made by the US Army in the 1840s. The remains of the Spanish and US forts, concealed behind formidable defensive earthworks, are linked by a tunnel. The fort is a few minutes' walk from the museum, where you can arrange to go on a guided tour of the area.

View of the earthworks surrounding Fort Barrancas

Gulf Breeze ❹

Road map A1. Santa Rosa Co. 👥 *6,300.* 🚆 *Pensacola.* 🚌 *Pensacola.* ℹ *1170 Gulf Breeze Parkway, (850) 932-7888.*

THE AFFLUENT community of Gulf Breeze lies at the western end of a promontory reaching out into Pensacola Bay. The area east of the town is heavily wooded and once formed part of the huge swathes of southern woodlands that were earmarked in the 1820s to provide lumber for shipbuilding *(see p217)*.

The **Naval Live Oaks Reservation**, off US 98, was originally a government-owned tree farm and now protects some of the remaining woodland. Visitors can follow trails through 1,300 acres (500 ha) of oak hammock woodlands, sand-hill areas, and wetlands, where wading birds feast off an abundance of marine life. A visitor center dispenses maps and information on local flora and fauna, and also has historical exhibits.

Ten miles (16 km) east of Gulf Breeze, **The Zoo** is a favorite family excursion, with more than 700 animals in residence. You can take a ride on the Safari Line train through 30 acres (12 ha) of land where animals roam freely, catch a show by Ellie the elephant, or stroll through the botanical gardens. Visitors even get the chance to look a giraffe in the eye from the high-rise feeding platform.

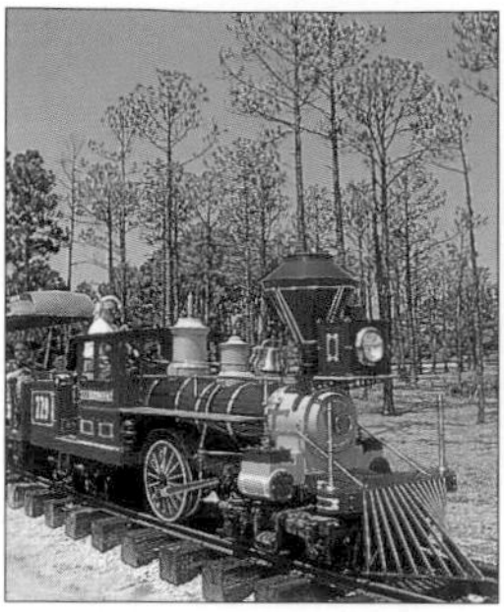

The Safari Line train, on its tour around The Zoo, Gulf Breeze

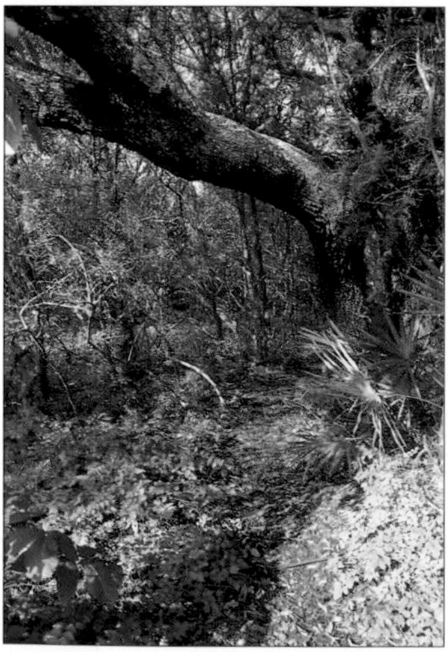

The nature trail, Naval Live Oaks Reservation

🦌 Naval Live Oaks Reservation

1801 Gulf Breeze Parkway. ☎ *(850) 934-2600.* ○ *daily.* ● *Dec 25.* ♿

🦌 The Zoo

5701 Gulf Breeze Parkway. ☎ *(850) 932-2229.* ○ *daily.* ● *Thanksgiving, Dec 25.* 💲 ♿ [w] www.the-zoo.com

Santa Rosa Island ❺

Road map A1. Escambia Co, Okaloosa Co, Santa Rosa Co. 🚆 *Pensacola.* 🚌 *Pensacola or Fort Walton Beach.* ℹ *8543 Navarre Parkway, Navarre, (850) 939-2691.*

A LONG, THIN STREAK of sand, Santa Rosa stretches all the way from Pensacola Bay to Fort Walton Beach, a distance of 45 miles (70 km). At its western tip **Fort Pickens**, completed in 1834, is the largest of four US forts constructed in the early 19th century to defend Pensacola Bay.

The Apache chieftain Geronimo was imprisoned here from 1886–8, during which time people came from far and wide to see him; the authorities supposedly encouraged his transformation into a tourist attraction. The fort remained in use by the US Army until 1947. Now, you are free to explore the brick fort's dark passageways and small museum.

Santa Rosa has several fine white beaches. Pensacola Beach and Navarre Beach are both popular, each with a fishing pier and plenty of water sports activities. Between them is a beautiful, undeveloped stretch of sand where you can relax away from the crowds. There is a campground at the western end of the island, near Fort Pickens.

🏛 Fort Pickens

1400 Fort Pickens Rd (Route 399). ☎ *(850) 934-2621.* ○ *daily.* 💲 ♿ ⛺

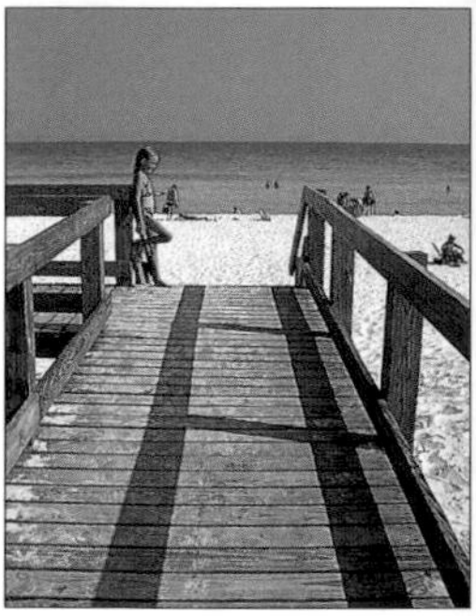

Boardwalk leading onto Pensacola Beach on Santa Rosa Island

Blackwater River ❻

Road map A1. Santa Rosa Co. 🚆 *Pensacola.* 🚌 *Pensacola.* ℹ *5247 Stewart St, Milton, (850) 623-2339.*

THE BLACKWATER RIVER starts in Alabama and flows for 60 miles (95 km) south to the Gulf of Mexico. One of the purest sand-bottomed rivers in the world, its dark, tannin-stained waters meander prettily through the forest, creating oxbow lakes, natural levees, and sand beaches.

The river's big attraction is its canoeing: one of the state's finest canoe trails runs for 31 miles (50 km) along its course. Canoe and kayak trips can be arranged through several operators in Milton, the self-styled "Canoeing Capital of Florida." These trips range from half-day paddles to three-day marathons, with the option of tackling the more

The Blackwater River, well known for its canoeing trail

challenging Sweetwater and Juniper creeks to the north.

The small **Blackwater River State Park**, located at the end of the canoe trail, offers swimming, picnicking areas, and the Chain of Lakes Trail. This 1-mile (1.5-km) nature trail runs through woodlands thick with oak, hickory, southern magnolia, and red maple trees, and ends up at a clutch of oxbow lakes.

Blackwater River State Park
Off US 90, 15 miles (24 km) NE of Milton. **(** (850) 983-5363. **◯** daily.

Fort Walton Beach **◯**

Road map A1. Okaloosa Co.
22,000. ✕ **Crestview.**
ℹ 34 Miracle Strip Parkway SE, (850) 244-8191, (800) 322-3319.

FORT WALTON BEACH lies at the western tip of the so-called Emerald Coast, a 24-mile (40-km) strip of dazzling beach stretching east to Destin and beyond. Diving shops and marinas line US 98, which skirts the coast and links Fort Walton to Santa Rosa Island. Known locally as Okaloosa Island, this is where most local people and visitors go. The clear water offers superb swimming as well as pier and deep-sea fishing, and this is a prime location for water sports too.

You can also swim or go sailing or windsurfing off the island's north shore, on sheltered Choctawhatchee Bay. Boat trips can be arranged at the numerous marinas. For those who prefer dry land, the Emerald Coast boasts a dozen golf courses.

Performing dolphins and sea lions star in daily shows at the popular **Gulfarium** marine park. The glass walls of the Living Sea aquarium reveal sharks, rays, and huge sea turtles. There are also seal and otter enclosures, as well as alligators and exotic birds. There's not a great deal to

Indian pot, Temple Mound Museum

lure you downtown except for the informative **Indian Temple Mound Museum**, which stands in the shadow of an ancient Indian earthwork. This former ceremonial and burial site of the Apalachee Indians *(see pp38–9)* dates from about AD 1400. The museum exhibits artifacts recovered from the mound and other Indian sites nearby, while well-illustrated displays trace more than 10,000 years of human habitation in the Choctawhatchee Bay area.

Three miles (5 km) north of town at Shalimar is the vast Eglin Air Force Base, the largest air force base in the world. Here, the **US Air Force Armament Museum** displays aircraft, missiles, and bombs dating from World War II to the present day. Visitors can snoop around a SR-71 "Blackbird" spy plane and inspect antique side-arms and high-tech laser equipment. Tours of the 720-sq mile (1,865-sq km) base are available.

Gulfarium
1010 Miracle Strip Parkway. **(** (850) 243-9046. **◯** daily. **●** public hols.
w www.gulfarium.com

Indian Temple Mound Museum
139 Miracle Strip Parkway. **(** (850) 833-9595. **◯** daily. **●** public hols.

US Air Force Armament Museum
100 Museum Drive (Route 85).
((850) 882 4062. **◯** daily.
● public hols.

People strolling along the Gulf of Mexico's white powder sands at Fort Walton Beach

Destin ❽

Road map A1. Okaloosa Co.
12,000. ✈ 🚉 *Fort Walton Beach.* ℹ
1021 Highway 98 E, (850) 837-6241.

SITUATED BETWEEN the Gulf of
Mexico and Choctawhatchee
Bay, Destin is a narrow strip of
a town that runs parallel to
the coastal highway, US 98. It
started out in 1845 as a fishing
camp but the town has since
grown into what is claimed to
be the "most prolific fishing
village" in the United States.

**Fisherman at work on his catches
at the harbor in Destin**

Deep-sea fishing is the big
draw, for the numerous
fishermen, and a steady flow
of charter boats buzzes in and
out of the harbor. The waters
near Destin are particularly
rich in fish because of a 100-ft
(30-m) drop in the continental
shelf only 10 miles (16 km)
from the shore. The prime
catches include amberjack,
tarpon, and blue marlin.
There is a busy calendar of
fishing tournaments in Destin,
the most notable being
October's month-long Fishing
Rodeo. Another important
date is early October, when
people flock to Destin for the
annual Seafood Festival.
Cockles, mussels, shrimp, and
crab tempt the crowds.

With its stunning beaches
and the clear waters so
typical of the Emerald Coast,
Destin has also become a
very popular seaside resort.
There are plenty of good
opportunities for diving, and
for snorkeling too.

🏛 **Destin Seafood Festival**
Destin *(Early Oct).*

**A wooden tower characteristic of
Seaside's gulfshore homes**

Seaside ❾

Road map B1. Walton Co. 200.
ℹ *(850) 231-4224.*

WHEN ROBERT DAVIS decided
to develop Seaside in the
mid-1980s, the vanished resorts
of his childhood provided his
inspiration. Davis's vision was
of a nostalgic vacation town of
traditional northwest Florida-
style wooden cottages, with
wraparound verandas, steeply
pitched roofs, and white picket
fences. The original style was
rapidly hijacked, however, by

The Beaches of the Panhandle

BETWEEN PERDIDO KEY and Panama City Beach lie
some of the most beautiful beaches in Florida. The
finely ground sand – 90 percent quartz, washed down
from the Appalachian mountains – sweeps into broad
beaches and can be nearly blinding in the sunlight.
The hordes descend in June and July, but the Gulf
waters are still pleasantly warm as late as November.
You can choose between quiet, undeveloped
beaches and the more dynamic resorts;
there is also plenty of opportunity
for diving and other water sports.

Pensacola Beach ③ has
miles of pristine sand overlooked by a string of shops,
hotels, and bars. A large
crowd gathers on
weekends. *(See p220.)*

Perdido Key ①
Some of the state's most
westerly shores, on Perdido
Key, are inaccessible by car
and are therefore quieter
than most. *(See p217.)*

Quietwater Beach ② is on the inland
shore of Santa Rosa Island. While not
the Panhandle's finest beach it is at
least an easy hop from Pensacola.

Navarre Beach ④ is one of
the quieter of the island's beach
It has good facilities, including a
pier for fishing. *(See p220.)*

0 kilometers   15
0 miles

quaint gingerbread detailing, turrets, and towers *(see p29)*.

The town's pastel painted, Neo-Victorian charms have an unreal, Disneyesque quality, and if you're driving along US 98 it's hard to resist stopping for a quick peek. And then, of course, there is the additional appeal of the beach.

Environs: Just 1 mile (1.5 km) west of Seaside, the **Grayton Beach State Recreation Area** boasts another magnificent stretch of Panhandle shoreline, and one that regularly features high in the rankings of the nation's top beaches.

In addition to its broad strand of pristine quartz-white sand, the park offers good surf fishing, boating facilities, a nature trail, and also a campground. During the summer, campers can take part in ranger-led programs that are suitable for the whole family.

Grayton Beach SRA
County Rd 30A , off US 98, (1 mile) 1.5 km W of Seaside. ☎ *(850) 231-4210.* 🕐 *daily.* 🎟 ♿

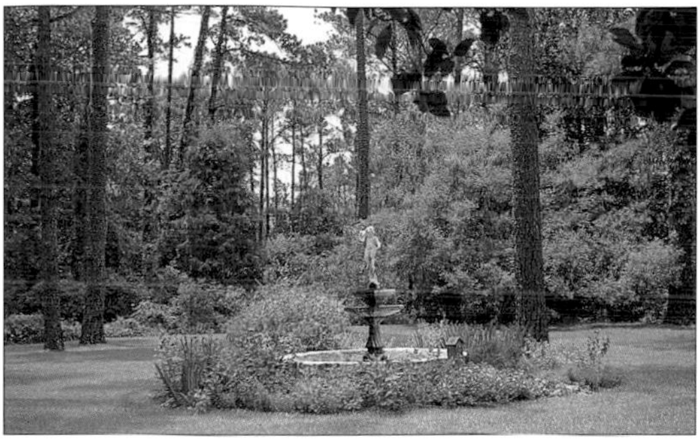

Statue amid the lush surroundings of the Eden State Gardens

Eden State Gardens and Mansion [10]

Road map B1. Walton Co. Point Washington. ☎ *(850) 231-4214.* 🚌 *Fort Walton Beach.* **Gardens** 🕐 *daily.* **House** 🕐 *Thu–Mon.* 🎟

Lumber baron William H. Wesley built this fine Greek Revival mansion overlooking the Choctawhatchee River in 1897. The gracious two-story wooden building, styled after an antebellum mansion, with high-ceilinged rooms and broad verandas, is furnished with antiques. Equally appealing are the gardens, planted with camellias and azaleas, and shaded by southern magnolia trees and live oaks; these lead to picnic tables by the river, near where the old lumber mill once stood. Whole trees were once floated from inland forests downriver to the mill, where they were sawed into logs. From there they were sent by barge along the Intracoastal Waterway to Pensacola.

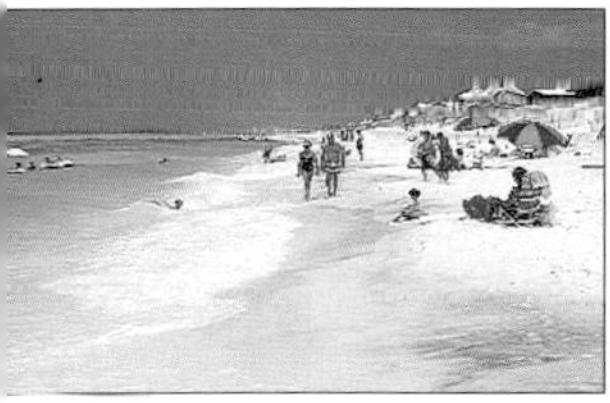

Santa Rosa Beach [7]
This undeveloped sandy beach is backed by dunes and marshlands teeming with birds and other wildlife.

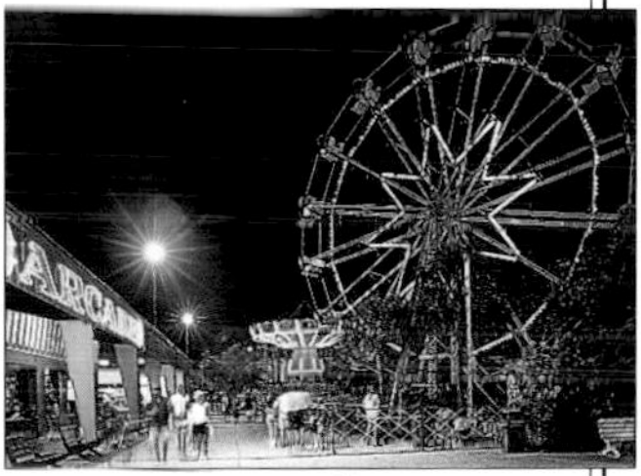

Panama City Beach [9]
Condos, hotels, and amusement and water parks line buzzing Panama City Beach. Diving and water sports are popular pastimes. *(See p224.)*

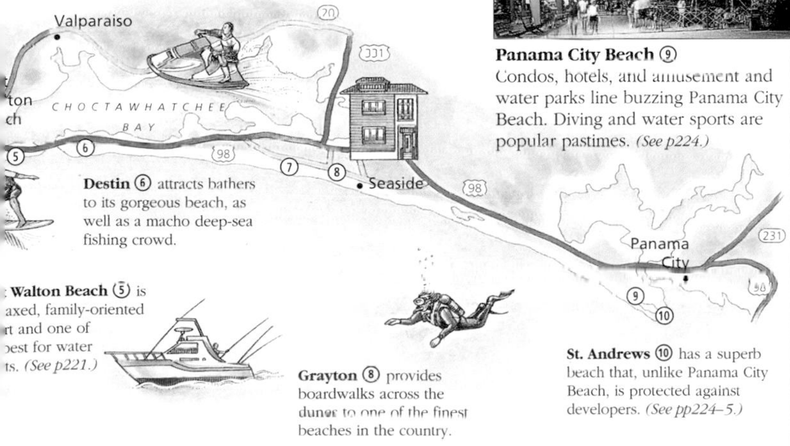

Destin [6] attracts bathers to its gorgeous beach, as well as a macho deep-sea fishing crowd.

: **Walton Beach** [5] is
axed, family-oriented
rt and one of
best for water
ts. *(See p221.)*

Grayton [8] provides boardwalks across the dunes to one of the finest beaches in the country.

St. Andrews [10] has a superb beach that, unlike Panama City Beach, is protected against developers. *(See pp224–5.)*

Panama City Beach, the liveliest seaside resort in the Panhandle

Panama City Beach ⓫

Road map B1. Bay Co. 🏛 *6,000.*
✈ 🚌 ℹ *12015 Front Beach Rd,
(850) 233-5070.* **Captain Anderson's**
📞 *(850) 234-3435.* **Treasure Island
Marina** 📞 *(850) 234-8944.*

A BRASH, CHEEKY postcard sort
of a place, Panama City
Beach is a 27-mile (43-km)
"Miracle Strip" of hotels,
amusement parks, and arcades,
bordered by a gleaming quartz
sand beach. The Panhandle's
biggest resort, it caters both to
the young crowds that swamp
the place at Spring Break *(see
p32)* and to families, who
dominate in summer. The
sports facilities are excellent.
   Panama City Beach, nicknamed the "wreck capital of
the south," is a famous diving
destination. Besides natural
coral reefs, it has more than
50 artificial diving sites created
by wrecked boats – providing
some of the best diving in the
Gulf. Dive operators offer
scuba and snorkeling trips
and lessons. For the less
energetic, Captain Anderson's
and Treasure Island Marina
offer dolphin feeding trips
and glass-bottomed boat tours.

🐬 Gulf World
15412 Front Beach Rd. ℹ *(850) 234-
5271.* ⭘ *daily.* ⬤ *Thanksgiving,
Dec 25–Jan 1.* 📷 ♿
🆆 *www.gulfworldmarinepark.com*
Dolphin and sea lion shows
are the highlights here. The
aquariums and a walk-through
shark tank are set in lush
tropical gardens with a
resident troupe of delightful
performing parrots.

🏛 Museum of Man in the Sea
17314 Panama City Beach Parkway.
📞 *(850) 235-4101.* ⭘ *daily.*
⬤ *Thanksgiving, Dec 25, Jan 1.* 📷 ♿
The Museum of Man in the
Sea provides a homespun but
educational look at the history
of diving and marine salvage.
It has exhibits ranging from
ancient diving helmets to
salvaged treasures from the
17th-century Spanish galleon
Atocha (see p26), and there is a
parking lot full of submarines.
A favorite among the latter is
Moby Dick, a whale rescue
vessel painted to resemble a
killer whale.

🦁 ZooWorld
9008 Front Beach Rd. 📞 *(850) 230-
1243.* ⭘ *daily.* ⬤ *Dec 25.* 📷 ♿
ZooWorld is home to more
than 350 animals, including
bears, big cats, alligators,
camels, giraffes, and orang-
utans, as well as more than
15 endangered species.
   The Gentle Jungle Petting
Zoo, which offers plenty of
opportunity to come face to
face with and touch the wildlife, is particularly popular
with young children.

**An orangutan, one of ZooWorld's
more entertaining residents**

🌊 Shipwreck Island Water Park
12000 Front Beach Rd.
ℹ *(850) 234-0368.* ⭘ *Apr–May:
Sat, Sun; Jun–Aug: daily.* 📷 ♿
This water park, next to the
Miracle Strip Amusement Park,
will have no trouble keeping
the family entertained for the
entire day. The 1,600-ft (490-m)
Lazy River tube ride is great
and there are higher-energy
options for the more adventurous: try the 35-mph (55-
km/h) Speed Slide, the Rapid
River, or the 370-ft (110-m)
White Water Tube. There are
gentler rides for youngsters
too, as well as a kids' pool.
Other attractions include a
wave pool and sunbathing
areas. Lifeguards keep watch.

**Fun on the Lazy River ride at
Shipwreck Island Water Park**

🌊 Miracle Strip Amuse-
ment Park
12000 Front Beach Rd. ℹ *(850)
234-5810.* ⭘ *Mar–Jun: Fri & Sat;
Jun–Aug: daily.* 📷 ♿
The beach by night is about
as vibrant and gaudy as you
would expect, with snack bars
and discos galore. Top of the
bill is the Miracle Strip Amusement Park, an amusement park
with a world-class 2,000-ft
(600-m) roller coaster, a Ferris
wheel, and dozens of other
rides, games, and sideshows.

ENVIRONS: An easy 3-mile
(5-km) hop southeast of the
main Strip, **St. Andrews State
Recreation Area** is a good
antidote to Panama City Beach,
though it can get very busy in
summer. The preserve has a

A replica of a turpentine still in St. Andrews State Recreation Area

fabulous white sand beach – named the best beach in the US in 1995. The swimming is good, and there is excellent snorkeling around the rock jetties. Behind the dunes, marshland areas and lagoons are home to alligators and wading birds.

Also within the park, not far from the fishing pier, is a modern re-creation of an early turpentine still, similar to those found throughout the state in the early 1900s *(see p217)*; a woodland trail starts nearby.

St. Andrews SRA
4607 State Park Ln. *(850) 233-5140.* daily.

Florida Caverns State Park ⑫

Road map B1. Jackson Co. 3345 Caverns Rd, off Route 166, 3 miles (5 km) N of Marianna. *Marianna.* *(850) 482-9598.* daily.

THE LIMESTONE that underpins Florida is laid bare in this series of underground caves hollowed out of the soft rock and drained by the Chipola River. The filtering of rain water through the limestone rock over thousands of years has created a breathtaking subterranean cavescape of stalactites, stalagmites, columns, and glittering rivulets of crystals. Wrap up warm for the guided tours, since the caverns maintain a cool 61–66 °F (16–19 °C).

The park also offers hiking trails and horseback riding, and you can swim and fish in the Chipola River. A 52-mile (84-km) canoe trail slips through the high limestone cliffs along the river's route south to Dead Lake, just west of Apalachicola National Forest *(see p226)*.

Torreya State Park ⑬

Road map C1. Liberty Co. Route CR 1641, 13 miles (21 km) N of Bristol. *Blountstown.* *(850) 643-2674.* daily. limited.

MORE OFF THE beaten track than most other parks in Florida, Torreya State Park is well worth seeking out. Named after the torreya, a rare type of yew tree that once grew here in abundance, the park abuts a beautiful forested bend in the Apalachicola River. High limestone bluffs, into which Confederate soldiers dug gun pits to repel Union gunboats during the Civil War, flank the river, offering one of the few high natural vantage points in Florida.

Gregory House, a fine 19th-century Classical Revival mansion, stands on top of the 150-ft (45-m) bluff. In 1935 it was moved here from its first site downriver by conservationists and has since been restored. Inside, it is simply furnished with period antiques.

It is a 25-minute walk from Gregory House down to the river and back, or you can take the 7-mile (11-km) Weeping Ridge Trail. Both paths run through woodland and offer a chance to spot all kinds of birds, deer, beaver, and the unusual Barbours map turtle (so-called for the maplike lines etched on its shell).

St. Joseph Peninsula State Park ⑭

Road map B1. Gulf Co. Route 30E. *Blountstown.* *(850) 227-1327.* daily. open all year.

AT THE TIP of the slender sand spit that extends north from Cape San Blas to enclose St. Joseph's Bay, this beautifully unspoiled beach park is ideal for those in search of a little peace and quiet. The swimming is excellent, and snorkeling and surf fishing are also popular activities. Bird-watchers should pack their binoculars, since the bird life is prolific along the shoreline: over 200 species of birds have been recorded here. You can stay in cabins overlooking the bay, and there are basic camping facilities, too.

You might want to venture away from the beach to explore the saw palmetto and pine woodlands, where you may see deer, raccoons, bobcats, and even coyotes.

The forested course of the Apalachicola River in Torreya State Park

Restored houses on the water's edge in Water Street, Apalachicola

Apalachicola ⓯

Road Map B1. Franklin Co.
🏃 3000. 🚌 Tallahassee. ℹ 99
Market Street, (850) 653-9419.

A RIVERSIDE CUSTOMS station established in 1823, Apalachicola saw its finest days during the first 100 years of its existence. It boomed first with the cotton trade then, later on, sponge divers and lumber barons made their fortunes here. Today, a swath of pines and hardwoods still stands as the Apalachicola National Forest, extending from 12 miles (19 km) north of Apalachicola right to the outskirts of Tallahassee.

At the end of the lumber boom in the 1920s, the town turned to oystering and fishing in the waters at the mouth of the Apalachicola River. Oyster and other fishing boats still pull up at the dockside, which is lined with refrigerated seafood houses and old brick-built cotton warehouses. Among the seafood houses on Water Street there are several places to sample fresh oysters.

The old town is laid out in a neat grid with many fine historic buildings dating from the cotton boom era. A walking map, available from the chamber of commerce, takes in such privately owned treasures as the 1838 Greek Revival Raney House.

Devoted to the town's most notable resident, the **John Gorrie State Museum** has a model of Gorrie's patent ice-making machine. Designed to cool the sickrooms of yellow fever sufferers, Dr. Gorrie's 1851 invention was the vanguard of modern refrigeration and air conditioning.

🏛 **John Gorrie State Museum**
46 6th Street (Gorrie Square).
【 (850) 653-9347. ◯ Thu–Mon.
⬤ Thanksgiving, Dec 25, Jan 1. 🌐

St. Vincent, St. George, and Dog Islands ⓰

Road Map B2, C2, C1. Franklin Co.
🚌 Tallahassee. ℹ 99 Market St,
Apalachicola, (850) 653-9419. **Jeannie's Journeys** 【 (850) 927-3259.
ⓦ www.sgiislandjourneys.com

THIS STRING of barrier islands separates Apalachicola Bay from the Gulf of Mexico. St. George, linked by a bridge to Apalachicola is developing fast and has a growing number of vacation homes. However, a 9-mile (14-km) stretch of beautiful dunes at its eastern end is preserved as the **St. George Island State Park**; the main expanse of beach is on the gulf side.

To the west, the **St. Vincent National Wildlife Refuge** is uninhabited and accessible only by boat: Jeannie's

Surf fishing, a popular activity on the quiet sands of St. George Island

---

Journeys, on East Gorey Drive, runs tours. There are two official tours, one in May, the other in October. Visitors can watch nesting ospreys in spring, sea turtles laying their eggs in summer, and migrating waterfowl in winter.

To the east, little Dog Island must be reached by boat from Carrabelle on the mainland. It has a small inn, big dunes, and excellent shell hunting.

🦌 **St. George Island State Park**
【 (850) 927-2111. ◯ daily.
🦌 **St. Vincent National Wildlife Refuge**
【 (850) 653-8808. ◯ daily.

Fun in the pool at Wakulla Springs

Wakulla Springs State Park ⓱

Road map C1. Wakulla Co. 550.
Wakulla Park Drive, Wakulla Springs.
【 (850) 922-3633. 🚌 Tallahassee.
◯ daily. 🌐 ♿

ONE OF THE WORLD'S largest freshwater springs, the Wakulla pumps 700,000 gal (2.6 million liters) of water a minute into the large pool which is the big appeal of this park.

You can swim or snorkel in the beautifully clear, limestone-filtered water, or take a ride in a glass-bottomed boat. There are also trips on the Wakulla River, with a good chance of seeing alligators, ospreys, and wading birds, and you can follow woodland trails.

Do not leave without visiting the Spanish-style Wakulla Springs Lodge hotel and restaurant, built in the 1930s.

Fishing for Shellfish in Apalachicola Bay

APALACHICOLA BAY is one of the most productive estuarine systems in the world. Fed by the nutrient-rich Apalachicola River, the bay is a valuable nursery, breeding, and feeding ground for many marine species. The warm, shallow waters of the salt marshes between Apalachicola Bay and Cedar Key *(see p231)* are important feeding grounds too, and the fishing tradition extends all along the coast.

A blue crab

Oysters, blue crab, shrimp, and other crustaceans, as well as a large variety of fish, all contribute to the local fishing industry, which is worth about $15 million a year. Apalachicola Bay is most famous for its oysters, which account for 90 percent of the state's total catch. The oysters grow rapidly in the bay's ideal conditions and reach a marketable size of 3 inches (8 cm) in under two years.

"Tongs," a pair of rakes joined like scissors, are used to lift the oysters from the sea.

A "culler" separates the oysters by size, throwing back any that are too small.

OYSTER FISHING

Oystermen, known locally as "tongers" after the tools they use, fish from small wooden boats, primarily in public grounds called oyster bars. The oysters can be harvested all year, but there is usually a lull in the summer and autumn, when fishermen focus on other species.

Fishing for oysters in Apalachicola Bay

Fresh oysters, best served on ice

Fresh seafood is sold throughout the year around Apalachicola. On the first weekend of November, seafood lovers converge on the town for the annual Florida Seafood Festival.

White, brown, and pink shrimps are fished both from small boats in the bay, and off-shore in the Gulf of Mexico from larger vessels, which may be out for a week or more. The catch is brought back to seafood houses on land for sorting and distribution.

Blue crabs, both the hard-shell and soft-shell varieties (the latter known as "peelers"), are caught in baited wire traps, which are dropped and collected by small boats. The crabs appear in warm weather, sometimes as early as February.

Tallahassee ⓲

JUST 14 MILES (23 KM) FROM the Georgia border, encircled by rolling hills and canopy roads, Tallahassee is the epitome of "The Other Florida" – gracious, hospitable, and uncompromisingly Southern. The former site of an Apalachee Indian settlement and a Franciscan mission, this remote spot was an unlikely place to found the new capital of Territorial Florida in 1824 *(see p211)*. However, from its simple beginnings, Tallahassee grew dramatically during the plantation era and after Florida's elevation to full statehood in 1845. The elegant town houses built by politicians, plantation owners, and businessmen during that period can still be enjoyed today.

Exploring Tallahassee

The historic district, where you'll find the city's fine 19th-century homes, is focused around Park Avenue and Calhoun Street, both quiet, shady streets planted with century-old live oak trees and southern magnolias. The Brokaw-McDougall House on Meridian Street is a splendid Classical Revival building. Similar influences are evident in The Columns, an 1830 mansion on Duval Street. The city's oldest building, it now houses the Chamber of Commerce, where you can pick up walking-tour maps. The Capitol Complex is at the very heart of downtown Tallahassee. Here, the venerable Old Capitol building has been beautifully restored to its 1902 state, with a pristine white dome and striped awnings. Inside, you can visit the Supreme Court chamber, the old cabinet meeting room, and also the Senate. The 22-floor New Capitol building behind, where the March–May legislative sessions take place, casts a shadow over its predecessor. But although it is a grim 1970s structure, it does at least offer a lovely view of Tallahassee from its top floor.

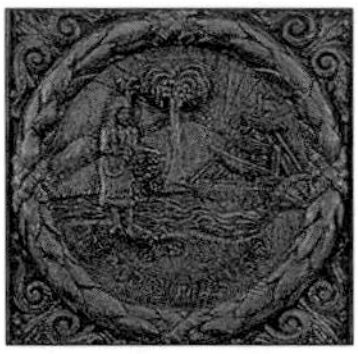

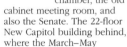

Wood carving in the Old Capitol Senate

VISITORS' CHECKLIST

Road map C1. Leon Co. 👥 *137,000.* ✈ *8 miles (13 km) S.* 🚆 *918 Railroad Avenue, (800) 872-7245.* 🚌 *112 W Tennessee Street, (850) 222-4240.* ℹ *New Capitol Building (first floor), Duval Street, (850) 413-9200, (800) 628-2866.* 🎉 *Springtime Tallahassee (Mar–Apr).*

🏛 Knott House Museum

301 East Park Ave. ☎ *(850) 922-2459.* 🕐 *Wed–Sat.* ● *Thanksgiving, Dec 25, Jan 1.* ♿

This house is unusual for the claim that it was built by a free black in 1843 – 20 years prior to the emancipation of Florida's slaves. Now one of the most beautifully restored Victorian homes in Tallahassee, it is named after the Knotts, who moved here in 1928 and completely refurbished the house. The lovely interior is evocative of the former owners. Poems

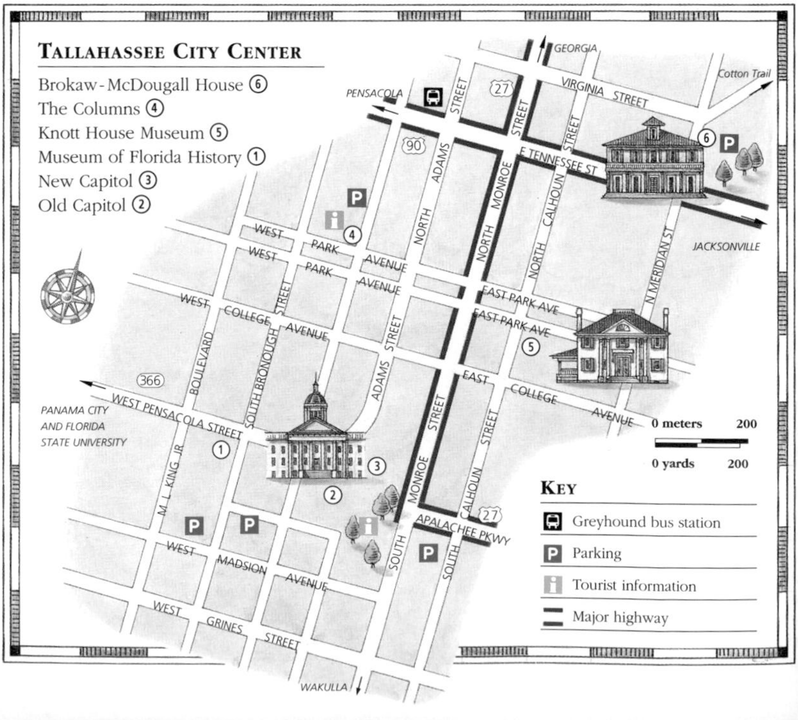

TALLAHASSEE CITY CENTER
Brokaw-McDougall House ⑥
The Columns ④
Knott House Museum ⑤
Museum of Florida History ①
New Capitol ③
Old Capitol ②
GEORGIA
Cotton Trail
PENSACOLA
VIRGINIA STREET
E TENNESSEE ST
NORTH ADAMS STREET
NORTH MONROE STREET
NORTH CALHOUN STREET
N MERIDIAN ST
JACKSONVILLE
WEST PARK AVENUE
EAST PARK AVE
WEST COLLEGE AVENUE
EAST COLLEGE AVENUE
SOUTH BRONOUGH STREET
BOULEVARD
ADAMS STREET
MONROE STREET
CALHOUN STREET
WEST PENSACOLA STREET
PANAMA CITY AND FLORIDA STATE UNIVERSITY
M L KING JR
APALACHEE PKWY
WEST MADSION AVENUE
WEST GRINES STREET
SOUTH
WAKULLA
0 meters 200
0 yards 200
KEY
Greyhound bus station
Parking
Tourist information
Major highway

that Luella Knott composed for and tied to her favorite antique furnishings are still in place to this day.

🏛 Museum of Florida History

500 S Bronough St. 📞 (850) 488-1484. ⬜ daily. ⬤ Thanksgiving, Dec 25. ♿ W www.flheritage.com

The museum tackles 12,000 years of the region's history in entertaining style. Varied dioramas feature elements of paleo-Indian culture, massive armadillos, and a mastodon skeleton made of bones found in Wakulla Springs (see p226). Numerous artifacts and succinct storyboards provide an excellent history from the colonial era up to the "tin can" tourists of the 1920s (see p49).

Boardwalk in the Museum of History and Natural Science

ENVIRONS: Three miles (5 km) southwest of the city, Lake Bradford Road leads to the **Tallahassee Museum of History and Natural Science**, which is very popular with children. The centerpiece is Big Bend Farm – a superb recreation of late 19th-century rural life; employees dressed as farmhands tend goats and geese among authentic 1880s farm buildings. Bellevue, a small plantation home built in the 1830s, is among the other attractions. On the shores of Lake Bradford, this woodland area provides natural habitat enclosures for black bears and bobcats, while alligators lurk amid the water lilies and cypress swamp areas.

Goodwood Plantation, on the northeastern edge of Tallahassee, was a major

producer of cotton and corn in the 19th century (see pp44–5). The main house, built in the 1830s, retains many original features inside, including a mahogany staircase and marble fireplaces from Europe. After years of neglect, the plantation buildings are being restored. Visitors can already explore the grounds, as well as some of the outbuildings.

🏛 Tallahassee Museum of History and Natural Science

3945 Museum Drive. 📞 (850) 576-1636. ⬜ daily. ⬤ Thanksgiving, Dec 24–25, Jan 1. 📷 ♿

🏛 Goodwood Plantation

1600 Miccosukee Rd. 📞 (850) 877-4202. ⬜ Mon–Fri. W www.goodwoodmuseum.org

A. B. Maclay State Gardens ⓳

Road map C1. 3540 Thomasville Rd, Leon Co. 📞 (850) 487-4556. 🚌 Tallahassee. 🚌 Tallahassee. ⬜ daily. 📷 ♿ W www.ssnow.com/maclay

A. B. Maclay State Gardens near Tallahassee, at their best in the spring

THESE GORGEOUS GARDENS, 4 miles (6 km) north of Tallahassee, were originally laid out around Killearn, the 1930s winter home of New York financier Alfred B. Maclay. More than 200 varieties of plants are featured in the land-scaped gardens that surround the shores of Lake Hall. They remain eye-catching even in winter, when the magnificent camellias and azaleas are in full

Unadorned Presbyterian church, Monticello

bloom (from January to April). Visitors can also swim, fish, go boating, or enjoy a stroll along the woodland Big Pine Nature Trail.

Monticello ⓴

Road map C1. Jefferson Co. 🏘 2,800. 🚌 Tallahassee. 🚌 Tallahassee. 🛈 420 W Washington St, (850) 997-5552.

FOUNDED IN 1827, Monticello (pronounced "Montisello") was named after the Virginia home of former President Thomas Jefferson. Lying at the heart of northern Florida's cotton-growing country, the town prospered and funded the building of elegant homes. Some of these are now bed-and-breakfasts, making the town a good base for exploring the Tallahassee area.

Monticello radiates from the imposing courthouse on US 90. The historic district lies to the north, where you'll find tree-canopied streets and a wealth of lovely old buildings, ranging from 1850s antebellum mansions to Queen Anne homes with decorative woodwork and Gothic features. Every year at the end of June, the town hosts its Watermelon Festival to celebrate a mainstay of the local agricultural economy. Pageants, dancing, rodeos, and the traditional watermelon seed spitting contest are among the festival's many attractions.

Suwannee River State Park ㉒

Road map D2. Suwannee Co.
13 miles (21 km) W of Live Oak.
🚌 *Live Oak.* 📞 *(904) 362-2746.*
⭘ *daily.* ♿ 🛏 🅿

MADE FAMOUS the world over by the song *Old Folks at Home*, written by Stephen Foster in 1851, the Suwannee has its sources in Georgia, from which it runs 265 miles (425 km) to the Gulf of Mexico.

Suwannee River State Park offers some of the best backcountry canoeing in Florida. The river is easy flowing here, and its low banks support a high forest of hickory, oak, southern magnolia, and some cypress trees. Canoeists have a good chance of encountering a broad range of wildlife, including herons, American coots, hawks, and also turtles. Canoe rental is available, and there is a boat ramp and a shady campground.

Enjoying the sun at a wharf in Suwannee River State Park

Steinhatchee ㉓

Road map D2. Taylor Co. 🏠 *1,000.*
🚌 *Chiefland.* 🅸 *428 N Jefferson, (850) 584-5366.*

SET BACK FROM THE mouth of the Steinhatchee River, this is a sleepy old fishing town, strung out along the riverbank. To get a flavor of the place, ignore the trailer parks and

stroll among the jumble of fish camps, bait shops, and boats tied up to the cypress wood docks. Trout fishing is big here, and you may also find people crabbing along the coast.

About 26 miles (42 km) northwest of Steinhatchee is **Keaton Beach**, a tiny but popular coastal resort surrounded by woodlands and marshes.

Cedar Key ㉔

Road map D2. Levy Co. 🏠 *750.*
🚌 *Chiefland.* 🅸 *2nd Street, (352) 543-5600.*

AT THE FOOT of a chain of little bridge-linked keys jutting out into the Gulf of Mexico, Cedar Key is a picturesque, weathered Victorian fishing village. In the 19th century it flourished as the gulf terminal of Florida's first cross-state railroad and from the burgeoning lumber trade. However, within a few decades

Cotton Trail Tour ㉑

IN THE 1820S AND '30S, the area around Tallahassee was the most important cotton-growing region in Florida. From the outlying plantations, horse-drawn wagons creaked along red clay roads to market in the capital. Today, these old roads pass through one of the last corners of unspoiled rural Florida.

This tour follows the old Cotton Trail, along canopied roads and past cattle pastures and paddocks carved out of deep green woodlands. It takes about 3.5 hours, or it could be done en route between Tallahassee and Monticello (see p229).

Bradley's Country Store ④
Famous for its homemade sausages this traditional country store is stil run by the Bradleys, who established the business in 1927

Old Pisgah United Methodist Church ③
This unadorned Greek Revival church, built in 1858, is the oldest Methodist building in Leon County.

Miccosukee Road ②
Originally an Indian trail, this canopy road was used by 30 local plantations in the 1850s.

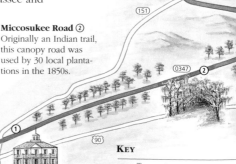

Goodwood Plantation ①
This former cotton plantation (see p229) retains its lovely 1840s mansion shaded by live oak trees.

KEY

▬ Tour route

═ Other roads

its namesake stands of cedar forest had been transformed into pencils, and the logging boom ended. A few of the old lumber warehouses have been turned into shops and restaurants, but the Cedar Key of today is blissfully quiet.

You can take a boat from the docks to an offshore island beach in the Cedar Keys National Wildlife Refuge, or take a bird-watching trip along the salt-marsh coast. Various boats run trips from the docks.

Alternatively, visit the entertaining **Cedar Key Historical Society Museum**, in which eclectic exhibits include some fossilized tapir teeth, Indian pottery shards, and crab traps. At the museum you can also pick up a map for touring the town's historic buildings.

Cedar Key Historical Society Museum

Corner of D and 2nd Streets. ☎ *(352) 543-5549.* ○ *daily.* ● *Thanksgiving, Dec 25, Jan 1.*

Environs: Thirty miles (50 km) to the north of Cedar Key is **Manatee Springs State Park**, where a spring gushes from a cave mouth more than 30 ft (9 m) below the surface of an azure pool. The swift-running spring water, which feeds the Suwannee River, is as clear as glass and is very popular with divers and snorkelers. Sightings of manatees, which occasionally winter here, are unreliable, but it is easy to spot dozens of turtles, fish, and egrets feeding in the shallows, and the ubiquitous turkey vultures hovering over head. You can also swim, rent a canoe, take a boat tour, or follow one of the many hiking trails; you may be lucky enough to see an armadillo in the undergrowth.

Manatee Springs State Park

Route 320, 6 miles (10 km) W of Chiefland. ☎ *(352) 493-6072.* ○ *daily.*

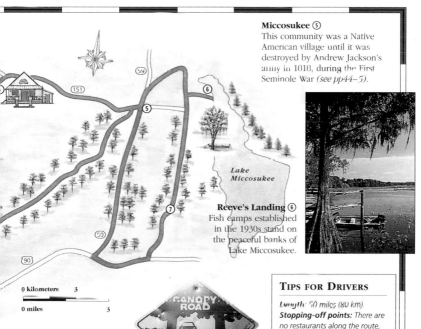

Weather-beaten hut on stilts off the coast of Cedar Key

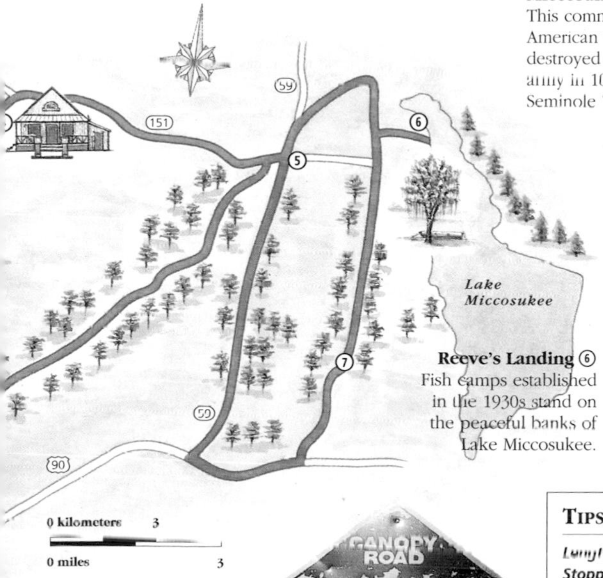

Miccosukee 5
This community was a Native American village until it was destroyed by Andrew Jackson's army in 1818, during the First Seminole War *(see pp44–5)*.

Reeve's Landing 6
Fish camps established in the 1930s stand on the peaceful banks of Lake Miccosukee.

Magnolia Road 7
One of Florida's last unpaved canopy roads, this track led to the now-vanished port of Magnolia, from which cotton was shipped to New York.

Tips for Drivers

Length: *50 miles (80 km).*
Stopping-off points: *There are no restaurants along the route, so take your own provisions or buy a snack at Bradley's Country Store, and enjoy a picnic on the banks of Lake Miccosukee.*

THE GULF COAST

OR MANY VISITORS *the Gulf Coast begins and ends with its fabulous beaches, bathed by the warm, calm waters of the Gulf of Mexico, and their accompanying resorts. However, with only a little effort you can kick the sand from your shoes and visit some of Florida's most interesting cities or explore wilderness areas that have been left virtually untouched by the vagaries of time.*

Ever since the Spanish colonization, the focus of activity along the Gulf Coast has been around Tampa Bay, the large inlet in Florida's west coast. Pánfilo de Narváez anchored in the bay in 1528, and Hernando de Soto *(see p41)* landed nearby in 1539. The bay was a perfect natural port and became a magnet to pioneers in the 19th century. The favorable climate even drew the odd sugar-grower: Gamble Plantation near Bradenton is the southernmost plantation house in the US *(see p252)*.

After the Civil War, the Gulf Coast became a significant center for trade between the US and the Caribbean. This was due in part to Henry Plant, whose rail line from Virginia, laid in the 1880s, helped to fuel both Tampa's and the region's greatest period of prosperity. Pioneers flooded in, from ethnic groups such as the Greek sponge fishermen who settled in Tarpon Springs, to wealthier American immigrants – chief among whom was circus king John Ringling, whose splendid Italianate home and impressive European art collection is the city of Sarasota's top attraction.

Henry Plant, like Flagler in eastern Florida *(see pp46–7)*, used the promise of winter sunshine to lure wealthy travelers from the north. The west coast's much-advertised average of 361 days of sunshine a year still helps attract great hordes of package tourists to the generous scattering of beaches. Lively beach scenes are the norm around St. Petersburg and Clearwater, but you can easily escape the cosmopolitan vacation atmosphere: only a short distance inland are quirky cattle towns, rivers perfect for canoeing, and swamps and forests where wild animals reside undisturbed.

The high-rise downtown skyline of Tampa, the most important city along the Gulf Coast

◁ The boardwalk giving access to the broad beach at Sand Key, near Clearwater Beach

Exploring the Gulf Coast

THE BEACHES THAT RUN in an almost continuous line along the Gulf Coast, interrupted only by a series of bays and inlets, are hard to resist. But the joy of this region is that it is easy to spice up a Gulf Coast vacation with some sightseeing. The abundant accommodations by the water, from quaint cottages to no-expense-spared resorts, makes this the natural place to base yourself, and all the main cities and inland sights are within easy reach. You'll find some of Florida's best museums in St. Petersburg, Tampa, and Sarasota, as well as high-profile attractions like Busch Gardens and the Florida Aquarium in Tampa. There are also other interesting sights: from the world's largest concentration of Frank Lloyd Wright buildings at Florida Southern College to the weird and wonderful mermaids of Weeki Wachee Spring.

The glistening towers and dome of the old Tampa Bay Hotel *(see p244)*

SEE ALSO

• *Where to Stay* pp308–310

• *Where to Eat* pp326–8 & p331

Tallabassee
Lake City
CRYSTAL RIVER **1**
HOMOSASSA SPRINGS STATE WILDLIFE PARK **2**
WEEKI WACHEE SPRING **3**
TARPON SPRINGS **4**
HILLSBOR R **11**
DUNEDIN **5**
BUSCH GARDENS **10**
CLEARWATER BEACH **6**
9 TAMPA
ST PETERSBURG BEACHES **7**
ST PETERSBURG **8**
TAMPA BAY
GAMBLE PLANTATION **13**
BRADENTON **14**
SARASOTA **15**
MYAKKA R STATE **16**
VENICE **17**
PORT CHARLOTT
GASPARILLA ISLAND **18**
LEE ISLAND COAST **23**
SAN

Exploring the pristine landscapes of Myakka River State Park

GETTING AROUND

The region is easy to get around by car. US 19 runs along the coast north of Tampa Bay, crossing the mouth of the bay over the magnificent Sunshine Skyway Bridge, while US 41 links the coastal communities south of Tampa. If speed is of the essence you'll want to use I-75, which runs farther inland. As in every other region of Florida, life is hard without a car. Greyhound buses link the main towns, but rail services are more limited; Amtrak trains run only as far as Tampa, but its connecting "Thruway" buses *(see p360)* provide a link to St. Petersburg and south along the coast as far as Fort Myers.

Deserted Clearwater Beach at sunset

Orlando

KEY

	Interstate highway
	Toll road
	Major highway
	Secondary route
	Scenic route
	River
	Vista

**IDA SOUTHERN
OLLEGE**
2
ELAND

98

Fort Pierce

70

31

CADIA

**BABCOCK WILDERNESS
ADVENTURES**

Caloosahatchee *Clewiston*

80

RT MYERS *29*

75 *82*

**KORESHAN STATE
HISTORIC SITE**

Naples

0 kilometers 30

0 miles 25

The old-fashioned pier on Anna Maria Island, a well-known local landmark west of Bradenton

SIGHTS AT A GLANCE

Crystal River ❶

Road map D2. Citrus Co. 🏠 *5,000.*
🚉 🛈 *28 NW US 19, (352) 795-3149.*

CRYSTAL RIVER has two main attractions. In winter people come to watch the manatees, which gather in herds of up to 300 to bask in the warm local springs, between January and March. You need to make a reservation with one of the boat operators in the area for an early morning trip around the **Crystal River National Wildlife Refuge**, which was set up specifically to protect the manatees. Manatees are active only in the very early morning hours, and the clear water makes spotting them easy.

A year-round attraction is the **Crystal River State Archaeological Site**, a complex of six Indian mounds 2 miles (3 km) west of the town. The site is thought to have been occupied for 1,600 years, from 200 BC to AD 1400, one of the longest continually occupied sites in Florida. An estimated 7,500 Native Americans visited the complex every year for ceremonial purposes, frequently traveling large distances to do so. Excavation of 400 of the possible 1,000 graves at the site has also revealed that local tribes had trade links with peoples north of Florida.

Climb up to the observation deck for a bird's-eye view of the site. Just below is the main temple mound, built in around

Pottery at Crystal River

AD 600. Beyond, two stelae or carved ceremonial stones, erected in around AD 440 can be seen flanking two of the site's three burial mounds. This stone is typical of the pre-Columbian cultures of Mesoamerica, but no evidence exists to link them with Crystal River. On the western edge of the site is a large village area marked by two midden mounds *(see p38)* on a midden ridge. A model of the site in the visitor center has examples of the pottery found.

⚔ Crystal River National Wildlife Refuge
1502 SE Kings Bay Drive. 📞 *(352) 563-2088.* ⭘ *daily. Boat trips at 6am.*
⋔ Crystal River State Archaeological Site
3400 N Museum Point. 📞 *(352) 795-3817.* ⭘ *daily.* 📷 ♿

THE MANATEE IN FLORIDA

You cannot go far in Florida without hearing about the sea cow, or manatee, an animal in serious risk of extinction. It is believed that there are only about 2,500 manatees left in the US, concentrated in the warm waters of Florida. Once plentiful, the animals were extensively hunted for meat and sport until the beginning of the 20th century, since when habitat destruction and boat accidents have done most of the damage.

The manatee, which grows to an average length of 10 ft (3 m), is a huge but gentle creature. It lives in shallow coastal waters, rivers, and springs, spending about five hours a day feeding; Seagrass is its favorite food.

The manatee, an inhabitant of both salt and fresh water

Homosassa Springs State Wildlife Park ❷

Road map D2. Citrus Co. 4150 South Suncoast Blvd, Homosassa.
🚉 *Crystal River.* 📞 *(352) 628-2311.*
⭘ *daily.* 📷 ♿

ONE OF THE BEST places to see manatees is at Homosassa Springs State Wildlife Park, where a floating observatory enables visitors to get close up to the animals.

Injured manatees, usually the victims of boat propellers, are treated and rehabilitated here before being released into the wild. There are often half a dozen in the recovery pool, and in winter more gather outside the park fence: as at Crystal River, in cold weather the manatees are attracted by the warm spring water.

Weeki Wachee Spring ❸

Road map D2. Hernando Co. Junction of US 19 & SR 50. 📞 *(352) 596-2062.*
🚉 *Brooksville.* ⭘ *daily.* 📷 ♿
🌐 www.weekiwachee.com

THIS LONG-STANDING theme park is built on one of Florida's largest freshwater springs. In the 1940s, ex-Navy frogman Newton Perry hit on the idea of using women swimmers to take the part of "live mermaids" performing

A performing "mermaid" at Weeki Wachee Spring

a kind of underwater ballet. A theater was built 15 ft (5 m) underwater with strategically placed air pipes for the swimmers to take in air.

Other attractions include Buccaneer Bay water park, a children's zoo, and a popular wilderness river cruise.

Tarpon Springs ❹

Road map D3. Pinellas Co.
🏠 20,000. 🚉 Clearwater. 🛈 11 E Orange St, (727) 937-6109.

The nature trail through unspoiled woodland on Caladesi Island

THIS LIVELY TOWN on the Anclote River is most famous as a center of Greek culture – the legacy of the immigrant fishermen lured here at the start of the 20th century by the prolific local sponge beds. You'll find restaurants specializing in Greek food, an Athens Street, a Poseidon gift shop, and a Parthenon bakery.

Alongside Dodecanese Boulevard are the Sponge Docks, which are busy once more – thanks to the recovery of the nearby sponge beds, decimated by bacterial blight in the 1940s. Boat trips organized by local sponge fishermen include a demonstration of sponge diving by a diver fitted out in a traditional suit.

The old **Spongeorama** museum and shopping village is housed in former dockside sheds, and the Sponge Exchange, now refurbished, is an upscale complex with galleries, boutiques, and quaint restaurants.

Two miles (3 km) south

rises **St. Nicholas Greek Orthodox Cathedral**, the most striking symbol of Tarpon Springs' Greek heritage. The Byzantine Revival church, a replica of St. Sophia in Istanbul, was erected in 1943 using marble transported all the way from Greece. It is the starting point for the Epiphany Festival, an important date in the local calendar *(see p35)*.

🏛 **Spongeorama**
510 Dodecanese Blvd.
📞 (727) 943-9509. 🚪 daily.

⛪ 🏛 **St. Nicholas Greek Orthodox Cathedral**
36 N Pinellas Ave. at Orange St.
📞 (727) 937-3540. 🚪 daily. ♿

Dunedin ❺

Road map D3. Pinellas Co.
🏠 36,000. 🚉 Clearwater. 🛈 301 Main St, (727) 733-3197.

DUNEDIN WAS founded by a Scotsman, John L Branch, who in 1870 opened a store to supply ships on their way down the Gulf Coast to Key West. Passing sea and rail routes brought trade and prosperity, and this soon attracted a number of his compatriots. Dunedin's Scottish heritage is still expressed in its annual Highland Games festival held in late March or early April.

The renovated properties on and around Main Street impart the authentic flavor of early 20th-century small-town Florida. The **Historical Museum**, which occupies Dunedin's former railroad

Trimming natural sponges before sale in Tarpon Springs

station, has a fine collection of photographs and artifacts from the town's early days. Nearby Railroad Avenue is now part of the Pinellas Trail, a paved walking and cycling path running for 47 miles (76 km) from Tarpon Springs to St. Petersburg, along the route of the former railroad.

🏛 **Historical Museum**
349 Main St. 📞 (727) 736-1176.
🚪 Tue –Sat. 🔴 public hols. ♿

ENVIRONS: Three miles (5 km) north of Dunedin, a causeway crosses to **Honeymoon Island State Recreation Area**. You can swim and fish there, but this barrier island is largely undeveloped, in order to preserve its status as an important osprey nesting site. It is also the departure point for the passenger ferry to the even more alluring **Caladesi Island State Park**, which can also be reached from Clearwater Beach *(see p238)*.

Caladesi's 3-mile (5-km) beach, fronting the Gulf of Mexico, was rated in 1995 as the second best in the country. The glorious beach gives way to dunes fringed by sea oats, which lead in turn to pine, cypress, and mangrove woods traversed by a 3-mile (5-km) nature trail. Maps are available from the visitor center.

🏕 **Honeymoon Island SRA**
Route 586, 3 miles (5 km) NW of Dunedin. 📞 (727) 469-5942.
🚪 daily. 🅿️ ♿ limited.
🏕 **Caladesi Island State Park**
1 Causeway Blvd. 📞 (727) 469-5918.
🚪 daily. 🅿️ ♿ limited.

Interior of the McMullen Log House, Pinellas County Heritage Village

Clearwater Beach ❻

Road map D3. Pinellas Co. 🏛 23,000.
✈ 🚌 Clearwater. 🚐 tourist trolley
from Cleveland St. 🛈 1130 Cleveland
St, Clearwater, (727) 461-0011.

THE SATELLITE of Clearwater city, this lively resort marks the start of the vacation strip that extends as far as Tampa Bay. Hotels and bars, often filled with European tourists, dominate the waterfront, but Clearwater Beach manages to retain some character. If you can't afford to stay on the Gulf side, there are cheaper hotels by the Intracoastal Waterway.

The broad sandy beach is very impressive, and the water sports facilities are excellent. Boat trips of all kinds depart from the marina: from diving or sports fishing expeditions to sunset cruises on the Gulf.

Screech owls in the Suncoast Sanctuary

ENVIRONS: Across Clearwater Pass is Sand Key, which runs south for 12 miles (19 km). **Sand Key Park**, near the top, has a popular palm-fringed beach ranked in the top 20 in the country, and offers a more down-to-earth scene than throbbing Clearwater Beach.

About 7 miles (11 km) to the south – beyond the chic residential district of Belleair, complete with a hotel built by Henry Plant (see pp46–7) – is the much-visited **Suncoast Seabird Sanctuary**. Up to 500 injured birds live at this sanctuary in Indian Shores.

Pelicans, owls, herons, egrets, and other species are all on view, while Ralph Heath, who runs the sanctuary, and his helpers offer guided tours.

It is well worth making the diversion inland to Largo, 8 miles (12 km) southeast of Clearwater Beach, to visit the **Pinellas County Heritage Village**. This consists of 16 historic buildings, brought here from various sites and restored. The highlights include the McMullen Log House (see p28) and the Seven Gables Home (1907), which offers a taste of the lifestyle of a wealthy Victorian family. Spinning, weaving, and other skills typical of Florida's pioneers are demonstrated in the museum at the center of the park.

🦅 Suncoast Seabird Sanctuary
18328 Gulf Blvd, Indian Shores.
🕻 (727) 391-6211. 🔘 daily. ⚕ ✓
🎟 **Pinellas County Heritage Village**
11909 125th Street N. 🕻 (727) 582-2123. 🔘 Tue–Sun. ⚫ public hols. ⚕

St. Petersburg Beaches ❼

Road map D3. Pinellas Co. ✈
🚌 Tampa. 🚌 St. Petersburg. 🚐 many
services from St. Petersburg. 🛈 St. Pete
Beach Chamber of Commerce, 6990
Gulf Blvd, (727) 360-6957.

SOUTH OF Clearwater you enter the orbit of the St. Petersburg Beaches. Until you reach Madeira Beach the waterfront scenes are rather disappointing. **Madeira Beach**, however, is a good place to stay if you prefer a laid-back atmosphere to the buzzing scenes of the bigger resorts. Johns Pass Village, a re-created fishing village nearby, also offers a quirkier-than-average choice of restaurants and shops. There is also a fishing pier and a marina, where fishing and other boats gather.

Farther south, monotonous ranks of hotels characterize Treasure Island. Next in line, **St. Pete Beach** (St. Petersburg was officially shortened to St. Pete because it was considered more evocative of a fun-filled resort) has a 7-mile (11-km) strip of white sand and a buzzing scene along the waterfront. At its southern end towers the Don CeSar Resort (see p309). Built in the 1920s, the hotel's scale and roll call of celebrity guests are typical of the grand hotels of that era.

At the southern tip of the barrier island group, **Pass-a-Grille** is a breath of fresh air after crowded St. Pete Beach. Skirted by the main coastal road, this sleepy community has some lovely homes from the early 1900s and beaches still in their natural state. A word of warning: take lots of change for the parking meters.

The extravagant Don CeSar Resort overlooking St. Pete Beach

Gulf Coast Beaches

With an average of 361 days of sunshine a year and just two hours' drive from Orlando, the coast between St. Petersburg and Clearwater is the busiest resort area along the Gulf Coast, attracting hordes of overseas visitors. Known variously as the Holiday Isles, the Pinellas Coast, or the Suncoast, the strip encompasses 28 miles (45 km) of superb barrier island beaches. Due to the high quality of the sand and water, plus the relative scarcity of pests, litter, and crime, the Suncoast regularly appears in lists of the nation's top beaches. Farther south, Sarasota's barrier island beaches are of an equally high standard: they attract more Floridians than package tourists. Wherever you are, expect a more laid-back mood than on the east coast.

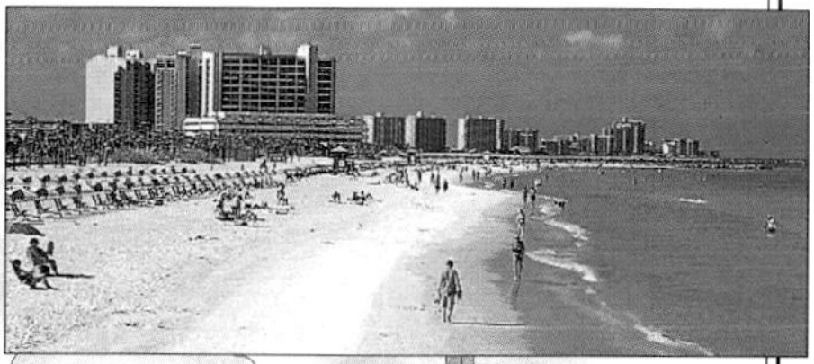

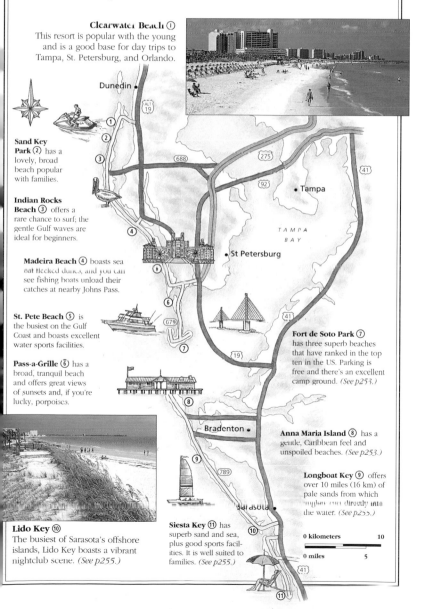

Clearwater Beach [1]
This resort is popular with the young and is a good base for day trips to Tampa, St. Petersburg, and Orlando.

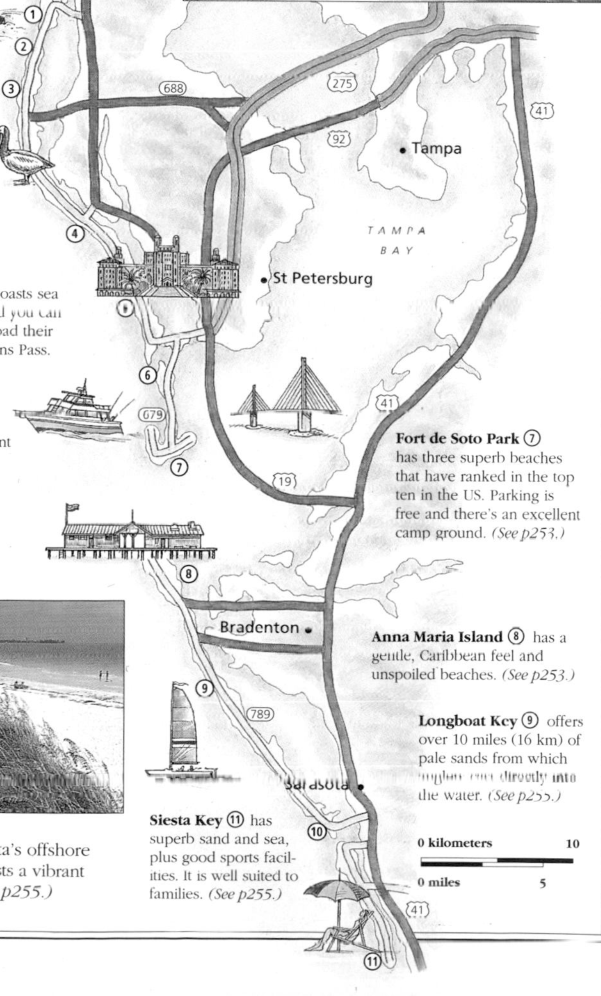

Dunedin
ALT 19
688
275
92
41
Tampa
TAMPA BAY
St Petersburg
679
19
Bradenton
789
Sarasota
0 kilometers 10
0 miles 5

Sand Key Park [2] has a lovely, broad beach popular with families.

Indian Rocks Beach [3] offers a rare chance to surf; the gentle Gulf waves are ideal for beginners.

Madeira Beach [4] boasts sea oat flecked dunes, and you can see fishing boats unload their catches at nearby Johns Pass.

St. Pete Beach [5] is the busiest on the Gulf Coast and boasts excellent water sports facilities.

Pass-a-Grille [6] has a broad, tranquil beach and offers great views of sunsets and, if you're lucky, porpoises.

Fort de Soto Park [7] has three superb beaches that have ranked in the top ten in the US. Parking is free and there's an excellent camp ground. *(See p253.)*

Anna Maria Island [8] has a gentle, Caribbean feel and unspoiled beaches. *(See p253.)*

Longboat Key [9] offers over 10 miles (16 km) of pale sands from which anglers cast directly into the water. *(See p255.)*

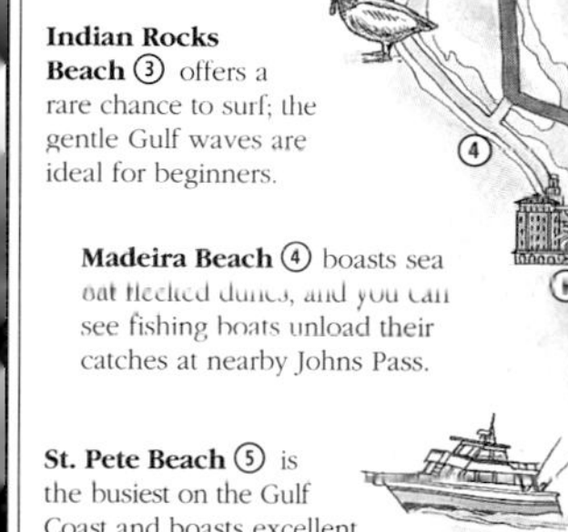

Lido Key [10]
The busiest of Sarasota's offshore islands, Lido Key boasts a vibrant nightclub scene. *(See p255.)*

Siesta Key [11] has superb sand and sea, plus good sports facilities. It is well suited to families. *(See p255.)*

St. Petersburg [8]

This city of broad avenues grew up in the great era of 19th-century land speculation. In 1875, Michigan farmer John Williams bought a plot of land beside Tampa Bay, with a dream of building a great city. An exiled Russian nobleman called Peter Demens soon provided St. Petersburg with both a railroad and its name – the latter in honor of his birthplace.

"St. Pete," as it is often called, used to be best known for its aging population. But times have changed, and the city now has a much more vibrant image. Extensive renovation has brought new life to the waterfront area downtown, and St. Petersburg's claim to be a lively cultural center is greatly boosted by the presence of the prestigious Salvador Dali Museum *(see pp242–3)*.

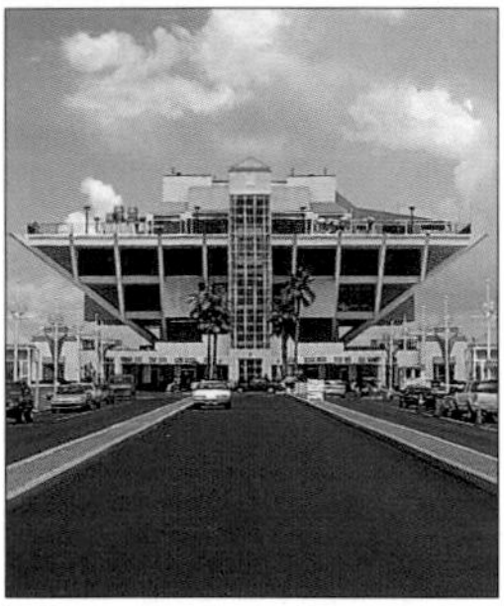

St. Petersburg's eye-catching Pier, its best known landmark

Exploring St. Petersburg

The landmark that appears in every tourist brochure about the city is **The Pier**. Its distinctive upside-down pyramid contains shops, restaurants, a disco, an aquarium, and an observation deck, and acts as a magnet for visitors heading for the downtown area. A tourist trolley service runs from the pier down to Great Explorations, stopping at all the major attractions en route.

Looking north from the pier, the handsome **Renaissance Vinoy Resort** *(see p309)*, built in the 1920s as the Vinoy Hotel and much modernized, dominates the downtown skyline. Away from the waterfront is the massive **Tropicana Field**, St. Petersburg's other main landmark. This is a popular place for large-scale activities ranging from rock concerts to sports events *(see p339)*.

🏛 St. Petersburg Museum of History

335 2nd Avenue NE. ☎ *(727) 894-1052.* ○ *daily.* ● *Thanksgiving, Dec 25, Jan 1.* 📷 ♿

[W] www.museumofhistoryonline.org

This museum tells the story of St. Petersburg from prehistoric times to the present. Exhibits range from mastodon bones, fossils, and native pottery to an entertaining mirror gallery, which gives visitors a comic taste of how they would have looked in Victorian fashions.

A special pavilion houses a replica of a sea plane called the *Benoist*, which marks St. Petersburg as the birthplace of commercial aviation. This aircraft made the first flight with a paying passenger across Tampa Bay in 1914.

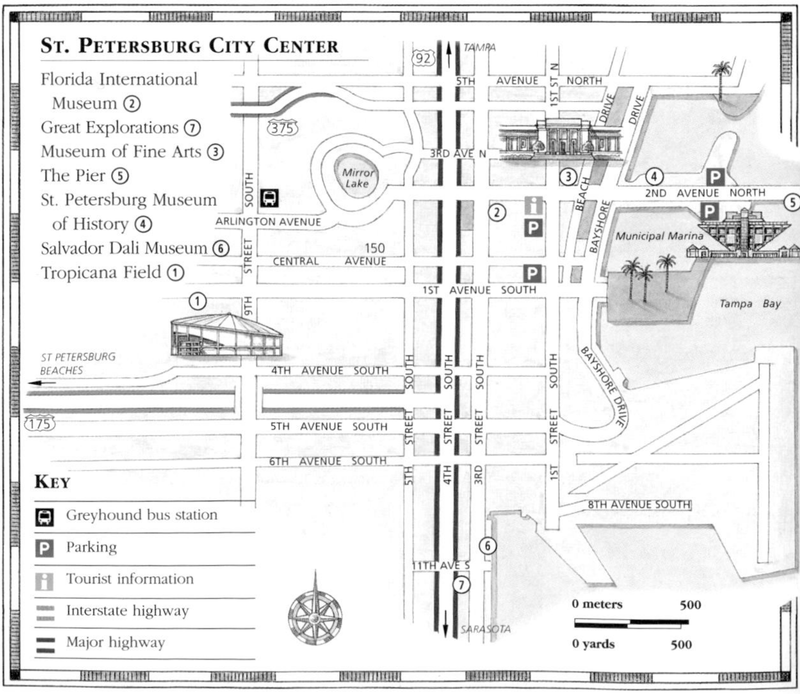
ST. PETERSBURG CITY CENTER
Florida International Museum ②
Great Explorations ⑦
Museum of Fine Arts ③
The Pier ⑤
St. Petersburg Museum of History ④
Salvador Dali Museum ⑥
Tropicana Field ①
KEY
Greyhound bus station
Parking
Tourist information
Interstate highway
Major highway
TAMPA
92
375
175
5TH AVENUE NORTH
1ST ST N
3RD AVE N
2ND AVENUE NORTH
BEACH DRIVE
BAYSHORE DRIVE
Mirror Lake
ARLINGTON AVENUE
CENTRAL AVENUE
150
1ST AVENUE SOUTH
9TH STREET SOUTH
Municipal Marina
Tampa Bay
ST PETERSBURG BEACHES
4TH AVENUE SOUTH
5TH AVENUE SOUTH
6TH AVENUE SOUTH
5TH STREET SOUTH
4TH STREET SOUTH
3RD STREET SOUTH
1ST STREET SOUTH
BAYSHORE DRIVE
8TH AVENUE SOUTH
11TH AVE S
SARASOTA
0 meters 500
0 yards 500

Poppy, one of Georgia O'Keeffe's acclaimed flower paintings, in the Museum of Fine Arts

🏛 Museum of Fine Arts

255 Beach Drive NE. 📞 *(727) 896-2667.* ⏰ *Tue–Sun.* 🚫 *Jan 1, Thanksgiving, Dec 25.* 📷 ♿ 📷
🌐 www.fine-arts.org

Housed in a striking modern Palladian-style building overlooking the bay, the Museum of Fine Arts is renowned for its wide-ranging collection of European, American, pre-Columbian, and Asian works. Supreme among the French Impressionist paintings are *A Corner of the Woods* (1877) by Cézanne and Monet's classic *Parliament, Effect of Fog, London* (1904). Other prominent works are the vivid *Poppy* (1927) by Georgia O'Keeffe, *La Lecture* (1888) by Berthe Morisot, and Auguste Rodin's *Invocation* (1886), which stands in the sculpture garden.

A large collection of photographs, dating from the early 1900s to the present, rounds off the collection.

🏛 Florida International Museum

100 2nd Street N. 📞 *(727) 821-1448.* ⏰ *daily.* 🚫 *Dec 25.* 📷 ♿
🌐 www.floridamuseum.org

Two blocks inland from St. Petersburg's pier, this museum occupies the former Maas Brothers department store, built in the 1950s. Behind an unprepossessing facade, the spacious interior provides excellent exhibition space. The museum has no permanent collection, but instead hosts a couple of large exhibitions each year, featuring items from some of the world's top museums. It opened in 1995 with the renowned "Treasures of the Czars" from the Kremlin.

🏛 Great Explorations

2nd Ave NE, The Pier
🏢 *(727) 821-8992.* ⏰ *daily.* 🚫 *Thanksgiving, Dec 25, Jan 1.* 📷 ♿ 🌐 www.greatexplorations.org

"Hands on" is the ethos at this museum, which is aimed at children but is equally fascinating to adults. It has six exhibit areas, focusing on the arts, sciences, and health.

Highlights include the Body Shop, where visitors can measure their strength and flexibility through a series of physical tests, and the Think Tank, with brain-teasers and problem-solving games. In the Touch Tunnel, you can check your reactions as you clamber and slide through a 90-ft (27-m) pitch-black maze.

🌿 Sunken Gardens

1825 4th Street N. 📞 *(727) 551-3100.* ⏰ *Wed–Sun.* 📷 ♿

Thousands of tropical plants and flowers flourish in this large walled garden, which descends to 10 ft (3 m) below the street outside. The site was

once a water-filled sinkhole *(see p20)*; its soil is kept dry by a network of hidden pipes.

Wander among the bougainvillea and hibiscus, and visit the extensive orchid garden. Other features include bird and alligator shows and a walk-through aviary full of parrots and macaws.

VISITORS' CHECKLIST

Road map D3. Pinellas Co.
🏠 *265,000.* ✈ *St. Petersburg/ Clearwater International Airport, 10 miles (16 km) N of Downtown.* 🚌 *180 9th St North, (727) 898-1496; also Amtrak bus to Pinellas Square Mall, Pinellas Park, (800) 872-7245.* ℹ *100 2nd Ave N, (727) 821-4715.* 🎭 *Festival of the States.* 🌐 *www.stpete.com*

Lush tropical plants flanking a stream at the Sunken Gardens

ENVIRONS: Five islands in Boca Ciega Bay south of St. Petersburg make up **Fort De Soto Park**. The park offers great views of the Sunshine Skyway Bridge and superb beaches, especially along the southern and western coasts. The islands are thick with vegetation and bird colonies and are popular with campers.

History fans should head for the chief island, Mullet Key, where massive gun emplacements concealed by high concrete walls mark the remains of Fort De Soto. The fort was begun during the Spanish-American War *(see p47)* but was never finished.

🏛 Fort De Soto Park

Pinellas Bayway, off Route 693, 9 miles (14 km) S of St. Petersburg.
📞 *(727) 866-2484.* ⏰ *daily.* ♿

The Sunshine Skyway Bridge, which spans the mouth of Tampa Bay

Salvador Dali Museum

ALTHOUGH FAR from the native country of Spanish artist Salvador Dali (1904–89), this museum boasts the most comprehensive collection of his work in the world, spanning the years 1914–70. The museum opened in 1982, 40 years after Ohio businessman Reynolds Morse first met Dali and began collecting his works. In addition to 95 original oil paintings, the museum has more than 100 watercolors and drawings, along with 1,300 graphics, sculptures, and other objects. The works range from Dali's early figurative paintings to his first experiments in Surrealism and the mature, large-scale compositions described as his "masterworks." The galleries and artworks are rotated regularly.

Masterworks Gallery
This focal point of the museum contains six of Dali's 18 masterworks, such as the Hallucinogenic Toreador, *which he painted in the years 1969–70.*

Nature Morte Vivante
This 1956 work is an example of Salvador Dali's use of a mathematical grid and the DNA spiral (as shown in the cauliflower) as the basis of a composition.

Museum Shop

★ The Sick Child
This early painting was composed in 1914, when Dali was just ten years old and already showing huge talent.

Entrance

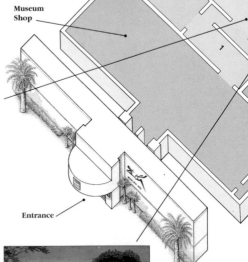

View of Cadaques
Impressionist influences are evident in this view, painted in 1917, of the shadow of Mount Pani stretching toward Dali's family home and other houses around the bay.

STAR PAINTINGS

- ★ **The Sick Child**

- ★ **The Discovery of America**

- ★ **Daddy Longlegs of the Evening–Hope!**

Don Quixote and Sancho
This 1968 etching is just one of over 1,000 drawings and other illustrations produced during Dali's Classic Period. Examples from the museum's collection appear in temporary exhibitions.

Raymond
James
Room

★ **The Discovery of America**
Inspired by a "cosmic dream," this work (1958–9) pays homage to the Spanish painter Velázquez while predicting man's first step on the moon.

5b

★ **Daddy Longlegs of the Evening– Hope!**
This bizarre image was the foundation stone of the collection. Painted in 1940, it shows a daddy longlegs crawling over the face of a hideously distorted violinist.

KEY TO FLOOR PLAN
- Introductory Gallery
- Early Works 1914–28
- Surrealism 1929–40
- Classic Period 1943–89
- Masterworks 1948–70
- Temporary exhibitions
- Nonexhibition space

GALLERY GUIDE
The collection is divided into five main galleries, ordered chronologically, with an introductory room. Temporary displays of Dali's many other works normally occupy the Raymond James Room.

HOW DALI'S ART CAME TO ST. PETERSBURG

Reynolds Morse and his fiancée Eleanor were fascinated by Salvador Dali from the time they saw an exhibition of his art in 1941. They bought their first Dali work, *Daddy Longlegs of the Evening–Hope!*, two years later and met the artist soon after. Thus began the Morses' lifelong friendship with Dali and his wife, Gala. Over the next 40 years the Morses amassed the largest private collection of Dali's art in the world. After a nationwide search, Morse chose the present waterfront site for the collection because of its resemblance to the artist's home town of Cadaques. The collection, bought by the Morses for about $5 million, is now worth in excess of $350 million.

Tampa ⑨

T AMPA IS ONE OF THE fastest-growing cities in Florida. Modern skyscrapers have replaced many original buildings, but vestiges of a colorful history remain – mainly in the old Cuban quarter, Ybor City *(see pp246–7)*, where Tampa's famous cigar industry took root in the 1880s, and in some quirky architecture downtown. The Spanish arrived here in 1539, but Tampa was just a small town until the late 1800s, when Henry Plant *(see pp46–7)* extended his railroad here. Today, Tampa's big attraction is Busch Gardens *(see pp250–51)*, one of the top theme parks in the US, but the sleek Florida Aquarium in the new Garrison Seaport Center is drawing more and more people into the heart of Tampa.

Greek vase, Museum of Art

View across Tampa with the university in the foreground

Exploring Downtown

You can easily explore Tampa's compact downtown area on foot. The main thoroughfare is the partly pedestrian Franklin Street, where you'll find the historic Tampa Theater and several examples of the public art on which the city justifiably prides itself.

Situated at the mouth of the Hillsborough River, Tampa can also be enjoyed from the water. The old paddlewheeler *Starlite Princess (see p339)* runs daytime and evening trips, while the Tampa Town Ferry, anchored near the Florida Aquarium, has regular hour-long tours, costing about $10. A water taxi covers a similar route, providing a view of the city's chief sights, including the old Tampa Bay Hotel and the Museum of Art.

For another view of downtown, take the free "People-mover" monorail from near the Hyatt Regency Hotel on Franklin Street across the water to Harbour Island.

🚻 Henry B. Plant Museum

401 W Kennedy Blvd. ☎ *(813) 254-1891.* ☐ *Tue–Sun.* ● *Thanksgiving, Dec 25, Jan 1. Donation requested.* ♿ Ⓦ www.plantmuseum.com

The luxurious Tampa Bay Hotel, which houses the Henry B. Plant Museum, is Tampa's most famous historic landmark, its Moorish minarets visible from all over the city.

Henry Plant commissioned the building in 1891 as a hotel for the well-to-do passengers

of his newly built railroad The construction alone cost $3 million, with an additional $500,000 spent on furnishings. The hotel was not a success, and it fell into disrepair soon after Plant's death in 1899. The hotel was bought by the city in 1905 and became part of the University of Tampa in 1933. The south wing of the ground floor was set aside and preserved as a museum.

Complete with a solarium, the museum is splendidly furnished and equipped, with 90 percent of the exhibits on display original to the hotel. Wedgwood china, Venetian mirrors, and 18th-century French furniture effortlessly evoke a lost age. Visitors are also welcome to walk around what is now the university campus to appreciate the sheer size of the building.

🏛 Tampa Museum of Art

600 N Ashley Drive. ☎ *(813) 274-8130.* ☐ *Tues-Sun.* ● *Easter, Thanksgiving, Dec 25, Jan 1.* 📷 ♿ Ⓦ www.ci.tampa.fl.us/museum

This museum exhibits everything from Greek, Roman, and Etruscan antiquities to 20th-century American fine art. The collection is too extensive to be displayed all at once, so the pieces are shown in rotation; the ancient pottery stands out among the antiquities. A large outdoor sculpture garden is the museum's most recent addition, and there is also a gallery devoted to local artists.

On the second Saturday of each month, the museum conducts free walking tours of the city's sculptures and other works of public art.

The elegant solarium at the Henry B. Plant Museum

Exterior of the Florida Holocaust Museum in St. Petersburg

⛫ Florida Holocaust Museum

55 Fifth St. S , St. Petersburg
📞 (727) 820-0100. ⭕ Mon–Fri.
⬤ public hols. 📷 ♿
ⓦ www.flholocaustmuseum.org

This museum, originally in Tampa Bay, reopened on February 21, 1999 in nearby downtown St. Petersburg.

There are no displays depicting the atrocities that took place; instead the exhibits focus on tolerance, education, and the history of anti-Semitism. There are many exhibits illustrating daily and religious Jewish life as it was before the Holocaust and after *Kristallnacht* (the Night of Broken Glass) in 1938. There is an introductory film, an interactive Tolerance and Learning Center, and an impressive memorial area.

🎭 Tampa Theater

711 Franklin St. 📞 (813) 274-8981.
⭕ daily. ⬤ Dec 25. 📷 ♿
📷 ⓦ www.tampatheatre.org

In its day, the Tampa Theater was one of the most elaborate movie theaters in America. The building was designed in 1926 by the architect John Eberson in an architectural style known as Florida-Mediterranean. The lavish result was described by the historian Ben Hall as an "Andalusian bonbon."

In an attempt to create the illusion of an outdoor location, Eberson fitted the ceiling with lights designed to twinkle like stars. Other effects included artificial clouds, produced by a smoke machine, and lighting designed to simulate the rising sun.

The easiest way to visit the beautifully restored theater, is to see a movie here *(see p339)*. Movie festivals, plays, and special events are all held here. Guided tours, which take place twice a month, include a 20-minute movie about the theater and a mini-concert on a traditional 1,000-pipe theater organ.

(see p339)

VISITORS' CHECKLIST

Road map D3. Hillsborough Co.
🏠 300,000. ✈ 5 miles (8 km) NW. 🚆 601 Nebraska Ave, (800) 872-7245. 🚌 610 Polk St, (800) 231-2222. ⛴ Channelside Drive, (813) 272-0555. 🚌 HARTline buses, (813) 254-4278. 🚤 Tampa Town Ferry and water taxi, (813) 223-1522. ℹ 400 N Tampa St, (813) 228-7777. 🎉 Gasparilla Festival (early Feb).

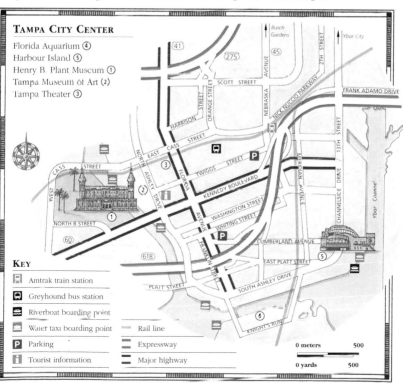

TAMPA CITY CENTER

Florida Aquarium ④
Harbour Island ⑤
Henry B. Plant Museum ①
Tampa Museum of Art ②
Tampa Theater ③

KEY

🚉 Amtrak train station

🚌 Greyhound bus station

🚤 Riverboat boarding point

🚤 Water taxi boarding point

🅿 Parking

ℹ Tourist information

🚊 Rail line

🚗 Expressway

═ Major highway

0 meters 500
0 yards 500

Street-by-Street: Ybor City

A CUBAN NAMED Don Vicente Martinez Ybor moved his cigar business from Key West to Tampa in 1886. About 20,000 migrant workers, mostly from Cuba and Spain, eventually joined him. The legacy of the cigar boom of the late 1800s and early 1900s is still visible in Ybor City. Its main street, 7th Avenue, with its Spanish-style tiles and wrought-iron balconies, looks much as it did then. Today the district is enjoying a new lease on life. What were once cigar factories and workers' cottages now house shops, restaurants, and clubs. Quiet during the day, Ybor City comes to life in the evening.

★ Ybor Square
The three enormous brick building of V.M. Ybor's original cigar factory once the largest in the world, are now occupied by a shopping mall, where you can buy quirky antique crafts, and gifts.

The Pleasure Dome has a tapas bar and three dance floors playing everything from jazz to high energy dance music.

Café Creole and Oyster Bar
You can enjoy Cajun and Creole food here, and eat alfresco in the courtyard. Jazz musicians entertain diners on weekends.

9TH AVENUE

8TH AVENUE

13TH STREET

15TH STREET

7TH AVENUE

AVENIDA / REPUBLICA DE CUBA

Masquerade at the Ritz,
a stunning 1917 movie theater, now houses one of Ybor's top nightclubs.

José Martí Park
A statue commemorates José Martí, the Cuban freedom fighter who made several visits to Ybor City to rally support for Cuba's independence campaign (see p47).

STAR SIGHTS

★ Ybor Square

★ Cigar Worker's House

0 meters	100
0 yards	100

KEY

– – – Suggested route

★ Cigar Worker's House
This tiny house (attached to Ybor City State Museum) is furnished to look like a cigar worker's home. "La Casita" is a fine example of the shotgun houses (see p287) built for the flood of immigrants who came to work in Ybor city in the late 1800s.

Little Sicily, an Italian-style deli, is a good place for lunch-time snacks.

Ybor City State Museum, housed in a former bakery, explores the history of Ybor City and also organizes walking tours of the district. There is a small ornamental garden attached.

9TH AVENUE
19TH STREET
18TH STREET
17TH STREET
LA SEPTIMA
Columbia Restaurant

Columbia Restaurant
Florida's oldest restaurant takes up a whole block on 7th Avenue. The Latino food and lively flamenco dancing make it popular with tourists (see p327).

La Tropicana serves traditional Cuban fare to its crowd of regulars.

El Sol Cigars
Although Ybor's oldest cigar store (opened in 1929) no longer rolls its cigars by hand, it is a good place to buy them.

THE CIGAR INDUSTRY IN TAMPA

With ships able to bring a regular supply of tobacco from Cuba to its port, Tampa was ideally located for cigar-making. Several huge cigar factories sprang up soon after V.M. Ybor moved here, and by 1900 Ybor City was producing over 111 million cigars annually. Each cigar was skillfully rolled by hand by workers who were often entertained by a lector reading aloud to them. Automation and the growing popularity of cigarettes changed all this. Cigars are still made in Tampa (mostly with leaves grown in Honduras), but now usually by machine. The Tampa Rico Company in Ybor Square is one of the few companies to hand roll cigars.

Workers in an Ybor City cigar factory, 1929

A diver amid reefs and exotic fish at the Florida Aquarium

🐠 Florida Aquarium

701 Channelside Drive. 📞 *(813) 273-4000.* ⭕ *daily.* ⬤ *Thanksgiving, Dec 25.* 🅿️ ♿ ⬛ *www.flaquarium.org*

This enormous aquarium, which opened in 1995 at a cost of $84 million, is located on the waterfront, and unmistakable with its blue, shell-shaped dome, it is a state-of-the-art interpretation of a modern aquarium. Inside, visitors will not only find tanks of fish but will also come face to face with baby alligators, birds, otters, and all kinds of other creatures living in their authentic habitats.

The purpose of the Florida Aquarium is to enable visitors to follow the passage of a drop of water from its first appearance in an underground spring to its arrival in the sea, passing through various habitats along the way.

The conditions of each habitat are re-created in separate galleries. The Florida Coral Reefs Gallery, for instance, takes visitors underwater for a panoramic view of a coral colony and its schools of colorful tropical fish. You can rent recorded commentaries by experts at different stages of the tour, and there are regular hands-on labs, with special projects and activities, and biologists and botanists standing by to explain them.

🏛 Hyde Park

Across the river, southwest of Downtown off Bayshore Boulevard, Hyde Park is a rare historic area in Tampa. Dating from the late 19th century, its houses display a striking mix of architectural styles from Colonial to Gothic Revival.

The quiet residential streets of Hyde Park are best explored by car. The one part to tempt people out of their vehicles is Old Hyde Park Village, off Snow Avenue, where you'll find several upscale shops and restaurants. On some days, musicians come out to entertain the shoppers.

An open-air concert for visitors to Old Hyde Park Village

🏛 Museum of Science and Industry

4801 E Fowler Ave. 📞 *(813) 987-6100.* ⭕ *daily.* 🅿️ ♿ ⬛ *www.mosi.org*

This excellent museum is another distinctive addition to the Tampa skyline; its Art Nouveau-style dome houses an IMAX® cinema, and the museum features all kinds of interactive displays. The Amazing You is an exploration of the human body and how it works, and in the hurricane room visitors can create their own tropical storm. The GTE Challenger Learning Center is a living memorial to the crew of the space shuttle Challenger *(see p185),* with simulators of a space station and a mission control room. Another major attraction is the Focus Gallery, which houses visiting exhibits.

MOSI is also home to the Saunders Planetarium, which hosts regular astronomical shows. On every Friday and Saturday evening, there are special star-viewing sessions at which, weather permitting, telescopes are set up in the parking lot so that visitors can observe the night sky.

🦒 Lowry Park Zoo

7530 N Blvd. 📞 *(813) 932-0245.* ⭕ *daily.* ⬤ *Thanksgiving, Dec 25.* 🅿️ ♿ ⬛ *www.lowryparkzoo.com*

This zoo, 6 miles (10 km) north of downtown Tampa, is one of the best in North America. One of the main attractions is the manatee center, which has up to 20 animals in residence at any one time and a rehabilitation pool. You can learn more about this endangered species by taking part in the "Manatee Sleepover," a special program that offers the chance to explore the zoo after closing time, learn about the rehabilitation program, and spend the night at the manatee center.

The zoo's Florida Wildlife Center, a special sanctuary for native animals such as alligators and the Florida panther, is another highlight. Other areas to visit are Primate World, the Asian Domain, home to Sumatran tigers and

The eye-catching dome of the Museum of Science and Industry

THE LEGEND OF GASPAR

José Gaspar was a legendary pirate who preyed on ships and communities between Tampa and Fort Myers in the 19th century. His stronghold was among the isles of the Lee Island Coast *(see pp264–5)*, many of whose modern names recall the association – including Gasparilla and Captiva, where Gaspar is said to have kept his female captives. The story goes that the pirate was eventually cornered by a US warship, and that he drowned himself in anchor chains rather than be taken prisoner.

Tampa suffered from several of Gaspar's raids, and now holds a Gasparilla Festival each February *(see p35)*. The highlight of this celebration is a mock invasion of the city by hundreds of rowdy villains aboard the world's only fully-rigged "pirate ship."

"Pirates" celebrating Tampa's Gasparilla Festival in the 1950s

A Sumatran tiger lounges at Asian Domain, Lowry Park Zoo

an extremely rare Indian rhino, and a free-flight aviary. There is also a children's museum, an amusement center, and a pleasant picnic area.

Busch Gardens ⓾

See pp250–51.

Hillsborough River ⓫

Road map D3. Hillsborough Co. 🚂 *Tampa.* 🚌 *Tampa.*

EXTENDING THROUGH the countryside northeast of Tampa, the Hillsborough River provides a pleasant respite from the hustle and bustle of the city. It is flanked on both sides by dense backwoods of live oak, cypress, magnolia, and mangrove trees, which once covered great swathes of Florida's terrain.

One of the best ways to experience the Hillsborough River is by canoe: **Canoe Escape** organizes trips along a stretch of the river about 15 minutes' drive from downtown Tampa. Located just beyond the city line, the area is surprisingly wild, and you have a good chance of spotting a great variety of wildlife, including herons, egrets, alligators, turtles, and otters. Canoeing conditions are ideal for beginners. You can choose from three main itineraries, each of which covers about 5 miles (8 km) – involving roughly two hours' paddling and allowing you plenty of time to absorb the surroundings; longer day trips are also available.

A section of the river is protected as **Hillsborough River State Park**. Canoeing is a popular way to explore here too; there are also walking trails, and you can swim and fish. The park has a large and popular campground,

which is open all year round, and there are also numerous picnic sites.

Developed in 1936, the Hillsborough River State Park became one of Florida's earliest state parks partly due to the historic significance of Fort Foster, built during the Second Seminole War *(see p44)* to guard a bridge at the confluence of the Hillsborough River and Blackwater Creek. The fort and bridge have been reconstructed, and a battle is re-enacted here annually in March. Tours visit the fort every weekend and on holidays; a shuttle bus runs to it from the park's entrance.

Canoe Escape
9335 E Fowler Ave, Thonotosassa, 12 miles (19 km) NE of Tampa. 🅲 *(813) 986-2067.* 🔾 *daily.* ⬤ *Thanksgiving, Dec 24 & 25.* 🈶

🎋 Hillsborough River State Park
15402 US 301, 12 miles (19 km) NE of Tampa. 🅲 *(813) 987-6771.* 🔾 *daily.* 🈶 🅱 🅰

Re-created buildings at Fort Foster in Hillsborough River State Park

Busch Gardens ❿

Busch Gardens is one-of-a-kind – a theme park that incorporates one of America's top zoos. To fulfill its unusual aim of re-creating life in colonial-era Africa, the park supports over 2,600 animals, with giraffes and zebras roaming freely over the "Serengeti Plain"; lions gorillas, and other African animals can be seen from a safari ride. Timbuktu's Dolphin Theater stages a popular dolphin show, and Bird Gardens features macaws, cockatoos, and birds of prey. Animals are the main attraction, but there are thrill rides too. The newest addition is Gwazi, an enormous dueling double roller coaster. Adventure Island, adjacent to Busch Gardens, is Florida's largest water park, offering water coasters and fun in the sun.

Congo River Rapids
Rapids, geysers, waterfalls, and a dark cave await rafters set adrift on a swift river current.

★ Kumba
The largest and fastest roller coaster in Florida, Kumba is Busch Gardens' top thrill ride. Participants plunge 135 ft (41 m) at speeds of more than 60 mph (100 km/h).

Dolphin Theater

Timbuktu

Stanleyville

Land of the Dragons
This children's play area has scaled-down rides for young visitors and a three-story tree-house, complete with bridges and a winding staircase.

Mystic Sheiks of Morocco
A marching band called the Mystic Sheiks gives impromptu performances at a variety of locations throughout the day.

Gwazi

| 0 meters | 100 |
| 0 yards | 100 |

Bird Gardens

KEY

🚊 Train station

💳 ATM (cash machine)

STAR ATTRACTIONS

★ Kumba

★ Edge of Africa

★ Egypt

★ Edge of Africa
This safari experience, on the southern edge of the Serengeti Plain, offers visitors a chance to have a close-up view of lions, hippos, hyenas, and other African animals.

VISITORS' CHECKLIST

Road map 3D. Busch Boulevard, Tampa. ☎ *(813) 987 5082.*
✈ *Tampa.* 🚆 *Tampa.* 🚌 *5, 14 & 18 from Marion St, downtown Tampa.* ○ *9:30am–6pm daily, extended hours for summer and holidays.* 🖾 🛦 🍴 🛒
W www.buschgardens.com
W www.adventureisland.com

Serengeti Plain

★ Egypt
The new hair-raising Akbar's Adventure Tours is found here, as well as a replica of Tutankhamun's tomb, a museum, and a bazaar.

A train can be taken around all the major areas within the park.

Entrance

Guest Relations

Myombe Reserve
This simulated rain-forest is the habitat of six western lowland gorillas and seven chimpanzees, both of which are endangered species.

World Rhythms on Ice
A 19th century German castle is the starting point for this new world-class ice-skating extravaganza, which focuses on a whirlwind tour of the countries of the world with incredible sets and spectacular special effects.

Florida Southern College [12]

Road map E3. Polk Co. 111 Lake Hollingsworth Drive, Lakeland. ☎ *(863) 680-4110.* 🚆 *Lakeland.* 🚌 *Lakeland.* ○ *Mon–Fri.* ● *Jul 4, Thanksgiving, Dec 25, Jan 1.* **Visitor Center** ○ *Tue–Sat, Sun (pm only).* ♿

This small college has the world's largest collection of buildings designed by Frank Lloyd Wright. Amazingly, the college president managed to persuade Wright (probably the most eminent architect of his day) to design the campus at Lakeland with the promise of little more than the opportunity to express his ideas – and payment when the money could be raised.

The light and spacious interior of the Annie Pfeiffer Chapel

Work began in 1938 on what Wright, already famous as the founder of organic architecture, termed his "child of the sun." His aim of blending buildings with their natural surroundings made special use of glass to bring the outdoor light to the interiors. The original plan was for 18 buildings, but only seven had been completed by the time Wright died in 1959; five were finished or added later.

The Annie Pfeiffer Chapel is a particularly fine expression of his ideas. Windows of stained glass break the monotony of the building blocks, and the entire edifice is topped by a spectacular tower in place of the traditional steeple; Wright called it a "jewel box."

As a whole, the campus has the light and airy feel that Wright sought to achieve. The buildings are linked to each other by the Esplanades – a covered walkway, stretching for 1.5-miles (2 km), in which light, shade, and variations in height draw attention from one building to the next.

You can wander around the campus at any time, but the interiors can be explored only during the week. The Thad Buckner Building, complete with clerestory windows, now houses a visitor center, where you can see drawings and furniture by Wright and photographs of the building work.

The antebellum Gamble Mansion

Gamble Plantation [13]

Road map D3. Manatee Co. 3708 Patten Ave, Ellenton. ☎ *(941) 723-4536.* 🚆 *Tampa.* 🚌 *Bradenton.* ○ *Thu–Mon.* ● *Thanksgiving, Dec 25, Jan 1.* 👥 ♿ *limited.* ☕

The only antebellum home left in southern Florida, this whitewashed mansion stands a little incongruously behind a picket fence on the main road into Bradenton.

It was built in 1845–50 by Major Robert Gamble, one of the most successful of the sugar planters who settled along the fertile Manatee River after the Second Seminole War *(see p44)*. Gamble built up his holding to cover 3,500 acres (1,416 ha), but only a fraction of this remains. The

Florida Southern College

Annie Pfeiffer Chapel [6]
Benjamin Fine Building [2]
Emile Watson Building [1]
J. Edgar Wall Waterdome [3]
Lucius Pond Ordway Building [9]
Polk County Science Buildings [8]
Raulerson Building [4]
Thad Buckner Building [5]
William Danforth Chapel [7]

Key

Esplanades
[P] Parking
[i] Information

0 meters 100
0 yards 100

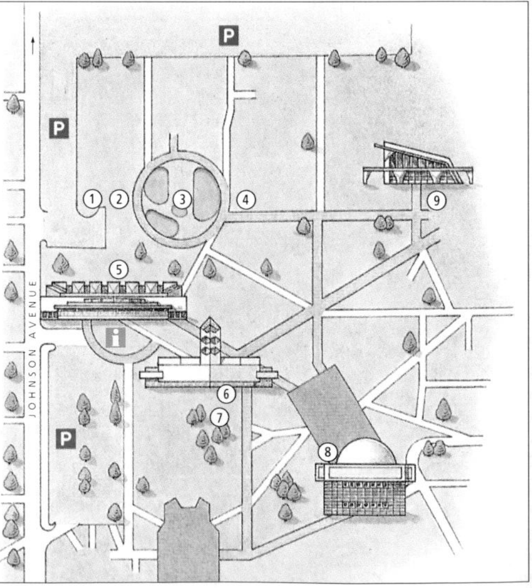

site of the old slave quarters, for instance, is now a school. The house is furnished just as it was in its heyday, and the garden, flourishing with live oak trees draped with Spanish moss, is pure Deep South.

However, romantic notions about Gamble's life are swept away in the small museum in the visitor center. Gamble got into financial difficulties and was forced to sell the house to pay his debts; among the artifacts on display in the museum is a document showing that the plantation, along with the grounds and 191 slaves, was sold in 1856 for the sum of $190,000.

Bradenton ⓮

Road map D3. Manatee Co.
🏠 *48,000.* ✈ 🚌 *including Amtrak Thruway bus.* ℹ *5030 Highway 301 N, (941) 729-7040.*

THE SEAT OF Manatee County, Bradenton is best known as the home of the Nick Bollettieri Tennis Academy *(see p343)*, the school that has nurtured the early promise of such world tennis stars as Andre Agassi and Pete Sampras.

The local beaches are a big attraction, but a couple of sights deserve a visit before you head off to the beach. **Manatee Village Historical Park** recounts the story of the Florida frontier a century ago through a fascinating collection of restored buildings. These include a boat house, a general store, and an early settler's house, and all have been furnished as they would have looked originally.

The **South Florida Museum** is both educational and fun. "Florida from Stone Age to Space Age" is the theme, with exhibits ranging from dinosaur dioramas to life-size replicas of 16th-century Spanish-style buildings and early cars. Laser shows add excitement to the Bishop Planetarium program, while the Parker Aquarium gives a lively overview of local marine life.

The kitchen of an early settler's house at Manatee Village Historical Park

🚩 **Manatee Village Historical Park**
604 15th St E. ☎ *(941) 749-7165.* ⭘ *Mon–Fri (Winter: Sun pm).* ● *public hols.* ♿

🏛 **South Florida Museum**
201 10th St W. ☎ *(941) 746-4131.* ⭘ *daily.* ● *public hols.* 🎫 ♿
ⓦ *www.sfmbp.org*

ENVIRONS: Five miles (8 km) west of central Bradenton, the **De Soto National Memorial** commemorates the landing near here in 1539 of Hernando de Soto *(see pp40–41).* He and his 600 men set out on an epic four-year 4,000-mile (6,500-km) trek into the southeastern US in search of gold. They discovered the Mississippi, but the trek was disastrous and de Soto and half his army died.

A monument recalls the luckless explorers and marks the start of the De Soto Trail, which follows part of the route they took. The park also has a replica of de Soto's

Stone monument to explorer De Soto

base camp; this is staffed by costumed volunteers, who give a memorable insight into the daily routines of the Spanish conquistadors. A visitor center has a museum, a bookstore, and exhibits of 16th-century weapons and armor. There is also a half-mile (1-km) nature trail through mangroves.

Two bridges link Bradenton to **Anna Maria Island**, whose sandy shoreline, backed by dunes, is largely undeveloped but is washed by breakers big enough to attract a handful of surfers. There is a scattering of small resorts based around the three main communities of Anna Maria, Holmes Beach, and Bradenton Beach. In the north stands the picturesque Anna Maria Pier, which was built in 1910. It has a small restaurant, snack bar, and shop at its seaward end.

🚩 **De Soto National Memorial**
75th Street NW. ☎ *(941) 792-0458.* ⭘ *daily.* ● *Thanksgiving, Dec 25, Jan 1.* ♿

Sunset on Anna Maria Island's beautiful, unspoiled beach

Sarasota 🏛

Hibiscus in the Selby Gardens

THIS CITY IS KNOWN AS Florida's cultural center, a fact often credited to John Ringling *(see p255)*, who was one of many influential people attracted to the up-and-coming town in the early 1900s. Ringling poured money into the area, and his legacy is all around, nowhere more so than in his house and fine art collection, the city's biggest attraction *(see pp256–9)*. Sarasota's other great asset is that it seems to have escaped the worst excesses of the state's other cities. Promoted as "Florida's Mild Side," Sarasota is an attractive and clean community, with the bonus of a waterfront setting. You can join its affluent and conservative inhabitants browsing around its stylish shops or lying on the beach. Fabulous barrier island beaches are just a short drive from downtown Sarasota and are the best places to stay.

Exploring Sarasota

The most pleasant area of downtown Sarasota focuses on Palm Avenue and Main Street, where restored storefronts dating from the early 20th century house antique shops, bars, and restaurants. Shopping and eating are also the main activities at nearby Sarasota Quay, and you can sign up for dinner cruises and other boat trips at the adjacent marina.

Dominating the waterfront to the north is the striking Van Wezel Performing Arts Hall *(see p29)*. Opened in 1970, this distinctive pink and lavender building is worth a visit both to admire its sweeping, seashell-inspired lines, and to attend one of the many events, including concerts and Broadway shows, which are staged here *(see p339)*.

🏛 Museum of Cars and Music of Yesterday

5500 N Tamiami Trail. **🗎** *(941) 355-6228.* **◯** *daily.* **●** *Dec 25.* **⊠** **₺** **✓**
Ⓦ www.sarasotacarmuseum.org

This museum is a strange mixture, with 120 old cars and over 1,000 music boxes, organs, and other musical novelties all under one roof.

Highlights of the collection, described by expert guides, are a rare 1954 Packard Model 120 convertible, a 1955 Rolls-Royce Silver Wraith, and a 1981 De Lorean in mint condition. The Great Music Hall contains pianos, phonographs, and a musical chair (which plays when you sit on it), available on a guided tour.

A favorite among young and old alike is the antique arcade, with dozens of working slot machines.

An 1890s carousel organ at the museum

Flamingos gather at a small lake at Sarasota Jungle Gardens

♣ Sarasota Jungle Gardens

3701 Bayshore Rd. **🗎** *(877) 861-6547.* **◯** *daily.* **●** *Dec 25.* **⊠** **₺**
Ⓦ www.sarasotajunglegardens.com

Originally developed as a botanical garden, this 10-acre (4-ha) former banana grove offers an oasis of tropical plants, trees, and flowers from around the world, with palm forests and gardens of hibiscus, ferns, roses, gardenias, and bougainvillea. The flamingo lagoon is a big attraction.

Other attractions, including a children's zoo and butterfly museum, place an emphasis on education and conservation. Simple and unsophisticated entertainment is offered by the exotic bird shows and a reptile show. There are also a cafe and a bookstore.

♣ Marie Selby Botanical Gardens

811 S Palm Ave. **🗎** *(941) 366-5730.* **◯** *daily.* **●** *Dec 25.* **⊠** **₺**
Ⓦ www. selby.org

You needn't be a gardener to appreciate the former home of wealthy Sarasota residents William and Marie Selby. Set among laurel and banyan trees overlooking Sarasota Bay, the estate was designed by Marie during the early 1920s as an escape from the modern world: you can still see the bamboo curtain she had planted to obscure the growing Sarasota skyline.

The gardens have more than 20,000 tropical plants and are particularly famous for their collection of orchids and epiphytes *(see p276)*. There are also display areas devoted to all kinds of exotic plants, from

Christy Payne House in the Marie Selby Botanical Gardens

tropical foods and herbs to colorful hibiscus plants. The Tropical Display House has an impressive array of jungle vegetation.

The Spanish-style house, now a gift shop, is of less interest than the 1930s Christy Payne House. This delightful plantation-style mansion holds a Museum of Botany and Arts.

🏛 St. Armands Circle

This upscale shopping and dining complex on St. Armands Key was one of John Ringling's creations. He purchased the island in 1917 and produced an adventurous plan for a housing development, which centered on a circular shopping mall featuring gardens and classical statues. The area flourished briefly before being caught up in the Depression but was revived in the 1950s. It now looks much as Ringling planned, with shady avenues radiating from a central point.

St. Armands Circle, well placed between Downtown and the beaches, is popular both during the day and at night. The shops are mostly expensive, but anyone can enjoy the street entertainers who often congregate here.

🚤 Mote Marine Aquarium

1600 Ken Thompson Parkway.
📞 (941) 388-2451. ⬤ daily.
⬤ Dec 25. 🎫 ♿ 📷
🖥 www.mote.org

This aquarium is located on City Island, between Lido and Longboat Keys. It has a bay walk with an excellent view of the Sarasota skyline, but

Young visitors observe tropical fish at the Mote Marine Aquarium

the real attractions can be found inside. Among the most popular exhibits is a huge shark tank, complete with underwater observation windows, and a "touch tank," where you can come to grips with all kinds of marine creatures, from horseshoe crabs and whelks to stingrays. More than 30 other aquariums are stocked with local fish and plants; there is a display on the rivers, bays, and estuaries of the surrounding area.

Explanatory leaflets provide a useful insight into every exhibit, while guides explain how the aquarium ties in with the work of the attached laboratory, prominent in the study of sharks and pollution.

🐦 Pelican Man's Bird Sanctuary

1708 Ken Thompson Parkway.
📞 (941) 388-4444. ⬤ daily.
⬤ public hols. ♿
🖥 www.pelicanman.org

Pelican Man's Bird Sanctuary treats more than 5,000 injured birds annually in its hospital.

VISITORS' CHECKLIST

Road map D3. Sarasota Co.
🏛 60,000. ✈ 2 miles (3 km) N.
🚌 575 N Washington Blvd,
(941) 955-5735; Amtrak bus,
(800) 872-7245. ℹ 655 N
Tamiami Trail, (941) 957-1877.
🎪 Circus Festival (Jan)
🖥 www.sarasotafl.org

Most of the birds are returned to the wild once they have been rehabilitated, but those too badly hurt to fend for themselves join the permanent residents; these can be seen in the sanctuary's pens.

The Pelican Man himself is Dale Shields, a self-taught bird expert who is happy to share his knowledge with visitors to the sanctuary.

Dale Shields, alias Pelican Man, at his sanctuary

🦩 Sarasota Beaches

The nearby barrier islands, Longboat Key, Lido Key, and Siesta Key, boast superb sandy beaches facing the Gulf of Mexico, and they are understandably popular (see p239). Development has been intense, with condos along the shore in places, but there are several quieter areas too. The beach in South Lido Park, on Lido Key, is peaceful during the week and has a pleasant woodland trail too.

On Siesta Key the main residential area is in the north, focused around a network of canals. The broad Siesta Key Beach nearby is lively at any time. You'll find a quieter scene at Turtle Beach, which also has the only campground on these Keys. Longboat Key is well known for its golf courses. Wherever you are, the water sports are excellent.

South Lido Park beach, with a view south of nearby Siesta Key

Ringling Museum of Art

Majolica
jar (c.1550)

JOHN RINGLING was an Ohio-born circus manager whose phenomenally successful show *(see p258)* made him a multimillionaire. His money and his regular trips abroad gave him many opportunities to purchase European art, and when he moved his winter home to Sarasota in 1910 he built a museum to house his vast collection. He and his wife, Mable, had a particular affection for Italy, and their magnificent Italian Baroque paintings are the cornerstone of the collection. Their estate, which includes the palatial Ca' d'Zan *(see pp258–9)*, was bequeathed to the state following John Ringling's death in 1936.

Statuary
The courtyard is dotted with copies of Classical sculpture, such as this bronze chariot.

A replica of
Michelangelo's
David

West Galleries
Built in the 1960s, these rooms contain temporary exhibits of mostly contemporary art; photography, painting, and sculpture are all represented. John Chamberlain's Car Parts *stands at the entrance to the galleries.*

12
13
14
15
16
17

GALLERY GUIDE

The galleries are arranged around a sculpture garden, with the West Galleries and Asolo Theater dominating one end of the courtyard. Starting with the galleries to the right of the entrance hall, the rooms roughly follow a chronological order counterclockwise, ranging from late medieval European painting to 18th-century American art; 16th- and 17th-century Italian painting is well represented. Modern art and special exhibitions are displayed in the West Galleries.

★ Astor Rooms
These lavish 19th-century interiors came from a New York mansion. Displays include a series of exquisite majolica jars from the early 16th century.

PLAN OF RINGLING MUSEUM

P — Ca' d'Zan — Circus Museum
Entrance
Sarasota Bay
Rose Garden
Exit
Museum of Art

41

STAR FEATURES

★ Astor Rooms

★ Courtyard

★ Rubens Gallery

The Asolo Theater
is an ornate 18th-
century theater,
brought over in
1947 from a
castle near
Venice.

VISITORS' CHECKLIST

5401 Bay Shore Road, Sarasota.
📞 *(941) 359-5700.* 🚌 *2, from
the corner of 1st St and Lemon
St, Downtown.* **House, Galleries
and Circus Museum** ◻ *10am–
5:30pm daily.* ● *Thanksgiving,
Dec 25, Jan1.* 📷 ♿ *1st floor
only of the Ca' d'Zan.* 🎫 🍴 🛍
W️ www.ringling.org

★ **Courtyard**
*A gallery of 91 antique columns of
various styles surrounds the courtyard.
Some of them date from the 11th century.*

The Building of a Palace
*This early Italian Baroque painting by Piero di Cosimo
is one of the gallery's proudest possessions. Painted in oil
on a wooden panel, it dates from around 1515.*

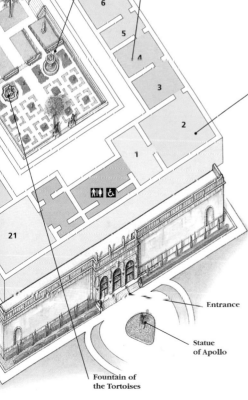

**Fountain of
Oceanus**

11
10
9
8
7
6
5
4
3
2
1
21

Entrance

**Statue
of Apollo**

**Fountain of
the Tortoises**

★ **Rubens Gallery**
*This gallery has the museum's
greatest treasures, including*
Abraham and Melchizedek,
painted in 1625.

KEY TO FLOOR PLAN

◻ Dutch and Flemish 1600–1700
◻ Rubens Gallery
◻ Medieval and Renaissance
◻ Italian 1500–1700
◻ French and Spanish 1600–1700
◻ European and American 1700–1800
◻ Astor Rooms
◻ Temporary exhibitions
◻ Rubens/Educational Installation

Ringling Museum: Ca' d'Zan

THE RINGLINGS' WINTER RESIDENCE, Ca' d'Zan, was the first part of the Ringling estate to be completed, providing a spectacular foretaste of what was to come. The Ringlings' love of Italy, nurtured during frequent visits to Europe, was displayed for all to see in the building's design as well as in its Venetian name, meaning "House of John." The property, which overlooks Sarasota Bay, was modeled after a typical Venetian palace, but there are also features drawn from French and Italian Renaissance architecture, as well as Baroque and more modern styles.

Set off by a 200-ft (60-m) marble terrace and crowned by a distinctive tower, Ca' d'Zan took two years to build and was finished in 1926. The ballroom, kitchen, bedrooms, and exercise room all provide glimpses of the life of the American super-rich of the period, and much of the original furniture is still in place.

★ **Ceramic Decoration**
The exterior of Ca' d'Zan boasts some of the finest examples of ceramic work in the country.

Solarium

★ **Ballroom**
The dominant feature of the ballroom is the extraordinary ceiling painting Dances of the Nations. *Depicting a variety of national dance costumes, it was painted by Willy Pogany, a 1930s' Hollywood set and costume designer.*

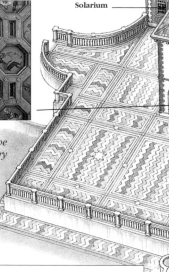

THE RINGLING CIRCUS

What started as a traveling wagon show, founded in 1884 by the five Ringling brothers, developed into one the most successful circuses of the era. The Ringlings' varied bill of entertainment proved more enduring than their rivals' offerings, and the brothers gradually bought up their competitors. In 1907, they formed a partnership with Phineas T. Barnum, whose taste for Siamese twins and exotic animals gave the circus a new slant from its more traditional origins.

The Circus Museum, opened in 1948, was not Ringling's idea, but with its models, carved circus wagons, and other rare items it gives a colorful insight into circus life.

Barnum's *Five Graces* circus wagon, 1878

The court, with its marble floors and onyx columns, was the Ringlings' living room and is the focal point of the house.

STAR FEATURES

★ **Ballroom**

★ **Ceramic Decoration**

Taproom

With its vaulted ceiling and stained-glass windows, the Taproom illustrates Ringling's love of collecting objects from far afield; he bought the bar from Cicardi's Restaurant in St. Louis, Missouri.

Exercise room

The tower was lit up when the Ringlings were at home.

Servants' rooms

Mable Ringling's bedroom features an elegant 1920s Louis XV-style suite and pillow cases she made herself.

Kitchen

John Ringling's Bedroom

The handsome Empire-style mahogany furniture, made in 1880, lends an austere air to this room. Jacob de Wit's Dawn Driving Away the Darkness *(1735) adorns the ceiling.*

John Ringling's Office

Bathroom

A barber's chair is the centerpiece of the bathroom, where the walls are faced with Siena marble; the tub is carved from a single block of stone.

Breakfast Room

This simply decorated room was used mainly for informal family occasions. The Venetian blinds are original.

Lush vegetation overhanging the river in Myakka River State Park

Myakka River State Park ⑯

Road map D3. Sarasota Co. 13207 SR 72, 9 miles (14 km) E of Sarasota. ⛟ *Sarasota.* 🅲 *(941) 361-6511.* ⬤ *daily.* 🅟 ♿ 🅖 🅒 🅐

IN SPITE OF ITS PROXIMITY to the city of Sarasota, in the Myakka River State Park you can enjoy a taste of how the region must have looked to its first settlers. Dense oak, palm thickets, pine flatwoods, and an expanse of dry prairie are interspersed with marshland, swamps, and lakes.

The parkland's 28,000 acres (11,300 ha), which stretch along the Myakka River and around Upper Myakka Lake, form an outstanding wildlife sanctuary. More than 200 species of birds have been recorded here, including egrets, blue herons, vultures, and ibis, all of which are plentiful, as well as much rarer ospreys, bald eagles, and wild turkeys. Alligators and deer can usually be seen, though other denizens such as foxes are glimpsed only rarely. Observation platforms, from which you can view the wildlife, are dotted throughout the park.

Ambitious explorers can take to the park's 39 miles (63 km) of marked hiking trails or 15 miles (24 km) of bridle trails; alternatively, there are guided tours by tram between December and May, the best time to visit, and narrated river tours by airboat all year round.

Venice ⑰

Road map D4. Sarasota Co. 🏃 *20,000.* ⛟ 🅸 *257 Tamiami Trail N, (941) 488-2236.*

VENICE IS a sleepy seaside town, situated slightly off the beaten track and awash with flowers and palm trees, which run down the center of the main shopping street, Venice Avenue. The town also has a fine collection of carefully restored historic buildings, including the Venice Little Theater on Tampa Avenue, which dates from 1927.

Caspersen Beach, fringed by sea oats and palmettos, lies at the southern end of Harbor Drive. It is a popular place to swim and fish, and to collect shells, although the

Fossil hunting, Caspersen Beach

main shelling beaches are further south *(see pp264–5)*. The area is famous for the fossilized sharks' teeth brought in by the tide; stocks were recently replenished by bringing in new sand from offshore sandbars.

Gasparilla Island ⑱

Road map D4. Lee Co, Charlotte Co. ⛟ *Venice.* 🅸 *5800 Gasparilla Rd, Boca Grande, (941) 964-0568.*

DISCOVERED originally by fishermen, and later by the wealthy fleeing northern winters, Gasparilla is a perfect island hideaway midway between Sarasota and Fort Myers.

Activity is centered around the community of Boca Grande, which is joined by a causeway to the mainland. The restored former railroad station, the San Marco Theater, and the grand Gasparilla Inn are eloquent reminders of times past. Many old wooden buildings have been saved and given a fresh coat of paint, giving the place a pleasant, tropical feel. Fishing has been big business here for a long time – Boca Grande is known as the "tarpon capital of the world" – and there are a number of marinas where you can arrange boat trips, some of which go to nearby barrier islands *(see pp264–5)*. Another way to explore is to

The Range Light, which warns off ships from Gasparilla Island's coast

follow the bike trail that runs down the island along the route of an old train track.

At the island's southern tip, the **Gasparilla Island State Recreation Area** has generally quiet beaches where you can fish and swim as well as hunt for shells. A squat late 19th-century lighthouse overlooks Boca Grande Pass, but its function is fulfilled by the more modern Range Light.

Gasparilla Island SRA
880 Belcher Rd. *(941) 964-0375.*
☐ *daily.*

The colorful 1920s Schlossberg-Camp Building in Arcadia

Arcadia ⑲

Road map E3. De Soto Co.
6,500. 16 S Volusia Ave, (863) 494-4033.

IT'S A PLEASURE to stroll around the old cattle ranching town of Arcadia. Local cowboys are more likely to ride around in a pickup truck than on horseback, but the horse is still very much part of the local culture. Cowboy fever reaches a peak twice a year, in March and July, when competitors and devotees from all over the US converge for the All-Florida Championship Rodeo, the oldest rodeo in the state.

Arcadia's flamboyant and sometimes colorful architecture recalls the prosperity and confidence of the 1920s. The best examples are the Florida Mediterranean-style Koch Arcade Building, on West Oak Street, and the Schlossberg-Camp Building, on West Magnolia Street.

Many earlier buildings were destroyed by a fire in 1905; the striking J.J. Heard Opera House on Oak Street was constructed the following year. Only a few buildings from the late 1800s survive; these can be seen by arrangement with the Chamber of Commerce.

Babcock Wilderness Adventures ⑳

Road map E4. Charlotte Co. SR 31, 6 miles (10 km) S of Babcock. *(800) 500-5583.* Punta Gorda. ☐ *daily* Dec 25. compulsory. www.babcockwilderness.com

THE HUGE Crescent B Ranch was originally owned by lumber baron, E.V. Babcock, who bled the cypress swamp for timber in the 1930s. It is still run by the phenomenally rich Babcock family, and part of the 90,000-acre (36,420-ha) working ranch is open as the Babcock Wilderness Adven-

Swamp buggy exploring Babcock Wilderness Adventures

tures. During 90-minute trips led by trained naturalists, swamp buggies take visitors through deep woods and a dense patch of cypress swamp, with plenty of opportunities to see wildlife. Panthers, which are bred successfully here, are in a specially designed paddock; alligators cruise just a short distance away. The ranch's herds of bison, horses, and cattle are also on view. Babcock's tours are very popular and must be booked well in advance.

RODEOS IN FLORIDA

Much of Florida's interior scrubland is ranching country, focused around cattle towns such as Arcadia, Kissimmee (see p177), and Davie (see p133), where rodeos are a feature of everyday life. Speed is the key during competitions. In events such as calf roping and steer wrestling (in which the cowboy must force the animal to the ground), the winner is the one with the fastest time – usually well under ten seconds. In bareback or saddle bronco riding the cowboys must stay on the bucking horse for at least eight seconds, but they are also judged on their overall skill and technique. During the competition a commentator keeps the audience informed of the cowboys' current form, giving details of any titles held.

Steer wrestling at Arcadia's All-Florida Championship Rodeo

Fort Myers ㉑

THE APPROACH to Fort Myers across the Caloosahatchee River is stunning, a fine introduction to a city that still has an air of old-time Florida. Following the sweep of the river is McGregor Boulevard, lined with ranks of royal palms; the first of these were planted by the inventor Thomas Edison, who put Fort Myers on the map in the 1880s, when it was just a small fishing village.

In addition to Edison's home and a few other sights, the old downtown area around First Street, with its many shops and restaurants, is worth exploring; a trolley service runs regularly through the downtown area linking the main sights. When you have had your fill of the city, there are beaches only a short distance away.

The original equipment on show in Thomas Edison's laboratory

🏛 Edison and Ford Winter Estate

2350 McGregor Blvd. ☎ (941) 334-3614. ◯ daily. ⬤ Thanksgiving, Dec 25. ◰ ☗ ⬤ ⬤ W www.edison-ford-estate.com

The waterfront retreat of one of America's most famous inventors, the Edison Winter Home is Fort Myers' most enduring attraction. Thomas Edison (1847–1931) built the estate in 1886, and the house, laboratory, and botanical gardens are much as he left them.

The two-story house and adjoining guesthouse were among the first prefabricated buildings in the US, built in sections to Edison's specifications in Maine and shipped to Fort Myers by schooner. This precluded extravagance, but the house is large and comfortable, and spacious overhanging porches around the ground floor kept the buildings cool. Many of the original furnishings are inside.

Edison was the holder of more than 1,000 patents, and his interests ranged from the light bulb to the phonograph, which recorded on wax cylinders. His laboratory, on the opposite side of McGregor Boulevard from the house, contains the equipment he used in his later experiments in synthetic rubber production. It is still lit by carbon filament light bulbs (his own invention), which have been in constant use since Edison's day. The museum displays personal items, dozens of phonographs, and a 1916 Model T car that was given to Edison by Henry Ford.

Thomas Edison was also an enthusiastic horticulturalist, and the gardens around the house and laboratory contain a great variety of exotic plants. The giant banyan tree, which was given to Edison by the tire magnate Harvey Firestone in 1925, boasts a circumference in excess of 400 ft (120 m).

Edison was a popular man locally, and tours of the home are notable for the breadth of knowledge and enthusiasm shown by the guides.

🏛 Ford Winter Home

2350 McGregor Blvd. ☎ (941) 334-3614. ◯ daily. ⬤ Thanksgiving, Dec 25. ◰ ☗ ⬤

Next to the Edison home (and viewable only on the same ticket) is Mangoes, the small estate bought in 1916 by the car manufacturer Henry Ford. The Fords were great friends of the Edisons, and following Thomas Edison's death in 1931 they never returned here.

The rooms have been faithfully re-created with period furnishings and still have the homey air favored by Clara Ford. Some early Ford cars are displayed in the garage.

🏫 Burroughs Home

2505 First St. ☎ (941) 332-6125. ◯ Tue–Fri. ⬤ public hols. ◰ ☗ ⬤

This Georgian Revival-style mansion was Fort Myers' first luxury home. Built for $15,000 in 1901, it was bequeathed to the city in 1983 in memory of Mr. and Mrs. Burroughs, the building's original proprietors. Nelson Burroughs, a cattle trader who had served under Custer in the Civil War, made his fortune in the late 19th century, when the city's proximity to Cuba made it vital as a cattle port during the Spanish-American War (see p47).

The elegant Burroughs Home, evocative of Fort Myers' heyday

Young visitors on the boardwalk at the Calusa Nature Center

The house is fully furnished as it was in the early 1900s, down to the smallest detail, with clothes in the bedrooms laid out as if for a night at the ball. Enjoyable 45-minute tours are conducted by historically costumed guides playing the parts of the Burroughs' two daughters, Mona and Jeddie.

Tours include the garden alongside the Caloosahatchee River, brimming with lady-finger, sleeping hibiscus, and Washingtonia palms; the old tennis court is still there too.

🏛 **Fort Myers Historical Museum**
2300 Peck St. ((941) 332-5955.
○ Tue–Sat. 🎫 &
Housed in the former railroad station, this museum recalls Fort Myers' heyday as a cattle town and delves into the area's early history as represented by the Calusa Indians and Spanish explorers. Highlights include a scale model of Fort Myers in 1900 and a refurbished 1930 private railroad car – the type used to bring wealthy northerners to the area for the winter sunshine. There is also a P-39 bomber that crashed into Estero Bay in the 1940s.

🦜 **Calusa Nature Center and Planetarium**
3450 Ortiz Ave. ((941) 275-3435.
○ daily (the planetarium Wed–Sun).
● Thanksgiving, Dec 25, Jan 1. 🎫
& 🚻 W www.calusanature.com
This 105-acre (42-ha) patch of wilderness is an excellent introduction to the flora and fauna of southwest Florida. There is a large aviary, and you can follow wooden walkways past ferns and mangrove, where it is often possible to

spot herons, egrets, and the occasional ibis. The museum provides illustrated talks on snakes and alligators, and there are also regular guided nature walks and tours of the aviary. There is also a re-created Seminole Indian village.

The planetarium features star and laser shows, for which there is a separate charge.

ENVIRONS: A souvenir shop on a massive scale, **The Shell Factory** lies 4 miles (6 km) north of Fort Myers. Not everyone will be tempted by the shell ornaments and shell jewelry, but the collection of shells and coral, claimed to be the largest in the world, is impressive. There are also sponges, natural and sculpted driftwood, paintings, posters, books, and numerous other gift items.

🐚 **The Shell Factory**
2787 N Tamiami Trail. ((941) 995-2141. ○ daily 10am–9pm. &

Koreshan State Historic Site ⓱

Road map E4. Lee Co. Estero, 14 miles (23 km) S of Fort Myers. ((941) 992-0311. 🚌 Fort Myers. ○ daily.
🎫 & 🚻 △

THOSE INTERESTED in obscure religions mix with nature lovers at the Koreshan State Historic Site, the former home of the Koreshan Unity sect.

In 1894 the sect's founder, Dr. Cyrus Teed, had a vision telling him to change his name to Koresh (Hebrew for Cyrus) and to move to southwest Florida, where he was to establish a great utopian city with streets 400 ft (122 m) wide. He chose this beautiful location on the Estero River, where members pursued a communal lifestyle, with equal rights for women and shared ownership of property.

Far from the city of ten million people that Teed had envisaged, the Koreshan Unity sect had a mere 250 followers at its peak, and membership dwindled after his death in 1908. The last four members donated the site to Florida in 1961. Twelve of the sect's 60 buildings and their gardens survive; they include Cyrus Teed's home, which has been completely restored.

The park has canoe and nature trails, camping facilities, opportunities for fresh and saltwater fishing, and also arranges guided tours.

Shell Factory

Cyrus Teed's restored home at the Koreshan State Historic Site

Lee Island Coast ㉓

THE LEE ISLAND COAST offers an irresistible combination of sandy beaches (famous for their shells), exotic wildlife, lush vegetation, and stupendous sunsets. Most people head for Sanibel and Captiva islands, with their chic resorts, marinas, and golf courses. However, other less developed islands – where there are few distractions from the beaches and natural beauty – are just a short boat trip away. Boat tours and charters can be picked up at many places, and there are also some regular boat services, whose routes are marked on the map below.

VISITORS' CHECKLIST

Road map D4, E4. Lee Co.
SW Florida International Airport, 15 miles (24 km) E. 2275 Cleveland Ave, Fort Myers, (800) 231-2222. 1159 Causeway Rd, Sanibel, (941) 472-1080.
Boat services: Tropic Star (941) 283-0015; Captiva Cruises (941) 472-5300; North Captiva Island Club Resort (941) 395-1001.

Tranquil beachfront cottages on Sanibel island

Sanibel and Captiva Islands

Despite being more accessible than the other islands, Sanibel and Captiva have a laid-back, Caribbean air. They are famous both as havens for lovers of the good life and for their shells. Most visitors soon get drawn into the shell-collecting culture, which has given rise to the expressions "Sanibel Stoop" and "Captiva Crouch" for the posture adopted by avid shell hunters. Sanibel may not be most people's idea of an island retreat – with its manicured gardens and rows of shops and restaurants along Periwinkle Way, the hub of Sanibel town – but there are no condos, and two areas are protected as preserves. Most of the beaches with public access are along Gulf Drive, the best being Turner and Bowman's beaches.

Captiva is less developed than Sanibel, but you'll still find the odd resort, including the South Seas Plantation Resort (see p308), with its busy marina – a starting point for boat trips to Cayo Costa.

✕ Sanibel Captiva Conservation Foundation

Mile Marker 1, Sanibel-Captiva Rd. (941) 472-2329. May–Nov: Mon–Fri; Dec–Apr: Mon–Sat. This private foundation oversees the protection of a chunk of Sanibel's interior wetland. Its 4 miles (6 km) of boardwalk trails are much quieter than those in the better known "Ding" Darling refuge nearby. An observation tower provides a perfect vantage point for viewing the island's birds.

🏛 Bailey-Matthews Shell Museum

3075 Sanibel-Captiva Rd. (941) 395-2233. Tue–Sun. W www.shellmuseum.org
Even if you aren't interested in shelling, this museum is well worth a visit. The centerpiece Great Hall of Shells includes displays grouped according to habitat, from barrier islands to the Everglades. It claims to have one-third of the world's 10,000 shell varieties.

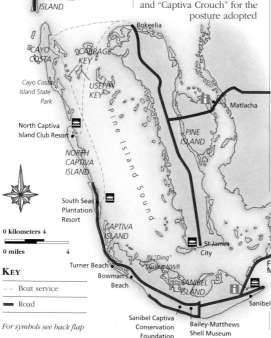

Boca Grande
GASPARILLA ISLAND
Bokeelia
CAYO COSTA
CABBAGE KEY
Cayo Costa Island State Park
USEPPA KEY
Pine Island Sound
Matlacha
North Captiva Island Club Resort
PINE ISLAND
NORTH CAPTIVA ISLAND
South Seas Plantation Resort
CAPTIVA ISLAND
St James City
FORT MYERS
Turner Beach
"Ding" Darling NWR
SANIBEL ISLAND
Bowman's Beach
Sanibel
Sanibel Captiva Conservation Foundation
Bailey-Matthews Shell Museum

0 kilometers 4
0 miles 4

KEY

– – Boat service

■ Road

For symbols see back flap

🦅 JN "Ding" Darling National Wildlife Refuge

1 Wildlife Drive. **(** *(941) 472-1100.* ◯ *Sat–Thu.* ● *public hols.* 📷 ▓

This refuge occupies two-thirds of Sanibel and is the island's leading attraction. Resident wildlife, including raccoons, alligators, and birds such as roseate spoonbills, bald eagles, and ospreys, are surprisingly easy to spot. The popular 5-mile (8-km) scenic "Wildlife Drive" can be covered by bike as well as by car, and there are tram tours too. Paths and canoe trails are lined with sea grape, red mangrove, and cabbage palm. Canoes, fishing boats, and bikes can all be rented within the refuge.

Yachts at anchor in the peaceful marina of Cabbage Key

Roseate spoonbills in the JN "Ding" Darling National Wildlife Refuge

🦅 Cayo Costa Island State Park

Cayo Costa Island. **(** *(941) 964-0375.* ◯ *daily.* 📷 ♿ ▲

Cayo Costa Island is one of the state's most unspoiled barrier islands. Much of it is planted with non-native Australian pine and Brazilian pepper trees. These were originally imported during the 1950s for their shade and wood, but are now gradually being cleared to let domestic species take over.

There are 9 miles (14 km) of dune-backed beach and, on the eastern side, several mangrove swamps to explore. Inland, there is a mix of pine flatwoods, grassy areas, and hammocks. The whole island offers plenty of bird-watching opportunities and excellent shelling, especially in winter.

Boat trips take visitors to Cayo Costa all year round; Tropic Star, from Bokeelia on Pine Island, offers the most frequent service. A tram links the bayside dock to the gulf side, and if you want to prolong your stay, there is a basic campground with 12 cabins.

Cabbage Key

This island was chosen by the novelist Mary Roberts Rhinehart for her home in 1938. Her house, built in the shade of two 300-year old Cuban laurel trees, is now the Cabbage Key Inn. This is best known for its restaurant, which is decorated with around 30,000 autographed one-dollar bills. The first bill was left by a fisherman anxious to make sure he had funds to buy drinks on his next visit. When he returned, he had money to spare and left the bill where it was. Other visitors then took up the idea.

A 40-ft (12-m) water tower nearby provides a lovely view of the small island, and there is also a short nature trail. Tropic Star from Pine Island and Captiva Cruises from Captiva Island run the most regular trips to the island.

Pine Island

This island, fringed with mangrove rather than beaches, is useful mainly as an access point to nearby islands. You can arrange all kinds of boat trips at the marina in Bokeelia; allow time to enjoy its fine collection of fishing piers.

SHELLS AND SHELLING

Junonia

The beaches of Sanibel and Captiva are among the best in the US for shelling. The Gulf of Mexico has no offshore reef to smash the shells, and the waters are relatively shallow and warm, with a flat bed – all factors that encourage growth. The wide plateau off the southern tip of Sanibel also acts as a ramp, helping to roll the shells ashore. Live shelling is a federal offense on Sanibel and subject to restrictions elsewhere, so collect only empty shells.

The best advice is to go early, and look just beneath the surface of the sand where the surf breaks. Seabirds feeding along the shore are a good indication of a good crop of shells. Shelling is best in winter or directly following a storm. The junonia and the lion's paw scallop are particularly sought after.

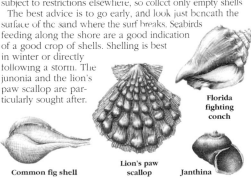

Florida fighting conch

Common fig shell

Lion's paw scallop

Janthina

THE EVERGLADES AND THE KEYS

*S*OUTHWEST FLORIDA *is mostly occupied by the world-famous Everglades – low-lying wetlands of huge ecological importance. Resorts and towns pepper the Keys, where Floridians and visitors alike come to enjoy the region's other natural wonder, the coral reef.*

Before the arrival of the Europeans, south Florida was home to tribes such as the Calusa and the Matecumbe *(see pp38–9)*. From the 1500s on, the Keys were visited by a succession of settlers, pirates, and wreckers *(see p289)*, but the mosquito-infested mainland was not settled until the mid-19th century, with the establishment of what is now the thriving coastal resort of Naples.

The first road to open up the area by linking the Atlantic and Gulf coasts was the Tamiami Trail, built in 1928. Pioneer camps located off it, such as Everglades City and Chokoloskee, have barely changed since the late 1800s and today seem caught in a time warp. They mark the western entrance of the Everglades National Park. This broad river of sawgrass, dotted with tree islands, possesses a peculiar beauty and is a paradise for its thrilling and prolific wildlife. Running southwest off the tip of the peninsula are the Keys, a chain of jewel-like islands protected by North America's only coral reef. Henry Flagler's Overseas Railroad once crossed the Keys; it has since disappeared and been replaced by the Overseas Highway – the route of one of the country's classic road trips. The farther south you go, the easier it is to agree with the saying that the Keys are more about a state of mind than a geographical location. At the end of the road is legendary Key West, where there is plenty to see and do, but where the relaxed Keys approach to life reigns supreme.

A vibrant mural in Key West's Bahama Village, reflecting the Caribbean origins of its inhabitants

◁ The mangrove swamps and tree islands of the Everglades, where meandering channels meet the ocean

Exploring the Everglades and the Keys

NAPLES AND MARCO ISLAND in the northwest are the best bases for enjoying the Gulf-shore beaches, and they boast some superb golf courses too. They also offer easy access to the wild and expansive scenery of Big Cypress Swamp and Everglades National Park, which together take up a great proportion of the region. The Florida Keys are justifiably famous for their activities focused on the nearby coral reef, such as fishing, diving and snorkeling. Islamorada and Key Largo in the Upper Keys both have plenty of accommodations to choose from, while bustling Marathon and colorful Key West, with its picturesque bed-and-breakfast inns, are excellent bases for exploring the more laid-back Lower Keys.

The Overseas Highway, the main artery through the Florida Keys

SIGHTS AT A GLANCE

Ah-Tha-Thi-Ki Museum ❸
Big Cypress Swamp ❷
Biscayne National Park ❻
Dolphin Research Center ❶❸
Dry Tortugas National Park ❶❽
Everglades National Park pp272–7 ❺
Indian and Lignumvitae Keys ❶❷
Islamorada ❶❶
John Pennekamp Coral Reef State Park ❽

Key Largo ❼
Key West pp284–9 ❶❼
Lower Keys ❶❻
Marathon ❶❹
Miccosukee Indian Village ❹
Naples ❶
Pigeon Key ❶❺
Tavernier ❾
Theater of the Sea ❶⓪

SEE ALSO

• *Where to Stay* pp310–11

• *Where to Eat* pp328–9 & p331

DRY TORTUGAS NATIONAL PARK

KEY WEST

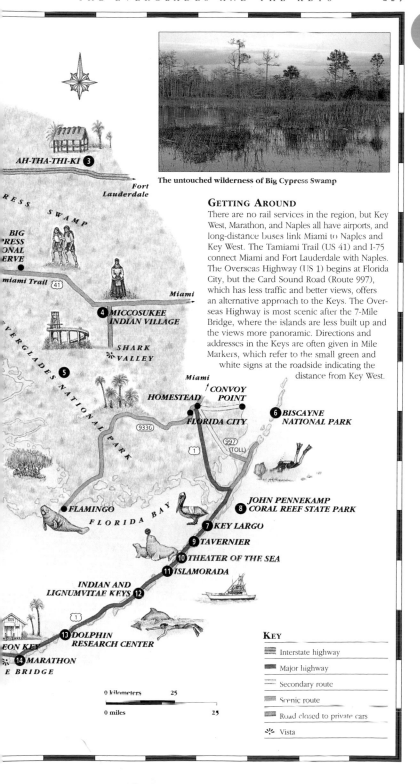

The untouched wilderness of Big Cypress Swamp

AH-THA-THI-KI ❸

Fort
Lauderdale

RESS SWAMP

BIG
PRESS
ONAL
ERVE

miami Trail (41)

Miami

❹ MICCOSUKEE
INDIAN VILLAGE

SHARK
VALLEY

EVERGLADES NATIONAL PARK

❺

Miami

HOMESTEAD

CONVOY
POINT

FLORIDA CITY

(9336)

(997)
(TOLL)

❻ BISCAYNE
NATIONAL PARK

● FLAMINGO

FLORIDA BAY

JOHN PENNEKAMP
CORAL REEF STATE PARK

❼ KEY LARGO

❾ TAVERNIER

❿ THEATER OF THE SEA

⓫ ISLAMORADA

INDIAN AND
LIGNUMVITAE KEYS ⓬

(1)

⓭ DOLPHIN
RESEARCH CENTER

EON KEY

⓮ MARATHON
E BRIDGE

GETTING AROUND

There are no rail services in the region, but Key
West, Marathon, and Naples all have airports, and
long-distance buses link Miami to Naples and
Key West. The Tamiami Trail (US 41) and I-75
connect Miami and Fort Lauderdale with Naples.
The Overseas Highway (US 1) begins at Florida
City, but the Card Sound Road (Route 997),
which has less traffic and better views, offers
an alternative approach to the Keys. The Overseas Highway is most scenic after the 7-Mile
Bridge, where the islands are less built up and
the views more panoramic. Directions and
addresses in the Keys are often given in Mile
Markers, which refer to the small green and
white signs at the roadside indicating the
distance from Key West.

0 kilometers 25

0 miles 25

KEY

▬ Interstate highway

▬ Major highway

═ Secondary route

▬ Scenic route

▬ Road closed to private cars

☀ Vista

Naples ❶

Road map E4. Collier Co.
🚶 *21,000.* ✈ 🚉 ℹ *895 5th Ave S,*
(941) 262-6141.

A CONSERVATIVE and affluent
beach city, Naples prides
itself on its manicured appearance and on its golf courses;
with 55 of them, it has the
greatest per capita concentration of courses in the state.

Downtown, most of what is
called "historic" Naples dates
from the early 20th century,
and with its pastel-colored
buildings is a pleasant area to
explore. Many of the 19th-
century houses were destroyed
by hurricane Donna in 1960,
which also claimed the original
1887 pier. Rebuilt in 1961, this
is now a popular spot for both
anglers and pelicans; the latter
are a common sight perched
upon the railings.

A beautiful white sandy
beach stretching for 10 miles
(16 km) is flanked mostly by
condos, but it offers easy
public access and safe swimming in warm Gulf waters.

The informative **Collier
County Museum** focuses on
local history and includes a
re-created Seminole village.
Exhibits range from ancient
indigenous Indian artifacts to
those connected with the
region's pioneering past and
the building of the Tamiami
Trail (US 41), on which the
museum stands.

The popular gulf shore beach alongside Naples pier

🏛 **Collier County Museum**
3301 Tamiami Trail E. 📞 *(941) 774-
8476.* ☐ *Mon – Fri.* ⬤ *public hols.*
♿ 🆆 www.colliermuseum.org
ENVIRONS: Developed as a
resort since the 1960s, **Marco
Island** is the most northerly
of the Ten Thousand Islands
chain and a good base for
exploring the western fringe
of the Everglades *(see p272)*.
Outstanding archaeological
finds, some 3,500 years old,
were discovered here. These
are now kept in museums
elsewhere, but dotted around
the island you can still see the
remains of midden mounds –
accumulations of discarded
shells and bones that give
important clues to the lifestyle
and diet of the ancient local
Calusa Indians *(see pp38–9)*.

Big Cypress Swamp ❷

Road map E4. Collier Co, Monroe Co.

H OME TO SEVERAL hundred
species such as the en-
dangered Florida panther *(see
p123)*, this vast, shallow wetland basin is not, in fact, a true
swamp. It features a range of
habitats, determined by only
slight differences in elevation,
which include sandy islands of
slash pine, wet and dry prairies,
and hardwood hammocks *(see
p273)*. One-third of the swamp
is covered by cypress trees,
growing in belts and long
narrow forests ("strands"). It
is the scale of these strands as
opposed to the size of the trees
that gives the area its name.

The swamp functions as a
wet season water storage area
for the greater Everglades
system and as a buffer zone
for the Everglades National
Park *(see pp272–7)*. Finished
in 1928, the Tamiami Trail,
also known as US 41, cuts
through the swamp and was
responsible for opening up
the area. The road skirts the
Everglades and stretches from
Tampa to Miami, hence its
name. Today, such engineer-
ing feats are environmentally
questionable, as they block
the natural movement of water
and wildlife essential to the
fragile balance of southern
Florida's unique ecosystem.

**Big Cypress National
Preserve** is the largest of the
protected areas located within

Boardwalk winding through Fakahatchee Strand, Big Cypress Swamp

THE SEMINOLES OF FLORIDA

Seminole (meaning "wanderer" or "runaway") was a term first used in the 1700s for members of several Creek Indian tribes, who were forced to flee south to Florida by land-hungry Europeans and later retreated into the Everglades (see p45). Today, the Seminole tribe is officially distinct from the other main grouping, the Miccosukee tribe, but members of both are known as Seminoles.

Historic land disputes led the US Government to allocate reservation lands to the Florida Indians in 1911. Here, Seminoles maintain their traditions but also incorporate elements of modern American life. Recently, they have built bingo halls in the hope that this will significantly increase tribal wealth (see p133).

Seminole dress in the late 1800s, showing European influence

Ah-Tha-Thi-Ki Museum ❸

Road map F4. Hendry Co. Snake Rd, 17 miles (27 km) N of Exit 14 off I-75. ☎ (863) 902-1113. ◷ 9am–5pm Tue–Sun. ● public hols. 🅿 ♿ 🆆 www.seminoletribe.com

THIS MUSEUM is located on 64 acres (26 ha) of the Big Cypress Seminole Reservation. The first, main building and a boardwalk opened in 1997, and new themed exhibition areas have now opened.

The museum is dedicated to the understanding of Seminole culture and history; Ah-Tha-Thi-Ki means "a place to learn." As well as exhibits, there's an impressive 180-degree, five-screen film.

Miccosukee Indian Village ❹

Road map F5. Dade Co. US 41, 4 miles (6.5 km) E of Forty Mile Bend. ☎ (305) 223-8380. ◷ daily. 🅿 ♿

MOST OF THE Miccosukee tribe live in small settlements along US 41. The best way to find out more about them is to visit the Miccosukee Indian Village, the only place open to the public, near Shark Valley (see p273).

Here, visitors can see traditional chickees (see p28) and watch demonstrations of crafts like basket-weaving, palmetto palm doll-making, and traditional beadwork. There is also a small heritage center and a restaurant where the more adventurous can try "swamp fare," such as frogs' legs, corn bread, and alligator tails.

Wood storks nesting in the trees of Corkscrew Swamp Sanctuary

the swamp, although its size means it is somewhat difficult to explore. Most visitors enjoy the views from US 41 and stop at the Oasis Visitor Center for information.

On the western edge of the swamp is the **Fakahatchee Strand State Preserve**, one of Florida's wildest areas. A huge natural drainage ditch or slough (pronounced "slew"), it is 20 miles (32 km) long and 3–5 miles (5–8 km) wide.

Logging ceased here in the 1950s, having destroyed 99 percent of old growth cypresses; the Preserve's only remaining examples, some of which are 600 years old, are found at Big Cypress Bend. Here, a short trail passes through a mosaic of plant communities, including magnificent orchids and nestlike epiphytes (see p276). Here too is the US's largest stand of native royal palms.

Route 846, running northeast from Naples, takes you to the popular **Corkscrew Swamp Sanctuary**. A 2-mile (3-km) boardwalk traverses various habitats, including Florida's largest stand of old growth cypress trees. The sanctuary is famous for its many birds and is an important nesting area for endangered wood storks, which visit almost every year during the winter months.

🏛 Big Cypress National Preserve
Oasis Visitor Center, US 41. ☎ (941) 695-4111. ◷ daily. ● Dec 25. ♿
🏛 Fakahatchee Strand State Preserve
Big Cypress Bend, US 41. ☎ (941) 695-4593. ◷ daily. ♿
🏛 Corkscrew Swamp Sanctuary
375 Sanctuary Rd, off Route 846. ☎ (941) 348-9151. ◷ daily. 🅿 ♿

Palmetto dolls and beadwork for sale in the Miccosukee Indian Village

Everglades National Park ❺

Park ranger

COVERING 1.4 MILLION acres (566,580 ha), this huge park still makes up only one-fifth of the entire Everglades area. The main entrance on its eastern boundary is 10 miles (16 km) west of Florida City. The park's boardwalk trails are mostly elevated, about half a mile (0.8 km) long and clearly marked; some are suitable for bicycles. Park rangers can help plan your visit and advise on guided tours and programs, which are organized daily. Boats and canoes can be rented, and there's a variety of boat trips to choose from. Lodgings consist of a hotel and campgrounds, including more primitive sites where visitors stay in chickees *(see p28)*, most of which are accessible only by canoe. There's a small charge for backcountry camping permits; reservations can be made only in the 24 hours prior to departure.

Chokoloskee
The Ten Thousand Islands archipelæ and the national park's west coast a accessible from the docks this tiny island.

GULF OF MEXICO

Whitewater Bay
Only where the sheet river of the Everglades meets the Gulf of Mexico and Florida Bay does open water, in the form of rivers, tidal creeks, and shallow lakes like Whitewater Bay, appear.

| 0 kilometers | 15 |
| 0 miles | 10 |

SAFETY TIPS

Protection against biting insects is vital, especially during the summer months. Follow the advice given by rangers and on information boards, and respect all wildlife: alligators can jump and move quickly on land; some trees and shrubs like the Brazilian pepper tree are poisonous, as are some caterpillars and snakes. If planning to go off the beaten path, let someone know your itinerary. Always drive slowly: much wildlife can be seen from the road – and may also venture onto it.

Coral snake

Canoeing in the Everglades
Along the western coast and around Florida Bay are countless opportunities to explore the park's watery tra These range from short routes to the week-long adventu of the challenging and remote Wilderness Waterway.

Shark Valley

Take a narrated tram ride or cycle along this 15-mile (25-km) loop road. At its end is a 60-ft (18-m) tower that offers great views.

Anhinga Trail

Starting at the Royal Palm Visitor Center, this is one of the most popular trails in the park. Its namesake, the anhinga bird, is often seen drying its distinctive plumage in the sun after diving for fish.

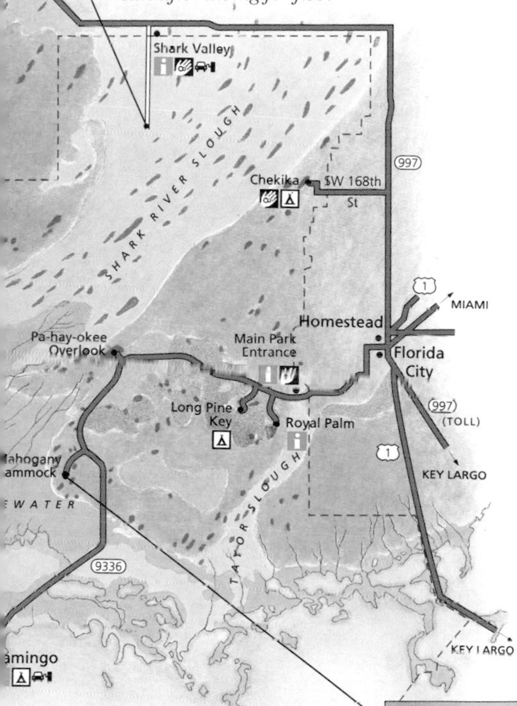

VISITORS' CHECKLIST

Road map E4, E5, F5. Monroe Co, Dade Co, Collier Co. ◯ *daily.*
🛈 *all visitor centers open Dec–May: 8am–5pm daily; during rest of year, call in advance to check.*
Main Visitor Center ☏ *(305) 242-7700.* ◯ *all year round.*
Gulf Coast Visitor Center *(in Everglades City)* ☏ *(941) 695-3311; for boat tours and canoe rental call (941) 695-2591.*
Shark Valley Information Center ☏ *(305) 221-8776; for tram tour reservations and bicycle rental (305) 221-8455.*
Royal Palm Visitor Center ☏ *(305) 242-7700.*
Flamingo Visitor Center ☏ *(941) 695-3092; for canoe, boat, or bicycle rental, boat tours, marina, call (941) 695-3101.*
🚻 *most park boardwalks are accessible. Call (305) 242-7700.*
🅰 *call (800) 365-2267 to book.*
🆆 *www.nps.gov/ever*

KEY

☐	Mangrove
☐	Saltwater prairie
☐	Cypress trees
☐	Freshwater prairie
☐	Freshwater slough
☐	Pinelands
☐	Hammock
– –	Wilderness Waterway
– –	Park boundary
▬▬	Paved road
═══	Road closed to private vehicles
🛈	Visitor information center
🚲	Entrance station
🅰	Campground
🚉	Gas station

Map labels: Shark Valley · SHARK RIVER SLOUGH · Chekika · SW 168th St · (997) · (1) MIAMI · Homestead · Pa-hay-okee Overlook · Main Park Entrance · Florida City · Long Pine Key · Royal Palm · (997) (TOLL) · KEY LARGO · (1) · Mahogany Hammock · SAWATER · TAYLOR SLOUGH · (9336) · KEY LARGO · Flamingo · FLORIDA BAY

Flamingo has the park's only hotel and its largest campground. Several hiking and canoe trails are in its vicinity.

Mahogany Hammock Boardwalk

This trail meanders through a large, dense tropical hardwood hammock. It is noted for its colorful tree snails (see p275) and epiphytes (see p276) and for being the home of the largest mahogany tree in the country.

The Wildlife of the Everglades

THE EVERGLADES is a vast sheet river system – the overspill from Lake Okeechobee *(see p124)* that moves slowly across a flat bed of peat-covered limestone. Some 200 miles (322 km) long and up to 50 miles (80 km) wide, its depth rarely exceeds 3 ft (1 m).

Tropical air and sea currents act on this temperate zone to create combinations of flora that are unique in North America. Clumps of vegetation, such as cypress domes *(see p23)*, tropical hardwood hammocks, and bayheads, break the expanse of sawgrass prairie. And there are hundreds of animal species – including 400 species of birds, for which the Everglades is particularly renowned. This unique ecosystem, with its rich vegetation and associated wildlife, can only be sustained by the cycle of dry (winter) and wet (summer) seasons – the Everglades' life force.

Osprey
This fish-eating bird is seen around the park's coast, bays, and ponds. Its large nests are easily recognizable.

The strangler fig starts life as a seed carried in bird droppings to a crevice of another tree. In time, it completely engulfs the host tree.

Green Tree Frog
This endearing amphibian has a resonant call that can be heard throughout the Everglades.

Snowy Egret
Beautiful breeding plumage, yellow feet, and a black bill identify this bird.

Bromeliad *(see p276)*

Bayheads are hammocks dominated by bay trees, that thrive on rich organic soil.

Sweet bay

Wax myrtle

Sawgrass

Cattail

TREE ISLANDS

Hammocks or tree islands are areas of elevated land found in freshwater prairie. They support a fantastic variety of flora and fauna.

Alligator flag

Bladderwort

Water Lily

'Gator holes are made by alligators hollowing out ponds and depressions during the dry season to reach the water below. The water-filled holes sustain many species during the winter.

American Alligator
With its rough hide and toothy grin, the alligator is one of the park's best known (and most feared) residents.

Royal palm

Great Blue Heron
Found all over Florida, this wading bird has a 6-ft (2-m) wingspan. In south Florida its plumage can sometimes be completely white.

Roseate Spoonbill
These striking birds winter in the park and use their spatulate bills to fish for food in shallow water.

The mahogany is just one of the West Indian species that predominates in tropical hardwood hammocks.

The gumbo limbo's bark is red and peeling, hence its nickname the "tourist tree."

Saw palmetto

Peat

Red mangrove trees are easily recognized by their distinctive roots. Salt-tolerant, they play a crucial role in protecting the shoreline and act as a nursery for marine animals.

[Tre]e Snail
[The]re are 58 varieties of [this] colorful tree snail, [wh]ich live in hammocks [an]d move around only [dur]ing the wet season.

Otter
Related to the weasel, this delightful animal is often seen frolicking in freshwater ponds.

Exploring Everglades National Park

MOST VISITORS COME TO Everglades National Park on a day trip, which can easily be spent exploring just one or two of the trails. However, a popular excursion involves stopping at the different boardwalk trails along the Main Park Road (Route 9336); it is an easy drive down and back to Flamingo on Florida Bay. Try to include at least one of the less-visited trails and ponds located off the southern part of the road between Mahogany Hammock and Flamingo. Information boards abound to help you identify the flora and fauna. Remember to bring insect repellent and protection against the sun.

Long Pine Key, which boasts a lovely campsite and shady trails

Rangers and visitors examining wildlife on a "slough-slog"

Around the Royal Palm Visitor Center
The highly informative Royal Palm Visitor Center and two nearby boardwalk trails are located on the site of Florida's first state park, created in 1916. The popular **Anhinga Trail**, passing over Taylor Slough, contains slightly deeper water than the surrounding terrain; in the dry winter months it attracts wildlife to drink. Its open site means there are

better photo opportunities and fewer insects, but the intense sun can be hazardous. Alligators congregate at the 'gator hole *(see p274)* at the beginning of the trail, and a wide range of fauna, including deer, raccoons, and the splendid anhinga bird, can be spotted.

The shady **Gumbo Limbo Trail**, on the other hand, is mosquito paradise even in winter. However, it is an easy walk, and, if your visit is confined to the park's eastern half, it offers the best chance to explore a tropical hardwood hammock. Watch for bromeliads, members of the pineapple family and a type of epiphyte.

Bromeliads on a mahogany tree

This nonparasitic plant grows on other plants but gets its nourishment from the air and rainwater. There are also many types of orchids and the trail's namesake, the gumbo-limbo tree *(see p275)*.

Long Pine Key
This area takes its name from a large stand of slash pines that are unique to southern Florida. Insect- and rot-proof, they have long been a popular building material. Pinelands need fire for survival; without it, they progress to hardwoods. As roads and canals act as fire breaks, park rangers set controlled fires to encourage the pinelands' regeneration and that of associated species like the saw palmetto.

The campsite here occupies a stunning position and is one of the main reasons for people to stop at Long Pine Key. Several shady trails lead off from it, and there's a half-mile (0.8-km) loop of the Pinelands Trail, located 2 miles (3 km) to the west. Don't stray from the path: the limestone bedrock contains "solution holes" created by rain eroding away the rock. These can be quite deep and difficult to spot.

TRAILS AROUND FLAMINGO

As a general rule, canoe trails through open water are a good way to escape the summer's insects, while the hiking trails are undoubtedly most agreeable during the winter months.

KEY

--- Hiking trail

--- Canoe trail

▬ Paved road

= Unpaved road

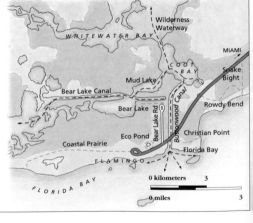

From Pa-hay-okee to Flamingo

The open expanse of sawgrass prairie that can be viewed from the elevated **Pa-hay-okee Overlook** is the epitome of the Everglades. The observation tower here is a perfect spot to watch the fluid light changes dancing across this sea of grass, especially in the late afternoon. Tree islands or hammocks break the horizon, and you will see a multitude of wading birds, hawks, and snail kites, whose only food, the apple snail, lives on the sawgrass. This prairie is also home to cattails and other wetland plants.

The **Mahogany Hammock Trail** *(see p273)*, by contrast, leads through one of the park's largest hammocks. This area is home to a wide variety of fauna and flora; the bromeliads here are very impressive, and the junglelike vegetation is especially dense during the wet summer months.

The various trails and ponds between Mahogany Hammock and Flamingo tend to attract fewer people but are no less rewarding, especially for the bird life. Try exploring West Lake Trail or Snake Bight Trail, which ends on Florida Bay.

The settlement of **Flamingo** lies 37 miles (60 km) from the main park entrance. In the late 1800s, it was a remote outpost and hideaway for hunters and fishermen; today, a few park rangers are the only long-term

The sawgrass prairie stretching away from the Pa-hay-okee Overlook

residents. Its position on Florida Bay gives visitors a wide choice of activities such as hiking, fishing, boating, and watching wildlife. An overnight stay at the campsite or lodge is recommended – especially for bird-watching, which is most rewarding in the early morning and late afternoon.

Apart from countless species of birds and animals, the bay and creeks around Flamingo contain manatees *(see p236)* and the endangered American crocodile. This is easily distinguished from the alligator by its gray-green color and the fact that the teeth of both jaws show when its mouth is shut. Your chance of seeing one, however, is slight.

Flamingo's visitor center has wildlife guides and information about local ranger-led activities. These include evening slideshows and talks, and daytime "slough-slogs" – intrepid walks through the swamp.

Biscayne National Park ❻

Road map F5. Dade Co. 9700 SW 328th St, Convoy Point. 🚉 *Miami* 🚌 *Homestead.* 📞 (305) 230-7275. ⏰ *daily.* ⬤ *Dec 25.* **Visitor Center** ⏰ 8:30am– 5:00pm. **Boat tours** 📞 (305) 230-1100. ♿ 🅰 W www.nps.gov/bisc

DENSE MANGROVE swamp protects the shoreline of Biscayne National Park, which incorporates the northernmost islands of the Florida Keys. Its shallow waters hold the park's greatest draw – a living coral reef with myriad forms and around 200 types of tropical fish. The barrier islands are untouched, so the coral here is healthier and the water even clearer than in the more popular underwater parks farther south around Key Largo.

You can take glass-bottomed boat tours, and there are also diving and snorkeling trips; these all leave from the visitor center, and it is advisable to reserve in advance.

Elkhorn coral and tropical fish in Biscayne National Park

THE EVERGLADES UNDER THREAT

Everglades National Park enjoys good protection within its boundaries, but threats from outside are more difficult to control. Since it was created in 1947, the park's greatest problems have been water related. The Everglades ecosystem and Florida's human population are in direct competition for this priceless commodity: irrigation canals and roads disrupt the natural through-flow of water from Lake Okeechobee *(see p124)*, and the drainage of land for development has also had

Agriculture near the Everglades uses great quantities of water

detrimental effects on wildlife. Agriculture in central Florida uses vast amounts of water, and high levels of chemical fertilizers promote the unnatural growth of swamp vegetation. Furthermore, local fish are often found to be suffering from mercury poisoning, which then enters the food chain.

Key Largo [7]

Road map F5. Monroe Co. 👥 *16,000.* 🚌 ℹ *MM 106, (305) 451-1414, (800) 822-1088.* **African Queen** ☎ *(305) 451-4655.*

The first of the inhabited Keys, this is the largest island in the chain and was named "long island" by Spanish explorers. Its proximity to Miami makes it also the liveliest, especially on weekends when it is crowded.

The island's greatest draws are the diving and snorkeling opportunities along the coral reef found just offshore, in the John Pennekamp Coral Reef State Park and the National Marine Sanctuary.

Another Key Largo attraction is the *African Queen*, the boat used in the 1951 film of the same name. This makes short pleasure trips (by reservation only). It is moored at MM 100, which is also the base for a casino ship offering a different kind of trip – one that provides a rare chance to gamble *(see p338)*.

Local legend tells of a mysterious and secretive former government official who lives in the hammocks and returns to civilization only when an ecological need arises. His various exploits over the years have resulted in land, once slated for development, being returned to pristine wilderness. Much of Florida's wetlands, hammocks, and beaches have gone under the bulldozer for high-rise apartments, new beachfront resorts, and shopping malls, but with the help of concerned citizens throughout the state, there is hope for keeping Florida's delicate ecosystem intact.

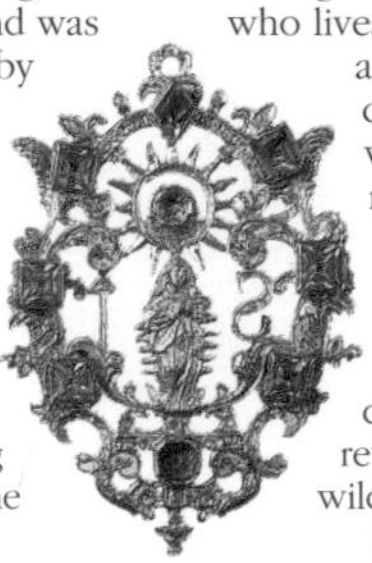

Gold ornament from a treasure ship

John Pennekamp Coral Reef State Park [8]

Road map F5. Monroe Co. MM 102.5. 🚌 *Key Largo.* ☎ *(305) 451-1202.* 🕒 *daily.* 🎟 ♿

Just under five percent of this park is on dry land, and its facilities include a visitor's center, a small museum covering the ecology of the reef, three swimming areas, and woodland trails. The park is best known for its fabulous underwater reaches, which extend 3 miles (5 km) east from Key Largo and provide an unforgettable glimpse of the vivid colors and extraordinary forms of coral reef life.

Visitors can rent canoes, dinghies, or motorboats, as well as snorkeling and scuba gear. Alternatively, snorkeling, and diving trips can easily be arranged, and there's a diving school that offers certified courses. Those who are less inclined to get wet can take a

Florida's Coral Reef

North America's only live coral reef system extends 200 miles (320 km) along the length of the Keys, from Miami to the Dry Tortugas. A complex and extremely delicate ecosystem, it protects these low-lying islands from storms and heavy wave action emanating from the Atlantic Ocean. Coral reefs are created over thousands of years by billions of tiny marine organisms known as polyps. Lying 10–60 ft (3–18 m) under the surface, the reef is an intricate web of countless cracks and cavities and is home to a multitude of plants and diverse sea creatures, including more than 500 species of fish.

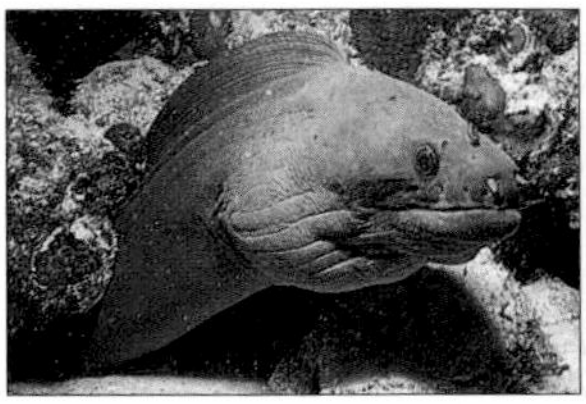

The scaleless green moray, fearsome in looks but generally harmless to humans

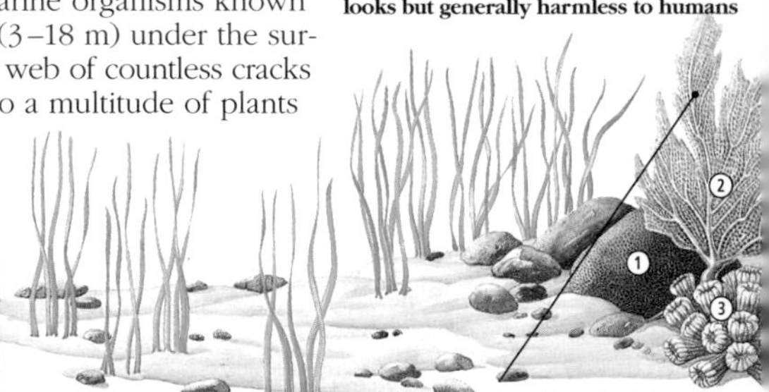

Sea fans, "soft" corals that have no skeleton

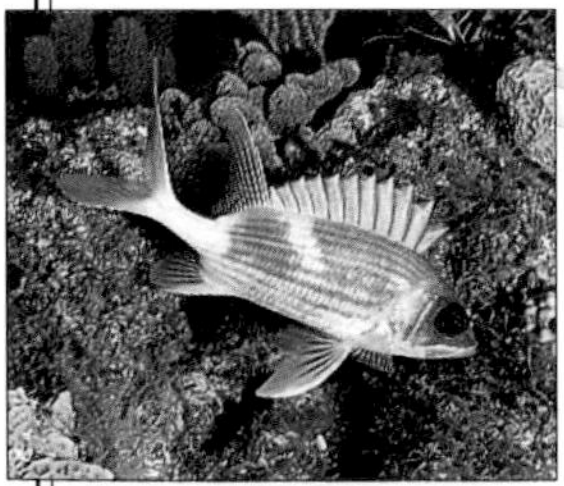

A large-eyed squirrelfish, best suited to a nocturnal existence

Key to Corals

[1] Smooth starlet coral
[2] Sea fan
[3] Flower coral
[4] Elliptical star coral
[5] Sea rod
[6] Pillar coral
[7] Orange tube coral
[8] Elkhorn coral
[9] Brain coral
[10] Staghorn coral
[11] Large flower coral
[12] Sea plume

Diver and spiny lobster, John Pennekamp Coral Reef State Park

Tavernier ❾

Road map F5. Monroe Co. 🏠 *2,500.*
ℹ️ *MM 92, (305) 451-1414.*

HENRY FLAGLER's railroad *(see pp46–7)* reached this part of the Keys around 1910. Today, a number of buildings, constructed in the 1920s and '30s as the settlement grew, are located around MM 92; of these only the Tavernier Hotel is open to the public.

Tavernier's most notable attraction is the **Florida Keys Wild Bird Rehabilitation Center**. Here, sanctuary is offered to injured birds, most of whom have been harmed by humans, involving cars or fishing tackle. They recuperate in spacious cages set in tranquil surroundings, contrasting with the bustle of the rest of the island.

🦅 **Florida Keys Wild Bird Rehabilitation Center**
MM 93.6. 📞 *(305) 852-4486.*
⭕ *daily.* ♿ Ⓦ www.fl-key.fl.us/flkeyswildbird

glass-bottomed boat trip. Most tours go to destinations that are actually located in the neighboring section of the Florida Keys National Marine Sanctuary, known as the Key Largo National Marine Sanctuary, which extends 3 miles (5 km) farther out to sea.

Some parts of the reef here are favored by snorkelers, such as the shallow waters of White Bank Dry Rocks, with its impressive array of corals and colorful tropical fish. Nearby Molasses Reef offers areas for both snorkelers and divers, who may encounter a myriad fish such as snapper and angelfish. Farther north, French Reef has various swim-through caves where divers can find darting shoals of glassy sweepers. At Key Largo Dry Rocks, the *Christ of the Deep* statue lies submerged at 20 ft (6 m) and is a popular underwater photo stop.

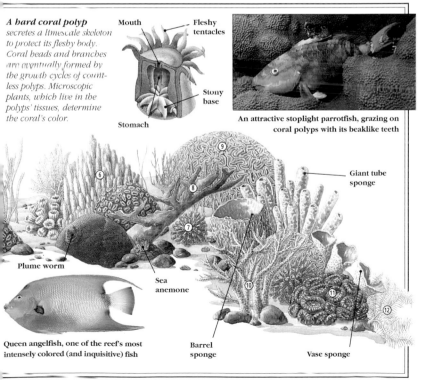

A hard coral polyp secretes a limescale skeleton to protect its fleshy body. Coral heads and branches are eventually formed by the growth cycles of countless polyps. Microscopic plants, which live in the polyps' tissues, determine the coral's color.

Mouth — Fleshy tentacles — Stony base — Stomach

An attractive stoplight parrotfish, grazing on coral polyps with its beaklike teeth

Giant tube sponge

Plume worm

Sea anemone

Queen angelfish, one of the reef's most intensely colored (and inquisitive) fish

Barrel sponge

Vase sponge

Theater of the Sea ⑩

Road map F5. Monroe Co. MM 84.5.
📞 *(305) 664-2431.* ⭕ *daily.* 📷 ♿

WINDLEY KEY is home to the Theater of the Sea, which opened in 1946 and is Florida's second oldest marine park. Situated in a former quarry created during the construction of Flagler's railroad *(see pp46–7)*, the attraction is famous for its traditional sea lion and dolphin shows. It is also possible to take boat trips to investigate wildlife in the local lagoons, and to enroll in sessions such as the "Trainer for a Day" program.

The Dolphin Adventure package includes a swim with the dolphins and two hours of continuous shows, but to be sure of a place you must reserve well in advance.

Triumphant fishermen in Whale Harbor Marina, Islamorada

Islamorada ⑪

Road map F5. Monroe Co. 🏄 *8,500.*
🚍 ℹ️ *MM 82.5, (800) 322-5397.*

PROUDLY DECLARING itself "The Sport fishing Capital of the World," Islamorada, pronounced "Eye-luh-mo-rada," encompasses seven islands and is best known for its outstanding big game fishing.

Whale Harbor Marina in the town of Islamorada, on Upper Matecumbe Key, bristles with impressive deep-sea charter craft used to catch blue-water fish. Fishing party boats based here take people of all levels of experience, so even if you are not a dedicated angler, these trips can be a great way to spend half a day out at sea.

Back in town at MM 82, the Art Deco Hurricane Monument marks the grave of 500 people killed by a tidal surge in the hurricane of 1935 *(see p24)*.

Indian and Lignumvitae Keys ⑫

Road map F5. Monroe Co.
🚤 *Islamorada.* 🚢 *Lower Matecumbe Key.* ℹ️ *Islamorada, (800) 322-5397.*

THESE UNINHABITED islands, on opposite sides of the Ocean Highway, are accessible only by boat.

Tiny Indian Key has a surprising amount of history for its size. An early Indian site, it was settled in 1831 by Captain J. Houseman, an opportunistic wrecker *(see p289)*. A small community flourished under his autocratic rule, but in 1840 Seminole Indians attacked, killing these settlers. The key was abandoned and today only the outlines of the village and its cisterns remain, amid vegetation impressive for both its variety and rampant growth. An observation tower provides splendid views of the island.

Larger Lignumvitae Key, which can be explored only on a guided tour, is of even greater botanical interest. It boasts 133 native tree species, including its namesake, a blue-flowering tree that can live for 1,000 years. Scientists believe that other vegetation here is as much as 10,000 years old. Notable wildlife includes some colorful tree snails *(see p275)* and impressively large spiders. Come prepared for mosquitoes, especially in summer.

Dolphins playing in protected waters, Dolphin Research Center

Dolphin Research Center ⑬

Road map E5. Monroe Co. MM 59.
📞 *(305) 289-1121.* ⭕ *daily.*
⬤ *public hols.* 📷 ♿
🌐 *www.dolphins.org*

A NONPROFIT-MAKING concern, the Dolphin Research Center on Grassy Key is a serious establishment whose main function is to research dolphin behavior. The Center also acts as a rest home for sick and injured dolphins, or those just worn out from the stresses of a busy life as a theme park attraction.

There are exhibits, regularly scheduled lagoon-side walking tours, and special programs like the college-credit Dolphin Lab and the "Dolphin Encounter," which allows you to swim with these amazing marine mammals. All events are very popular; reservations must be made only from the first day of the month preceding your intended visit.

The observation tower and original ruined water cisterns on Indian Key

Fishing in the Florida Keys

THERE ARE THREE main fishing zones in South Florida, each offering its own type of experience and rewards. Near the warm Gulf Stream, offshore gamefish such as marlin abound in conditions excellent for deep-sea (or blue-water) angling. The Atlantic coastal waters up to and including the coral reef itself contain tropical species like snapper and grouper. And to the north of the Keys, the shallow backcountry flats of the Gulf are home to game fish such as tarpon.

Fishing lure

Islamorada, Marathon, and Key West are the area's major fishing centers, and small marinas throughout the region have boats for rent. There are enough options to suit most tastes, budgets, and abilities, but you might have a greater chance of success if you book a place on a fishing party boat or hire an experienced guide. Weather conditions and seasonal variations determine the available species, but you can fish the waters of the Florida Keys all year round.

DEEP-SEA VERSUS BACKCOUNTRY

Deep-sea fishing, one of the most exhilarating options available, appeals to the Hemingway spirit of the trophy angler. Renting your own sports boat, however, is expensive. Skiffs fish the tranquil and scenic backcountry reaches, where cunning and stealth help secure a catch.

Flat-bottomed skiffs are poled through inshore waters; motors can get snarled up in the seagrass.

Fishermen in sports boats fitted with fighting chairs wear harnesses to battle deep-sea fish.

Bait and tackle shops are found along the Overseas Highway and in marinas. They not only rent and sell equipment and licenses (see p341) but are often the best places to find out about guides and fishing trips offered locally.

Big game fish are the ultimate trophy. Local restaurants can clean and cook your catch for you, but for a long-lasting memento, let a taxidermist prepare and mount your fish (see p341).

Fishing party boats are a popular and economical way to fish around the reef. The per-person price usually includes a fishing license, tackle, and bait, as well as the crew's expertise.

Marathon's Boot Key Harbor, with the 7-Mile Bridge in the distance

Marathon ⑭

Road map E5. Monroe Co.
🏠 13,000. ✈ 🛈 MM 53.5, (305)
743-6555.

Mᴀʀᴀᴛʜᴏɴ was originally named Vaca ("cow") Key by the Spanish settlers, probably for the herds of manatees or sea cows (see p236) once found offshore. It was renamed in the early 1900s by the men who had the grueling task of laying the Overseas Railroad (see p267).

The main center of the Middle Keys, this island is rather heavily developed and at first glance appears to be an uninviting strip of shopping plazas and gas stations. Marathon's principal appeal lies in the surrounding fishing grounds; those located under the bridges where the Atlantic Ocean and the Gulf of Mexico meet are considered to be particularly fertile.

Devotees can choose from a broad range of angling techniques (see p281). These include spear-fishing (illegal in the Upper Keys but allowed here) and line-fishing off what may be the longest pier in the world – a 2-mile (3-km) stretch of the old 7-Mile Bridge. There are several pleasing waterfront resorts with small beaches, created artificially from imported sand; turn south off the Overseas Highway for these. Definitely worth a visit is **Crane Point Hammock**,

Door detail, Crane Point Hammock

consisting of 64 acres (26 ha) of tropical hardwood forest and wild mangrove wetlands. There are nature trails and a traditional conch-style house (see p287) built out of tabby – a type of local homemade concrete, made of burned seashells and coral rock. The entrance to the hammock is via the **Museum of Natural History of the Florida Keys**, opened on Earth Day in 1991. The interesting collection explains the history and geology as well as the ecology of the islands, and is designed to appeal in particular to younger visitors.

🏛 **Museum of Natural History of the Florida Keys**
MM 50.5. 📞 (305) 743-9100.
⭘ daily. ⬤ Dec 25. 🏷 ♿
🌐 www.cranepoint.org

Pigeon Key ⑮

Road map E5. Monroe Co. MM 47.5, via the old 7-Mile Bridge. 📞 (305) 289-0025. ⭘ daily. 🏷 ♿

Tʜɪs ᴛɪɴʏ ᴋᴇʏ was once the construction base for Henry Flagler's 7-Mile Bridge, described by some as the eighth wonder of the world when it was eventually completed in 1912. Seven wooden structures, originally used by building and maintenance crews, are today part of a marine research and educational foundation and form one of the last intact railroad villages from the Flagler era.

There's a historical museum in the Bridge Tender's House, but many people visit simply to enjoy the island's tranquil surroundings. The old bridge, running parallel to the "new" 7-Mile Bridge built in 1982, marches across the Key on concrete piles and provides a stunning backdrop to the island. It is also the only way to reach the Key. No cars are allowed on the Key, so go by foot or by bicycle, or take the shuttle bus from the foundation's headquarters at MM 48.

Lower Keys ⑯

Road map E5. Monroe Co. 🚗 Key West. 🛈 MM 31, (305) 872-2411.

Oɴᴄᴇ ʙᴇʏᴏɴᴅ the 7-Mile Bridge, the Keys appear to change. The land is rugged and less developed than in the Upper Keys, and the

The Negro Quarters, an example of Pigeon Key's original dwellings

Bahia Honda's beautiful beach, one of the few natural sand beaches in the Florida Keys

vegetation more wooded, supporting different flora and fauna. But by far the most striking change is in the pace of life; this slows right down, and upholds the local claim that the Lower Keys are more about a state of mind than a geographical location.

Just 37 miles (60 km) from Key West is **Bahia Honda State Park**, a protected area of 524 acres that boasts the finest beach in all the Keys – and the second best in the US according to a recent survey. Brilliantly white sand is backed by a dense, tropical forest crossed by a number of trails. If you follow these you will find various unusual species of tree, such as silver palm and yellow satinwood, and there are lots of birds. The usual water sports equipment is available to rent, but visitors should remember that the current here can be very strong.

Trips out to the **Looe Key National Marine Sanctuary** are also available from the park. Both snorkelers and divers agree that this 5 mile (8-km) section of the reef is a spectacular dive location, with unique coral formations and abundant marine life.

From Bahia Honda, the highway swings north and reaches the next major point of interest, and second largest island in

Perky's Bat Tower

the chain, **Big Pine Key**. This island is the Lower Keys' main residential community and the best place to see the diminutive Key Deer, most often spotted at dusk or in the early morning. Take the turning for Key Deer Boulevard near MM 30 to reach the **Blue Hole**, a flooded quarry set in woodlands. The viewing platform here is ideal for watching the deer and other wildlife that come to drink. Nearby, the one-mile (1.6-km) looped path of the Jack Watson Nature Trail has markers to help in identifying the trees and plants. Continuing on down the Overseas Highway, as you cross Cudjoe Key keep a lookout for **"Fat Albert,"** a large white

surveillance blimp. Tethered at a height of 1,400 ft (427 m), Fat Albert's job is to monitor anything from hurricanes and drug smugglers to political activities in Cuba.

Neighboring Sugarloaf Key, once the location of a sponge-farming enterprise, is now famous for its **Bat Tower**, reached by turning north off the Overseas Highway just after MM 17. It was built in 1929 by Richter C. Perky, a property speculator, for the purpose of attracting the bats that he believed would rid the island of its ferocious mosquitos, allowing him to develop it as a resort. Unfortunately, not a single bat came and the tower remains as a testament to his plan's resounding failure.

✗ Bahia Honda State Park
MM 37. **☎** *(305) 872-2353.*
☐ *daily.* 🖼 🚹

KEY DEER

Related to the white-tailed deer, Florida's endangered Key Deer are found only on Big Pine Key and the surrounding islands. They swim between these keys, but are more often sighted as they roam around the slash pine woodlands. Despite the enforcement of strict speed restrictions, and the establishment of a refuge on Big Pine Key, around 50 deer are killed in road accidents each year. The number of deer has stabilized at around 300. It is strictly forbidden to feed them.

A fully grown Key Deer, no bigger than a large dog

Street-by-Street: Key West ⑰

THE SOUTHERNMOST SETTLEMENT in the continental US, Key West is a city like no other and a magnet for people who want to leave the rest of Florida, and even America, behind. This is a place to join in with locals busy dropping out and to indulge in the laid-back, tropical lifestyle.

First recorded in 1513, the island soon became a haven first for pirates and then for "wreckers" *(see p289)*, both of whom preyed on passing merchant ships and their precious cargos. Key West grew to be the most prosperous city in Florida, and the opportunistic lifestyle on offer lured a steady stream of settlers from the Americas, the Caribbean, and Europe; you'll find their legacy in the island's unique architecture, cuisine, and spirit. A large gay community, writers, and new-agers are among the more recent arrivals who have added to Key West's cultural cocktail.

The Curry Mansion
This opulent 19th-century home's interior reflects the wealth of Key West's wreck captains (see p288).

Sloppy Joe's was Ernest Hemingway's favorite haunt. The bar moved here from its former site on Greene Street in 1935.

Pier House Resort
Just off Mallory Square, this resort has a popular terrace where people gather to watch the famous Key West sunsets.

DUVAL STREET

GREENE STREET

CAROLINE STREET

Mallory Square

WHITEHEAD STREET

★ Mel Fisher Maritime Museum
All kinds of shipwreck treasures, and the gear used to find them, are displayed in this excellent museum (see p288).

Audubon House, built in the 1840s, contains period pieces and ornithological prints by John James Audubon *(see p44).*

The Wreckers' Museum *(see p288)*

KEY

– – – Suggested route

STAR SIGHTS

★ **Mel Fisher Maritime Museum**

★ **Bahama Village**

Duval Street
Key West's main thoroughfare, Duval Street is lined with souvenir shops and is often busy with tourists. Several of the Old Town's sights are located here.

Fleming Street
Typical of the quiet, shady residential roads of the Old Town, Fleming Street boasts many beautiful wooden houses. These are fine examples of traditional Key West architecture (see p287).

VISITORS' CHECKLIST

Road map E5. Monroe Co.
28,000. ✈ 2 miles (3 km) E of Duval St. 🚌 615 Duval St, (305) 296-9072. 🚢 Mallory Sq, (305) 292-8158. ℹ️ 402 Wall Street, (305) 294-2587. Walking tours (305) 293-9291. **Audubon House** 📞 (305) 294-2116. ⬜ daily. 🎭 Conch Republic Independence Celebration (Apr), Hemingway Days Festival (Jul), Fantasy Fest (mid-Oct).

St. Paul's Episcopal Church
This 1912 church is dedicated to the patron saint of shipwrecked sailors. Some of its 49 stained-glass windows feature nautical imagery.

Margaritaville
Jimmy Buffet, the Floridian singer, owns this café and adjoining shop, where T-shirts and memorabilia are on sale.

The San Carlos Institute
was founded by Cubans in 1871. Today it occupies a beautiful Baroque-style building, which dates from 1924 and functions as a Cuban heritage center.

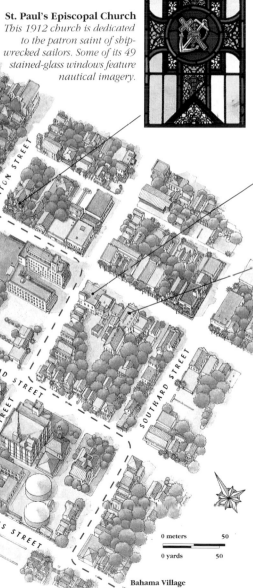

EATON STREET

SOUTHARD STREET

EAD STREET

G STREET

MAS STREET

| 0 meters | 50 |
| 0 yards | 50 |

Bahama Village

★ Bahama Village
As yet relatively undeveloped, this old Key West neighborhood is filled with brightly painted clapboard buildings.

Exploring Key West

Hemingway's boxing glove

MOST OF THE SIGHTS are either on or within two or three blocks of Duval Street, which links the Gulf of Mexico with the Atlantic and is the main axis of Old Key West. Focused between Whitehead and White streets, this district boasts the largest concentration of 19th-century wooden buildings in Florida. Simple shotgun houses, which were erected to house Cuban cigar-workers, contrast with the whimsically Romantic style of the homes of wealthier citizens. To get your bearings, take the Conch Train or Old Town Trolley tour, rent a bicycle, or just wander around the back streets. In the south of the island, you'll find lovely sandy beaches.

Shady palms lining a subtropical beach in southern Key West

A Tour of Key West

On the northern edge of the old town, **Mallory Square** is the famous place to watch the sunset, when performance artists vie with each other to amuse the crowds. During the day, to get the feel of the city, head down Duval Street and take side streets at random. These pretty streets are lined with Key West's distinctive gingerbread houses, set among shady tropical trees and drooping bougainvillea.

Even more rewarding, and named after Key West's earliest settlers, is **Bahama Village**. This historic neighborhood on the western fringe of the old town is bordered by Fort, Virginia, Petronia, and Whitehead streets. Life here is lived outside, with animated domino games on street corners and chickens wandering freely – a taste of the Caribbean in North America. The typical shotgun houses have largely escaped the enthusiastic renovations found elsewhere.

🏛 East Martello Museum and Gallery

3501 S Roosevelt Blvd. 📞 *(305) 296-3913.* ⬤ *daily.* ⬤ *Dec 25.* 🎟 ♿

Located in the east of the island, the East Martello tower was begun in 1861 to protect Fort Zachary's defensive position *(see p288).* It was never completed, as its design quickly became outmoded.

Today, the squat tower is an informative museum that gives the visitor an excellent introduction to Key West and its checkered past. Everything is included here, from stories about Key West's many literary connections to the island's changing commercial history. You can also see one of the unbelievably flimsy rafts used by Cubans to flee Castro's regime *(see pp50–51).*

The tower itself offers fine views and houses works of art by a number of local artists, including appealing primitive paintings by Mario Sanchez.

🦆 Hemingway House

907 Whitehead St. 📞 *(305) 294-1575.* ⬤ *daily.* 🎟 ♿ 🅆 www.hemingwayhouse.com

Probably the town's major (and most hyped) attraction, this Spanish colonial-style house built of coral rock is where Ernest Hemingway lived from 1931–40. Above the carriage house is the room where the novelist penned several works; *To Have and Have Not* was the only book set in Key West. His library and mementos from his travels are displayed, as are memorabilia such as the cigar-maker's chair upon which he sat and wrote. Guides describe the hard-living writer's nonliterary passions of fishing and hell-raising in Sloppy Joe's *(see p284).*

Descendants of his six-toed cats still prowl around the house and its luxuriant garden.

🏛 Lighthouse Museum

938 Whitehead St. 📞 *(305) 294-0012.* ⬤ *daily.* ⬤ *Dec 25.* 🎟

Across the road from Hemingway House stands the town's lighthouse, built in 1848. The clapboard keeper's cottage at its foot houses a modest museum containing lighthouse and other historical artifacts. For many people the greatest attraction is the tower itself. Make the 88-step climb, and you will be rewarded by panoramic views and the chance to step inside and look through the old lens, once capable of beaming light some 25 miles (40 km) out to sea.

Original Lighthouse flag

***Boza's Comparsa* (1975), Duval Street by M Sanchez, East Martello Museum**

Key West Style

THE ARCHITECTURE of Key West is striking above all for its simplicity, a response to the hot climate and the limited materials available – principally wood, which was either salvaged or imported. Early "conch" houses, built at the beginning of the 19th century, were often built by ships' carpenters who introduced elements they had seen on their travels. From the Bahamas came various devices to increase shade and ventilation against the Florida sun.

Elaborately carved wooden brackets

Later, Classical Revivalism filtered in from the north, while the Victorian style of the late 1800s introduced a highly decorative influence. Key West's prosperous inhabitants favored often extravagant ginger-bread details, but carvings also adorn humbler dwellings. Since the 1970s, when the town's architectural legacy was first properly acknowledged, many houses have been renovated, especially inside. But their essential flavor remains.

Large sash windows admit cooling breezes.

Shutters keep out the sun and give protection during storms; originally some windows had no glass.

Wide verandas provide much needed shade.

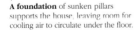

Gingerbread-style fretwork often decorates balustrades; rarely do you find two houses with identical styles of carving.

THREE BAY HOUSE
The most common type of Key West house, the three bay, is only a little more refined than the "shotgun" style, named for the fact that a bullet fired through the front door would exit cleanly out the back. Orienting the gable toward the street maximized the number of houses that could be fitted on one block.

A foundation of sunken pillars supports the house, leaving room for cooling air to circulate under the floor.

Roof hatches, inspired by a similar device found on ships, bring extra ventilation to the building's top floor.

Colored paintwork is popular today, although the more traditional whitewash remains the most common.

Doorways often display the most obvious Classical Revival influences.

The "eyebrow" virtually obscures the upper windows from view.

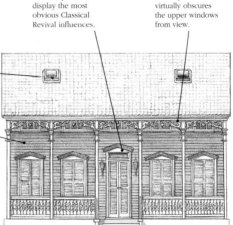

FIVE BAY "EYEBROW" HOUSE
Classic Key West symmetry is much in evidence in this five-bay house. Unique to the island is the "eyebrow" feature or roof over-hang, which shades the top-floor rooms from the heat of the sun.

The impressive brick vaulting of Fort Zachary Taylor

♠ Fort Zachary Taylor State Historic Site

End of Southard St. ((305) 292-6713. ◯ daily. 📷 ♿ limited.

Part of the national coastal defense system begun in the mid-19th century, this brick fort was completed in 1866. During the Civil War, Union troops were stationed here to keep the island loyal to the north. Originally, the fort was three stories high and had toilets that were flushed by the tides. It was remodeled in the 1890s.

Today, it houses a military museum which contains a fine collection of Civil War artifacts. Visitors can also explore the grounds and enjoy the view from an observation deck. Nearby is Key West's best public beach, which has shady picnic areas and is a perfect spot for a relaxing swim.

🏛 The Mel Fisher Maritime Museum

200 Greene St. 📘 (305) 294-2633, (800) 434-1399. ◯ 9:30am–5pm. 📷 ♿ 🅦 www.melfisher.com

A plain stone exterior belies the opulence of some of the treasures this museum holds. The late Mr. Fisher grabbed the headlines in 1985 when he discovered the wrecks of the Spanish galleons *Nuestra Señora de Atocha (see p26)* and *Santa Margarita*, about 40 miles (64 km) west of Key West; inside were 47 tons of gold and silver bars and 70 lbs (32 kg) of raw emeralds that sank with them in 1622.

Items on display include jewelry, coins, and crucifixes. The story of the salvage operation is also told, but check the awesome website.

🏛 The Wreckers' Museum

322 Duval St. ((305) 294-9502. ◯ daily. 📷 ♿ limited.

Originally the home of wreck captain, Francis B. Watlington, this is thought to be the oldest house in Key West. Built in 1829, its design reveals some rather idiosyncratic maritime influences, such as the hatch used for ventilation in the roof. The house is stuffed full of nautical bric-a-brac, ships' models and paintings, and an array of documents concerning wrecking – the industry that first made Key West (and Captain Watlington) rich. Visitors are greeted by volunteer staff, whose anecdotes make the history of the house come alive.

Don't miss the separate kitchen house in the backyard, the oldest of the few examples that still remain in the Keys. Located away from the main building, it minimized the risk of fire and in addition helped to keep the temperature down in the rest of the house.

The ship-style hatch in the attic of the Wreckers' Museum

🏠 The Curry Mansion

511 Caroline St. ((305) 294-5349. ◯ daily. 📷 ♿ 🅦 www.currymansion.com

This grand and embellished mansion was begun in 1855 by William Curry, a Bahamian wreck captain who became Key West's first millionaire. His son Milton completed the work 44 years later.

In addition to its sweeping verandas, the house boasts many original features, including wood-paneled rooms and electrical fittings. The rooms are furnished with Victorian and later objects, from Tiffany stained glass to a rifle once owned by Ernest Hemingway – all collected by the present owner. It is said that key lime pie *(see p315)* was first made here by Aunt Sally, the cook, using canned condensed milk (first available in 1895). The Curry Mansion is also a guest house *(see p311)*.

The charming Robert Frost Cottage in the garden of Heritage House

🏛 Heritage House Museum

410 Caroline St. ((305) 296-3573. ◯ daily. ● Thanksgiving, Dec 25, Jan 1. 📷 ♿

Built in 1834 and originally the home of a British captain, this house is one of Key West's oldest buildings. It is in near-original condition and contains period furnishings and travel curios that belonged to the Porters, a wealthy Key West family. The garden contains an outdoor kitchen house and, beneath a fine banyan tree, the Robert Frost cottage; this is named after the American poet who stayed here during his many visits to Key West. A freshwater well in the garden was allegedly used by early mariners and Indians.

🪦 Key West Cemetery

701 Passover Lane. 📞 (305) 292-8177. ⬜ daily. ♿

Due to the proximity of the limestone bedrock and water table, most of the tombs here are above ground. Laid out on a grid system, the cemetery holds the remains of many of Key West's earliest residents. Within the compound there are separate areas for Jews and Roman Catholics, while many of the Cuban crypts are crowned with a statue of a chicken, probably associated with the Santería religion *(see p75)*. There is even a special burial area devoted to pets.

A statue of a single sailor commemorates the loss of 252 crewmen on the battleship USS *Maine*, which was sunk in Havana's harbor at the onset of the Spanish-American War in 1898 *(see p47)*. Stroll around to read the often amusing inscriptions and epitaphs, "I told you I was sick" among others. Many of the town's early settlers were known simply by their first or nicknames, and this Key West informality followed them to their graves. There are references to Bunny, Shorty, Bean, and so forth. Dismissive of this tradition, Ernest Hemingway is reported to have said "I'd rather eat monkey manure than die in Key West."

Statue of the Lone Sailor

THE BUSINESS OF WRECKING

In the late 1700s, the waters off the Keys were fished mainly by Bahamians of British descent, who patrolled the reef in order to salvage shipwrecks. Lookouts, or "Wreckers," at their vantage points would shout "Wreck ashore!" to send salvage vessels racing toward the reef to be the first to claim a grounded ship. In this way, goods from around the world ended up in the Keys; these ranged from basics such as timber to luxury goods like lace, wine, and silver. This opportunistic scavenging came to be known as "wrecking." It grew so popular that in 1825 an act of the US Congress legislated for much tighter control and decreed that only US residents could have such salvage rights. Key West boomed, and in the years that followed, it became the richest city in Florida.

Facsimile of a wrecker's license

Dry Tortugas National Park ⑱

Road map D5. Monroe Co.
🚤 Key West. 🛈 402 Wall St, (305) 242-7700.

THE DRY TORTUGAS consist of seven reef islands lying 68 miles (109 km) west of Key West. Of these, Garden Key is the most visited, being the site of **Fort Jefferson**, the largest brick fortification in the US. The hexagonal design included a moat 70 ft (21 m) wide, and walls up to 8 ft (2.5 m) thick and 50 ft (15 m) high. It was originally envisaged that the fort would control the Florida Straits with a garrison of 1,500 men and 450 cannons. Beginning in 1845, construction continued for the next 30 years, but the fort was never completed or involved in any battle. During the Civil War, after being occupied by Union forces, it was downgraded to a prison for captured deserters.

The only access is by boat or seaplane. Most people come on organized trips from Key West, which often include an opportunity to snorkel in the crystal-clear water. The bird-watching is especially good between March and October, when the islands are home to migrant and nesting birds, such as boobies, sooty terns, and magnificent frigatebirds with their 7-ft (2-m) wingspan.

Remote Garden Key in Dry Tortugas National Park, occupied by the imposing 19th-century Fort Jefferson

TRAVELERS' NEEDS

WHERE TO STAY

FLORIDA HAS a huge variety of places to stay suitable for all budgets and tastes – from rustic wooden cabins with minimal facilities to luxurious resort hotels that cater to their guests' every need. In between, you can choose from ordinary hotels, more charming bed and breakfasts, convenient motels, or fully equipped apartments. Campsites, where you can pitch a tent or hook up an RV or mobile home, are also plentiful. On the whole you get a good deal for your

Sign outside the Coombs House Inn *(see p306)*

money in Florida, though prices fluctuate greatly according to the season and location. The listings on pages 296–311 recommend more than 200 places around the state, all representing the best of their kind and in all price ranges. The *Florida Accommodation Directory*, available from the tourist board, lists hotels, motels, and other lodgings all over the state, and local tourist offices can provide more detailed information about places in their particular area.

The lobby of the stylish Eden Roc Resort and Spa in Miami *(see p297)*

HOTELS AND RESORTS

UNLESS YOU STAY in one of Miami Beach's superb Art Deco establishments, you'll find that most hotels in the state are large, modern buildings, with excellent facilities and a swimming pool but minimal atmosphere and often rather impersonal service.

Chain hotels are common and extremely popular here, and have the advantage of at least being predictable – although prices vary depending on the location. They range from the upscale Marriott and Inter-Continental hotels through the mid-range Holiday Inns and Howard Johnsons (HoJo's) to the budget Days Inn chain.

Resorts are large hotel complexes generally located by the water and often set in immaculately kept grounds. Prices are high, but these resorts provide all manner of amenities, from swimming

pools (sometimes Olympic-size) to shops and usually a choice of restaurants. Many have excellent sports facilities, including golf courses and tennis courts, and may provide instructors for individual lessons. Health clubs are increasingly popular, with daily fitness classes and spa diets often available.

These shady gardens and pool typify many plush Florida resorts

With their well-equipped games rooms, special children's programs, and other facilities, these resorts can be a good option for families.

BED AND BREAKFASTS

ANYONE IN SEARCH of a more traditional sense of hospitality might stay in a bed and breakfast (B & B). Sometimes referred to as "homestays," these are private homes where the owner is your host. Breakfast is usually excellent with homemade breads and coffee, and guests often eat together in an informal atmosphere. The ambience and personal touch usually make up for the absence of traditional hotel facilities – although some B & Bs are quite luxurious.

Any place called an "inn" tends to be bigger and pricier than the average B & B and may even have a restaurant, but it is still likely to be more friendly than a chain hotel.

Rural areas and historic towns have the best choice of bed and breakfasts. In Key West and St. Augustine, for example, you can stay in beautiful old homes with antique furnishings.

The main drawbacks with B & Bs are that they may have restrictions on children, and may require a minimum stay in tourist season; since most have just a few rooms, you also need to book well in advance.

Several agencies specialize in arranging B & B accommodation. They include **Florida B&B Inns**, which specializes

Cedar Key Bed and Breakfast *(see p306)* in the Panhandle

in historic establishments across the state, and the **Key West Innkeepers Association**. The southeast edition of the *Bed and Breakfast USA* guide and the AAA publication *Bed and Breakfasts, Country Inns, and Historical Lodgings,* are also useful sources. There may be local listings for B&Bs, so check the Yellow Pages.

HOW TO RESERVE

To SECURE A ROOM in the hotel of your choice in season, particularly in Orlando or Miami, reserve several months in advance; in off season, you can usually get a room on short notice. At any time of year you should always be able to find a room, even if the hotel is not your ideal choice.

You can book by phone with a credit card (a deposit may be required) and should give advance notice if you plan to arrive after 5pm; otherwise you may lose your reservation

FACILITIES

COMPETITION in Florida's hotel trade is fierce so facilities are generally good. Rooms without a TV, attached bathroom, and air conditioning are rare, even in B & Bs, and most have a refrigerator and desk; some hotels also provide kitchen facilities *(see p294)*. Bedrooms usually have two queen-size beds.

People with disabilities will be best provided for in a conventional hotel or resort. In addition to elevators and ramps, a few hotels have rooms especially designed for people in wheelchairs. If you have special needs, inform the hotel when you reserve.

PRICES

ROOM RATES VARY enormously depending on the time of year, with prices in tourist season often 30–50 percent more than in off season. In South Florida the tourist season runs from mid-November to Easter, while in the Panhandle and the Northeast, where it is cooler in winter, hotels charge their highest rates in summer. Wherever you are, however, expect to pay peak rates at Christmas, Easter, and Thanksgiving. At any time of year, you can pay up to 25 percent more for a room facing the water, so it's worth asking for the full range of prices.

Rooms that cost less than about $70 tend to offer similar facilities, and it is only above $70 (less in rural areas) that the standard is noticeably different. Rates are usually calculated per room rather

than per person. This means that only a small reduction is made on the cost of a double room when calculating the price of a single.

It is always worth inquiring about any special deals. For example, you may get a lower price on your room if you eat in the hotel (ask about meal plans), or if you plan to stay for a week or more. Many hotels also offer discounts for senior citizens and families.

The fashionable Delano Hotel in South Beach, Miami *(see p297)*

HIDDEN EXTRAS

ROOM RATES are generally quoted exclusive of both sales tax *(see p332)* and the so-called resort tax, which is 2–5 percent of the price of the room (depending on the area). So taxes can add as much as 12 percent to the rate quoted.

The cost of making phone calls from a hotel room is extortionate. A few places offer free local calls from rooms, but as a rule using a pay phone in the lobby is much cheaper. You are often charged for receiving faxes too.

Many hotels charge for valet parking: a fee of anything from $2 to $17 a day (as at the Delano Hotel) is not unusual, not counting the optional tip for the attendant.

Given the inflated price of most hotel breakfasts, you'd do well to go out to a nearby café or diner. Be warned too that you must pay for watching certain in-room movies: read the screen before pressing your remote control button.

A Deco room in the Brigham Gardens Guest House, Miami *(see p296)*

Cabins for rent by the ocean at Bahia Honda in the Keys *(see p283)*

MOTELS

FEW VACATIONERS are likely to go out of their way to stay in a motel, but motels are a good last-minute option, particularly during tourist season. The outskirts of towns and cities are classic motel territory, but in Florida they are also common in beach resorts, where they provide a good alternative to conventional hotels, especially at the busiest times of year.

Motels are cheaper than many hotels and more convenient too. You can park your car (for free) near your room, unload your bags, and be off to the beach or out sightseeing in minutes. Rooms are usually simple but adequate. Inspect the room before checking in, however, since some rooms might not be clean.

Colorful neon sign for a motel in Orlando

ACCOMMODATIONS IN ORLANDO

FOR ANYONE PLANNING to visit the theme parks, proximity is a major consideration: arriving early is the best way to avoid the worst lines *(see p163)*. Waiting in traffic for an hour or more to get into the park can take up precious time. Furthermore, you will have the option to return to your hotel if you need a break during the day, or while you wait for lines to die down.

Universal Orlando has two on-site hotels, Disneyland Resorts offers one on-site and two adjacent hotels. Rooms at these mega-resorts are costly, convenient, and offer great package deals. However, both Universal and Disney have "good neighbor hotels," which are nearby, less expensive, and also offer admission packages.

Lodgings are in big demand at the resorts and must be booked six months to a year in advance if you wish to visit at Easter or Christmas. There are so many hotels in Greater Orlando, though, that you need never worry about finding a room. When choosing where to stay ask how long it takes to get to the parks, whether shuttle buses are available, and how often they run.

APARTMENT RENTALS

WITH FLORIDA being such a big family destination, apartment accommodations are very popular. Rooms with cooking facilities, known as "efficiencies," are provided in some hotels and motels. These may cost more than standard rooms but enable families to avoid expensive restaurant meals. In rural areas you find efficiency (self-catering) cabins attached to campgrounds.

Condominiums ("condos"), consisting of complete apartments, are found mainly in beach resorts. They may seem expensive ($1,200 per week is on the low side), but can be a good value if you have a large family. **Villa/Overseas Connection** and **Vacation Home Rentals Worldwide** are among the many agencies to arrange condo rental, and they can normally organize rental of a private apartment or house, too. Tour operators that specialize in Florida can provide the same service if you request it.

Finally, you can stay in a private home for free by doing a house swap. To arrange this, you can enroll as a member of a home-exchange organization: **HomeLink**, for example, has members worldwide.

CAMPING

FLORIDA HAS A HUGE number of campsites. These range from the basic, where there may be no running water, to the luxurious, with swimming pools, restaurants, shops, and

A camper enjoying privacy and quiet in Torreya State Park *(see p225)*

boat rental outlets. People more often stay in mobile homes or RVs than camp in tents, but even RV parks have space for tents; some rent out trailers and cabins too. State parks charge $10–25 per site, while private camp ground charges go up to about $40 per night. Most sites take advance bookings, but state parks hold back some spaces for people who arrive on the day.

The **Florida Association of RV Parks and Campgrounds** (ARVC) produces the annual *Florida Camping Directory*, listing its licensed members; copies can be ordered directly from the ARVC, and you can sometimes get the directory free from the tourist board. Contact the **Department of Environmental Protection,**

A trailer in a tranquil spot in a Panhandle park

The well-kept gardens and pool at the youth hostel in Kissimmee

Parks and Recreation for a list of campsites in the state parks. You may also want to contact **KOA Kampgrounds of America**, which runs about 30 good quality sites in Florida and issues its own directory.

YOUTH HOSTELS

FLORIDA HAS several youth hostels, including ones in South Beach, Orlando, and Fort Lauderdale. **Hostelling International – American Youth Hostels** issues a list of its members. The **Florida Council of Hostelling International** will also provide information.

Facilities are often excellent, often with swimming pools and game rooms , and rates are very low: around $15 per night, slightly more for nonmembers. You should book ahead in tourist season.

TRAVELING WITH CHILDREN

MOST HOTELS provide basic facilities for families, such as cribs (cots); a babysitting service may also be available. Some places, however, particularly in Orlando and popular beach locations, put children higher on their list of priorities and provide kids' swimming pools and play areas; some have children's programs too, with organized activities and day trips (you may have to pay extra).

Most hotels do not charge for children under 12 sharing a room with their parents; in some cases (at Walt Disney World, for example) this is extended to those under 18. Some rooms have a sofa that folds out into a bed; otherwise an extra bed may be set up for a small additional fee.

DIRECTORY

BED AND BREAKFASTS

AAA Auto Club South
w www.aaasouth.com

Key West Innkeepers Assn.
922 Caroline St,
Key West, FL 33040.
C (800) 492-1911.
w www.keywestinns.com

Florida B&B Inns
PO Box 6187, Palm Harbor,
FL 34684
C (800) 524-1880. w
www.florida-inns.com

APARTMENT RENTALS AND HOME EXCHANGE

Villa/Overseas Connection
PO Box 1800,
Sag Harbor, NY 11963.
C (631) 725-9308.

HomeLink
Tampa, FL 33647.
C (800) 638-3841.
w www.homelink.org

Vacation Home Rentals Worldwide
235 Kensington Ave,
Norwood, NJ 07648.
C (201) 767-9393.
w www.vhrww.com

CAMPING

Department of Environmental Protection, Parks and Recreation
3900 Commonwealth Blvd,
Tallahassee, FL 32399.
C (850) 488-9872.
w www.myflorida.com

Florida Association of RV Parks and Campgrounds
1340 Vickers Drive,
Tallahassee, FL 32303.
C (850) 562-7151. w
www. floridacamping.com

KOA Kampgrounds of America
PO Box 30558,

Billings, MT 59114.
C (106) 248 7444.
C (0990) 143610 for
bookings in the UK.
w www.koa.com

YOUTH HOSTELS

Hostelling International
PO Box 37613,
Washington DC 20013.
C (202) 783-6161.
w www.iyhf.org
(international)
w www.hiayh.org (US)

Youth Hostel Association
14 Southampton St,
London WC2.
C (20) 7836-1036.

Choosing a Hotel

THE HOTELS IN THIS GUIDE have been selected across a wide price range for their good value, facilities, and location. This chart highlights some of the factors that may influence your choice. Entries are listed by region, beginning with Miami. For Miami map references see pages 96–101; for road map references see pages 12–13.

MIAMI

	Credit Cards	Children's Facilities	Swimming Pool	Good Restaurant	Kitchen Facilities
MIAMI BEACH: *Clay Hotel and International Youth Hostel* $ 1438 Washington Ave, FL 33139. **Map** 2 E3. 〔 *(305) 534-2988.* FAX *(305) 673-0346.* Booking is essential for this youth hostel, housed in a lovely Spanish Revival building. Unbeatably cheap for such a prime location. ***Beds:** 220*	MC V				■
MIAMI BEACH: *Kenmore* $$ 1050 Washington Ave, FL 33139. **Map** 2 E3. 〔 *(305) 674-1930.* FAX *(305) 534-6591.* Jointly run with the Park Washington and popular with a gay crowd, the Kenmore is distinctively Deco, both inside and out. 🛈 ***Rooms:** 60*	AE MC V		■		
MIAMI BEACH: *Lido Spa* W www.lidospa.com $$ 40 Island Ave, FL 33139. **Map** 1 C1. 〔 *(305) 538-4621.* FAX *(305) 534-3680.* A favorite spa for locals who know a bargain, the Lido is located on Belle Isle close to South Beach. ⧉ ⧉ ⧉ ⧉ ⧉ ⧉ ⧉ *May–Oct.* ***Rooms:** 120*	AE MC V		■	●	■
MIAMI BEACH: *Park Washington* $$ 1020 Washington Ave, FL 33139. **Map** 2 E3. 〔 *(305) 532-1930.* FAX *(305) 672-6706.* One of a trio of Deco hostelries (with neighbors Kenmore and Bel Air). Lemon-toned rooms house original 1930s furnishings. 🛈 ***Rooms:** 50*	AE MC V		■		■
MIAMI BEACH: *Brigham Gardens* W www.brighamgardens.com $$$ 1411 Collins Ave, FL 33139. **Map** 2 F3. 〔 *(305) 531-1331.* FAX *(305) 538-9898.* Two 1930s buildings and a gorgeous garden with caged singing birds nestle peacefully in the heart of buzzing South Beach. The rooms are individually decorated with a Deco mix of color and art. ⧉ 🛈 ***Rooms:** 21*	AE MC V				■
MIAMI BEACH: *Dorchester* W www.dorchesterhotel.net $$$ 1850 Collins Ave, FL 33139. **Map** 2 F2. 〔 *(305) 531-5745.* FAX *(305) 673-1006.* A big pool, a tropical garden, and better than average service are among the attractions of the Dorchester. ⧉ ⧉ ⧉ 🛈 ***Rooms:** 94*	AE DC MC V		■		
MIAMI BEACH: *The Governor* W www.governorsouthbeach.com $$$ 435 21st St, FL 33139. **Map** 2 F1. 〔 *(305) 532-2100.* FAX *(305) 532-9139.* Secluded but well situated on a side street, this is an undiscovered Deco gem. Rooms are comfortable and the decor unfussy. ⧉ ⧉ 🛈 ***Rooms:** 124*	AE DC MC V		■	●	
MIAMI BEACH: *Indian Creek* W www.indiancreekhotelmb.com $$$ 2727 Indian Creek Drive, FL 33139. 〔 *(305) 531-2727.* FAX *(305) 531-5651.* This small, friendly hotel retains its 1936 look, with sepia photos, period furniture, and original features. There is a delightful tropical garden and a tiny Asian-Caribbean restaurant. ⧉ ⧉ ⧉ 🛈 ***Rooms:** 61 **Suites:** 6*	AE DC MC V		■	●	
MIAMI BEACH: *Marseilles* W www.marseilleshotel.com $$$ 1741 Collins Ave, FL 33139. **Map** 2 F2. 〔 *(305) 538-5711.* FAX *(305) 673-1006.* The family-run Marseilles isn't fancy but is well located in SoBe. Thanks to the unusual design, most rooms have two views. ⧉ ⧉ ***Rooms:** 111*	AE DC MC V		■	●	
MIAMI BEACH: *Mermaid Guest House* $$$ 909 Collins Ave, FL 33139. **Map** 2 E4. 〔 *(305) 538-5324.* FAX *(305) 538-2822.* Flowering banana trees hide this South Beach hangout, popular with models and actors. Each room has unique decor. ⧉ ⧉ 🛈 ***Rooms:** 10*	AE DC MC V				■
MIAMI BEACH: *Avalon Majestic* W www.southbeachhotels.com $$$$ 700 Ocean Drive, FL 33139. **Map** 2 F3. 〔 *(305) 538-0133.* FAX *(305) 534-0258.* You're right at the heart of the action at this trendy 1930s hotel. Rooms are Deco-style, the restaurant lively *(see p316)*. ⧉ 🛈 ⧉ ***Rooms:** 106*	AE DC MC V			●	
MIAMI BEACH: *Betsy Ross* W www.betsyrosshotel.com $$$$ 1440 Ocean Drive, FL 33139. **Map** 2 F3. 〔 *(305) 531-3934.* FAX *(305) 531-5282.* A cocktail of Deco and Colonial styles, this hotel has very comfortable rooms with great views of the beach and ocean. ⧉ ⧉ 🛈 ***Rooms:** 61*	AE DC MC V		■		

Price categories for a standard double room per night in high season, including tax and service charges:

$ under $60
$$ $60–$100
$$$ $100–$150
$$$$ $150–$200
$$$$$ over $200

CHILDREN'S FACILITIES
A child-friendly hotel, with cribs, high chairs, and other facilities that may include a baby-sitting service and special children's programs.

SWIMMING POOL
The hotel has a swimming pool for use by residents.

GOOD RESTAURANT
There is a particularly good restaurant, which is normally also accessible to nonresidents.

KITCHEN FACILITIES
The hotel has some rooms with cooking and other kitchen facilities, usually known as "efficiencies."

	Credit Cards	Children's Facilities	Swimming Pool	Good Restaurant	Kitchen Facilities
MIAMI BEACH: *Breakwater* W www.breakwater/hotel.com $$$$ 940 Ocean Drive, FL 33139. **Map** 2 F3. (305) 532-1220. **FAX** (305) 532-4451. Guests get a gracious welcome at this oceanfront hotel. The colorful rooms reflect the hotel's original Deco charm. **Rooms:** 60	AE DC MC V		■	●	
MIAMI BEACH: *Pelican* W www.pelicanhotel.com $$$$ 826 Ocean Drive, FL 33139. **Map** 2 F4. (305) 673-3373. **FAX** (305) 673-3255. Designer-kitsch in the extreme, this hip hostelry has theme rooms ranging from a pink satin brothel chamber to one filled with church art and furnishings. No expense is spared on the details. **Rooms:** 26	AE DC MC V			●	
MIAMI BEACH: *Radisson Deauville Resort* $$$$ 6701 Collins Ave, FL 33141. (305) 865-8511. **FAX** (305) 865-8154. Between SoBe and Bal Harbour, this oceanfront hotel is well equipped with a huge pool, tennis courts, and solarium. **Rooms:** 476	AE DC MC V	●	■	●	
MIAMI BEACH: *Shelborne Beach Resort* W www.shelbourne.com $$$$ 1801 Collins Ave, FL 33139. **Map** 2 F2. (305) 531-1271. **FAX** (305) 531-2206. Directly on the ocean in South Beach, the Shelborne has an impressive marble lobby and rooftop fitness center **Rooms:** 225	AE DC MC V	●	■		■
MIAMI BEACH: *Astor* W www.hotelastor.com $$$$$ 956 Washington Ave, FL 33139. **Map** 2 E3. (305) 531-4056. **FAX** (305) 531-3193. This Art Deco showpiece has marble bathrooms, a four-star restaurant, and a very stylish clientele. **Rooms:** 40	AE MC V		■	●	
MIAMI BEACH: *Casa Grande* W www.islandoutpost.com $$$$$ 834 Ocean Drive, FL 33139. **Map** 2 F4. (305) 672-7003. **FAX** (305) 673-3669. Elegantly furnished, this hotel is one of the best in South Beach. Every room has a VCR and CD-player. **Rooms:** 34	AE DC MC V				■
MIAMI BEACH: *Delano* $$$$$ 1685 Collins Ave, FL 33139. **Map** 2 F2. (305) 672-2000. **FAX** (305) 532-0099. SoBe's best hotel – where staff dress all in white and match the gorgeous, if stark, rooms. **Rooms:** 208	AE DC MC V	●	■	●	
MIAMI BEACH: *Eden Roc Resort and Spa* W www.edenrocresort.com $$$$$ 4525 Collins Ave, FL 33140. (305) 531-0000. **FAX** (305) 674-5555. Built to look like a beached cruise liner, this star of 1950s flamboyance has been completely renovated. It now has contemporary rooms and myriad facilities, including a stylish spa. **Rooms:** 350	AE DC MC V	●	■	●	
MIAMI BEACH: *Fontainebleau Hilton Resort and Towers* $$$$$ 4441 Collins Ave, FL 33140. (305) 538-2000. **FAX** (305) 673-5351. The most prestigious resort in Miami Beach *(see p67)*, the Fontainebleau has every amenity imaginable, from children's activities to the famous Tropigala floor show *(see p95)*. **Rooms:** 1,206	AE DC MC V	●	■	●	
MIAMI BEACH: *Impala* W www.hotelimpalamiamibeach.com $$$$$ 1228 Collins Ave, FL 33139. **Map** 2 F3. (305) 673-2021. **FAX** (305) 673-5984. You'll see plenty of limos pull up at this busy Deco hotel. The restrained but exquisite sandy-toned rooms house beautiful wooden and wrought-iron furniture, majestic beds, and original artworks. **Rooms:** 17	AE DC MC V			●	
MIAMI BEACH: *Raleigh* W www.raleighhotel.com $$$$$ 1775 Collins Ave, FL 33139. **Map** 2 F2. (305) 534-6300. **FAX** (305) 538-8140. The Raleigh boasts classy, minimalist rooms (some with ocean views), a trendy pool area, and a hip restaurant. **Rooms:** 107	AE DC MC V	●	■	●	
MIAMI BEACH: *The Tides* W www.tideshotel.com $$$$$ 1220 Ocean Drive, FL 33139. **Map** 2 F3. (305) 604-5000. **FAX** (305) 604-5070. The tallest building on Ocean Drive, this is another Art Deco masterpiece. All the rooms have great views of the water. **Rooms:** 45	AE DC MC V		■	●	

Price categories for a standard double room per night in high season, including tax and service charges:

$ under $60
$$ $60–$100
$$$ $100–$150
$$$$ $150–$200
$$$$$ over $200

CHILDREN'S FACILITIES
A child-friendly hotel, with cribs, high chairs, and other facilities that may include a baby-sitting service and special children's programs.
SWIMMING POOL
The hotel has a swimming pool for use by residents.
GOOD RESTAURANT
There is a particularly good restaurant, which is normally also accessible to nonresidents.
KITCHEN FACILITIES
The hotel has some rooms with cooking and other kitchen facilities, usually known as "efficiencies."

	CREDIT CARDS	CHILDREN'S FACILITIES	SWIMMING POOL	GOOD RESTAURANT	KITCHEN FACILITIES
MIAMI BEACH: *Wyndham Resort* W www.wyndham.com $$$$ 4833 Collins Ave, FL 33140. ((305) 532-3600. FAX (305) 532-2334. This big but relatively quiet hotel offers proximity to the exclusive shops in Bal Harbour plus countless water sports and children's activities. 24 ⚡ ❄ 🛏 🍴 P 🛁 *Rooms: 424*	AE DC MC V	●	▦	●	
DOWNTOWN: *Hampton* W www.hampton.com $$ 2500 Brickell Ave, FL 33129. **Map** 4 D4. ((305) 854-2070. FAX (305) 856-5055. The Hampton offers easy access to Downtown, Coconut Grove, and Coral Gables. Rooms are bright, and breakfast is included. ⚡ 🍴 🛏 🛁 *Rooms: 69*	AE DC MC V		▦		
DOWNTOWN: *Miami River Inn* W www.miamiriverinn.com $$$ 118 SW South River Drive, FL 33130. **Map** 4 D1. ((305) 325-0045. FAX (305) 325-9227. Built in 1906 and restored to its early Miami charm, the building features period decor and airy rooms. ⚡ ❄ 🍴 P 🛁 *Rooms: 40*	AE DC MC V		▦		▦
DOWNTOWN: *Doubletree Grand* W www.doubletreehotels.com $$$ 1717 N Bayshore Drive, FL 33132. ((305) 372-0313. FAX (305) 372-9455. Here you get great views of Biscayne Bay, a marina, a health club, and boats for rent. ⚡ ❄ 🛏 🍴 P 🛁 *Rooms: 154*	AE DC MC V		▦	●	▦
DOWNTOWN: *Wyndham Hotel* W www.wyndham.com $$$$ 1601 Biscayne Blvd, FL 33132. ((305) 374-0000. FAX (305) 374-0020. Rising high above the 125-store Omni shopping mall, this central hotel is near Bayside and offers panoramic views. ⚡ ❄ 🛏 🍴 P *Rooms: 528*	AE DC MC V	●	▦		
DOWNTOWN: *Doral Golf Resort and Spa* W www.doralgolf.com $$$$$ 4400 NW 87th Ave, FL 33178. ((305) 592-2000. FAX (305) 594-4682. Located on a championship golf course, this hotel is beautifully land-scaped and has a world-class spa. ⚡ ❄ 🛏 🍴 P 🛁 *Rooms: 693*	AE DC MC V	●	▦	●	
DOWNTOWN: *Inter-Continental Miami* W www.interconti.com $$$$$ 100 Chopin Plaza, FL 33131. **Map** 4 F1. ((305) 577-1000. FAX (305) 577-0384. A short walk from Bayside Marketplace, this luxury hotel has city views and a gourmet restaurant *(see p317)*. 24 ⚡ ❄ 🛏 🍴 P *Rooms: 633*	AE DC MC V	●	▦	●	
CORAL GABLES: *Riviera Court Motel* $$ 5100 Riviera Drive, FL 33146. **Map** 6 F3. ((305) 665-3528. FAX (305) 667-8993 This cheap and cheerful 1950s-style hotel is on Dixie Highway, with easy access to area attractions. Rooms are pleasant and homey. *Rooms: 31*	AE DC MC V		▦		▦
CORAL GABLES: *Omni Colonnade* W www.omnihotel.com $$$$$ 180 Aragon Ave, FL 33134. **Map** 6 D1. ((305) 441-2600. FAX (305) 445-3929. This plush hotel just off Miracle Mile incorporates a 1920s George Merrick rotunda *(see p80)*. The period theme echoes throughout, with mahogany furniture and marble floors. 24 ⚡ ❄ 🛏 🍴 P 🛁 *Rooms: 157*	AE DC MC V	●	▦	●	
CORAL GABLES: *Place St. Michel* W www.hotelplacestmichel.com $$$$ 162 Alcazar Ave, FL 33134. **Map** 5 C1. ((305) 444-1666. FAX (305) 529-0074. This romantic 1926 hotel, a short walk from Miracle Mile, is evocative of Paris: dark wood paneling, 1930s French furniture, and Deco fittings create the illusion. It also boasts a fine French restaurant. ⚡ 🍴 *Rooms: 27*	AE DC MC V			●	
CORAL GABLES: *The Biltmore* W www.biltmorehotel.com $$$$$ 1200 Anastasia Ave, FL 33134. **Map** 5 A2. ((305) 445-1926. FAX (305) 913-3159. Rich in history (Al Capone gambled here in the 1920s), the grande dame of Miami's hotels will pamper you with every modern amenity in opulent, antique-filled suites. 24 ⚡ ❄ 🛏 🍴 P 🛁 *Rooms: 300*	AE DC MC V	●	▦	●	
COCONUT GROVE: *Hampton Inn* W www.hampton.com $$$ 2800 SW 28th Terrace, FL 33133. **Map** 6 F3. ((305) 448-2800. FAX (305) 442-8655. Located under a mile (1.5 km) from Coconut Grove's cafés and nightlife. Continental breakfast is included. ⚡ 🛏 🍴 *Rooms: 136*	AE DC MC V		▦		

COCONUT GROVE: *Doubletree* W www.doubletreehotels.com $$$$$
2649 S Bayshore Drive, FL 33133. **Map** 6 F4. ((305) 858-2500.
FAX (305) 858-5776. A stroll from the cafés and boutiques of "the village,"
this sleek hotel offers beautiful views of Biscayne Bay marina. There's
marble and modern art throughout. 24 ♦ ⌹ ♦ ♦ ♦ *Rooms: 192*
AE DC MC V

COCONUT GROVE: *Miami Coconut Grove* $$$$$
2669 S Bayshore Drive, FL 33133. **Map** 6 F4. ((888) 472-6229, (305) 858-
9600 FAX (305) 859 2026. Among the world's finest hotels, with crystal
chandeliers, designer furnishings, and original art. Pavarotti's suite can be
rented when he's not in residence. 24 ♦ ♦ ♦ ♦ P ♦ *Rooms: 177*
AE DC MC V

COCONUT GROVE: *Mayfair House* W www.mayfairhouse.com $$$$$
3000 Florida Ave, FL 33133. **Map** 6 E4. ((305) 441-0000. FAX (305) 447-9173.
Perched on top of an exclusive shopping mall, Mayfair House provides
opulent lodgings. Large rooms have rich mahogany furniture and private
balconies; some even have antique pianos. 24 ♦ ♦ ♦ P ♦ *Rooms: 179*
AE DC MC V

FARTHER AFIELD: *Paradise Inn Motel* $$
8520 Harding Ave, Surfside, FL 33141. ((305) 865-6216. FAX (305) 865-9028.
This budget motel isn't fancy, but it's clean and located just a block
from the beach and the huge North Shore Park. *Rooms: 96*
AE MC V

FARTHER AFIELD: *Suez Oceanfront Resort* $$
18215 Collins Ave, Sunny Isles, FL 33160. ((305) 932-0661. FAX (305) 937-0058.
Located on the beach, and with good amenities, the Suez is child friendly
with a kids' pool and playground. ♦ ♦ ♦ ♦ *Rooms: 196*
AE DC MC V

FARTHER AFIELD: *Beach House Bal Harbour* $$$$$
9449 Collins Ave, Bal Harbour, FL 33154. ((305) 865-3551. FAX (305) 861-6596.
The service is friendly, there is a white sand beach for guests, a good restaurant,
and a cocktail lounge. Good sports facilities include a golf course, jai alai, and
tennis courts. ♦ ♦ ♦ ♦ P ♦ *Rooms: 170* W www.rubellhotels.com
AE DC MC V

FARTHER AFIELD: *Newport Beachside Resort* $$$$$
16701 Collins Ave, Sunny Isles, FL 33160. ((305) 949-1300. FAX (305) 947-5873.
Best known for its entertainment, from comedy shows to Las Vegas-style
revues, the Newport offers huge rooms, many with balconies, and a
fishing pier. ♦ ♦ ♦ ♦ P *Rooms: 295* W www.newportbeachsideresort.com
AE DC MC V

FARTHER AFIELD: *Sheraton Bal Harbour* W www.starwood.com $$$$$
9701 Collins Ave, Bal Harbour, FL 33154. ((305) 865-7511, (800) 999-9898. FAX (305)
864-2601. If you want proximity to the Bal Harbour shops, deluxe rooms overlooking the ocean, and a 10-acre tropical garden, then this is the place to stay.
24 ♦ ♦ ♦ ♦ P ♦ *Rooms: 642*
AE DC MC V

FARTHER AFIELD: *Sonesta Beach* W www.sonesta.com $$$$$
350 Ocean Drive, Key Biscayne, FL 33149. ((305) 361 2021. FAX (305) 361 3096.
Stylish but casual, this resort has kids' activities, tennis courts, and live
music in the lounge. The hallmarks of the rooms are soft pastel colors
and tremendous ocean views. 24 ♦ ♦ ♦ ♦ P ♦ *Rooms: 292*
AE DC MC V

THE GOLD AND TREASURE COASTS

BOCA RATON: *Ocean Lodge* $$
531 N Ocean Blvd, FL 33432. **Road map** F4. ((561) 395 7772. FAX (561) 395 0554.
No more than a shell's throw from the beach, this motel is also close to
restaurants and shops. It has a shady barbecue area. ♦ ♦ *Rooms: 18*
AE MC V

BOCA RATON: *Shore Edge Resort* $$
425 N Ocean Blvd, FL 33432. **Road map** F4. ((561) 395-4491. FAX (561) 347-8759.
At this quaint, cozy motel across the street from the ocean the rooms
are small but tidy, and the proprietors are very friendly. *Rooms: 16*
AE MC V

BOCA RATON: *Boca Raton Resort* W www.bocaresort.com $$$$$
501 E Camino Real, FL 33431. **Road map** F4. ((561) 395-3000. FAX (561) 447-3183.
The most chic and pretentious place in town *(see p126)*, this Spanish-
style hotel boasts rooms in a choice of decor, from dark woods to
Oriental rugs and sleek marble. 24 ♦ ♦ ♦ ♦ P ♦ *Rooms: 963*
AE DC MC V

CLEWISTON: *Clewiston Inn* W www.clewinn.com $$$
108 Royal Palm Ave, FL 33440. **Road map** E4. ((863) 983-8151.
FAX (863) 983-4602. This traditional inn with the look of a colonial mansion
provides comfortable lodging and good Southern cooking. *Rooms: 57*
AE DC MC V

Price categories for a standard double room per night in high season, including tax and service charges:

$ under $60
$$ $60-$100
$$$ $100-$150
$$$$ $150-$200
$$$$$ over $200

CHILDREN'S FACILITIES
A child-friendly hotel, with cribs, high chairs, and other facilities that may include a baby-sitting service and special children's programs.

SWIMMING POOL
The hotel has a swimming pool for use by residents.

GOOD RESTAURANT
There is a particularly good restaurant, which is normally also accessible to nonresidents.

KITCHEN FACILITIES
The hotel has some rooms with cooking and other kitchen facilities, usually known as "efficiencies."

	CREDIT CARDS	CHILDREN'S FACILITIES	SWIMMING POOL	GOOD RESTAURANT	KITCHEN FACILITIES

DELRAY BEACH: *Seagate Hotel and Beach Club* $$$$
400 S Ocean Blvd, FL 33483. **Road map** F4. **(** (561) 276-2421. **FAX** (561) 243-4714
This friendly oceanfront hotel with a 400-ft. (122-m) private beach offers well-furnished rooms in earthy tones, and two pools. ⚡ ❄ 🍴 **P** *Rooms:* 69
Credit cards: AE DC MC V — Children's ●, Swimming ▦, Good Restaurant ●

FORT LAUDERDALE: *Holiday Inn Beach* [w] www.holiday-inn.com $$$
999 Ft. Lauderdale Beach Blvd, FL 33304. **Road map** F4. **(** (954) 563-5961.
FAX (954) 564-5261.Located right across from the beach, this hotel offers every amenity, plus a heated pool and a galleria ⚡ ❄ 🍴 ⦿ *Rooms:* 240
Credit cards: AE DC MC V — Swimming ▦, Good Restaurant ●

FORT LAUDERDALE: *A Little Inn by the Sea* $$$$
4546 El Mar Drive, FL 33308. **Road map** F4. **(** (954) 772-2450. **FAX** (954) 938-9354.
Swiss-run and popular with Europeans, this beachfront B&B north of downtown has a relaxed family feel. Fine fabrics, quality wicker furniture, and canopy beds adorn the attractive rooms. ⚡ ❄ ⦿ *Rooms:* 29
Credit cards: AE DC MC V — Swimming ▦, Kitchen ▦

FORT LAUDERDALE: *Holiday Inn Lauderdale-By-The-Sea* $$$
4116 N Ocean Drive, FL 33308. **Road map** F4. **(** (954) 776-1212.
FAX (954) 776-1411. In a quiet spot just across the street from the beach, this hotel is perfect for families. ⚡ ❄ 🍴 ⦿ *Rooms:* 186
Credit cards: AE DC MC V — Children's ●, Swimming ▦, Good Restaurant ●, Kitchen ▦

FORT LAUDERDALE: *Riverside* [w] www.riversidehotel.com $$$$
620 E Las Olas Blvd, FL 33301. **Road map** F4. **(** (954) 467-0671.
FAX (954) 462-2148. Built in 1936 in a now-trendy area of restaurants and shops, this hotel has ceiling fans, terra-cotta floors, and a tasteful mix of wicker and oak. ⚡ 🍴 **P** *Rooms:* 105
Credit cards: AE DC MC V — Swimming ▦, Good Restaurant ●

FORT LAUDERDALE: *Hyatt Regency Pier 66 Marina* $$$$$
2301 SE 17th St Causeway, FL 33316. **Road map** F4. **(** (954) 525-6666.
FAX (954) 728-3541. This high-rise hotel offers great views and a fitness center and spa. 24 ⚡ ❄ 🍴 🍴 **P** ⦿ *Rooms:* 388. [w] www.hyatt.com
Credit cards: AE DC MC V — Children's ●, Swimming ▦, Good Restaurant ●

FORT PIERCE: *Dockside Harbor Light Resort* [w] www.docksideinn.com $$
1160 Seaway Drive, FL 34949. **Road map** F3. **(** (561) 468-3555. **FAX** (561) 465-8009.
On the Intracoastal Waterway and with two private piers, this inn is good for boating and fishing. Inside, nautical themes dominate. ❄ ⦿ *Rooms:* 73
Credit cards: AE DC MC V — Swimming ▦, Kitchen ▦

HOLLYWOOD: *Holiday Inn Sunspree Resort* $$$
2711 S Ocean Drive, FL 33019. **Road map** F4. **(** (954) 923-8700.
FAX (954) 923-7059. Located by the beach, this family-oriented resort has a kids-eat-free policy. ⚡ ❄ 🍴 🍴 **P** ⦿ *Rooms:* 201
Credit cards: AE DC MC V — Children's ●, Swimming ▦, Good Restaurant ●, Kitchen ▦

HUTCHINSON ISLAND: *Marriott Beach and Marina* $$$$$
555 NE Ocean Blvd, FL 34996. **Road map** F3. **(** (561) 225-3700.
FAX (561) 225-0003. A good family resort with lots going on, such as children's activities, tennis, swimming, golf, and nature walks.
24 ⚡ ❄ 🍴 🍴 **P** ⦿ *Rooms:* 298. [w] www.floridatreasures.com
Credit cards: AE DC MC V — Children's ●, Swimming ▦, Good Restaurant ●, Kitchen ▦

JUPITER: *Wellesley Inn Jupiter* [w] www.wellesleyinnsandsuites.com $$
34 Fisherman's Wharf, FL 33477. **Road map** F4. **(** (561) 575-7201. **FAX** (561) 575-1169.
Right on the Loxahatchee River Preserve, this family-friendly hotel offers an outdoor pool and Continental breakfast. ⚡ ❄ 🍴 ⦿ *Rooms:* 105
Children's ●, Swimming ▦

JUPITER: *Jupiter Beach Resort* [w] www.jupiterbeachresort.com $$$$$
5 North A1A, FL 33477. **Road map** F4. **(** (561) 746-2511. **FAX** (561) 747-3304.
This plush but unpretentious resort has relatively simple rooms with marble baths and colorful furnishings. Private balconies afford terrific ocean and sunset views. ⚡ ❄ 🍴 🍴 **P** ⦿ *Rooms:* 153
Credit cards: AE DC MC V — Children's ●, Swimming ▦, Good Restaurant ●

PALM BEACH: *Beachcomber Apartment Motel* $$$
3024 S Ocean Blvd, FL 33480. **Road map** F4. **(** (561) 585-4646, (800) 833-7122.
FAX (561) 547-9438. This basic but very comfortable motel is only a couple of steps from its own private beach. ❄ ⦿ *Rooms:* 48
Credit cards: AE MC V — Swimming ▦, Kitchen ▦

Palm Beach: *Palm Beach Hawaiian Ocean Inn* [$][$][$][$] 3550 S Ocean Blvd, FL 33480. **Road map** F4. ☎ *(561) 582-5631.* [FAX] *(561) 588-4563.* About 7 miles (11 km) south of downtown, this inn is good value, with large, bright rooms. 🚭 ❄ 🏊 [P] 🍴 ***Rooms:*** *58*	AE DC MC V		■	●	■
Palm Beach: *Heart of Palm Beach* [$][$][$][$] 160 Royal Palm Way, FL 33480. **Road map** F4. ☎ *(561) 655-5600.* [FAX] *(561) 832-1201.* Located only a few blocks from Worth Avenue and the beach, this hotel offers ample suites but small rooms. 🚭 ❄ 🏊 🍴 ***Rooms:*** *88*	AE DC MC V	●	■	●	
Palm Beach: *Plaza Inn* [W] www.plazainnpalmbeach.com [$][$][$][$] 215 Brazilian Ave, FL 33480. **Road map** F4. ☎ *(561) 832-8666.* [FAX] *(561) 835-8776.* This Deco gem has four-poster beds, hand-crocheted spreads, and cooked-to-order breakfasts. 🚭 ❄ 🍴 ***Rooms:*** *50*	AE MC V		■		
Palm Beach: *The Breakers* [W] www.thebreakers.com [$][$][$][$][$] 1 South County Rd, FL 33480. **Road map** F4. ☎ *(561) 655-6611.* [FAX] *(561) 655-3577.* Sumptuous and classy, this "Italian palace" is Palm Beach's finest hotel *(see p117).* Not a classic family establishment, but the children's facilities are great. [24] 🚭 ❄ 🏋 🏊 [P] 🍴 ***Rooms:*** *569*	AE DC MC V	●	■	●	
Palm Beach: *Four Seasons Palm Beach* [W] www.fourseasons.com [$][$][$][$][$] 2800 S Ocean Blvd, FL 33480. **Road map** F4. ☎ *(561) 582-2800.* [FAX] *(561) 547-1557.* The elegant lobby filled with antiques and tapestries gives way to huge, beautifully furnished rooms with every modern amenity. The balconies offer fine ocean views. [24] 🚭 ❄ 🏋 🏊 🐕 [P] 🍴 ***Rooms:*** *210*	AE DC MC V	●	■	●	
Palm Beach Gardens: *Heron Cay* [W] www.heroncay.com [$][$][$] 15106 Palmwood Rd, FL 33410. **Road map** F4. ☎ *(561) 744-6315.* [FAX] *(561) 744-0943.* This Caribbean islands-style B & B lazes beside the Intracoastal Waterway. 🚭 ❄ 🍴 ***Rooms:*** *3*	MC V		■		
Palm Beach Gardens: *PGA National Resort and Spa* [$][$][$][$][$] 400 Avenue of the Champions, FL 33418. **Road map** F4. ☎ *(561) 627-2000.* [FAX] *(561) 622-0261.* Here, the fabulous spa boasts mineral-rich pools; tennis and golf instruction is also available. 🚭 ❄ 🏋 🏊 [P] 🍴 ***Rooms:*** *339*	AE DC MC V	●	■		■
Pompano Beach: *Ronny Dee Motel* [$][$] 717 S Ocean Blvd, FL 33062. **Road map** F4. ☎ *(954) 943-3020.* [FAX] *(954) 783-5112.* Nothing fancy here, but the Ronny Dee is clean and convenient for the beach. A coffee and doughnut breakfast is included. ***Rooms:*** *35*	AE MC V		■		■
Stuart: *Harborfront Inn Bed & Breakfast* [$][$][$] 310 Atlanta Ave, FL 34994. **Road map** F3. ☎ *(561) 288-7289.* [FAX] *(561) 221-0474.* Harborfront's blue-trimmed cottages on the riverside are within walking distance of downtown. Enjoy the home-cooked breakfast. 🚭 ❄ 🍴 ***Rooms:*** *6*	AE MC V				■
Vero Beach: *Islander Resort* [W] www.verobeachfl.us/islander [$][$][$] 3101 Ocean Drive, FL 32963. **Road map** F3. ☎ & [FAX] *(561) 231-4431.* Here you're just 300 ft (100 m) from the beach, near restaurants and shops, and can barbecue your own food by the pool. Each room has its own unique decor. ❄ 🍴 ***Rooms:*** *16*	AE MC V		■		■
Vero Beach: *Disney's Vero Beach Resort* [$][$][$][$][$] 9250 Island Grove Terrace, FL 32963. **Road map** F3. ☎ *(800) 359-8000.* [FAX] *(561) 234-2030.* Hallmark Disney quality abounds in luxury bedrooms and timeshare cottages; the pool is centered around a Spanish galleon, and activities include campfire sing-alongs. 🚭 ❄ 🏋 🏊 🍴 ***Rooms:*** *204*	AE MC V	●	■		■
West Palm Beach: *Fairfield Inn* [$][$] 5981 Okeechobee Blvd, FL 33417. **Road map** F4. ☎ *(561) 697-3388.* [FAX] *(561) 697-2834.* Beyond the airport, adjacent to Florida's Turnpike, this is a clean, comfortable inn. Breakfast is included. 🚭 🏊 🐕 ***Rooms:*** *114*	AE DC MC V		■		
West Palm Beach: *Hibiscus House* [W] www.hibiscushouse.com [$][$][$] 501 30th St, FL 33407. **Road map** F4. ☎ & [FAX] *(561) 863-5633.* Built in 1922, this historic home has been lovingly restored. Decor is Victorian and breakfast arrives on beautiful china and crystal. There is a free shuttle bus into town. 🚭 🍴 ***Rooms:*** *5*	AE MC V		■		
West Palm Beach: *Palm Beach Polo and Country Club* [$][$][$][$][$] 11199 Polo Club Rd, FL 33414. **Road map** F4. ☎ *(561) 798-7000.* [FAX] *(561) 790-7114.* This private resort has condos, villas, or studios to rent for a minimum of four weeks, and offers tennis, golf, and polo. 🚭 ❄ 🏋 🏊 🍴 ***Rooms:*** *60*	AE MC V	●	■		■

For key to symbols see back flap

Price categories for a standard double room per night in high season, including tax and service charges:

$ under $60
$$ $60-$100
$$$ $100-$150
$$$$ $150-$200
$$$$$ over $200

CHILDREN'S FACILITIES
A child-friendly hotel, with cribs, high chairs, and other facilities that may include a baby-sitting service and special children's programs.

SWIMMING POOL
The hotel has a swimming pool for use by residents.

GOOD RESTAURANT
There is a particularly good restaurant, which is normally also accessible to nonresidents.

KITCHEN FACILITIES
The hotel has some rooms with cooking and other kitchen facilities, usually known as "efficiencies."

ORLANDO AND THE SPACE COAST

	CREDIT CARDS	CHILDREN'S FACILITIES	SWIMMING POOL	GOOD RESTAURANT	KITCHEN FACILITIES
CAPE CANAVERAL: *Radisson Resort at the Port* W www.radisson.com $$$ 8701 Astronaut Blvd, FL 32920. **Road map** F2. (321) 784-0000. FAX (321) 784-3737. Ceiling fans and wicker give this resort a Caribbean feel. Ten minutes' drive from Kennedy Space Center. **Rooms:** 285	AE DC MC V	●	▨	●	
COCOA: *Econo Lodge Space Center* $$ 3220 N Cocoa Blvd, FL 32926. **Road map** E3. (321) 632-4561, (888) 721-9423. FAX (321) 631-3756. Nothing spectacular, but adequate, clean, and well located just 8 miles (13 km) from the Kennedy Space Center. **Rooms:** 142	AE DC MC V		▨	●	
COCOA BEACH: *Comfort Inn and Suite Resort* $$$ 3901 N Atlantic Ave, FL 32931. **Road map** E3. (321) 783-2221. FAX (321) 783-0461. A hop, skip, and jump from the beach, this inn opens onto a palm-shaded pool-side area with barbecue grills. **Rooms:** 144	AE DC MC V		▨		▨
COCOA BEACH: *Inn at Cocoa Beach* $$$$ 4300 Ocean Beach Blvd, FL 32931. **Road map** E3. (321) 799-3460. FAX (321) 784-8632. Patios and balconies give sea views at this B & B, where room decor ranges from modern to traditional. **Rooms:** 50	AE MC V		▨		
CYPRESS GARDENS: *Best Western Admiral's Inn* $$ 5665 Cypress Gardens Blvd, FL 33884. **Road map** E3. (863) 324-5950. FAX (863) 324-2376. Just steps from the beautiful Cypress Gardens, this inn has comfortable (though not fancy) rooms. **Rooms:** 156	AE DC MC V		▨	●	
DOWNTOWN ORLANDO: *Four Points Hotel* W www.fourpoints.com $$$ 151 E Washington St, FL 32801. **Road map** E2. (407) 841-3220. FAX (407) 849-1831. This newly renovated hotel is in walking distance of Church Street Station and offers an inclusive all-you-can-eat breakfast. **Rooms:** 250	AE DC MC V		▨	●	
DOWNTOWN ORLANDO: *The Courtyard at Lake Lucerne* $$$$ 211 N Lucerne Circle E, FL 32801. **Road map** E2. (407) 648-5188. FAX (407) 246-1368. This well-run B & B in a quiet garden beside Lake Lucerne comprises four historic houses, one of which is the oldest in town. **Rooms:** 30 W www.orlandohistoricinn.com	AE DC MC V			●	▨
DOWNTOWN ORLANDO: *The Veranda Bed & Breakfast* $$$$ 115 N Summerlin Ave, FL 32801. **Road map** E2. (407) 849-0321. FAX (407) 849-0321. Two 1920s wooden homes nestled in a pretty garden in the old district. Verandas, hardwood floors, and ceiling fans create a Key West look. Period furnishings add charm to the rooms. **Rooms:** 12	AE DC MC V		▨		▨
INTERNATIONAL DRIVE: *La Quinta Inn* W www.laquinta.com $$ 8300 Jamaican Ct, FL 32819. **Road map** E2. (407) 351-1660. FAX (407) 351-9264. This low-price inn 9 miles (14 km) from Walt Disney World offers well-kept rooms and a free continental breakfast. **Rooms:** 200	AE DC MC V		▨		▨
INTERNATIONAL DRIVE: *Best Western Plaza International* $$$ 8738 International Drive, FL 32819. **Road map** E2. (407) 345-8195. FAX (407) 352-8196. Walt Disney World is ten minutes' drive away and Sea World is even closer. Family suites are good for kids. **Rooms:** 672	AE DC MC V	●	▨		▨
INTERNATIONAL DRIVE: *Ramada Inn* $$ 4855 S Orange Blossom Trail, FL 32839. **Road map** E2. (407) 851-3000. FAX (407) 859-8972. Within reach of downtown Orlando and busy "I-Drive," this inn has large suites and a tropical pool area. **Rooms:** 132	AE DC MC V		▨		▨
INTERNATIONAL DRIVE: *Country Hearth Inn* W www.countryhearth.com $$ 9861 International Drive, FL 32819. **Road map** E2. (407) 352-0008. FAX (407) 352-5449. This mansion-style inn has a lovely front porch lounge and quiet rooms with balconies. Breakfast is included. **Rooms:** 150	AE DC MC V	●	▨		▨

INTERNATIONAL DRIVE: *Holiday Inn Express* (S)(S)(S)
6323 International Drive, FL 32819. **Road map** E2. [(407) 351-4430.
FAX (407) 345-0742. Close to Walt Disney World, the Inn is geared to children.
They stay and eat for free and enjoy a special "comedy zone." **Rooms:** 218
AE DU MC V

INTERNATIONAL DRIVE: *Clarion Plaza Hotel* [W] www.clarionplaza.com(S)(S)(S)(S)
9700 International Drive, FL 32819. **Road map** E2. [(407) 996-9700.
FAX (407) 996-9119. An expansive marble lobby welcomes you to this
efficiently run hotel with airy rooms. **Rooms:** 809
AE DC MC V

INTERNATIONAL DRIVE: *Renaissance Orlando Resort* (S)(S)(S)(S)(S)
6677 Sea Harbor Drive, FL 32821. [(407) 351 5555.
FAX (407) 351-9991. Across the street from SeaWorld, this resort has an
outstanding children's program. The marble bathrooms and golf
privileges are there to please the adults. **Rooms:** 780
AE DC MC V

LAKE WALES: *Chalet Suzanne* [W] www.chaletsuzanne.com (S)(S)(S)(S)
3800 Chalet Suzanne Drive, FL 33853. **Road map** E3. [(863) 676-6011.
FAX (863) 676-1814. This pleasant hotel set in orange groves has rooms
decorated with eclectic souvenirs. The in-house restaurant is superb.
There's even an airstrip for your private plane. **Rooms:** 30
AE DC MC V

WALT DISNEY WORLD: *Super8 Maingate* [W] www.super8.com (S)
7571 W Irlo Bronson Hwy, FL 34747. **Road map** E3. [(407) 396-7500.
FAX (407) 396-7497. This clean and comfortable hotel is located one mile
(1.5 km) west of Walt Disney World. **Rooms:** 281
AE DC MC V

WALT DISNEY WORLD: *Disney's All-Star Music Resort* (S)(S)
1801 W Buena Vista Drive, FL 32830. **Road map** E3. [(407) 939-6000.
FAX (407) 939-7222. Musically themed throughout, from the bedspreads to
walk-through jukebox. The rooms are pleasant. **Rooms:** 1,920
AE MC V

WALT DISNEY WORLD: *Disney's All-Star Sports Resort* (S)(S)
1701 W Buena Vista Drive, FL 32830. **Road map** E3. [(407) 939-5000.
FAX (407) 939-7333. Fans will enjoy the sports decor. Facilities, including huge
pools, are shared with the adjacent Music Resort. **Rooms:** 1,920
AE MC V

WALT DISNEY WORLD: *Perri House* [W] www.perrihouse.com (S)(S)
10417 Centurion Court, FL 32836. **Road map** E3. [(407) 876-4830.
FAX (407) 876-0241. Perfect for families, this is a quiet country inn secluded
on a 16-acre nature preserve adjacent to Walt Disney World. Comfortable
rooms feature cherry and oak furnishings. **Rooms:** 8
AE DC MC V

WALT DISNEY WORLD: *Days Inn, Days Suites* [W] www.thhotels.com (S)(S)(S)
5820 W Irlo Bronson Hwy, FL 34746. **Road map** E3. [(407) 396-7900.
FAX (407) 396-1789. Here you can enjoy four pools, a children's playground, and
a picnic area. Just 2 miles (3 km) from Walt Disney World. **Rooms:** 604
AE DU MC V

WALT DISNEY WORLD: *Disney's Caribbean Beach Resort* (S)(S)(S)
900 Cayman Way, FL 32830. **Road map** E3. [(407) 934-3400 **FAX** (407) 934-3288
Five cheerful "villages" with attractive rooms are situated around a lake
where water birds congregate. Pools and artificial white sand beaches dot
the property and contribute to a tropical feel. **Rooms:** 2,112
AE MC V

WALT DISNEY WORLD: *Grosvenor Resort* (S)(S)(S)
1850 Hotel Plaza Blvd, FL 32830. [(407) 828-4444.
FAX (407) 828-8192. This elegant, colonial-theme hotel features pleasant
rooms and a wide range of facilities. **Rooms:** 626
AE DC MC V

WALT DISNEY WORLD: *Holiday Inn Hotel and Suites Maingate* (S)(S)(S)
5678 W Irlo Bronson Hwy, FL 34746. **Road map** E3. [(407) 396-4488
FAX (407) 396-1296. Children rule here – there is even a kids' check-in desk.
Clowns make up rooms and lead activities at a children's camp, 3 miles (5
km) outside Walt Disney World. **Rooms:** 614.
AE DC MC V

WALT DISNEY WORLD: *Buena Vista Palace* (S)(S)(S)(S)
1900 Buena Vista Drive, FL 32830. **Road map** E3. [(407) 827-2727.
FAX (407) 827-6034. This resort features a host of restaurants and facilities.
Room decor is in earthy tones. **Rooms:** 1,014
AE DC MC V

WALT DISNEY WORLD: *Disney's BoardWalk Villas* (S)(S)(S)(S)(S)
2101 N Epcot Resorts Blvd, FL 32830. **Road map** E3. [(407) 939-5100.
FAX (407) 939-5150. Opened in 1996, these New England-style "seaside"
cottages offer comfy family lodgings. **Rooms:** 532
AE MC V

<table>
<tr><td>

Price categories for a standard double room per night in high season, including tax and service charges:

$ under $60
$$ $60-$100
$$$ $100-$150
$$$$ $150-$200
$$$$$ over $200

</td><td>

CHILDREN'S FACILITIES
A child-friendly hotel, with cribs, high chairs, and other facilities that may include a baby-sitting service and special children's programs.
SWIMMING POOL
The hotel has a swimming pool for use by residents.
GOOD RESTAURANT
There is a particularly good restaurant, which is normally also accessible to nonresidents.
KITCHEN FACILITIES
The hotel has some rooms with cooking and other kitchen facilities, usually known as "efficiencies."

</td></tr>
</table>

	CREDIT CARDS	CHILDREN'S FACILITIES	SWIMMING POOL	GOOD RESTAURANT	KITCHEN FACILITIES
WALT DISNEY WORLD: *Disney's Wilderness Lodge* $$$$ 901 Timberline Drive, FL 32830. **Road map** E3. 【 *(407) 824-3200.* **FAX** *(407) 824-3232.* Wind down at this isolated but romantic "mountain retreat" with wooden floors and crackling fires. 🚲 🕸 **P** *Rooms: 728*	AE MC V	●	■	●	
WALT DISNEY WORLD: *Disney's Beach Club Resort* $$$$$ 1800 Epcot Resorts Blvd, FL 32830. **Road map** E3. 【 *(407) 934-8000.* **FAX** *(407) 934-3850.* Echoing the style of New England's grand hotels of the 1870s, this resort has exquisite rooms, extensive facilities, and one of the best restaurants in Walt Disney World. 24 🚲 🕸 🍽 🛗 **P** 🅿 *Rooms: 583*	AE MC V	●	■	●	
WALT DISNEY WORLD: *Disney's BoardWalk Inn* $$$$$ 2101 N Epcot Resorts Blvd, FL 32830. **Road map** E3. 【 *(407) 939-5100.* **FAX** *(407) 939-5150.* This elegant inn, with its floral rugs and hardwood floors, evokes an old-world B & B. 24 🚲 🕸 🍽 🛗 🅿 **P** *Rooms: 378*	AE MC V	●	■		
WALT DISNEY WORLD: *Disney's Contemporary Resort* $$$$$ 4600 N World Drive, FL 32830. **Road map** E3. 【 *(407) 824-1000.* **FAX** *(407) 824-3539.* A monorail ride from Epcot and the Magic Kingdom, this slick, lively resort has Deco-style rooms. 24 🚲 🕸 🛗 **P** 🅿 *Rooms: 1,041*	AE MC V	●	■	●	
WALT DISNEY WORLD: *Disney's Grand Floridian Resort* $$$$$ 4401 Grand Floridian Way, FL 32830. **Road map** E3. 【 *(407) 824-3000.* **FAX** *(407) 824-3186.* Verandas, oak beds, and Victorian-style opulence offer a taste of old Florida just next door to the Magic Kingdom. Enjoy total indulgence with a host of facilities. 24 🚲 🕸 🍽 🛗 **P** 🅿 *Rooms: 900*	AE MC V	●	■	●	
WALT DISNEY WORLD: *Disney's Vacation Club Resort* $$$$$ 1510 N Cove Rd, FL 32830. **Road map** E3. 【 *(407) 827-7700.* **FAX** *(407) 827-7710.* Ceiling fans, picket fences, and palm trees re-create the atmosphere of old Key West. Recreational facilities abound. 🚲 🕸 🍽 🅿 *Rooms: 709*	AE MC V	●	■	●	■
WALT DISNEY WORLD: *Disney's Yacht Club Resort* $$$$$ 1700 Epcot Resorts Blvd, FL 32830. **Road map** E3. 【 *(407) 934-7000.* **FAX** *(407) 934-3450.* Styled like a posh Cape Cod yacht club, with brass fittings and charts on the walls, this lavish resort shares its wide range of facilities with the adjacent Beach Club. 24 🚲 🕸 🍽 🛗 **P** 🅿 *Rooms: 631*	AE MC V	●	■		
WALT DISNEY WORLD: *Walt Disney World Dolphin* $$$$$ 1500 Epcot Resorts Blvd, FL 32830. **Road map** E3. 【 *(407) 934-4000.* **FAX** *(407) 934-4099.* Architecturally arresting and close to Epcot, the urbane Dolphin caters to a business crowd. 24 🚲 🕸 🍽 🛗 **P** 🅿 *Rooms: 1,510*	AE DC MC V	●	■		
WALT DISNEY WORLD: *Walt Disney World Swan* $$$$$ 1200 Epcot Resorts Blvd, FL 32830. **Road map** E3. 【 *(407) 934-3000.* **FAX** *(407) 934-4499.* Topped by two swans, five-stories high, and with the swan theme found throughout, this hotel offers colorful rooms and some of the best dining in the park. 24 🚲 🕸 🍽 🛗 **P** 🅿 *Rooms: 758*	AE DC MC V	●	■	●	
WALT DISNEY WORLD: *The Villas at the Disney Institute* $$$$$ 1960 Magnolia Way, FL 32830. **Road map** E3. 【 *(407) 827-1100.* **FAX** *(407) 827-4100.* Ideal for families, this resort and campus *(see p161)* has great sports and entertainment facilities. 🚲 🕸 🍽 🛗 🅿 **P** *Rooms: 585*	AE MC V	●	■	●	■
WINTER PARK: *The Fortnightly Inn* $$ 377 E Fairbanks Ave, FL 32789. **Road map** E2. 【 *(407) 645-4440.* Built in 1922, this prim B & B is furnished with handsome antiques. A delicious home-cooked breakfast is a treat for guests. 🚲 *Rooms: 5*	AE MC V				
WINTER PARK: *Park Plaza* 🆆 www.parkplaza.com $$$ 307 Park Ave S, FL 32789. **Road map** E2. 【 *(407) 647-1072.* **FAX** *(407) 647-4081.* Wooden floors and oriental rugs set the tone here. Rooms are furnished with antiques. There is a restaurant next door. 🚲 🕸 **P** *Rooms: 27*	AE DC MC V				

THE NORTHEAST

DAYTONA BEACH: *Coquina Inn Bed & Breakfast* $$
544 S Palmetto Ave, FL 32114. **Road map** E2. ▐ & FAX *(904) 254-4969.*
This 1912 home, on a quiet tree-lined street in the historic district, has
beautifully furnished rooms with oak floors and ceiling fans. The
bountiful breakfast is a delight. **Rooms: 4**
AE MC V

DAYTONA BEACH: *Inn on the Beach* $$
1615 S Atlantic Ave, FL 32118. **Road map** E2. ▐ *(904) 255-0921.* FAX *(904) 255-3849.*
This budget oceanfront hotel has spacious efficiencies, a sundeck, and
both full-sized and kids' swimming pools. **Rooms: 195**
AE DC MC V

DAYTONA BEACH: *Bahama House* $$$
2001 S Atlantic Ave, FL 32118. **Road map** E2. ▐ *(904) 248-2001.*
FAX *(904) 248-0991.* This friendly Bahamas-themed establishment offers
efficiencies with bleached-wood furnishings. There are daily children's
activities and some units have Jacuzzis. **Rooms: 95**
AE DC MC V

DAYTONA BEACH: *Adam's Mark* W www.adamsmark.com $$$$
100 N Atlantic Ave, FL 32118. **Road map** E2. ▐ *(904) 254-8200.*
FAX *(904) 253-0275.* Overlooking the beach boardwalk, this is Daytona's
most stylish resort. It has several restaurants, a health club, disco, and
children's playground. **Rooms: 437**
AE DC MC V

FERNANDINA BEACH: *The Bailey House* W www.bailey-house.com $$$
28 S 7th St, FL 32034. **Road map** E1. ▐ *(904) 261-5390.* FAX *(904) 321-0103.*
Stained glass, antique beds, and fireplaces evoke a Victorian ambience at
this 1895 home. A veranda complete with porch swing and rocking chairs
encircles the house. Bikes are provided for exploring. **Rooms: 10**
AE MC V

FERNANDINA BEACH: *The Amelia Island Williams House* $$$$
103 S 9th St, FL 32034. **Road map** E1. ▐ *(904) 277-2328.* FAX *(904) 321-1325.*
Rated one of the South's best B & Bs, this 1856 mansion has exquisite
rooms with clawfoot baths. Priceless antiques range from 16th century
Japanese prints to a carpet owned by Napoleon. **Rooms: 8**
MC V

FERNANDINA BEACH: *Amelia Island Plantation* $$$$$
3000 First Coast Hwy, FL 32034. **Road map** E1. ▐ *(904) 261-6161.*
FAX *(904) 277-5159.* At the southern end of Amelia Island, surrounded by live
oak forests and towering dunes, this golf resort offers spacious rooms,
condos, and villas. Facilities are extensive. **Rooms: 680**
AE DC MC V

GAINESVILLE: *Magnolia Plantation* W www.magnoliabnb.com $$$
309 SE 7th St, FL 32601. **Road map** D2. ▐ *(352) 375-6653.* FAX *(352) 338-0303.*
Decked with verandas and countless windows, this charming, antique-filled
1880s mansion offers a warm welcome. Imaginative breakfasts are served
indoors or alfresco under the magnolias. **Rooms: 5 Cottages: 6**
AE MC V

GAINESVILLE: *Residence Inn by Marriott* $$$
4001 SW 13th St, FL 32608. **Road map** D2. ▐ *(352) 371-2101, (800) 331-3131.*
FAX *(352) 377-2247.* This centrally located inn offers airy suites with well-equipped
kitchens and living areas. **Rooms: 80**
AE DC MC V

JACKSONVILLE: *House on Cherry Street* $$
1844 Cherry St, FL 32205. **Road map** E1. ▐ *(904) 384-1999.* FAX *(904) 384-5013.*
This early 20th-century clapboard house provides an attractive, relaxed
alternative to staying downtown (15 minutes' drive away). A porch
overlooks a croquet lawn leading down to the river. **Rooms: 4**
AE MC V

JACKSONVILLE: *Omni Jacksonville Hotel* W www.omnihotel.com $$$
245 Water St, FL 32202. **Road map** E1. ▐ *(904) 355-6664.* FAX *(904) 791-4812.*
Located just east of downtown, this stylish hotel features good, friendly
service and an excellent restaurant. **Rooms: 354**
AE DC MC V

JACKSONVILLE: *Radisson Riverwalk Hotel* W www.radisson.com $$$
1515 Prudential Drive, FL 32207. **Road map** E1. ▐ *(904) 396-5100.*
FAX *(904) 396-7154.* Enjoy an awesome view of the St Johns River and city
skyline from rooms with cheerful decor. **Rooms: 321**
AE DC MC V

JACKSONVILLE BEACH: *Sea Turtle Inn* W www.seaturtle.com $$
1 Ocean Blvd, FL 32233. **Road map** E1. ▐ *(904) 249-7402.* FAX *(904) 247-1517.*
This oceanfront inn offers great views from private balconies. Wake up to
coffee and newspapers brought to your room. **Rooms: 193**
AE MC V

Price categories for a standard double room per night in high season, including tax and service charges:

$ under $60
$$ $60-$100
$$$ $100-$150
$$$$ $150-$200
$$$$$ over $200

CHILDREN'S FACILITIES
A child-friendly hotel, with cribs, high chairs, and other facilities that may include a baby-sitting service and special children's programs.

SWIMMING POOL
The hotel has a swimming pool for use by residents.

GOOD RESTAURANT
There is a particularly good restaurant, which is normally also accessible to nonresidents.

KITCHEN FACILITIES
The hotel has some rooms with cooking and other kitchen facilities, usually known as "efficiencies."

	CREDIT CARDS	CHILDREN'S FACILITIES	SWIMMING POOL	GOOD RESTAURANT	KITCHEN FACILITIES
MICANOPY: *The Herlong Mansion* w www.herlong.com $$$ 402 NE Cholokka Blvd, FL 32667. **Road map** D2. (& **FAX** *(352) 466-3322*. Imposing columns front this splendid 1845 house set in beautiful gardens. Breakfasts are served *en famille*. ⬛ 🔲 **Rooms:** *11*	MC V				
MOUNT DORA: *Lakeside Inn* w www.lakeside-inn.com $$$ 100 N Alexander St, FL 32757. (*(352) 383-4101*. **FAX** *(352) 385-1615*. Built in 1883 and refurbished a century later, the tranquil Lakeside Inn is popular with anglers, bird-watchers, and antique hunters. ⬛ 🔲 🔲 **Rooms:** *89*	AE DC MC V		▪	●	
OCALA: *Holiday Inn* $$$ 3621 W Silver Springs Blvd, FL 34478. **Road map** D2. (*(352) 629-0381*. **FAX** *(352) 629-8813*. Clean and comfortable, this budget inn has a heated pool, tennis courts, and an exercise center. ⬛ 🔲 🔲 **Rooms:** *270*	AE DC MC V		▪		
ORMOND BEACH: *Comfort Inn Beachside* $$ 507 S Atlantic Ave, FL 32176. **Road map** E2. (*(904) 677-8550*. **FAX** *(904) 673-6260*. At this beachside inn, close to restaurants and shops, the rooms are light and airy, and all have ocean views. ⬛ 🔲 🔲 **Rooms:** *47*	AE MC V		▪		▪
ST. AUGUSTINE: *Howard Johnson Lodge* $$ 137 San Marco Ave, FL 32084. **Road map** E1. (*(904) 824-6181*. **FAX** *(904) 825-2774*. Close to the historic district, this hotel has spacious units, all with kitchenettes. There is a tram to local attractions. ⬛ 🔲 🔲 **Rooms:** *78*	AE DC MC V		▪		▪
ST. AUGUSTINE: *Alexander Homestead* w www.alexanderhomestead.com $$$ 14 Sevilla St, FL 32084. **Road map** E1. (*(888) 292-4147*. **FAX** *(904) 823-9503*. Lace curtains and wooden floors are the motif at this 1880s home turned B & B. Guests are treated to after-dinner liqueurs. ⬛ 🔲 🔲 **Rooms:** *4*	AE DC MC V				
ST. AUGUSTINE: *Casablanca Inn B&B* w www.casablancainn.com $$$ 24 Avenida Menendez, FL 32084. **Road map** E1. (*(800) 826-2626*. **FAX** *(904) 826-1892*. Elegantly furnished throughout, this classy B & B provides stunning bay views from private balconies, two of which are equipped with hammocks. Breakfast is unforgettable. ⬛ 🔲 🔲 **Rooms:** *20*	AE MC V				
ST. AUGUSTINE: *Kenwood Inn B&B* w www.oldcity.com/kenwood $$$ 38 Marine St, FL 32084. **Road map** E1. (*(904) 824-2116*. **FAX** *(904) 824-1689*. Built in the 1880s, this charming inn in the historic district has a secluded courtyard and individually decorated rooms with period features. A tasty continental breakfast is served indoors or out. ⬛ 🔲 🔲 **Rooms:** *14*	MC V		▪		
ST. AUGUSTINE: *Southern Wind* w www.southernwindinn.com $$$ 18 Cordova St, FL 32084. **Road map** E1. (*(904) 825-3623*. **FAX** *(904) 810-5212*. This colonnaded house has rooms decorated with period pieces and Flagler-era antiques. Breakfast is served on vintage china. ⬛ 🔲 **Rooms:** *10*	MC V				

THE PANHANDLE

	CREDIT CARDS	CHILDREN'S FACILITIES	SWIMMING POOL	GOOD RESTAURANT	KITCHEN FACILITIES
APALACHICOLA: *Coombs House Inn* w www.coombshouse.com $$$ 80 6th St, FL 32320. **Road map** B1. (*(850) 653-9199*. **FAX** *(850) 653-2785*. In two 1900s clapboard homes, this B & B offers lovely antiques, full breakfasts, and bike rentals. ⬛ 🔲 **Rooms:** *18*	AE MC V				
CEDAR KEY: *Cedar Key Bed & Breakfast* $$ 810 3rd St, FL 32625. **Road map** D2. (*(877) 543-5051*. **FAX** *(352) 543-8070*. Gingerbread woodwork adorns this 1880 home by the water. Antiques please the eye and hearty breakfasts fill the stomach. ⬛ 🔲 **Rooms:** *7*	MC V				
CEDAR KEY: *The Island Hotel* w www.islandhotel-cedarkey.com $$ 373 2nd St, FL 32625. **Road map** D2. (*(352) 543-5111*. **FAX** *(352) 543-6949*. This 1859 hotel has thick tabby walls *(see p282)*, original wooden floors, and nautical murals. Dine on the veranda in good weather. ⬛ **Rooms:** *13*	MC V			●	

DESTIN: *Village Inn* $$
215 Hwy 98 E, FL 32541. **Road map** A1. ☎ (800) 821-9342. **FAX** (850) 837-7893.
Just over the street from Destin harbor and its fishing boats, this family-oriented motel has spacious rooms. The beaches, restaurants, and shops are all within ten minutes' drive. **Rooms:** 100
AE DC MC V

DESTIN: *Holiday Inn* W www.holidayinn-destin.com $$$
1020 Hwy 98 E, FL 32541. **Road map** A1. ☎ (850) 837-6181. **FAX** (850) 837-1523.
This circular hotel gives some rooms a grand view of the Gulf. It has children's activities and a friendly staff. **Rooms:** 233
AE DC MC V

DESTIN: *Henderson Park Inn B&B* W www.hendersonparkinn.com $$$$$
2700 Hwy 98 E, FL 32541. **Road map** A1. ☎ (850) 654-0400. **FAX** (850) 654-0405.
Pricey and quite large for a B & B, the rooms in this New England-style inn are beautiful and the breakfast is a treat. Private balconies afford views of the Gulf and the uncluttered white beach. **Rooms:** 36
AE MC V

FORT WALTON BEACH: *Sound Sight Inn* $$
314 Miracle Strip Parkway, FL 32548. **Road map** A1. ☎ (877) 763-7433.
FAX (850) 664-2735. Stately oak trees fill the courtyard of this friendly lodge, 2 miles (3 km) from downtown and the beach. **Rooms:** 140
AE MC V

FORT WALTON BEACH: *The Four Points Hotel* W www.sheraton4pts.com $$$
1325 Miracle Strip Parkway, FL 32548. **Road map** A1. ☎ (850) 243-8116.
FAX (850) 244-3064. The Sheraton has large, brightly decorated rooms, many with Gulf views and some right on the beach. **Rooms:** 217
AE DC MC V

GULF BREEZE: *Bay Beach Inn* $$
51 Gulf Breeze Parkway, FL 32561. **Road map** A1. ☎ (850) 932-2214.
FAX (850) 932-0932. Overlooking Pensacola Bay, this hotel offers spacious rooms and a waterfront eatery with great pastries. **Rooms:** 168
AE DC MC V

NAVARRE: *Comfort Inn* $$
8680 Navarre Parkway, FL 32566. **Road map** A1. ☎ (800) 868-1761.
FAX (850) 939-2084. A small, comfortable B & B inn, conveniently located across the bridge from uncrowded white beaches. **Rooms:** 63
AE DC MC V

PANAMA CITY BEACH: *Best Western Del Coronado* $$$
11815 Front Beach Rd, FL 32407. **Road map** B1. ☎ (850) 234-1600.
FAX (850) 235-1645. Smack on the Gulf, this small complex is a delight, with its friendly staff and well-furnished lodgings. **Rooms:** 106
AE DC MC V

PANAMA CITY BEACH: *Marriott's Bay Point Resort* $$$
4200 Marriott Drive, FL 32408. **Road map** B1. ☎ (850) 234-3307.
FAX (850) 233-1308. Nestled in a quiet wildlife preserve away from the beach, the Bay Point is considered one of the country's top golf and tennis resorts. The rooms are elegantly furnished. **Rooms:** 355
AE DC MC V

PANAMA CITY BEACH: *Edgewater Beach Resort* $$$$
11212 Front Beach Rd, FL 32407. **Road map** B1. ☎ (800) 874-8686.
FAX (850) 235-6899. Tropically themed both inside and out, this lavish sea-side resort offers condos with one, two, or three bedrooms. Sports and recreational facilities are extensive. **Rooms:** 520
AE DC MC V

PENSACOLA: *New World Landing* W www.newworldlanding.com $$
600 S Palafox St, FL 32501. **Road map** A1. ☎ (850) 432-4111. **FAX** (850) 432-6836.
Small, warm, and cozy describes this B & B in the historic area. Furnishings reflect the five periods of Pensacola's past, and there are photos of the inn's famous guests in the front hall. **Rooms:** 14 **Suites:** 1
AE MC V

PENSACOLA: *Residence Inn by Marriott* W www.residenceinn.com $$$
7230 Plantation Rd, FL 32504. **Road map** A1. ☎ (850) 479-1000. **FAX** (850) 477-3399.
This pleasant inn with spacious rooms is in a quiet area 7 miles (11 km) from downtown. Breakfast is included. **Rooms:** 64
AE DC MC V

PENSACOLA BEACH: *Five Flags Inn* W www.fiveflagsinn.com $$
299 Fort Pickens Rd, FL 32561. **Road map** A1. ☎ (850) 932-3586.
FAX (850) 934-0257. Right on the beach with all rooms overlooking the Gulf, the Five Flags is friendly and well furnished. **Rooms:** 49
AE MC V

PENSACOLA BEACH: *Best Western Pensacola Beach* $$$
16 Via de Luna, FL 32561. **Road map** A1. ☎ (850) 934-3300. **FAX** (850) 934-9780.
This relaxed, Gulf-side hostelry has bright, airy rooms, some with marine views. A continental breakfast is included. **Rooms:** 122
AE DC MC V

For key to symbols see back flap

Price categories for a standard double room per night in high season, including tax and service charges:

$ under $60
$$ $60-$100
$$$ $100-$150
$$$$ $150-$200
$$$$$ over $200

CHILDREN'S FACILITIES
A child-friendly hotel, with cribs, high chairs, and other facilities that may include a baby-sitting service and special children's programs.

SWIMMING POOL
The hotel has a swimming pool for use by residents.

GOOD RESTAURANT
There is a particularly good restaurant, which is normally also accessible to nonresidents.

KITCHEN FACILITIES
The hotel has some rooms with cooking and other kitchen facilities, usually known as "efficiencies."

	CREDIT CARDS	CHILDREN'S FACILITIES	SWIMMING POOL	GOOD RESTAURANT	KITCHEN FACILITIES
SEASIDE: *Josephine's Bed and Breakfast* W www.josephinesinn.com $$$$$ 101 Seaside Ave, FL 32459. **Road map** B1. (850) 231-1940. FAX (850) 231-2446. Visit the unique town and stay at this 1990s, antebellum-style mansion. Antiques and lace blend imperceptibly with modern conveniences. The restaurant is a local favorite. *Rooms:* 9	AE MC V			●	▪
TALLAHASSEE: *Ramada Inn North* $$ 2900 N Monroe St, FL 32303. **Road map** C1. (850) 386-1027. FAX (850) 422-1025. Just a short drive from downtown, this efficiently run hotel provides spacious rooms and friendly service. *Rooms:* 200	AE DC MC V		▪	●	
TALLAHASSEE: *Radisson Hotel* $$$ 415 N Monroe St, FL 32301. **Road map** C1. (850) 224-6000. FAX (850) 222-0335. This elegant, cheerful hotel provides complimentary airport and city center transportation. *Rooms:* 116	AE DC MC V			●	
TALLAHASSEE: *Governors Inn* $$$$ 209 S Adams St, FL 32301. **Road map** C1. (850) 681-6855. FAX (850) 222-3105. Beams from a stable that once stood here are built into this modern inn. Some rooms have open fireplaces, all feature antiques. *Rooms:* 40	AE DC MC V				

THE GULF COAST

	CREDIT CARDS	CHILDREN'S FACILITIES	SWIMMING POOL	GOOD RESTAURANT	KITCHEN FACILITIES
ANNA MARIA ISLAND: *Haley's Motel* W www.haleysmotel.com $$ 8102 Gulf Drive, FL 34217. **Road map** D3. (800) 367-7824. FAX (941) 778-1991. Just a short stroll from the beach, Haley's offers either simple, comfortable one-bed efficiencies or two-bed apartments. *Rooms:* 17	AE DC MC V		▪		▪
CAPTIVA ISLAND: *South Seas Plantation Resort* $$$$$ 5400 Plantation Rd, FL 33924. **Road map** D4. (941) 472-5111. FAX (941) 481-4947. Once a coconut plantation, the 330 acres (130 ha) at this lavish resort contain villas, cottages, condos, and hotel rooms. Countless sports facilities are also on site. *Rooms:* 600	AE DC MC V	●	▪	●	▪
CLEARWATER BEACH: *Howard Johnson Express Inn* $$ 656 Bayway Blvd, FL 33767. **Road map** D3. (727) 442-6606. FAX (727) 461-0809. This small hotel is set back from the beach but overlooks the bay. It has a fishing deck, unfussy rooms, and shops nearby. *Rooms:* 39	AE DC MC V		▪		
CLEARWATER BEACH: *Clearwater Beach Hotel* $$$$ 500 Mandalay Ave, FL 33767. **Road map** D3. (727) 441-2425. FAX (727) 449-2083. Run by the same family for 40 years, this grand hotel on the Gulf offers an old-fashioned, homey atmosphere. *Rooms:* 210	AE DC MC V	●	▪		
CLEARWATER BEACH: *Holiday Inn SunSpree Resort* $$$$ 715 S Gulfview Blvd, FL 33767. **Road map** D3. (727) 447-9566. FAX (727) 446-4978. At this modern, family-oriented resort, the under-12s eat free, and there are activities for teenagers. *Rooms:* 216	AE DC MC V	●	▪	●	
DUNEDIN: *Inn on the Bay* W www.innonthebay.net $$ 1420 Bayshore Blvd, FL 34698. **Road map** D3. (800) 759-5045. FAX (727) 734-0972. Clean and comfortable, the accommodations here offer sweeping bay views. Breakfast is included. *Rooms:* 40	AE MC V		▪	●	
FORT MYERS: *Amtel Marina Hotel* W www.amtelmarinahotel.com $$$$ 2500 Edwards Drive, FL 33901. **Road map** E4. (800) 833-1620. FAX (941) 337-1530. This fancy high-rise has fine views of the yacht basin and river. Downtown sights are just a walk away. *Rooms:* 419	AE DC MC V		▪		
LONGBOAT KEY: *The Resort at Longboat Key Club* $$$$$ 301 Gulf of Mexico Drive, FL 34228. **Road map** D3. (941) 383-8821. FAX (941) 383-0359. Ideal for golf and tennis, this luxurious resort has large suites with balconies overlooking the Gulf. *Rooms:* 232	AE DC MC V	●	▪		▪

ST. PETERSBURG: *Beach Park Motel* $$
300 Beach Drive NE, FL 33701. **Road map** D3. ☎ *(800) 657-7687.* FAX *(727) 894-4226.*
Located downtown, with a view of the pier, this motel is ideally placed
for sightseeing. The rooms have small balconies. **Rooms: 26**
AE MC V

ST. PETERSBURG: *Bayboro House* w www.bayborohousebandb.com $$$
1719 Beach Drive SE, FL 33701. **Road map** D3. ☎ *(727) 823-4955.*
FAX *(727) 823-4955.* This gracious Queen Anne home, built in 1907 and filled
with lace and antiques, is only 2 miles (3 km) south of downtown. There's a
panoramic view of Tampa Bay from the veranda. **Rooms: 5 Suites: 2**
MC V

ST. PETERSBURG: *Renaissance Vinoy Resort* $$$$$
501 5th Ave NE, FL 33701. **Road map** D3. ☎ *(727) 894-1000.* FAX *(727) 894-2270.*
Dating from 1925, this elegantly restored hotel offers lovely bay views
and imaginatively furnished rooms. Most downtown attractions are within
walking distance. **Rooms: 360**
AE DC MC V

ST. PETE BEACH: *Travelodge* $$$
6300 Gulf Blvd, FL 33706. **Road map** D3. ☎ *(727) 367-2711.* FAX *(727) 367-7068.*
Popular with families and right on the beach, this inn offers rooms and
efficiencies decorated with floral prints. **Rooms: 200**
AE DC MC V

ST. PETE BEACH: *Dolphin Beach Resort* $$$
4900 Gulf Blvd, FL 33706. **Road map** D3. ☎ *(727) 360-7011.* FAX *(727) 367 5909.*
Located on the ocean, the Dolphin offers sailboats for rent, bus tours to
attractions, nightly entertainment, and free parking. **Rooms: 173**
AE DC MC V

ST. PETE BEACH: *Don CeSar Resort and Spa* $$$$$
3400 Gulf Blvd, FL 33706. **Road map** D3. ☎ *(727) 360-1881.* FAX *(727) 367-6952.*
Once the haunt of the likes of Scott Fitzgerald, this 1928 Mediterranean-style
"pink palace" is breathtaking. Each room is different, and the walls are
hung with original art. **Rooms: 277**
AE DC MC V

SANIBEL ISLAND: *Island Inn* w www.islandinnsanibel.com $$$$
3111 W Gulf Drive, FL 33957. **Road map** E4. ☎ *(941) 472-1561.*
FAX *(941) 472-0051.* Built around 100 years ago, this inn has a genteel, old-
world air. Comfy, wicker-filled cottages and rooms overlook the Gulf.
Guests return year after year, so book well ahead. **Rooms: 57**
AE MC V

SANIBEL ISLAND: *Sanibel Inn* w www.sanibelinn.com $$$$$
937 E Gulf Drive, FL 33957. **Road map** E4. ☎ *(941) 472-3181.* FAX *(941) 472-5234.*
With a choice of rooms or condos, this beachside inn has accommodations
to suit most needs, and offers sports facilities aplenty. **Rooms: 96**
AE DC MC V

SANIBEL ISLAND: *Sanibel's Seaside Inn* $$$$$
541 E Gulf Drive, FL 33957. **Road map** E4. ☎ *(941) 472-1400.* FAX *(941) 472-6518.*
In a peaceful location, right on the shell-strewn beach, this "olde Florida"
inn has a choice of brightly decorated accommodations from rooms to
cottages. Bicycles are available for island exploration. **Rooms: 32**
AE DC MC V

SARASOTA: *Best Western Golden Host Resort* $$
4675 N Tamiami Trail, FL 34234. **Road map** D3. ☎ *(941) 355-5141.*
FAX *(941) 355-9286.* The resort is set in lovely tropical grounds, close to local
attractions and the beach. Breakfast is included. **Rooms: 80**
AE DC MC V

SARASOTA: *Wellesley Inn* $$$
1803 N Tamiami Trail, FL 34234. **Road map** D3. ☎ *(941) 366-5128.*
FAX *(941) 953-4322.* This friendly inn just north of downtown overlooks
a marina. The rooms are colorful and airy. **Rooms: 106**
AE DC MC V

SARASOTA: *Hyatt Sarasota* $$$$
1000 Blvd of the Arts, FL 34236. **Road map** D3. ☎ *(941) 953-1234.*
FAX *(941) 952-1987.* This bayfront hotel is convenient for downtown
Sarasota. Most rooms have balconies. **Rooms: 297**
AE DC MC V

TAMPA: *Days Inn Airport* $$
2522 N Dale Mabry Hwy, FL 33607. **Road map** D3. ☎ *(813) 877-6181.*
FAX *(813) 875-6171.* Situated between downtown and the airport, this motel
offers comfortable rooms. Breakfast is included. **Rooms: 293**
AE DC MC V

TAMPA: *Gram's Place* w www.grams-inn-tampa.com $$
3109 N Ola Ave, FL 33603. **Road map** D3. ☎ & FAX *(813) 221-0596.*
Basically a youth hostel with some private rooms, this music-filled B & B is
promoted as a bohemian retreat. **Rooms: 14**
AE MC V

For key to symbols see back flap

Price categories for a standard double room per night in high season, including tax and service charges:

$ under $60
$$ $60-$100
$$$ $100-$150
$$$$ $150-$200
$$$$$ over $200

CHILDREN'S FACILITIES
A child-friendly hotel, with cribs, high chairs, and other facilities that may include a baby-sitting service and special children's programs.
SWIMMING POOL
The hotel has a swimming pool for use by residents.
GOOD RESTAURANT
There is a particularly good restaurant, which is normally also accessible to nonresidents.
KITCHEN FACILITIES
The hotel has some rooms with cooking and other kitchen facilities, usually known as "efficiencies."

	CREDIT CARDS	CHILDREN'S FACILITIES	SWIMMING POOL	GOOD RESTAURANT	KITCHEN FACILITIES
TAMPA: *Holiday Inn City Center* $$$ 111 W Fortune St, FL 33602. **Road map** D3. [(813) 223-1351. FAX (813) 221-2000. On the Hillsborough River downtown, within walking distance of most attractions, this is a modern hotel with large rooms. *Rooms: 312*	AE DC MC V		■	●	
TAMPA: *Hyatt Regency Westshore* $$$$$ 6200 Courtney Campbell Causeway, FL 33607. **Road map** D3. [(813) 874-1234. FAX (813) 281-9168. Secluded on a bayside nature preserve, this slick hotel has airy rooms overlooking the water. *Rooms: 445*	AE DC MC V	●	■	●	
TAMPA: *Wyndham Harbour Island Hotel* $$$$$ 725 S Harbour Island Blvd, FL 33602. **Road map** D3. [(813) 229-5000. FAX (813) 229-5322. On an island overlooking the river mouth, this exclusive hotel is linked to downtown Tampa by the Peoplemover *(see p244)*. Dark wood and floral fabrics in the rooms. *Rooms: 300*	AE DC MC V	●	■		
TARPON SPRINGS: *Spring Bayou Inn* w www.floridasecrets.com $$ 32 W Tarpon Ave, FL 34689. **Road map** D3. [& FAX (727) 938-9333. Built in 1905, this homey B & B has wooden floors and an eclectic mix of furnishings, which includes antiques. *Rooms: 5*					
VENICE: *The Banyan House* w www.banyanhouse.com $$$ 519 S Harbor Drive, FL 34285. **Road map** D4. [(941) 484-1385. FAX (941) 484-8032. A grand old Mediterranean-style home, this B & B has splendid Victorian furnishings and high, beamed ceilings. *Rooms: 10*	MC V		■		■
VENICE: *Holiday Inn Venice* $$$ 455 US 41 Bypass N, FL 34292. **Road map** D4. [(941) 485-5411. FAX (941) 484-6193. A buffet dinner, Broadway-style show, and relaxed atmosphere put this Holiday Inn a cut above the rest. *Rooms: 159*	AE DC MC V		■	●	■

THE EVERGLADES AND THE KEYS

	CREDIT CARDS	CHILDREN'S FACILITIES	SWIMMING POOL	GOOD RESTAURANT	KITCHEN FACILITIES
BIG PINE KEY: *Barnacle Bed and Breakfast* $$$ 1557 Long Beach Drive, FL 33043. **Road map** E5. [(305) 872-3298. FAX (305) 872-3863. Swamped by lush foliage, this architectural delight has a rooftop sundeck. One room faces the private beach. *Rooms: 4*	MC V				■
ISLAMORADA: *Breezy Palms Resort* $$ MM 80, Overseas Hwy, FL 33036. **Road map** F5. [(305) 664-2361. FAX (305) 664-2572. Sunny rooms and apartments are dotted around the grounds of this resort, which has its own moorings. *Rooms: 40*	AE MC V		■		■
ISLAMORADA: *Cheeca Lodge* $$$$$ MM 82, Overseas Hwy, FL 33036. **Road map** F5. [(800) 327-2888. FAX (305) 664-2893. This tranquil low-rise resort offers a plethora of seaside activities for both kids and adults. Bamboo-furnished rooms include subtle touches such as hand-painted mirror frames. *Rooms: 203*	AE DC MC V	●	■		■
KEY LARGO: *Holiday Inn* w www.holidayinnkeylargo.com $$$$ MM 100, Overseas Hwy, FL 33037. **Road map** F5. [(800) 843-5397. FAX (305) 451-5592. Located close to fishing boats and maritime attractions, this pretty resort has bright, modern rooms. *Rooms: 132*	AE DC MC V		■	●	
KEY LARGO: *Westin Beach Resort Key Largo* $$$$ MM 97, Overseas Hwy, FL 33037. **Road map** F5. [(305) 852-5553. FAX (305) 852-8669. Hidden in a grove of trees crossed by nature trails, this resort has rooms with private balconies. *Rooms: 200*	AE DC MC V	●	■	●	
KEY WEST: *Key West International Youth Hostel* $ 718 South St, FL 33040. **Road map** E5. [(305) 296-5719. FAX (305) 296-0672. At this simple but well-maintained hostel, the cosmopolitan backpacking crowd have the use of pool tables and rented bicycles. *Beds: 80*	MC V				■

KEY WEST: *La Pensione* W www.lapensione.com $$$$
809 Truman Ave, FL 33040. **Road map** E5. **(** (800) 893-1193. **FAX** (305) 296-6509.
Built in 1891 by a local cigar family, this gracious house has unfussy rooms
with firm beds and no TV: for some an added bonus. ⚓ *Rooms: 9*
AE DC MC V

KEY WEST: *La Te Da* W www.lateda.com $$$
1125 Duval St, FL 33040. **Road map** E5. **(** (877) 528-3320. **FAX** (305) 296-3981.
Famous for its drag shows, adults-only La Te Da provides plush lodgings
for its largely gay clientele. Harry's poolside bar is fun. 🛏 ⚓ *Rooms: 15*
AE MC V

KEY WEST: *Nancy's William Street Guesthouse* $$$
329 William St, FL 33040. **Road map** E5. **(** (305) 292-3334. **FAX** (305) 296 1740.
Beautifully renovated, this Key West home is furnished with wicker and
antiques. The two rooms and four apartments have outside access and
descendants of Hemingway's cats frequent the garden. 🏊 ⚓ *Rooms: 6*
AE DC MC V

KEY WEST: *Southernmost Motel* $$$$
1319 Duval St, FL 33040. **Road map** E5. **(** (305) 296-6577. **FAX** (305) 294-3380.
Within walking distance of the Old Town, this motel is always busy. It
has beautiful tropical rooms with balconies. 🏊 🛏 ⚓ *Rooms: 127*
AE MC V

KEY WEST: *Wicker Guesthouse* W www.wickerkw.com $$$$
913 Duval St, FL 33040. **Road map** E5. **(** (305) 296-4275. **FAX** (305) 294-7240.
This friendly complex of new and restored houses in the historic district
has a range of rooms and spacious suites. 🏊 ⚓ *Rooms: 18*
AE DC MC V

KEY WEST: *Curry Mansion Inn* $$$$$
511 Caroline St, FL 33040. **Road map** E5. **(** (305) 294-5349. **FAX** (305) 294-4093.
This historic house, just off Duval Street, is also a museum *(see p284)*. Most
rooms are in a lovely annex and very comfortable. 🏊 🛏 🍴 ⚓ *Rooms: 28*
AE DC MC V

KEY WEST: *Holiday Inn La Concha* W www.keywest.com/laconcha $$$$
430 Duval St, FL 33040. **Road map** E5. **(** (305) 296-2991. **FAX** (305) 292 3213.
Mentioned by Hemingway and once home to Tennessee Williams, this
1925 hotel is a local landmark. The rooms have original features, and the
rooftop affords some of the best views in town. 🏊 🍴 ⚓ *Rooms: 160*
AE DC MC V

KEY WEST: *Casa Marina Resort* W www.casamarinakeywest.com $$$$$
1500 Reynolds St, FL 33040. **Road map** E5. **(** (305) 296-3535. **FAX** (305) 296-4633.
Built in the 1920s by Henry Flagler, Key West's first grand hotel is set in
beautiful grounds. Opulent public areas lead to relatively simple rooms,
many with balconies facing the sea. 🏊 🍴 🅿 ⚓ *Rooms: 311*
AE DC MC V

MARATHON: *Faro Blanco Marine Resort* $$$
1996 (MM48.5) Overseas Hwy, FL 33050. **Road map** E5. **(** (800) 759-3276.
FAX (305) 743-2918. Choose from 1950s garden cottages, houseboats, as well as
apartments in a real lighthouse and condos. 🍴 *Rooms: 100*
AE MC V

MARCO ISLAND: *Boat House Motel* W www.theboathousemotel.com $$$
1180 Edington Place, FL 34145. **Road map** E4. **(** (941) 642-2400.
FAX (941) 642-2435. Situated in the old town, beside the river, this
comfortable motel has a variety of rooms and a two-bedroom cottage.
There are picnic tables and grills, plus 3 condos. ⚓ *Rooms: 20*
MC V

NAPLES: *Holiday Inn* $$
1100 9th Ave N, FL 34102. **Road map** E4. **(** (941) 262-7146. **FAX** (941) 261-3809.
This quiet chain motel is quieter than most and convenient for
sightseeing. The friendly bar is popular at happy hour. *Rooms: 137*
AE MC V

NAPLES: *Vanderbilt Beach* W www.vanderbiltbeachresort.com $$$
9225 Gulfshore Drive N, FL 34108. **Road map** E4. **(** (941) 597-3144.
FAX (941) 597-2199. This small, friendly inn on the beach has rooms and 16
condos. Complimentary breakfast for room guests only. ⚓ *Rooms: 66*
AE MC V

NAPLES: *Inn By The Sea* W www.innbythesea-bb.com $$$$
287 11th Ave S, FL 34102. **Road map** E4. **(** (941) 649-4124. **FAX** (941) 434-2842.
Patchwork quilts, pine floors, and wicker fill this 1937 clapboard home,
two blocks from the beach in the heart of Old Naples. 🏊 ⚓ *Rooms: 5*
AE MC V

NAPLES: *The Registry Resort* $$$$$
475 Seagate Drive, FL 34103. **Road map** E4. **(** (941) 597-3232.
FAX (941) 566-7919. This deluxe resort caters to families and has an excellent children's program and the best Sunday brunch in town. The beach is
a stroll away through the mangroves. 🕐 🏊 🍴 🛏 🅿 ⚓ *Rooms: 474*
AE DC MC V

For key to symbols see back flap

WHERE TO EAT

Sign of the Green Turtle Inn *(see p328)*

FAST FOOD IS as much a staple here as anywhere in the US, but the joy of Florida is the abundant fresh produce, from tropical fruit to seafood, which restaurants of every description use to great effect. Fierce competition also helps to ensure that food is usually of both excellent quality and good value. Restaurants cater to every palate and budget, from the trendy establishments in Miami, which set or follow the latest culinary fashions, to simpler places in the interior, where the food tends to be more homey and traditional. Wherever you are, the most enjoyable meals are often to be had in the most down-to-earth local restaurants. The restaurants listed on pages 316–29 are recommended for their quality of food, service, and value for money. Cafés and bars, for drinking and more informal eating, are listed separately on pages 330–31.

The restaurant at South Beach's Art Deco Cardozo Hotel *(see p61)*

TYPES OF RESTAURANTS

FLORIDA'S BEST restaurants, mostly located in cities or attached to resort hotels, tend to serve European (often French) or elaborate regional cuisine. A breed of innovative chefs has combined Florida's fine local produce with zesty Caribbean flavors to create what people call New Florida or "Floribbean" cuisine. This kind of food is also served in smaller, more casual bistro-style restaurants, which are very popular and whose menus often change daily.

Miami and the cities of the Gold and Gulf coasts have a good reputation for their restaurants. The quality of the food in Walt Disney World is also surprisingly well regarded.

Miami is home to the state's greatest concentration of ethnic restaurants and cafés. Here, you can eat your way around the world from Asia to Europe and the Caribbean. Florida has the US's best choice of Hispanic food, which you can eat anywhere from a budget diner to a formal supper club.

Restaurants of every size and shape serve seafood. In one Florida institution, the "raw bar," you can enjoy deliciously fresh raw oysters or clams and steamed shrimp.

EATING HOURS

URBAN DWELLERS like to eat out, even for breakfast. This is an especially popular tradition on Sundays, when a leisurely brunch, often served buffet style, can be eaten from around 10am to 2pm.

On weekdays lunch is eaten from noon to 2:30pm and supper from 6pm onward. Away from the resorts and buzzing districts like South Beach in Miami, where many people prefer to dine at around 11pm, Floridians tend to eat early – usually between 7 and 9pm.

RESERVATIONS

TO AVOID disappointment, it is wise to reserve a table, especially on weekends or at the more upscale or popular restaurants. At some places, like Joe's Stone Crab in South Beach *(see p316)*, you cannot book ahead and instead must wait in line for a table.

TIPS ON EATING OUT

DINING OUT in Florida is mostly an informal affair. Very few restaurants require a jacket and tie, and those that do will provide jackets for diners without. "Casual but neat" is the general rule.

All restaurants have separate areas for smokers and non-smokers. If you book ahead, you will often be asked which section you'd prefer; if not, be sure to specify.

Tips range from 15 to 20 percent. At sophisticated places, diners frequently tip the higher amount if the service has

The informal surroundings of the Blue Desert Café, Cedar Key *(see p325)*

been exceptionally good. The state sales tax of 6 percent will be added to your bill automatically.

Travelers' checks and credit cards are accepted in most restaurants, but neighborhood diners, fast food chains, coffee shops, and delis tend to accept only cash.

VEGETARIAN FOOD

VEGETARIANS WHO eat fish and seafood will have no problem at all in Florida. The rest, however, will often scour menus in vain for meat- and fish-free dishes. Unless you encounter one of the few truly vegetarian restaurants, prepare yourself for a diet in which salads, pasta dishes, and pizzas will feature strongly.

Cheap eats at a picnic site in one of Florida's state parks

DINING ON A BUDGET

THERE ARE SEVERAL easy ways to cut your food budget. First, as a rule, helpings in restaurants are huge, so order less than you would normally; an appetizer is often enough for a light meal. Diners may share dishes, but there is usually a small charge for this.

All-you-can-eat buffets are a bargain, and some restaurants have cheaper meals on a "prix-fixe" menu. In addition, "early bird" menus or specials feature set meals at a reduced price for those who eat early, usually from 5 to 6pm: these are a great boon for families. In this way, a full meal can be discounted by up to 35 percent. Check the listings for restaurants which offer early bird specials: call ahead for

McGuire's Irish Pub in Pensacola, serving food as well as beer *(see p326)*

details since the times and conditions usually vary.

It is less expensive to eat out at lunchtime than in the evening if you want to do so in a chic restaurant. Hotel dining, however, is always pricey. For breakfast, you'd do well to join the locals in a nearby deli or diner for what may be a much livelier and probably superior meal.

Bars often serve reasonably priced food, and during happy hour many serve hot hors d'oeuvres – enough for a meal if you aren't feeling ravenous.

Some restaurants, especially in the Keys, will cook your own fish for a reduced price. Also, many state parks have barbecued where you can grill your catch or whatever food you care to bring along. Delis and supermarkets are good for picnic provisions; delis also have prepared cooked dishes and sandwiches that you can eat on or off the premises.

MENUS

MENUS THROUGHOUT the state rely heavily on fresh fish and other seafood items, such as clams, lobsters, shrimp, crab, and conch. You can also find crawfish, blackened fish (coated with Cajun spices and cooked quickly in a smoking hot pan), and gumbos, if Cajun-style food appeals to you. Beef, chicken, and pork are readily available, from prime fillet of beef and tenderloin cuts to southern fried chicken, roast pork, or fried pork chops. Surf 'n' Turf is a popular combination of

seafood and beef, usually steak and lobster. If "dolphin" appears on a Florida menu, it refers to mahimahi, a white-fleshed fish. If you're unsure of what anything is, or if you need a special menu, the staff will be pleased to help. It's all part of the service.

CHILDREN

MOST RESTAURANTS are happy to accommodate the needs of younger diners. Some places provide small portions at about half the regular price, while others have special menus featuring child-sized meals of things kids like to eat such as hot dogs and fries. Some also provide high chairs or booster chairs; call ahead to check what is available.

Children are not allowed in bars, but if food is served on the premises they can accompany adults and have a meal in an area away from the bar.

Jaws hot dog stand at Keaton Beach in the Panhandle

What to Eat in Florida

Hot sauce

T HE FOOD IN FLORIDA is more culturally diverse than in any other state – above all in south Florida, where the Latin American and Caribbean influence is strong. In the north, where links to the Southern states run deep, more homey meals feature staples such as cornbread and black-eyed peas. Thanks to the state's long coastline you can enjoy fine fresh fish and seafood wherever you are, and Florida's benign climate means that fresh fruit and vegetables are available all year. For tips on interpreting a Florida menu see page 313.

Bacon

Bisc

Eggs

Grits

Southern Breakfast
A classic breakfast includes grits, a white corn porridge best served with lots of butter, salt, and black pepper.

Crab cakes

Cocktail sauce

Conch fritters

Gator bites

Fritters
Anything from shrimp to alligator can be fried in batter, ready for dipping in a spicy sauce.

Conch Chowder
This creamy soup is made with a giant sea snail, or conch – a popular ingredient in Florida. Other seafood may also be used.

Melted butter

Mustard sauce

Stone Crab Claws
Served chilled, usually as an appetizer, the claws are the only part of the stone crab to be eaten. They are harvested from October to April.

U-Peel Shrimp
This simple dish consists of shrimp cooked in a spicy broth. They are peeled and eaten with the fingers, ideally with a glass of cold beer.

Hush puppies

Black-eye pea sala

Fish fried in batter

Sweet potato

Ribs
Spicy, barbecued ribs, usually served with fries, are best when gnawed directly off the bone.

Heart of palm salad

Hush Puppies
Southern-style cornmeal fritters are eaten primarily in the Panhandle, traditionally with fried catfish.

Seared Tuna
Tuna is served here New Florida style, with a mango salsa and grilled chayote, a kind of squash.

Chicken Tropicana
This sautéed chicken dish comes with a tropical fruit sauce, coconut, and cashews.

Jerk Pork
Marinaded pork served with roasted corn on the cob is a classic Caribbean meal.

Key Lime Pie
Filled with a tangy custard flavored with Florida's own tiny key lime, this is the most famous dessert in the state.

FLORIDA FRUITS

Tropical and citrus fruits are grown in lush abundance in Florida. They are used in both sweet and savory dishes but are perhaps best when served unadorned in fruit salads or when whipped up with ice to make shakes.

Star fruit

Kiwi fruit

Kumquat

Lime

Rice Pudding
Sweet, creamy, and enriched with nutmeg and lemon, this homey dessert is popular in city diners and cafés.

Orange   Papaya   Fruit shake

HISPANIC FOOD

Menus in all kinds of establishments, from smart restaurants to no-frills diners, reflect the spread of Latin American dishes – above all those of Cuban origin – into Florida's mainstream cuisine: the Cuban sandwich, filled with generous amounts of cheese, ham, and pork, and *moros y cristianos* ("Moors and Christians," after the white rice and black beans) are seen everywhere; more unusual combinations such as the guava and cheese dessert are found only in the most authentic restaurants.

Cuban sandwich

Strong, sweet café cubano

Flan, crème caramel Hispanic style

Moros y cristianos (rice and beans)

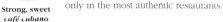

Vaca frita (fried beef)

Fried plantains

Tomato relish

Moros y cristianos, vaca frita (literally "fried cow"), and fried plantains – a classic Cuban combination

Guava paste with white cheese, an acquired taste

Choosing a Restaurant

THE RESTAURANTS in this guide have been selected for their good value or exceptional food. This chart highlights some of the factors that may influence your choice, such as the style of food and whether you can opt to eat outdoors. Entries are alphabetical within each price category. Information on cafés and bars is given on pages 330–31.

	CREDIT CARDS	CHILDREN'S FACILITIES	EARLY BIRD SPECIALS	GOOD REGIONAL CUISINE	BAR

MIAMI

MIAMI BEACH: *China Moon* 134 21st St. **Map** 2 F1. ((305) 532-8758. Open for lunch and dinner, this small place serves the best Chinese food in the area at budget prices. Open all the time.	$					
MIAMI BEACH: *11th Street Diner* 1065 Washington Ave. **Map** 2 E3. ((305) 534-6373. This top-notch 24-hour diner occupies a 1948 steel dining car. Dynamic staff serves traditional food (try the key lime pie) and modern dishes.	$	AE DC MC V	●			■
MIAMI BEACH: *Nexxt* 700 Lincoln Rd. **Map** 2 E2 ((305) 532-6643. An encyclopedia menu, an eclectic mix, and outside tables in this cafeteria-style eatery make this spot your best bet for a quick, cheap meal.	$	AE MC V				■
MIAMI BEACH: *Puerta Sagua* 700 Collins Ave. **Map** 2 E4. ((305) 673-1115. Serving staples like black beans, rice, and plantain, this diner is nothing fancy but offers tasty Cuban cuisine in an informal atmosphere. ▯	$	AE DC MC V				
MIAMI BEACH: *Wolfies* 2038 Collins Ave. **Map** 2 E4. ((305) 538-6626. A well-known Jewish deli, in business since 1947, where waitresses dispense good-sized portions of New York-style food 24 hours a day.	$	DC MC V	●	■		
MIAMI BEACH: *Stephan's Gourmet Market and Café* 1430 Washington Ave. **Map** 2 E3. ((305) 674-1760. Downstairs, a glorious Italian deli has delicious food to take away or to eat at sidewalk tables; upstairs is a tiny restaurant frequented by locals. ▯	$$	AE DC MC V	●			
MIAMI BEACH: *Tap Tap* 819 5th St. **Map** 2 E4. ((305) 672-2898. Serving real Haitian food such as grilled conch with manioc and shrimp in coconut sauce, this unusual restaurant attracts a vibrant, multicultural crowd. There's even an art gallery upstairs. ▯ 🎴 ♪	$$	AE DC MC V			●	■
MIAMI BEACH: *Astor Place Bar and Grill* Hotel Astor, 956 Washington Ave. **Map** 2 E3. ((305) 672-7217. One of the in-places of South Beach, this stylish restaurant features modern dishes such as corn-crusted yellowtail snapper. **P** ▯ 🎴 ♪ *Sun brunch.*	$$$$	AE DC MC V			●	■
MIAMI BEACH: *Tuscan Steak* 433 Washington Ave. **Map** 2 E5. ((305) 534-2233. One of Miami Beach's best. A flashy crowd goes for the giant antipasto, the T-bone with garlic puree, and the pricey drinks. ▯	$$$	AE MC V				■
MIAMI BEACH: *A Fish Called Avalon* Avalon Hotel, 700 Ocean Drive. **Map** 2 E4. ((305) 532-1727. In the heart of the Art Deco district, this seafood grill is known for its delicious Floribbean cuisine and lively atmosphere. **P** ▯ 🎴 ♪ ● *L.*	$$$	AE DC MC V		■	●	■
MIAMI BEACH: *The Forge* 432 Arthur Godfrey Rd. ((305) 538-8533. Celebrities abound at this Miami Beach landmark. Its glitzy decor has opulent American cuisine to match; the desserts are sublime, and The Forge boasts the longest wine list in the city. **P** **V** ▯ 🎴 ♪ ● *L.*	$$$$	AE DC MC V			●	■
MIAMI BEACH: *Joe's Stone Crab* 11 Washington Ave. **Map** 2 E5. ((305) 673-0365. This Miami institution is a must. There's lobster, shrimp, and fish as well as the signature stone crab claws. No reservations. **P** **V** ▯ ● *Mon L; May–Oct.*	$$$	AE DC MC V	●		●	■

Price categories include a three-course meal for one, a glass of house wine, and all unavoidable extras including service and tax.
$ under $20
$$ $20–30
$$$ $30–45
$$$$ $45–60
$$$$$ over $60

CREDIT CARDS
Indicates which credit cards are accepted: AE American Express; DC Diners Club; MC MasterCard; V VISA.

CHILDREN'S FACILITIES
Small portions and high chairs available, and there may also be a special children's menu.

EARLY BIRD SPECIALS
Meals offered at a discounted price if you eat early, usually before 7pm.

GOOD REGIONAL CUISINE
Florida specialties, such as seafood or dishes with Hispanic or Caribbean influence.

Restaurant	Price	Credit Cards	Children's Facilities	Early Bird Specials	Good Regional Cuisine	Bar
MIAMI BEACH: *Nemo Restaurant* 100 Collins Ave. ☎ *(305) 532-4550.* The music is loud, but there is a patio for quieter dining. New American multicultural cuisine, plus a magnificent Sunday brunch. 🍷 🪑 ♫	$$$	AE MC V			●	■
MIAMI BEACH: *Osteria del Teatro* 1443 Washington Ave. **Map** 2 F3. ☎ *(305) 538-7850.* This Italian restaurant serves traditional and more modern dishes, such as crab-stuffed ravioli with lobster sauce. Book ahead. [P] 🍷 ⬤ *L.*	$$$	AE DC MC V			●	
MIAMI BEACH: *The Tiger Oak Room* Raleigh Hotel, 1775 Collins Ave. **Map** 2 F2. ☎ *(305) 534-6300.* The menu here offers a most eclectic mix of traditional American fare alongside exotic meat and fish dishes from Japan and Vietnam. Choose the elegant dining room or the terrace overlooking the pool. [P] 🍷 🪑 ⬤ *Mon & Tue D.*	$$$	AE DC MC V	●		●	■
MIAMI BEACH: *YUCA* 501 Lincoln Rd. **Map** 2 E2. ☎ *(305) 532-9822.* YUCA, an acronym for "young upwardly mobile Cuban Americans," earns rave reviews for its Nuevo Cubano cuisine. Traditional dishes with new twists include sweet plantain stuffed with dried, cured beef. 🍷 🪑	$$$$	AE DC MC V			●	■
MIAMI BEACH: *Blue Door* Delano Hotel, 1685 Collins Ave. **Map** 2 F2. ☎ *(305) 674-6400.* A highly sophisticated and expensive restaurant, where deft waiters in cream uniforms serve French cuisine with a tropical accent. [P] 🪑	$$$$	AE DC MC V	●		●	■
MIAMI BEACH: *China Grill* 404 Washington Ave. **Map** 2 E4. ☎ *(305) 534-2211.* Gathering flavors and techniques from around the globe, this place serves world cuisine in a futuristic setting. Sake and vodka bar. [P] 🍷 ⬤ *Sat & Sun L.*	$$$$	AE MC V			●	■
MIAMI BEACH: *Pacific Time* 915 Lincoln Rd. **Map** 2 E2. ☎ *(305) 534-5979.* The menu changes daily at this pleasant restaurant. The Pan-Asian cuisine here is a unique experience. Vegetarians are not forgotten. [V] 🍷 🪑 ⬤ *L.*	$$$$	AE DC MC V			●	■
MIAMI BEACH: *Steak House at the Fontainebleau Hilton* 4441 Collins Ave. ☎ *(305) 538-2000.* Perfect for a romantic dinner, this upscale steakhouse produces outstanding seafood and pasta. Candlelight, soft music, superb service. [P] 🍷	$$$$	AE DC MC V			●	■
DOWNTOWN: *S & S Restaurant* 1757 NE 2nd Ave. **Map** 4 E1. ☎ *(305) 373-4291.* A no-frills diner serving a good selection of staple American dishes around a counter. Specials include pot roast and meat loaf.	$					
DOWNTOWN: *Fishbone Grille* 650 S. Miami Ave. **Map** 4 D1. ☎ *(305) 530-1915.* Plain and simple, this is a great catch for seafood lovers. Tuna, snapper, or conch – whatever you want, they'll cook and serve it. 🍷 🪑	$$$	AE MC V	●		●	■
DOWNTOWN: *The Fish Market* Wyndham Hotel, 1601 Biscayne Blvd. ☎ *(305) 374-0000.* One of Miami's best kept secrets, this seafood restaurant, decorated with mirrors and marble, serves excellent Floribbean seafood. [P] 🍷 ⬤ *L; Sun & Mon.*	$$$	AE DC MC V			●	■
DOWNTOWN: *The Royal Palm Court* Inter-Continental Hotel, 100 Chopin Plaza. **Map** 4 F2. ☎ *(305) 577-1000.* Try the bargain buffets served at lunch and dinner, or one of the filling pasta dishes. Popular with the locals. [P] 🍷	$$$	AE DC MC V	●		●	■

<table>
<tr><td>

Price categories include a three-course meal for one, a glass of house wine, and all unavoidable extras including service and tax.
$ under $20
$$ $20–30
$$$ $30–45
$$$$ $45–60
$$$$$ over $60

</td><td>

CREDIT CARDS
Indicates which credit cards are accepted: AE American Express; DC Diners Club; MC MasterCard; V VISA.
CHILDREN'S FACILITIES
Small portions and high chairs available, and there may also be a special children's menu.
EARLY BIRD SPECIALS
Meals offered at a discounted price if you eat early, usually before 7pm.
GOOD REGIONAL CUISINE
Florida specialties, such as seafood or dishes with Hispanic or Caribbean influence.

</td></tr>
</table>

	CREDIT CARDS	CHILDREN'S FACILITIES	EARLY BIRD SPECIALS	GOOD REGIONAL CUISINE	BAR
LITTLE HAVANA: *La Carreta I* $ 3632 SW 8th St. 【 *(305) 444-7501.* From its menu to its clientele, this popular family restaurant is thoroughly Cuban. Come for good food and good fun: La Carreta draws a fine crowd on weekend nights. Open 24 hours a day. 🍴	AE DC MC V	●		●	▦
LITTLE HAVANA: *Varilles* $ 3555 SW 8th St. 【 *(305) 445-0240.* Little Havana's most famous restaurant is as vast as its menu and portions. You'll find every Cuban specialty imaginable, though some dishes are a bit stodgy. The atmosphere is informal and welcoming to non-Cubans. 🍴	AE DC MC V	●			
LITTLE HAVANA: *Casa Juancho* $$ 2436 SW 8th St. 【 *(305) 642-2452.* Deservedly famous for its superlative Spanish cuisine, this restaurant is very popular with Miami's Hispanic community. The decor evokes rural Spain, and troubadours entertain in the evenings. 🅿 🍴 🎴 🎵	AE DC MC V	●			▦
CORAL GABLES: *John Martin's* $ 253 Miracle Mile. **Map** 6 C1. 【 *(305) 445-3777.* A lovely dining room, charming hospitality, and good food (including a few Irish dishes) make this a local favorite. 🍴 🎵 *Fri, Sat & Sun.* ● *Dec 25.*	AE DC MC V	●			▦
CORAL GABLES: *La Bussola Ristorante* $$$ 264 Giralda Ave. **Map** 6 C1. 【 *(305) 445-8783.* A gracious restaurant serving Italian fare such as gnocchi and pasta. The fabulous desserts are recommended. 🅿 🍴 🎵 *Tue–Sat.* ● *Sat & Sun L; Dec 25.*	AE DC MC V				▦
CORAL GABLES: *Caffè Abbracci* $$$ 318 Aragon Ave. **Map** 6 C1. 【 *(305) 441-0700.* This café serves tempting north Italian dishes. Innovative pastas, grilled goose liver, and fried calamari are house specialties. 🍴 🅿 ● *Sat & Sun L.*	AE DC MC V	●			▦
CORAL GABLES: *Christy's* $$$ 3101 Ponce de Leon Blvd. **Map** 6 C2. 【 *(305) 446-1400.* A very popular steak house featuring succulent beef and seafood in a club-like setting. A tasty Caesar salad accompanies each entrée. 🍴 ● *Sat–Sun L.*	AE DC MC V				▦
CORAL GABLES: *Restaurant St. Michel* $$$ Hotel Place St. Michel, 162 Alcazar Ave. **Map** 6 C1. 【 *(305) 446-6572.* New American cuisine with a Caribbean zing is dished up in this delightfully French environment. Specialties include sesame-coated tuna. 🆅 🍴 🎴 🎵	AE DC MC V	●	▦	●	▦
CORAL GABLES: *Norman's* $$$$ 21 Almeria Ave. **Map** 6 A1. 【 *(305) 446-6767.* Chef Norman Van Aken is famous for his new World Cuisine, and the menu here shows his skill to the maximum. 🆅 🍴 🅿 ● *Sun*	AE DC MC V			●	▦
COCONUT GROVE: *Café Tu Tu Tango* $ CocoWalk, 3015 Grand Ave. **Map** 6 E4. 【 *(305) 529-2222.* This lively informal café has a tapas-style menu; order a few light snacks or one more substantial dish. Great for people-watching. 🆅 🍴 🎴 🎵	AE DC MC V	●		●	▦
COCONUT GROVE: *Cheesecake Factory* $$ CocoWalk, 3015 Grand Ave. **Map** 6 E4. 【 *(305) 447-9898.* A taste of California in Miami, offering a vast menu from burgers to pasta and over 30 types of cheesecake. Special Sunday brunch menu. 🆅 🍴 ● *Dec 25.*	AE DC MC V	●			▦
COCONUT GROVE: *Señor Frog's* $$ 3480 Main Highway. **Map** 6 E4. 【 *(305) 448-0999.* Expect traditional food at this Mexican eatery. Only fresh produce is used and sauces are prepared daily. Try the sizzling *fajitas*, stuffed *enchiladas*, or one of the unusual savory chocolate *mole* dishes. 🆅 🍴 🎴	AE DC MC V	●			

Coconut Grove: *Bicé* $$$$ AE DC MC V
Grand Bay Hotel, 2669 S Bayshore Drive. **Map** 6 F4. [C] (305) 858-9600.
Setting a new trend in Floribbean cuisine, this unashamedly upscale
restaurant also boasts impeccable service and elegant decor. P ▯ ▯ ♫

Farther Afield: *Here Comes the Sun* $ AE DC MC V
2188 NE 123rd St, North Miami. [C] (305) 893-5711.
This bistro is biased toward vegetarian dishes, but fish and chicken are also
available. Vegetables are organic and there are daily specials. V ● Sun.

Farther Afield: *Rusty Pelican* $$$ AE DC MC V
3201 Rickenbacker Causeway, Key Biscayne. [C] (305) 361-3818.
You'll get the best view of the Miami skyline from this elegant waterfront
bistro. Local seafood dishes are recommended. P ▯ ▯ ♫ Fri–Sat.

Farther Afield: *Sunday's On The Bay* $$$ AE DC MC V
5420 Crandon Blvd, Key Biscayne. [C] (305) 361-6777.
A good family restaurant that offers seafood and water views. There
is a huge and varied choice for Sunday brunch. ▯ ▯ ♫ Sun.

Farther Afield: *Chef Allen's* $$$$$ AE DC MC V
19088 NE 29th Ave, North Miami Beach. [C] (305) 935-2900.
Sleek and chic, this Miami landmark is known for its high quality,
daring New Florida cuisine. The activity in the kitchen, framed by
a huge picture window, is fascinating. P ▯ ● L, Super Bowl.

THE GOLD AND TREASURE COASTS

Boca Raton: *TooJay's* $ AE DC MC V
5030 Champion Blvd. **Road map** F4. [C] (561) 241-5903.
There's usually a line outside this deli but it's worth the wait. Choose from
overstuffed pastrami and corned beef sandwiches, salmon bagels, and
massive portions of cheesecake. Not for weight watchers. ● Dec 25.

Boca Raton: *Max's Grille* $$ AE DC MC V
404 Plaza Real, Mizner Park. **Road map** F4. [C] (561) 368-0080.
A place to see and be seen at Mizner Park, where you can enjoy some
excellent regional cuisine in classy surroundings. P V ▯ ▯

Boca Raton: *La Vieille Maison* $$$$ AE DC MC V
770 E Palmetto Park Rd. **Road map** F4. [C] (561) 391 6701.
Built by Addison Mizner (see p116), this home is now an intimate
five-star French restaurant, ideal for romantic dinners. P ▯ ▯

Dania: *Martha's Supper Club* $$$ AE DC MC V
6024 N Ocean Drive. **Road map** F4 [C] (954) 923-5444.
Known for its superb seafood (the coconut fried shrimp are very good),
Martha's also enjoys great views of the Intracoastal Waterway. ▯ P ♫

Davie: *Armadillo Café* $$$ AE DC MC V
4630 SW 64th Ave. **Road map** F4. [C] (954) 791-4866.
Southwestern food at its best with delicious dishes from smoked duck
to tacos, served up in a casual atmosphere. ▯ ▯ ● L; public hols.

Deerfield: *Pal's Charley's Crab* $$$ AE DC MC V
1755 SE 3rd Court. **Road map** F4. [C] (954) 427-4000.
Located on the Intracoastal Waterway, this restaurant has different
menus for lunch and dinner with the emphasis on seafood. A special
sunset menu is available from 4–5:30pm. ▯ P ▯

Deerfield Beach: *Brooks* $$$ AE MC V
500 S Federal Hwy. **Road map** F4. [C] (954) 427-9302.
Brooks tempts you with Floribbean dishes created from wonderfully fresh
ingredients. Prix fixe or à la carte. A local favorite. P ▯ ● L; Dec 25.

Fort Lauderdale: *Aruba* $ AE MC V
1 E. Commercial Blvd. **Road map** F4. [C] (561) 776-0001.
The best on the beach, this always crowded spot is known for its lobster salad
sandwich and huge servings. Live music Friday and Sunday. ▯ ▯ ♫

Fort Lauderdale: *Café Europa* $ AE MC V
726 E Las Olas Blvd. **Road map** F4. [C] (954) 763-6600.
This buzzing self-service café serves excellent pizzas, salads, and sand-
wiches, plus cappuccinos in 52 regular and unusual flavors. ▯

For key to symbols see back flap

Price categories include a three-course meal for one, a glass of house wine, and all unavoidable extras including service and tax.
$ under $20
$$ $20–30
$$$ $30–45
$$$$ $45–60
$$$$$ over $60

Credit Cards
Indicates which credit cards are accepted: AE American Express; DC Diners Club; MC MasterCard; V VISA.

Children's Facilities
Small portions and high chairs available, and there may also be a special children's menu.

Early Bird Specials
Meals offered at a discounted price if you eat early, usually before 7pm.

Good Regional Cuisine
Florida specialties, such as seafood or dishes with Hispanic or Caribbean influence.

Restaurant	Credit Cards	Children's Facilities	Early Bird Specials	Good Regional Cuisine	Bar
Fort Lauderdale: *The Floridian Restaurant* $ 1410 E Las Olas Blvd. **Road map** F4. ☎ *(954) 463-4041.* Sunday mornings are especially busy at this trendy neighborhood meeting place, when devotees enjoy three-egg omelettes, buttermilk pancakes, and steak. Lunches and dinners are also very reasonable. Open 24 hours. 🍷 ⛱					
Fort Lauderdale: *Bobby Rubino's* $$ 4100 N Federal Hwy. **Road map** F4. ☎ *(954) 561-5305.* One of Florida's first rib restaurants; you can't beat their onion loaf and special recipe barbecue sauce. Fabulous ribs and grills. [P] 🍷 ● *Sun L.*	AE DC MC V	●			■
Fort Lauderdale: *California Café* $$ 2301 SE 17th St Causeway. **Road map** F4. ☎ *(954) 728-3500.* Sweet potato crusted-salmon is one of the dishes offered at this restaurant, which uses the flavors of California and Florida. The innovative seasonal menu also includes pizza and pasta dishes. [P] [V] 🍷 ⛱ ♫ *Thu–Sat.*	AE DC MC V	●		●	■
Fort Lauderdale: *Mango's* $$ 904 E Las Olas Blvd. **Road map** F4. ☎ *(954) 523-5001.* Mango's has a wide choice of dishes from tasty appetizers to pastas and specialties such as the shrimp pepperpot. 🍷 ⛱ ♫ ● *Thanksgiving, Dec 25.*	AE MC V			●	■
Fort Lauderdale: *Burt & Jack's* $$$ Berth 23, Port Everglades. **Road map** F4. ☎ *(954) 522-5225.* Hidden away in Port Everglades, this formal restaurant offers panoramic views as you chew on man-sized portions of steak and seafood. The wine list and service are excellent. [P] 👔 🍷 ⛱ ♫ ● *L; Dec 25.*	AE DC MC V			●	■
Fort Pierce: *Mangrove Mattie's* $$ 1640 Seaway Drive. **Road map** F3. ☎ *(561) 466-1044.* Delectable seafood, including pasta sauces, is the mainstay at this pleasant restaurant. Meaty steaks and ribs are also available. 🍷 ⛱ ● *Dec 25.*	AE DC MC V	●	■	●	■
Hollywood: *Bavarian Village* $$ 1401 N Federal Hwy. **Road map** F4. ☎ *(954) 922-7321.* This welcoming restaurant is definitely for those with a hearty appetite and a yen for German food. Traditional American dishes (steak and fish) are also on the menu, and it's very family friendly. 🍷 ♫ ● *Mon–Sat L.*	AE DC MC V	●	■		■
Hutchinson Island: *Scalawags* $$ 555 NE Ocean Blvd. **Road map** F3. ☎ *(561) 225-6818.* Ceiling fans and wicker furniture give Scalawags a tropical flavor that complements its Floribbean dishes. Seafood buffets on Wednesdays. ⛱ ♫	AE DC MC V	●	■	●	■
Jupiter: *Charley's Crab* $$$ 1000 N US 1. **Road map** F4. ☎ *(561) 744-4710.* Overlooking Jupiter River, this is one in the chain of Charley's Crab eateries and prides itself on expertly prepared Floribbean seafood. [P] 🍷 ⛱	AE DC MC V	●	■	●	■
Palm Beach: *Chuck & Harold's* $$ 207 Royal Poinciana Way. **Road map** F4. ☎ *(561) 659-1440.* The porch tables are the best for celebrity-spotting while you enjoy dishes such as conch chowder or one of the blackboard specials. [P] 🍷 ⛱ ♫	AE DC MC V	●	■	●	■
Palm Beach: *Bice Ristorante* $$$$ 313½ Worth Ave. **Road map** F4. ☎ *(561) 835-1600.* Seriously good Italian food is served in this formal restaurant. The dress code matches the elegant decor. [P] 👔 🍷 ⛱	AE DC MC V				■
Palm Beach: *Florentine Dining Room* $$$$ Breakers Hotel, 1 South County Rd. **Road map** F4. ☎ *(561) 655-6611.* For a truly memorable experience, try the refined setting of this restaurant and the lavish New Florida cuisine served here. [P] 👔 🍷 ♫	AE DC MC V	●		●	■

PALM BEACH: *Renato's* $$$ AE DC MC V
07 Via Mizner. **Road map** F4. [(561) 655-9752.
Tucked away in one of Palm Beach's alleys, Renato's offers European
dishes, carefully prepared and faultlessly served. **P** **T** **?** 🎵 ● *Sun L.*

POMPANO BEACH: *Flaming Pit* $$ AE DC MC V
1150 N Federal Hwy. **Road map** F4. [(954) 943 3484.
Locals flock here for the prime rib and steak, great chicken, and the salad
bar, which comes with all the fixings. Low prices and friendly service.

STUART: *The Ashley* $$ AE MC V
61 SW Osceola St. **Road map** F3. [(561) 221-9476.
A varied breakfast menu is available and, later on, dishes like coco-mango
shrimp, salads, fresh fish, and pasta are served. **V** 🎵 *Tue–Sat.*

VERO BEACH: *Ocean Grill* $$ AE DC MC V
1050 Sexton Plaza. **Road map** F3. [(561) 231-5409.
Decorated with antiques, this 1940s waterfront restaurant offers flavorful
seafood and meat dishes such as Indian River crab cakes and roast
duckling. **V** ● *Sat & Sun L; Jul 4, first 2 weeks in Sep, Thanksgiving.*

WEST PALM BEACH: *Randy's Bageland* $ MC V
911 Village Blvd, Village Commons. **Road map** F4. [(561) 640-0203.
Randy's Jewish deli-style cooking produces mouthwatering *knishes* (stuffed
dumplings), *pirogis* (pies) and, of course, bagels. Also a few fish dishes. **V**

WEST PALM BEACH: *Aleyda's Tex Mex* $$ AE DC MC V
1890 Okeechobee Blvd. **Road map** F4. [(561) 688-9033.
Sink your teeth into good old-fashioned Tex-Mex food at this popular joint.
You'll find *tacos, fajitas, tamales,* and the weekday buffet lunch is great. **V**

ORLANDO AND THE SPACE COAST

COCOA BEACH: *The Mango Tree Restaurant* $$$ AE MC V
118 N Atlantic Ave. **Road map** F3. [(321) 799-0513.
This gourmet restaurant serves local dishes, with seafood as a specialty.
Situated just yards from the Atlantic Ocean, there is a tropical garden with
waterfowl, Japanese carp, and lush foliage. **V** **?** 🎤 🎵 ● *Mon.*

DOWNTOWN ORLANDO: *Crackers Seafood Restaurant* $$ AE DC MC V
Church Street Station, 129 W Church St. **Road map** E2. [(407) 422-2434.
A Victorian saloon-style restaurant serving Creole food with the emphasis
on seafood. Try the gumbo, oysters, or the blackened gator tail. **?**

DOWNTOWN ORLANDO: *Le Coq au Vin* $$ AE DC MC V
4800 S Orange Ave. **Road map** E2. [(407) 851-6980.
Welcoming surroundings and consistently fine rustic French cuisine are
the draw at this popular restaurant. **?** ● *Mon; Sat & Sun L; most public hols.*

DOWNTOWN ORLANDO: *Lili Marlene's at Church Street Station* $$$ AE DC MC V
Church Street Station, 129 W Church St. **Road map** E2. [(407) 422-2434.
Brass, stained glass, and antique fittings from around the world set the
mood at this brasserie, which serves meat, fish, and pasta dishes. **?**

INTERNATIONAL DRIVE: *The Crab House* $$ AE DC MC V
8291 International Drive. **Road map** E2. [(407) 352 6140.
Choose from no less than nine crab dishes at this informal restaurant. The
seafood salad bar is loaded with freshly shucked oysters, shrimp, marinated
mussels, and crawfish, and other seafood dishes. **?** 🎤

INTERNATIONAL DRIVE: *Damon's The Place For Ribs* $$ AE DC MC V
Mercado, 8445 International Drive. **Road map** E2. [(407) 352-5984.
Just follow your nose to some of the best ribs in town at this no-frills eatery
that also serves steak, seafood, and monster sandwiches. ● *Dec 25.*

INTERNATIONAL DRIVE: *Bergamo's Italian Restaurant* $$$ AE DC MC V
Mercado, 8445 International Drive. **Road map** E2. [(407) 352-3805.
This trattoria serves up excellent Italian cuisine and operatic waiters. Try the
osso buco with risotto or pasta dishes. **V** **?** 🎵 ● *L; Thanksgiving, Dec 25.*

INTERNATIONAL DRIVE: *The Butcher Shop Steakhouse* $$$ AE DC MC V
Mercado, 8445 International Drive. **Road map** E2. [(407) 363-9727.
Here, you'll get the biggest and best steaks along I Drive, and you
can even cook your own at the grill if you like. **?** ● *L; Thanksgiving, Dec 25.*

Price categories include a three-course meal for one, a glass of house wine, and all unavoidable extras including service and tax.
(S) under $20
(S)(S) $20–30
(S)(S)(S) $30–45
(S)(S)(S)(S) $45–60
(S)(S)(S)(S)(S) over $60

CREDIT CARDS
Indicates which credit cards are accepted: AE American Express; DC Diners Club; MC MasterCard; V VISA.
CHILDREN'S FACILITIES
Small portions and high chairs available, and there may also be a special children's menu.
EARLY BIRD SPECIALS
Meals offered at a discounted price if you eat early, usually before 7pm.
GOOD REGIONAL CUISINE
Florida specialties, such as seafood or dishes with Hispanic or Caribbean influence.

	CREDIT CARDS	CHILDREN'S FACILITIES	EARLY BIRD SPECIALS	GOOD REGIONAL CUISINE	BAR
INTERNATIONAL DRIVE: *Hard Rock Café* (S)(S) 6050 Universal Blvd, Universal Orlando. **Road map** E2. ((407) 351-7625. This huge round building in CityWalk is festooned with pop memorabilia and murals. The burgers, sandwiches, and sundaes are great, and there is live music in the concert hall at an extra charge. **P** ♫	AE DC MC V	●			■
INTERNATIONAL DRIVE: *Everglades* (S)(S)(S) 9840 International Drive. **Road map** E2. ((407) 996-9840. This better-than-average upscale hotel restaurant serves creative gourmet dishes inspired by Florida cuisine. Try the 'gator chowder. **P** **Y**	AE DC MC V			●	■
KISSIMMEE: *Pacino's Italian Ristorante* (S)(S) 5795 W Highway 192. **Road map** E3. ((407) 396-8022. Charbroiled food is the focus of this comfortable and friendly family restaurant. If you prefer, there's a free delivery service to any nearby hotel. ▦ ● *L.*	AE DC MC V	●			■
WALT DISNEY WORLD: *California Grill* (S)(S) Disney's Contemporary Resort. **Road map** E3. ((407) 939-3463. A stylish restaurant with good views and an open-plan kitchen, serving creative West Coast fare like smoked salmon pizza, and pork and polenta. **P** **Y**	AE MC V	●			■
WALT DISNEY WORLD: *Cape May Café* (S)(S) Disney's Beach Club Resort. **Road map** E3. ((407) 939-3463. The buffet breakfast proceedings here are conducted by Admiral Goofy. At dinner, a bell announces the start of the clam bake buffet, laden with a great array of food to choose from. **P** ● *L.*	AE MC V	●		●	
WALT DISNEY WORLD: *Chef Mickey's* (S)(S) Disney's Contemporary Resort. **Road map** E3. ((407) 939-3463. Very much a family-oriented place offering breakfast and dinner buffets. Enjoy the antics of your favorite Disney characters as you eat. **P** ♫ ● *L.*	AE MC V	●			
WALT DISNEY WORLD: *Coral Café* (S)(S) Walt Disney World Dolphin Hotel. **Road map** E3. ((407) 934-4000. One for all the (health conscious) family – the menu here even counts the calories and fat content of each dish. Themed dinner buffets nightly. **P** **V**	AE MC V	●		●	
WALT DISNEY WORLD: *Ohana* (S)(S) Disney's Polynesian Resort. **Road map** E3. ((407) 939-3463. This buzzing, open-plan dining room is the setting for Polynesian-style cuisine. Set-price dinners include meat and shellfish roasted over a fire pit and served on 3-ft (1-m) long skewers. **P** ♫ ● *L.*	AE MC V	●			
WALT DISNEY WORLD: *Planet Hollywood Orlando* (S)(S) 1506 E Buena Vista Drive. **Road map** E3. ((407) 827-7827. Located within a purple neon globe, you'll find video screens and masses of movie memorabilia to gaze at while you munch on mainstream fare such as meaty burgers and tasty pizzas. ♫	AE MC V	●			■
WALT DISNEY WORLD: *Olivia's Café* (S)(S) Disney Old Key West. **Road map** E3. ((407) 939-3463. You'll think you're in old Key West at this café serving conch-style meals. Check out the Florida paella, conch chowder, and mojo chicken. **P**	AE MC V	●		●	
WALT DISNEY WORLD: *Whispering Canyon Café* (S)(S) Disney Wilderness Lodge. **Road map** E3. ((407) 939-3463. Snap on your six-guns and settle in for an all-you-can-eat campfire cookout buffet in a Wild West setting. Also open for frontier-style breakfasts. **P** **V**	AE MC V	●			■
WALT DISNEY WORLD: *Yacht Club Galley* (S)(S) Disney Yacht Club Resort. **Road map** E3. ((407) 939-3463. Open all day for "down home" favorites including fish, steak, and pasta in nautical surroundings. The dinner buffet has scrumptious desserts. **P**	AE MC V	●			■

WALT DISNEY WORLD: *Gulliver's Grill* $$$ AE DC MC V
Walt Disney World Swan Hotel. **Road map** E3. (*(407) 934-1609.*
Try the tastes of *Brobdingnag,* the legendary land of giants, at this
lovely plant-filled restaurant. It serves well-prepared American cuisine,
and vegetarian dishes are available upon request. P V Y

WALT DISNEY WORLD: *Narcoossee's* $$$ AE MC V
Disney's Grand Floridian Resort. **Road map** E3. (*(407) 824-1400.*
This restaurant in an octagonal chalet right alongside the Seven Seas lagoon
serves delicious meat and fish dishes with fresh local vegetables. P ● *L*

WALT DISNEY WORLD: *The Outback* $$$ AE DC MC V
Wyndham Palace, 1900 Buena Vista Drive. **Road map** E3. (*(407) 827-3430.*
An indoor waterfall creates a soothing atmosphere at this down-under
chain bistro. Feast on jumbo stuffed shrimp and steaks. P V Y ● *L.*

WALT DISNEY WORLD: *Reflections* $$ AE MC V
The Disney Institute. **Road map** E3. (*(407) 939-3463.*
This on-site cafe offers box lunches, deli sandwiches, coffee, and great
desserts. Ideal for those attending the Institute. V Y ♫

WALT DISNEY WORLD: *Arthur's 27* $$$$$ AE DC MC V
Wyndham Palace, 1900 Buena Vista Drive. **Road map** E3. (*(407) 827-3450.*
There's a fabulous view and a meal to match at this 27th-floor restaurant.
Probably some of Orlando's finest Floribbean cuisine. P Y ♫ ● *L.*

WALT DISNEY WORLD: *Victoria & Albert's* $$$$$ AE MC V
Disney's Grand Floridian Resort. **Road map** E3. (*(407) 824 1089.*
Reservations are a must at this lavish restaurant. The six-course fixed-price
menu is superlative, and you're waited on by a butler and a maid. Ask for
the chef's table, the most exclusive one in the house. P T V Y ♫ ● *L.*

WINTER PARK: *Café de France* $$$$ AE DC MC V
526 Park Ave S. **Road map** E2. (*(407) 647-1869.*
A cozy French bistro serving lighter meals such as crêpes at lunchtime; at
dinner try the rack of lamb or the daily special. Y ▦ ● *Mon; public hols.*

WINTER PARK: *Park Plaza Gardens* $$$$ AE DC MC V
319 Park Ave S. **Road map** E2. (*(407) 645-2475.*
An airy courtyard in a plant-filled atrium provides the setting at this elegant
restaurant. The consistently delicious and award-winning American cuisine
is served with panache. Y ♫ *Fri & Sat, Sun brunch.* ● *Dec 25, Jan 1.*

THE NORTHEAST

DAYTONA BEACH: *Hog Heaven* $ MC V
37 N Atlantic Ave. **Road map** E2. (*(904) 257-1212.*
The inviting aroma of meat cooking on a traditional pit barbecue pervades
this friendly, casual dining spot. Bring a hearty appetite. Y

DAYTONA BEACH: *Aunt Catfish's* $$ AE MC V
4009 Halifax Drive. **Road map** E2. (*(904) 767-4768.*
This popular eatery located on the Intracoastal Waterway is especially
renowned for its fried catfish and other Southern-style dishes such as crab
cakes and clam strips. Also open for Sunday brunch. ▦

DAYTONA BEACH: *Down the Hatch* $$ AE MC V
4894 Front St, Ponce Inlet. **Road map** E2. (*(904) 761-4831.*
A homey, family-oriented restaurant serving beautifully fresh fish and a few
meat dishes. Set right on the water, you can watch the boats unload their
catch at the end of the day. ▦ ♫ *Wed–Sun.* ● *Thanksgiving, Dec 25.*

FERNANDINA BEACH: *Florida House Inn* $ AE MC V
20–22 S 3rd St. **Road map** E1. (*(904) 261-3300.*
At this lovely gingerbread house (Florida's oldest surviving hotel), diners
sit at long trestle tables laden with generous servings of good American
home cooking. Always "all-you-can-eat"! ● *Sun, Mon D; Dec 24 D.*

FERNANDINA BEACH: *Beech Street Grill* $$$ AE DC MC V
801 Beech St. **Road map** E1. (*(904) 277-3662.*
Occupying a gorgeous 1889 building, the Grill offers a progressive
menu of contemporary Florida cuisine and an excellent wine list.
Daily specials showcase the innovative seafood dishes. Y ♫ *Thu–Sat.*
● *L; Thanksgiving, Dec 25, Super Bowl Sunday.*

Price categories include a three-course meal for one, a glass of house wine, and all unavoidable extras including service and tax.
$ under $20
$$ $20–30
$$$ $30–45
$$$$ $45–60
$$$$$ over $60

CREDIT CARDS
Indicates which credit cards are accepted: AE American Express; DC Diners Club; MC MasterCard; V VISA.

CHILDREN'S FACILITIES
Small portions and high chairs available, and there may also be a special children's menu.

EARLY BIRD SPECIALS
Meals offered at a discounted price if you eat early, usually before 7pm.

GOOD REGIONAL CUISINE
Florida specialties, such as seafood or dishes with Hispanic or Caribbean influence.

	CREDIT CARDS	CHILDREN'S FACILITIES	EARLY BIRD SPECIALS	GOOD REGIONAL CUISINE	BAR
FERNANDINA BEACH: *The Grill* $$$$$ — Ritz Carlton Hotel, 4750 Amelia Island Parkway. **Road map** E1. (904) 277-1100, x1269. An upscale restaurant that offers a minimum three-course menu and a generous Sunday brunch. The menu changes daily. 🅿 🍴 ♪ ● L.	AE DC MC V	●		●	■
GAINESVILLE: *The Chuck Wagon* $ — 3483 Williston Rd. **Road map** D2. (352) 336-5677. This country-style eatery, complete with rocking chairs, offers dishes like honey-glazed ham and catfish fillets. 🅥 🍴 ● Thanksgiving, Dec 25.	AE MC V	●			
JACKSONVILLE: *Café Carmon* $$ — 1986 San Marco Blvd. **Road map** E1. (904) 399-4488. This bistro tempts diners with excellently prepared foods from tomato and basil pasta to grilled or blackened fresh catch of the day. 🅥 🍴	AE DC MC V	●		●	
JACKSONVILLE: *Juliette's, A Florida Bistro* $$$ — Omni Jacksonville Hotel, 245 Water St. **Road map** E1. (904) 355-6664. The menu here promises treats such as fresh grilled tuna and salmon steaks and other regional specials. Make the most of the excellent service and the gourmet desserts. 🅿 🍴	AE DC MC V	●		●	■
JACKSONVILLE: *The Wine Cellar* $$$ — 1314 Prudential Drive. **Road map** E1. (904) 398-8989. One of Jacksonville's top restaurants, the Wine Cellar features 200 wines and dishes like grilled salmon with dill sauce. 🍴 ● Sat L; Sun; public hols.	AE DC MC V			●	■
JACKSONVILLE BEACH: *Dolphin Depot* $$ — 704 N 1st St. **Road map** E1. (904) 270-1424. Once a gas station, this Art Deco building contains one of the Northeast's best restaurants. Its small size ensures a quieter meal, and the blackboard menu changes daily. Reservations are advised. 🍴 ● L; public hols, Super Bowl.	AE DC MC V	●		●	
OCALA: *Arthur's* $$ — Ocala/Silver Springs Hilton, 3600 SW 36th Ave. **Road map** E2. (352) 854-1400. Arthur's is known for its lunch and dinner buffets: there's a different special every day, plus a lavish brunch on Sundays. 🅿 🍴	AE DC MC V	●	■		■
ORMOND BEACH: *Barnacle's Restaurant & Lounge* $$ — 869 S Atlantic Ave. **Road map** E2. (904) 673-1070. This beachside eatery is always packed; the casual atmosphere, seafood, succulent ribs, and splendid views make it a popular choice. 🍴 ● L.	AE DC MC V	●	■	●	■
ORMOND BEACH: *La Crepe en Haut Restaurant* $$$$ — 142 E Granada Blvd. **Road map** E2. (904) 673-1999. This elegant French restaurant with crisp white tablecloths, ornate crystal, and fine cuisine is off the beaten path but worth the trip. 🍴 ● Sat & Sun L; Mon; public hols.	AE MC V	●		●	■
ST. AUGUSTINE: *Salt Water Cowboy's* $ — 299 Dondanville Rd. **Road map** E1. (904) 471-2332. Set in a reconstructed fish camp, this informal restaurant serves local dishes such as alligator tail, oysters, and jambalaya. ● L; Super Bowl Sunday; Dec 24 & 25.	AE DC MC V	●		●	■
ST. AUGUSTINE: *Santa Maria* $$ — 135 Avenida Menendez. **Road map** E1. (904) 829-6578. Seafood is the specialty here, but dishes such as black bean soup, steaks, and ribs are also recommended. Located on a pier in the marina. 🍴	AE DC MC V	●		●	■
ST. AUGUSTINE: *Raintree* $$$ — 102 San Marco Ave. **Road map** E1. (904) 824-7211. Occupying one of the street's remaining historic buildings, Raintree is renowned for its award-winning food. Round off a meal of superb seafood or traditional meat dishes with a crêpe at the dessert bar. 🍴 ● L; Dec 25.	AE MC V	●	■	●	■

THE PANHANDLE

APALACHICOLA: *Seafood Grill & Steakhouse* $$
100 Market St. **Road map** B1. 📞 *(850) 653-9510.*
Located downtown, this friendly grill features a good range of meals. Tuck
into the "world's largest" fried fish sandwich, the area's famous oysters, and
pick one of the 30 or more beers offered. 🍷 ⬤ *Sun; public hols.*
AE MC V

CEDAR KEY: *Blue Desert Café* $
12518 Hwy 24. **Road map** D2. 📞 *(352) 543 9111.*
In this shotgun home, efficient staff serve an eclectic mix of Tex-Mex,
Cajun, and Asian dishes. The decor is Western kitsch, the ambience fun
and friendly, and it's the only place in town open late. 🔲 🆅 ⬤ *L; Sun & Mon.*

DESTIN: *The Donut Hole* $
635 Hwy 98. **Road map** A1. 📞 *(850) 837-8824.*
Good, hearty basic food at modest prices make this eatery a great bargain.
Breakfast, sandwiches, and key lime pie are the specialties here.

DESTIN: *The Back Porch* $$
1740 Old Hwy 98. **Road map** A1. 📞 *(850) 837-2022.*
This seafood and oyster house dishes up succulent chargrilled, broiled, and
fried fish and shellfish. Try the lobster specials. 🔲 ⬤ *Thanksgiving, Dec 25.*
AE DC MC V

DESTIN: *Marina Café* $$$
404 E Highway 98. **Road map** A1. 📞 *(850) 837-7960.*
A jewel on the Emerald Coast, this restaurant combines excellent service,
a spectacular location, and creative, internationally inspired cuisine. Early
diners benefit from two-for-one dinners 🍷 🔲 🎵 ⬤ *L; Dec 25, Jan.*
AE DC MC V

DESTIN: *Morgan's* $$
W. Highway 98. **Road map** A1. 📞 *(850) 654-3320.*
Family restaurant and entertainment center at Silver Sands factory stores.
Seafood and other regional cuisine at bargain prices. 🔲 🎵
AE DC MC V

FORT WALTON BEACH: *Staff's Seafood Restaurant* $$
24 Miracle Strip Parkway. **Road map** A1. 📞 *(850) 243-3482.*
Opened in 1913, Staff's has been well-known for its fine local recipes ever
since. The menu also offers steak, roast beef, and pork dishes.
🔲 🎵 ⬤ *L; public hols, Super Bowl.*
AE MC V

GRAYTON BEACH: *Criolla's* $$$
170 E County 30-A. **Road map** A2. 📞 *(850) 267 1267.*
Criolla's signature is an enterprising menu of elaborately concocted dishes.
The Creole set meal is unusual and very reasonable. 🍷 ⬤ *L; Sun & Mon Sep–Apr*
AE MC V

GULF BREEZE: *Bon Appetit Waterfront Café* $$
Holiday Inn, 51 Gulf Breeze Parkway. **Road map** A1. 📞 *(850) 932-3967*
This waterfront café offers appetizing Floribbean food and complimentary
beer or wine. Choose one of the mouthwatering desserts to round off your
meal. 🔲
AE DC MC V

PANAMA CITY BEACH: *Bayview Restaurant* $$$
Marriott's Bay Point Resort, 4200 Marriott Drive. **Road map** B1.
📞 *(850) 234-3307.* This establishment offers a family-oriented environment.
The new Friday night seafood buffet is sumptuous. 🍷
AE DC MC V

PANAMA CITY BEACH: *Capt. Anderson's* $$$
5551 N Lagoon Drive. **Road map** B1. 📞 *(850) 234 2225.*
Great for seafood, the menu at this huge 5-star dockside restaurant also
includes meat dishes and Greek specialties. 🍷 ⬤ *L; Nov–Jan.*
AE DC MC V

PANAMA CITY BEACH: *The Treasure Ship* $$$
3605 S Thomas Drive. **Road map** B1. 📞 *(850) 234-8881.*
Housed in a replica of a 16th-century galleon, this three-level restaurant has
open-air decks, water views, and tasty fresh seafood. Try the grilled tuna,
salmon, or mahi steaks. 🔲 🎵 ⬤ *Nov–Feb.*
AE DC MC V

PENSACOLA: *Cracker Barrel Old Country Store* $
0050 Lavelle Way. **Road map** A1. 📞 *(850) 944-2090.*
This chain family restaurant serves homecooked Southern dishes in large
portions. Try grain-fed catfish, corn bread, and collard greens. There's also a
"country store" where you can browse for souvenirs. 🆅 ⬤ *Dec 25.*
AE MC V

Price categories include a three-course meal for one, a glass of house wine, and all unavoidable extras including service and tax.
$ under $20
$$ $20–30
$$$ $30–45
$$$$ $45–60
$$$$$ over $60

CREDIT CARDS
Indicates which credit cards are accepted: AE American Express; DC Diners Club; MC MasterCard; V VISA.
CHILDREN'S FACILITIES
Small portions and high chairs available, and there may also be a special children's menu.
EARLY BIRD SPECIALS
Meals offered at a discounted price if you eat early, usually before 7pm.
GOOD REGIONAL CUISINE
Florida specialties, such as seafood or dishes with Hispanic or Caribbean influence.

	CREDIT CARDS	CHILDREN'S FACILITIES	EARLY BIRD SPECIALS	GOOD REGIONAL CUISINE	BAR
PENSACOLA: *Landry's Seafood House* $$ 905 E Gregory St. **Road map** A1. (*(850) 434-3600.* Here, tasty Cajun-style meals with a hint of the Caribbean include gumbos and freshly cooked seafood with a variety of sauces. ▯ ▦ ♫ ● *Dec 25.*	AE DC MC V	●		●	▪
PENSACOLA: *McGuire's Irish Pub* $$ 600 E Gregory St. **Road map** A1. (*(850) 433-6789.* A visit to Pensacola isn't complete without a stop at McGuire's, where huge portions of steak, pasta, pizza, and pub fare are served. Wash it down with one of their home-brewed beers. ▮ ▯ ♫ ● *Thanksgiving, Dec 25.*	AE DC MC V	●		●	▪
PENSACOLA: *Skopelos on the Bay* $$$ 670 Scenic Hwy. **Road map** A1. (*(850) 432-6565.* Famous for award-winning food, this restaurant serves seafood and meat dishes with a European twist. The Greek appetizers such as *dolmades* are delicious. ▯ ▦ ● *Sun, Mon; Dec 25, Jan 1.*	AE MC V	●		●	▪
PENSACOLA: *Barnhill's Country Buffet* $$ 10 S. Warrington Rd. **Road map** A1. (*(850) 456-2760.* Another family-style buffet where children are more than welcome. Open every day for lunch and dinner.	AE MC V	●	▪		
PENSACOLA BEACH: *Boy on a Dolphin* $$ 400 Pensacola Beach Blvd. **Road map** A1. (*(850) 932-7954.* Three decades of Greek-influenced cuisine. The catch of the day is always excellent, as are the steaks. ▯ ▦ ● *Dec 24.*	AE MC V	●		●	▪
SEASIDE: *Bud & Alley's* $$$ County Rd 30 A. **Road map** B1. (*(850) 231-5900.* This unpretentious, friendly meeting place offers an innovative menu of regional food that changes seasonally. The open-air rooftop bar has spectacular Gulf views. ▯ ▦ ♫ ● *Tue; Jan, most public hols.*	MC V	●		●	▪
TALLAHASSEE: *Chez Pierre* $$ 1215 Thomasville Rd. **Road map** C1. (*(850) 222-0936.* Southern hospitality plus good French food make this bistro a local favorite. Delicious pastries too. ▯ ♫ ● *Sun; Dec 25, Jan 1.*	AE DC MC V	●			▪
TALLAHASSEE: *Andrew's 2nd Act* $$$ 228 South Adams St. **Road map** C1. (*(850) 222-3444.* This gourmet restaurant is one of three at this address; here the set menu is excellent, and the flavor is Mediterranean dishes. Service is attentive. ▣ ▮ ▯ ♫ ● *Sat L; Sun.*	AE MC V				▪
THE GULF COAST					
ANNA MARIA ISLAND: *Sign of the Mermaid* $$$ 9707 Gulf Drive. **Road map** D3. (*(941) 778-9399.* A good spot for Sunday brunch, the Mermaid is always busy so book ahead. The seafood gumbo is recommended. No license so BYO. ▯ ● *Mon L.*	MC V	●	▪	●	
CAPTIVA ISLAND: *The Bubble Room* $$$ 15001 Captiva Rd. **Road map** D4. (*(941) 472-5558.* Here, gigantic portions of seafood and steaks and outrageous desserts are served by high-energy staff. The fun activity and funky decor make it popular with children. ● *Dec 25.*	AE DC MC V	●		●	▪
CAPTIVA ISLAND: *Chadwick's at South Seas Resort* $$$ 5400 Plantation Rd. **Road map** D4. (*(941) 472-7575.* This restaurant is laid out on several levels, with special areas for family dining. It serves an excellent Sunday brunch, and there are daily themed buffets The Porter House next door serves great steaks. ▯ ♫	AE DC MC V	●		●	▪

CAPTIVA ISLAND: *The Old Captiva House at 'Tween Waters Inn* $$$
15951 Captiva Rd. **Road map** D4. (*(941) 472-5161.*
Regional cuisine is served in fine old Florida style, in a casual atmosphere, with a choice of four price brackets for dinner entrées. 🍴 ⛿ ♫ ● *L.*

AE MC V

CLEARWATER BEACH: *Alley Cat's Café* $$
2475 McMullen Booth Rd. **Road map** D3. (*(727) 797-5555.*
The fish here is either cooked to a special house recipe, such as swordfish with ancho chili and avocado salsa, or according to taste, for example, pan-roasted or blackened. 🍴 ⛿ ● *Easter, Thanksgiving, Dec 25.*

AE MC V

CLEARWATER BEACH: *Seafood & Sunsets at Julie's Café* $$
351 S Gulfview Blvd. **Road map** D3. (*(727) 441-2548.*
This casual café across the street from the beach is a great place to enjoy the sunsets and the reasonably priced local cuisine. 🍴 ⛿ ● *Thanksgiving.*

AE MC V

DUNEDIN: *Bon Appetit* $$
148 Marina Plaza. **Road map** D3. (*(727) 733-2151.*
Consistently good food with an American flavor is dished up here and accompanied by breathtaking views of St. Joseph's Sound. 🅿 🍴 ⛿

AE DC MC V

FORT MYERS: *The Veranda* $$$
2122 2nd St. **Road map** E4. (*(941) 332-2065.*
This charming restaurant housed in a 1902 building offers original culinary creations like artichoke fritters stuffed with blue crab. The decor is Deep South and the service attentive. 🅿 🍴 ⛿ ♫ ● *Sat L; Sun; public hols.*

AE MC V

ST. PETERSBURG: *Columbia Restaurant* $$$
800 2nd Ave NE. **Road map** D3. (*(727) 822-8000.*
One in a chain of Columbia restaurants in Florida offering fine Spanish cuisine, this one also has spectacular views of Tampa Bay. 🅿 🍴

AE DC MC V

ST. PETERSBURG: *Keystone Club* $$
320 4th St N. **Road map** D3. (*(727) 822-6600.*
This eatery has an informal atmosphere, is popular with locals, and serves the best prime rib steak for miles around. 🍴 ● *L; some public hols.*

AE DC MC V

ST. PETERSBURG: *Merchand's Bar & Grill and Terrace Room* $$$
Renaissance Vinoy Resort, 501 5th Ave. **Road map** D3. (*(727) 894-1000, x511.*
Located in a beautiful 1920s hotel, this elegant restaurant features largely Mediterranean-style food. The bouillabaisse is recommended. 🅿 🍴 ♫

AE DC MC V

ST. PETE BEACH: *Hurricane Seafood Restaurant* $
807 Gulf Way. **Road map** D3. (*(727) 360-9558.*
Set right on the beach, this restaurant prides itself on its crab cakes and fresh Florida grouper, which comes blackened, grilled, broiled, or in a sandwich. The cocktail deck is especially popular at sunset. 🍴 ⛿

MC V

ST. PETE BEACH: *Maritana Grille* $$$$
Don CeSar Beach Resort, 3400 Gulf Blvd. **Road map** D3. (*(727) 360-1882.*
A winner of several culinary awards, the Maritana Grille boasts elaborate dishes using local and organic produce. The atmosphere is relaxed and the decor tropical. 🅿 🍴 ● *L*

AE DC MC V

SANIBEL ISLAND: *Windows On The Water* $$$
Sundial Beach Resort, 1451 Middle Gulf Drive. **Road map** D4 (*(941) 395-6014.*
In a beautiful location overlooking the Gulf of Mexico, this rather elegant restaurant features delicious Floribbean cuisine. 🍴

AE DC MC V

SARASOTA: *Bart's Bayside* $$
230 Sarasota Quay. **Road map** D3. (*(941) 954-3839.*
Choose the steak or tasty seafood such as stuffed lobster. Dine indoors or on the terrace overlooking the bay. 🅿 🍴 ⛿ ♫ *Fri & Sat.*

AE DC MC V

SARASOTA: *Michael's On East* $$$
1212 East Avenue S. **Road map** D3. (*(941) 366-0007.*
One of Sarasota's premier restaurants, Michael's has innovative regional cuisine and a large selection of microbrewed beers. 🍴 🅿 ● *Sat & Sun L.*

AE DC MC V

TAMPA: *Columbia Restaurant* $$
2117 E 7th Ave, Ybor City. **Road map** D3. (*(813) 248-4961*
This is the original Columbia restaurant and has been serving Spanish and Cuban food since 1905. There are several dining rooms with beautiful tiled floors and a nightly flamenco show. 🍴 🅿 ♫

AE DC MC V

Price categories include a three-course meal for one, a glass of house wine, and all unavoidable extras including service and tax.
§ under $20
§§ $20–30
§§§ $30–45
§§§§ $45–60
§§§§§ over $60

CREDIT CARDS
Indicates which credit cards are accepted: AE American Express; DC Diners Club; MC MasterCard; V VISA.
CHILDREN'S FACILITIES
Small portions and high chairs available, and there may also be a special children's menu.
EARLY BIRD SPECIALS
Meals offered at a discounted price if you eat early, usually before 7pm.
GOOD REGIONAL CUISINE
Florida specialties, such as seafood or dishes with Hispanic or Caribbean influence.

	CREDIT CARDS	CHILDREN'S FACILITIES	EARLY BIRD SPECIALS	GOOD REGIONAL CUISINE	BAR
TAMPA: *Lauro Ristorante Italiano* §§ 3915 Henderson Blvd. **Road map** D3. 📞 (813) 281-2100. This restaurant offers delicious traditional Italian food in pleasant surroundings. Good service, moderate prices. 🍴 ● *Sat L; Sun.L*	AE DC MC V				●
TAMPA: *Bern's Steak House* §§§ 1208 S Howard Ave. **Road map** D3. 📞 (813) 251-2421. A must for meat lovers, Bern's has made steak cuisine a fine art. Each order is prepared to your specifications, and accompanied by organic vegetables. It is very popular and reservations are essential. 🅿 🍴 🎵 ● *L; Dec 25.*	AE DC MC V				●
TAMPA: *Oystercatchers* §§§ 6200 Courtney Campbell Causeway. **Road map** D3. 📞 (813) 281-9116. Right in the Hyatt Regency Westshore hotel, this place specializes in seafood. Choose from the menu or the catch of the day on display. 🅿 🍴 🎵 ● *Dec 25.*	AE DC MC V	●		●	●
TAMPA: *Mis en Place* §§§§ 442 W Kennedy Blvd. **Road map** D3. 📞 (813) 254-5373. The innovative menu of this busy bistro changes daily but never fails to please. Locals love this place so reserve ahead. 🍴 ● *Sat L, Mon D; Sun.*	AE DC MC V			●	●
VENICE: *Sharky's on the Pier* §§ 1600 S. Harbor Drive. **Road map** D4. 📞 (941) 488-1456. Fish, cooked in a variety of styles, is the house specialty; your choice can be broiled, blackened, chargrilled, or fried. 🍴 �"🎵 ● *Thanksgiving, Dec 25.*	AE MC V	●		●	●

THE EVERGLADES AND THE KEYS

	CREDIT CARDS	CHILDREN'S FACILITIES	EARLY BIRD SPECIALS	GOOD REGIONAL CUISINE	BAR
ISLAMORADA: *Manny and Isa's Kitchen* § MM 81.6, Overseas Hwy. **Road map** F5. 📞 (305) 664-5019. Nothing fancy, but this place serves authentic Cuban dishes and tasty fried lobster at budget prices. 🍴 ● *Tue; Oct; Thanksgiving, Dec 25 & Jan 1.*	AE MC V	●		●	
ISLAMORADA: *Green Turtle Inn* §§ MM 81.5, Overseas Hwy. **Road map** F5. 📞 (305) 664-9031. A Keys tradition since 1947; locals flock to eat the famous turtle chowder and alligator steak. A pianist entertains in the evenings. 🍴 🎵 ● *Mon.*	AE DC MC V	●		●	●
ISLAMORADA: *Marker 88* §§§ MM 88, Overseas Hwy. **Road map** F5. 📞 (305) 852-9315. This gourmet restaurant overlooking Florida Bay offers creative Keys seafood as well as classic European cuisine. 🍴 ● *Mon; Thanksgiving, Dec 25.*	AE DC MC V	●		●	●
KEY LARGO: *The Fish House Restaurant and Seafood Market* §§ MM 102.4, Overseas Hwy. **Road map** F5. 📞 (305) 451-4665. It looks like a shack, but this is the place locals depend on for the freshest fish and conch salad. No frills, just good seafood.	MC V			●	●
KEY LARGO: *Mrs. Mac's Kitchen* §§ MM 99.4, Overseas Hwy. **Road map** F5. 📞 (305) 451-3722. A local institution, this unpretentious diner, serving overstuffed sandwiches, bowls of chili, and fresh seafood, is great. 🍴 ● *Sun; most public hols.*		●			
KEY WEST: *Blue Heaven* §§ 729 Thomas St. **Road map** E5. 📞 (305) 296-8666. Housed in a wonderful old Key West building, this friendly restaurant offers delicious seafood in a laid-back atmosphere. The seating at painted wooden tables is basic. 🆅 🍴 🚗 🎵 ● *Thanksgiving, Dec 25.*	MC V	●		●	
KEY WEST: *Mangia Mangia Pasta Café* §§ 900 Southard St. **Road map** E5. 📞 (305) 294-2469. Superb freshly made pasta and the tasty accompanying sauces have earned this centrally located café an enviable reputation. 🍴 ● *L; most public hols.*	AE MC V				

KEY WEST: *Banana Cafe* $$ — AE DC MC V
1211 Duval St. **Road map** E5. ☎ (305) 294-7227.
A fabulous variety of crepes heads the menu here, and the intimate. beachside tables only add to the ambience. 🍴 🕏

KEY WEST: *Mangoes* $$$ — AE DC MC V
700 Duval St. **Road map** E5. ☎ (305) 292-4606.
Choose from fabulous salads (most of which are suitable for vegetarians) and innovative Floribbean dishes at this Duval Street bistro. Sidewalk tables are perfect for people-watching. 🕏 🅥

KEY WEST: *Louie's Back Yard* $$$$ — AE DC MC V
700 Waddell Ave. **Road map** E5. ☎ (305) 294-1061.
The menu at this beautifully restored conch house restaurant features the freshest seafood blended with Caribbean and Thai flavors. Set amid tropical vegetation, this may be the best place on the island. 🍴 🕏 ● 10 days in Sep.

KEY WEST: *Pier House Resort* $$$$ — AE DC MC V
Pier House Resort, 1 Duval St. **Road map** E5. ☎ (305) 296-4600.
This exclusive waterfront restaurant, one of the best in the Keys, serves fancy Florida cuisine such as lobster with marinated plantain. Reserve an outside table for the best sunset views (see p284). 🍴 🕏 🎵 ● Mon–Sat L.

MARATHON: *Brian's in Paradise* $ — AE DC MC V
MM 52, Overseas Hwy. **Road map** E5. ☎ (305) 743-3183.
Family-style dining with a long menu and many specials under $10. Choose from burgers, fish dishes, and home-style meals. 🍴 ● Thanksgiving, Dec 25.

MARATHON: *Kelsey's Fine Dining* $$$ — AE MC V
MM 48.5, Overseas Hwy. **Road map** E5. ☎ (305) 743-9018.
Located on the docks of Faro Blanco Resort, Kelsey's offers seafood and steaks and will also prepare your own catch for you. 🍴 🕏 🎵 ● L; Mon.

MARCO ISLAND: *Konrad's* $$ — AE DC MC V
Mission San Marco. **Road map** E4. ☎ (941) 642 3332.
Konrad's boasts stylish decor and one of the best salad bars on the island. The early bird dinners and the scampi are very popular. 🅿 🕏 ● Dec 24, 25.

MARCO ISLAND: *Snook Inn* $$ — AE DC MC V
1215 Bald Eagle Drive. **Road map** E4. ☎ (941) 394-3313.
Seafood and steaks are the specialty at this waterfront eatery, and they'll also cook your own fish for you. Great sunset views from the separate bar. 🕏 🎵

MARCO ISLAND: *Olde Marco Island Inn & Suites* $$$ — AE MC V
100 Palm St. **Road map** E4. ☎ (941) 394-3131.
There are six dining rooms at this upscale restaurant, built as a lodge in 1883. Fine Continental cuisine and a lovely setting. 🍴 🕏 🎵 ● L.

NAPLES: *First Watch* $ — AE MC V
1400 Gulf Shore Blvd N. **Road map** E4. ☎ (941) 434-0005.
The best place in town for breakfast, this family-oriented country kitchen just opposite Lowdermilk Park is always busy. 🕏 ● D; Thanksgiving, Dec 25.

NAPLES: *Remy's Bistro* $ — AE DC MC V
2300 Pine Ridge Rd. **Road map** E4. ☎ (941) 403-9922.
Remy's offers fresh fish, burgers, and great sandwiches. Try the grilled tuna sesame. Happy hour has two-for-one specials. 🅿 🍴 ● Dec. 25, Jul 4.

NAPLES: *The Dock at Crayton Cove* $$ — AE MC V
12th Ave S, on Naples Bay. **Road map** E4. ☎ (941) 263-9940.
Seafood dishes predominate at this restaurant next to the marina. Try the generous sandwiches or the raw bar. 🍴 🕏 ● Thanksgiving, Dec 25

NAPLES: *Bistro 821* $$$ — AE DC MC V
821 5th Ave S. **Road map** E4. ☎ (941) 261-5821.
Try this stylish bistro for creative World cuisine. Choose from the menu or a selection of daily specials featuring dishes such as lemon sole stuffed with scallop and lobster mousse. 🍴 🕏 ● L, Thanksgiving, Dec 25, Super Bowl.

NAPLES: *Opus* $$$ — AE MC V
5200 Tamiami Trail N, Suite 103. **Road map** E4. ☎ (941) 261-2555.
This brand new restaurant specializes in Continental and American dishes. The daily specials always include fresh seafood. The atmosphere is friendly, and the food delicious. 🅿 🍴

Bars and Cafés

Florida's easy-going lifestyle helps to ensure an abundance of bars and cafés. The term café often denotes an informal, bistro-style restaurant but can also refer to a coffee house or, indeed, a bar. Sports bars are very popular and usually have several television sets, each tuned to a different station – but frequently the sound is turned off while loud music plays in the background. Many bars and cafés have a happy hour, generally from 4 to 7pm, when drinks are less expensive and snacks are often served free of charge; those included here are good for just a drink as well as a meal, or a coffee and a snack.

MIAMI

Miami Beach: *News Café*
800 Ocean Drive. **Map** 2 F4.
📞 *(305) 538-6397.*
With ample sidewalk tables, this laid-back café is the top meeting place in South Beach and is open 24 hours a day. People gather to drink, eat, and take in the Ocean Drive scene. The eclectic menu features good breakfasts and huge bowls of pasta as well as light, healthy meals. There are a dozen kinds of coffee, and the pastry list is equally long. 🍴 🍴 *AE DC MC V*

Miami Beach: *Van Dyke Café*
846 Lincoln Rd. **Map** 2 E2.
📞 *(305) 534-3600.*
This popular SoBe hangout, with tables inside and out, occupies a lovely restored Mediterranean-style building. House specialties are bread pudding and zabaglione with fresh berries. There is a good choice of coffees and herbal teas, and a jazz trio performs in the evenings. 🍴 🍴 🎵 *AE DC MC V*

Downtown: *Hard Rock Café*
401 Biscayne Blvd. **Map** 4 F1.
📞 *(305) 377-3110.*
Tourists and locals alike fill the Hard Rock Café, which is festooned with rock memorabilia and throbs with loud music. There's a bar for those intent on drinking and soaking up the atmosphere, but reserve ahead if you want to eat. The food is American, from juicy burgers to hot, tasty apple pie, and the portions are generous. 🍴 🎵 *AE DC MC V*

Coral Gables: *Café Books & Books*
265 Aragon Ave. **Map** 5 C1.
📞 *(305) 448-9544.*
Located in the courtyard of Books & Books, this European-style deli serves soup and sandwiches and fantastic desserts, all made from scratch by Lyon & Lyon Caterers. There's a full coffee bar, and it's open 7 days, 9am til 11pm. 🍴 🍴 *AE MC V*

Coral Gables: *Doc Dammers Saloon*
180 Aragon Ave. **Map** 5 C1.
📞 *(305) 441-2600.*
Inside the Omni Colonnade Hotel, this well-stocked, mahogany Deco bar is frequented by a sophisticated, 30-plus set. Tasty food is served, the Latin American and Caribbean specialties being the highlights. 🍴 *AE MC V*

Coconut Grove: *Fat Tuesday's*
CocoWalk, 3015 Grand Ave. **Map** 6 E4.
📞 *(305) 441-2992.*
This former sports bar has three satellite dishes, 51 TVs, and five pool tables. It is now one of the Fat Tuesday's chain bar/cafes, which serves as a meeting place for the young at heart. US and imported beer are available, and the menu offers light meals and snacks, such as buffalo wings, veggie pizza, fajita burgers, giant burgers, and Mississippi mud pie. 🍴 *AE DC MC V*

THE GOLD AND TREASURE COASTS

Boca Raton: *Pete Rose's Ballpark Café*
8144 W Glades Rd. **Road map** F4.
📞 *(561) 488-7383.*
There's plenty of Cincinnati Reds memorabilia at the Ballpark Café, as well as the usual videos and bar games. You can also shoot a game of pool or watch TV at your table. A live sports radio show is broadcast from 6 to 8 pm, when the place is packed with people on their way home from work. 🍴 *AE DC MC V*

Fort Lauderdale: *Pier Top Lounge*
Pier 66, 2301 SE 17th St.
Road map F4.
📞 *(954) 525-6666.*
It takes one hour for the revolving rooftop lounge in the Hyatt Regency Pier 66 Hotel to rotate a full 360-degree turn. Customers are treated to some breathtaking views of Fort Lauderdale's skyline

and its waterways – a spectacular sight at sunset. There's live music and dancing, but no cover charge. 🎵 *AE DC MC V*

Fort Lauderdale: *Shooters*
3033 NE 32nd Ave. **Road map** F4.
📞 *(954) 566-2855.*
This waterfront bar and restaurant is a people-watcher's paradise. It is always packed with a casual crowd eating, drinking, and watching the boats sail by. The menu is quite extensive and reasonably priced. You can nibble on dishes such as shrimp and crab cakes, or tuck into more substantial food like seared tuna salad or a Florida grouper sandwich. 🍴 🍴 *AE DC MC V*

Palm Beach: *The Leopard Lounge*
363 Cocoanut Row. **Road map** F4.
📞 *(561) 659-5800.*
Located in the Chesterfield Hotel, the Leopard Lounge is strikingly decorated with scarlet and black drapes, and the leopard theme is picked out in the plush carpeting and tablecloths. On weekends the place is jammed with locals who dance to the sounds of the "big band" era, performed live. A full menu is served. 🍴 🎵 *AE DC MC V*

ORLANDO AND THE SPACE COAST

Orlando: *Blazing Pianos*
8445 International Drive.
Road map E2.
📞 *(407) 363-5104.*
One of Orlando's most popular night spots, this large piano bar offers musical entertainment every night, drawing a steady crowd of mixed ages. The stage has three Yamaha grand pianos and musicians play requests and conduct a sing-along. Food is served, and the full bar offers imported and local beers, but the real attraction here is the music. 🍴 🎵 *AE DC MC V*

Orlando: *Cheyenne Saloon and Opera House*
Church Street Station, 129 W Church St.
Road map E2.
📞 *(407) 422-2434*
This is downtown Orlando's best country and western music venue. The tri-level saloon has balcony seating in restored church pews that overlook the stage. The entertainment ranges from country music to demonstrations of clog dancing. You can snack on the excellent appetizers or feast on barbecued ribs, grilled chicken, and steaks. 🍴 🎵 *AE DC MC V*

THE NORTHEAST

JACKSONVILLE: *River City Brewing Company*
835 Museum Circle. **Road map** E1.
(*(904) 398-2299.*
Home-brewed beer and a varied selection of food at reasonable prices make this a popular spot with the locals. On Friday there's a live band, and Saturday nights offers a local DJ. There is no cover charge. 🖼 🍴 🎵 *AE DC MC V*

St. Augustine: *A1A Ale Works*
1 King St. **Road map** E1.
(*(904) 829-2977.*
Situated at the foot of the Bridge of Lions, this friendly pub and restaurant has a microbrewery on site. Ale aficionados come for the seven varieties of home-brewed ale that are available. Live bands play at weekends. 🖼 🍴 🎵 *AE DC MC V*

St. Augustine: *OC White's Seafood and Spirits*
118 Avenida Menendez. **Road map** E1.
(*(904) 824-0808.*
In an 18th-century building found across the street from St. Augustine's marina, OC White's offers a great view and live entertainment nightly. The interior is decorated with wax figures of pirates, and a full menu of seafood, steaks and burgers is served. 🖼 🍴 🎵 *AE MC V*

Daytona Beach: *Oyster Pub*
555 Seabreeze Blvd. **Road map** E2.
(*(904) 255-6348.*
Just one block from the beach, this pub has a raw bar serving fresh oysters, shrimp, and other seafood. During happy hour, prices are cut for both drinks and seafood. There is sports coverage on 27 TVs, a pool room, and a disc jockey on weekends. 🍴 🎵 *AE MC V*

Gainesville: *Purple Porpoise Oyster Pub*
1728 W University Ave. **Road map** D2.
(*(352) 376-1667.*
This is a long-established college bar for students at Gainesville's University of Florida. What it lacks in sophistication it makes up for in atmosphere, and the staff is very friendly. A band plays on Thursday evenings. 🍴 🎵 *AE DC MC V*

THE PANHANDLE

Panama City Beach: *Shuckum's Oyster Pub*
15614 Front Beach Rd. **Road map** B1.
(*(850) 235-3214.*
The bar at this unpretentious and popular watering hole is covered with signed dollar bills left by satisfied customers. Shuckum's is

best known for its local oysters, which are served raw, baked, steamed, or fried in a sandwich. Other seafood dishes are also available. 🖼 🍴 🎵 *MC V*

Pensacola Beach: *Sidelines Sports Bar and Restaurant*
2 Via de Luna Drive. **Road map** A1.
(*(850) 934-3660.*
This informal meeting place in Pensacola Beach has a different special for each night of the week; on "Cajun Night," for example, they serve up Cajun Bloody Marys. There's seating in booths, and the ubiquitous sports memorabilia and giant-screen televisions adorn the walls. 🍴 🎵 *AE MC V*

Tallahassee: *Banjo's Steakhouse*
2335 Apalachee Pkwy. **Road map** C1.
(*(850) 877-8111.*
Just a few miles from the center of Tallahassee on US 27 is this casual steakhouse and bar. Banjo's is famous for its barbecued ribs, steaks, and chicken, and the salad bar is enough for a meal by itself. There's a kid's menu too; this is the place for good, old-fashioned BBQ. 🖼 🍴 🎵 *AE, MC*

THE GULF COAST

Lee Island Coast: *The Mucky Duck*
11546 Andy Rosse Lane, Captiva Island. **Road map** D4.
(*(941) 472-3434.*
This British-style pub occupies a charming 1930s building in Captiva town. Its creator, a former British policeman, named it after his favorite pub back home. You can play darts, enjoy a beer, and watch the sunset. The eclectic menu has English meals such as fish and chips and vegetarian platters. 🖼 🍴 *AE DC MC V*

Tampa: *Elmer's Sports Café*
2003 E 7th Ave, Ybor City. **Road map** D3.
(*(813) 248-5855.*
Ybor City's original sports bar is renowned for its thick and chewy pizzas, great wings, and good beers. Elmer's has giant-screen TVs scattered all around the café, and there's also a pool table. This place is far from fancy, but the homemade food is tasty and the atmosphere pleasant. 🍴 *AE MC V*

Tampa: *Ovo Café*
1901 E 7th Ave, Ybor City. **Road map** D3.
(*(813) 248-6979.*
With freshly cut flowers on every table, fine art on the walls, and cabinets displaying jewelry, this informal bistro offers food for the

eyes as well as the stomach. One of the house specialties is potato-stuffed pasta shells, but the salads and puddings, such as Belgian waffles, are also recommended. There's a separate bar too. 🍴 *AE MC V*

THE EVERGLADES
AND THE KEYS

Naples: *HB's On The Gulf*
851 Gulf Shore Blvd N.
Road map E4.
(*(941) 261-9100.*
Sophisticated HB's On The Gulf, opened in 1946, is located in the Naples Beach Hotel on Naples Pier. It is a fine place for watching the sun go down, although you need to arrive early to get a seat. After sunset, the huge outside bar is packed with people, and a live band provides musical entertainment. HB's serves a full menu, but the food is not the highlight here. 🖼 🍴 🎵 *AE DC MC V*

Key West: *Hog's Breath Saloon*
400 Front St. **Road map** E5.
(*(305) 292-2032.*
The original Hog's Breath Saloon was established by an Alabama expatriate in Fort Walton Beach in 1976, but it moved down to Key West in 1988. It is now a local favorite, offering a raw bar, local seafood dishes, and tasty desserts (including a fine version of the famous key lime pie). There is live music every day from 1pm until 2am. 🖼 🍴 🎵 *AE MC V*

Key West: *Jimmy Buffet's Margaritaville Café*
500 Duval St. **Road map** E5.
(*(305) 292-1435.*
There are plenty of Jimmy Buffet trinkets here, both on display and for sale *(see p285)*, though the local singer-songwriter is rarely seen. Frosty Margaritas are the house specialty, and light meals, sandwiches, burgers, and local seafood such as conch fritters are also available. 🍴 🎵 *AE MC V*

Key West: *Sloppy Joe's*
201 Duval St. **Road map** F5.
(*(305) 294-5717.*
Formerly Ernest Hemingway's favorite drinking place *(see p284)*, Sloppy Joe's is more commercial than in the novelist's day, attracting mainly tourists. However, it retains its Key West character, and when bands play it can be hard to get a seat. The menu includes typical bar fare, with jalapeño or conch fritters, chicken fingers and fries, and the renowned "original Sloppy Joe" burger. 🍴 🎵 *MC V*

SHOPPING IN FLORIDA

**Hammock shop sign
in Cedar Key**

SHOPPING IS probably the most popular pastime in Florida, and Miami in particular attracts many overseas shoppers. The state is known for its discount stores, but at the other end of the scale also boasts some extraordinarily upscale shops, usually clustered in shopping districts or malls.

For first-time visitors to Florida, the shopping culture may take some getting used to. Rather than shopping in town or city centers, Floridians generally gravitate toward the huge out-of-town shopping malls, where department stores and all kinds of other shops sell everything from clothes to computers. If you're after souvenirs and gifts, the small specialty shops are your best bet.

For a taste of Florida's souvenirs and other good buys, see pages 334–5. If you're looking for something specific, local tourist offices can provide listings of stores in their area. Shops in Miami are described on pages 92–3.

Mizner Park in Boca Raton, with shops as elegant as its architecture

WHEN TO SHOP

MOST STORES open from 10am to 6pm Monday to Saturday, often staying open late once a week. Shopping mall stores may keep longer hours. Some stores open on Sundays too, typically noon to 6pm, while some (mainly in cities) never close.

SALES TAX

FLORIDA LEVIES a 6 percent sales tax (may vary in different counties) on all goods except children's clothes, drugs, and groceries. Tax is not included in displayed prices but is automatically added to the bill.

SHOPPING MALLS

SHOPPING MALLS are a quintessential feature of the shopping scene in Florida. As well as shops, malls provide all kinds of facilities from movies to restaurants, so in theory you can spend a whole day in the mall and want for nothing. Parking is easy, and out-of-town malls can normally be reached by public bus.

As well as department stores, there is often a daunting array of smaller one-of-a-kind shops and chains, from bookstores such as Barnes & Noble to clothes shops like The Gap.

Miami is well known for its malls, such as the posh Bal Harbour Shops (see p92), and affluent Gold Coast towns like Boca Raton and Palm Beach also have a good selection. Malls, however, are part of the scenery all over Florida.

SHOPPING DISTRICTS

FOR THOSE horrified by the idea of shopping malls, Florida's open-air shopping districts are a fine alternative. Some of these have breathed new life into historic districts, such as St. Armands Circle in Sarasota (see p255) and Hyde Park Village in Tampa (see p248). Palm Beach's Worth Avenue (see pp114–15), one of the world's most exclusive shopping streets, has been fashionable since the 1920s. By contrast, pristine Mizner Park in Boca Raton (see p126) is new but built in an old style.

Shops in these districts are predominantly upscale, but you find more down-to-earth places too, particularly those geared to the tourist market – such as the quaint Johns Pass Village near Madeira Beach on the Gulf Coast (see p238).

DEPARTMENT STORES

MOST SHOPPING MALLS include at least one department store. These are often huge affairs, offering an amazing range of goods and services, from complimentary gift-

**A stylish fashion boutique in Bal
Harbour Shops in Miami**

wrapping to assistants to help you with your shopping.

Most of the department stores can be found throughout the US, and all have a particular reputation for their quality or merchandise. For example, Bloomingdale's has a good name for its stock of new fashions and also its gourmet food. Some stores deal in fashion, such as the elegant Saks Fifth Avenue, most famous for its designer clothes, Neiman Marcus and the conservative Lord and Taylor. Florida's own, long-established Burdines chain has branches throughout the state, but it has lost out to the nationwide chains.

For essentials, from pencils to toothpaste, you need look no further than the no-frills supermarkets such as Target, K Mart, and Wal-Mart, which you'll find everywhere. Sears and JC Penney also deal in general merchandise.

SHOPPING FOR BARGAINS

FOR SOME PEOPLE, the chief appeal of Florida's shops are their cut-price goods. Discount stores carry all kinds of general merchandise, but electronic equipment, household goods, and clothes are the biggest draw. Some stores specialize in inexpensive designer clothes, chief among them being Ross, TJ Maxx, and Marshalls, with branches in all major cities.

Particularly popular among bargain-hunters are the factory outlet malls, where slightly imperfect or discontinued merchandise is sold at 50 to 75 percent below the retail price. At most of these you

One among Micanopy's collection of quaint antique shops

find brand-name stores selling household items and all types of clothing, such as Levi's jeans and Benetton sweaters.

Orlando's International Drive (see p176) is lined with a multitude of discount and outlet stores. You can even find cut-price Disney souvenirs here, but be warned that the quality may not be up to that found in the theme parks themselves.

Flea markets, usually large, lively affairs that function on weekends, are popular territory for bargains. Used goods may not interest you, but at most markets you'll find crafts, antiques, and other things you might consider taking home, and plenty of food stands. Some markets are equally good for their entertainment value, such as the Fort Lauderdale Swap Shop (see p130), the state's largest flea market and allegedly its most popular attraction after Walt Disney World.

GIFTS AND SOUVENIRS

FRESH ORANGES are a popular buy for Florida's visitors. The best quality fruit is grown by the Indian River on the east coast (see p111), where shops and stalls sell oranges by the sackful. Shops can normally send the fruit home for you if you live within the US.

Seashells have wider appeal, but always check the origins of these. The Lee Island Coast (see pp264–5) is most famous for its shells, and you can buy legally harvested specimens in the Shell Factory near Fort Myers (see p263). The shells and coral touted by roadside stalls along US 1 in the Keys are mostly imported. The same stalls

Sponges for sale in Key West

often sell natural sponges, but the classic place for these is Tarpon Springs (see p237).

Native Americans sell crafts made on their reservations at Miccosukee Indian Village (see p271) and in Hollywood (see p132), but Florida is not a great place for crafts. Antiques are more plentiful. Several towns are famous for their antique shops, including Micanopy (see p208) and Dania (see p132).

Disney has turned merchandising into a fine art, and shopping is a major activity at Walt Disney World and at Orlando's other theme parks. More mundane museum stores are good for souvenirs too, from reproductions of artifacts to educational games.

One of Florida's many factory outlets, advertising its bargain prices

What to Buy in Florida

Chocolate
sea shells

PEOPLE WILL PROBABLY TELL YOU that you can buy just about anything you could ever want in Florida, from a designer bikini to a state-of-the art CD player – or even a new home. Indeed some overseas visitors go to Florida specifically to shop. Even if you are searching for more humble souvenirs or gifts, you will have your choice in the state's theme parks and seaside tourist centers. You may have to search around if you want to avoid kitsch memorabilia – though, in fact, this is what Florida probably does best and is what evokes more than anything else the flavor of the Sunshine State.

Miami Dolphins cap

Unmistakably Florida
All over Florida you can buy fun (and tacky) souvenirs from towels to ashtrays, often at reasonable prices. They are frequently emblazoned with "Florida," a palm tree, alligator, or some other characteristic image.

Keyring

**Dried meal from the
Kennedy Space Center**

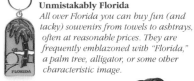

Theme Park Fare
All the theme parks, from Universal Studios to Busch Gardens, produce their own merchandise, designed to appeal to all ages.

**Fake Oscar from
Universal Studios**

**Tile with flamingos –
a favorite motif**

**Alligator
money bank**

Seminole Crafts
Crafts made by Florida's Seminole Indians are available in a few places (see p333). You can pick up dolls and jewelry for just a few dollars, and brightly colored clothes, bags, and blankets can be a good buy too.

Hand-Rolled Cigars
The Cuban tradition of hand-rolling cigars survives in Ybor City in Tampa (see pp246–7) and in Miami's Little Havana (see p93), though many are now made by machine. They make a fine gift for cigar-smoking friends.

Books
Books about Miami's Art Deco district often feature superb photos and make a lasting souvenir of the city. Or take home the flavors of Florida in the form of a cookbook.

Latin Music
If you get a taste for the Latin rhythms of Miami's Hispanic community, there is plenty of locally produced music to buy.

INEXPENSIVE GOODS

Many overseas visitors to the US will find that because of lower taxes a whole range of goods are cheaper than they are at home, including jeans, sunglasses, running shoes, CDs, cameras, books, and so on. Florida also has many discount stores *(see p333)* that offer lower prices still; small electrical appliances are often a good buy. Downtown Miami is famous for its bargain shops *(see pp92–3)*, which sell primarily low-cost gold, jewelry, and electronic equipment. Feel free to bargain if you have the nerve. Note that if you buy electronic equipment you will need to get a transformer for it to work outside the US. Most shops are used to foreign visitors and can send bulky purchases back home for you.

T-Shirts
Sold everywhere from gift shops to ordinary discount stores, T-shirts can be very cheap – but you should check the quality before buying.

Authentic cowboy boots

Leather belt

Western Gear
The leather goods sold in stores such as JW Cooper are not necessarily made in Florida, and may not appeal to visitors from Texas. However, they are often a good value by international standards.

THE FLAVORS OF FLORIDA

Florida is famous worldwide for its citrus fruits, which you can buy either fresh (all year round in the case of some varieties) or preserved – as colorful candies, jams, or jellies, or as tasty marinades and oils for cooking. For those with a sweet tooth there are all sorts of sugary goodies, from sticky coconut patties to chewy sweets like salt water taffy. Locally made chocolate is not of great quality, but often comes in fun shapes.

Coconut patties

A basket of jellied citrus fruit, a favorite edible souvenir

Florida-grown oranges, sold by the sack

Colorful salt water taffy, popular among visitors

Lime marmalade

Tangerine jam or "butter"

Hot jalapeño pepper jelly

Mango marinade

Key lime oil for cooking

ENTERTAINMENT IN FLORIDA

Whether your preference is for a Broadway drama, a lavish Las Vegas-style floorshow, a night in a disco, or a bit of gambling, Florida has something for everyone. You'll find the greatest range of entertainment in South Florida, particularly along the Gold Coast and in Miami *(see pp94–5)*, but Sarasota and Tampa are also major cultural centers. Walt Disney World and Orlando offer the best choice of family entertainment, with theme parks galore to thrill the children during the daytime and dinner

Performer at Wild Bill's dinner show

shows at night. In the Northeast and the Panhandle the entertainment is more limited, being best in resorts like Panama City Beach and university cities such as Gainesville and Tallahassee.

Wherever you are, in cities with distinct mainland and beach areas, such as Fort Lauderdale, the liveliest nightlife is on the waterfront. As far as the performing arts are concerned, most high-quality shows take place between October and April, although there is a good choice of events all year round.

The Raymond F. Kravis Center for the Performing Arts, West Palm Beach

SOURCES OF INFORMATION

Most regional newspapers in Florida have a special weekend section that lists all local attractions and events, as well as details of venues. Local Convention and Visitors' Bureaus and chambers of commerce are also chock-a-block with brochures.

MAKING RESERVATIONS

The easiest way to purchase tickets for a concert, play, football game, or other event is to call the relevant box office and pay by credit card. Some places, however, will require you to make your reservation through **Ticketmaster**. This company runs an extensive pay-by-phone operation and also has outlets in music and discount stores. It charges a commission of $2–8 per ticket above the ticket's face value, depending on the event.

MAJOR VENUES

Florida's largest venues, some of which are known as performing arts centers, are used for a whole range of performances, from operas to rock concerts, as well as for special events including, in some cases, sports events. This is where major national touring companies or artists usually perform, though you can sometimes see local productions here too.

The following are among the most important venues in Florida: the **Raymond F. Kravis Center for the Performing Arts** in West Palm Beach; Fort Lauderdale's **Broward Center for the Performing Arts**; the huge **Tampa Bay Performing Arts Center** in Tampa; and the **Van Wezel Performing Arts Hall** in

Theatre emblem, Pensacola

Sarasota. Other major theaters with large arenas include St. Petersburg's **Tropicana Field**, Florida's only domed stadium, and the **Florida Citrus Bowl** in Orlando, a 70,000-seat arena where stars from Paul McCartney to George Michael perform. The huge **All-tel Stadium** in Jacksonville hosts major rock concerts, too.

THEATER

Road shows, often lavish productions with extravagant sets and big casts, originate on Broadway and are the highest-quality productions you are likely to see in Florida. The state has several good theater companies of its own, whose shows are performed in smaller, more atmospheric spots such as the **Mann Performing Arts Hall** in Fort Myers or Key West's **Red Barn Theater**. The **Florida State University Center for the Performing Arts** is home to Sarasota's own Asolo Theater Company. The building, originally the opera house of Dunfermline in Scotland, was brought to Sarasota in the 1980s. The **Players of Sarasota** is the city's longest established theater company, such famous actors as Montgomery Clift launched their careers. Its performances of musicals and plays usually earn high praise.

CLASSICAL MUSIC, OPERA, AND DANCE

MOST MAJOR cities have their own symphony orchestra. The **Florida Philharmonic Orchestra**, which performs mainly in Miami and in the cities along the Gold Coast, is the best in the state – but Miami's New World Symphony *(see p94)* is better known internationally. Keep an eye open for performances by the **Concert Association of Florida** (in Fort Lauderdale and Miami) and the Jacksonville Symphony Orchestra, which is based at the city's **Times-Union Center for the Performing Arts**.

The state's largest opera company is the **Florida Grand Opera**, the fruit of a merger in 1994 of Miami's and Fort Lauderdale's own opera companies. It puts on about five major productions every year in Broward and Dade counties. **Gold Coast Opera** presents classical opera at four locations in southeast Florida. For a more intimate experience, visit a small venue such as the **Monticello Opera House**, which hosts opera between September and May.

The best ballet company is the Miami City Ballet *(see p94)*, whose choreographer is Edward Villela, a protégé of the late George Balanchine.

MOVIES

FOR ARTS MOVIES you'll do better in New York or Los Angeles, but Florida has plenty of multiscreen cinemas showing blockbuster films. The state's most famous cinema is the historic **Tampa Theatre** *(see p245)*, which hosts a variety of live acts but serves up mainly a mixture of classic and foreign films.

Also watch out for annual film festivals: Sarasota has one in November, and the Miami International Film Festival takes place in February, when films are shown at the Gusman Center for the Performing Arts *(see p94)*.

DINNER SHOWS

DINNER SHOWS are a popular form of family entertainment in Florida, especially in Orlando *(see p177)*. Here, diners sit at communal tables and are served huge meals that are generally themed to the show that you are watching. Audience participation is normally *de rigueur*.

Outside Orlando, the dinner shows tend to be less raucous but still provide varied entertainment, from conventional plays to comedies and musicals. The **Mystery Dinner Theater** in Clearwater Beach invites diners to solve a murder mystery as the drama is acted out on stage, and the **Mai Kai** in Fort Lauderdale, a long-running and superbly tacky Polynesian revue, entertains with dancers dressed in grass skirts, fire eaters, and the like. Jacksonville's **Alhambra Dinner Theater** puts on ambitious musicals of the *Oklahoma* and *South Pacific* school.

A singer entertains at Miami's Latin Carnival *(see p32)*

LIVE MUSIC AND NIGHTCLUBS

SOME OF THE MOST entertaining places to dance are clubs where you can dance to live instead of canned music. The best are often clubs where the music is provided by a big band or orchestra; "supper clubs" offer food as well as a band. The music can be varied: the **Coliseum Ballroom**, a Moorish-style gem in St. Petersburg, draws a crowd for both ballroom and country dancing. South Beach has the greatest choice of conventional discos *(see p95)*, but you'll find good clubs in popular vacation spots. **Razzles** in Daytona Beach offers high-energy music, and **Cheers** in Fort Lauderdale showcases current rock bands and has a busy dance floor. Jacksonville's **T-Birds** plays 60s, 70s, and 80s tunes until 2am. Nightclubs require you to show ID to prove that you are over 18 or, in some cases, 21.

Festivals are fertile territory for live music, and there are also countless spots where dancing to the music isn't compulsory. Key West has several well-established places, like the Hog's Breath Café *(see p331)*. Ybor City's **Skipper's Smokhouse** offers reggae and blues. Country and western music is popular, for which Panama City Beach's **Ocean Opry Theater** is a major venue. Some of the bars listed on pages 330–31 also offer live entertainment.

Sign for Hog's Breath Café in Key West

The lavish interior of the Tampa Theatre, an historic cinema

Street performers in Mallory Square, providing nightly entertainment at sunset

CRUISE AND BOAT TRIPS

FLORIDA IS THE world's leading departure point for cruises to the Caribbean, and ships set off regularly from Miami, Port Everglades, and other, smaller ports. But you can also go on mini-cruises, for a day or just an evening – the cost of which starts at around $40.

Evening cruises usually entail dinner and dancing, but the new rage is a casino cruise. **Cunard's *Princess*** and the **Discovery Cruise Line**, operating out of Miami and Port Everglades, have casinos on board. In Jacksonville, the **La Cruise Casino** offers on-board gambling.

If you are happy with a more modest cruise, pleasure boat trips are available all over Florida. The Jungle Queen in Fort Lauderdale *(see p131)*, the **Manatee Queen** in Jupiter *(see p113)*, and St. Petersburg's **Starlite Princess** are popular tour boats. The **Rivership Romance** offers trips on the St. Johns River starting from Sanford *(see p206)*.

The Rivership Romance on the St. Johns River

GAMBLING

GAMBLING ON cruise ships is popular because conventional casinos are illegal on the mainland: once a ship is in international waters, about 3 miles (5 km) from shore, the law no longer applies. On land, you can visit one of the state's four legal **Seminole Indian Casinos**: one is in Hollywood *(see p133)*, another in Immokalee near Naples, one near Tampa, and one in Okechobee. You can play poker, and there are slot machines, but the main activity is bingo. Poker is played at race tracks too, where you can also bet on the horses.

CHILDREN'S ENTERTAINMENT

KIDS ARE CATERED to all over Florida, not just at the theme parks. Museums often have excellent hands-on exhibits, and in many zoos and some parks you find "petting zoos," where children can enjoy direct contact with the animals. Kids can also have great fun at the water parks *(see p341)*, found all over the state. With **Walt Disney World Resort**, **Universal Orlando**, **SeaWorld**, and other big attractions, Orlando has no shortage of family entertainment; keep an eye out for what's on at the **T.D. Waterhouse Center**, which hosts everything from ice-skating shows to circuses and NBA games.

There is also plenty of free entertainment. Kids often enjoy street entertainers, and there are festivals to choose from all year round *(see pp32–5)*.

GAY ENTERTAINMENT

SOUTH BEACH in Miami is well known for its vibrant gay scene *(see p95)* that is attracting more and more gay visitors from home and abroad. Key West has been a gay mecca for a number of years, as has Fort Lauderdale, where **The Copa** club is the most popular gay stomping ground. There is a less developed scene in Tampa, but the **Pleasure Dome** in Ybor City has a good bar, a wild dance floor, and offers the best in live drag shows.

For additional information, buy *The Out Pages*, an excellent book listing a wide variety of gay venues and businesses in Florida. Listings information is provided in the Southern edition of the US *Gay Yellow Pages* and in selected books published by the **Damron Company**.

Festivities during the Gay Pride celebration in Fort Lauderdale

DIRECTORY

TICKETMASTER OUTLETS

Central Florida
(407) 839-3900.

Fort Lauderdale
(954) 523-3309.

Fort Myers
(941) 334-3309.

Miami
(305) 358-5885.

North Florida
(904) 353-3309.

St. Petersburg
(727) 898-2100.

Tampa
(813) 287-8844.

West Palm Beach
(561) 966-3309.

MAJOR VENUES

Broward Center for the Performing Arts
201 SW Fifth Ave,
Fort Lauderdale.
(954) 462-0222.

Florida Citrus Bowl
1610 W Church St,
Downtown Orlando.
(407) 849-2020.

All-tel Stadium
1 Stadium Blvd,
Jacksonville.
(904) 633-6100.

Raymond F. Kravis Center for the Performing Arts
701 Okeechobee Blvd,
West Palm Beach.
(561) 832-7469

Tropicana Field
1 Tropicana Drive,
St. Petersburg.
(727) 825-3120.

Tampa Bay Performing Arts Center
1010 N MacInnes Place,
Tampa.
(800) 955-1045.

Van Wezel Performing Arts Hall
777 N Tamiami Trail,
Sarasota.
(941) 953-3366.

THEATER

Florida State University Center for the Performing Arts
5555 N Tamiami Trail,
Sarasota.
(941) 351-8000.

Players of Sarasota
838 N Tamiami Trail,
Sarasota.
(941) 365-2494.

Red Barn Theater
319 Duval St, Key West.
(305) 296-9911.

Mann Hall
8099 College Park SW,
Fort Myers.
(941) 489-3033.

CLASSICAL MUSIC, OPERA, AND DANCE

Times-Union Center for the Performing Arts
300 W Water St,
Jacksonville.
(904) 633-6110.

Concert Association of Florida
555 17th St, Miami Beach.
(305) 532-3491.

Florida Grand Opera
1200 Coral Way, Miami.
(305) 854-7890.

Florida Philharmonic Orchestra
3401 NW 9th Ave,
Fort Lauderdale.
(954) 561-2997.

Gold Coast Opera
1000 Coconut Creek Blvd,
Pompano Beach.
(954) 973-2323.

Monticello Opera House
West Washington St,
Monticello.
(850) 997-4242.

MOVIES

Tampa Theatre
711 N Franklin St,
Tampa.
(813) 274-8981.

DINNER SHOWS

Alhambra Dinner Theater
12000 Beach Blvd,
Jacksonville.
(904) 641-1212.

Mai Kai
3599 N Federal Highway,
Fort Lauderdale.
(954) 563-3272 or
(800) 262-4524.

Mystery Dinner Theater
25 Belleview Blvd,
Clearwater.
(727) 584-3490.

LIVE MUSIC AND NIGHTCLUBS

Cheers
941 W Broward Blvd, Fort Lauderdale.
(954) 771-6337.

Coliseum Ballroom
535 4th Ave North,
St. Petersburg.
(727) 892-5202.

Ocean Opry Theater
8400 Front Beach Rd,
Panama City Beach.
(850) 234-5464.

Razzles
611 Seabreeze Blvd,
Daytona Beach,
(904) 257-6236.

Skipper's
910 Skipper Rd,
Ybor City, Tampa.
(813) 971-0666.

T-Birds
9039 Southside Blvd,
Jacksonville.
(904) 363-3399.

CRUISE AND BOAT TRIPS

Cunard Line's *Princess*
6100 Blue Lagoon Dr,
Miami Beach.
(800) 458-9000.

Discovery Cruise Line
PO Box 527544,
775 NW 70th Ave,
Miami
(800) 937-4477

Rivership Romance
433 N Palmetto Ave,
Sanford.
(407) 321-5091.

Starlite Princess Cruises
3400 Pasadena Ave South,
St. Petersburg.
(813) 229-1200.

Manatee Queen
1065 N Ocean Blvd,
Jupiter.
(561) 744-2191.

GAMBLING

Seminole Indian Casino
5223 N Orient Rd,
I-4 Exit 5, Tampa.
(813) 621-1302.

Seminole Indian Casino
506 South 1st St,
Immokalee.
(800) 218-0007.

CHILDREN'S ENTERTAINMENT

Waterhouse Center
600 W Amelia St,
Orlando.
(407) 849-2020

SeaWorld/Busch Gardens
(407) 363-2613.
w www.seaworld.com

Universal Orlando
(407) 363-2613. w
www.universalorlando.com

Walt Disney World
(407) 824-4321.
w www.disney.com

GAY ENTERTAINMENT

The Copa
624 SE 28th St,
Fort Lauderdale.
(954) 463-1507.

Damron Company
PO Box 422458,
San Francisco, CA 94142.
(415) 255-0404.

Pleasure Dome
1430 E 7th Ave,
Ybor City, Tampa.
(813) 247-2711.

Sports and Outdoor Activities

THANKS TO FLORIDA'S CLIMATE, you can take part in many sports and outdoor activities all year round, making the state a top destination for all sports enthusiasts, from golfers and tennis players to canoeists and deep-sea divers; some people even base their entire vacation around the sports opportunities available. Water sports of all kinds are well represented, with wonderful beaches on both the Atlantic and Gulf coasts. Florida also boasts approximately 10 million acres (4 million ha) of protected land, which can be explored on foot, horseback, bicycle, or boat. For those who prefer to watch rather than take part, Florida has a wide range of spectator sports to offer; these are described on pages 30–31.

A seaside golf course at Boca Raton on the Gold Coast

SOURCES OF INFORMATION

THE TWO BEST sources of general information are the **Florida Sports Foundation** and the **Department of Environmental Protection (DEP)**, which can provide information on most outdoor activities. The *Florida Vacation Guide*, available from Florida tourist board offices abroad, gives useful addresses, or you can contact local tourist offices for information about specific areas. Further sources are given in individual sections.

GOLF

FLORIDA IS A GOLFER'S paradise; with over 1,100 courses, it is the country's top golfing destination. Palm Beach offers so many courses (150 total) it claims to be the "golfing capital of the world," even though Naples boasts the greatest concentration.

Courses in Florida are flat by most standards, but landscaping provides some relief. Many of the most challenging courses are attached to resort hotels along the coast (some of which offer special golf vacation packages); you'll find courses inland too, including at Walt Disney World *(see p162)*. About two-thirds of courses are open to the public.

Golf is a year-round sport, but winter is the busiest season. If you play in summer, start early in the day to avoid late afternoon thunderstorms and lightning. Greens fees vary from under $20 to over $75 per person and are highest in the peak winter season.

The *Fairways in the Sunshine* golf guide, from the Florida Sports Foundation, lists all public and private courses.

TENNIS

TENNIS, LIKE GOLF, is very popular in Florida. Many hotels have courts, and some resorts offer vacation packages that include lessons. Contact the **United States Tennis Association (Florida Section)** for information on coaching, clubs, and competitions. The state's most famous tennis school is the **Nick Bollettieri Tennis Academy** *(see p253)*, which offers weekly training programs for $800 and up, as well as one-day sessions.

DIVING AND SNORKELING

FLORIDA IS SUPERB diving and snorkeling territory. The country's only living coral reef skirts the state's southeast coast, stretching the length of the Keys, where there is a magnificent variety of coral and fish *(see pp278–9)*. The reef lies 3–5 miles (5–8 km) offshore and is easily accessible to amateur snorkelers. Guided snorkeling trips are available throughout the Keys and are generally excellent.

The state's estimated 4,000 diving sites have increased, thanks to the artificial reefs program. All over Florida, from Panama City Beach to Fort Lauderdale, everything from bridge spans to freighters have been used to create a habitat for coral and colorful fish; there is even a Rolls Royce in the waters off Palm Beach. Sunken Spanish galleons also provide fascinating dive sites, mainly in south Florida.

If you don't have a Certified Divers Card you'll need to take a course. Recognized NAUI or PADI courses are widely available, and novices can learn in just four days for $300–400.

For more information, Florida Sports Foundation's *Florida Boating and Diving Guide* is helpful, or you can call the **Florida Association of Dive Operators**.

Freshwater swimming at Wakulla Springs in the Panhandle

Colorful jet ski and boat rental outlet in the Panhandle

SWIMMING AND WATER SPORTS

SWIMMING is as natural as breathing to most Floridians. Many hotels have pools, but the joy of Florida is the chance to swim in the ocean or in the many lakes, springs, and rivers.

The Atlantic provides the best waves and Florida's only surfing beaches, including Cocoa Beach (see p181). The warm, gentle swells of the Gulf of Mexico are better for kids. These western beaches are beautiful, with white sands and dunes in the Panhandle, even though the waters can be less clear than on the Atlantic side. Coastal erosion means that the southeastern beaches are often quite narrow, while there are only a couple of sandy beaches in the Keys.

Beach access is sometimes controlled: many lie within parks, which charge admission. Some hotels like to give the impression that their beach is for guests only, but they can't stop public access. Lifeguards monitor the most popular beaches in high season.

Many inland parks have freshwater swimming areas, including some beautifully clear spring water holes, such as in Blue Spring State Park (see p206). Another alternative for families are the water parks, found throughout the state, which have all kinds of rides and pools.

The full range of water sports, from windsurfing to jet skiing, is offered at Florida's resorts; water-skiing can also be enjoyed on freshwater lakes and inland waterways.

FISHING

FLORIDA'S NUMEROUS lakes and rivers are overflowing with fish, and fishing is not so much a sport as a way of life for a great many Floridians. The opportunities are endless both inland and all along the coast.

The Atlantic and Gulf shores are both dotted with the haunts of dedicated fishermen. Fishing right off the pier is popular at many coastal spots, but for those who enjoy angling on a different scale there is plenty of sport fishing for which the state is probably best known.

Deep-sea fishing boats can be chartered at many seaside resorts. The biggest fleets are in the Panhandle, especially around Fort Walton Beach and Destin, and in the Keys. With the Gulf Stream nearby, the waters off the Keys offer the most varied fishing in the state (see p281). Organized group excursions are an excellent

Fishing fleet sign, Destin

option for novices. If you want to take your big fish home, a taxidermist will preserve it for you; the more eco-conscious alternative these days is to have a model made of your catch. Bait and tackle shops or the charter boat operator can give you the names of local taxidermists.

Florida has thousands of lakes, as well as rivers and canals, for freshwater fishing. Boat rentals and fishing guides are available along the larger rivers, such as the Anclote and the St. Johns, and in other popular fishing areas like Lake Okeechobee (see p124). Fishing is also permitted in many state and other parks. In rural parts, fish camps offer simple accommodations and basic supplies, though some are open only during the summer.

Licenses, costing from $12 to $30, are required for both freshwater and saltwater fishing. The *Fishing Handbook,* available from the **Florida Game and Fresh Water Fish Commission**, gives information on locations and licensing. It also gives details of the entry dates, fees, regulations, and prizes of Florida's fishing tournaments; one of the best known is Destin's Fishing Rodeo (see p34).

For more information on fishing or hunting, contact the Department of Environmental Protection, or the Florida Game and Fresh Water Fish Commission (see p343).

Pelicans observing anglers on a pier on Cedar Key

The Intracoastal Waterway at Boca Raton, on the Gold Coast

BOATING

FLORIDA'S WATERWAYS attract boats of every description, from state-of-the-art yachts to wooden skiffs. With over 8,000 miles (12,870 km) of tidal coastline and 4,500 sq miles (11,655 sq km) of inland waters, the state is a paradise for boaters. Having a boat is as normal as having a car for some Floridians; the state has over 700,000 registered boats, and this doesn't include the 300,000 brought in annually from outside Florida.

The Intracoastal Waterway, extending 500 miles (800 km) down the east coast to the tip of the Keys (see pp20–21), is very popular. Often sheltered from the Atlantic Ocean by barrier islands, the route runs through rivers, creeks, and dredged canals. Although most of the west coast is open, the most interesting territory for boaters is where the Intra-coastal Waterway resumes among the islands of the Lee Island Coast (see pp264–5).

The 135-mile (217-km) Okeechobee Waterway, which cuts through the state, is ano-ther popular route, becoming positively busy during the summer. It runs along the St. Lucie Canal from Stuart, across Lake Okeechobee and then on to Sanibel Island via the Caloosahatchee River.

These inland waterways, like many of the state's 166 rivers, are suitable for small boats or houseboats. Many of the latter are more like float-ing apartments, often being equipped with air conditioning, microwave ovens, and even television. Houseboats can be rented from several marinas, in Sanford on the St. Johns River, for example (see p206), while small to medium-sized boats are available at many fish camps or marinas.

Florida has an astonishing 1,250 marinas. Those along the coast usually have excellent facilities, with accommodations and rental outlets for boats and fishing tackle; inland marinas tend to be more basic. *Florida Boating and Diving*, a brochure available from the **Florida Sports Foundation**, lists most marinas in the state, with details of their facilities.

BACKCOUNTRY PURSUITS

FLORIDA'S PROTECTED areas vary from popular beaches to much wilder areas like the Everglades. The provision of facilities varies too, but most parks have some kind of visitors' center, dispensing maps and other information.

Some also organize guided tours. Winter is the best time to explore, when the summer rains and mosquitos are over.

Over 110 areas are protected by the state, classified variously as State Parks, State Recreation Areas, and State Preserves. They all charge admission and usually open from 8am to sunset daily. The Department of Environmental Protection (DEP) issues a free guide, *Florida State Parks*, which lists them all plus their facilities.

Information on the fewer federally run national parks is available from the **National Park Service** in Georgia. Many other parks are private, in-cluding sanctuaries run by the **Florida Audubon Society**; these are particularly good for bird life. The *Florida Trails* guide, issued by the national tourist board (see p347), has a com-plete list of private, state, and national parks.

Florida State Park emblem

As a result of the Florida Rails-to-Trails Program, old train tracks have been turned into trails, suitable for hiking, biking, in-line skating, and riding. Best are the 16-mile (26-km) Tallahassee–St. Marks Historic Railroad State Trail, south of Tallahassee, and the Gainesville–Hawthorne State Trail (see p209) in the Northeast. The DEP's Office of Greenways and Trails has information on these and many other trails.

Outdoor adventure tours are organized by a few companies. One is **Build a Field Trip**, which arranges trips all over the state including in the Everglades and the Keys.

Visitors on a boardwalk in the Everglades National Park

BIKING

THERE IS PLENTY of opportunity for both on-road and off-road biking in Florida, where the flatness of the landscape makes for easy cycling territory – though avid bikers may find it rather dull. The rolling countryside of the Panhandle is by far the most rewarding area to explore, while the Northeast has some good trails too, for example in Paynes Prairie *(see p209)*.

If you don't bring your own, bicycles can usually be rented on site or from a local source. For general biking information, contact the **State Bicycle Office** or the DEP.

Canoeing in the Blackwater River State Park

WALKING

FLORIDA MIGHT not seem ideal walking country, but the variety of habitats makes up for the flat landscape. Most state parks have hiking trails, and there is a project currently underway to create the National Scenic Trail – starting at the Big Cypress National Preserve *(see p270)* in south Florida and ending near Pensacola. So far, 1,000 miles (1609 km) of the planned 1,292-mile (2,079-km) route have been completed.

The **Florida Trail Association** is the best place to get information on hiking trails.

CANOEING

THERE IS ample opportunity for canoeing in Florida; the Florida Canoe Trail System is made up of 36 routes along creeks and rivers totaling 950 miles (1,520 km). A number of parks are known for their canoe runs, the most famous being the exhilarating, 99-mile (160-km) Wilderness Waterway in the Everglades National Park *(see pp272–7)*. Some of the best rivers, such as the Blackwater River *(see p220)*, can be found in the North, while the Hillsborough River on the Gulf Coast is also popular *(see p249)*. Always

Enjoying the countryside near Ocala on horseback

check the water level before setting off, as both high and low levels can be dangerous.

HORSEBACK RIDING

THE OCALA NATIONAL FOREST in the Northeast *(see p207)* has over 100 miles (160 km) of trails suited to horseback riding. There are 15 state parks with riding trails, including Myakka River *(see p260)*, Jonathan Dickinson *(see p113)*, and the Florida Caverns *(see p225)*; about half the parks have facilities for overnight stays.

Information is available from the *Florida Horse Trail Directory*, issued by the **Department of Agriculture and Consumer Services**, or from the DEP.

SURVIVAL
GUIDE

PRACTICAL INFORMATION

The State Seal of Florida

WITH MORE THAN 40 million visitors a year, Florida is very well geared to catering to tourists' needs. It is the ultimate family vacation destination. A strong emphasis is placed on entertaining children, and the informal lifestyle and excellent facilities make traveling with youngsters a real pleasure. The only complaint a child is likely to have is if the line to see Mickey Mouse is too long or the sun too hot. Given its warm climate, for most Americans Florida is a winter destination. The peak season runs from December to April, when rates for flights and hotels are at their height, and the beaches and attractions are at their busiest. Anyone visiting Walt Disney World or the other theme parks should be prepared for long waiting times during any holiday period.

A roadside tourist information center in Kissimmee

VISAS

BRITISH CITIZENS, members of many EU countries, and citizens of Australia and New Zealand do not need a visa provided they have a return ticket and their stay in the US does not exceed 90 days. All that is required is a completed "visa waiver" form, issued by flight attendants either before or during the flight.

Other citizens must apply for a nonimmigrant visa from a US consulate, while Canadians need only proof of residence.

US immigration officers are known for their stringency. On entering the country it is quite possible that you may be asked to prove that you have sufficient funds to cover your stay.

CUSTOMS ALLOWANCES

CUSTOMS ALLOWANCES for visitors over 21 years of age entering the US are: 1 liter (2 pints) of alcohol, gifts worth up to $100, and 200 cigarettes, 100 cigars (as long as they're not made in Cuba), or 3 pounds (1.4 kilograms) of tobacco. A number of goods are prohibited, including cheese, fresh fruit, meat products, and, of course, illegal drugs.

TOURIST INFORMATION

MOST LARGE CITIES in Florida have a Convention and Visitors' Bureau (CVB), where you'll find a huge array of brochures. In smaller places go to the Chamber of Commerce, but since these offices cater mainly to the business community, some can be of only limited help. Most hotels have free "WHERE" magazines that list entertainment, museums, shopping, and dining. Also, there is usually a brochure rack in the hotel lobby.

For information before you leave home, call or write off for a vacation pack, issued by the Florida Tourism Corp. both in the US and abroad. This will include a list of all the tourist offices in Florida, which can then be contacted directly.

ADMISSION CHARGES

MOST MUSEUMS, parks, and other attractions charge an admission fee. This can vary enormously, from $2 at a small museum to over $40 for a day pass into Walt Disney World's Magic Kingdom.

Children and card-carrying students and senior citizens can often claim a discount, and anyone can use the coupons found in brochures available at tourist offices. These can cut the price of admission fees and also buy budget meals in local restaurants. Coupons from the information center on International Drive near Orlando (see p176) can save you hundreds of dollars.

OPENING TIMES

SOME ATTRACTIONS close once a week, often on Monday, but the majority open daily. State parks are usually open every day from sunrise to sunset, though attached visitor centers may close earlier. The theme parks have extended opening hours during the high season. Most sights close on major national holidays: typically New Year, Thanksgiving, and Christmas (see p35).

TRAVELING WITH CHILDREN

AS A TOP FAMILY destination, Florida places the needs of children high on its list of priorities. You can rent strollers or small wagons at

A boy enjoying a ride in a dolphin stroller, for rent at SeaWorld

the major theme parks; car rental firms must supply children's seats, and many restaurants offer special menus *(see p313)*. On planes, buses, and trains, children under 12 usually pay only half the standard fare, less if they are very young.

The main thing to worry about if you have children is the sun. Just a few minutes' exposure to the midday sun can burn tender young skin; use sunblock and hats.

Florida's theme parks are vast, and it is well worth agreeing on a place to meet in the event that someone gets lost; most parks also have a special "lost kids area."

For information on hotel facilities for children, see page 295; for entertainment for children, see page 338.

SENIOR CITIZENS

FLORIDA IS A MECCA for senior citizens, both to visit and to settle. Anyone over 65 (less in some instances) is eligible for all kinds of discounts – at attractions, hotels, restaurants, and public transit.

The **American Association of Retired Persons** can help members plan their vacation and offers discounts on air fares, car rental, and rooms.

ETIQUETTE

DRESS IN FLORIDA is casual, except in a few top restaurants *(see p312)*. Shorts and T-shirts are acceptable in most beachside bars. On the beach itself it is illegal for women to go topless, except in a few places, such as Miami's South Beach. Drinking alcohol on beaches and in other public places is also illegal.

It is against the law to smoke in buses, trains, taxis, and in most public buildings; there are usually separate areas for smokers and nonsmokers in restaurants and cafés.

Unless a service charge is imposed, in restaurants you should tip 15 to 20 percent of the bill. Taxi drivers expect a similar tip. For hotel porters, $1 per bag is usual.

TRAVELERS WITH DISABILITIES

AMERICA IS WAY AHEAD of most nations in the help it gives people with disabilities. Federal law demands that all public buildings be accessible to people in wheelchairs, although some old buildings have remained exempt. This guide specifies whether or not a sight is accessible, but you are advised to call ahead for details. For example, in nature preserves wheelchair-friendly boardwalks may make some areas accessible, while others remain out of bounds.

Accessible to wheelchairs

A few rental companies have cars adapted for people with disabilities, and some buses have wheelchair access – watch for a sticker on the windshield or by the door. Amtrak and Greyhound offer reduced fares.

Mobility International offers general advice for travelers with disabilities. The Florida Tourism Corporation issues a useful services directory, and Walt Disney World has its own special guide too.

ELECTRICAL APPLIANCES

YOU WILL NEED a voltage converter and an adapter to use the American 110–120 volts AC system; adapters for the two-prong plugs used in the US can be bought abroad or locally. Many hotels, however, have plugs that power both 110- and 220-volt electric shavers, and often supply wall-mounted hair dryers.

DIRECTORY

CONSULATES

Australia
1601 Massachusetts Ave, NW, Washington, DC 20036.
((202) 797-3000.

Canada
200 S Biscayne Blvd, Suite 1600, Miami, FL 33131.
((305) 579-1600.

UK
1001 Brickell Bay Drive, Suite 2110, Miami, FL 33131.
((305) 374-1522.
Suntrust Center, Suite 2110, 200 S Orange Ave, Orlando 32801.
((407) 426-7855.

TOURIST INFORMATION

Canada
((416) 928 3139.

Florida
FLAUSA Guide Book,
www.flausa.com.
((800) 735-2872.

UK
((0891) 600555.

OTHER NUMBERS

American Association of Retired Persons
601 E St, NW,
Washington, DC 20049.
((202) 434-2277.

Mobility International
PO Box 10767, Eugene, OR 97440.
((541) 343-1284.

Customers in casual dress at the bar in the Columbia Restaurant, Tampa

Personal Security and Health

Publicity about attacks on tourists in the early 1990s was considered exaggerated by the Florida authorities given the small number of assaults relative to the vast number of visitors. Even so, the police responded quickly, introducing extra security measures and offering new safety guidelines to visitors. Crimes against tourists have since fallen. You must still be alert in urban areas, above all in Miami or if you are driving, but anyone who takes precautions should enjoy a trouble-free trip.

LAW ENFORCEMENT

Enforcement of the law is shared by three agencies: the city police forces, sheriffs (who police country areas), and the Florida Highway Patrol, which deals with traffic accidents and offenses outside the cities. Major tourist centers are well policed, and Miami and Orlando also have a special Tourist Oriented Police (TOP), a recent arrival on the scene, and one that may well be copied elsewhere.

Given Florida's eagerness to both attract and protect tourists, police officers are friendly and helpful to visitors.

GUIDELINES ON SAFETY

Most cities in Florida, like elsewhere in the world, have "no-go" areas that should be avoided. The staff at the local tourist office or in your hotel should be able to advise. Note that downtown areas are generally unlike city centers elsewhere; they are first and foremost business districts, which are dead at night and often unsafe. If in doubt, take a taxi rather than walk.

Burglaries within hotels are not unheard of. Leave your best jewelry at home and lock other valuables in the safe in your room, or hand them in at the reception desk; few hotels will guarantee the security of belongings kept in your room.

If someone knocks on your door claiming to be hotel staff, you may want to check with reception before letting the person in.

Carry as little money as possible when you go out, keep your passport separate from your travelers' checks, and leave your duplicate room key with the desk clerk. If you are unlucky enough to be attacked, hand your wallet over immediately. Do not try to resist.

STAYING SAFE IN MIAMI

Although visitors are rarely the victim, Miami has one of the highest crime rates in the US. Certain districts are to be avoided at all costs. These include Liberty City and Overtown, both located between the airport and Downtown. Farther north, Little Haiti and Opa-Locka are interesting areas to visit, but they should be treated with caution *(see pp87–9)*. Avoid all deserted areas at night, including the transit terminals and Downtown. Lively night spots such as Coconut Grove and South Beach are the safest areas to hang out in after dark, but even here you should not venture into quiet back streets (such as south of 5th Street in South Beach). Whatever time of day you go out, be sure to carry a decent map with you.

In addition to the regular police patrols, Miami's Tourist Oriented Police provide extra

Police officers on patrol, Florida-style, in St. Augustine

cover in the area around the airport, especially around car rental outlets. Rental staff should be able to advise motorists on the best route into town and will also supply drivers with a map. See page 358 for safety tips for drivers.

In an emergency dial 911, or contact **Metro-Dade Police Information** if you don't need immediate help.

LOST PROPERTY

Even though you have only a slim chance of retrieving stolen property, you should report all lost or stolen items to the police. Keep a copy of the police report carefully if you are planning to make an insurance claim.

Most credit card companies have toll-free numbers for reporting a loss, as do Thomas Cook and American Express for lost travelers' checks. If you lose your passport, contact your embassy or consulate immediately *(see p347)*.

TRAVEL INSURANCE

Travel insurance coverage of a minimum of $1 million is highly recommended, mainly because of the high cost of medical care. Prices depend on the length of your trip, but make sure the policy covers accidental death, emergency medical care, trip cancellation, and baggage or document loss. Your insurance company or travel agent should be able to recommend a suitable policy, but it's worth shopping around for the optimum deal.

A county sheriff, in the regulation dark uniform, and his patrol car

Emergency ambulance

Orange County fire engine

MEDICAL TREATMENT

Larger cities in the state, and some smaller towns, have 24-hour walk-in medical and dental clinics, where minor casualties and ailments can be treated. For less serious complaints, drugstores (many of which stay open late or for 24 hours), should be sufficient.

If you have a serious accident or illness, you can rely on high-quality treatment at a hospital. Stories of medics making accident victims wait while they haggle over money are largely apocryphal; even so, guard your insurance documents with your life. Nothing comes for free: a straightforward visit to the doctor can cost about $50. Hospitals accept most credit cards, but doctors and dentists will often want cash. Those without insurance may need to pay in advance.

Anyone on prescribed medication should take a supply with them and ask their doctor to provide a copy of the prescription in case of loss or the need for more.

NATURAL HAZARDS

Hurricanes are infrequent but devastating when they do strike (see pp24–5). There are tried and tested emergency procedures, and if the worst should happen, follow the announcements on local television and radio. You can call the **National Hurricane Center** in Miami, which gives out information

on impending hurricanes, and a Hurricane Hotline may also be established.

The climatic hazard to affect most visitors is the sun. Use sun screen or sun block, and try to wear a hat; make sure that your children are well protected, too. Remember that heat can be as big a problem as sunlight; drink plenty of fluids to prevent dehydration.

Florida may be famous for its man made attractions, but there are places where the natural world still dominates. While the Everglades holds potentially more danger than other areas, you should be careful wherever you go. Alligators are a thrilling sight, but they can and do kill – so treat them with respect. There are also several venomous snakes native to Florida, including the water moccasin, whose bite can be fatal. It is best not to touch unfamiliar vegetation, and steer clear of Spanish moss; it houses the red mite, which causes skin skin irritation. Also, be on the lookout for poisonous spiders and scorpions.

Biting and stinging insects, including mosquitos, are a real nuisance between June and November, particularly in areas close to fresh water. Visits to

Road sign indicating alligators are nearby

A lifeguard keeps watch over a beach in the Panhandle

DIRECTORY

LOST CREDIT CARDS AND TRAVELERS' CHECKS

American Express
(800) 528-4800 (cards).
(800) 221-7282 (checks).

Diners Club
(800) 234-6377.

MasterCard
(800) 826-2181.

Thomas Cook
(800) 223-7373 (checks).

VISA
(800) 336-8472.

OTHER EMERGENCY NUMBERS

All Emergencies
911 to alert police, fire, or medical services.

Metro-Dade Police Information
(305) 595-6263.

Moneygram
(800) 926-9400.

National Hurricane Center
(305) 229-4483 recorded message with hurricane details.

parks and preserves can be uncomfortable if you don't wear insect repellent.

Florida's beaches are usually well supervised by lifeguards, but still, keep a close eye on young children. Riptides are a danger in some places.

EMERGENCIES

In an emergency, the police, ambulance, or fire services can be reached by dialing 911. The call is free from public phones, and on expressways there are emergency call boxes roughly every half-mile (1 km). If you are robbed in the street, go directly to the closest police station – dial 911 should you need help in locating it.

If you need emergency cash, ask someone to transfer this from your bank at home to a specified bank in Florida; or use the **Moneygram** service, a more tourist-friendly option offered by American Express.

Banking and Currency

FOREIGN CURRENCY EXCHANGE is available at the main branches of any large city bank. In addition, most of the major airports have exchange desks. For the convenience of residents and visitors alike, cash machines (ATMs) throughout the state allow transactions 24 hours a day. The best rule is to take plenty of travelers' checks with you, and keep your credit cards ready.

BANKING

BANKS ARE GENERALLY open from 9am to 3 or 4pm on weekdays, but some keep slightly longer hours. **Bank of America**, one of the country's major banks, offers foreign exchange in all its branches. Other banks include Amsouth, SunTrust, and First Union National Bank, all of which have branches throughout the state.

TRAVELERS' CHECKS

TRAVELERS' CHECKS are the best way to carry money around, both for ease of use and security (lost or stolen checks can be refunded). In many instances you can use them as if they were cash: US dollar travelers' checks are commonly accepted in shops, restaurants, and hotels; those issued by American Express or Thomas Cook are the most widely recognized. Change will be given in cash; if your checks are in large denominations, be sure to ask the cashier if there is enough money in the register before you countersign on the dotted line.

To exchange your travelers' checks into cash directly, go to a bank or exchange bureau. Remember to inquire about

commission fees before starting your transaction. All banks cash dollar travelers' checks, but you'll get the best rates in a big city bank or at a private exchange office. The latter are not common, but **American Express** and **Thomas Cook**, for example, both have a branch in Miami and Orlando, as well as in a number of other cities around the state.

Travelers' checks in other currencies will be no use in shops, and only some banks and hotels will exchange them. Personal checks drawn on overseas banks, such as Eurocheques, cannot be used in Florida.

AUTOMATIC TELLER MACHINES

MOST BANKS in Florida have ATMs (Automatic Teller Machines) in their lobbies or in an external wall. These machines enable you to withdraw US bills, usually in $20s, from your bank or credit card account at home.

Before leaving home, ask your credit card company or bank which American ATM systems or banks will accept your bank card, and check the cost of each transaction. Make sure, too, that you have (and know) your PIN number.

Automatic teller machine (ATM)

The largest ATM systems are **Plus** and **Cirrus**, which accept VISA and MasterCard as well as various US bank cards.

ATMs allow you 24-hour access to cash, but take care when using them in deserted areas, especially after dark; robberies are not unheard of.

CREDIT CARDS

CREDIT CARDS are a part of everyday life in Florida, as in other parts of the country. Anyone not carrying one may have a difficult time buying items and renting a car. The most widely accepted credit cards are VISA, American Express, MasterCard, Diners Club, Japanese Credit Bureau, and Discover.

Credit cards enable you to avoid having to carry around large amounts of cash and can be used to pay for everything from admission fees to hotel bills. It is also standard practice for car rental companies to take an imprint of your card as security; often the only alternative is to pay a hefty deposit in cash. Some hotels adopt the same practice: a "phantom" sum of $200–300 may be debited for one night in a hotel. This should be automatically restored to your credit when you check out, but it's a good idea to remind the clerk when you leave; any delay could result in your having less credit available on your card than you think.

Credit cards are useful in emergencies – hospitals will accept most major cards. With MasterCard and VISA you can get cash at banks and ATMs.

One of many drive-in banks, for fast, user-friendly banking

Coins

American coins (actual size shown) come in 1-dollar, 50-, 25-, 10-, 5-, and 1-cent pieces. The new goldtone $1 coins are in circulation, as are the State quarters, which feature an historical scene on one side. Each coin has a popular name: 1-cent pieces are called pennies, 5-cent pieces are nickels, 10-cent pieces are dimes and 25-cent pieces are quarters.

25- cent coin
(a quarter)

10- cent coin
(a dime)

5- cent coin
(a nickel)

1- cent coin
(a penny)

Bank Notes (Bills)

Units of currency in the United States are dollars and cents. There are 100 cents to a dollar. Notes come in $1, $5, $10, $20, $50 and $100 denominations and all are the same color. The new $5, $10, $20, $50 and $100 bills are now in circulation. Paper bills were first issued in 1862, when coins were in short supply and the Civil War needed financing.

An American Eagle
from old currency

1- dollar bill ($1)

5- dollar bill ($5)

10- dollar bill ($50)

20- dollar bill ($20)

50- dollar bill ($50)

100- dollar bill ($100)

Communications

US stamp

COMMUNICATING WITH PEOPLE both within and outside Florida, whether by mail or telephone, rarely causes problems – though no one claims that the United States' postal system is the world's fastest (at least as far as domestic mail is concerned). There is more competition in the field of telecommunications: Southern Bell, for example, operates the majority of public telephones, but since there are a number of companies in the field it is often worth shopping around. An easy way to save money is to avoid making telephone calls from your hotel room, for which often exorbitant surcharges are imposed.

USING A COIN-OPERATED TELEPHONE

1 Lift the receiver and wait for the dial tone.

2 Insert the correct coin or coins.

3 Enter the number.

Coins
These coins are accepted by pay phones.

5 cents

10 cents

25 cents

4 If you decide not to make a connection, or if the call does not get through, you can retrieve your money by pressing the coin return.

5 If the call is answered and you talk for longer than the allotted time, the operator will interrupt and ask you to deposit some more coins into the phone. Pay phones do not give change.

REACHING THE RIGHT NUMBER

- Direct-dial calls to another area code: dial **1** followed by the area code and the 7-digit number. Since the 3-digit area codes can cover large areas, some "zone calls" (those within the same code area) also require you to dial 1 first.
- International direct-dial calls: dial **011**, then the code of the country (Australia 61, New Zealand 64, UK 44), followed by the local area/city code (minus the first 0) and the number.
- International operator assistance: dial **01**.
- International directory inquiries: dial **00**.
- Local operator assistance: dial **0**.
- Local directory inquiries: dial **411**.
- Long-distance information: dial **1**, then the appropriate area code, followed by **555-1212**.
- An **800**, **888**, or **877** prefix means the call will be free.
- For the police, fire or ambulance service, dial **911**.

PUBLIC TELEPHONES

PUBLIC PAY PHONES ARE everywhere in cities; elsewhere, you will find them mainly in gas stations, shops, and malls.

Most public telephones take coins – you'll need about $8 worth of quarters to make an international call. However, there is a growing number of card-operated phones. Some of these take special prepaid debit cards, which involve dialing a toll-free number to gain access to your required number. Alternatively, you can use your credit card from any phone. You must simply dial (800) CALLATT, key in your credit card number, and then wait to be connected; you will be charged at normal rates.

Telephone directories are supplied at most public phones and give details of rates.

Phone cards that can be used in selected public telephones

TELEPHONE CHARGES

TOLL FREE NUMBERS (which are prefixed by 800, 888, or 877) are common in the US and are well worth taking advantage of; some hotels have the gall to impose an access charge for these calls. While you can dial 800 or 888 numbers from abroad, note that they are not toll free.

When making a local call from a public telephone, the minimum charge, 25 cents, will buy you about three minutes. For long-distance domestic calls the lowest rate (which is 60 percent less than the standard rate) runs from 7pm to 8am on weekdays and on weekends (except 5 to 11pm on Sunday). These discounts also apply to calls to Canada, but they take effect an hour later. International rates vary depending on which country you are contacting: the cheapest rate for the UK is from 6pm to 7am.

Most telephone calls are possible without the aid of an

operator (whose intervention raises the price of a normal call). Collect calls can be made only by the operator and so can be very expensive.

FAX SERVICES

WORLDWIDE FAX services are available throughout the state. Most larger airports have business centers where you can send and receive faxes. In addition, hotels generally have business centers or mail-and-copy services; the concierge will direct you to the appropriate place. These days, many travelers carry a laptop personal computer. In order to send and receive e-mail you just need to have access to a phone line.

POSTAL SERVICES

POST OFFICE opening hours vary but are usually 9am to 5pm on weekdays, with some offices opening on Saturday mornings too. Drugstores and hotels often sell stamps, and some department stores and big transit terminals have stamp vending machines. Note that stamps not bought from a post office sometimes cost extra.

Surface mail sent overseas from the US takes weeks, so you'd do better to send letters air mail, which should take five to ten working days.

All domestic mail goes first class and takes one to five days – longer if you forget to include the zip code. You can

A rank of newspaper-dispensing machines in a Palm Beach street

pay extra for **Priority Mail**, for a delivery in two to three days, or **Express Mail**, which offers next-day delivery in the US and within two to three days to many foreign countries. Be sure to use the right mailbox. Mailboxes are painted blue; Express and Priority mailboxes are silver and blue and are clearly marked.

Many Americans use private courier services, such as UPS and Federal Express, for both domestic and international mail; they can offer next-day delivery to most destinations.

Many shops can mail your purchases home for you; mailing a parcel yourself involves the use of approved materials available from post offices.

TELEVISION AND RADIO

TELEVISION IN FLORIDA is the same as anywhere else in the US, that is, dominated by game shows, sit-coms, talk shows, and soaps. The cable channels offer more variety: ESPN is devoted to sports, CNN to news, for example. Hotel rooms usually have cable TV, but you may have to pay to see a movie *(see p293)*.

Most radio stations pump out pop and easy listening music, but if you hunt around (especially on the FM band) you can often pick up entertaining local stations, including Spanish-language ones in south Florida. More serious broadcasting is left to the likes of NBC, ABC, and PBS (Public Broadcasting System), which serve up a diet of documentaries, talk shows, and classical music.

NEWSPAPERS

EVERY LARGE CITY publishes its own daily newspaper. Most widely read is the *Miami Herald*, which provides good coverage of national and international news; it also has a widely read Spanish-language edition, *El Heraldo*.

You can usually pick up a national paper such as *USA Today* from street dispensers, but most of these are given over to local papers. For other national US dailies, such as the *New York Times*, and foreign newspapers, you will normally have to rely on bookstores and good newsstands.

Two of the most widely read daily newspapers in the state of Florida

FLORIDA TIME

MOST OF FLORIDA runs on Eastern Standard Time (EST). The Panhandle west of the Apalachicola River, however, is on Central Standard Time (CST), which is one hour behind the rest of the state.

EST is five hours and CST six hours behind Greenwich Mean Time (GMT). If you are making an international telephone call, add five hours for the United Kingdom, 15 hours for Australia, and 17 hours for New Zealand.

Standard mailbox

TRAVEL INFORMATION

FLORIDA IS the top tourist destination in the US, and is well served by flights from all over the world. The state's chief gateways are Miami, Orlando, and Tampa, and the growing number of charter flights is raising the profile of other airports. Flying is also worth considering if you plan to travel any distance within Florida. The hop

United Airlines flies to Florida from around the world

between Miami and Key West, for example, takes 40 minutes, compared with four hours by car. However, when it comes to getting around the state, the car reigns supreme, with fast interstates, major highways, and quieter county roads to choose from. Trains and buses provide an alternative for those willing to plan their routes carefully.

Clean and orderly interior of Orlando International Airport

ARRIVING BY AIR

ALL THE MAJOR US carriers, including **Continental**, **American Airlines**, **United Airlines**, **US Airways**, and **Delta Air Lines**, have hundreds of scheduled domestic services to Orlando and Miami, as well as to Florida's other main airports. Most offer direct flights from abroad too, but this will normally entail a stop at a US airport en route.

From the UK, **British Airways** and **Virgin Atlantic** have scheduled direct flights to Miami and Orlando; British Airways also has a service between London and Tampa. American Airlines runs daily flights to Miami from London's Gatwick and Heathrow airports. Delta Air Lines flies to Florida from Ireland via Atlanta, Georgia or New York.

European carriers such as Air France, KLM, and Iberia also offer a range of flights. Qantas

and several US airlines offer one- or two-stop flights from Australia and New Zealand.

For flights into one of Florida's smaller gateways, consult a travel agent, who can route you to wherever you wish to go.

Increasingly, charter flights are offering direct access to some of Florida's smaller resorts such as Palm Beach and Fort Myers. Most charter flights emanate from Canada, the Caribbean, and Latin America, but there is a growing number from Europe, offering service to Fort Lauderdale and Orlando from Gatwick, Manchester, and Prestwick in the UK. The choice of charter flights to Orlando has been further boosted by the upgrading of nearby Sanford airport.

AIR FARES

THE CHEAPEST round-trip fares to Florida are generally economy or APEX tickets on a scheduled flight (which must be booked in advance). The competition between travel agencies and between

AIRPORT	INFORMATION	DISTANCE FROM CITY	TAXI FARE TO CITY (APPROX)	SHUTTLE BUS FARE TO CITY (APPROX)
Miami	(305) 876-7000	10 miles (16 km) to Miami Beach	$20 to Miami Beach	$8–15 to Miami Beach
Orlando	(407) 825-2352	18 miles (28 km) to Walt Disney World	$40–45 to Walt Disney World	$15 to Walt Disney World, or 75c by Lynx bus
Sanford	(407) 322-7771	40 miles (64 km) to Walt Disney World	$45–50 to Walt Disney World	$50 to Walt Disney World
Tampa	(813) 870-8700	6 miles (9 km) to Downtown	$12–15 to Downtown	$13 to Downtown
Fort Lauderdale	(954) 359-1200	8 miles (13 km) to Fort Lauderdale, 30 miles (48 km) to Miami	$15–20 to Fort Lauderdale, $55 to Miami	$10 to Fort Lauderdale, $12 to Miami

A shuttle bus serving Miami airport

the numerous airlines serving Florida means that it is worth shopping around. Keep an eye out for promotional fares, and some specialty operators offer good deals on charter flights.

Fares can be surprisingly cheap in the off season, and you'll often get a better deal if you fly midweek. During vacation periods, by contrast, seats are in big demand and air fares can rocket to more than double their normal rates, being highest in December.

Note that US airlines sometimes offer discounted seats on domestic flights if you buy an inbound ticket from them.

PACKAGE DEALS

THE CHEAPEST vacation deal to Florida is a package that throws in car rental and/or accommodation with the cost of the flight. Fly-drive deals offer a rental car "free" or at a vast discount, but be warned: there are heavy surcharges to pay *(see p.357)*.

Flight and accommodation packages are common and often a good bargain. What you lose out in terms of flexibility, you may gain in peace of mind. Double deals are very popular – combining, for example, a week in Orlando with a week at a Gulf Coast resort. Package deals to all the major theme parks are worth considering if you're spending the whole time there; information is available from travel agencies.

FLORIDA AIRPORTS

FLORIDA'S TOP international airports are reasonably well equipped with information desks, banks, car rental desks, and other facilities. If you're collecting a rental car, you may be taken by bus to a pick-up point nearby. If you are heading into town, check out the shuttle buses (or "limos"), which offer a door-to-door

service to and from the airport; they operate like shared taxis but are cheaper than regular cabs. Major hotels usually offer a courtesy bus service to their guests.

MIAMI AIRPORT

MIAMI INTERNATIONAL AIRPORT is one of the busiest in the world, which can mean long lines at immigration. The walk between concourses and gates is often long too.

Tourist information desks are found outside all customs exits, and car rental counters, taxis, private limos, and shuttle buses are on the lower level concourse. Companies such as **SuperShuttle** run 24-hour shuttle bus services to all the main districts of Miami. City buses in theory serve the airport, but these services should not be relied upon.

ORLANDO AND SANFORD AIRPORTS

A RECENT SURVEY rated Orlando International Airport the country's number one airport for overall customer convenience. Moving walkways and the automated monorail system make getting around the two terminals easy. Multilingual tourist information centers by the security checkpoints are open from 7am to 11pm.

Many hotels have their own courtesy buses, but there are also shuttle buses; the **Mears Transportation Group** serves most destinations in the area.

A less expensive way to travel to International Drive or downtown Orlando is by Lynx bus *(see p363)*. Services leave from outside the "A Side" terminal every half hour. Both trips take about 50 minutes.

The newly revamped airport at Sanford is much quieter than the main Orlando airport. Facilities are still being developed, but there are taxis and several car rental outlets, which are conveniently located right outside the terminal building.

The People Mover monorail at Orlando International Airport

Driving in Florida

DRIVING IN FLORIDA is a delight. Most highways are uncrowded, and Floridians are generally courteous and considerate drivers. Gasoline is inexpensive and car rental rates are the lowest in the United States.

You can get by without a car in Orlando (see p363), but wherever you are life is much easier with one. Incidents of foreign motorists being victims of crime on the road have deterred some from driving, but safety measures are improving. Many rest areas on interstate highways are now covered by 24-hour armed security patrols, and direction signs have been improved in Miami (see p358).

Interstate Highway 4

US Highway 1, heading south

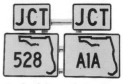

Overhead signs at the junction of two routes

ARRIVING BY CAR

THERE IS A GOOD choice of routes into Florida from the neighboring states of Georgia and Alabama. The advantage of using the main highways is that you will find welcome centers just over the border dispensing fresh orange juice and general information. They are located on the Florida side of the state line along I-95, I-75, I-10, and US 231.

ROADS IN FLORIDA

FLORIDA HAS AN excellent road network. The fastest and smoothest routes are the interstate highways, referred to as I-10, I-75, and so on. These usually have at least six lanes with rest areas located every 60 miles (100 km) or so.

Interstates form part of the expressway system of roads (sometimes called "freeways"), to which access is permitted only at specified junctions or exits. Among other expressways are turnpikes and toll roads. Chief among the latter are the Bee Line Expressway (between Orlando and the Space Coast) and the Florida

Turnpike, which runs from I-75, northwest of Orlando, to Florida City south of Miami. The toll you have to pay is dependent, logically, on the distance covered; if you travel the entire 329 miles (530 km) of the Turnpike, for example, the trip will cost around $20. Tolls can be paid to a collector in a booth or, if you have the right change and don't need a receipt, dropped into a collecting bin, where the money is counted automatically.

Be warned that local drivers change lanes frequently on expressways. Stick to the right to stay out of trouble and take care when approaching exits, which can be on both sides of the highway; most accidents occur during left turns.

Other routes include the US highways, which are usually (but not always) multilaned, but slower than expressways and often less scenic, lined with motels and gas stations. State Roads and County Roads are smaller and better for touring. Unpaved routes exist in some of Florida's more rural areas; note that some car rental companies may not permit you to drive on these.

City parking restrictions

Mile marker in the Keys

Speed limit (in mph)

Rest area, indicated off an interstate

ROAD SIGNS

MOST ROAD SIGNS are clear and self-explanatory. If you are caught disregarding instructions you might be fined.

Generally, road numbers or names rather than destinations are marked, and different types of roads are indicated by signs of different shapes and colors. Directional signs are usually green.

NAVIGATING

A GOOD ROAD MAP is vital for touring Florida by car. The *Florida Transportation Map*, available free from most Convention and Visitors' Bureaus and Florida tourist

The toll plaza on Florida's Turnpike at Boca Raton

offices abroad, is adequate for general purposes; it gives the location of rest areas on interstate highways and includes maps of the main cities. If you plan to spend any length of time in a city, however, you should try to pick up a local detailed map. The city maps in tourist offices are often inadequate for driving – in which case a good bookshop would be the best source.

Navigating your way around Florida is comparatively easy. East-west routes have even numbers and north-south routes odd numbers. Signs on the roadside, including mile markers in the Keys *(see p269)*, tell you which road you are on; while the name hanging over intersections is not the road you are on but the one you are crossing. Junctions have two numbers – when through routes follow the same course for a time.

A typical **Florida road intersection, in Tallahassee**

SPEED LIMITS

SPEED LIMITS in the US are set by individual states. The limits in Florida are as follows:
• 55–70 mph (90–105 km/h) on highways.
• 20–30 mph (32–48 km/h) in residential areas.
• 15 mph (24 km/h) near schools.

Speed limits can vary every few miles, so keep a close eye out for the signs. On an interstate you can be fined for driving slower than 40 mph (64 km/h). Speed limits are rigorously enforced by the Florida Highway Patrol, whose representatives issue tickets on the spot. A fine can set you back as much as $150.

CAR RENTAL

CAR RENTAL COSTS in Florida are already cheap by most standards, and you can save even more by booking and paying before leaving home. Fly-drive deals can knock more than 50 percent off the cost, but don't be fooled by offers of so-called "free" car rental. Hidden extras like state tax and insurance will not be included in these offers.

If you wait until you arrive to organize your car rental, it is usually cheaper to rent a vehicle at the airport rather than from a downtown outlet.

Highway Patrol insignia

All you need to rent a car is your driver's licence, passport, and a credit card. If you don't have the latter, you'll have to pay the deposit in cash. The minimum age for car rental is 21, but drivers under 25 may need to pay a surcharge.

Make sure your car rental agreement includes Collision Damage Waiver (CDW) – also known as Loss Damage Waiver (LDW) – or you'll be liable for any damage to the car, even if it was not your fault. Rental agreements include third party insurance, but this is rarely adequate. It is advisable to buy additional or supplementary Liability Insurance, which should provide coverage of up to $1 million. These extras, plus taxes, can add $35–40 to each day's rental.

Some companies add a premium if you want to drop the car off in another city, and all charge a lot for gas: if you return the car with less fuel than it had initially, the difference can cost you as much as $3 per gallon.

The majority of international car rental agencies *(see p359)* offer a reasonable range of vehicles, from economy models to convertibles. All rental cars come equipped with an automatic transmission, power steering, and air-conditioning.

TIPS FOR DRIVERS

• Traffic travels on the right-hand side of the road.
• Seat belts are compulsory for both drivers and passengers, and children under three must sit in a child seat.
• You can turn right on a red light unless there are signs to the contrary, but you must come to a stop first.
• A flashing amber light at intersections means slow down, look for oncoming traffic, and then proceed with caution.
• Passing is allowed on both sides on any multilane road, including interstate highways.
• It is illegal to change lanes across a double yellow or double white solid line.
• If a school bus stops on a two-way road to drop off or pick up children, traffic traveling in both directions must stop. On a divided highway, only traffic traveling in the same direction need stop.
• Don't drink even one beer. Driving under the influence (DUI) is treated very seriously; violators can be fined hundreds of dollars or even imprisoned for a short period.

One of many car rental agencies

Charming old-fashioned filling station on the Gold Coast

GASOLINE

U NLEADED gasoline is used by most modern cars and vans and comes in three grades – regular, super, and premium – and diesel fuel is usually also available.

Gasoline is inexpensive by most standards, but the price varies a great deal according to the location and service. Almost all gas stations are self-service; it is rare to find one that has an attendant to fill the tank, check the oil, and clean the windshield. Gas prices are marked inclusive of tax per gallon – the US gallon, that is, which is 3.8 liters, about a liter less than an Imperial gallon. At most gas stations you can pay with cash, a credit card, or travelers' checks, although some places (mainly in rural areas) take cash only. Occasionally you are expected to pay in advance.

If you drive along back roads, make sure the car is topped off with oil, gas, and water, as you won't come across many filling stations.

BREAKDOWNS

I F YOUR CAR breaks down, pull off the road, turn on the emergency flashers, and wait for the police. On expressways you can make use of the emergency phones *(see p349)*. If you are traveling alone, you may choose to rent a cell phone – offered at a small cost by most car rental firms.

If you have rented a car, you will find an emergency number on the rental agreement, so try that first; in the event of a serious breakdown, the rental agency will provide a new vehicle. The **American Automobile Association** (AAA) provides its own breakdown vehicles and will assist its members. Or, call the State Police or the emergency number on your gasoline credit card.

Time elapsed shown here

Insert coins here

Turn handle to register coins

Parking meter

PARKING

F INDING a parking space is rarely a problem at theme parks and other major tourist attractions, shopping malls, or in most downtown districts. The main places where you may have difficulty are in the vicinity of city beaches – for example in Fort Lauderdale or South Beach *(see p362)*.

You'll find small and multi-level parking lots in cities, but usually you'll have to use parking meters. When you find a space (ideally in the shade), feed the meter generously: the fee varies from 25c to $1 per hour. Overstay and you risk a substantial fine or the possibility of your car being clamped or towed away. Be sure to read parking signs carefully. Restrictions are normally posted on telephone poles, street lights, or roadside

---

SAFETY FOR DRIVERS

Miami has the worst reputation for crime against motorists, but take care wherever you are. Various measures have been introduced to safeguard foreign drivers. For example, the license plate code identifying rental cars was dropped, and in Miami road signs were improved: an orange sunburst sign guides drivers along the main routes to and from the airport. Here are a few tips to help you stay safe:

• If arriving in Florida by air at night, you could arrange to pick up your rental car the next morning in order to avoid driving in unfamiliar territory after dark.
• Avoid having handbags or other valuable items visible inside the car; pack them out of sight in the trunk.
• Keep car doors locked, especially in urban areas.
• Ignore any attempt by a pedestrian or motorist to stop you, e.g., by pointing out some alleged fault on your car or, less subtly, by ramming you from behind. Another ruse is to stand by a "broken-down" vehicle, signaling for help.
• If you need to refer to a map in a city, don't stop until you are in a well-lit and preferably busy area.
• Avoid sleeping in the car off the highway, although some rest areas on expressways have security patrols.
• Avoid taking short cuts in urban areas. Stick to the main highways if possible.

Sunburst signs for visitors to Miami

Tandems and bikes for rent in cycle-friendly Palm Beach

walls or curbs. Cars should not be parked within 10 ft (3 m) of a fire hydrant: this is the surest way to get towed away.

For those prepared to pay, valet parking is available at many hotels and restaurants.

BICYCLING

Bicycling is becoming more and more popular as recreation *(see p343)* or as a means of keeping fit, but on the whole bicycles are not used as a practical form of transportation. Cycling in most urban areas is not very agreeable, not least because drivers are not accustomed to sharing the road with bikes, and can be hazardous.

The places best suited to bikers are smaller cities or seaside resorts such as South Beach, Key West, Palm Beach, or St. Augustine – where the roads aren't too busy and where car parking can be a problem. Bikes can be rented for about $10–15 per day. In-line skating is also very popular in these vacation areas, and skates are easy to rent.

MOTORCYCLE RENTAL

If cruising florida's streets and highways on a Harley-Davidson is your dream, you may want to visit **Iron Horse Rentals**, which has branches in Fort Lauderdale, Orlando, Miami, and Tampa. Charges are about $135 for 24 hours, plus a deposit of $500; the minimum age is 21. **Harley-Davidson** in Ft. Lauderdale and Miami, offers a similar range of motorcycles for rent.

RV RENTAL

Recreational vehicles (RVs), or mobile homes are great for groups or families. It costs $300 and up to rent one for a week. RV rental outlets are surprisingly scarce. The largest in the United States is **Cruise America**, which also has agents abroad, or, for another good outlet offering RV rental, try **Sundance Motorhomes**.

Rental conditions are usually similar to those for car rental *(see p357)*. Size and facilities vary greatly, but most RVs have every imaginable convenience.

The car ferry at Mayport *(see p195)*, a shortcut across the St. Johns River

Traveling Around Florida

VISITORS TO FLORIDA who rely on public transportation will find their horizons rather restricted. The rail network is limited, leaving Greyhound buses – which link most sizable towns – as the main form of long-distance land transportation. Places outside the main urban areas will often elude those without cars. Some local bus services are good, but you'll need time and flexibility to make use of these. Public transportation within cities is more useful. Here, the emphasis is on serving commuters rather than visitors, but the main tourist centers have some services that cater to the needs of sightseers.

Spanish Revival-style Tri-Rail station in West Palm Beach

ARRIVING BY TRAIN

THE USE OF RAILROADS in the US is dwindling, but there are still connections between major cities. The national passenger rail company, **Amtrak**, serves Florida from both the east and west coasts. There are three daily services from New York City. The Silver Meteor and Silver Palm run south via Washington DC down to Jacksonville and Miami, taking about 25 hours. The Silver Star travels the same route as far as Orlando, where it then veers west to Tampa.

The Sunset Limited, complete with deluxe cabins and movie entertainment, covers the 3,066 miles (4,933 km) from Los Angeles to Sanford near Orlando, stopping at Phoenix and New Orleans.

If you want to travel by train but take your own car, there is Amtrak's Auto Train, which runs daily from Lorton in Virginia to Sanford, taking about 18 hours.

A bargain flight can work out cheaper than the equivalent rail fare. You'll often do best to buy a rail pass.

EXPLORING BY TRAIN

AMTRAK TRAINS serve only a limited number of towns and cities in Florida (see the map on pages 12–13). Other than Tampa, the Gulf Coast is linked only by Amtrak buses, known as "Thruway" buses. These run from Winter Haven, near Orlando, to Fort Myers via St. Petersburg and Sarasota, with guaranteed connections with Amtrak rail services.

Rail fares do not compete well with those of Greyhound, but trips are obviously more relaxing than on a bus. When traveling overnight, you can choose between the ordinary (but reclining) seats of "coach class" and a cabin.

Anyone planning to do more than a couple of trips by train might consider buying a rail pass, which gives unlimited travel during a set period of time; this must be bought from an Amtrak agent before you arrive; agents can also send out timetables for both national and regional services.

Florida's only other train service is **Tri-Rail**, which links 15 stations on the line between Miami airport and West Palm Beach, including Fort Lauderdale and Boca Raton. Intended primarily for commuters, the trains can also be useful for tourists. Services run more or less hourly, with reduced services on weekends. One-way fares range from about $2 to $6, depending on the number of zones you pass through, and transfers to Miami's Metrorail and Metromover services *(see p362)* are free.

Tri-Rail also runs guided tours, to South Beach and Worth Avenue, for example, as well as special trips to big games at the Orange Bowl Stadium in Miami.

LONG-DISTANCE BUSES

WHETHER YOU are traveling from other parts of the country or within Florida, **Greyhound** buses offer the cheapest way to get around. Some services are "express," with few stops en route, while others serve a greater number of destinations.

A few routes have "flag stops," where a bus may stop to deposit or collect passengers in places without a bus station. Pay the driver direct, or, if you want to reserve in advance, go to the nearest Greyhound agent – usually in a local store or post office.

An air-conditioned Greyhound bus, serving the Florida Keys

Passes provide unlimited travel for set periods of time (from between four and sixty days), but are useful only if you have a very full itinerary. Overseas visitors should also note that passes are cheaper if bought from a Greyhound agent outside the United States.

A complete bus timetable is not available, but agents can send out photocopies of requested services.

LOCAL AND CITY BUSES

Bus services operated by local authorities can be useful for short hops within county boundaries, although services are rarely frequent enough for sightseeing trips. You can travel between many of the cities of southeastern Florida by stringing together local buses, but you'll need to allow plenty of time.

There is more opportunity to take advantage of buses within cities, and shuttle buses are useful for traveling to and from the airports in Orlando and Miami (see p355). Buses in the US do not have conductors, so always have the right money, ticket, or token to give the driver (or put in the box) as you board.

TAXIS

Taxis (more often called "cabs") are easily found at airports, transit terminals, and major hotels. Taxi stands are rare elsewhere, and since cabs do not tend to cruise around city streets, it is best to order one by phone: numbers are listed in the *Yellow Pages.* Alternatively, ask someone at your hotel to call a taxi for you – although you may be expected to pay them a tip for doing this.

If you are traveling off the beaten track in a city, it will help to have your destination marked on a map. Not all drivers know their way

Horse and carriage, a pleasant way to go sightseeing in St. Augustine

around. All taxi fares should be metered according to the distance traveled. Some cabs accept credit cards, but you should check in advance.

WATER TAXIS

In several cities water taxis add a new dimension to urban travel. You'll find them in Miami, Jacksonville, Tampa, and Fort Lauderdale. Routes are generally geared to tourists, and as a result they are fairly limited in scope – linking hotels, restaurants, and shops, for example. However, they are fine for sightseeing.

Some operate as regular shuttle services, as is the case across the St. Johns River in Jacksonville, while others, such as those in Tampa and Miami, can be summoned only by phone. Fares are usually $5–10, which you pay on board.

TRANSPORTATION FOR TOURISTS

Most popular tourist centers provide special transportation for visitors. This often comes in the form of old-fashioned trolley buses: Tallahassee has a replica streetcar with wooden seats and brass handrails. In Daytona Beach and Fort Lauderdale trolleys are a useful link between downtown and the beach.

A familiar sight in Key West is the Conch Train, which consists of open-sided cars towed by a butane-powered jeep disguised as an old locomotive. St. Augustine has a similar train, and horse-drawn carriages, which can be rented in downtown Orlando too.

UNDERSTANDING CITIES

You should not think of "downtown" as the heart of a city; though it may be the hub of business, most people spend their leisure time elsewhere. Most large cities are arranged on a grid pattern, with numbered streets taking their orientation from the junction of two main axes downtown – as in Miami (see p363).

As a tourist, one of the best ways to sightsee is to walk. At pedestrian crossings be sure to pay attention to the "Walk" and "Don't Walk" or "Wait" signals.

Signals at a pedestrian crossing, ordering you to proceed or stop

A Key West taxi – painted pink rather than the usual yellow

Traveling Around Miami

Public transportation in Miami is run by the Metro-Dade Transit Agency, which operates the buses, the Metrorail commuter train network, and Downtown's elevated Metromover. There is also a limited water taxi service, which can be a pleasant way to get around, but it is hard to make the most of Miami without a car unless you're happy to stay in South Beach. However you travel, pay heed to the safety tips on pages 348 and 358.

The Metromover, which loops around downtown Miami

ARRIVING IN MIAMI

For information on getting away from Miami airport, see page 355. If you arrive at the **Amtrak** station, just north of the airport, or at one of the **Greyhound** terminals, there are no car rental outlets but plenty of taxis and a choice, if using of buses going to Downtown and Miami Beach.

Arriving by car is relatively hassle free. I-95, the main road from the north, heads straight through Downtown before joining US 1, which continues south skirting Coral Gables. Route A1A is a slower way in from the north but takes you directly into South Beach. From the west, US 41 runs through Little Havana to the coast, where it links up with the main north-south routes.

Amtrak Station
8303 NW 37th Ave.
☎ (305) 835-1222.

Greyhound Stations
Airport, 4111 NW 27th St.
☎ (305) 871-1810.
Bayside, 700 Biscayne Blvd.
☎ (305) 374-6160.
North Miami, 16560 NE 6th Ave.
☎ (305) 945-0801.

METRORAIL AND METROMOVER

Metrorail, a 21-mile (34-km) rail line between the northern and southern suburbs of Miami, is of limited use to visitors. However, it provides a useful link between Coral Gables or Coconut Grove and the downtown area. Services run daily every ten minutes or so from 6am until midnight.

You can transfer free from Metrorail to the Tri-Rail line *(see p360)* in Hialeah, and also to the Metromover system at Government Center station (where you can pick up transport maps and information on rail routes).

The Metromover connects the heart of Downtown with the Brickell and Omni business districts on two elevated loop lines. Although the service is underused by local people, the Inner Loop provides a good way to see the downtown area *(see pp70–71)*. Cars operate continually from 6am to midnight. Make sure that you have coins ready for the turnstile as you enter the station.

Metro-Dade Transit Information
☎ (305) 770-3131.

METROBUS

Miami's metrobus network serves most places of interest, but the frequency of services varies greatly and is much reduced on weekends. Many of the services converge on Flagler Street and Government Center, Downtown, which is a good place to pick up buses.

There are express routes, which cost about double the usual fare. If you need to change buses, ask for a free transfer when you get on the first bus; you pay as you board, so have the right change ready. Transfers to the Metrorail or Metromover cost extra.

Metrobus stop

TAXIS

Taxis are often the best way to get around at night, even if you have a car; you may feel nervous about navigating after dark, and parking can be a problem in some areas.

Taxis charge approximately $2 per mile; the trip from South Beach to Coconut Grove, for example, will cost around $15. Don't try to hail a passing cab from the curb *(see p361)*; it is best to order one by phone. **Metro Taxi** and **Central Cab** are both reliable.

Metro Taxi
☎ (305) 888-8888.

Central Cab
☎ (305) 532-5555.

A typical Metromover station, with a plan of the network by the entrance

WATER TAXIS

Miami's water taxi operates two routes from Bayside Marketplace: a request service (11am–12am) runs east to South Beach, with stops at Lincoln Road and the 5th Street marina, and a shuttle service goes up the Miami River as far as the Orange Bowl Stadium, stopping at various restaurants and hotels on the way every 30 minutes between 10am and midnight.

Water Taxi
☎ (954) 467-6677.
🅆 www.watertaxi.com

TRAVELING BY CAR

Driving in Miami is not as intimidating as you might think. Biscayne Bay is a useful reference point, and you can't go far wrong if you stick to the main through streets.

Parking is straightforward, but it can be a nightmare in South Beach. On weekends forget it; at other times bring change for the meters, which operate from 9am to 9pm, and pay heed to the signs threatening to tow away your vehicle. You can contact the **Miami Parking System** and the **Miami Beach Parking Department** for directions to specific parking lots.

Miami Beach Parking Department
☎ (305) 673-7505.

Miami Parking System
☎ (305) 373-6789.

STREET ADDRESSES

Miami is split into four by the junction of Miami Avenue and Flagler Street in Downtown. Avenues, which run north-south, and streets, running east-west, start their numbering here. The coordinates NE, SE, NW, and SW, which prefix street names in Miami, change depending on which side of the main two axes the road is.

In Miami Beach, the southernmost street is 1st Street; the numbers then simply increase as you move northward.

Traveling in Florida's Other Cities

In the most popular tourist centers, quaint trolley buses and carriages designed to cater to tourists provide a relaxing way to sightsee *(see p361)*. In the bigger cities of Jacksonville and Tampa and in the Orlando area, however, it is worth familiarizing yourself with some of the alternative forms of transportation.

ORLANDO

You can survive in Orlando better than in other areas without a car thanks to the excellent **Lynx Buses**, which serve the airport, downtown Orlando, International Drive, and Walt Disney World. If you need a transfer, ask for one when you board the first bus.

I-Ride minibuses ply International Drive between Wet 'n Wild and SeaWorld. Buses run every ten minutes from 7am to midnight. Passes are a good value and mean that you don't always have to have change handy. Passes and timetables are available from the Lynx bus station in downtown Orlando (near Church Street Station) and from Walgreens stores on International Drive. Taxis are plentiful but costly. Private shuttle buses are much less expensive, especially for the trip from International Drive to Walt Disney World, but you need to reserve ahead for these.

Lynx Buses
☎ (107) 841 8240.

JACKSONVILLE

Jacksonville is best suited to the driver. The fairly new **Automated Skyway Express**, or ASE, is a monorail line that currently serves only Downtown, although there are plans to extend the line.

Jacksonville also has a water taxi (marine) service between the north and south banks of the St. Johns River. Shuttles operate between 10–11am and

Jacksonville's SS *Marine Taxi*, ready to cross the St. Johns River

4 6pm, depending on the weather. For other destinations, rely on the buses operated by the **Jacksonville Transit Authority**, whose terminus downtown is on Kings Road, about eight blocks north of Jacksonville Landing.

Automated Skyway Express
☎ (904) 632-5531.

SS Marine Taxi
☎ (904) 733-7782.

Jacksonville Transit Authority
☎ (904) 630-3100.

TAMPA

Downtown Tampa is quite compact, but without a car you'll need to use the local HARTline buses *(see p245)* to travel to outlying sights such as Busch Gardens. These depart from the terminal on Marion Street and run roughly every half hour along most routes, from about 5am to 8pm. There is also a trolley bus connection to Ybor City.

Water taxis in Tampa run a request service, stopping at a number of downtown attractions *(see pp244–5)*.

A tourist trolley bus in Tampa

Orlando's Lynx buses logo

Miami Parking System

General Index

Acknowledgments

DORLING KINDERSLEY would like to thank the following people whose contributions and assistance have made the preparation of this book possible.

MAIN CONTRIBUTORS

RICHARD CAWTHORNE is a freelance travel writer who specializes in the United States.

DAVID DICK is a postgraduate at University College London, specializing in US history.

GUY MANSELL writes travel articles for British magazines and newspapers, including *The Sunday Telegraph*, as well as guidebooks.

FRED MAWER is a travel journalist who contributes regularly to the *Daily Telegraph* and the *Mail on Sunday*. He is also the author of half a dozen guidebooks and has contributed to various Eyewitness guides.

EMMA STANFORD has traveled extensively in Florida and has written several books and articles about the state. She has written guidebooks for Berlitz, the AAA, and Fodor's.

PHYLLIS STEINBERG lives in Florida. She writes about food, travel, and lifestyle for various Florida and US magazines and newspapers.

OTHER CONTRIBUTORS AND CONSULTANTS

Frances and Fred Brown, Monique Damiano, Todd Jay Jonas, Marlena Spieler, David Stone.

ADDITIONAL PHOTOGRAPHY

Dave King, Clive Streeter, James Stevenson.

ADDITIONAL ILLUSTRATIONS

Julian Baker, Joanna Cameron, Stephen Conlin, Gary Cross, Chris Forsey, Paul Guest, Stephen Gyapay, Ruth Lindsay, Maltings Partnership, Paul Weston.

DESIGN AND EDITORIAL

RESEARCHER Fred Brown
MANAGING EDITOR Vivien Crump
MANAGING ART EDITOR Jane Ewart
DEPUTY EDITORIAL DIRECTOR Douglas Amrine
DEPUTY ART DIRECTOR Gillian Allan
PRODUCTION David Proffit
PICTURE RESEARCH Monica Allende
DTP DESIGNERS Lee Redmond, Ingrid Vienings

Louise Boulton, Cathy Day, Fay Franklin, Donald Greig, Emily Green, Leanne Hogbin, Ian Kearey, Kim Kemp, Desiree Kirke, Harvey de Roemer, Paul Steiner, Ingrid Vienings, Michael Wise.

CARTOGRAPHY

Malcolm Porter, David Swain, Holly Syer and Neil Wilson at EMS Ltd. (Digital Cartography Dept), East Grinstead, UK.
MAP CO-ORDINATORS Emily Green, David Pugh

PROOF READER

Stewart Wild

INDEXER

Hilary Bird

SPECIAL ASSISTANCE

Dorling Kindersley would like to thank all the regional and local tourist offices in Florida for their valuable help. Particular thanks also to: Rachel Bell, Busch Gardens; Alison Sanders, Cedar Key Area Chamber of Commerce; Marie Mayer, Collier County Historical Museum, Naples; Mr. and Mrs. Charlie Shubert, Coombs House Inn, Apalachicola; Nick Robbins, Crystal River State Archaeological Site; Emily Hickey, Dali Museum, St. Petersburg; Gary B. van Voorhuis, Daytona International Speedway; James Laray, Everglades National Park; Sandra Barghini, Flagler Museum, Palm Beach; Ed Lane, Florida Geological Survey, Florida Department of Environmental Protection, Tallahassee; Dr. James Miller, Archaeological Research, Florida Department of State, Tallahassee; Florida Keys National Marine Sanctuary; Jody Norman, Florida State Archives; Damian O'Grady and Tanya Nigro, Florida Tourism Corporation, London; Larry Paarlberg, Goodwood Plantation, Tallahassee; Dawn Hugh, Historical Museum of Southern Florida; Ellen Donovan, Historical Society of Palm Beach County; Melissa Tomasso, Kennedy Space Center; Valerie Rivers, Marjorie Kinnan Rawlings State Historic Site, Cross Creek; Carmen Smythe, Micanopy County Historian; Bob McNeil and Philip Pollack, Museum of Florida History, Tallahassee; Frank Lepore and Ed Rappaport, National Hurricane Center, Miami; Colonel Denis J. Kiely, National Museum of Naval Aviation, Pensacola; Richard Brosnaham and Tom Muir, Historic Pensacola Preservation Board; Ringling Museum of Art, Sarasota; Ardythe Bromley-Rousseau, Salvors Inc., Sebastian; Arvin Steinberg; Wit Tuttell, Universal Studios; Holly Blount, Vizcaya, Miami; Melinda Crowther, Margaret Melia and Joyce Taylor, Walt Disney Attractions, London.

PHOTOGRAPHY PERMISSIONS

Dorling Kindersley would like to thank the following for their assistance and kind permission to photograph at their establishments: The Barnacle Historic Site; © 1996 FL Cypress Gardens, Inc.; all rights reserved, reproduced by permission; © Disney Enterprises, Inc.; Dreher Park Zoo: The Zoo of the Palm Beaches; Fish and Wildlife Service, Department of the Interior; Florida Park Service; Harry P. Leu Gardens, Orlando, FL; Key West Art and Historical Society: Lighthouse Museum and East Martello Museum; Metro-Dade Culture Center, Historical Museum of Southern Florida; Monkey Jungle Inc., Miami, FL; National Park Service, Department of Interior; Pinellas County Park Department; National Society of the Colonial Dames of America in the State of Florida; Suncoast Seabird Sanctuary Inc.,

Indian Shores, FL, and all other museums, churches, hotels, restaurants, stores, galleries, and sights too numerous to thank individually.

PICTURE CREDITS

t = top; tl = top left; tlc = top left center; tc = top center; trc = top right center; tr = top right; cla = center left above; ca = center above; cra = center right above; cl = center left; c = center; cr = center right; clb = center left below; cb = center below; crb = center right below; bl = bottom left; b = bottom; bc = bottom center; bcl = bottom center left; br = bottom right; d = detail.

DORLING KINDERSLEY would like to thank the following individuals, companies, and picture libraries for their kind permission to reproduce their photographs:

AFP: Stephen Jaffe-STF 51br; AISA, Barcelona: 193b; Museo de America 42cl; © Disney Enterprises, Inc. 146–7, 154–5; Vidler 109t, 122t; ALLSPORT, UK: Steve Swope 31b; Allsport, USA/Scott Halleran 94t; Shaquille O'Neal/Christian Laettner 31cr; APPLETON MUSEUM OF ART, Ocala: *Jeune Bergere (Young Sheperdess)*, William Adolphe Bouguereau (1825–1905), French. Oil on canvas 208t; ARCHIVE PHOTOS, New York: 47cla, 50clb; Bert & Richard Morgan 114b; MUSEUM OF ART, Fort Lauderdale: *Big Bird with Child*, Karel Appel (1972) © DACS 1997 128t; MUSEUM OF FINE ARTS, St. Petersburg: *Poppy*, Georgia O'Keeffe (1927) © ARS, NY and DACS, London 1998 241t; TONY ARRUZA: 21cb, 24cbl, 36, 124t, 136b, 276c, 283b, 337t; AVALON HOTEL, Miami: 59tl.

LARRY BENVENUTI: 279cr; BIBLIOTECA NACIONAL, Madrid: *Codice Osuna* 41cb; BRITISH MUSEUM: 39t, 43cr; THE BRIDGEMAN ART LIBRARY, London: *The Agony in the Garden (Christ in the Garden of Olives)*, 1889 by Gauguin, Paul (1848–1903), Norton Gallery, Palm Beach 123t; BUSCH ENTERTAINMENT CORP.: 2–3, 104b, 250b, 251t, 251bra, 251b. All Rights Reserved, Discovery Cove: 167c, 167b.

CAMERA PRESS: Steve Benbow 160b; JOHN CARTER: 19b, 354c; © Disney Enterprises, Inc. 140–41; Courtesy of THE CHARLESTON MUSEUM, Charleston, South Carolina: Osceola portrait 44ca; ROBERT CLAYTON: 52–53, 285t, 358b, 360b, 362tr, 362b, PAT CLYNE: 110t; BRUCE COLEMAN, London: Atlantide SDF 280t; Erwin & Peggy Bauer 275br; Raimund Cramm GDT 180cla; Jeff Foott Productions 23bl; © John Shaw 23cl; George McCarthy 23t; LIBRARY OF CONGRESS, LC-USF33 30491-M3 49cr; CORBIS: 41t, 42–3c; Jonathan Blair 142t; CULVER PICTURES, INC., New York: 46cl, 49t, 53 (inset).

SALVADOR DALI MUSEUM, St. Petersburg: 242t; All works of art by Salvador Dali © DEMART PRO ARTE BV/DACS 1997, *Nature Morte Vivante* 242ca, *The Sick Child* 242cb,

Cadaques 242b, *Don Quixote y Sancho Panza* 243t, *Discovery* 243ca, *Daddy Longlegs of the Evening–Hope* (1940) 243cb; Salvador Dali by Marc Lacroix 243b; © INTERNATIONAL SPEEDWAY CORPORATION, Daytona: 204t, 205c, 205b; Nascar 205cb; DAVID DYE, University of Memphis: South Florida Museum 38cl, 41cla.

MARY EVANS PICTURE LIBRARY: 103 (inset); C. Sheppard 9 (inset); ET ARCHIVE: Natural History Museum 43cla.

MEL FISHER MARITIME HERITAGE SOCIETY, Key West, Photograph by Dylan Kibler © 1993 40t; © HENRY MORRISON FLAGLER MUSEUM, Palm Beach: 47t, 120tl, 120c, 120b, 121t, 121ca, 121cb; Archives 120tr, 121b; by kind permission from FLORIDA HOLOCAUST MUSEUM: 245tl.

PET GALLAGHER: 18b; GENESIS SPACE PHOTO LIBRARY: NASA 184bl, 184br, 185bl, 185br, 186cb, 186c, 186tl; GIRAUDON, Paris: Bridgeman Sir Francis Drake portrait, Olivier Isaac (1540–1596) 41cr; Laurus 37b; THE GRANGER COLLECTION, New York: 44clb, 44crb, 44t, 47crb, 48cl, 48t; THE RONALD GRANT ARCHIVE. © King Feature Syndicated 168bl.

ROBERT HARDING PICTURE LIBRARY: Liason 50–51c; © THE MIAMI HERALD: © Al Diaz 31cl, 122b; Chuck Fadely & Art Gallery 90t; © Guzy 51cla; © Charlie Trainor 75cr; HENRY HIRD 200b; DIVISION HISTORICAL RESOURCES, STATE DEPARTMENT, Tallahassee: 39crb, 110c; Courtesy of HIBEL MUSEUM OF ART, Palm Beach, FL: *Brittany and Child*, oil, gesso, and gold leaf on silk, Edna Hibel 24 1/2" x 20 1/2" (1994) 117c; HISTORICAL MUSEUM OF SOUTHERN FLORIDA, Miami: 48cb, 49clb, 50c, 61bt, 72t, 271t;

THE IMAGE BANK, London: 10b, 19c, V. Chapman 48–9c; IMAGES COLOUR LIBRARY: 15t, 49cra, 55ba, 272br, 285b; INDEX STOCK PHOTOGRAPHY, INC., New York: 21b, 32c, 32t, 34t, 34b, 35c, 46t, 117b, 169b, 172c, 249t, 332c, 336c; © Bill Bachmann 22cl; © James Blank 15b, 268c; J. Christopher 25cr; © Henry Fichner 23cr; © Warren Flagler 51cra; Scott Kerrigan 281cr; Larry Lipsky 165bl, 277br; Wendell Metzen 30t, 30b, 180ca, 274t; © M Timothy O'Keefe 290–91; Jim Schwabel 16, 257t, 269t, 270t; Scott Smith 94c; Steve Starr 24bra, 246l; M. Still 277t; Randy Taylor 32b; ARCHIVO DE INDIAS, Seville: 40cb; INDIAN TEMPLE MOUND: 38cl.

MIAMI WORLD JAI-ALAI: 31t; Michael Fineman 133b

KENNEDY SPACE CENTER – VISITORS CENTER, Cape Canaveral: 182t, 183ca, 183cb, 184tr, 187c; KEN LAFFAL: 21t, 54b, 105t, 113b, 336t; FRANK LANE PICTURE LIBRARY: © Dembinsky 22bla, 279; © David Hosking 17b, 22br, 23br, 180t, 274cr; Maslowski 112c; © Leonard Lee Rue 23crb; LIGHTNER MUSEUM, St. Augustine, FL: 47bla; LOWE ART MUSEUM: 81c.

BARRY MANSELL: 271c; MACMILLAN PUBLISHERS: Pan
Books *Native Tongue* and *Tourist Season* Carl
Hiassen 82b; MARVEL ENTERTAINMENT GROUP, NY:
Spider-Man TM and © 1996, Marvel Characters,
Inc. All rights reserved 126t; FRED MAWER, London:
73t, 77t, 132b, 137t, 178t, 182cb.

© NASA: 186tr, 187t; MUSEO NAVAL, Spain: 26cl;
PETER NEWARK'S PICTURES: American Pictures 43clb;
Historical Pictures 27cb; Military Pictures 45cb; THE
NEW YORK PUBLIC LIBRARY: Print Collection, Miriam
and Ira D. Wallach Division of Art, Prints and
Photographs, Astor, Lenox and Tilden Foundations
40–41c; JESSE NEWMAN ASSOCIATES: 115br; GLENN VAN
NIMWEGEN, Wyoming: 276ca, 277bl; Northampton
Museums and Art Gallery: 42t. NOAA National
Hurricane Center, Miami: 24–5, 25t.

ORONOZ, Madrid: 40ca.

THE PALM BEACH POST, FL: © Allen Eyestone 51clb;
© Thomas Hart Shelby 114cl; © Greg Lovett 33c;
© Loren Hosack 115bl, 118b;
© E.A. Kennedy III 20b; © Mark Mirko 35b; ©
Bob Shanley 184t; © Sherman Zent 33b; PICTURES
COLOUR LIBRARY: 289b; PLANET EARTH PICTURES: 279t;
Kurt Amsler 236t; Peter Gasson 23bla; © Brian
Kenney 22cr, 22bl, 23cla, 180cra, 274cl, 272bl,
273ca, 275t, 275c, 275bl, David Maitland 22cra;
Doug Perrine 278cr, 279t; Mike Potts 274b; Nancy
Sefton 278bl.

QUADRANT PICTURE LIBRARY: © Anthony R. Dalton
51crb.

MIKE RASTELLI, Ocala: 261b; REX FEATURES:
© Sipa-Press 51t; Kevin Wisniewski 75t; THE JOHN
AND MABLE RINGLING MUSEUM OF ART, Sarasota:
258b, 259t; Bequest of John Ringling, *The*

Building of a Palace, Piero di Cosimo
(1515–1520) 257c, *Abraham and Melchizedek*,
Peter Paul Rubens (c.1625) 257b.

SEAWORLD ORLANDO: 5t, 114c, 164t, 164b, 165cra;
SMITHSONIAN INSTITUTION: Department
of Anthropology catalogue no. 240915 38clb;
FLORIDA STATE ARCHIVE, Tallahassee: 43t, 45t, 45ca,
46b, 49ca, 116br, 119t, 205ca, 217b, 247b, 249t:
Museum of Florida History 49crb, 111b; TONY
STONE IMAGES: Daniel McCulloch 50t; Stephen
Krasemann 266; Randy Wells 272c; SUPERSTOCK:
174t.

TAMPA THEATRE: 337b; FLORIDA DEPARTMENT OF
COMMERCE, DIVISION OF TOURISM: R. Overton 39cra.

UNIVERSAL ORLANDO © 2000. All Rights Reserved
173t. © UNIVERSAL STUDIOS: 169t, 171b. UNIVERSAL
STUDIOS ESCAPE © 1999. A Universal Studios/Rank
Group Joint Venture. All Rights Reserved 169t,
169br, 170b, 171t, 172cl, 173b.

© THE WALT DISNEY COMPANY: 148, 149, 156, 157,
162; WARREN ASSOCIATES: 172tl, 173cl; PROF L.
GLENN WESTFALL, FL: 46–7; BILL WISSER, Miami: 65t;
WOLFSONIAN FOUNDATION, Miami: Mitchell Wolfson,
J.R. Collection 65b; WORLD PICTURES: 160t.

Front endpaper: All special photography except
TONY STONE: Stephen Krasemann br.

Jacket: All special photography except INDEX
STOCK PHOTOGRAPHY, NY: back br; PLANET EARTH
PICTURES: Flip Schulke back bl; SEA WORLD:
front cr.

All other images © Dorling Kindersley. See
www.DKimages.com for further information.

EYEWITNESS TRAVEL GUIDES

COUNTRY GUIDES

AUSTRALIA • CANADA • CRUISE GUIDE TO EUROPE AND THE
MEDITERRANEAN • CUBA • EGYPT • FRANCE • GERMANY
GREAT BRITAIN • GREECE: ATHENS & THE MAINLAND
THE GREEK ISLANDS • IRELAND • ITALY • JAPAN
MEXICO • POLAND • PORTUGAL • SCOTLAND
SINGAPORE • SOUTH AFRICA • SPAIN
THAILAND • GREAT PLACES TO STAY
IN EUROPE • A TASTE OF SCOTLAND

REGIONAL GUIDES

BALI & LOMBOK • BARCELONA & CATALONIA • CALIFORNIA
EUROPE • FLORENCE & TUSCANY • FLORIDA • HAWAII
JERUSALEM & THE HOLY LAND • LOIRE VALLEY
MILAN & THE LAKES • MUNICH & THE BAVARIAN ALPS • NAPLES WITH
POMPEII & THE AMALFI COAST • NEW ENGLAND • NEW ZEALAND
PROVENCE & THE COTE D'AZUR • SARDINIA
SEVILLE & ANDALUSIA • SICILY • SOUTHWEST USA & LAS VEGAS
A TASTE OF TUSCANY • VENICE & THE VENETO

CITY GUIDES

AMSTERDAM • BERLIN • BOSTON • BRUSSELS • BUDAPEST
CHICAGO • CRACOW • DELHI, AGRA & JAIPUR • DUBLIN
ISTANBUL • LISBON • LONDON • MADRID
MOSCOW • NEW YORK • PARIS • PRAGUE • ROME
SAN FRANCISCO • STOCKHOLM • ST PETERSBURG
SYDNEY • VIENNA • WARSAW • WASHINGTON, DC

NEW FOR AUTUMN 2002

INDIA • MOROCCO • NEW ORLEANS • TURKEY

FOR INFORMATION ON OUR NEW EYEWITNESS TOP TEN POCKET SERIES
AND ON
DK TRAVEL MAPS & PHRASEBOOKS

VISIT US AT
www.dk.com

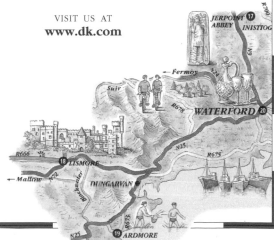

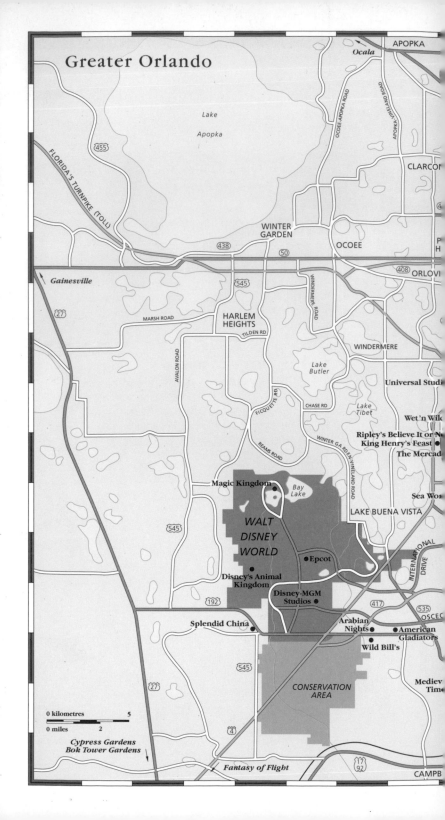